A CUP OF NEWS
The life of
Thomas Nashe

ALSO BY CHARLES NICHOLL

The Chemical Theatre

A CUP
OF NEWS

The life of
THOMAS NASHE

Charles Nicholl

Routledge & Kegan Paul

London, Boston, Melbourne
and Henley

First published in 1984
by Routledge & Kegan Paul plc
39 Store Street, London WC1E 7DD, England
9 Park Street, Boston, Mass. 02108, USA
464 St Kilda Road, Melbourne,
Victoria 3004, Australia, and
Broadway House, Newtown Road,
Henley-on-Thames, Oxon RG9 1EN, England

Set in Sabon, 10 on 12 pt by
Input Typesetting Ltd, London
and printed in Great Britain by
The Thetford Press Limited, Thetford, Norfolk

Library of Congress Cataloging in Publication Data

Nicholl, Charles.

A cup of news.
Bibliography: p.
Includes index.
1. Nash, Thomas, 1567–1601—Biography. 2. Authors, English—Early
modern, 1500–1700—Biography. 3. Pamphleteers—England—Biography.
I Title.
PR2326.N3Z78   1983   828'.309 [B]   83–19048

British Library CIP available

ISBN 0–7100–9517–1

CONTENTS

Acknowledgments   *ix*

1   THE PAMPHLETEER   *1*

2   CHILDHOOD   *11*

3   CAMBRIDGE   *23*

4   LONDON   *39*

5   THE WITS   *48*

6   CUTHBERT CURRYKNAVE   *62*

7   LORD STRANGE   *80*

8   PIERCE POLITIC   *99*

9   GREENE AND HARVEY   *122*

10   'IN THE COUNTREY'   *135*

11   JACK WILTON   *154*

12   THE CRACK-UP   *166*

13   THE CAREYS   *181*

14   MASTER MOTH   *203*

15   A SILENCE   *221*

16   THE *ISLE OF DOGS* AFFAIR   *242*

17   LENTEN STUFF   *257*

Notes   *275*

Bibliography   *324*

Index   *331*

ILLUSTRATIONS

Between pages 146 and 147

 1 Portrait of Thomas Nashe, 1597 (British Library)
 2 St Margaret's, Lowestoft
 3 All Saints', West Harling
 4 Christopher Marlowe, supposed portrait, 1585 (Corpus Christi College, Cambridge)
 5 Gabriel Harvey, woodcut portrait, 1596 (British Library)
 6 The ghost of Robert Greene, woodcut, 1598 (Bodleian Library, Oxford)
 7 Lord Strange, *c.* 1593 (collection of the Earl of Derby)
 8 (a) Croydon Palace (British Library);
   (b) The Great Hall, Croydon (British Library)
 9 Sir Robert Cotton at age 54 (Society of Antiquaries of London)
10 Sir George Carey by Hilliard, 1601 (Courtauld Institute of Art)

DOCUMENTS

Between pages 274 and 275

1 Thomas Nashe's christening, November 1567 (Lowestoft Parish Registers, St Margaret's, Lowestoft)
2 Margaret Nashe's will, 2 December 1589 (Archdeacon Court of Suffolk Register IC/AA2, bk xxxii, ff. 225–6, Suffolk Record Office)
3 Nashe's matriculation as sizar scholar of St John's, 13 October 1582 (University Matriculation Register, Cambridge)
4 Nashe's admission as Lady Margaret scholar of St John's, autograph entry, 1584 (St John's College Register of Officers, Fellows and Scholars)
5 Nashe's Latin verses on *Ecclesiasticus*, in text hand, part of a presentation copy by Lady Margaret scholars, 1585 (State Papers, Dom. Add. Eliz., vol. xxix, f. 167, Public Record Office)
6 List of students attending philosophy lectures in 1588 (Lansdowne MS 57, art. 92, British Library)
7 Signature, probably Nashe's, in a copy of Thomas Phaer, *The Seven First Bookes of the Eneidos of Virgill* (London, 1558), t-p verso (British Library, shelf mark C 56 e 2)
8 Nashe's signature and marginalia, *c.* 1592, in a copy of John Leland, *Principum ac Illustrum in Anglia Virorum Encomia* (London, 1589), t-p, pp. 130, 132 (Art Collection of the Folger Shakespeare Library)
9 Harvey's marginalia on Nashe and Greene, *c.* 1592, in a copy of Sir Thomas Wilson, *The Art of Rhetorike* (London, 1567), sigs K3, K5v (Rosenbach Library, Philadelphia)
10 (a) Nashe's autograph letter to William Cotton, August-September 1596 (Cotton MS Jul C III, f. 280, British Library);
(b) Address to Cotton and an Elizabethan shopping-list (ut supra, f. 280v)

11 Government directive to Richard Topcliffe *et al.*, concerning *The Isle of Dogs* and Nashe's seized papers, 15 August 1597 (Privy Council Register for the Reign of Elizabeth, vol. xii, 346, Public Record Office)

12 Nashe's epitaph in a manuscript copy of 'The Progress to Parnassus' [i.e. *2 Returne from Parnassus*], *c.* 1601 (Art Collection of the Folger Shakespeare Library, MS V a 355, f. 7)

ACKNOWLEDGMENTS

Illustrations and documents are reproduced by kind permission of the following: the Trustees of the British Museum, Figures 1, 5, 8(a) and 8(b), and Documents 6, 7, 10(a) and 10(b); the Master, Fellows and Scholars of Corpus Christi College, Cambridge, Figure 4, the authenticity of which is not guaranteed by them; the Bodleian Library, Oxford, Figure 6; the Earl of Derby, Figure 7; the Society of Antiquaries of London, Figure 9; the trustees of Berkeley Castle and the Courtauld Institute of Art, Figure 10; the rector of St Margaret's, Lowestoft, Document 1; the Suffolk Record Office, Ipswich, Document 2; the Syndics of Cambridge University Library, Document 3; the St John's College Library, Cambridge, Document 4; the Public Record Office, Documents 5 and 11; the Folger Shakespeare Library, Washington, Documents 8 and 12; the Rosenbach Museum and Library, Philadelphia, Document 9.

No biography of Nashe could be written without fully acknowledging the work of R. B. McKerrow. His *editio princeps* of Nashe's works, published some seventy-five years ago, is the bedrock on which this book is built. My debts to other Nashe scholars – F. P. Wilson, Donald J. McGinn, C. G. Harlow, *et al.* – are enumerated in the Notes and Bibliography.

More personally, I should like to mention some whose time and wisdom I have borrowed: the late Frances Yates; Josephine Nicholl; Muriel St Clare Byrne; Neil Rhodes; Hugh Lees of Lowestoft; Mr Roberts of the Old Palace School, Croydon. To these my thanks, as also to David Godwin and Jacqueline Korn for their faith in the book; to Sally for her apparent faith in me; and to the spirit of Tom Nashe for refusing to rest.

'Truth is ever drawne and painted naked, and I have lent her but a leathren patcht cloake at most, to keepe her from the cold . . .'

THOMAS NASHE   *The Terrors of the Night*

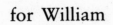
for William

1

THE PAMPHLETEER

'They have lyved long on the almsbasket of wordes . . .'

WILLIAM SHAKESPEARE *Loves Labors Lost*

Thomas Nashe came in on the crest of the last great Elizabethan wave. He arrived in London in 1588, an ambitious young wit fresh from Cambridge. His first major success as an author was with *Pierce Penilesse*, published in 1592. Further successes followed. He was prolific and controversial, the pamphleteer who precisely caught the time's flavour. He reigned pre-eminent among 'the riffe-raffe of the scribling rascality'.[1] But his bent for topical satire and lampoon also earned him trouble – 'let me but touch a peece of paper, there arise such stormes and tempestes about my eares as is admirable'[2] – and in the summer of 1597 he had to flee London to escape arrest. The rest is silence, punctuated only by his last bizarre masterpiece, *Nashes Lenten Stuffe* (1599), written in 'prayse of the Red Herring'. By the end of 1601 he was dead. His brief, turbulent, poverty-haunted career spans just a dozen years, from the defeat of the Armada to the writing of *Hamlet*. He was about 33 when he died.

In that short time, Nashe may be said to have made the 1590s his own. In literary circles he was *hic et ubique* as friend, foe, gossip or critic, a darting figure at the thick of the fray. He was the intimate friend of Christopher Marlowe and Robert Greene; he was the co-author of Ben Jonson's first venture as a playwright (the scandalous *Isle of Dogs*); his day-to-day colleagues were writers like John Lyly, Thomas Watson, Harry Chettle, the comedians Tarlton and Kemp, the disreputable printer John Danter, the 'king of the tobacconists' Humfrey King.[3] His path crossed often with Shakespeare's – in the circles around Lord Strange and the Earl of Southampton, and when Nashe was writing for the Lord Chamberlain's troupe in 1596 – but their relations are shadowy. Nashe appears in *Loves Labors Lost* (c. 1593), amiably caricatured as Master Moth, the knavish page-boy, 'that handfull of wit'.[4] Shakespeare's work of the mid-1590s is shot through with echoes and borrowings from Nashe's pamphlets: characters from Petruchio to Falstaff contain refractions of Nashe the satirist and Nashe the man.[5] Equally impressive is the list of Nashe's literary enemies. No-one emerges from his pamphlets

1

in more monstrous detail than his arch-enemy, Dr Gabriel Harvey, the Cambridge don, poet and rhetorician, with his two brothers in his wake, Richard the astrologer-parson and John, the physician of King's Lynn. Other writers who one way or another 'cast the begger in his dish' include Barnabe Barnes, Anthony Chute, Thomas Churchyard, Sir John Harington, George Chapman and Joseph Hall. There is a nervy intensity about Nashe's friendships and quarrels alike: he was unpredictable company.

Clinging, as every Elizabethan writer must, to the fringes of nobility and the court, 'folowinge a goutie patron by the smell',[6] Nashe also leads us through the back-doors of many great Elizabethan households. He moved in the curious circles surrounding Lord Strange, later 5th Earl of Derby. He turns up at Sir George Carey's castle on the Isle of Wight, at Archbishop Whitgift's palace at Croydon, at Robert Cotton's gloomy mansion in Huntingdonshire, where Ben Jonson later had a vision of his son's death. We shall hear of other big names – Leicester, Ralegh, the Countess of Pembroke, Lord Cobham – with whom Nashe dealt, though not in the way of service. Ingeniously veiled satire on the great and powerful is one of his specialities, libels none the less appetizing because based on some tittle-tattle he picked up from the Clerk of the Kitchens or over dice with the 'dapper Mounsier Pages of the Court'.[7]

Patronage was precarious and usually rather brief, and Nashe was soon back on the streets again, his true *milieu*, living to the full his most famous *persona*, Pierce Penniless, the half-starved malcontent young poet who petitions the Devil to spirit away those capitalist 'cormorants' who 'bung up all the welth of the land in their snap-haunce bags' while we poor scholars must 'wander in backe lanes and the out-shiftes of the Citie'.[8] In these seedy 'out-shiftes' of London Nashe took his lodgings – out in the 'liberties' of Shoreditch and Southwark, the Bohemian haunts where the play-houses and pleasure-dens were; in the back-streets of Smithfield, where he lodged with John Danter; at 'olde Mistresse Silver-pinnes' in Pickt-hatch Walk; in 'a Chamber in Cole-harbour, where they live in a continuall myst betwixt two Brew-houses'.[9] We glimpse him holding court among the book-stalls at St Paul's, packed into the Rose theatre for a performance of Shakespeare's *Henry VI*, dining on pickled herrings and Rhenish wine with Robert Greene. And, from time to time, we find him in the Counter, debtor's prison, cavalierly protesting that 'a Gentleman is never throughly entred into credit till he hath beene there' and that 'I should never have writ passion well, or beene a peece of a Poet, if I had not arriv'd in those quarters.'[10] He is not really joking, either. He recognized, not perhaps without reluctance, that this *demi-monde* of taverns and tenements was not only his lot as a writer, it was his life-blood. The verve, squalor and oddities of London 'low life' fired his imagination and invigorated his style. For all his scholarly aspirations and 'had I wist Court humors', Nashe's genius was urban, lurid, grotesque and low. It fed – 'alas, poore hungerstarved Muse' – on adrenalin, culled daily from the streets of Elizabethan London.

Nashe's ubiquity, his fleeting presence at so many levels of Elizabethan life, is one clue to the appeal of his pamphlets, both in the 1590s and now. His work has long been valued as vividly documentary. 'The light tracts of Tom Nash', wrote a historian in 1815, are a positive 'granary for commentators.'[11] His writings have, says the great modern editor of his works, R. B. McKerrow, 'a vividness of presentation which makes them more surely and entirely of their own time and country, more representative of the England of Elizabeth, than almost any others'.[12] This vein of reportage, this portraiture – warts and all, indeed warts especially – of Elizabethan life, is partly why Nashe is described as a 'pamphleteer' rather than a more respectable 'author'.

The term 'pamphleteer', in an Elizabethan context, demands some explanation. This feel of topicality and reportage in Nashe suggests that the closest modern equivalent is 'journalist'. Nashe had a newshound's instincts, certainly, and pamphlets like *An Almond for a Parrat* (1590) and *Have with you to Saffron-Walden* (1596) are the fruits of genuine 'investigative journalism', even if the final product (polemic and lampoon respectively) is not quite 'news'. News, in our sense, was in its infancy. The typical Elizabethan 'news letter' was some hastily translated propagandist piece about European wars and politics. John Wolfe, who published Harvey's tracts against Nashe, put out some 36 'French news' pamphlets in the early 1590s.[13] Home news was mainly confined to sensational accounts of trials and executions, murders, meteors and monstrous births, shading into the prophetic ware of the astrologers and almanac-men. 'State matters', as Nashe found to his cost, were not to be touched on, except in the most blandly jingoistic terms. State censorship – operated in well-oiled partnership by the Archbishop of Canterbury, the Privy Council and the London civic authorities – was vigilant and harsh. Nashe fought a continuous battle with intelligencers and informers, those 'mice-eyed decipherers' who would comb each new pamphlet for topical references and 'runne over al the peeres of the land in peevish moralizing and anatomizing it'.[14]

But despite his veins of clandestine political journalism, it would be misleading to think of Nashe solely as a journalist without a newspaper, printing 'truth' in the teeth of official suppression. He was no crusader. His pamphlets are nearer to our *Private Eye* magazine: they have the *frisson* of topicality, libel and snook-cocking laughter, but little sense of reformist zeal, or even compassion, behind them.[15] If the pamphleteer was essentially a journalist, he was one forced by circumstances – artistic, social, psychological – into various other literary roles, and these other roles are also included in the term 'pamphleteer'. In *The Anatomie of Absurditie*, Nashe speaks of his wit venturing forth 'in this satyricall disguise',[16] and it was undoubtedly the role of satirist which offered the pamphleteer his most valuable freedom. It was primarily as a penner of lampoons, harangues and 'bitter-sauced Invectives' that Nashe won such notoriety in his day (and long after: a pamphlet called *Tom Nash his Ghost*, published in 1644, professed to rekindle his 'yerking, firking, jerking, Satiricall and Poeticall veine').[17] He was the scourge of the Puritans, the guttersnipe antagonist of hypocrisy, pedantry, money-madness and officialdom, of 'pinchfarts', 'pennyfathers' and 'crusty cum-twangs' wheresoever. Greene called him 'young Iuvenall, that byting Satyrist'; to Thomas Lodge he was the 'true English Aretine'. Nashe himself frequently claimed kinship with Pietro Aretino, the great Italian satirist whose comedies were first published in England in the 1580s. 'We want an Aretine here among us,' he wrote, implying himself as chief candidate, 'that might strip these golden asses out of their gaie trappings.'[18] Satire was in Nashe's bones – he was quarrelsome, insubordinate, his typical mood one of confrontation – but also satire was a convenience, a vehicle for other messages. It afforded ancient, ingrained prototypes for his brand of journalism – sermons, homilies, morality plays; the licensed railing of fools and jesters; the classical satire of Juvenal, Martial and Ovid; the humanist critiques of Erasmus, Agrippa and Aretino. Nashe tested and often overstepped the acceptable frontiers of satire. As Jaques says in *As You Like It*,

> . . . I must have liberty
> Withal, as large a charter as the wind,
> To blow on whom I please, for so fools have;
> And they that are most galled with my folly,
> They most must laugh.[19]

This was written in about 1599. Perhaps Shakespeare had in mind the edict of that June, which ordered the suppression of various unseemly 'satyres and epigrams', including 'all Nasshes bookes'.[20] It was undoubtedly Nashe's intuitive enlarging of the satirist's 'charter' that sparked off the satirical vogue of the 1590s.

To 'journalist' and 'satirist' should be added a third, somewhat vaguer term like 'entertainer'. Nashe was a brilliant prose stylist, instantly recognizable: a 'swelling and boystrous' voice, a 'certayne nimble and climbinge reach of Invention'.[21] Whatever he wrote about, it was his special 'treatment' that won the readers, those 'proper phrases of pure Nasherie' that even his enemy Harvey was forced to recognize. The energy of his writing is prodigious. In his first published piece he pronounced: 'Give me the man whose extemporall veine in any humour will excell our greatest Art-maisters deliberate thoughts.'[22] It was a manifesto he stuck to: his 'extemporall veine' – racy, colloquial, peppered with fragments of scholarship – may be more 'deliberate' than it at first appears, but the whole feel of off-the-cuff spontaneity, of an almost unwholesome mental profusion and momentum, is vital to his performance. Nashe has recently been championed as the pioneer of 'Elizabethan grotesque',[23] and this too, with its blend of obsessive physical detail and wild metaphoric excess, seems to spring from an imagination momentarily unhinged, jolted into over-reaction. There is a sense of emergency in it, as in Hamlet's 'antick disposition'. None of this should obscure the prime fact of Nashe on song – he is very, very funny.

C. S. Lewis calls Nashe 'the perfect literary showman, the juggler with words who can keep a crowd spellbound by sheer virtuosity'.[24] The crowd was a paying public, and this too is a crucial aspect of the pamphleteer: his out-and-out commercialism. Nashe was a professional writer, the epitome of the Elizabethan free-lance: 'onely give mee a gentle hire for my durtie day labor, and I am your bounden Orator for ever'.[25] The idea of living off your pen was still a novelty. Here the influence of Robert Greene, prolific author of plays, 'love-pamphlets' and 'conny-catching' *exposés*, was decisive on Nashe. Patrons were still essential to the writer's living, but it was the popular press Nashe chose, preferring to remain (as Harvey sneered) 'humbly and thrise-affectionately bounden to the Right-honourable Printing-house for his poore shifts of apparell'.[26] The economics were hard – '40 shillings and an odde pottle of wine' was typical payment for a manuscript, with not a whiff of copyright thereafter – and the public's demand for novelty insatiable: 'newe herrings, new, wee must crye, every time wee make our selves publique, or else we shall bee christened with a hundred newe tytles of Idiotisme'.[27] But whatever his laments about the *magna opera* he had it in him to write, the role of the street-wise scribbler was one he played to perfection. He always had 'a pamphlet hot a-brooding', dashed it off over 'a pinte of wine & a pipe of tobacco', dedicated it with a careless shrug 'to his Readers, hee cares not what they be'.[28] There is a marvellous opportunism in Nashe. His casual, rapid, jazzy style was in a literal sense his trade-mark: it was fashioned out of the imperatives of Grub Street, where we 'must have our work dispatcht by the weeks end, or els we may go beg'. His pages savour of printing-house sweat, of the hard times when 'the fire of our wit is left, as our onely last refuge to warme us'.[29]

The journalist, the satirist, the showman and the hack: all these are part of Nashe's status as 'undoubtedly the greatest of the Elizabethan pamphleteers'. In a sense, the term 'pamphleteer' is right for him precisely because of its looseness. A pamphleteer writes pamphlets, and a pamphlet is whatever the reader will pay his threepence for.[30] As well as pure satire and lampoon, Nashe's published works include: a piece of pro-establishment propaganda, an end-of-summer 'shewe', a discourse on dreams and apparitions, an apocalyptic religious invective, a picaresque romance or novel, and a panegyric of Great Yarmouth. To these may be added a few prefaces and poems, some editing work, various unidentified bits of plays, and two major lost works (his elegy on Marlowe and the mysterious *Isle of Dogs*). Also lost are the private, occasional pieces he wrote for patrons. To these he refers when he says, in 1592, 'I have written in all sorts of humors privately, I am perswaded, more than any yoong man of my age in England.'[31] Only one has survived in manuscript: *The Choise of Valentines*, a long bawdy poem, notorious in its day under the popular title of 'Nashe's Dildo'.

All his literary 'humours' the catch-all pamphlet accommodated. Its formlessness, or informality, was perfect for his wayward butterfly mentality. It gave him room to be himself, to 'sprinkle his soul' into a chosen subject. Subjects, in fact, seem no more than pretexts for the performance, a starting-point soon lost from view as he plunges off down unlikely sideroads. As Lewis puts it: 'In a certain sense of the verb "say", if asked what Nashe "says", we should have to reply, "Nothing". He tells no story, expresses no thought, maintains no attitude.'[32] This perhaps is the crux. Nashe is the pamphleteer *par excellence*, not because he writes *about* Elizabethan life, but because he writes from *inside* Elizabethan life. He is more than topical: he is actual. For straight descriptive reportage one goes elsewhere: to Dekker's pamphlets, the 'city comedies' of Jonson and Middleton, Greene's 'conny-catching' tracts; to the great topographers, Harrison, Stow, Camden. These give us composed pictures of some sort, but with Nashe it is all unedited, like the 'rushes' of a movie. Figures shoulder up into view, caught in lurid detail – an 'old stradling Usurer' with a 'huge woorme-eaten nose'; a drunken Dane with 'a flaberkin face, like one of the foure winds'; sixpenny strumpets and their 'cut-purse paramours'; Harvey's unfortunate manservant, a 'big-board thresher' in a stolen blue coat too short for him. One stumbles over things, scuffed daily lumber: cap-cases and coney-skins, dust-boxes and dripping-pans, a Palermo razor, a 'twilted' tailor's cushion, a pair of old velvet slippers 'mangie at the toes, like an Ape about the mouth'. One overhears current jokes, scurrilous anecdotes, snatches of ballads, inconsequential gossip – Dexter's man Michael has moved to Exeter, Fol Long the fencer died drinking *aqua vitae*, the performing horse Morocco farts outrageously.[33]

Nashe's pamphlets are, in short, the real thing. They come straight from his nerve-ends, from what he called 'the slenderest twinckling reflexe' of his eyesight.[34] The world of the 1590s crowds in just the other side of his prose, a synaptic gap away. In the winter of 1592 he completed *Strange Newes*, his long-awaited riposte to Gabriel Harvey, and he offered it to his dedicatee, William Beeston, and to all the world thereafter, with the words: 'I am bolde, in steade of new wine, to carowse to you a cuppe of newes.'[35] This is the true kind of 'news', this cup of neat Elizabethan experience, which Nashe pours out to his readers.

Little has been written about the life and personality of the young man behind these pamphlets, surprisingly little for someone who steps out at us so vividly, and sheds such a casual, intimate light on his famous contemporaries. As with most Elizabethan writers, there are mysteries about him, both biographical and psychological. His life moves in and out of focus. In his heyday in the early 1590s he lived in a glare of self-generated publicity; elsewhere there are silences, unexplained movements, hints of dirty dealing. His pamphlets give the 'feel' of him, but also throw up questions about the sort of character that could write them, the mind behind the razzle-dazzle. Like his friend Marlowe, there is something unsettling about him, the unpredictable spark of high psychological voltage.

From his contemporaries, notably from his enemies, we get a strong idea of his physical presence, of how he looked and moved and shaped up. We have reason to be especially grateful to one Richard Lichfield, barber-surgeon at Trinity College, Cambridge, who published in the autumn of 1597 an extremely abusive pamphlet called *The Trimming of Thomas Nashe*. Halfway through this work, there appears the only extant contemporary portrait of Nashe (Figure 1). A rough woodcut caricature, wishfully presenting him as fettered in irons, it nevertheless captures many details of Nashe's appearance which are corroborated from verbal descriptions elsewhere. It was undoubtedly cut by someone who knew Nashe by sight, though as nothing is known of the publisher of the *Trimming*, Philip Scarlet, there is no way of knowing the identity of the artist. The real Nashe is close behind this strange little cartoon.

The dress of the figure is stereotypical, though certain details are meant to be suggestive. Leaving aside the leg-irons – the bulk of the *Trimming* was written in March 1597: Nashe may or may not have been in prison at the time – one notes the close-fitting, buttoned doublet, the shirt underneath having a wide 'falling band' collar turned over the neck of the doublet. Below he wears the conventional round or trunk hose, popularly known as 'Spanish kettledrums', decorated with vertical paning; plain, rather baggy 'canions' or 'nether-stocks' down to the knees; then stockings and what appear to be ankle-boots, perhaps leather 'pumps'. Even this tells its story: Nashe is in doublet and hose rather than, say, a scholar's gown, or a 'buff jerkin', or the rough 'leather pilch' that Ben Jonson favoured.[36] He is fashionable enough but a bit down-at-heel: the clothes look seedy, crumpled, worn too long. As Lichfield puts it, 'thou canst but get some old, greasie, cast fustian sute to weare'.[37] Two things particularly are meant to suggest a careless, disreputable air: his lack of a hat and his unbuttoned doublet. So Hamlet comes in wild-eyed to Ophelia, 'with his doublet all unbrac'd, no hat upon his head', and Frank Quicksilver, the mutinous apprentice in *Eastward Hoe*, enters with his doublet points unlaced, and proceeds to 'cast my coate and cap away'.[38]

The figure inside the clothes has a scrawny look – see especially the long skinny fingers, the 'leacherous hairie sinew on the calfe of the legge'[39] – and this is amply confirmed by all who knew him. He was, throughout his life, accounted an imp-like, boyish figure. Greene calls him 'sweete boy'; Lyly refers to him as 'a little wagg'; Henry Chettle also uses the word 'boy'.[40] Shakespeare presents him in *Loves Labors Lost* as Moth the mischievous page-boy, a 'halfpenny purse of wit'. In the Nine Worthies show at the end of the play, Moth gets the part of Hercules even though 'he is not quantitie enough for that Worthies thumb; he is not so big as the end of his Club'. The point seems to be that Nashe as biting satirist is a sort of Herculean shrimp, a wanton boy with a big stick. Nashe himself always stresses his youthfulness: even at age thirty he calls himself a 'stripling'. It is part of his whole style of pace and agility, and by contrast he paints Harvey as a lumbering, ursine figure, well past his best. Nashe's assault on him is 'a new kind of quicke fight, which your decrepite slow-moving capacitie cannot fadge with'.[41] Harvey, his patronizing temper goaded beyond endurance, retaliates by calling Nashe infantile and shrill – 'bratt of arrogancy . . . unmannerly puppy . . . master of impudency . . . curstest boy . . . baby of parchment . . . bombard goblin . . . gad-fly . . . gosling of the Printing-house . . . young haddock', etc.[42] None of this should be taken too literally – Nashe did not actually look like an Elizabethan schoolboy. But it tells us pretty clearly that he was someone small, sharp-edged and skinny.

It is in the face and hair that the artist has taken care to portray Nashe's actual features. 'I, being a youth of the English cut, ware my haire long,' says Nashe's Jack Wilton, and Nashe himself is clearly shown with a shock of shaggy dishevelled hair. Harvey, who had occasion to reprimand Greene for his 'fonde disguisinge of a Master of Arte with ruffianly haire', also gives us a glimpse of a Bohemian Nashe with his 'raunging eyes under that long haire'.[43] This too is a fashionable touch – long hair came in in the 1590s: Nashe speaks of 'the loose haird sort of yong Gentlemen & Courtiers' – but it looks too wild and untidy to be consciously elegant. The face itself is thin but rounded, with a high forehead. What is most noticeable, exceptional in Elizabethan times, is his total lack of beard. This too was often commented upon. It was part of Nashe's air of perennial boyishness. Lichfield ponders 'why thou hast so much haire on thy head, and so thinne or rather almost none at all on thy face'. His suggestion that Nashe is 'too effeminate, and so becomst like a woman, without a beard' is lame: Nashe's sexuality may be questionable, but there is no hint that he was effeminate or camp, and anyway Lichfield elsewhere announces that Nashe has lost his facial hair through syphilis ('by chacing after whores, his beard away hath chast').[44] What seems more probable is that Nashe was blonde, or at least fair-complexioned, and his beard was wispy and indistinct. He cheerfully spoke of his 'beardlesse yeeres', aged twenty-four, and of 'the minoritie of my beard', aged twenty-eight. Indeed he turned his smooth chin into an article of faith:

> Marry God forfend, for at no hand can I endure to have my cheeks muffled up in furre like a Muscovian, or weare any of this Welch freeze on my face. O it is a miserable thing to dresse haire like towe twixt a mans teeth, when one cannot drinke but hee must thrust a great spunge into the cup, & so cleanse his coole porridge, as it were through a strayner, ere it comes to his lippes.[45]

The beards of others are favourites with Nashe for telling detail or caricature. Harvey's, for instance: sometimes a spruce *pic-à-devant*, 'a prety polwigge sparrows tayle peake', sometimes more scruffy, 'like a Crow with two or three durtie strawes in her mouth, going to build her neast'. We hear of Robert Greene's 'iolly long red peake, like the spire of a steeple'; of an old usurer's 'gray beard cut short to the stumps, as though it were grimde'; of a college butler's 'grim triangle'; of the relative merits of 'the Swallowes taile cut & the round beard like a rubbing brush'.[46]

One last feature completes this contemporary portrait of Nashe. What at first appears to be some wispy hair over his upper lip is more probably the cutter's representation of Nashe's peculiar teeth. In *Pierces Supererogation* (1593) Harvey warns, 'Take heede of the man whom Nature hath marked with a gagtooth,' and an anonymous poem in the same pamphlet calls Nashe a 'gagtooth'd fopp'.[47] 'Gag' in this sense, apparently cognate with 'jagged', means 'to project or stick out'. Higgins' *Nomenclator* (1585) gives us 'gag teeth or teeth standing out', and Chapman describes a wild boar as 'gag-toothed', presumably referring to its tusks.[48] The idea seems to be of individual wayward teeth project-ing at angles, rather than an overall 'goofy' look. These the cutter's marks attempt to convey, and Lichfield completes the scene of dental disarray with his description of Nashe, on the page facing the woodcut: 'thy mouth distorted, thy lips ugly wrested, and thy nose hang hook-wise'.

It is not a pretty sight — skin and bones in a grubby doublet, snaggle

teeth and a mop of hair, the 'gentleman raggamuffin'. Nashe was not
one for prettiness, in his looks any more than in his writings. He cared
little 'for the false glistering of gay garments, or insinuating curtesie of
a carpet Peere'.[49] There was that compulsion in him towards the seedy,
unsettling side of things, the underbelly of Elizabethan life. Perhaps he
would argue, as John Donne once did, that 'foulnesse onely is a signe
of rigour'.[50] If it is hard to animate this woodcut into a living man, then
perhaps the elusiveness is right. Look once at his picture and he is a
mere boy, a smirking quipster. Look twice and he is the pamphleteer of
genius, who lived on the edge and conjured up laughter from 'forsaken
extremities'. It is his story that the following chapters have to tell.

2

CHILDHOOD

'My master beat me, my father beat me, my mother gave me bread and
butter . . .'

Summers Last Will and Testament

Thomas Nashe was a parson's son. He was born at Lowestoft, on the
coast of Suffolk, in November 1567. The neat hand of Robert Allen,
Lowestoft parish clerk, records his christening in the register (Document
1) but does not give the precise date.[1] His father was William Nashe (or
Nayshe, as it appears in local records). He – his son tells us – 'sprang
from the Nashes of Herefordshire',[2] but nothing is known of him before
the 1560s, when he appears as 'minester' of St Margaret's, the parish
church of Lowestoft. In February 1562, his first wife died, soon after
the birth of their daughter, Mary, and on 29 April he married a local
woman named Margaret Witchingham.[3] She was to bear him seven
children in fourteen years, of whom only two – Israel, born August
1565, and Thomas – survived childhood. The parents had a penchant
for biblical names (Israel, Martha, Rebecca) and did well to christen the
future pamphleteer after Thomas the doubter, for whom seeing was
believing.

It is not clear whether William Nashe himself migrated from Herefordshire to this easternmost edge of England. It is possible that John Nash
of Swainsthorpe in Norfolk, who died in 1548, represents an earlier
generation in East Anglia; he or his brother William may be the
pamphleteer's grandfather.[4] Nothing is known of the Herefordshire
family. Nashe was ready, when pressed, to defend 'the gentilitie of the
Nashes' and 'prove the extancy' of his ancestors, but he adds: 'wee can
vaunt larger petigrees than patrimonies'.[5] Well-bred but no longer very
well-off seems the idea. Like all Elizabethans, Nashe's sense of social
gradation was finely tuned. He pours satirical scorn on the *nouveaux
riches* of the age, 'these whelpes of the first Litter of Gentilitie'. Harvey,
the ropemaker's son, was a 'mushrumpe sprung up in one night'. For
all his restless temper, Nashe's social views were essentially orthodox:
he was no early champion of 'mungrel *Democratia*, in which one is
all & all is one'.[6] True to this orthodoxy he complained when the suffix
'Gent' was given him on title pages: 'it hath pleased M. Printer . . . to
intaile a vaine title to my name, which I care not for, without my consent

or privitie I here avouch'. He was no 'carterly upstart' but no true gentleman either.[7] Aside from mentioning his border-country origins, Nashe's only remarks about his father are that he put 'good meate in poore mens mouthes' and that he 'brought me up' at university.[8] Being able to afford charity (a social virtue Nashe tirelessly championed) and the expenses of university suggests that the Nashes were comfortable enough, even if Thomas did begin his Cambridge career as a humble 'sizar' scholar. Margaret Nashe's will – drawn up in 1589, William Nashe having died intestate – gives us a glimpse of the family household, furnished with a comfortable amount of Elizabethan 'goods and movables' (Document 2). We hear of the 'best bedsteade' in the hall, of pewter 'uppon my cubbord heade and in the butterie', of candlesticks, 'dyaper napkyns', tablecloths, silver spoons and featherbeds. It includes a bequest to 'one Gylian', probably a family servant.

This mild prosperity may not have always been the case. Nashe's earliest years, before the family moved to more profitable pastures than Lowestoft, were probably meagre and hard. The living of Lowestoft was extremely poor, and had recently (1553–9) been paired with the parish of Besthorpe, Norfolk, for that reason. Also, it seems that William Nashe was never formally instituted as vicar, but served as stipendiary curate for an absentee, John Blomevyle of Rollesby, Norfolk.[9] At these lower echelons, the clergy was an impecunious business. Nashe was doubtless exaggerating when he called Richard Harvey 'a dolefull foure nobles Curate' – four nobles (£1 6s 8d) was what a labourer or water-carrier might earn in a year – but the reality was little better: we hear of one Cleaton, curate of Buxton, earning £5 *per annum*, with all his tithes going to his patron, and Philip Stubbes claimed some churchmen earn as little as £2, 'yea, and table themselves also of the same'. It is unlikely that, as curate, William Nashe received the tithes of herring, or the 'Christ's dole' of 10s per fishing-boat, which were the Lowestoft vicar's ancient due.[10] There must have been some private wealth in the family for them to survive at all. Nashe's jibe at Richard Harvey – he has 'scarce so much ecclesiasticall living in all, as will serve to buy him cruell strings to his bookes, and haire buttons' – perhaps carries an echo of his own childhood.

The vicarage of St Margaret's, where Nashe was born and lived his first years, stood in the southwest corner of the old churchyard, looking down over Lowestoft and the sea. It was burned to the ground in 1606. The spot today is just brambles and old gravestones, though the path running up to the South Door of the church is probably one the Nashes took each day.[11] Among Nashe's earliest memories must have been the imposing bulk of the church (Figure 2) up on the rise above them, staunch Perpendicular Gothic in panelled flint, with a wooden spire 120 ft high. Formerly in the possession of St Bartholomew's priory, it still bore remnants of the old religion: the 'mass clock' on the South porch, the image of St Margaret of Antioch in its niche over the entrance. The little 'parvise' room above the porch was known as the 'Old Maids' Chamber' after two mediaeval anchoresses. The lectern, which dates from 1500, was in the form of a large brass eagle: it was hollow, for use as an alms-box, coins being deposited through the beak. In the chancel was a table with a chained *liber grammaticus*: here, no doubt, William Nashe eked out his stipend with some school-teaching. The church was generally in poor repair, and later, in 1592, over £200 had to be found for improvements. These were the first uneasy years of the Anglican settlement: the child would dimly hear dark talk of the recent Catholic terror, of the men burned at neighbouring Beccles by Bishop Hopton. He would sit through his father's sermons, learning perhaps (a good text for this sea-faring congregation) that 'the waves of the sea are mighty and rage horribly, but yet the Lord who dwelleth on high is mightier'.[12] Nashe's religion – his restless, vacillating, fearful faith – should never be under-estimated. It began here in the cradle, in the visible and mental shadow the church cast over his childhood.

But St Margaret's was also the centre of a very human world. Slightly apart from Lowestoft itself, there was a little straggling village along Church Road, opposite the vicarage. Church Farm stood next to the churchyard, built around an old manor house. In 1570, when Thomas was three, Lowestoft's first grammar school was set up in the close just east of the church. Founded by a local merchant, Thomas Annot, it provided for forty young scholars. The schoolmaster, competent in 'grammar and the Latin tongue, and other things incident and necessary', was paid £16 *per annum*, plus 20d down for each new boy. Its first master – 'Annot his Schoolmaster' – was Stephen Philip: he may have been a relative of the Nashes, since his wife was a Witchingham, like Margaret Nashe. There is a pleasant small wholeness about this community – village, farmyard, schoolhouse – clustered around St Margaret's. Down below was Lowestoft (or Leystofe, as Nashe invariably spells it), a small, busy, but none too prosperous fishing town of about 1800 people.[13] As a boy Nashe must have soon got to know its quays and shipyards, the fish-houses below the cliffs and the 'denes' above where the nets dried, the waterfront world of herringmen and oyster-catchers, salters and towers, 'makers of lines, roapes and cables, dressers of Hempe, spinners of thred and net weavers'. Here he could listen to the 'wither-fac'd' mariner that 'talks quakingly and shudderingly of a storme', and to another that tells of 'nothing but eating Tallow and yong black-amores, of five and five to a Rat in every messe'. Here he could watch 'a companie of lusty sailers', with their 'good big pop mouths to crie Port-a-helme Saint George', quaffing from 'large silver kans' and dancing 'a drunken Danish Lavolto or two'. Here perhaps he saw a drowned man, 'sodden to haddocks meate', with 'blew iellied sturgeon lips'. A novelty in town in the early 1570s was the 'Dutch folk', Protestant refugees from the Spanish-occupied Low Countries, a 'rabble rout of outlandishers' for the town to 'provant and victuall'.[14]

Under Elizabeth the fisheries were booming, the home market being boosted by the observance of three 'fish days' a week. There was talk in 1576 of an organized national herring-fleet of 400 ships. The principle was that a healthy fishing-fleet formed the basis of a strong navy. As Nashe puts it: 'not a slop of a ropehaler they send forth to the Queenes ships, but hee is first broken to the Sea in the Herring mans Skiffe or Cock-boate'.[15] For all this, Lowestoft remained a poor town, over-shadowed by its bigger neighbour, Great Yarmouth, with which it was always 'at wrig wrag' over boundaries and fishing rights. In 1588 the townsmen pleaded they were too poor to provide ships against the Armada, though they did eventually furnish the *Mathew*, a 35 tonner under Captain Michell. In 1592, they had to swallow their pride and borrow £100 from a Yarmouth merchant, one Bartlemewe, to help repair St Margaret's. The town boasted twenty large ships in Henry VIII's time, but by 1614 this was down to six or seven: the town was 'decayed' and people bought their fish off the Dutch instead of fishing themselves.[16]

Throughout his life, Nashe spoke with rare respect of fishermen. They win 'the treasure of fish out of those profundities', their low ships 'holding their owne pell-mell in all weathers'. They toil 'faythfully & painfully', are frugal in 'apparraile or dyet'. Christ's disciples, he notes, were 'but beggerly Fisher-men' that lived 'a hungerd and colde by the Sea-side'. He is moved by the struggles of those who 'live under the yoke of the Sea, or have their heads washt with his bubbly spume'. He knows the harsh lot of the sailor, who 'lyes in brine', is 'lamentable sick of the scurvies' and eats a 'hungry feast of Dogs & Cats, or Haberdine and poore Iohn at the most'.[17] He is casually at home with nautical terms: 'haling of bolings yare'; 'spreading their drabled sailes in the full clue abroad'; 'from the oreloope into the hold'; 'a round sticke fastned in the tacklings for skippers the better to climbe by'. The germs of all this are here in Lowestoft. In maritime, expansionist England, everyone was conscious of the sea, but few Elizabethan writers have it in their bones like Nashe. When he speaks of the sea the tempo of his language quickens. He calls it the 'roaring territory', the 'boiling desert', the 'rugged brine', the 'glassy fieldes of Thetis', the 'churlish frampold waves', the 'brackish suddes'.[18] In *Christs Teares over Ierusalem* (1593), a fraught Nashe puts these words into Christ's mouth:

Fooles be they that imagine it is the Windes that so tosse and turmoyle them in the deepe: they are no winds but insurrective sins which so possesse the waves with the spyrite of raging. I drowned all the sinnes of the first World in water: all the sinnes of the first World now welter, souse & beate unquietly in the Sea.[19]

In a moment of psychological crisis, the pamphleteer seems to trawl up some sunken childhood sensation of stormy waters and harrowing sermons.

Out of these fragments the infant Nashe pieced together his world. The people moving through the draughty vicarage and delapidated church, the farmyard and schoolhouse, the streets and shipyards of a small Elizabethan fishing-town, were the first trickle of performers in the great *comédie humaine* he would observe and anatomize with such gusto. The Nashes – albeit slightly sheltered by status and vestigial 'patrimonies' – lived the hard life of 'seaborderers', huddled between the 'roaring territory' of the North Sea and the flat, dreary inland marshes, 'imbristled' with reeds. The rhythms of the community – churchdays and holidays, christenings and funerals, seasons and tides, the mackerel fishing in the spring and the herring 'soon after Bartlemewe tyde' – were counterpointed by more intimate rhythms: before he was five Thomas had seen two sisters born, both christened Martha, both less than one year old when 'the soule bell towld them thence'.[20]

In 1573 the Nashes were on the move. The rectory of West Harling in Norfolk fell vacant that May, and on 8 October William Nashe was formally presented to the living by Bassingbourne and Anne Gawdy, lord and lady of the local manor. Margaret Nashe, pregnant again, remained awhile in Lowestoft, probably with the children. A daughter was born, christened Rebecca on 6 December. Sometime after this, perhaps in the early summer of 1574 when the danger of flooded roads was less, the family set off on the forty-mile journey to Harling: Mistress Nashe; her step-daughter Mary, nearly eleven; Israel, eight; Thomas, six; and the baby Rebecca. The road led along the narrow raised 'causey' between Lake Lothing and Oulton Fen, across the wooden bridge at Mutford built by Katherine Mayde, and out on the high road inland, through Beccles, Bungay and Diss.

The move from curate-in-charge to country rector was undoubtedly a step up for William Nashe and his family. From Domesday times the rector of West Harling was entitled to '*mansum cum xxvii acris terra*' – the rectory and glebe – and the living had been united with that of Middle Harling in 1457.[21] Today, All Saints', West Harling, is a pale, windswept little church, set on a grassy clearing among pine woods, and reached by unsigned tracks (Figure 3). In Nashe's day it was very different, for West Harling is one of those villages that have shrunk over the centuries. In Elizabethan times there were over a hundred communicants, by 1736 only seven houses and sixty inhabitants. Just east of the church stood Old Harling Hall, 'a fine old embattled stone building, moted round', built by the Berdewells in the mid-fifteenth century.[22] The memorial brasses of this ancient local family are there in the aisle of the church. Elizabeth Berdewell was a daughter of Edmund de Wychingham: perhaps a chance for Mistress Nashe, *née* Witchingham, to put on airs. The crest on William Berdewell's brass features a very priapic goat: adolescent Tom Nashe would spot the intrusion, no doubt with a giggle, perhaps also with an inkling of future obsessions. Only the foundations now remain of the old manor house. Also gone are the freestone spire and the separate South Chapel which the church boasted in Nashe's day, and the remarkable black poplar tree by the church gate, described as nearly 90 ft tall and some 15 yards 'about the root nigh the earth'. It was blown down about 1690.

The leet of West Harling belonged to Giltcross hundred and so both manor and church fell under the jurisdiction of the Howard family, Dukes of Norfolk. Two of William Nashe's recent predecessors at the rectory, Sir John and Sir Thomas Thompson, had been chaplains to the Duke. Even at this early stage we brush against this powerful, dramatic family, paramount among the English Catholic nobility: references to the Howards in some of Nashe's later writings have never been properly noticed. The Nashes arrived at a moment of great upheaval. Thomas Howard, the fourth Duke, had been executed in June 1572, attainted of high treason for his relations with Mary Queen of Scots. His father, Henry Howard, Earl of Surrey, and his aunt Catherine, Henry VIII's fifth queen, had also died on the scaffold. His teenage son, Philip, stripped of the Norfolk title, was shipped off to Audley End, Cambridgeshire. There, in 1574, he caused a minor scandal by attempting to seduce a fresh-faced country girl named Mercy Harvey – sister to none other than Nashe's great foe-to-be, Gabriel. Letters between 'Milord' and 'pore M' are still extant, transcribed by Gabriel, whose intervention apparently saved young Mercy's wavering virtue. Nashe got hold of the story, of course, and in *Have with you to Saffron-Walden* speaks of Harvey's 'baudy sister' and 'how shee is as good a fellow as ever turnd belly to belly'.[23]

Though tranquil when the grass is high and the sycamores in leaf, West Harling is a bleak, isolated spot. The East wind seethes through the trees, as if the sea itself were just the other side. A sense of threat and exposure percolates through to Nashe's adult writings about the countryside. In the country one is 'parched & broiled' in summer, 'quivering and quaking' in winter, 'all riveld and weather-beaten with the sharpe dryving shours'. The rains 'rough-enter through the crannies', the winds 'blow and batter', the child in bed hears 'roring and buffetting lullabies in stead of singing and dandling by-os'. Rural atmosphere is nocturnal, gothic, lurking: the 'Scritch-owle' with its 'lavish blabbing of forbidden secrets', the 'fearefull croking cry' of ravens that 'fluttred and clasht against the windowes', a 'dimme frostie circle' around the full moon, a 'dry rusty creeking' from the gate's 'hookes and gymmes'.[24] In works like *The Terrors of the Night* and *Christs Teares*, both written in 1593, Nashe reaches back to childhood fears for the dark, unsettling effects he wants. If 'in the dead of the night ... a dogge howle, we suppose we are transported into hell, where we heare the complaint of damned ghosts'; if 'wee bee troubled with too manie clothes, then we suppose the night mare rides us'.[25] One guesses a parallel in his mind between gloomy, haunted Conington (where the *Terrors of the Night* was written) and the windswept old rectory of his boyhood.

In sensing 'the country' as mainly a matter of discomfort, confinement and perils real or imagined, Nashe was no more than typical of his time. To write about the natural world the Elizabethan author tended to reach for his Pliny or his *Euphues*, rather than venture out into the actual countryside. He used landscape, packaged it for melodic, aphoristic, heraldic or symbolic uses, peopled it with arcadian swains and comic yokels. Only Shakespeare seems to give us rural England as it actually hit the eye – 'low farms, poor pelting villages, sheep-cotes and mills' ... 'the fold stands empty in the drowned field' ... 'light thickens and the crow makes wing to the rooky wood'.[26] Nashe detested the pastoral mode – 'Pan sitting in his bower of delights' tuning 'his miserable hornepipes'[27] – but not out of any contrary urge to landscape realism. His finest essay in purely descriptive prose offers a guided tour of the streets of Great Yarmouth. His longest single descriptive piece concerns an *artificial* garden in Renaissance Italy.[28] There are occasional glimpses of real country in his play, *Summers Last Will and Testament*, as in this robust description of winter:

> He over-bars the christall streames with yce,
> That none but he and his may drinke of them;
> All for a fowle Back-winter he layes up;
> Hard craggie wayes and uncouth slippery paths
> He frames ...[29]

But even here the prime effect is not visual, rather a sense of the inconvenience of winter. Throughout *Summers Last Will*, the personification of the seasons draws us away from their rural realities. Harvest's description of a poor crop is typical:

My oates grew like a cup of beere that makes the brewer rich: my rye like a Cavalier that weares a huge feather in his cap, but hath no

courage in his heart . . . ; my barley, even as many a novice is crosse-
bitten as soone as ever hee peepes out of the shell, so it was frost-
bitten in the blade.[30]

The urban similes – watered-down beer, cowardly cavaliers and gulled
greenhorns – are what come across, not the ancient imperatives of
harvest. This is deliberate – Nashe is giving a flighty modern twist to a
genre that looks clear back to vegetation rituals – but it is also telling
about his instinctive responses and preferences.

It tells us, in fact, where to look for country life in Nashe: not in
sensitivity to landscape, nor in the decoratively bucolic, but where one
always finds Nashe at his best – in his dealings with people. What come
out of his pamphlets are vivid particular glimpses of rural life and labour:
a saddler 'knocking in of tackes, iarring on them quaveringly with his
hammer a great while together'; reapers that 'run on the score with
Georges wife for their posset'; a 'countrie huswives banskin, which she
thirles hir spindle on'; masons using animal hair 'to mixe their lyme'; a
grindstone scouring a knife 'bright as the firmament'; the rough edges
of cool-staves and dung-forks, mattocks and adzes; the makeshifts of
poverty using a 'canker-eaten scull' for a chamber-pot; the meagre chewy
diet of 'sheepes trotters, porknells and butterd rootes' or 'wythred scal-
lions and greene cheese' or 'hedge wine and leane mutton'.[31] Above all
one senses his relish for the stories, superstitions and intuitive lore of
the countryside. Almost the only explicitly autobiographical recollection
of his rural childhood is this from the *Terrors*:

I have heard aged mumping beldams as they sat warming their knees
over a coale scratch over the argument verie curiously, and they would
bid yong folks beware on what day they par'd their nayles, tell what
luck everie one should have by the day of the weeke he was borne
on, show how many yeares a man should live by the number of
wrinkles on his forehead, and stand descanting not a litle of the
difference in fortune when they are turnd upward, and when they are
bent downward; him that had a wart on his chin, they would
confidently assertaine he should have no need of anie of his kin:
marry, they would likewise distinguish betweene the standing of the
wart on the right side and on the left. When I was a little childe, I
was a great auditor of theirs, and had all their witchcrafts at my
fingers endes, as perfit as good morrow and good even.[32]

These old cunning-women and their superstitions have an authenticity
which his knowing scepticism does not try to disguise. He remembers
the murky little firelit room, the shivers down his spine. There is local
material too in *An Almond for a Parrat*, where he spices his anti-

Martinist polemic with gobbets of gossip about East Anglian puritans: the vicar of Little Downham 'groaping his own hennes like a Cotqueane'; the Norwich cobbler who took the pulpit in St Andrew's when the preacher was late, and delivered 'a good thriftie exhortation in the praise of plaine dealing'; a 'woodcocke' at Great Yarmouth who preached that 'whosoever weares a vayle is an whore without exception'. Next

> I cut over to Ipswitch: there is a Cowdresser there that I am sure will entertaine me if she be not dead, great Iane of Ipswitch they call her, one that hath been a tender mother to many a Martinist in her time, and hath a very good insight in a canne of strong wine. A good vertuous Matrone is she and a wise, having no fault but this, that she will be drunke once a day, and then she lyes her downe on her bedde, and cryes, O my God, my God, thou knowest I am drunke, and why I should offend thee, my God, by spuing thus, as I doe.[33]

As with the mumping beldams, one senses an attachment deeper than attitudes. Nashe lets the satirical point slip because there is a ribald humanity in the story that is better and funnier. He does not disapprove of Great Jane any more than Shakespeare does of Falstaff.

Nashe lived at West Harling, presumably, from the age of six until he went up to Cambridge in late 1581, aged about fourteen. What comes out of these formative years is the sense of a boy fastening onto the shapes and textures of human life. Perhaps this appetite for people and their oddities, so marked in his adult writings, is partly a compensation, a product of the flat open countryside he grew up in – sea, marsh, wind and sky, the 'dull Northernly drosse of our clime', the whole agoraphobic experience of East Anglia. He crowds his pamphlets with life and activity, distinctions and edges. His interest in people is almost compulsive, a psychological mechanism geared up too high. In this sense the pamphleteer took shape not in Cambridge or London, but in lonely Harling, with his child's eye ranging round the big blank landscape for something to grab hold of.

So much for the first stages of Nashe's 'sentimental education'. What of more formal education, which must have occupied most of his time at Harling? Of his schooling we know nothing: it is probable he was largely taught by his father. Before the family left Lowestoft, young Thomas would have learned his 'hornbook', 'absey book' and 'primer', either at home or at the 'petty school' attached to Annot's Free School near St Margaret's. By the age of six or so, a child was expected to have the rudiments of the three r's – or *prosodia*, *orthographia* and *numeratio*, in the pedagogic parlance of the day – and so to be ready for grammar school proper.[34] It was just at this age that Thomas came with his family to West Harling. Their nearest town was Thetford, and while there was a flourishing new grammar school there, founded in 1566 by Sir Richard Fulmerston, it is unlikely that a young boy would be expected to trudge across seven miles of windswept heath to attend a school day that began at six in the morning. Nashe only mentions the town twice in his writings, once to call it 'ruinous and desolate' and once to recall the ranting 'tenne shillings Sermons' of a Puritan preacher there.[35] He would surely make more fuss of the place if he had been schooled there: compare his proud affection for Cambridge. In an area as isolated as Harling there was probably a village school. As rector, his father may well have served as local schoolmaster, and he may also have acted as tutor to Squire Gawdy's boys at the local manor – Bassingbourne junior, born in 1560, and his younger brother Philip.[36] The 'liber grammaticus' in the chancel of St Margaret's suggests he had done some teaching at Lowestoft, at least until the founding of Annot's School. Nashe *may* have described his father as a 'scholar' (the phrase in question is impossibly ambiguous)[37] and he certainly held strong beliefs that preachers should be scholars, learned alike in scripture and rhetoric. 'Dull-headed divines' and their 'balde Sermons' are roundly abused:

> Nothing comes from theyr mouthes but grosse full-stomackt tauto-logy. They sweat, they blunder, they bounce & plunge in the Pulpit, but all is voyce and no substance. . . . Scripture peradventure they come of thicke and three-folde with, but it is so ugly daubed, plaistred and patcht on, so peevishly speckt & applyde, as if a Botcher (with a number of Satten and Velvette shreddes) should cloute and mend Leather-doublets & Cloth-breeches.[38]

Whatever the precise circumstances, one guesses that Nashe was a bright but mischievous schoolboy. His mock-biography of Gabriel Harvey conveys a sense of the aching mechanical boredom of the standard curriculum: learning to 'write a faire capitall Romane hand', toiling through '6000 books of the Arte of Grammer', learning to 'parse and construe' and compose Latin verses, and generally feeling there was something better to do with one's youth than 'pick quarrells with old Gulielmus Lillies *Sintaxis* and *Prosodia* everie howre of the daye'. Nashe portrays the schoolmaster as a petty tyrant with 'a rodde in his hand for his scepter and horne-booke Pigmeis for his subiects'. He thinks of 'a boy new breetcht, who leapes and daunceth for ioy his pain is past', until his master 'seeing him so iocund and pleasant, comes and dooes as much for him againe, whereby his hell is renued'. He sees also a comic, parochial figure, who 'bites the lip, and winkes and smiles privily, and lookes pertly upon it' while his star-pupil makes 'an oration before a countrey Maior'.[39] Will Summers' virtuoso speech in praise of truancy in *Summers Last Will* perhaps contains an authentic glimpse of the schoolboy Nashe:

> Out upon it, who would be a Scholler? Not I, I promise you: my minde alwayes gave me this learning was such a filthy thing, which made me hate it so as I did: when I should have beene at schoole, construing *Batte, mi fili, mi fili, mi Batte*, I was close under a hedge, or under a barne wall, playing at spanne Counter, or Iacke in a box. . . . O, in what a mightie vaine am I now against Horne-bookes! Here, before all this companie, I professe my selfe an open enemy to Inke and paper. Ile make it good upon the Accidence body, that In Speech is the divels Pater noster: Nownes and Pronounes, I pronounce you as traitors to boyes buttockes: Syntaxis and Prosodia, you are tormenters of wit, & good for nothing but to get a schoole-master two pence a weeke. Hang copies; flye out, phrase books; let pennes be turnd to picktooths: bowles, cards & dice, you are the true liberal sciences; Ile ne're be Goosequil, gentlemen, while I live.[40]

This should not be taken too literally – it is a scholar's set-piece against scholarship – but it is hard to resist hearing echoes of hookey-playing Tom Nashe of Harling.

The clever country-boy became, at any rate, a scholar of sorts, one of the Bohemian 'university wits', a 'scholler and a good-fellow'. He was a voracious reader, an Autolycan 'snapper up of unconsidered trifles'. His scholarship is eclectic, disordered, showy. He crammed his 'tables' and notebooks with scraps of classical knowledge, and he made full use of compendiums, collections and 'epitomes' – McKerrow speaks of his 'systematic gutting' of Agrippa's *De Incertitudine et Vanitate Scientiarum*.[41] Of *Pierce Penilesse* Harvey says that Nashe 'searched every corner of his Grammar-schoole witte, for his margine is as deepelie learned as *Fauste precor gelida*', referring to the line from Mantuan's *Eclogues* conned by every schoolboy.[42] This is fair enough criticism: Harvey himself was genuinely and deeply learned, Nashe more an enthusiast than an academic. Like all educated Elizabethans Nashe loved and revered the classics, Latin more than Greek in these humanist days. His favourite was Ovid – over a hundred quotations appear in his works – and this he would certainly have read at school, if not the more *risqué Amores* and *Ars Amatoria* which he particularly enjoyed.[43] School would also have given him his first taste of Horace's *Epistles*, the comedies of Terence and Plautus, the rhetoric of Cicero: all grist to his stylistic mill. He would spice this with plenty of extra-curricular reading down the trashy, ephemeral end of the market: ballads, romances and prophecies.

Scarce nine yeres of age he attaind too, when, by engrossing al ballets that came to anie Market or Faire there-abouts, he aspired to bee as desperate a ballet-maker as the best of them.

'He' there is Harvey, but the cap fits Nashe well enough. So, perhaps, does his description of Harvey as a 'litigious' boy, 'a desperate stabber with pen-knives, and whom he could not overcome in disputation, he would be sure to break his head with his pen and ink-horne'.[44] On this temperamental note we leave Nashe's 'Grammer yeares' and imagine him 'rotten ripe for the Universitie'.

3

CAMBRIDGE

'At the Universitie of Cambridge, I light amongst wags as lewd as my
selfe, with whom I consumed the flower of my youth'

ROBERT GREENE   *The Repentance*

According to the University register (Document 3) Thomas Nashe matriculated as a sizar scholar of St John's College on 13 October 1582.
Other evidence makes it clear that he had been in residence for a term
or two before this: he probably came up in the winter of 1581–2, soon
after his fourteenth birthday.[1] A sizar was a poorer student who did
menial tasks – 'bed-making, chamber-sweeping and water-fetching' by
one account, also serving at table – in return for free 'sizes' or rations
from the college buttery. University life for the less well-off was hard:
in 1580 two Oxford students were found wandering the country with
a forged beggar's licence to 'get moneye . . . for their better exhibition'.
Nashe speaks of hungry students that 'capt and kneed' the college butler
for 'a chipping' (a crust of bread).[2] In *The Blacke Booke* (1604), Thomas
Middleton gives a brief impression of Nashe as undergraduate:

> Pierce-pennelesse, exceeding poore Scholler, that hath made cleane
> shooes in both Universities, and bene a pittifull Batler all thy life time,
> full often heard with this lamentable cry at the Buttry-hatch: Ho
> Lancelot, a Cewe of bread and a Cewe of beere; never passing beyond
> the confines of a farthing, nor once munching commons, but onely
> upon Gaudy dayes.[3]

As well as a meagre 'philosophycall diet', the student had to put up with
crowded makeshift lodgings. When Marlowe came up to Corpus Christi
in December 1580, he was chambered with three other scholars in a
converted store-room.[4] The old 'prizing books' of St John's give a
detailed account of accommodation there. Undergraduates lived three
or four to a 'set', under the eye and tutelage of a college fellow. Each
set had a communal bedchamber, a central 'keeping room' and a number
of tiny, partitioned-off studies. The fellow slept in the high bed, students
in 'truckle' or 'trundle' beds, often two or more sharing a bed. A typical
study was fitted out with 'a table lock & key, 5 shelves & a little hanging

23

deske, a little board to sit upon, with an iron casement'.[5] One is reminded of John Donne's claustrophobic cell as a law student at Lincoln's Inn:

> . . . in this standing woodden chest,
> Consorted with these few bookes, let me lye
> In prison, and here be coffin'd when I dye.[6]

It was a frugal, intimate, cloistered life. To 'keep term' the scholar had to attend college all but twenty days in a year. Apart from going to the 'Schools' or to church, he could only leave the college twice a week, and then never alone and never entering a townsman's house. It was a strictly male society: even the laundresses had to collect and deposit their washing outside the college gate. Discipline was hard – whippings, fines, bread and water, reading the bible in Hall: the college accounts mention 20s 'allowed to Mr Bayley for his punishments the last yeare'.[7] The daily academic routine was spartan. A typical day began at dawn, with the 'foure of the clocke bell' tolling; an hour later compulsory chapel, then into the public Schools for lectures and disputations in rhetoric, logic, dialectics or philosophy. The first proper meal was at 10 a.m., the standard fare being a farthingworth of beef and some 'porage' made of beef-broth and oatmeal; after that more work, more chapel, some time off. Supper was at five o'clock, after which it was the 'Colledge fashion' to read a 'chapter' of disputation, a vestige of the monastic *capitulum*. The college gates shut at 8 p.m. In the winter, chill and damp prevailed: 'the rheume' – catarrh – 'is the student's disease', says Nashe. When the college coalhouse was empty the scholars would 'runne up and downe halfe an houre, to gette a heate on their feete when they go to bed'.[8]

This – not to mention the freshman's ordeals of 'salting' and 'tucking'[9] – was the austere scholastic world which greeted the fourteen-year-old Nashe. For all that, Cambridge was undoubtedly the prestige university of the day. It was the seat of Tudor humanism, the intellectual bastion of the English Reformation: Protestant archbishops from Cranmer to Bancroft were Cambridge men, as were political supremos like Burghley, Walsingham, Gresham and the Bacons. And within Cambridge, St John's was still considered the pre-eminent college. Its hey-day had been the mid-sixteenth century, when it boasted scholars like Roger Ascham, Sir John Cheke, Dr John Dee and William Grindal. At that time, enthused Nashe,

> that most famous and fortunate Nurse of all learning, Saint Iohns in Cambridge, . . . was as an University within it selfe, shining so farre above all other houses, halles and hospitals whatsoever, that no Colledge in the Towne was able to compare with the tithe of her Students.[10]

Nashe never spoke of 'thrice fruitful S. Iohns' and the great minds 'nurst at thy paps' without affection and pride, yet he felt bound to contrast that *belle époque* with the current state of the college in the 1580s. 'How ill their precepts have prospered with our idle age', he wrote, especially complaining of 'the doting practice of our Divinitie Dunces, that strive to make their pupills pulpit-men before they are reconciled to Priscian'. His complaint is just: with a chronic shortage of educated ministers after the Reformation, the government regarded the universities as clerical breeding-grounds. This policy, Nashe argued, impoverished both university and ministry, filling the one with 'young hypocrites' and the other with 'cow-baby-bawlers and heavy-gated lumberers'. He was probably intended for holy orders himself, but soon found the theological atmosphere unbearably oppressive:

> Our Fathers are now growne to such austeritie, as they would have us straite of chyldren to become old-men. They will allowe no time for a gray bearde to grow in. If at the first peeping out of the shell a young Student sets not a grave face on it, or seemes not mortifiedly religious, (have he never so good a witte, be hee never so fine a Scholler,) he is cast of and discouraged.[11]

Closely associated with this, in Nashe's mind at least, was the predominance of the Puritan party at Cambridge. The great architects of Puritanism, Cartwright and Travers, had been ejected from the university in the 1570s, but the movement remained strong. Among Nashe's student contemporaries was the Welshman John Penry, who brought Puritan agitation to fever-pitch in 1588–9 with the brilliant 'Martin Marprelate' campaign (it was Nashe who first publicly identified Penry as 'Martin', in the *Almond for a Parrat*).[12] Despite the efforts of Drs Still and Howland – Masters of St John's, 1574–7 and 1577–87 – the college remained a hot-bed of faction. Cartwright himself had studied at John's, and fellows like Hugh Broughton, John Knewstub and Henry Alvey continued the tradition – any of these might be the 'good old fellow' of St John's twitted by Nashe in the *Almond*.[13] Cambridge may not have been Nashe's first taste of Puritanism – his native East Anglia was full of it – but it was where his attitude hardened into abhorrence.

Nor, probably, did Nashe sustain much pleasure in the official academic curriculum. The freshman's first year was mainly spent in the study of rhetoric. This, he complained, meant little more than the mechanical aping of Cicero – 'they count him excellent eloquent, who stealeth not whole phrases but whole pages out of Tully'; they have 'no invention or matter' of their own, but 'tack up a stile of his stale galymafries'. He recalls the dull, arid lectures, the 'humming and hawking' of a fidgety audience. Richard Harvey – at whose lectures Nashe 'purg'd rheume many a time' – read the Philosophy Lecture 'verie lentenlie and scantlie':

> Credite mee, any that hath but a little refuse *Colloquium* Latine, to interseame a Lecture with, and can saie but *Quapropter vos mei auditores*, may reade with equivalent commendation and liking.[14]

In logic the fashion was all for Ramus. The Ramist critique of Aristotle essentially questioned the whole scholastic base of university education. To many, Nashe included, the 'raylings of Ramus' went arm in arm with Puritanism.[15] A French Calvinist, Ramus had died in the St Bartholomew's Day slaughter of 1572. Marlowe's *Massacre at Paris* (*c.* 1590) has him murdered onstage, the 'flat dichotomist' who scoffed at the Aristotelean *Organon* and 'said it was a heap of vanities'. Ramus protests he only cut out the confusions, 'reduc'd it into better form'.[16] This sums up the controversy well enough.

In *The Unfortunate Traveller* (1594) Nashe gives a long comic description of a 'solemne scholasticall entertainment' at Wittenberg University. This is doubtless a satiric reflection of academic pomp and circumstance at Cambridge – it was instantly suspected as such, and Nashe's pious denial cuts little ice.[17] The occasion is a visit by the 'chief Patrone' of the university. First

> the heads of their universitie (they were great heads of certaintie) met him in their hooded hypocrisie and doctorly accoustrements, *secundum formam statuti*; where by the orator of the universitie, whose pickerdevant was verie plentifully besprinkled with rose water, a very learned or rather ruthfull oration was delivered (for it raind all the while). . . . A thousand *quemadmodums* and *quapropters* he came over him with; every sentence he concluded with *Esse posse videatur*; through all the nine worthies he ran with praising and comparing him . . . and with that crowe troden verse in Virgil, *Dum iuga montis aper*, hee packt up his pipes and cride *dixi*.

No sooner was this finished but

> there rusht upon him a miserable rablement of iunior graduats, that all cride uppon him mightily in their gibrige, lyke a companie of beggers, God save your grace, God save your grace, Iesus preserve your Highnesse, though it be but for an houre. Some three halfe penyworthe of Latine here also had he throwen at his face, but it was choise stuffe I can tell you.

Next came the 'burgers and dunsticall incorporationers' of the town, and a speech from their 'bursten belly inkhorne orator', a man with 'a sulpherous big swolne large face' and 'eyes lyke two Kentish oysters'. The following day there were 'solempne disputations', a tedious 'traine of opponents & respondents' minutely caricatured – one 'peckt with his forefinger at everie halfe sillable', another would 'twine up his mustachios twice or thrice over while they might have leasure to applaud him', a third 'waverd & wagled his head like a proud horse', another 'spread his armes like an usher' and 'thript with his finger and his thumbe when he thought he had tickled it with a conclusion', and so on. Behind it all is some dismal, rainy ceremonial at Cambridge, and a smirking student keenly attentive for the sole reason that 'their outwarde iestures would now and then afford a man a morsel of mirth'.

Cambridge was not all spartan regime, clerical dispute and academic fustian. The perennial bumptiousness of the student seems, in fact, to have risen to the occasion. In 1577 William Harrison spoke grimly of a growing spirit of licence, of students that 'ruffle and roist it out, exceeding in apparel and bantling riotous companie which draweth them from their bookes'. In 1578 the authorities feared that far from 'professyng to godlines, modesty, vertue and learning', the university was becoming a 'storehouse' for 'prodigall, wastfull, ryotous, unlerned, and insufficient persons'. Gowns were cast off in favour of velvets, silks, 'excessive ruffs', 'hoses of unsemely greatnes'. We hear of swearing, dicing, drinking, 'deformed long locks', spitting at 'holie exercises'.[18] Much of this was blamed on the rich *dilettante* element, who came to Cambridge as a matter of fashion, but a classic instance of this new flash and swagger is a young man of very middling origins, a saddler's son from Norwich named Robert Greene.[19] Nearly ten years older than Nashe, he also began as a sizar of St John's, but after his BA in 1579 he migrated downriver to Clare Hall. At Cambridge – according to his own sensationalist *Repentance* (1592) – he fell in with 'wags' and 'braggarts' and 'boon companions', young spendthrifts that 'practizd sundry superficiall studies'.[20] Setting aside his books, he travelled to Italy and Spain, where he learned 'all the villainies under heaven'. In 1580 he began his promiscuous literary career with *Mamillia*, a 'Looking-Glasse for the Ladies of England', closely modelled on John Lyly's *Euphues*. By the time Nashe came up, Greene was back at Cambridge – the second part of *Mamillia* (1583) is signed 'from my studie at Clare-hall'. 'At my return,' he says, 'I ruffeled out in my silkes, in the habit of Malcontent, and seemed so discontent that no place would please me to abide in.' He proceeded MA in 1583: his title-pages never fail to boast the fact. There is no proof Nashe actually knew him at Cambridge, though their close friendship in

London in the later 1580s makes it likely. Either way, the maverick Greene offered Nashe a model – the scholar as entertainer and wit, *homme du monde* rather than 'dromidote ergonist'.

Nashe was not especially one for silks and ruffs, but he was doubtless part of the wilder percentage of students. Richard Lichfield, barber-surgeon at Trinity College, gives a censorious account of Nashe's Cambridge career. He says that 'being distracted of his wits', Nashe 'fell into divers misdemeanors', and that in his 'fresh-time' he 'florished in all impudencie toward Schollers, and abuse to the Townsmen; insomuch that to this daye the Townes-men call everie untoward Scholler of whome there is great hope, *a verie Nashe*'.[21] This should not be taken unequivocally – Lichfield is probably punning on the dialect word 'nash', an impertinence, hence 'nash-gab', a 'pert and gossiping person' – but the general picture of waywardness, of kicking against the proprieties, is plausible. Nashe tasted freedom at Cambridge: he got his education *extra curriculum*, in the 'sundry superficiall studies' practised among Greene's set rather than the dour dialectics of Ramus. The Cambridge he cherished in later life was 'an excellent honourable assembly of sharpe iudiciall fierie wits and fine spirites'. He might remember one or two academics with respect – 'mellifluous' Thomas Playfere and 'eloquent' Eleazar Knox, both college fellows – and praise contemporary John's men like George Meriton as 'rare yong men' destined for academic eminence, but it was not in the lecture-halls or 'solempne' ceremonials that he found the fiery heart of university life.[22] An exception to this is perhaps the colourful figure of Everard Digby, senior fellow of St John's, who combined august philosophical studies like the *Theoria Analytica* (1579) with a flagrantly indecorous lifestyle. 'During the time of a sermon and communion he went about fishing openly in the back-side [i.e. on the 'backs'] with a casting-net', he would 'blow a horn and halloa after it' in the college court, and he 'threatened openly to set the president in the stocks in the hearing of the scholars'. Digby was deprived of his fellowship in 1587, nominally for failing to settle college debts. He was also accused of Catholic leanings, though the only real evidence of these is his open hostility towards the Puritan faction in the college (and towards Ramism: he published two refutations of Ramus in 1580).[23] It is interesting to find, in the context of Cambridge in the 1580s, the anti-Puritan equated with the pro-Catholic. This equation has, I hope to show later, a bearing on Nashe himself. There was certainly a strong Catholic presence at Cambridge – in 1583 the English seminary at Rheims was receiving disaffected students from Oxford and Cambridge at the rate of about twelve a month.[24] Unlike the vociferous Puritans, the Catholics were a silent underground presence, forced by various regulations into apparent conformity. The poet Henry Constable was probably still at St John's when Nashe arrived: he left in the early

1580s, openly converted to Catholicism and lived most of his life in France.[25] His *Spiritual Sonnets*, unpublished till the nineteenth century, catch the rich, heated tones of Elizabethan recusancy. So, in more knotted and bitter mood, do the early verse-satires of John Donne, another young Catholic and budding poet who studied at Cambridge later in the 1580s, though not formally affiliated to any college.[26] Among the more volatile and mutinous students the emotional appeal of Catholicism was strong, if only as the polar opposite to the 'plaine, simple, sullen, yong, contemptuous yet unhansome' Calvinism that predominated.[27]

Names like Greene, Constable and Donne suggest, in their different ways, the powerful literary stirrings at Cambridge in this decade. But the most explosively promising talent, and the one most closely contemporary with Nashe, was Christopher Marlowe. Born at Canterbury in February 1564 – so nearly four years older than Nashe – he was only a few terms senior at Cambridge. He came up to Corpus Christi in December 1580, matriculated in March 1581 and proceeded MA in 1587. Their friendship very probably began there, continuing later in literary London. Though there are hints of dispute between them in 1589,[28] there is no doubt they were close. Nashe invariably speaks of him with affection and, after his tragic death in 1593, with a keen sense of loss. In 1596, when things were at a low ebb for Nashe, he recalled 'poore deceased Kit Marlow' as among 'my frends that usde me like a frend'. In *Lenten Stuffe* he paid tribute to Marlowe's 'diviner Muse'.[29] His actual elegy on Marlowe – printed in certain copies of *Dido, Queene of Carthage* (1594) – is unfortunately lost, and with it, perhaps, details of their friendship. The title-page of *Dido* seems to credit Nashe as co-author of the play ('written by Christopher Marlowe and Thomas Nash, Gent'). The play is generally regarded as Marlowe's 'prentice-piece', penned at Cambridge. It may have been a student collaboration, perhaps for a college production – plays in English were performed, though Latin was more approved by the authorities – or it may only be that Nashe edited the play after Marlowe's death.[30] *Dido* is essentially a *virtuoso* exercise, a flexing of poetic muscle: Marlowe has taken that staple of the Elizabethan classroom, Virgil's *Aeneid*, and turned it into vibrant blank verse (compare the lumbering translations by Phaer and Stanyhurst then current). His sexual tastes – he reputedly claimed 'that all they that love not Tobacco and Boies were fooles'[31] – are suggested by the elegantly camp *tableau* which opens the play: 'Here the Curtaines draw; there is discovered Iupiter dandling Ganimed upon his knee'. Ganymede is Jupiter's 'sweete wagge', a 'female wanton boy' wheedling gifts out of his besotted old sugar-daddy:

I would have a iewell for mine eare,
And a fine brouch to put in my hat,
And then Ile hugge with you an hundred times.[32]

The cloistered male world of Cambridge helped to shape Marlowe's homosexuality, as did the theatre-world of London, with its pretty boy actors, 'ingles' for the players. As well as *Dido*, Marlowe's student writings include lengthy verse-translations from Ovid's *Elegies* (known as the *Amores*) and Lucan's *Pharsalia*. Nashe knew the former in manuscript: he quotes from it in *The Unfortunate Traveller*, written in 1593, and he was probably recalling the detumescent plight of the lover in Book III – 'It mocked me, hung down the heade, and suncke' – when he wrote his *Choise of Valentines*.[33] The *Amores* was the favourite *risqué* reading of cultured young Elizabethans: Marlowe was making a shrewd bid for popularity, a name for naughtiness, in Cambridge circles. He also translated Colonthus' *Helenae Raptus*, now lost. The poetry is extraordinary – his *Amores* looks forward to the 'enamelled perfection' of *Hero and Leander*, his *Pharsalia* to the 'barbaric splendour' of *Tamburlaine*[34] – and must have made an immediate impact on all who read it. None of the big names of the 1580s – Spenser, Sidney, Watson – could touch its best moments.

Already Marlowe's reputation was double-edged: a brilliant young poet with a 'wanton muse', a tinge of ambiguity and corruption. It is not only his early writings that suggest this. Nashe perhaps knew, as we do not, the full story behind Marlowe's MA degree in 1587, and why the university authorities at first refused to grant it, and were then forced to reverse their decision by express command of the Privy Council, which informed them that Marlowe had 'done her Majestie good service' and had been working for 'the benefitt of his Countrie' in certain secret 'affaires'. The Council minutes shed some light on this extraordinary intervention:

> Whereas it was reported that Christopher Morley was determined to have gone beyond the seas to Reames and there to remaine, their Lds [i.e. lordships] thought good to certefie that he had no such intent but that in all his accons he had behauved him selfe orderlie and discreetelie . . . Their Lds request was that the rumor thereof should be allaied by all possible meanes, and that he should be furtherd in the degree he was to take this next Commencement.[35]

It seems clear that Marlowe had been moving in Catholic circles in Cambridge, posing as a would-be emigrant to Cardinal Allen's seminary at Rheims, while in reality feeding back information to the government. When the university authorities swallowed his 'cover', withholding his degree in the belief that he really was a disaffected young Papist, the Council was forced to intervene, partly for Marlowe's sake but mainly to protect its operation. Government interest in the Jesuits' recruitment network had been sharpened by the Babington plot of the previous year, spearheaded by John Ballard, himself a Cambridge man who had defected to Rheims in 1581. This is not the last time that Marlowe was mixed up in shady government work: it is probable he was 'run' by Thomas Walsingham, who in turn reported to his older cousin, Sir Francis Walsingham, spy-master general. Marlowe was openly in Thomas Walsingham's service in the 1590s; his friend, the poet and translator Thomas Watson, who also had ambiguous Catholic connections, was another of Walsingham's *protégés*.[36] It is even possible that Marlowe was playing a double game, that his sympathies really did lie with the Catholics. Among the 'monstrous opinions' attributed to him by the government informer Richard Baines were 'that if there be any God or any good Religion, then it is in the Papistes, because the service of God is performed with more Cerimonies', and, more bluntly, 'that all protestantes are Hypocriticall asses'.[37] We shall never know the truth, because the spy's real face is just another mask.

This is the Marlowe Nashe knew at Cambridge: *poète maudit*, apparent Catholic extremist, undercover agent. He stares out with a quizzical, chilly gaze from the Corpus Christi portrait (Figure 4), painted in 1585, when he was 21. He has thick auburn hair, a pale, sardonic, thinly-bearded face. He wears a stylish doublet, black 'slashed' with orange, and a lace-trimmed collar. There is a touch of *mignon* sexuality in the rouged lips, not quite smiling. The Virgilian motto beside him is apt: '*Quod me nutrit me destruit*' – that which feeds me also destroys me.

No less notorious than Greene and Marlowe, though a very different kettle of controversy, were the three brothers Harvey, on whom Nashe was to spend, perhaps waste, so much energy in years to come. Gabriel, born in about 1550, was the eldest of this brood, sons of a prosperous rope-maker of Saffron Walden, Essex – the 'Hs of Hempe Hall', Nashe calls them.[38] He had been at Cambridge since the year before Nashe was born, first as a student at Christ's, then as a fellow of Pembroke Hall, and most illustriously as University Praelector in Rhetoric for three years running, 1574–6, two of his inaugural lectures being published in 1577 (*Ciceronianus* and *Rhetor*). In 1578 he took up a new fellowship at Trinity Hall and began to study Civil Law. He was then at the height of his prowess, a brilliant scholar apparently destined for academic, perhaps political, greatness. He was presented to the Queen at Audley End and commemorated the event with a volume of Latin hexameters.[39] He had a powerful patron in the Earl of Leicester and he counted among his friends Sidney, Spenser, Edward Dyer and Daniel Rogers. It is typical of his bent for self-advertisement that as soon as Spenser made his mark, with the *Shepheards Calendar* (1579), Harvey rushed out two editions of 'wittie familiar letters' between Spenser and himself.[40]

By the time Nashe arrived in late 1581, Harvey's star was beginning to fade, his huge intellectual powers more and more smothered by florid showmanship and overbearing conceit. In 1581 he failed, after much unseemly wrangling, to obtain the coveted post of Public Orator. During the campaign, he found himself 'miserably flouted' in a satirical college comedy called *Pedantius*, written by (or on behalf of) his rival, Anthony Wingfield. Nashe was not yet at Cambridge when it was first performed, at Trinity College on 6 February 1581, but he seems to have seen it later, delighting at Harvey 'full drawen & delineated' as the 'concise and firking finicaldo fine School-master':

> The iust manner of his phrase in his Orations and Disputations they stufft his mouth with, & no Buffianisme throughout his whole bookes but they bolsterd out his part with. . . . Not the carrying up of his gowne, his nice gate on his pantoffles, or the affected accent of his speach, but they personated. And if I should reveale all, I thinke they borrowd his gowne to playe the Part in, the more to flout him.[41]

News of a new university butt quickly travelled to Oxford: a student there penned a lampoon in his 'commonplace book', calling Harvey the 'Omnipotent Orator, famous Rhetorician Archpott' whose 'front' (face) shines brighter 'then a brasspott'.[42] Much of the material Nashe later used against Harvey he picked up in his early undergraduate days: 'there be them in Cambridge that had occasion to take note of it', he says of Harvey's behaviour before the Queen at Audley End, 'for he stood noted or scoard for it in their bookes manie a faire day after'.[43] Nashe's marvellous account of Harvey 'revelling & domineering at Audley-ende' gives us Gabriel at his most posturing and vain. He came 'ruffling it out, huffty tuffty, in his suite of velvet' and 'thrust himselfe into the thickest rankes of the Noblemen and Gallants'. He delivered an oration before the royal Maids of Honour, embarrassing all with its blend of 'maidenly scoffing', 'rude ruffianisme' and 'finicall complement'. He was permitted to kiss the Queen's hand, and she remarked on his swarthy good looks, saying he looked like an Italian.

> No other incitement he needed to rouze his plumes, pricke up his ears, and run away with the bridle betwixt his teeth. . . . Now he was an insulting Monarch above Monarcha, the Italian that ware crownes on his shooes; and quite renounst his naturall English accents & gestures, & wrested himselfe wholy to the Italian *puntilios*, speaking

our homely Iland tongue strangely, as if he were but a raw practitioner in it.[44]

This is extreme caricature, but its essential truth can be gauged from Harvey's own Latin preenings on the occasion, *De Osculo* ('The Kiss') and *De Vultu Itali* ('The Italian Face'). Nashe joins the factual with the burlesque almost seamlessly. It is true, for instance, that Leicester dispensed with Harvey's services in about 1580 '& sent for another Secretarie to Oxford' (Arthur Atey), but not necessarily true that it was because Harvey had appeared at court 'in all the coulours of the raine-bow, and a paire of moustachies like a black horse tayle tyde up in a knot'.[45] Other bits of Cambridge Harveiana gathered by Nashe have the same kind of truth-in-jest. 'A scoffe which longer dwelt with him than the rest', we learn,

> was that once he would needs defend a Rat to be *Animal rationale* . . . because she eate and gnawd his bookes, and, except she carried a braine with her, she could never digest or be so capable of learning. And the more to confirme it, . . . the next rat he seazd on hee made an Anatomie of, and read a lecture of 3 dayes long upon everie artire or mussckle in her, and after hangd her over his head in his studie, in stead of an Apothecaries Crocodile.[46]

We hear of Harvey the poetaster. His love for Mistress Widdowes, wife of the St John's college butler, was 'the first motive or caller foorth of Gabriels English Hexameters'; he wrote hexameters in praise of the yew tree at Trinity Hall and the weather-cock on All Hallows', even wrote home to his father in 'those ioulting Heroicks'; he wrote one hexameter with too many syllables, which a college wag sent back with a louse wrapped up in it, and a message saying 'This verse hath more feet than a lowse.' We hear of his poverty and college debts: he would 'cosen poore victuallers and pie-wives of Doctours cheese and puddinges' and abuse Jack at the Falcon Inn 'for that he would not lend him a messe of mustard to his red herrings'. We hear how he promenaded on Market Hill of an evening, 'holding his gowne up to his middle, that the wenches may see what a fine leg and a dainty foote he hath'. This is the Harvey of Cambridge folklore, an apocryphal elaboration of his real flaws. Also apocryphal, probably, is the woodcut portrait of Harvey in Nashe's *Have with you to Saffron-Walden* (Figure 5). Nashe claims it is a 'lively counterfet and portraiture', and the over-dressed, mustachioed figure looks 'huffty tuffty' enough. But Nashe is also suspiciously apologetic: the figure wears 'round hose' while Gabriel favoured 'Venetians'; he is 'plump and round' while Harvey was skinny, a mere 'lute pin put in a sute of apparell'. It seems probable that the portrait was not originally of Harvey, but that the printer, John Danter, had it to hand and Nashe considered it illustrative enough of 'his Gabrielship'.[47]

Through the 1580s, Harvey's university career slowly ran out of steam. He was elected Proctor in 1583 – a disciplinary role that would not have endeared him to the likes of Nashe – but in February 1585 he was out-manoeuvred for the Mastership of Trinity Hall. As Thomas Baker puts it, 'a flashy wit, a rambling Head & a factious spirit ruin'd his Interest here' and 'a man of a more peacable temper' was appointed. In a plaintive letter to Lord Burghley, chancellor of the university, Harvey says he feared 'even for very shame to shew my face in the Town'.[48] There was also some humiliating 'default' in doing his 'Doctors Actes' at Cambridge, and it was eventually at Oxford that he incepted as Doctor of Civil Law in July 1585. Nashe picks over this business in *Strange Newes*, but the details are unclear.[49] After this Harvey disappears from the limelight – part of the time practising civil law at the Court of Arches in London – until he bursts back on the scene in 1592, in public combat with Greene and Nashe.

If the Gabriel that Nashe first knew of at Cambridge was something of a has-been, a noted university 'character', his younger brother Richard was a more aggressive presence. As we shall see, it was Richard who actually started the whole Harvey-Nashe broil. Though less deeply learned than Gabriel, he also had a bright academic career. In 1581 he was elected fellow of Pembroke Hall, and in 1585 became University Praelector in Philosophy. He had early won a reputation as a violent partisan of Ramus – 'thou that hadst thy hood turnd over thy eares when thou wert a Batchelor, for abusing of Aristotle & setting him up on the Schoole gates, painted with Asses eares on his head'[50] – and in 1583 published his *Ephemeron* in praise of the Ramist 'reformed dialectic'. His other great passion was astrology. His *Astrologicall Discourse* appeared in January 1583, prophesying dire effects from an imminent 'conjunction' of Saturn and Jupiter. The fateful day (28 April) passed peacably, to Harvey's eternal embarrassment. As Nashe puts it, 'Saturne and Iupiter prov'd honester men than all the World tooke them for, whereupon the poore Prognosticator was ready to runne himselfe through with his Iacobs Staffe.' Harvey was denounced by Bishop Aylmer from the pulpit at Paul's Cross and refuted in learned works by the Earl of Northampton and the mathematician Thomas Heath. Elderton composed 'whole bundles of ballets' about him, and the great comic Tarlton 'made iests of him' at the Theatre in Shoreditch. At Cambridge, 'the whole Universitie hyst at him'.[51] Sometime later, apparently in 1586–7, a satirical 'shewe' was put on at Peterhouse – *Duns Furens*, or 'Dick Harvey in a frensie'. The title means 'the raging dunce', glancing at Duns Scotus, the great mediaeval critic of Aristotle. During its performance, Nashe claims, 'Dick came and broke the Colledge glasse

windowes', whereupon he was 'fetcht in and set in the Stockes till the
Shew was ended'.[52] He was a little man – Nashe calls him the 'Pigmie
Braggart', the 'pert Didimus', a 'demie divine, no higher than a Tailors
pressing iron' – but correspondingly ferocious. He was, says Nashe,
always 'in hate',

> either with Aristotle; or with the great Beare in the firmament, which
> he continually bayted; or with Religion, against which in the publique
> Schooles he set up Atheistical Questions.[53]

And the students cordially hated him back. Greene thought him 'a vaine
glorious asse' and, according to Nashe, 'Kit Marloe was wont to say
that he was an asse, good for nothing but to preach of the Iron Age.'[54]
   And then there was John, born in 1564 and now a student at Queens'
College. He too was a devotee of astrology, and published various
almanacs and prognostications in the 1580s. On the title-page of his
Astrological Addition (1583), he describes himself as a 'Student in Phisicke', and he did indeed go on to practise medicine at King's Lynn.
With the *Addition* he published his translation of *Iatromathematica* (or
'Phisical Mathematiques'), a text he ascribes to the legendary Egyptian
magus, Hermes Trismegistus. This must be one of the first English
versions of a Hermetic text. It is likely that John Harvey was an early
enthusiast of the new Hermetic medicine, or 'chymicall physick', of
Paracelsus – Gabriel too was fascinated by Paracelsus, and was a friend
of the chemist John Hester, chief translator of Paracelsist works.[55] The
Harveys were resolutely *avant-garde* in their intellectual enthusiasms. It
was their fiery young opponents who were the reactionaries: Nashe's
derision of astrology, alchemy, the whole fashionable interest in 'Renaissance magic', is a major plank in his anti-Harvey platform. John is the
shadowiest of the three Harveys, if only because his early death in July
1592 absented him from the actual Harvey-Nashe hostilities. Nashe half-
heartedly rakes up some Cambridge incidents – assignations with 'the
wenches in Queenes Colledge Lane', an altercation with one Wathe at
a Commencement dinner[56] – but John was mainly notorious by association. He received his due dose of satire in yet another college comedy,
this one performed at Clare Hall (Greene's college). Nashe records its
untranslatable title as *Tarrarantantara Turba Tumultuosa Trigonum,
Tri-Harveyorum, Tri-harmonia.*

Despite these manifold distractions, Nashe's academic career proceeded
smoothly enough. In 1584 he was officially enrolled as a scholar of the
Lady Margaret foundation.[57] His entry appears in the St John's admis-

sion books – 'Ego Thomas Nashe Suffolciensis admissus sum discipulus pro domina fundatrice' (Document 4). His handwriting – this is the earliest extant – has spikes and sharp angles suggestive of his disputatious temper, also a buoyancy in the way the line rises up against the falling one above. We see that Nashe had begun to write his entry on the line above and was checked after writing 'Ego T': the pen was handed to Master Coke of Derbyshire, perhaps a senior or richer student. A little moment of impatience, an elbowing forward, is frozen on the page. Another glimpse of Nashe's academic life is a collection of Latin verses penned in formal text-hand by eleven Lady Margaret scholars. These date from 1585; Nashe's is the ninth in the series (Document 5). The set theme is a verse from *Ecclesiasticus* (the apocryphal Book of Sirach) on the perils of peace and contentment – 'O death how bitter is the thought of you to the man content with his lot'. Its theme of smugness threatened seems not uncongenial to Nashe: the last couplet is somehow characteristic –

> Quos Arabi fortuna favet, quos copia Croesi,
>   hos mors pallenti perculit atra metu.
> (Those with the luck of the Arab and the wealth of Croesus,
>   even these black death strikes pale with fear.)

The Latin is polished, the calligraphy impressive. He graduated BA in March 1586.

In about 1586–7, Richard Lichfield tells us, Nashe

> had a hand in a Show called *Terminus & non Terminus*, for which his partener in it was expelled the Colledge: but this foresaid Nashe played in it (as I suppose) the Varlet of Clubs; which he acted with such naturall affection, that all the spectators tooke him to be the verie same.[58]

The performing of plays, revels and '*scenici ludi*' in the college halls and chapels was a vital part of university life. We have touched on the lampooning of the Harveys and the possibility that Marlowe's *Dido* began life on a college stage. Nashe undoubtedly saw Thomas Legge's Latin tragedy, *Richardus Tertius*, performed in the hall of St John's in about 1583 – he later recalled the 'codshead' who fluffed his only line in the play – and the *Persa* of Plautus given there that Christmas.[59] College plays were encouraged 'for the emboldening of their junior schollers' in oratorical arts: acting 'teacheth audacity to the bashfull grammarian'.[60] Productions were, if Nashe is to be believed, rudimentary. In the *Unfortunate Traveller* he describes a 'Comedie handled by scollers' being 'leathernly set forth'. The students 'stampingly trode the stage' and flung their arms 'lyke cudgels at a peare tree', in fact 'the onely thing they did well was the prodigall childs hunger, most of their schollers being hungerly kept'.[61] College plays were a chance to let off steam. Rowdy laughter warmed the long winter nights between Christmas and Shrovetide, when most of the shows went on. Dick Harvey's vandalism at Peterhouse was not unusual – windows, tables and benches were frequently broken, as the College accounts testify. Nothing is known of Nashe's *Terminus & non Terminus* beyond what Lichfield tells us. His account is plausible enough, though the bit about Nashe playing the 'Varlet of Clubs' is obviously an interpolation. The play was probably in Latin, and undoubtedly satirical. The title is puzzling, almost Beckettian: 'The End and Not the End'.[62] One wonders who Nashe's 'partener in it' was, presumably the main author as he and not Nashe was expelled for it. Could it possibly be Everard Digby, the mutinous fellow of St John's, who was indeed expelled in 1587?

In January 1587 Nashe's father died. He was buried at West Harling on the 24th of that month. It may have been sudden, for he died intestate: administration of his estate was granted to Margaret Nashe on 8 February at the Consistorial Court in Norwich.[63] Personal feelings aside, this was a severe blow to Nashe's university career. In the *Anatomie of Absurditie* he speaks bitterly of students 'withdrawne from theyr studies' while still 'raw', because of the death of their protector – 'where should they finde a friend to be unto them in steed of a father, or one to perfit that which their deceased parents begun?'[64] The *Anatomie* was written around this time, while 'idle in the Countrey' during a 'vacation', probably in summer 1587. It is a student piece through and through, clever, polished, shallow: he later shrugged it off as an 'Embrion' of his 'infancie'.[65] It is full of his dislike of Puritanism, Ramism, 'barbarisme', 'duncerie', and so on. It is stuffed with second-hand material from Erasmus' *Parabolae* and Agrippa's *De Incertitudine*, and much quoting of Ovid. Nashe had also been reading plenty of more popular, ephemeral literature – Lloyd's *Pilgrimage of Princes* (1573), Gosson's *Ephemerides of Phialo* (1579), Melbancke's *Philotimus* (1583), Greene's *Penelopes Web* (1587) and Doleta's *Strange Newes out of Calabria* (1587) are all used. The whole style is strongly 'euphuistic' – as Nashe says elsewhere, 'Euphues I readd when I was a little ape in Cambridge, and then I thought it was *Ipse ille*.'[66] The very title is calculatedly fashionable: Lyly subtitled *Euphues* an 'Anatomy of Wit', Greene's *Arbasto* (1584) was an 'Anatomie of Fortune', and there was Philip Stubbes' popular *Anatomie of Abuses* (1583). Nashe tilts at the latter, a Puritan invective, when he speaks of writers claiming 'to anatomize abuses and stubbe up sin by the rootes',[67] an early instance of his technique of identifying a target without naming him.

The last reference to Nashe at Cambridge is a list of students resident in 1588 (Document 6). Among the '*Auditores Philosophiae*' of St John's we find 'Do Nash' – Dominus Nashe – slated to attend philosophy lectures under Mr Rowly. Sometime in that year, however, probably in the summer, Nashe made the break. Lichfield says he 'forsooke Cambridge' for the 'higher Clime' of London when he was 'Batchelor of the third yere', in other words between March 1588 and March 1589. Nashe himself asserts that he 'took up his inn' at St John's for 'seven yere together lacking a quarter'. By 'quarter' he probably means 'term': a career running from late 1581 to summer 1588 would lack just the Michaelmas Term to make up seven years. As for his reasons for leaving, Lichfield claims it was for fear 'he should be staied for *egregie dunsus*, and not attain to the next Degree' (his MA). William Covell, writing in 1595, hints at some kind of expulsion, saying that Cambridge had been 'unkinde' to Nashe 'to weane him before his time'. Nashe, however, felt safe to boast: 'it is well knowen I might have been Fellow if I had would'.[68] The immediate truth was probably lack of money after his father's death, though this may only have sealed a mounting dissatisfaction with academic life. Greene was the literary lion of London; Marlowe had gone down in 1587 and caused a sensation with his *Tamburlaine the Great*, starring Edward Alleyn in the title-role.[69] The promise of 'Lady London', dreams of literary fame and fortune, were irresistible. Nashe packed his meagre baggage, his promising manuscript, and sallied forth. Marlowe's lines from Edward II catch the mood of nervy ambition – 'you must cast the scholler off, And learne to court it like a Gentleman'; no more 'black coate' faced with serge, no more 'holding of a napkin' and 'saying a long grace at a tables ende', no more 'smelling to a nosegay all the day'.

> You must be proud, bold, pleasant, resolute,
> And now and then stab as occasion serves.[70]

4

LONDON

'one vast, unwieldie and disorderlie Babel of buildings which the world
calls London . . .'

THOMAS MILLES *The Customers Alphabet*

On the high road from Cambridge to London in 1588, the traveller's
pulse began to race somewhere around Shoreditch. It was there, still a
mile north of the city gates, that he hit the outer rind of London's
notorious 'noysom and disorderly' suburbs. He passed St Leonard's
church – hearing perhaps how the vicar, one Hanmer, was melting down
the brasses to coin base silver[1] – and then the smithy at the crossroads.
Away to his right, above a huddle of houses, he could see the pennants
and thatched roofs of the Theatre and Curtain play-houses, and beyond
them the three windmills on Finsbury Fields. The road became a teeming
street. Where old men could remember fields and spacious priories –
Holywell and St Mary Spital – there was now 'continuall building of
small and base tenements', a tangle of 'poor cottages' and 'alleys backe-
ward', of 'stables, ins, alehowses, tavernes, garden houses converted
into dwellings, ordinaries, dicyng howses, bowling alleyes and brothel
houses'.[2] Amidst this ragged development could be glimpsed leafy, secretive gardens where the well-to-do had their 'summer houses for pleasure',
and then the green marshy stretch of Moorfields, haunt of washer-
women, prostitutes, beggars ('Zoons, methinks I see myself in Moorfields, upon a wooden leg, begging threepence'[3]), animals grazing,
archers at practice, fullers bringing cloth to the tenteryards, and anyone
whom business or pleasure brought to these 'liberties' beyond the civic
pale. Crossing the bars into Bishopsgate Street Without, hearing the
sound of gunfire from the Artillery Yard, the traveller passed on by the
gates of St Mary Bethlehem, the 'hospitall for distracted people' better
known as Bedlam, and at last found himself before Bishopsgate, there
to alight for lodging at the Dolphin, 'a common Inne for receipt of
travellers', or at the classier White Hart opposite, or to press on into
the great city itself.

These straggling suburbs of Shoreditch and Bishopsgate, the northern
'skirts and out-shifts' of London, were to be a familiar stamping-ground
for Nashe in his early days as a struggling young author. Official records
and such works as Stow's *Survay of London* (1598) paint these areas

as virtual ghettoes, riddled with plague, vice and crime. But they were also the Bohemian haunt, the *quartier latin* of Elizabethan London. In the streets around the Theatre and Curtain, London's first public play-houses, lived the theatrical crowd. James Burbage, who built the Theatre in 1576, and his son Richard, later Shakespeare's leading actor, lived on Holywell Street. In this same street, in the late summer of 1588, the great comic actor Dick Tarlton lay dying, nursed by 'one Em Ball', a Shoreditch woman 'of verye bad reputacion'.[4] Christopher Beeston, later Shakespeare's colleague in the Lord Chamberlain's troupe, lived on Hog Lane: Nashe's friend William Beeston, the 'pottle-pot Patron' of *Strange Newes*, was perhaps a kinsman. Another resident of Hog Lane was the hot-blooded Gabriel Spenser, the player who died on Hoxton Fields, run through with a rapier by Ben Jonson. Many years later, Christopher Beeston's son, still living in the area, told Aubrey that Shakespeare had 'lived in Shoreditch'[5] – he was probably there by 1588, a provincial player with a talent for knocking together blank verse. Where the player-folk gathered, so did the young writers of the day, some because drama was their vocation, others for merely commercial reasons. Our first sight of Marlowe in London comes one September afternoon in 1589, when he and his friend Thomas Watson were arrested on Hog Lane, after a brawl in which an innkeeper's son, William Bradley, was stabbed to death. They were hauled off to Newgate: the prison list refers to them both as *'nuper de Norton ffowlgate'* – lately resident in the liberty of Norton Folgate, just south of Shoreditch. Marlowe was released after a fortnight, though Tom Watson languished in 'the Stink' till February 1590. Marlowe had another brush with the local law in May 1592, this time on Holywell Street, where he was run in for threatening Constable Nicholls and Sub-constable Helliott, and bound over to keep the peace.[6] This is the volatile, half-delinquent world of the poets out in these shanty-town suburbs. Another of Marlowe's Shoreditch neighbours was the spy Robert Poley, whose sinister presence at Marlowe's death has never been fully explained.[7] Robert Greene, though known for his 'continuall shifting of lodgings' and 'beggerly departing in every hostisses debt', was another familiar figure in Shoreditch. He was a friend of Tarlton's and must also have known the Em Ball with whom the old clown lived his last days on Holywell Street. Greene's own girl was surnamed Ball. She was the sister of a thief nicknamed 'Cutting' Ball, who died at Tyburn, and she bore Greene's bastard son, Fortunatus. Harvey calls her a 'sorry ragged queane'. Fortunatus – little Lucky Greene – died a child in 1593 and was buried at St Leonard's, Shoreditch: his mother was then living on Holywell Street.[8] Perhaps she was a sister of Tarlton's Em, perhaps they were one and the same lady.

Thomas Nashe, like Greene, would be branded as a restless, shifty moonlight-flitter, 'so haunted with an earthquake, that in what house soever you are one daye, you are shaken out the next'. Richard Lichfield, pretending to search for him to present him with a copy of *The Trimming of Thomas Nashe*, complains:

> you (the Worlds Citizen) are heere and there, you may dine in this place, & goe supperlesse to bed, if you know where to have your bed: you maye bee in one prison to-day and in another to-morrow. . . . Of your owne you have not so much as one of Diogenes his poore cottages. . . . Now sir, for the uncertaintie of your mansion house, . . . my little Booke might kill three or four porters, that must run up and downe London to seeke you.[9]

For all Nashe's 'fleeting incorporeall substaunce', it is a fairly safe bet that in these early days he was to be found out in these same liberty alleys that lodged the likes of Greene, Marlowe, Watson, Shakespeare and Tarlton. 'Poore Scholers and souldiers', he complained, must 'wander in backe lanes and the out-shiftes of the Citie, with never a rag to their backes', while respectable folk never 'come neere the liberties by five leagues and above'.[10] His pamphlets contain many glimpses of life on the edge of the city – the cunning-man hanging out his 'rat-banners' over a cobbler's stall; the 'Aqua vitae sellers and stocking menders'; the sixpenny whores with faces 'sodden & perboyld with French surfets'; old Megge Curtis of Shoreditch for whom the pages of a pamphlet served 'to stop mustard pots with'; Mother Livers of Newington, the fortune-teller; the lecherous 'grosse-pencild Painter' who 'drawes more into his shady Pavilion then depart pure vestals'; the pleasure-seekers streaming across the fields to an afternoon play, a bout of 'bowzing and beere-bathing' or an assignation at 'the signe of the smock'; and in the same fields the plague-infected poor turned out to die, 'in . . . Finsbury & Moore-fieldes wyth myne owne eyes have I seene halfe a dozen of such lamentable out-casts'.[11]

Nashe must have been in London by July or August 1588, since he had time to get to know Dick Tarlton – he boasted in *Strange Newes* that the great comic had deferred to his 'simple judgement' in certain 'matters of wit' – and Tarlton was dead by 5 September.[12] Nashe was probably one of the throng who gathered at the open-air pulpit outside St Paul's on 20 August to hear the defeat of the Armada proclaimed. Little did he realize that a few years later 'the preacher at Poules Crosse' would be incited to 'preach manifestly against Maister Lilly [John Lyly] and mee', with a text of 'Woe to the Printer, woe to the Seller, woe to the

Buyer, woe to the Author'.[13] If the backstreets of Shoreditch were his
lodgings, the precincts of St Paul's Cathedral were the hub and centre
of his day-to-day life. Elizabethan St Paul's was much more than a
cathedral – in fact *qua* cathedral it was in poor shape, delapidated by
Reformation iconoclasm and the burning of the steeple in 1561. It was
the great popular forum and promenade of the city. In vain the bishops
deplored its degeneration into a 'house of talking, of walking, of brawling, of minstrelsy, of hawkes and of dogs'; the aisles a 'horse-fair' for
'bargains, meetings, brawlings, murders, conspiracies' and a 'common
passage' for colliers and other 'burden-bearing people'; the font desec-
rated as a counter for 'ordinary payment'. Within the huge, echoing
cathedral, lawyers and moneylenders met their clients, tailors displayed
their wares, scriveners wrote copies in a fair 'text-hand', the unemployed
thronged the '*si quis*' pillar where vacancies were posted, and cut-purses
practised 'the foist and the nip' in the midst of the crowd. On Saturdays
the dog-whipper was busy at his 'unsavery visitation', clearing the
cathedral for Sunday's devotions.[14] One went 'to Poules to learne some
news': it was the place of assignation, gossip and deals. Jonson's Captain
Bobadil was a 'Pauls man'; Falstaff 'bought' Bardolph 'in Pauls'; Dekker
devoted a whole chapter of his *Guls Hornbook* to advising 'How a
Gallant should behave himself in Powles Walkes'. A favourite rendezvous
for adventurers, gallants and needy wits was in the walk near the tomb
of 'good Duke Humphrey' (a mediaeval Duke of Gloucester). Those
who failed to cadge some supper were said to be 'dining with Duke
Humfrey'. Thus Nashe's Pierce Penniless, 'like a careless malecontent,
that knew not which way to turne, retired me to Paules, to seeke my
dinner with Duke Humfrey'.[15]

There is no doubt that Paul's was a daily haunt of Nashe's, indeed in
Lenten Stuffe it springs to his mind as a simile for frequency – 'I have
traded them as frequently as the middle walke in Poules, or my way to
bed every night'.[16] He was drawn there not only by his love of the
milling disreputable pageantry it afforded, but also because it was his
place of business. The twelve-acre precinct of St Paul's Churchyard was
the city's book-mart and hub of the literary profession, 'the peruser of
everie mans works, & Exchange of all Authors'.[17] Along the North wall
by Paternoster Row, the stationers had their 'dwelling houses, ware
houses and sheades', and all round the churchyard were shops with title-
pages nailed on every post and stalls laden with pamphlets, plays, learned
Latin texts, sermons, almanacs, ballads and jigs. Here the writers held
court and the readers browsed amid calls of 'Honest man what booke
lacke you?' and 'Buy some new booke sir, there are the last newes from
Fraunce, what bookes buy you?' – the answer might be anything from
'the new Testament in the Assirian tongue' to 'some pretie little booke
to read in the chimnie corner'.[18] These were boom years for publishers

and printers. Some 550 new titles were registered at Stationers' Hall in
the four years 1591–4, with perhaps as much as a third more appearing,
for one reason or another, unauthorized: a rough average of nearly 200
books a year.[19] Nashe professed to rail on the effusion of ephemera this
partly entailed:

> For who can abide a scurvie pedling Poet to plucke a man by the
> sleeve at everie third step in Paules Churchyard, & when he comes
> in to survey his wares, theres nothing but purgations and vomits
> wrapt uppe in wast paper. . . . Looke to it you Booksellers and
> Stationers, and let not your shops be infected with any such goose
> gyblets or stinking garbadge as the Iygs of newsmongers.[20]

There are ironies behind this kitchen-stuff rhetoric, the tasteless depiction
of literary output as vomit or offal. Nashe is himself buttonholing the
reader, peddling his wares (the passage comes from an address to the
'Gentle Reader' in *Pierce Penilesse*). It is his share of the market, not
literary decorum, he wishes to protect, or if decorum only because the
'base inck-dropper' and his tenth-rate products dragged the whole
market down: 'let them be circumspect what dunghill papers they bring
thither, for one bad pamphlet is enough to raise a damp that may poison
a whole Tearme'. There is this huckstering element in many of his literary
pronouncements. It is part of the intimacy of the Elizabethan literary
scene: not only did the writers all know one another, but the readers
knew them too, the showy young men with bad reputations who loitered
among the bookstalls and tobacco-shops of Paul's.

To St Paul's Churchyard, no doubt, the unknown Thomas Nashe bent
his steps in the summer of 1588, hoping to sell his manuscript of
the *Anatomie of Absurditie*. He had succeeded sometime before
19 September, for on that date the publisher Thomas Hackett paid 6d
at Stationers' Hall to license his copy of the work.[21] Master Hackett
was an old and respected member of the book-trade, a member of the
Stationers' Company since 1569. He had recently published a pamphlet
by William Rankins, a translation by Arthur Golding, Greepe's *Exploites
performed by Syr F. Drake*, and the first printed work by Thomas Kyd,
whose *Spanish Tragedy* was currently enjoying huge success on stage.
Nashe had clearly found himself a fairly 'upmarket' publisher. Though
Hackett undoubtedly did business at Paul's, his main premises were in
Lombard Street, 'under the signe of the Popes heade', and thus another
fragment of Nashe's London comes into view. Hackett's shop was in
the complex of rented tenements round the Pope's Head tavern, opposite
St Mary Woolnoth church: a prosperous, mercantile area associated
with the wool-trade.[22] The printer of the *Anatomie*, as of many of
Hackett's publications, was John Charlewood. Nashe probably spent

time correcting the proofs at Charlewood's printing house at the sign of the Half-Eagle and Key in the Barbican, though it was not until the early months of 1590 that the *Anatomie* was finally printed up and put on sale.[23] By then he had already made some mark as a cocky, controversial young wit, and was on intimate terms with the city which he loved and mirrored, which made him and broke him.

What Nashe lived off in these early days in London is something of a mystery. With his father dead he can have had little or no private money. Whatever he made from the sale of the *Anatomie* to Hackett would soon be spent. His dedication of the pamphlet to Sir Charles Blount perhaps elicited some reward – £2 was the standard 'dedication fee' – but there is no evidence that Blount actively patronized him.[24] He no doubt touted for penny-a-line work with the theatre companies, but competition in this burgeoning literary market was fierce: the famous Greene might get 20 nobles (£6 13s 4d) from the Queen's Men for *Orlando Furioso*, but an unknown piece-worker like Nashe would have sweated for the lowest rates.[25] One possible source of support for our struggling young author in the late 1580s is William Beeston. Dedicating *Strange Newes* to Beeston in 1592, Nashe thankfully remarks:

> Verily, all poore schollers acknowledge you as their patron, providi-
> tore and supporter, for there cannot a threed-bare Cloake sooner
> peepe forth, but you strait presse it to be an outbrother of your
> bounty: three decayed Students you kept attending upon you a long
> time.[26]

It seems plausible that Nashe himself was one of these threadbare scholars for whom Beeston provided. If so it was early enough in his London career for him still to class himself as a 'decayed student'. We know nothing of Beeston beyond what Nashe tells us. He was a jovial, hard-drinking fellow, elderly and wealthy. He wore a 'round cap' and a 'dudgen dagger', drank at the Stillyard and the Blue Boar in Spitalfields, and spent 'many pounds' on that 'durt of wisedome called Alcumie'. He adored poetry and ballads, and was a 'copious Carminist' himself: Nashe recalls him winning breakfast off Master Vaux of Lambeth 'one morning at an unlawful game called riming'. Another of Beeston's circle was Sir John Davies, the poet of *Astraea* and *Nosce Teipsum*.[27] Davies was a 'bencher' at the Middle Temple at this time, and Beeston himself seems to have had legal connections, for Nashe says he moved 'amongst Grave Doctors and men of iudgement in both Lawes [i.e. Canon and Civil] everie daie'. We quickly find Nashe on the fringes of the Inns of Court, a lively, fashionable, intellectual *milieu*. This was virtually London's university: here future greats like Francis Bacon and Robert Cotton studied, together with a strong contingent of well-breeched young *dilettantes*, rounding their education off with 'a smattering of the law and some experience of the metropolis'.[28] Here, in years to come, would be the staple of Nashe's reading public, as also the intelligentsia who applauded the subtleties of Shakespeare, that 'caviary' too delicate for 'the general'. Among the writers, Thomas Lodge, Matthew Roydon, Everard Guilpin and John Donne studied at the Inns. Ben Jonson dedicated his satirical comedy, *Every Man Out of his Humour* (1599), to those 'noblest nurseries of humanity and liberty in the Kingdom, the Inns of Court', in honour of his 'friendship with divers in your Societies'.[29] It was a raucous world too, as accounts of the Gray's Inn *gesta* and the 'Prince of Purpoole' revels show. In a letter to a legal friend in 1596, Nashe speaks of someone having 'revived an old innes a court tricke of turning [   ] out in a paper, & framed close stooles for them to carry in there pockets, as gentlewomen do there spunges'.[30] The edge of the paper has torn away, but the missing word is almost certainly 'turds'.

Beeston's well-stocked cellar may have relieved him for a while, but the plain fact is that Nashe was perennially hard up, and that before his career began to take off he must have been drastically so, living from day to day, cadging and hustling, frequenting the usurers and commodity-brokers, dining 'with Sir Iohn Best-betrust at the signe of the Chalk and the Post'[31] – i.e. on credit – or 'with Duke Humfrey' himself. In *Pierce Penilesse* and *Strange Newes*, the earliest of his pamphlets to feature strong autobiographical veins, he looks back at these hard times when he 'liv'de a long time without mony' and was often 'pinched with want':

> All in vaine I sate up late and rose earely, contended with the colde and conversed with scarcitie: for all my labours turned to losse, my vulgar Muse was despised & neglected, my paines not regarded or slightly rewarded, and I my selfe (in prime of my best wit) laid open to povertie.

He admits he has 'dealt upon spare commodities of wine and capons' and 'sung George Gascoignes Counter-tenor' – done time, in other words, in one of the Counter prisons, Wood Street or the Poultry, for defaulting on debts. He complains bitterly that 'such a franke Gentleman as I should want', that 'Coblers, Hostlers and Carmen should be worth so much and so much, and I, a scholler and good-fellow, a begger'.[32] His enemies were quick to jibe at his straitened circumstances. In the *Trimming*, Richard Lichfield gives this apocryphal account of the young Nashe *in extremis*:

You remember the time when your fellowe Lusher and you lay in cole-harbour together, when you had but one payre of breeches betweene you both, but not one penie to blesse you both, and how by course hee wore the breeches one day, and went cunny-catching about for victuals, whilest you lay in bedde, and the next day you wore the breeches to goe begge whilest he lay in bed: for all the worlde like two bucketes in one well.[33]

In *The Blacke Booke* (1604), Thomas Middleton gives us a vivid impression of Nashe down and out in London.[34] Visiting London in disguise, the Devil resolves to call on 'Pierce Penniless', who had written the famous 'supplication' to him. He searches for him among 'roosting Inns and frothy Ale-houses', and eventually meets a 'summer' who knows him:

Who? Pierce, honest Pennilesse? hee that writ the Mad-cappes Supplication? Why, my very next neighbour, lying within three leane houses of mee, at olde Mistresse Silver-pinnes, the onely doore-keeper in Europe.

Pierce's lodgings are, we learn, in the Pickt-hatch, an unsavoury location in Clerkenwell named after a famous brothel.[35] In a 'garden house' down Pickt-hatch Walk, the visitor is directed up to the little back-chamber where the author rooms:

I stumbled up two payre of stayres in the darke, but at last caught in mine eyes the sullen blaze of a melancholy lampe, that burnt very tragically uppon the narrow Deske of a halfe Bedstead, which descryed all the pittifull Ruines throughout the whole chamber. The bare privities of the stone-walls were hid with two pieces of painted cloth, but so ragged and tottred that one might have seene all neverthelesse. . . . The Testerne or the shadow over the bed was made of four Elles of Cobwebs, and a number of small spinners Ropes hung downe for Curtaines.

Pierce lies stretched out asleep on the bed, on a pillow 'stuft with horsemeate' and sheets 'smudged so durtily as if they had bene stolne by night out of Saint Pulchers Church-yard'. He wears a 'lamentable' old doublet of Kendal Green wool. Beside him lie some crumpled papers 'in foule written hand'. The noise of the visitor disturbs him. He begins to 'stretch and grate his nose against the hard Pillowe' and 'after a rowze or two' he wakes, muttering drunkenly that 'the divell is a mad knave still'.

This is fiction, of course, but it has a documentary core. We do not know if Nashe actually lodged in Clerkenwell – though we do know that his friend Greene frequented the Red Lattice, which stood near the Pickt-hatch on Turnmill Street.[36] But even if the address is wrong, the essential dingy scenario, the whiff of squalid rooming-houses, is authentic. So too the whole 'Pierce Penniless' persona: a mere literary pose in itself, essence of needy scribbler, but behind it real hardships and bitterness.[37] Championing Nashe as a pioneer journalist we must remember the 'deadlines' – poverty, hunger, sickness, imprisonment. If his writings sometimes seem two-dimensional, these are a kind of third dimension. For a young man brought up in rural Norfolk and schooled in claustrophobic Cambridge, the impact of Elizabethan London must have been immense. Its teeming visions assaulted his senses, its dangerous pleasures emptied his purse. The gulf between the slick, vapid *Anatomie* he brought with him, and the racy, bristling, brash *Almond for a Parrat* he wrote in late 1589, is a measure of the changes that London wrought in him.

5
THE WITS

'Never give me credit, if Sanguine Witt put not Melancholy Arte to bedd'

JOHN ELIOT (QUOTED BY GABRIEL HARVEY)   *Pierces Supererogation*

The literary figure most closely associated with Nashe in his early years in London was the redoubtable Robert Greene. It was Greene who gave Nashe his first big break, for in the summer of 1589 the latest romance from his prolific pen, *Menaphon*, appeared complete with a twelve-page preface by Nashe, addressed 'to the Gentlemen Students of both Universities' and signed 'how ever, yours ever, Thomas Nash'.[1] This was a remarkable literary *coup* by Nashe. In the late 1580s Greene reigned supreme as the popular author of the day, 'Greene with the running Head and the scribling Hand, that never linnes putting-forth new, newer & newest bookes of the maker'.[2] His output was prodigious: some 30 pamphlets and half a dozen plays, written in little over a decade. As Nashe admiringly puts it, 'in a night & a day would he have yarkt up a Pamphlet as well as in seaven yeare, and glad was that Printer that might bee so blest to pay him deare for the very dregs of his wit'.[3] He had an intuitive nose for literary fashions, for sniffing out a market and supplying it. While *Euphues* was still *de rigeur* Greene came out with a 'sequel', *Euphues his Censure* ('Gentlemen, by chance some of Euphues loose papers came to my hand. . .'). When the vogue was pastoral Greene set to work on *Pandosto*, with its lost princess Fawnia among the shepherds, and *Menaphon*, which soon became known as 'Greene's Arcadia'. Scarcely had the debris of the Armada settled before Greene was penning *The Spanish Masquerado*, disclosing the 'pride and insolencie' of Spain in certain 'breefe Sentences and Mottos'. He used his title-pages as advertisements, his prefaces to 'puff' forthcoming works, and the Horatian motto that adorned his title-pages – '*Omne tulit punctum qui miscuit utile dulci*' ('He who mixes profit with pleasure bears off every prize') – soon became shortened to a simple swagger, '*Omne tulit punctum*', as much as to say, 'I'm the greatest'. It was above all Greene's catch-penny commercial skills which Nashe learnt from him, his adaptability and nonchalance. These virtues were inseparable from certain artistic vices: he was facile, derivative, sloppy – his handwriting too, complained one of his editors, was 'none of the best'.[4] Harvey dismissed him as 'the Ape of Euphues', parading in 'borrowed & filched plumes of some little Italianated bravery'. Nashe too had to 'graunt that Greene came oftner in print than men of iudgement allowed', but nevertheless 'he was a daintie slave to content the taile of a Tearme, and stuffe Serving mens pockets'. In the melancholy of his last days Greene summed up:

> Many things I have wrote to get money, which I could otherwise wish to be supprest. Povertie is the father of innumerable infirmities. In seeking to salve private wantes I have made my selfe a publique laughing stocke.[5]

For all this he was a genuinely gifted writer. The best of his writings have a grace and sleekness to them, a style (as Nashe describes it) 'not so stately yet comely'.[6] His versatility, if commercially inspired, was also a commendable restlessness. Indeed no sooner had he mined the romantic and arcadian vein of the late 1580s than he discarded it. In 1590 he put out *Greenes Mourning Garment*, announcing his 'farewell to fond desires' and wanton romancing. This ushered in a new batch of autobiographical work, full of sensational repentances and prodigal-son motifs, with a new motto, '*Sero sed serio*', roughly translatable as 'better late than never'.[7] Another vein of the early 1590s, perhaps Greene's finest, was the 'conny-catching' series, detailing the lore and language of the Elizabethan underworld. The strong journalistic element in the latter, together with the topical satire in the *Quip for an Upstart Courtier* (1592), suggests that Greene in turn learned from his young 'discovery', Nashe.

Greene's was not a solely literary reputation: he acquired and no doubt cultivated a huge personal notoriety. 'Who in London hath not heard of his dissolute and licentious living', his 'unseemely apparell and more unseemely company', his 'scandalous and blasphemous raving'?[8] In his *Repentance* (1592), Greene describes himself as a 'mirrour of mischief', a man addicted to 'wantonnes' and 'riot'. He tells of his 'inordinate quaffing', of the alehouses where he chalked up 'more than ever I meant to pay by twenty nobles thick', of the 'harlots whose throates are as smooth as oyle', whose 'sweete inchaunting notes soothed me up in all kind of ungodlines'.[9] He had briefly married, in about 1585, 'a Gentlemans daughter of good account' named Dorothy, or Doll, but soon grew restless:

> For as much as she would perswade me from my wilful wickednes, after I had a child by her, I cast her off, having spent up the marriage money which I obtained by her.

Leaving her and the baby 'at six or seaven' he returned to his dissolute life in London. His callous behaviour haunted him in his last days: 'Oh my deare Wife, whose company and sight I have refrained these sixe yeares: I aske God and thee forgivenesse for so greatly wronging thee.'[10]

Much of our picture of Greene as rake-hell comes, admittedly, from his own repentance-tracts or from Harvey's tirade against him in the *Foure Letters* (1592). Both are probably exaggerating in the interests of good copy. Nashe's comments in *Strange Newes* are cooler, more human. He neither denies nor censures Greene's womanizing (he 'hath beene in so many hote skirmishes') or his boozing ('in one year he pist as much against the walls as thou [i.e. Harvey] and thy two brothers spent in three'). Instead he shrugs it all off: Greene 'inherited more vertues than vices' and as for the latter, 'debt and deadly sinne, who is not subiect to?'[11] We shall return to Nashe's defence of the dead Greene in due time. He was undoubtedly a man of great charm: 'he was of singuler pleasaunce the verye supporter', says Henry Chettle, who transcribed his deathbed pamphlet, *Greenes Groatsworth of Wit*: 'of face amible, of body well-proportioned, his attire after the habit of a schollerlike gentleman, onely his haire somewhat long'. Nashe sketches in a cavalier figure sporting a long red beard, from which 'a man might hang a Iewell, it was so sharpe and pendant', and a 'very faire Cloake with sleeves, of a grave goose turd greene'.[12] Greene's only extant portrait, in John Dickenson's *Greene in Conceipt* (1598), unfortunately adds little (Figure 6). It shows us Greene's ghost, complete with winding-sheet, hard at work on a pamphlet. The jutting beard may be intended as a trait, but the cut's main interest is in its casual enumeration of the pamphleteer's tools: pen, inkhorn, note-books and paper-knife.

The publisher Cuthbert Burby said that Greene's 'loose behaviour' was 'odious to God and offensive to men', but he added ruefully that Greene would have been 'wise, learned and polliticke' had his 'lascivious life' not seduced him from more 'profitable' studies.[13] The note of self-destruction is right, that fast-burning fuse which most of these young writers shared. One hears again the motto on Marlowe's portrait, '*Quod me nutrit me destruit*'. Greene's repentance pamphlets may play up his depravities but they accurately suggest his instability, the violent oscillations of his character. The first of his many religious crises dates back to his early twenties: recently home from Italy, he wandered into St Andrew's church, Norwich, where the sermon, probably by John More, struck 'the terrour of Gods iudgementes' into him – 'I should bee wipte out of the booke of life, if I did not speedily repent my loosenes.' A ballad bearing his name was entered on the Register in March 1581: 'Youth recalleth his former Follies with an Inward Repentance', the first of his many confessionals. However, this 'good motion lasted not long in mee'. His old 'copesmates' demanded to know the reason for his new 'solemne humour', and when he explained,

> they fell upon me in ieasting manner, calling me Puritane and Presizian, and wished I might have a Pulpit, with such other scoffing tearmes, that by their foolish perswasion the good and wholesome lesson I had learnt went quite out of my remembrance.

Thereupon 'I fel againe with the Dog to my olde vomit'.[14] This became the recurrent pattern for Greene, lurching between extremes of debauchery and agonized religiosity.

Behind the *grand guignol* which came as second nature to these men, one glimpses a familiar type: gifted, weak, alcoholic. That easy, chatty style — 'To be briefe, Gentlemen, I have seene the world & rounded it' — is so often just Roberto in his cups with another tavern-tale to tell. Greene was a kind of Elizabethan pop star, one whose success exposed him to parasites and exploiters:

> for those my vaine discourses I was beloved of the more vainer sort of people, who beeing my continuall companions, came still to my lodging, and there would continue quaffing, carowsing and surfeting with me all the day long.[15]

This was the flamboyant, flawed figure whom Nashe called, in 1589, his 'sweet friend'. In giving Nashe the prime spot at the forefront of *Menaphon* Greene was being shrewd as well as friendly. In return he got something more than well-turned prefatory complements to his pamphlet ('thy Arcadian *Menaphon*') and himself. He also got the services of a bright young talent, enlisted under his banner in the factious literary world of 'quarrels, frayes and continuall controversies'. In taking up the cudgels against Greene's rivals, Nashe had a problem, for foremost among them at this time was his own Cambridge friend Marlowe. The earliest hint of this controversy came in early 1588, when Greene sounded off, in his preface to *Perimedes the Blacke-smith*, against writers whose 'verses iet upon the stage in tragicall buskins, everie worde filling the mouth like the fa-burden of Bo-Bell, daring God out of heaven with that Atheist Tamburlan'. The obvious allusion to Marlowe's *Tamburlaine* is compounded by another to 'mad and scoffing poets that have poeticall spirits as bred of Merlins race' — punning on 'Marlin', a variant of Marlowe's name frequently used at Cambridge.[16] It is not clear whether Greene was simply resenting Marlowe's spectacular success or whether, as he implies, he was himself reacting to some previous 'derision'. His own play, *Alphonsus, King of Aragon*, clearly modelled on *Tamburlaine*, was probably onstage by 1588 and suffering from adverse comparison. Whatever the exact circumstances, the quarrel was still simmering when Greene wrote *Menaphon*: a remark about a foolish 'Canterbury tale' told by 'a Cobblers eldest sonne' seems to glance at Marlowe, who was indeed a Canterbury cobbler's son. The follower of literary fashion, then, would have little difficulty in identifying the target when he read, on the first page of Nashe's preface, of certain playwrights who 'intrude themselves to our eares as the Alcumists of eloquence'; who 'mounted on the stage of arrogance, think to out-brave better pennes with the swelling bumbast of bragging blanke verse'; and whose huge conceit 'overcloyeth their imagination' and 'commits the digestion of their cholericke incumbrances to the spacious volubilitie of a drumming decasillabon'.[17] But though Marlowe is the obvious candidate as arrogant, blank-versifying tragedian, it is notable that Nashe nowhere insists on the identification. There are none of the punning little signposts at which he was so adept. He keeps the butt of his remarks plural, thus steering an agile course between the expediency of taking Greene's side and the loyalty he owed to his friend Marlowe. In fact when he does get down to snide particulars, it is not Marlowe but Thomas Kyd who swims into focus:

> It is a common practise now a dayes amongst a sort of shifting companions, that runne through every Art and thrive by none, to leave the trade of *Noverint*, whereto they were borne, and busy themselves with the indevours of Art. . . . English *Seneca* read by Candlelight yeelds many good sentences, as *Blood is a begger*, and so forth; and if you intreate him faire in a frostie morning, hee will affoord you whole Hamlets, I should say handfuls of Tragicall speeches. But . . . *Seneca*, let blood line by line and page by page, at length must needes die to our Stage; which makes his famished followers to imitate the Kid in Aesop, who, enamoured with the Foxes newfangles, forsooke all hopes of life to leape into a new occupation; and these men, renouncing all possibilities of credite or estimation, to intermeddle with Italian translations.

The pun on Kyd's name confirms other hints: Kyd's father was a scribe or scrivener ('the trade of *Noverint*'); his famous *Spanish Tragedy* was an epitome of English Senecan drama; and he had recently published some Italian translations (Tasso's *Householders Philosophie*, issued in 1588 by Nashe's own publisher, Thomas Hackett). The reference to 'whole Hamlets' may suggest that Kyd was the author of the so-called 'Ur-Hamlet', the lost early version of the play on which Shakespeare drew for his version of *c.* 1601.[18] It is possible that Kyd was involved in the original 'derision' of Greene: he and Marlowe were certainly sharing a chamber, and writing for the same troupe, a couple of years later.[19] It is equally possible that Kyd got egg on his face simply because Nashe did not want to attack Marlowe. These literary squabbles were, one suspects, skin-deep anyway – real in terms of rivalry, expressive of the touchy, quick-flaring temper of these men, but in the main thoroughly overplayed in the interests of publicity. A good quarrel got them talking at Paul's, stoked the *enfant terrible* mystique: what better plug for Marlowe and his *Tamburlaine* than to be tilted at in public by Robert Greene? Among these university-bred wits dispute was a way of life, both with one another and with their non-university rivals such as Kyd and, somewhat later, Shakespeare. The college 'chapter of disputation' surfaced in London as a demotic repartee of quips, scoffs and satirical broadsides. Even the Harvey-Nashe quarrel, though more complex and bitter, has this element of self-advertisement in it, as also a literary awareness of polemic itself as a genre, looking back to the mediaeval traditions of 'flyting' and the great humanist controversies like Poggio and Valla's. There were genuine moments of loathing in it, but also the kinship of the double-act. It is worth noting, incidentally, that a passage in Nashe's *Anatomie of Absurditie* reads very like a hit at Greene himself. Scoffing at romancers in general, all 'fabulous follie' and 'love passions', Nashe especially refers to 'prefixed posies . . . of profit mixt with pleasure' (Greene's '*miscuit utile dulci*' motto); to constant metaphorical harping on the properties of 'minerals, stones and herbes' (a Euphuistic habit Nashe elsewhere explicitly associates with Greene); and to blotting 'many sheetes of paper in the blazing of Womens slender praises' (Greene's *Penelopes Web*, issued in summer 1587 – just when Nashe was writing the *Anatomie* – was expressly a 'Christall Myrror of faeminine perfection' setting forth the virtues of womankind).[20] Greene must surely have seen the *Anatomie* in manuscript, and seen himself, the great 'penner of Love pamphlets', ragged in it. If Nashe regretted the passage, he did not withdraw it: he even uses the *Menaphon* preface to puff the forthcoming publication of the *Anatomie*.[21] A bit of good healthy satire was all in the game.

With the publication of *Menaphon*, probably in the late summer of 1589 – it was entered on the Stationers' Register on 23 August – Nashe could congratulate himself on having 'arrived'. He had staked his claim near the centre of the London literary world and its commotions. His preface to *Menaphon* is essentially a review of contemporary English writing: polished, acrid, acute and, to some, insufferably arrogant. He hits a light, fluent, humorous tone, what the Elizabethans called 'facetious' –

'that affabilitie which our Latinists entitle *facetus*, & we more familiarlie describe by the name of discoursing'.[22] The addressing of the piece to 'the Gentlemen Students of both Universities' is no empty formality. Nashe is, in a sense, speaking for a whole circle of writers, university men themselves − 'fellowe Schollers about this Cittie', as Greene puts it[23] − who were driven by choice or circumstance into the intellectually less salubrious world of the London play-houses and popular press. This group of writers, to which Nashe was the newest and youngest recruit, is generally known as the 'University Wits'. By the late 1580s Greene was its leading star and Marlowe its explosive young genius: together with Nashe they make up the Cambridge axis of the group. The original nucleus, however, was a group of Oxford men − John Lyly, Thomas Watson, George Peele, Thomas Lodge and Matthew Roydon − who had been associated together in London since about 1581, when they constituted the 'Holborn Set', so called because Lyly then rented chambers in the old Savoy hospital, near the Strand, while Lodge and Roydon studied at the Inns of Court. Two other writers belonged to this earlier set: the poet Thomas Acheley, or Atchelow, as Nashe spells it; and George Buc, later to become Master of the Revels. There are no records of either having studied at university, but they seem to be honorary 'Wits'. Nashe praises Acheley for his 'deepe witted schollership', and Buc may well be the 'G.B., Cant' who provided complimentary verses for three of Greene's pamphlets (he could call himself *Cantabrigiensis* by virtue of hailing from Ely).[24]

Nashe seems to have known two of the Oxonian 'Wits' particularly well: John Lyly and Thomas Watson. It was ten years since Lyly had triumphed with the two *Euphues* books: their esteem is scarcely exaggerated by the publisher Blount when he says 'our Nation are in his debt for a new English which hee taught them'.[25] His was a courtly as well as a popular success − 'that Beautie in Court which could not parley *Euphueisme*' was 'little regarded' − and his career had prospered. He was variously secretary to the Earl of Oxford, 'vice-master' of the boy actors of St Paul's School, Clerk Controller of the Office of Tents and Toyles, and, in February 1589, Member of Parliament for Hindon, Wiltshire. Gabriel Harvey, writing in November 1589, puts another side to his reputation:

> an odd, light-headded fellow, . . . a professed iester, a Hick-scorner, a scoff-maister, a playmunger, an Interluder; once the foile of Oxford, now the stale of London, and ever the Apesclogg of the presse.[26]

During the 1580s Lyly produced a series of glittering comedies, performed by the 'chyldren of Paules', often before the Queen: some years later, during the suppression of the boys' company, Nashe recalled

the merriments of *Mother Bombey* and wished 'the Playes at Powles up
againe'.[27] Lyly comes across as a small, spruce, dandified figure. Harvey
calls him 'a dapper & deft companion' full of 'prettie sentences'. Nashe
asserts, 'hee is but a little fellow, but hee hath one of the best wits in
England'. It has been thought that Ben Jonson caricatures him as
Fastidious Brisk in *Every Man out of his Humour* (1599). We know
from Nashe he was a smoker ('in as much time as hee spendes in taking
Tobacco one weeke . . .') and from other sources that he lived in the
precincts of Bartholomew's Hospital, handy for his work in the Tents
and Toyles department of the Revels Office in Smithfield.[28] Nashe speaks
of Lyly with respect as well as affection, even asserting that he himself
had 'but a mite of wit in comparison of his talent'. He often refers to
him with the prefix 'Maister' (or 'M.'), a deference he does not accord
to Greene or Marlowe. Lyly was older, and somewhat more courtly and
respectable, than the other Wits. Nonetheless, as we shall see, he threw
himself with gusto into pamphleteering against the Puritans, together
with Nashe, and the pair were allies against the Harveys, though Lyly
never actually published against them ('he flieth from such inferiour
concertation'). Gabriel Harvey bore an ancient grudge against Lyly. Back
in 1580 Harvey had penned a 'bolde Satyriall' poem entitled *Speculum
Tuscanismi*, ridiculing fashionable Italianate affectations. This was
immediately suspected as a satire on the Earl of Oxford, who had
recently snubbed Harvey's hero Sidney on the tennis court. According
to Harvey it was Oxford's 'minion secretary', Lyly, whose 'smooth
glossing & counterfait suggestion' first stirred up the Earl's suspicions
about the poem.[29] Harvey also alleged that it was through Lyly's
'procurement or encouragement' that Greene and Nashe first attacked
him in 1592: there may be some truth in this, though they had their
own motives as well.

Of Thomas Watson Nashe wrote: 'a man he was that I dearely lov'd
and honor'd, and for all things hath left few his equalls in England'.
This was in 1596, four years after Watson's untimely death, but Nashe
doubtless knew him from early days in London, and in the preface to
Menaphon he lauded Watson as a 'singuler' translator whose versions
of Sophocles' *Antigone* (1581) and Tasso's *Amintas* (1585) 'may march
in equippage of honour with any of our ancient Poets'.[30] Of all the Wits,
Watson was perhaps the most genuinely scholarly. After Oxford he had
spent some seven years on the continent, 'worshipping the Muses' and
studying law: his title-pages announce him as '*J.V. studiosus*', a student
of canon and civil law.[31] His translations show him at home with Latin,
Greek, Italian and French. His sonnet-sequence, *Ekatompathia* (1582),
is a refined, cosmopolitan collection, as influential as Sidney's more
famous *Astrophel and Stella* on the sonneteering boom of the 1590s. In
1595 Shakespeare's *Venus and Adonis* won him praise as 'Watsons

heyre'.[32] But for all his more elevated writings, Watson's name was also associated with more dubious, catch-penny literature. William Cornwallis, who employed Watson as tutor to his children, described him disapprovingly as one who 'could devise twenty fictions and knaveryes in a play, which was his daily practyse and his living'.[33] In 1596 a critic says that Sir John Harington's *Metamorphosis of Ajax* merely creams off 'the froth of witty Tom Watsons jests', adding 'I heard them in Paris fourteen years ago', which implies that Watson's plays (lost like so much Elizabethan drama) went on at Paris Gardens, on the south bank of the Thames, in the early 1580s.[34] Like all his colleagues, Watson had a wild reputation, which his spell in Newgate prison with Marlowe in 1589 did little to improve. He had already figured in official enquiries in 1587, summoned before the Privy Council for his involvement with the eccentric Anne Burnell, who claimed to be the natural daughter of King Philip of Spain. Watson had apparently fuelled her delusions with some scholarly mumbo-jumbo – a witness describes him as 'one Watson a wise man in St Ellenes [St Helen's, Bishopsgate] that could tell strange thinges' – and he probably earned a few shillings into the bargain.[35] We see these hard-up scholars ready to turn their wits to anything. And, since Mistress Burnell ended up being 'whipped through the Citty of London', we sense the callousness of their japes. Thomas Kyd said that Marlowe was 'intemperate & of a cruel hart' and reproved his 'rashnes in attempting soden pryvie iniuries to men'.[36] Marlowe is a law unto himself but there is this cruel edge, this potential for viciousness, among all the Wits. It may be that Nashe, as 'byting Satirist', sublimated it into his art more effectively than most.

Watson had a long history of Catholic connections. During his continental travels he resided at least twice, in 1576 and again the following year, at the Catholic seminary at Douai. One of his books is dedicated to the young Earl of Arundel, son of the executed Duke of Norfolk; another to the Earl of Oxford, suspected as a closet papist. His employer Cornwallis was a wealthy London Catholic. His remarks to Mistress Burnell included the potentially seditious assertion that Philip II was 'the best spaniard that ever came in England'. Yet Watson was also, like Marlowe, a *protégé* of Thomas Walsingham's. In his dedication of *Meliboeus* (1590) to Walsingham, he dates their friendship back to Paris in the 1570s.[37] Was he, like Marlowe at Cambridge, playing the informer, using his Catholic connections to ferret out intelligence for Walsingham? It may have been through him that Marlowe was first recruited into Walsingham's service. Whatever his murkier dealings, Watson was much beloved of his fellow Wits. His *Ekatompathia* was prefaced by a letter from John Lyly – 'my good friend, I have read your new passions and they have renewed mine old pleasures' – and commendatory verses by Peele, Roydon and Acheley. Watson in turn contributed Latin verses in praise of Greene in the front of *Ciceronis Amor* (1589), Greene's follow-up to *Menaphon*. Nashe recalled at least one night on the town with Tom Watson, telling how, over 'supper at the Nags Head in Cheape' in the company of 'divers Gentlemen', Watson had entertained him with tales of Gabriel Harvey. It was Watson that 'first told me of his vanitie', says Nashe. He recited some 'Hexameters' that night about Harvey being 'knowne to the world for a foole and clapt in the Fleet for a rimer'. They were probably composed *extempore* – their scansion is heinous and the information false. There is no other evidence that Harvey was imprisoned in the Fleet for his libel against Oxford, and when challenged to back up his allegations to that effect Nashe can only weakly say that Watson's verse 'prooves it'.[38] Was Watson perhaps playing Nashe along just a little – the eager young journalist, ten years his junior, scribbling it all down in his notebook – just as the 'wise man' played along poor Mistress Burnell, and the confidential agent his Catholic acquaintances?

Another of the Wits to whom Nashe paid tribute in 1589 was George Peele. Nashe calls him 'the chiefe supporter of pleasaunce now living, the *Atlas* of Poetrie and *primus verborum Artifex*'. He praises Peele's early play, *The Arraignment of Paris* (*c.* 1581), for 'dexteritie of wit and manifold varietie of invention', qualities wherein Peele 'goeth a steppe beyond all that write'.[39] All these writers had a speciality: Peele's was the poetic occasional piece. His 'device' for Lord Mayor Dixie's pageant in 1585 was the first such to be printed; his publications of 1589–90 included celebrations of Sir Francis Drake, the Earl of Essex and the Accession Day tilts. These paid a bit – the Earl of Northumberland gave him £3 for *The Honour of the Garter* in 1593 – but, like the others, Peele mainly depended on the popular stage. His *Battle of Alcazar*, also known as 'Muly Mulocco', was probably onstage in 1589: like Greene's *Alphonsus*, it was clearly designed to cash in on *Tamburlaine*. His country comedy, *The Old Wives Tale*, contributes briefly to the scathing of Gabriel Harvey, satirized in the hexameter-wielding character of Huanebango.[40] Peele shared the same rakish, dissipated image as the other Wits, in fact he outdid them all by becoming that paradigm of witty rascality, the 'hero' of a jest-book – *The Merry Conceited Jests of George Peele* (the earliest edition extant is 1607 but it was probably out earlier). Much of this merely appends Peele's name to various time-honoured *facetiae*: other jest-collections of the time bear the names of Scogin, Skelton and Tarlton.[41] But the compiler seems also to have thrown in occasional *vraisemblable* glimpses of Peele himself. In one tale, for instance, George sends his ten-year-old daughter – a 'pretye' girl with her father's 'reddy witte' – with a message to a gentleman. Peele did indeed have daughters by his first marriage (to Anne Christian of Oxford) and the eldest one did, in January 1596, carry a message for

her father – not the deceitful message of the *Jests* but a begging letter
to Lord Burghley, written in poverty and sickness:

> Pardon greate Patrone of learning & Vertue this rude encounter, in
> that I presume, A Scholler of so meane meritt, to present your
> wisdome with this small manuell [*The Tale of Troy*] by this simple
> messengr my eldest Daughter & necessities servant. Longe sicknes
> havinge so enfeebled me maketh bashfullnes allmost become
> impudency.[42]

The same 'jest' describes Peele as then living on the Bankside. This too
is corroborated: at the time of his second marriage, in December 1591,
Peele was living in the parish of St Olave, Southwark, close to the Rose
theatre where his plays were intermittently performed.[43] The glimpse we
are given of Peele at his Bankside house, wrapped in a blanket, hard at
work on a translation while his wife and daughter roast larks for supper,
may just be authentic. So too, perhaps, that Peele had (like Nashe) 'a
beard of indifferent size', that he spoke in a voice 'more woman than
man', that his favourite haunt was a 'blinde' alehouse in Sea-Coal Lane,
and that he was 'of the poeticall disposition, never to write so long as
his mony lasted'.[44] Thus flecked with authenticity, the *Jests* cannot quite
be ignored. The dissolute, cheating wastrel they depict is not, of course,
the real George Peele. On the other hand, the compiler did not choose
Peele's name because he was a pattern of clean living.

Matthew Roydon is an altogether shadowier figure. He is nowadays
chiefly remembered for his exquisite elegy on Sidney, 'A Frends Passion
for his Astrophel'. Nashe praises this in *Menaphon*: he must have known
it in manuscript, since it was first published, anonymously, in *The
Phoenix Nest* anthology of 1593.[45] Nashe mentions 'other most absolute
Comike inventions' of Roydon's, probably referring to pleasant poetry
rather than stage plays: if the latter, they are lost. Despite a scanty
output, Roydon was very much part of the Wits' clique. He has prefatory
verses before Watson's *Ekatompathia*, and Nashe speaks of him in the
same breath as Peele and Acheley. As late as 1599 his name is linked
with Acheley's, though the document in question – a 'surety of the peace'
– shows that relations were then none too cordial.[46] Most interestingly,
Kyd speaks of Roydon as one of Marlowe's familiar friends, 'such as he
conversed withal'. Kyd also asserts that in about 1593 Roydon quit
England 'to goe unto the King of Scotts' – an action with dissident
implications – though he admits this is only hearsay.[47] Along with
Marlowe and George Chapman – another friend, who dedicated two
volumes of poetry to 'sweet Mathew' – Roydon seems to have had
connections with Sir Walter Ralegh's circle, whose free-thinking temper
and occultist dabblings became a talking-point in the early 1590s. It has

been argued that he wrote the anonymous *Willobie his Avisa* (1594), with its obscure pro-Ralegh propaganda and its riddling references to 'the poet W.S.', probably Shakespeare.[48] Nashe has a finger in the Ralegh pie, and we shall hear mention of Matthew Roydon again.

The only member of the set not explicitly mentioned in Nashe's pamphlets is Thomas Lodge, though since he was Greene's collaborator and friend in the late 1580s, Nashe must surely have known him well enough. Greene's political pamphlet, *The Spanish Masquerado*, published in early 1589, is prefaced by Lodge's French verses in praise of his '*doux ami*'. At about this time they collaborated on a play, *A Looking Glass for London and England*, which offered a portrait of decadent ancient Nineveh as a cautionary model for contemporary London:

> London look on, this matter nips thee near:
> Leave off thy riot, pride and sumptuous cheer.[49]

Lodge's most famous work, the romance *Rosalynde* (1590), is written in the Euphuistic vein which Greene also mined: some critics have discerned revisions by Greene himself.[50] Greene certainly edited Lodge's follow-up, *Euphues Shadow* (1592), and issued it 'in the behalfe of my absent friend' who 'nowe is gone to sea' – Lodge had sailed with Cavendish's expedition to South America in August 1591.[51] Though Nashe never refers to Lodge by name, there is one passage in *Pierce Penilesse* that reads very like an unflattering sketch of Lodge's younger days. It describes 'the prodigall young Master':

> A yoong Heyre or Cockney, that is his Mothers Darling, if hee have playde the waste-good at the Innes of the Court or about London, and that neither his Students pension, nor his unthrifts credite, will serve to maintaine his Colledge of whores any longer, falles in a quarrelling humor with his fortune, because she made him not King of Indies, and sweares and stares, after ten in the hundreth, that nere such a such Pesant as his Father or brother shall keepe him under: he will to the sea, and teare the gold out of the Spaniards throats, but he will have it, byrlady: And when he comes there, poore soule, hee lyes in brine, in Balist, and is lamentable sicke of the scurvies: his dainty fare is turned to a hungry feast of Dogs & Cats . . .[52]

This is typical of Nashe's satirical subterfuge: on one level innocuously general, a 'type', but to those that knew full of bitingly personal details. Lodge was just such a 'yoong Heyre' and 'waste-good' who had squandered his fortune on loose living. The son of a former Lord Mayor and master grocer, Sir Thomas Lodge, he had inherited lands and money upon the death of his mother, Lady Anne, in 1579. By 1583, however, we find him in dire straits, selling off the last of his properties to supply his 'present neede of money': he had spent his way through some £1000 in four years, an incredible feat.[53] His *Alarum against Usurers* (1584) recounts the miseries of debt which 'as an eye-witness I avowe'. No longer able to indulge his expensive vices, Nashe's young prodigal determines to seek his fortune at sea. This was Lodge's course too: he sailed under Captain Clarke in 1585, bound for the Canaries. One of the products of the voyage, or so Lodge claimed, was his popular romance, *Rosalynde*. He offered it as 'the fruits of his labors that he wrought in the ocean, when everie line was wet with a surge, and everie passion countercheckt by a storme'.[54] Nashe seems to undercut Lodge's stylish seafaring image by presenting the prodigal's voyage as a grisly catalogue of discomforts and diseases. Other details help the reader to focus on Lodge. He had, like Nashe's young heir, studied at the Inns of Court (1578–80). The business about his father and brother trying to 'keepe him under' is exactly right – from legal records we hear of Sir Thomas' determination to dispossess him ('because his sonne Tho Lodge did take such a disordred Corse of lyffe as he did, & that he sawe no lykelyhood that yt wold be otherwyse with him') and of long bitter litigation with his elder brother, William.[55] This brings us back to *Rosalynde* again, which is strongly autobiographical in its depiction of young Rosader being cheated and mistreated by his elder brother Saladyne. *Rosalynde* was the major source of Shakespeare's *As You Like It*, whose hero Orlando is thus a filtered reflection of Lodge himself. To be satirized by Nashe and dramatized by Shakespeare was no mean distinction in the 1590s. Why did Nashe jibe at him? Perhaps they simply did not like each other, though there is nothing from Lodge to confirm this, in fact his *Wits Miserie* (1596) is shot through with borrowings from *Pierce Penilesse*, and compliments Nashe as 'true English Aretine'.[56] As noted before, these bouts of literary in-fighting were none too serious: they enhanced more *kudos* than they damaged. But as Nashe must have had some motives, two suggest themselves: rivalry for Greene's literary favours in and around 1589; and disgruntlement at the success of romances like *Rosalynde* and *Euphues Shadow*, which Nashe no doubt considered trite, derivative and *démodé*. A third factor may have precipitated the scoff. In 1591 there appeared a pamphlet entitled *Catharos*: its author, 'T.L. of Lincolns Inne, Gent', was almost certainly Lodge.[57] It was a humorous satirical production. The title-page promised a 'merrie baighting fit' and a 'nettle for nice noses'. Lodge was, in short, poaching on Nashe's preserve: crime enough to earn him this little burlesque – the rich boy who ran away to sea – from the true 'yoong master' of the satirical field.

This was Nashe's circle in the late 1580s, these men among his companions at Paul's Churchyard and the Theatre, at the Red Lattice and the Nag's Head, in printing-houses and cheap rented chambers 'at the townes end'. The notoriety which clings to the Wits is partly mythic – because they and their publishers played up their roaring reputation, and because the forces of law and order took every opportunity to vent their disapproval. But the Wits *were* a kind of threat. It was not just that they drank too much, consorted with tarts, fought in the backstreets and took the 'divine drugge' tobacco. It was not even their subversive temper and supposed blasphemy. It was, above all, their elusive free-lance status. They were scholars that chose to be hirelings, gentlemen that lived like rogues. They moved in this strange *demi-monde* whose borders touched both the underworld and the heights of nobility. They seemed to have kicked away all the social *points d'appui* on which the respectable Elizabethan rested his world-view. The Puritan controversial-ist, Stephen Gosson, said that Lodge was 'little better than a vagrant, looser than liberty, lighter than vanity', and this catches the key-note of vagrancy and vertigo.[58] There was also that feel of extremism about them, excitable and drastic, poets with (as Nashe puts it) 'muses so mutinous as every stanzo they pen after dinner is full pointed with a stabbe'.[59] Nashe was really the last of the Wits. As a literary group their popularity was waning by the early 1590s: by the latter half of the decade only Nashe and Lodge were still active. Nashe seems to catch something of these early vertiginous days in London when he says, 'Wee scoffe and are iocund, when the sworde is ready to goe through us; on our wine-benches we bid a *Fico* for tenne thousand plagues.'[60] This sense of doomed bravado is a fitting epitaph for the Wits. They sparkled briefly, amid much moral and actual squalor, yet with their intellectual passion and their devotion to the literary craft, they created a climate, a freedom, for more profound and stable writers who followed.

6

CUTHBERT CURRYKNAVE

'Mirth I used as a covert, wherein I would bring the truth into light'

'MARTIN MARPRELATE'   *Hay any Worke for Cooper*

In the summer of 1589 Nashe was drawn into an enterprise which deeply influenced his whole literary career. He became, for the first and last time, a paid government propagandist, engaged in pamphlet-war with the Puritan militants who published a series of clandestine tracts under the *nom de guerre* of 'Martin Marprelate'. It is somehow typical of Nashe that, as stylist and satirist, he learned more from his professed enemy Martin than from any one of his fraternity of Wits.

The origins of this spicy theological fray stretch back to the earliest years of Elizabeth's reign. Ever since the Settlement of 1559 there had been protests that the Anglican church was still clouded with the 'dregs of popery'. By the early 1570s the Puritan movement was in top gear, aimed at demolishing the hierarchies of Anglicanism and taking as its prime target those figureheads of church power and conformity, the bishops. These were corrupt 'petty popes', denying the people a 'godly learned ministry'. Their authority had no backing in the Scriptures, which alone the Puritan recognized as canonical. Their 'tyrannous lordship', announced the anonymous *Admonition to Parliament* (1572), 'cannot stand with Christ's kingdom'.[1] Fanned by the oratory of Cartwright, Travers, Field and Wilcox, Puritan principles spread through the ministry, notably in the South East and Midlands. Preachers abandoned their surplices, doctored the Prayer Book, held informal 'prophesyings' and set up local synods based on the Genevan '*classis*'. Despite the sprouting of breakaway, inspirational sects, the mainstream of Puritan-Presbyterian reform grew broad and powerful, championed by civic authorities, debated in parliament and the universities, and cultivated in high places by the likes of Burghley, Walsingham and the Earl of Leicester.[2]

This was the splintered state of the Church when John Whitgift was appointed Archbishop of Canterbury in 1583. He was already known as a formidable foe of Puritanism: as Master of Trinity, Cambridge, he had engineered the expulsion of Cartwright, and rebutted his doctrines in a series of establishmentarian tracts.[3] A staunch Calvinist himself,

Whitgift defended orthodoxy more on pragmatic than spiritual grounds, linking religious 'quietness and order' with political security, and arguing (as an anti-Martinist pamphleteer later put it) 'that to the rule of the Church the whole state of the Realme is linckt, & that they filching away Bishop by Bishop seeke to fish for the Crowne'.[4] Under Whitgift's vigorous prosecution, this argument cost many Puritans their liberty and some their lives. Succeeding the mild Grindal, he swiftly made his intentions clear: his proclamation of conformity, the Six Articles, was followed by the suspension of some 200 ministers. His prime weapon was the dreaded Court of High Commission, which operated secretly, required neither legal formalities nor parliamentary sanction, and bound all examinees by the oath *ex officio*, demanding an answer to all questions even to the point of self-incrimination. In vain Burghley protested, in 1584, that Whitgift was creating a new Inquisition, his Commission 'a device to seek for offenders rather than to reform any'.[5] The religious police – run by Whitgift's brilliant adjutant, Richard Bancroft, then Canon of Westminster – began the round-up, the secret interrogations 'in some close chamber at Lambeth or some obscure gallerie in London Pallace' where 'they may juggle & foyst in what they list without controlment'.[6] It was Bancroft who later hit on the idea of hiring the stylists of the day – among them Lyly, Greene and Nashe – as propagandists with a popular touch.

In 1587 a new force appeared among the beleaguered Puritan ranks: John Penry. A 24-year-old Brecon man – 'a person full of Welsh blood, of a hot restless head'[7] – Penry had already made his name as a preacher at Cambridge and Oxford and a leading light of the *classis* at Northampton. In March 1587 he presented parliament with a 'humble supplication in the behalf of the country of Wales', known as *The Aequity*, in which he lamented the decayed state of the Welsh ministry. Recklessly he buttonholed the Queen herself: 'will not the enemies of Gods truth with uncleane mouthes avouch that shee had little regarde unto true or false religion anie further than it belonged unto hir profite?'[8] Official reaction was swift. Five hundred copies of the *Aequity* were seized. Penry was hauled before the Commission, and denounced as a 'factious slanderer', a 'lewde boy', a purveyor of 'flat treason and heresie'. Whitgift thundered, 'Ere you depart the court we will finde sufficient matter to emprison you', but they could not and after a month Penry went free, his missionary zeal redoubled: 'I see you my dere and native countrymen perish; it pitieth me; I come with the rope around my necke to save you.'[9] Early in 1588 he published his *Exhortation*, further indicting the bishops as 'soule-murtherers'. This work was clandestinely printed by Robert Waldegrave, a printer of pronounced Puritan leanings. In April Waldegrave followed this up by issuing, again without licence, *The State of the Church of England Laide Open*, written by another of this new generation of Puritan militants, John Udall, a preacher at Kingston, Surrey. This work too was ordered to be seized, and on 16 April Waldegrave's press and type were impounded by agents of the Stationers' Company and destroyed.[10] In the summer of 1588 this renegade trio – Penry, Waldegrave and Udall – went underground, and 'Martin Marprelate' was born.

During the raid on his printing-shop, Waldegrave had concealed some type 'in a boxe under his cloke', and taken it to the London house of Elizabeth Crane, widow of a preacher who had died in Newgate. More type and a press were assembled and furtively conveyed to Mistress Crane's country house at East Molesey, a short run upriver from London and close to Udall's home at Kingston. Confused rumours filtered back to the authorities and on 10 June Stationers' Company wardens swooped on a tinker's house in Kingston. They found only an irate housewife, whom they pacified with two shillings; their informant, one Draper, was thrown in the Counter for his pains.[11] Three miles away in Molesey the secret press began to roll. By the end of October 1588 five books had been prepared: two under Penry's name, two under Udall's, and the first cackling broadside from 'Martin Marprelate', generally known as the *Epistle*. Martin's specific target was *The Defence of the Government Established*, 1400 pages of lumbering orthodoxy issued in 1587 by Dr John Bridges, Dean – or, as Martin has it, 'Drone' – of Sarum. But the pamphlet quickly moves into the main Martinist theme: a virulent assault on the 'pettie Anti-christs' of the episcopacy, and on their loathed leader Whitgift, who throughout Martin's campaign is cajoled with such nicknames as 'Iohn of Cant', 'the pope of Lambehithe', 'my Lords grease' and 'Maister Iohn Kankerbury'. Martin promises to 'kindle such a fire in the holes of these foxes as shall never be quenched as long as there is a l.B. [Lord Bishop] in England'. His weapon will not be theological theorizing, but an armoury of raucous jests, anecdotes and libels:

> You see, my worshipfull priestes of this crue to whom I write, what a perilous fellow M. Marprelate is: he understands of all your knaverie, and it may be he keepes a register of them.

And behind the promise of 'smear' he lets play a more sinister threat of a nation undermined: 'I will place a young Martin in everie parish, . . . every one of them able to mar a prelate.'[12] The flaunting, scandalmongering tone went straight for the establishment nerve. Martin threatened, as Nashe later put it, to 'iustle our governement forth of doores with a iest'.[13]

The *Epistle* burst on the scene sometime shortly before 14 November 1588, on which day a citizen reported that certain 'bookes or libells' were on sale, price twopence, at two Kingston houses. That same day

Burghley and Hatton, Lords Treasurer and Chancellor, addressed an urgent *communiqué* to Whitgift about this 'lewd and seditious' matter being 'secretly dispersed by persons of unquiet spyrrites'. Interrogations at Kingston turned up little, as did a raid on Waldegrave's house in London (they 'violently rusht into his house, breaking through the maine wall thereof after midnight').[14] The authorities were left staring at a pamphlet professedly 'printed oversea within two furlongs of a Bounsing Priest', and dated at the end, 'Betweene twelve and twelve of the clocke, *Anno pontificatus vestri quinto*', i.e. the fifth year of Whitgift's 'papacy'. This was the first of the fantastic locatives and dedications which became Martin's trademark; they were copied by the anti-Martinists and refined *ad absurdum* by Nashe in his later works. In reality, the Martinist cell had left Molesey about a fortnight before the *Epistle* broke, and by mid-November it was established at the house of Sir Richard Knightley at Fawsley, near Northampton.[15] Sir Richard's housekeeper recalls Penry's secretive arrival, bearing the master's ring and letter of introduction. His man carted in various 'stuff' in baskets, and 'one thing like a black Stone' – presumably the imposing-stone of the press – and piled them up in 'the Nursery'. Two days later Waldegrave came, under 'a feigned name of Sheme or Shamuel'. His cover was 'the pretence of sorting' Sir Richard's 'evidences' (documents, deeds, etc.). At Fawsley, Martin's follow-up pamphlet, known as the *Epitome*, was printed and sewn by Waldegrave, corrected by Penry and distributed by a London cobbler, Humfrey Newman, code-name 'Brownbread', who had joined up as 'common disperser and carrier of Martins Books'. Another new member of the cell was Henry Sharpe, Northampton bookbinder: it would be from his disclosures, after arrest in September 1589, that the authorities first learned the full story of Martin's secret press.[16] Udall fades from the scene at this point, taking up a post in Newcastle in December. He took no further part in the 'martinizing', though this stood him in little stead when he was brought to trial in 1590. This was now the classic Martinist cell: Penry, Waldegrave, Newman and Sharpe, and in and amongst them 'Martin the Metropolitane' himself, a figment so real that a servant of Sir Richard's stated 'that Martin was there and went apparelled in greene'.[17] Was this Penry himself, who another witness said 'went disguised in a long sky-coloured Cloake', or was there another, unknown figure there?

The *Epitome* opens with more provocation. Martin taunts his pursuers:

Why my cleargie masters, is it even so with your terriblenes? May not a pore gentleman signifie his good will unto you by a Letter, but presently you must put your selves to the paines and charges of . . . posting over citie and countrie for poore Martin?

He admits that most Puritans think him extreme, 'because I am too open, because I iest', but asserts that his shock-tactics are really a diversion. The bishops' futile effort to track him down leaves them unguarded against more articulate challenges:

> Your dealing therein is but to holde my dishe while I spill my pottage: you defend your legges against Martins strokes, while the Puritanes by their *Demonstration* [i.e. Udall's *Demonstration of Discipline*, one of the books printed at Molesey] crushe the very braine of your Bishopdomes.[18]

The *Epitome* was out by the first week in December. In early January the outlaw press was on the move again, first to a deserted farmhouse at Norton, and then by cart along the back-roads to Coventry, to the house of John Hales, zealous Puritan and a relative of Knightley's.

By now the authorities were rallying their counter-attack. In January 1589, Thomas Cooper, Bishop of Winchester, published his *Admonition to the People of England*, an official riposte to the 'slaunderous untruethes reprochfully uttered by Martin the libeller'. On 9 February, Richard Bancroft delivered a bitter philippic from Paul's Cross, which was swiftly printed. Four days later a Royal Proclamation against these 'schismatical' libels and 'fantasticall' writings 'in rayling sorte' was posted up. All copies were to be given up to the authorities to be 'utterly defaced': it was henceforth a crime to possess one, and those actually involved were risking the 'uttermost perils' and 'paines' reserved for traitors.[19] The Queen can have been little pleased when, a few days after the Proclamation, her beloved Earl of Essex pulled out a copy of Martin from beneath his cloak and said, in effect, 'What then shall become of me?'[20] And even less pleased when, on about 20 February, the third of Martin's publications appeared. A single-sheet broadside known as the *Mineralls*, it set forth 37 'minerall and metaphisicall Schoolpoints to be defended by the reverend Bishops', thus offering a satirical 'Quintessence' of all 'Catercorner divinitie'.[21] The *Mineralls* was (as Penry told Sharpe) just a 'pretty thing to be set out before the other Bookes', and so duly appeared from the Coventry hide-out the fourth of Martin's railleries, *Hay any Worke for Cooper*, which answered Bishop Cooper's *Admonition* with a jeering street-cry ('hay' = 'have ye'). In this 'briefe Pistle directed by way of hublication to the reverend Bysshops', Martin perfects his *persona*. He cavorts and abuses, splintering his propaganda with manic interjections:

> whau, whau, but where have I bin al this while. Ten to one among some of these puritans. Why Martin, why Martin I say, hast tow forgotten thy selfe? Where hast ti bene? Why man, cha bin a seeking

for a Samons nest, and cha vound a whol crue, either of ecclesiasticall traitors, or of bishops of the Divel, of broken and maimed members of the church; never winke on me good fellow, for I will speke the truth.

He writes with unflagging energy, the missionary desperado: 'What though I were hanged, do you thinke your cause shalbe the better?' Some thousand copies of the pamphlet were abroad by the end of March. It was another round to Martin. 'Farewell, farewell, farewell, olde Martin, and keepe thee out of their handes for all that. For thou art a shrewd fellowe, thou wilt one day overthrow them. Amen.'[22]

The valediction was not inappropriate, for now the cracks appeared in the Martinist cell. Months of flight, secrecy and gruelling nocturnal labour were beginning to tell. Penry came seldom to Hales' house for fear of drawing suspicion; Hales was anxious to be rid of the press; Sharpe was in daily fear of arrest and was 'purposeing to have offered himself of his owne accord into their hands'. In April Waldegrave and Sharpe dined together at Wolston, near Coventry. Waldegrave was pale and haggard. He complained of bad diet and of being kept 'so closely at worke' that he 'lyved as in a Prison'. After dinner the two men walked out into the fields. Sharpe asked, 'What newes?' Waldegrave answered that 'now all was despatched and the Milne was not going' (the 'mill' was their code for the printing-press). Then he announced he was quitting. He 'wolde no longer meddle or be a dealer in this course', partly because all moderate Puritans did 'mislike yt', and partly because he had acquired a new manuscript of Cartwright's and 'wolde go prynt it in Devonshire'.[23] A month later, around Whitsun (18 May), the Martinists learned that Waldegrave had slipped out of the country and was setting up a press at Rochelle. Martin had lost his printer and chief henchman, and silence fell while he regrouped.

It was about this time, the spring of 1589, that the flouted authorities began to consider a new tactic. Proclamations, pursuivants and official rhetoric had failed: it was time to bring on the professionals. The idea was Bancroft's: 'by his advice', Whitgift later explained, 'that Course was taken wch did principally stop Martin & his Fellow's mouths, viz: to have them answered after their own vein in writing'.[24] Thus the martinizing of Martin began, turning against him his own weapons of lampoon and jocular abuse. Among the writers who contributed plays, doggerel poems and pamphlets to the establishment cause – lurking behind such names as 'Mar-Martine', 'the Cavaliero Pasquill',

'Marforius', 'Double V' and 'Cutbert Curryknave' – were the three Wits,
Lyly, Greene and Nashe, and probably Anthony Munday.

First in this new campaign were the anti-Martinist shows, put on at
the Theatre and other play-houses. We hear of Martin 'attired like an
Ape on ye Stage', and presented 'with a cocks combe, an apes face, a
wolfs bellie, cats clawes, &c'. In one show Martin was put to 'the paine
of worming and launcing': physicians 'opened the vaine that feeds his
head' and pronounced that 'he would spit out his lunges within one
yere'.[25] These were obviously coarse, sensational performances, full of
violent antics. A tract by 'Pasquill' gives another glimpse – the players

> brought foorth Divinitie wyth a scratcht face, holding of her hart as
> if she were sicke, because Martin would have forced her, but myssing
> of his purpose, he left the print of his nayles uppon her cheekes, and
> poysoned her with a vomit which he ministred unto her, to make her
> cast uppe her dignities and promotions.[26]

Another entertainment, mentioned separately in three anti-Martinist
pamphlets, was apparently called *The Maygame of Martinisme*. It was
'verie defflie set out, with Pompes, Pageants, Scutchions, Emblems,
Impreases, strange trickes and devises'. It featured a mock maying-dance:
'Penry the welchman is the fore-gallant of the Morrice', and 'Martin
himself is the Mayd-Marian, trimly drest uppe in a cast Gowne', with
'his face handsomely muffled with a Diaper-napkin to cover his beard'.
This was played at the Theatre, probably in May 1589.[27] None of these
shows survives in written form: who penned or played them is uncertain.
It is possible that the comic actor John Lanham was involved, for one
pamphleteer says, after clear references to the *Maygame*, 'let old Lanam
lash him [Martin] with his rimes'.[28] Will Kemp may also have contributed his famous comic talents: a later Martinist tract mentions a 'Kemp'
among the 'haggling and prophane' detractors of Martin, and Nashe
dedicated his own effort, *An Almond for a Parrat*, to Kemp.[29] Both
Lanham and Kemp were old members of Leicester's troupe, which had
dispersed on the death of its patron in 1588 and joined ranks with Lord
Strange's Men. The latter company was specifically mentioned by Lord
Mayor Hart in November 1589, when the authorities were moving to
suppress the unseemly plays they had originally encouraged. It seems
probable that Strange's Men, including Kemp and Lanham, were responsible for some of these gruesome travesties of Martin.[30]

The first of the popular broadsides against Martin to be actually
printed were two anonymous pamphlets in rhyme, *A Whip for an Ape*
and *Mar-Martine*, both published sometime before July 1589.[31] These
poems – crude, knock-about stuff – have been attributed to John Lyly,
who undoubtedly wrote the prose pamphlet *Pappe with a Hatchet*, under

the pseudonym of 'Double V'; and who may have had a hand in the anti-Martinist shows in his capacity as play-master of Paul's Boys. A more likely candidate as 'Mar-Martine', however, is Anthony Munday, an unsavoury character who long combined the roles of spy and pamphleteer in that half-lit world where we have glimpsed Marlowe and Watson. Back in 1578 he had infiltrated the English seminary at Rome, returning to pen anti-Catholic pamphlets and earn the praise of Richard Topcliffe, chief persecutor of the Catholics, as an agent 'who wants no sort of wit'.[32] Now he was working as informer and pursuivant in the hunt for Martin. Imagining 'an oration of Iohn Canturburie to the pursuvants', Martin has Whitgift barking at 'Maister Munday':

Ah thou Iudas, thou that hast alreadie betrayed the Papistes, I thinke meanest to betray us also. Diddest thou not assure me, without all doubt, that thou wouldest bring mee in Penry, Newman, Waldegrave, presse, letters and all, before Saint Andrewes day last. And nowe thou seest we are as farre to seeke for them as ever we were.[33]

St Andrew's Day last is 30 November 1588. This may suggest that the raid on Waldegrave's house at about that time was at Munday's instigation. Perhaps he was one of the pursuivants who, *teste* Martin, rifled Waldegrave's books that night and sold them 'up and down the streets to watchmen and others'. It was certainly Munday who brought in Giles Wigginton, a preacher suspected of involvement with Martin, on 6 December.[34] As a prolific hack, Munday would be a natural choice for Bancroft's literary campaign against Martin. His efforts in such volumes as *A Banquet of Daintie Conceits* (1588) show him capable of writing poetry as bad as that in the *Whip* and *Mar-Martine*.

By July 1589 the authorities were at last gaining the upper hand. Londoners flocked to the theatres to see Martin whipped and wormed, and to Paul's to buy the doggerel broadsides (the *Whip* quickly went into a second edition). The stage shows went on tour through the provinces: Pasquill, writing in October, says they had been 'long in the Country'.[35] Other more respectable counter-blasts, like Leonard Wright's *Admonicion to Martin Marprelat* and Tobias Bland's *Baite for Momus*, were issued. It seemed clear too that Martin was in disarray. His press had been silent since the end of March, Waldegrave had fled the country, and Sharpe shown himself ready to make a deal, his wife petitioning Chancellor Hatton to that effect in mid-June. But if Whitgift was beginning to rest easier, he was seriously under-estimating his opponent. On 22 July he awoke to a rude shock: *Theses Martinianae*. It was in a different type and it was professedly by a different author, a 'pretty stripling' called 'Martin junior'. It was affectionately addressed to 'good

neame and nuncka' (i.e. uncle) Whitgift. Martin was back in a new suit
of clothes:

> You see, nunckle Canterburie, that though I bee but young, yet I
> beginne prettily well to followe my fathers steppes; for I promise you
> I am deceived unlesse I have a pretty smattering gift in this Pistle-
> making.

He makes light of the 'flim flam' rumours that his 'father' – Martin
himself – has been silenced: 'the reporte abroad goeth that you are
drawen drie, and can say no more; they are fooles that so thinke, say
I'. He exhorts old Martin to 'feare none of these beastes, these persu-
vants, these Mar-Martins, these stage players, these prelates, these popes,
these divels'.[36] A week later, to complete the revival, his elder brother,
'Martin senior', came forth with *The Iust Censure and Reproofe of
Martin Iunior*.

The drift of these two brilliant pamphlets is to suggest Martin as
Hydra-like and irrepressible: 'I could have told tis long agoe', says
Martin senior, 'that my father would get him so many sons as Iohn
Canturbury would have no cause to sitte quiet at dinner'.[37] It was
indeed something of a resurrection that Penry had accomplished. He had
recruited a new team of printers – a saltpetre man named John Hodgkins
(or Hoskins), and two assistants, Tomlyn and Simmes – and he had
established a new headquarters, at Wolston Priory near Coventry. Here
Hodgkins was installed 'very privately in a low Parlour, and was kept
there under the name of an Imbroyderer, that the servants might know
nothing of the matter'.[38] Above all, Penry had a new right-hand man:
Job Throckmorton, squire of Hasely, Warwickshire, and MP for
Warwick, who henceforth acted as proof-reader, financier and 'principal
agent in all these libels'.[39] Internal tensions and subterfuges dog these
latest defiances from Martin. Hodgkins was an unknown quantity: he
could be the bishops' man. Care was taken that he knew nothing of the
actual authorship of the pamphlets. He was only told that 'a Booke
should come into his hands'. One day, walking with Penry near Throckmorton's house, he 'saw lying before him in ye way a Roll of paper
wrapped up together'. He picked it up and found it was the 'copie' of
Theses Martinianae.[40] This elaborate ploy is reflected in the text itself,
where Martin's own 'scrabled and weatherbeaten papers' are found by
Martin junior 'besides a bush'. The instinctive theatricality, Martin's
relish for **this** deadly game, is amazing.

In these two pamphlets the 'rimers and stage plaiers' on the episcopal
pay-roll are roundly abused. Mar-Martin is called a mere 'ribaulder',
brought up in a 'brothel-house' and thence 'promoted into the service
of some laundresse in a bishoppes house'. He is probably, thinks Martin

junior, a 'Londoner or an universitie man', a dubious 'youth' whose dishonest dealings will 'see him, one of these odd dayes, carted out of the town'. Apparently unable to name him, Martin hits shrewdly at the disreputable literary *demi-monde* out of which he springs. The business about him entering the bishops' service via the laundry suggests the rather dubious, subfusc relationship, the back-room dealing, between the churchmen and the pamphleteers. As for the actors, 'being stage players, that is plaine rogues', they can do Martin little harm. Such 'seelie hunger starved wretches' are, he concludes, 'merveilous fitte upholders of Lambehithe palace and the crowne of Canturburie'.[41] The sarcasm is pitched just right to play on the bishops' doubts as to whether their 'haggling and prophane' hacks really were the proper spokesmen for 'their hierarchie'.

In the second week of August, in swift response to this new effrontery, appeared the first anti-Martinist work which could genuinely claim to answer Martin in his 'own vein in writing'. Entitled *A Countercuffe given to Martin Iunior*, written by 'the venturous, hardie and renowned Pasquill of England, Cavaliero', and printed 'betweene the skye and the grounde, within a myle of an Oake', it is a short 'butterfly pamphlet', a single sheet folded in quarto to give a title-page and six pages of text.[42] The metaphor – countercuffs and cavalieros – is one of challenge and combat: 'Pasquill hath taken up your Glove, and desires you to charge your weapon at him like a Man.' He will fight as dirty as Martin: 'if you barke like a Curre and bite behind, he will have a tricke with his heele to strike out your teeth'. He will answer Martin smear for smear: 'Pasquill hath posted very diligently over all the Realme, to gather some fruitfull Volume of *The Lives of the Saints*' (i.e. of scandals and anecdotes about the Puritans). The whole pamphlet breathes an air of business-like detection. Pasquill speeds from Kent to Essex to Hertfordshire, wherever there are 'tidings' of Martinism. At St Albans

he staid one whole Saboath at the Christopher, and having there pestered a new pair of writing-tables with profitable Notes for that quarter, he set forward the Munday following to North-hampton-shire.

There he encounters one of the 'Brother Preachers', with

a little Hatte like a Sawcer uppon hys crowne, a Filch-man in his hande, a swapping Ale-dagger at his back, containing by estimation some two or three pounds of yron in the hyltes and chape, and a Bandogge by his side to commaunde forty foote of grounde wheresoever he goes.

These passages have a strong flavour of Nashe: the writer 'pestering' his notebooks; the pun on Anthony Munday as pursuivant; the swift visual sketch of the Puritan. Does this mean that Nashe *is* 'Pasquill', the author of this 'countercuff' and its two sequels, *The Returne of Pasquill* and *Pasquils Apologie*? The answer, I think, is yes and no. There is certainly material from Nashe in them but he was not their main author (McKerrow included them in his edition of Nashe, but later doubted they were his).[43] What seems likely is that Nashe was at this time engaged more as a roving researcher than a writer, gathering material in the Puritan strongholds of the South, including his native East Anglia, some of it filtering *verbatim* into the tracts themselves. Nashe himself says – in the one anti-Martinist pamphlet accepted as entirely his, *An Almond for a Parrat* – 'I am more than halfe weary of tracing too and fro in this cursed commonwealth.' He speaks of stories written up in his 'tables', of his 'blacke booke' which the Puritans should beware. Even by the end of the *Almond*, which has more hard fact – stories, incidents, names, etc. – than any other anti-Martinist work, he has still 'not halfe emboweled' his 'register'.[44] The locations mentioned in the Pasquill tracts – the Christopher Inn at St Albans; an 'assemblie of the brotherhood' infiltrated at Ashford, Kent; the road 'betweene Bifield and Fawseley' – may actually record Nashe's movements in the summer of 1589, in this curious role of ecclesiastical journalist. Well might Pasquill threaten the Martinist sympathizers that he 'hath excellent Ferrets to followe them in their owne Boroughs'.

But if Nashe was the news-hound, who actually wrote the Pasquill tracts? A plausible answer is Robert Greene. He was certainly a member of the anti-Martinist clique: Nashe explicitly includes him when he recalls (in 1592) the controversy 'twixt Martin and us' – 'us' being 'Paphatchet, Pasquill & others' that opposed 'that mightie Platformer of Atheisme'.[45] Greene and Nashe were closely associated this summer of 1589, which saw their appearance together in *Menaphon*. Their collaboration may well extend to the Pasquill tracts – Greene, the foremost scribbler of the day, being hired to write them, with Nashe, his lesser-known associate, as co-author and chief supplier of piping hot 'informations'. Earlier in the year, Greene's *Spanish Masquerado* had shown him capable of the kind of politico-religious writing required. His new mood of seriousness, announced in *Greenes Mourning Garment* (1590), would be well suited by this role of establishment polemicist: *'nascimur pro patria'* would be the motto adorning his 'conny-catching' tracts – 'we are born to serve our country'. It is hard to adduce stylistic evidence, since all these writers were avowedly echoing Martin's own style. As Lyly puts it, in *Pappe with a Hatchet*, 'whatsoever shall seeme lavish in this Pamphlet, let it be thought borrowed of Martins language'.[46] But looking, for instance, at the opening of Pasquill's *Returne*, with its taut, dramatic dialogue between Pasquill and Marforius, one can confidently say that Nashe could not have written it and Greene certainly could.

On 14 August, just a few days after the appearance of Pasquill's *Countercuffe*, the Martinists received a more real and crippling blow. In a 'gunpowder house' on the outskirts of Manchester, whither the press had been moved from Wolston, the three Martinist printers, Hodgkins, Tomlyn and Simmes, were arrested by the officers of the Earl of Derby. They were printing *More Work for the Cooper* – Martin's promised sequel to *Hay any Worke* – and had completed 'six Quires of one side before they were apprehended'.[47] They were brought down to London, thrown in the Tower and interrogated with 'rackinge and great torments'. On the 24th Whitgift wrote grimly to Lord Burghley: 'I assuer my self that they shalbe Delt with acording to there Desertes. . . . I dowt not but that the author of those unchristian Libles may by them be detected.'[48] What exactly the printers revealed is uncertain. One thing the authorities learned was that the Martinist cell had another press at its disposal and a cache of type at a 'Marchants Howse in London'. So, even after the arrest of Henry Sharpe at Wolston in mid-September, they knew that Penry and Throckmorton were still on the loose, and still capable of pamphleteering. Their fears were answered when, in mid-October, appeared the latest (and last) of Martin's defiances: *The Protestatyon of Martin Marprelate*. The ragged printing of its title-page and first sheet is a vivid typographic memento of the stresses and dangers under which it was produced: it was probably set up by Penry himself. Martin does not disguise his fears – 'these events I confes doe strike me, and give me iuste cause to enter more narrowly into my selfe, to see whether I bee at peace with god or no'. He returns again and again to 'the state of the poor men that are taken', dwelling on the horrors of capture and interrogation: 'halter, axe, bonds, scourging and racking'. But the main feeling, as with Martin junior, is one of breathtaking brinkmanship. At the centre of the book, in large type, is the 'protestation' itself, in which Martin offers 'personally to appear' in 'open disputation' with the bishops. His conditions are that he 'be not delt with or molested' and that if he wins the argument, Whitgift and his crew are 'to trusse up and be packing to Rome & to trouble our church no longer'.[49]

With the luck of the desperate, Martin had timed his *Protestatyon* perfectly. Three new anti-Martinist pamphlets were on the bookstalls by late October – *Martins Months Minde* by 'Marforius', *The Returne of Pasquill*, and Lyly's *Pappe with a Hatchet* – and not one of them dealt adequately with the *Protestatyon*. Marforius makes no mention of it at all, while Pasquill and Lyly can only refer to it in hurried post-scripts.[50] Even with his last gasp Martin had upstaged them. It was also becoming increasingly clear that a new note of hesitation was creeping into the

bishops' campaign, and that the authorities were beginning to look
askance on the playwrights and pamphleteers they had commissioned.
Both *Pappe* and the *Returne* speak of the official suppression of the anti-
Martinist stage shows. Pasquill says he has 'a tale to tell' of 'the slye
practise that was used in restraining' them.[51] Lyly complains, more
openly: 'would those comedies might be allowed to be plaid that are
pend, and then I am sure he [Martin] would be decyphered'. Lyly had
probably written these later comedies himself: they would, he says,
present a more realistic portrait of Martin, not dressed up as an ape,
'but in a cap'de cloake' and all the usual clothes he would wear 'on
some rainie weeke daie'.[52] In early November the authorities sealed their
displeasure, and ordered the closure of all theatres in London. Lord
Strange's Men defied the ban, we learn: they snubbed the Lord Mayor
'contemptuously' and played at the Cross Keys, for which two of them
were imprisoned. On 12 November the Privy Council ordered a general
clean-up of theatrical practice, primarily because 'the players take uppon
them to handle in their plaies certen matters of Divinytie and of State
unfit to be suffred'. A committee of censors was set up and the players
ordered to present their prompt-books for scrutiny.[53] The anti-Martinist
shows, with their riotous treatment of 'matters of Divinytie', were no
doubt the cause (or, at least, the excuse) for this clamp-down. The
anti-Martinist pamphleteers too were feeling the pinch. Much of the
clandestine drama at the opening of Pasquill's *Returne* comes from his
sense of enemies on both sides: 'Peace, Cavaliero, your tongue will be
slitte if you take not heede: I have heard some say you should wring for
this geare if the Queene were dead.' And by the time of his last pamphlet
– *Pasquils Apologie*, issued July 1590 – the backlash is even clearer.
Many consider it distasteful to 'see us runne one at another like furious
Bulles, foming and casting out those reproches'. He has been accused of
Catholic leanings – 'this fellow', they say, 'seems to have a Pope in his
bellie'. Certain 'small rubs' have been 'cast in my way to hinder my
coming forth'.[54]

These 'rubs' – obstacles, as in Hamlet's 'there's the rub' – refer to
books being written in late 1589, which attacked the anti-Martinists as
little more edifying than Martin himself. Pasquill refers to a 'Common
Counsellor' and 'student at the Lawe' who has 'undertaken to be a
stickler betweene us all'. This is probably Francis Bacon, whose *Advertisement touching the Controversies of the Church of England* was
written at this time.[55] Another voice being raised was Gabriel Harvey's,
who completed his *Advertisement for Papp-hatchett and Martin Marprelate* on 5 November. Harvey's immediate motive was personal – his
old enemy Lyly had glanced at him in *Pappe*, calling him a pedant 'full
of latin endes', who 'cares as little for writing without wit as Martin
doth for writing without honestie'. Harvey begins with abuse of Lyly

and his pamphlet – 'a few morsels of fly-blowne Euphuisme, somewhat nicely minced for puling stomacks' – but soon moves into a broader complaint about the anti-Martinist propaganda:

What scholler or gentleman can reade such alehouse and tinkerly stuffe without blushing? . . . What good could grow out of it but to make every man madbrayned and desperate, but a generall contempt of all good order in Saying and Dooing, but an universall Topsy-Turvy?[56]

The pamphleteers are dismissed as 'a Synode of Diapason Fooles', debasing the ecclesiastical cause with their 'ruffianly scoffes'. At about the same time Harvey's brother Richard entered the fray under the guise of 'Plaine Percevall the Peace-maker', ostensibly trying to 'botch up a reconciliation between Mar-ton and Mar-tother'. His abuse of the anti-Martinists in *Plaine Percevall*, and of Nashe in *The Lamb of God*, was the spark which ignited the Nashe-Harvey quarrel. He calls the anti-Martinists literary yobs: 'Hufsnufs, Roisters, and the residew of light fingerd Younkers, which make every word a blow and every booke a bobbe'.[57] The anonymous author of *A Myrrour for Martinists*, registered in December 1589, completes the denigration of the pamphleteers: they are 'men of uncircumcised lips, whose evill wordes corrupt good manners'.[58]

By the close of 1589, one long polemical year after Martin's first *éclat*, the war had reached a curious plateau. Martin's press had been seized but Martin not silenced; the anti-Martinist shows had drawn the crowds but were now suppressed; the pamphleteers had risen to the challenge, but they too were being disowned by their pay-masters, and attracting critical notices from the likes of Bacon and the Harveys. It was at this edgy, ambivalent stage that Thomas Nashe set to work on the *Almond for a Parrat*. He called himself 'Cutbert Curryknave', to 'curry' meaning to soak, scrape or beat leather (the job of a 'currier'), hence figuratively to give someone a drubbing or beating, to 'tan his hide'. Probably written in November 1589, the *Almond* was specifically intended as the riposte to Martin's *Protestatyon*, which had only been glancingly dealt with by Pasquill and Lyly.[59] But also – whether by design, timing or simply Nashe's relish for the fray – it has the feel of being the anti-Martinists' *coup de grâce*. It gives full details of the capture of the press; it is the first openly to put the finger on Penry as Martin, and the first to implicate John Udall. There is a density of material, a plenty of scurrilous 'news', a satirical sureness, which suggest a writer at last in control of Martin, possessed of his secrets: 'I am a shreud fellow at the uncasing of a fox and have cats eyes to looke into everie corner of a Puritans house.'[60]

He opens, in response to the *Protestatyon*:

> Welcome, Mayster Martin, from the dead, and much good ioy may you have of your stage-like resurrection. It was told me by the undanted persevants of your sonnes, and credibly beleeved in regard of your sinnes, that your grout-headed holinesse had turnd uppe your heeles like a tired iade in a medow, and snorted out your scornefull soule, like a mesled hogge on a mucke-hill, which had it not beene false, as the devill would have it . . .

And on he races, the crescendo straightaway arrived at but then sustained, the reader swept along with no time to dwell on those reverberant little touches ('stage-like', 'grout-headed') before the idea of Martin's death throws up other sketches and images – of Margaret Lawson, Puritan scold of St Paul's, using her 'Parrats tong in stead of a winde-clapper to scarre the crowes from thy carrion'; of Cuthbert Cliff the 'ecclesiastical cobbler', weeping into his blacking tub and stitching 'your traytourshippe' a tomb of untanned leather – and then, still on the theme of death, we are into a mischievous tale of a Northamptonshire preacher, who took a precedent 'piping hot from the primitive church' and, to save on funeral expenses,

> tombled his wife naked into the earth at high noone, without sheete or shroude to cover her shame, breathing over her in an audible voice: Naked came I out of my mothers wombe, and naked shall I returne again.[61]

Of all the anti-Martinists it was Nashe who took most readily to Martin's polemic 'vein', caught its effervescence and bite, revelled in its ranging freedom. The comic phraseologies bustle across the page – 'I praie thee, good hedge-creeper', 'master sauce malapert', 'good munckie face Machivell'. The satirical synopses of Puritanism are swiftly etched – 'a balde eloquent brother', 'those reverend elders of the church, Hicke, Hob and Iohn'; 'old true-pennie Marprelate' himself, 'writing of pamphlets in some spare out-house', and 'ruminating under an oake or in the bottom of a haystacke, whose bloud shall be first spilte in the reformation of the Church'.[62]

Beneath the bubbling surface of the *Almond* is the hard core of Nashe's understanding of Puritanism, a knowledge imbibed as a boy in Norfolk, deepened by his years at Cambridge, and now finely honed by his months of anti-Martinist sleuthing. He rounds on the Puritans' intellectual dourness – 'our reformatorie Churchmen, who account wit vanitie and poetry impietie' – with the anger of one who has suffered from it. He scoffs at the artisan-provincial base of the movement with an ingrained snobbishness. Yet also, as so often with Nashe, there are more tangled responses beneath the polemical veneer. He cannot quite dissociate his own insubordinations from Martin's. When he puts a tirade against Academe into Martin's mouth – 'What is Logicke but the highe waie to wrangling, containing in it but a world of bibble-babble? . . . Go to, you are a great companie of vaine men that stand upon your degrees and tongues'[63] – it seems little more than an exaggeration of his own anti-academic stance, that derision of deliberating 'Art-maisters' and 'quadrant crepundios' which is so noticeable in his preface to *Menaphon*. As one reads into the *Almond* one glimpses a kind of covert allegiance between the antagonists. They speak the same language – 'M. Martin, how like you my stile, am I not old *Ille ego qui quondam* at ye besleeving of a sichophant?' In the outlaw Martin, the budding satirist finds his own venturings beyond the pale of propriety writ large. The air of official disapproval now brooding over the anti-Martinists becomes a frustration which only Martin can release:

> If authority do not moderate the fiery fervence of my enflamed zeale, Ile assaile thee from terme to terme . . . .
> O God, that we two might bee permitted but one quarter, to try it out by the teeth for the best benefice in England, then would I distill my wit into incke and my soule into arguments.[64]

'We two' fight, and find life in the fight. The real enemy is 'authority', moderating its fervence and wit. Compared to his lavishing of abuse on Martin, Nashe's commendation of Whitgift's 'mildnes and gravity' is damp indeed.

In open complaint at fastidiousness in the episcopal camp Nashe says, 'it is our English policy to advauntage our enemies by delaies' and so let sedition 'seede'. This was apparently the case with the *Almond*, for it seems that publication was delayed until the spring of 1590. In his dedication to the comedian Will Kemp, Nashe apologizes that his 'tidings' are already stale, adding: 'impute it to the intercepting of my papers, that have stayed for a good winde ever since the beginning of winter'.[65] The pamphlet was, in other words, sat on by the authorities – perhaps because its unmasking of Penry as Martin accorded ill with their failure to catch him. In dedicating the *Almond* to 'that most comical and conceited Cavaliere, Monsieur du Kempe, Iestmonger and Vicegerent generall to the Ghost of Dicke Tarlton', Nashe again shows an instinctive allegiance. Kemp might, he says, prefer not to be his patron, for fear of those disapproving 'Citizens' who 'cannot away with argument'. If so he will dedicate it to the soul of Tarlton himself, imitating

that merry man Rablays, who dedicated most of his workes to the
soule of the old Queene of Navarre many yeares after her death, for
that she was a maintainer of mirth in her life. Marry, god send us more
of her making, and then some of us should not live so discontented as
we do: for now a dayes a man cannot have a bout with a Balletter,
or write *Midas habet aures asininas* in great Romaine letters, but hee
shall bee in daunger of a further displeasure. Well, come on it what
will, Martin and I will allow of no such doinges; wee can cracke half
a score blades in a backe-lane though a Constable come not to part
us.[66]

Again the secret cameraderie. In one corner the citizens and constables,
the Harveys and Bacons, the dispensers of 'further displeasure'. In the
other the entertainers, a motley crew of odd-balls and malcontents, the
clowns Kemp and Tarlton, the gargantuan Rabelais, the renegade Martin
and the pamphleteer Curryknave.

The *Protestatyon* and the *Almond* constitute the last exchange in the
Marprelate war. Pasquill's last pamphlet – the *Apologie*, July 1590 – is
directed at Penry *per se* and scarcely mentions Martin. It has no
distinctive traces of Nashe, or of any other Wit: the *nom de plume* may
have been handed over to another writer, possibly Munday. Penry
himself had escaped to Scotland shortly after the completion of the
Protestatyon. There he was protected by King James and reunited with
Waldegrave: he continued to publish, under his own name, from Edinburgh. He was eventually captured, in London, in March 1593, and on
29 May he was hanged at St Thomas a Watering on the Southern
outskirts of London. John Udall was arrested in 1590 and died in prison
two years later. Henry Sharpe told all he knew and probably gained his
liberty thereby. Newman the distributor and Hodgkins the printer were
still in prison, 'condemned of felonie', in May 1591: their eventual fate
is unknown. Strangely, Job Throckmorton, deeply implicated in the later
Martinizing, escaped any punishment – this despite a trial at Warwickshire assizes in 1590 and a detailed indictment drawn up against him
by Matthew Sutcliffe in 1595.[67]

One question remains. Was Nashe right in identifying Penry as Martin
himself? There is no doubt that Penry was the *animus* of the whole
Martinist adventure, 'a principal Dealer in all the action every where',
as the Attorney General's brief put it. But no-one, not even the other
Martinists, could prove that he actually wrote the tracts. Sharpe testified
that when he challenged Penry, 'I think this Booke [the *Epitome*] to be
of your making', Penry 'gave no aunswere but laughed'; and that when
he warned that the type of Martin junior being the same as Penry's
Supplication 'wolde descry him to be Martin', Penry returned 'a careless
answere and so they past yt over'.[68] At every point Penry refused to be

drawn, just as he devised elaborate ploys to convey copy to Hodgkins anonymously. At his trial John Udall said: 'I think there is never minister in this land that doth know who Martin is; and I for my part have been inquisitive but could never learn.' Throckmorton said: 'I am not Martin, I knewe not Martin.' Penry himself went to the gallows denying that he was Martin: 'I answer that my name is John Penri and not Marten Marprelate: I answer that I desier to be called to my triall in this poynt.' The authorities declined to charge him as such: they had enough to hang him anyway. They took Penry's own advice, in a letter from prison to Lord Burghley: 'it were meetest for them to lett Martin dy of himself and not rayse up his ghost after this sort. . . . The man will dy whosoever he was.'[69] Martin had the last laugh after all. We shall never be quite sure who it was that wrote these daring, scintillant tracts, lighting a torch which Nashe carried on in his comic prose and which thence irradiated the comedies of Shakespeare and Jonson.

7

LORD STRANGE

'Meanewhile yett rests, yow smile at what I write,
Or, for attempting, banish me your sight'

NASHE (TO 'LORD S.')   *The Choise of Valentines*

In the early months of 1590, the *Anatomie of Absurditie* and the *Almond for a Parrat* were both published. Thomas Nashe, aged twenty-two, was a fully-fledged author at last. He was fledged also in a more personal sense, for his mother had died that winter: perhaps he was there, among the ghosts of his childhood, when she was buried at St Margaret's, Lowestoft, on 10 December 1589. In her will — proved by brother Israel at Ipswich the following February[1] — it is Thomas who is mentioned first, before the elder and chief legatee Israel, and Thomas who gets her own 'fetherbedde' and the 'coverlett which I do laye on' (Israel gets the 'best bedsteade in the hall'). Nothing very unusual, but perhaps a hint of her feelings for the younger and wilder son. She probably knew that the silver spoons, pewter and candlesticks she bequeathed him would soon be stocking some London pawnshop.

With publication came publicity, for in the spring of 1590 appeared the first printed reference to Nashe, an unfriendly notice by Richard Harvey in the prefatory epistle to *The Lamb of God*.[2] After holding forth extensively on the 'odious iester' Martin, Harvey pauses to apologize for his presumption, saying:

> It becummeth me not to play that part in Divinitie that one Thomas Nashe hath lately done in humanitie, who taketh uppon him in civill learning, as Martin doth in religion, peremptorily censuring his betters at pleasure, Poets, Orators, Polihistors, Lawyers, and whome not, and making as much and as little of every man as himselfe listeth.

The target here is Nashe's preface to *Menaphon*. Harvey's tetchiness at the stripling Nashe dispensing scoffs and disdain is, perhaps, not unjustified. He treats Nashe as an upstart, in love with 'the aboundance of his own swelling sense'. He advises him, 'either study more or presume less'. He says he had never heard of Nashe before this, 'for I cannot imagine him to be Thomas Nashe our Butler at Pembrooke Hall, albeit peradventure not much better learned'. Having already censured the

80

anti-Martinists in *Plaine Percevall*, he makes much of equating Nashe's 'rash presumption' with Martin's: 'the iolly man will needes be playing the douty Martin in his kinde'. He warns, 'let not Martin, or Nash, or any other such famous obscure man, or any other piperly makeplay or makebate, presume overmuch of my patience'.

Thus Nashe's early reputation: an impudent wit, a secular Martin, a 'makebate' (stirrer up of 'bate' or strife). It must have been around this time that he in some way insulted Thomas Churchyard, an indefatigable old Grub Streeter who had been churning out pamphlets and doggerel poems since before Nashe was born. Gabriel Harvey tells us that 'in the ruffe of his freshest iollitie' Nashe was 'faine to cry M. Churchyard a mercy in printe'.[3] No such apology is identifiable in Nashe's early works but the squabble was real enough: addressing Churchyard in 1592, Nashe speaks of 'our old quarrel' and 'that unadvised indammagement I have done you heretofore'. It was by then far in the past – 'deepe buried in the grave of oblivion' – and the differences patched up. 'Ile be your champion henceforward', Nashe promises, and Churchyard returns the compliment in his *Pleasant Conceit* (1593):

> The Angell bright, that Gabrill is in sky
> Shall know that Nashe I love and will doe still.[4]

Richard Harvey's epistle in *The Lamb of God* – or the Harveys', if Nashe was right in suspecting that 'the elder brothers hand was in it'[5] – is the opening shot in Nashe's next 'civill war of wittes'. For more than two years after this brief flurry of publicity, however, his movements are obscure – until September 1592, in fact, when the publication of *Pierce Penilesse* and the events surrounding the death of Greene bring him suddenly back into the limelight. What then was Nashe up to in these first years of the 1590s? *Pierce Penilesse* itself tells us something – more than has hitherto been noticed – and there are other fragments and suppositions to sift. It has been supposed, for instance, that Nashe was the 'Robin Goodfellow' who penned *Tarltons Newes out of Purgatorie* (1590).[6] Despite his association with Tarlton, and the assertion by Harvey and others that he owed his comic style to Tarlton, the work lacks Nashe's distinctive flair. More plausible is that Nashe wrote the *Wonderfull, Strange and Miraculous Astrologicall Prognostication* for the year 1591, under the guise of 'Adam Fouleweather, Student in Assetronomy'. This was one of a trio of mock-prognostications, the others being by 'Francis Fayre-weather' and 'Simon Smell-knave'.[7] The identification of Nashe as 'Fouleweather' assumes he is using the pamphlet to tilt at Richard Harvey and his much-ridiculed *Astrologicall Discourse*. The title-page promises, 'if there be found one lye, the Author will loose his credit for ever' – not unlike Harvey's rash assurance that if his predictions failed, 'let me lose the credit of my astrologie'. Fouleweather is clearly a Londoner and his casual movements about town – 'from Poules to the Counter', 'betwixt the Old Swanne and Westminster', among the 'butchers of East Cheape' – might perhaps anticipate the sharply realized London ambiance of *Pierce Penilesse*. References to 'Martin the kill-hog' and 'Brownists, Barowists & such balductum devises' look back to the Marprelate controversy. But none of this is conclusive: the prognostication, and the parody of it, are too constant a formula for any particular satire on Harvey to be effective. Where the writer sounds Nashe-like he may only be drawing on a shared stock of Elizabethan catch-phrases, jokes and conversational small change. The humour lacks the range and bite which the *Almond* had already shown. With a stylist as distinctive as Nashe, 'not to be convinced that it is his is almost to be certain that it is not'.[8] But while these two attributions are questionable, the general conception behind them – of Nashe as someone knocking around the literary scene, ready to turn his pen to such hack formats as the 'news from . . .' and the spoof-prognostication – is authentic enough.

This leaves us with just one undoubted piece of Nashe's in the years between the *Almond* and *Pierce Penilesse*: his preface, jauntily titled 'Somewhat to Reade for them that List', to the first edition of Sir Philip Sidney's sonnet-cycle, *Astrophel and Stella*, published in 1591.[9] In terms of prestige this was every bit as effective as his earlier appearance at the prow of Greene's *Menaphon*. Sidney was still, five years after his death, a magic name, and his *Arcadia* (1590) had enjoyed huge success. Of all Nashe's writings this is the glossiest, tailored to the cultivated tastes of its audience as neatly as it is trimmed to fit four quarto pages. He bids the reader leave the 'puppet play' of inferior poets, and

> turn aside into this Theater of pleasure, for here you shal find a paper stage streud with pearle, an artificial heav'n to overshadow the faire frame, & christal wals to encounter your curious eyes, whiles the tragicommody of love is performed by starlight.

This last phrase is often quoted, as is Nashe's shapely little synopsis of *Astrophel*: 'the argument cruell chastitie, the Prologue hope, the Epilogue dispaire'. Nashe effortlessly hits that decorative lyrico-critical vein deemed appropriate for these poetic prefaces. The whole piece has a somewhat mechanical feel: a polished piece of literary day-labour. Nor does he miss his chance to deliver a fulsome tribute to the 'most rare Countesse of Pembroke', the 'fayre sister of Phoebus & eloquent secretary to the Muses', a 'second Minerva' whom 'Poets extoll as the Patronesse of their invention'. Mary Herbert, Countess of Pembroke, was Sidney's sister and literary executrix, and a highly active patron of literature. With one eye on the Countess and the other on his public, Nashe winningly signs off, 'Yours in all desire to please, Tho: Nashe'.

It all seems innocuous enough. But Nashe's preface failed to please. Within a few months a new edition of *Astrophel* was out, with no preface by Nashe. To understand this sudden guillotining we must look more closely at the brief and stormy history of the first quarto of *Astrophel*.[10] The main problem was that Sidney's poems were printed without permission. The publisher, Thomas Newman, says as much in his introductory epistle, preceding Nashe's preface. He speaks of his 'fortune' to 'light upon' a manuscript copy of the poems, his distress that 'anie thing proceeding from so rare a man shoulde bee obscured', and his 'bold' decision to publish it. There is nothing exceptional in this: there were no regulations and few scruples about publishing MSS without the consent of the author or his 'assigns'. In this case, however, the assign was the powerful Countess of Pembroke, who guarded her brother's memory fastidiously. The personal nature of the poems, the errors and corruptions of Newman's edition, sheer seigniorial pique: these combined and the Countess took action. On 18 September 1591 the book was impounded. The Stationers' Register records the payment of fourpence to porters, 'for carryeinge of Newmans bookes to the hall'. A few days later the Stationers' Company beadle 'ryd with an answere to my Lord Treasurer [Burghley] beinge with her maiestie in progress for the takeinge in of bookes intituled Sir P:S: Astrophell and Stella'. The clerk's phrasing is opaque, but it seems clear that the suppression of Newman's edition had been ordered by the great Burghley himself, who now received 'answere' that it was done. Burghley was not normally involved in censorship matters: he undoubtedly intervened at the request of the Countess.

It was not only the matter of *Astrophel* itself that had touched the Countess. Also included in the first edition were 'sundry other rare Sonnets of divers Noblemen and Gentlemen'. Prominent among these were twenty-eight sonnets by Samuel Daniel, who was one of the Countess's most favoured *protégés*, residing at Wilton House as literary adviser and as tutor to the Pembrokes' son William, the future 3rd Earl. Daniel's sonnets had also been acquired and published without permission. All but three of them appear the following year in his sonnet-cycle, *Delia*, and here he complains, in the dedication to the Countess, that it is Newman's piracy that has forced him into print. His private poems – 'things uttered to my selfe and consecrated to silence' – have been 'bewraide to the world, uncorrected'. He has been 'betraide by the indiscretion of a greedie Printer'. The purloining of Daniel's work doubtless added fuel to the Countess's displeasure over *Astrophel*. On purely literary grounds, the plaintiffs have a point. Newman's second edition of *Astrophel* – issued some time before April 1592, presumably from an authorized MS – is far superior to the first. One modern critic has counted some 350 alterations, 'almost always for the better'.[11] Daniel's official sonnets in *Delia* also show careful revision from their earlier 'uncorrected' state.

Publisher Newman, we note, suffers little in all this. He retains his copyright on *Astrophel*, acquires a new MS, publishes an orderly second edition. If anyone, it is Nashe, whose preface goes down with the first edition, who suffers. What was his role in all this? Newman says, in his epistle to the first edition, that he has engaged literary experts of 'skill and experience' to advise him in 'correcting and restoring' Sidney's work to its 'first dignitie' – in other words, editors. It seems likely that Nashe was one of these: indeed, since publishers can sometimes exaggerate, he may simply have been *the* editor of the unauthorized *Astrophel*. Here we can take some bearings, for Sidney's other great work, the *Arcadia*, has a broadly similar textual history. An unauthorized edition appeared in 1590 and, though not actually suppressed, it was supplanted in 1593 by an 'official' second edition. The editor of the latter – the Pembrokes' chief secretary, Hugh Sanford – makes it clear that the Countess considered the first edition 'disfigured' and 'blemished'. As in the case of *Astrophel*, the publisher continued unabashed: William Ponsonby published both editions of the *Arcadia*. It is the editor – almost certainly the Italian *littérateur* and lexicographer, John Florio – who gets a flea in his ear for his meddlesome additions to Sidney's original: he must learn 'from wiser judgements then his owne' that 'Sir Philip Sidneis writings can no more be perfected without Sir Philip Sidney, then Apelles pictures without Apelles.' If Nashe was the editor of *Astrophel* he was probably pronounced, like Florio, *persona non grata*. The excision of his preface may in part reflect this. Florio's hatred of Hugh Sanford surfaces finally in 1598, with his drubbing of 'Master H.S.' in the preface to his Italian dictionary. A few months later, in *Lenten Stuffe*, Nashe has a go at 'H.S.' and his 'Maid-marrian' (i.e. the Countess).[12] These later squibs doubtless refer back to Sanford's role in these editorial controversies.

Turning afresh to Nashe's preface, at least one passage seems to touch on this vexed subject of the appropriation of manuscripts. Like Newman, Nashe asserts that it is a service to present these great poems to a wider public, to 'open the gate' to Sidney's 'glory'. '*Fama poetis*', he says, is

> oftentimes imprisoned in Ladyes casks & the president bookes of such as cannot see without another mans spectacles, yet at length it breakes foorth in spight of his keepers, and useth some private penne (in steed of a picklock) to procure his violent enlargement.

The metaphor is one of liberation. His 'private' pen – as prefacer and, probably, editor – has rescued *Astrophel* from the clutches of a cultural

elite. Here, carefully held in check, is the professional writer's half-
envious contempt for the aristocratic *coterie*. Nashe's pen is 'private'
because independent: it survives on its own merits, as Sidney's surely
will. With hindsight one detects the note of defiance, and a bit of cheek,
surely, in the way Nashe invites us to think of one particular lady from
whose 'casks' *Astrophel* has been burgled. Similarly double-edged are
Nashe's scoffs at Nicholas Breton. His dismissal of pastoral poetry –
'Pan sitting in his bower of delights, & a number of Midasses to admire
his miserable hornepipes' – is unmistakably aimed at Breton's recent
volume, the *Bowre of Delights*. Another taunt confirms this. Nashe says,
mock-modestly, 'my stile is somewhat heavie gated, and cannot daunce
trip and goe so lively, with *oh my love, ah my love, all my loves gone*,
as other Sheepheards that have been fooles in the Morris time out of
minde.' The italicized line is quoted direct from 'Amoris Lachrimae', the
opening poem in Breton's *Bowre*. This may be plain market-place rivalry
– the *Bowre* was registered on 3 May 1591, and so probably appeared
around the same time as *Astrophel* – but it has also some curious
sidelights. For one thing, Breton was yet another of the Countess of
Pembroke's poets, as a string of dedications shows. To attack him, in
this Sidney-Pembroke context, is also to flout her: she is, by implication,
chief among the 'Midasses' who admire Breton's 'miserable hornepipes'.
One assumes that Nashe knew she was Breton's patroness and that the
implied insolence was deliberate. The other curious point is that Breton's
Bowre was yet another case of purloined manuscripts. The publisher,
Richard Jones, claimed to be printing the poems 'in the Authours
absence'. For 'absence' read 'ignorance', as Breton makes clear in his
next work, *The Pilgrimage to Paradise*, dedicated, yet again, to the
Countess. In the preface, dated 12 April 1592, he protests that the *Bowre*
was 'donne altogether without my consent or knowledge', and that many
of the poems in it were not his. As for the genuine pieces – a few 'toies' –
including 'Amoris Lachrimae' and an epitaph on Sidney – 'I know not
how he [Jones] unhappily came by' them.[13] In mid-1591, it would seem,
manuscript poems from the Pembroke circle were fetching a good price
in St Paul's, with no questions asked as to provenance. Nashe is openly
involved with two batches, Sidney's and Daniel's, and he is at pains to
haul a third, Breton's, into some kind of limelight. Nashe had no
recorded dealings with Richard Jones in 1591, but he certainly did a
year later: it was Jones who published the first edition of *Pierce Penilesse*.
While there is no proof that Nashe was actually involved in any underhand business, the drift of this half-submerged story is somehow very
typical of him. Tales of Grub Street piracy lurk beneath his preface's
polished veneer, and his flattering overtures to the Countess of Pembroke
are compromised by a vein of oblique but self-damaging insolence, as if
thumbing his nose when her back is turned.[14]

Such brief employments in the publishing trade were one source of income for Nashe in the early years of the 1590s. To keep the wolf from the door he also turned, like most of his fellow Wits, to the play-houses. Even the prolific proser Greene relied on plays as his 'chiefest stay of living', a servitude he bitterly resented. Whatever Nashe wrote is now lost, or at least unidentified, but he clearly did turn his hand to playwriting, since Greene addresses him – along with Marlowe and Peele – as one of those 'fellow Schollers about this Cittie' that 'spend their wits in making Plaies'. Greene calls them fools for depending on 'so meane a stay', and urges them: 'Seeke you better Maisters, for it is pittie men of such rare wits should be subiect to the pleasures of such rude groomes.' Nashe himself, by 1592 at least, had swallowed any snobbery on this point, for he inserts a handsome 'Defence of Playes' into *Pierce Penilesse*. It was probably motivated by the closure of the London theatres, by order of the Privy Council, on 22 June 1592. This was after a riot by some apprentices in Southwark, who had gathered under the 'pretence of their meeting at a Play'.[15] Nashe seems to refer to this in his 'confutation of citizens obiections against players', where he says: 'some Petitioners of the Counsaile against them obiect, they corrupt the youth of the Cittie, and withdraw Prentises from theyr worke'. He answers that apprentices will be rowdy anyway – 'the ruder handicrafts servants never come abroade but they are in danger of undoing' – and that no play in itself encourages 'tumults or rebellion', but 'layes before such the halter and the gallows'. On the contrary, plays are 'a rare exercise of vertue'. They kindle a healthy nationalism, their subjects being 'borrowed out of our English Chronicles'. They show the 'ill success' of treason and usurpation: 'all the cankerwormes that breede on the rust of peace are most lively anatomiz'd'. They offer a sharp 'reproofe to these degenerate effeminate dayes of ours'. Suppress the playhouses and the malcontent will flourish: 'faith, when Dice, Lust and Drunkennesse and all have dealt upon him, if there be never a Playe for him to goe too for his pennie, he sits melancholie in his Chamber, devising upon felonie or treason'. Thus Nashe challenges the powerful 'censurers' who 'oppugn' plays, the municipal Puritans to whom 'all Artes' are 'vanitie'.

Nashe mentions various actors – Tarlton, William Bentley, William Knell[16] – but one in particular has pride of place: Edward Alleyn. Neither Roscius nor Aesop, 'those admyred tragedians', could 'performe more in action than famous Ned Allen'. Nashe also singles out one play for praise: Shakespeare's *Henry VI* –

How would it have ioyed brave Talbot (the terror of the French) to thinke that after he had lyne two hundred yeares in his Tombe, hee should triumphe again on the Stage, and have his bones newe embalmed with the teares of ten thousand spectators at least (at severall times) who, in the Tragedian that represents his person, imagine they behold him fresh bleeding.

This conveys something of the emotive impact of Elizabethan theatre: the triumphs and tears, the crush of the crowd. It also means that Nashe was the first person *ever* to praise Shakespeare in print, indeed the first to refer to him at all, since *Pierce Penilesse* appeared a few days before Greene's *Groatsworth*, with its famous smear against the 'upstart Crow', William 'Shake-scene'.[17] It is possible there is an ulterior motive in Nashe's praise. It has been argued that Nashe himself contributed some scenes to the first two parts of *Henry VI*. There are, certainly, some striking parallels with phrases in Nashe's own pamphlets, though these could equally be Nashe echoing Shakespeare. The Jack Cade scenes in *2 Henry VI* have the atmosphere of Nashe's comic prose but, as Rhodes suggests, they could be Shakespeare's own exploiting of 'the stylistic innovations of the Marprelate controversy'. An early collaboration between Shakespeare and Nashe remains tantalizingly possible but unprovable. Nashe has also been claimed as part-author of a lost version of *Henry V* that can be glimpsed behind Shakespeare's Falstaff comedies.[18] On somewhat safer ground, Nashe's championing of Alleyn and *Henry VI* points to one particular theatre-company: Lord Strange's Men. Though technically still a member of the Lord Admiral's troupe, Alleyn is known to have starred in Strange's Men productions in 1592–3. It was the leading company of the day, and a popular item in its repertoire was 'harey the vi' which – impresario Henslowe notes in his account books – played fourteen times at the Rose theatre between 3 March and 20 June 1592. Whether or not Nashe is discernible in *Henry VI*, he may well have been writing for Lord Strange's Men, hacking out scenes for *Machiavel*, or *Harry of Cornwall*, or the picaresque tale of *Bindo and Richardo*, all lost plays from the Strange's Men repertoire of 1592.[19] Some professional involvement with Lord Strange's troupe would certainly link up – either as cause or effect – with another, more elevated connection. Sometime before the early summer of 1592 Nashe had at last found himself a noble patron. He was Ferdinando Stanley, Lord Strange.

Born in about 1559, this 'talented and popular young nobleman' was the eldest son of Henry Stanley, 4th Earl of Derby and King of Man, and he was blood-related to the Queen on both sides of his family.[20] The Stanleys were an old and entrenched family, classic Northern Earl stock, nostalgic for baronial autonomy and deeply tinged with the old religion. At the family seats in Lancashire – Knowsley, Lathom, New

Park – the Earl kept a huge retinue of 140 servants and dependants, lived in 'princely style' with much 'hospitality and magnificence', and presided over the Council of the North.[21] From this distant mini-court, the young Lord Strange graduated to the royal court itself. In January 1580, and often thereafter, his troupe of boy acrobats entertained the Queen with 'feates of Tumbling and activity'[22] – out of this nucleus emerged, after many changes and mergers, the great acting company of the early 1590s. Strange and his wife Alice, youngest daughter of Sir John Spenser of Althorp, swiftly won a reputation as cultivated and generous literary patrons. Greene dedicated *Tullies Love* (1589) to him, hoping to be 'shrowded under the protection of so honourable a Maecenas'. George Peele celebrated the performance of 'Derby's son and heir, brave Ferdinand' at the Accession Day Tilts of 1590. Spenser called him 'the very Paterne of right Nobilitie' in *The Teares of the Muses* (1591), dedicated to Lady Strange, with whom Spenser claimed kinship. Marlowe claimed himself to be 'very well known' to Lord Strange in 1592. Among other writers who expressed their gratitude and admiration were Thomas Newton, Barnabe Barnes, George Chapman, Matthew Roydon, William Covell, Sir John Harington, John Davies of Hereford, Henry Lok and John Marston.[23] Strange's untimely death in April 1594 was lamented by Spenser in *Colin Clouts Come Home Again* (1595). Calling him 'Amyntas', the same pastoral name Nashe uses for him, Spenser says:

> He whilest he lived was the noblest swaine
> That ever piped in an oaten quill:
> Both did he other which could pipe maintaine,
> And eke could pipe himselfe with passing skill.[24]

This praises Strange as a poet as well as a patron of poets: some of his efforts appear in the anthology, *Belvedere* (1600), though the poems are not individually identified. As well as a courtier, patron and poet, Strange seems to have been a scholar whose enthusiasm was for the fashionable occult studies. He is sometimes claimed as a member of Ralegh's esoteric clique – the so-called School of Night – but there is no real evidence of this.[25] His general occultist leanings, and Nashe's attitude to them, will emerge in the course of this book.

How and when Nashe gained Lord Strange's favour is unknown. One possibility is the anti-Martinist connection. From the 'household books' kept by the Earl of Derby's steward, William ffarington, we know that Strange was in London from January 1589, when he was summoned to parliament, till about July.[26] As his players were performing anti-Martinist shows around then, Strange himself might have met the writers involved in the campaign – Greene, who dedicated *Tullies Love* to him later in the year; Lyly, who was a member of the same parliament

(though not, of course, of the same House); and Nashe. Strange was
back up in Lancashire in August, when his father's officers captured the
Martinist press at Manchester. He may have been involved in the operation – he was often acting-deputy in the Earl's lieutenancy of Lancashire.
Is it possible that Nashe got the 'inside story' of the capture – how the
printers 'were shrouded under the name of salt-petermen', how they
'pretended the printing of Accidences when my L. of Darbies men came':
two details found only in the *Almond* – through some connection with
Strange and his circle? In this general context, an entry in the Derby
'household books' catches the eye. At the end of February 1590, at
Lathom while Strange was there,

> this Saturdaie my L. [Earl of Derby] came home, Mr ffoxe [Derby's
> 'clerk comptroller'] came & a s'vant of the B. of Canterbury. Players
> played at nyght.[27]

This unidentified 'servant' of the Archbishop's, dismounting on a
winter's day at Lathom, could be one of any number of people. He
could be Thomas Nashe, who, as anti-Martinist pamphleteer and sleuth,
could well be described as Whitgift's 'servant'; and who was later actually a member of the Archbishop's household at Croydon, described as
Whitgift's 'gentleman'.[28] The *Almond* was soon to appear at this time,
with its dedication to Will Kemp, one of Lord Strange's Men. Perhaps
he was one of the players who played that night at Lathom.

That is conjecture. There is, in fact, no hard evidence to link Nashe
with Strange until the summer of 1592, when he rounds off *Pierce
Penilesse* with a resounding panegyric of 'thrice noble Amyntas', i.e.
Lord Strange.[29] He speaks of his 'private experience' of Strange's
generosity, says he is 'thankfull' for 'benefits received' from him, and
describes a sonnet he includes as 'wholie intended to the reverence of
this renoumed Lord, to whom I owe the utmoste powers of my love and
dutie'. Later in the year, warning against too precise an identification
between 'Pierce' and himself, Nashe asserts: 'Neither was I pincht with
any ungentleman-like want when I invented *Pierce Penilesse*', and he
adds: '*Pauper non est cui rerum suppetit usus*' – he who has the use of
things is not a poor man.[30] '*Usus*' is employed here technically to mean
the use as opposed to the possession of property, as in the legal term
'usufruct' (Latin *usus et fructus*). Nashe clearly implies he was being
'kept' while he wrote *Pierce*: his benefactor was doubtless that 'magnificent rewarder of vertue', Lord Strange. The bulk of *Pierce* was composed
in May-July 1592 – it was registered at Stationers' Hall in early August,
but Richard Harvey had seen at least part of the manuscript by 14
June.[31] During these months, at least, Nashe received hospitality, casual
'doles' and occasional errands from a courtier on the highest rung of

the Elizabethan ladder. The period of Strange's patronage may stretch back some while before this, but not long after: by September 1592 Nashe was in the Archbishop's service at Croydon, and there is no evidence of any connection with Strange thereafter. The Derby household books for 1591–2 have unfortunately perished, so we have no details of Strange's movements. Nor is it clear where his London residence was – Derby House itself, on Paul's Wharf Hill, had been given over the 'Heraults and Persevantes of Armes' since Queen Mary's time, while the house on Canon Row, Westminster, owned by the 6th Earl – Strange's younger brother, William – was not being built till about 1602.[32] But we see the man himself, in the Knowsley portrait (Figure 7), probably painted after his accession as 5th Earl of Derby in September 1593.[33] The face is precise, intelligent, refined; not a hearty figure, but sympathetic; there are hints of ill-health and bookish melancholia, but also he is ready to laugh, as Nashe must so often have made him do.

Pierce was not Nashe's only dedication to Lord Strange (the 'Amyntas' panegyric is essentially a dedication, though 'inserted conceitedly in the matter' rather than at the front). Strange is undoubtedly the 'Lord S' to whom Nashe addressed his bawdy poem, *The Choise of Valentines* or 'Nashes Dildo'.[34] The date of composition is uncertain, but it seems likely it was presented to Strange in 1592. Its bawdiness implies a certain familiarity – not even Nashe would offer his 'Dildo' to an untried patron. He signs off, 'Thus hath my penne presum'd to please my friend', suggesting relaxed and amicable relations with his 'Dear Lord'. It was certainly abroad before April 1593, when Gabriel Harvey threatened to 'decipher thy unprinted packet of bawdye and filthy Rymes' and denounce the 'ruffianisme of thy Brothell muse'.[35] The piece acquired some notoriety in its day. The Puritan satirist Joseph Hall refers to 'those ribald rymes of thine' in his *Virgidemiarum* (1597): his portrait of the obscene poet 'Labeo' may be partly aimed at Nashe.[36] The poet and calligrapher, John Davies of Hereford, twice denounces the 'Gomorrahs filth' of Nashe's poem. In his *Scourge of Folly* (1611), a personified 'Paper' complains how that 'patch' (fool) Pierce Penniless 'made me . . . beare suits to the Devill' and then

> Abusde me further, in the Devills name,
> And made [me] *Dildo* (dampned *Dildo*) beare,
> Till good-mens hate did me in peeces teare.

Davies' outrage at the 'Dildo' is part of a general dislike of Nashe, evident throughout this twenty-two-line passage. Elsewhere in this same volume, Davies laments the long-dead Lord Strange and recalls him as 'my Deere Lord, sole Master of mine all'.[37] Nashe the *risqué* entertainer clearly had his enemies in Strange's circle.

The Choise of Valentines survives in three separate manuscripts, one

of them transcribed in cypher.[38] It is one of the few pieces of Elizabethan
erotica extant. It tells of the amorous misadventures of young 'Tomalin'
on St Valentine's Day. Finding his lover, Mistress Frances, has been
forced to enter a 'house of venerie', Tomalin repairs thither, posing as
a punter. The *madame* – 'a foggie three-chinned dame' – leads him up
into a 'shadie loft', sets him in a 'leather chaire' and puts some 'prettie
Trulls' on parade. He declines their favours and insists the bawd gives
him her latest attraction, 'gentle mistris Francis'. She is no half-a-crown
hackster, says the bawd; Tomalin promises to pay 'tenne good gobbs'
of gold for her; the deal is struck and

> Hey-ho, she coms, that hath my heart in keepe,
>   Sing lullabie my cares, and fall asleepe.
> Sweeping she comes, as she would brush the ground,
>   Hir ratling silkes my sences doe confound.

Once they are alone, she 'sprung full lightlie to my lips'. She lays back
on the bed, 'shutts her eyes and waggles with hir tongue', and so begins
the classic slow strip:

> Softlie my fingers, up theis curtaine, heave
> And make me happie stealing by degreese.
>   First bare hir leggs, then creepe up to hir kneese.
> From thence ascend unto hir mannely thigh
>   (A pox on lingring when I am so nighe)
> Smocke climbe a-pace, that I maie see my ioyes.

The *pièce de resistance* is duly bared: a 'prettie rysing wombe', a 'dusky
nett of wyres' and a 'loftie buttock'. But all is not well: so delicious are
these peek-a-boo thrills that Tomalin 'spends' his all before the 'fight'
begins. The disappointment is keen:

> I kisse, I clap, I feele, I view at will,
>   Yet dead he lyes not thinking good or ill.
> Unhappie me, quoth shee, and wilt not stand?
>   Come, lett me rubb and chafe it with my hand.

Under Frank's vigorous attentions, the 'sillie worme' revives from its
'swoune' and the business begins in earnest, continuing for some sixty
lines of breathless erotic rhyme –

> With Oh and Oh, she itching moves hir hippes,
>   And to and fro, full lightlie starts and skips.
> She ierks hir leggs, and sprauleth with hir heeles,
>   No tongue maie tell the solace that she feeles

– intermingled with some witty burlesques of neo-Platonic love poetry.
But once again the masculine '*noctis equi*' gallop the faster. Tomalin

comes and Frank does not. 'Leave me not forlorne', she pleads, but he
is useless – 'the well is drye . . . the glasse is runne' – and so she reaches
for the eponymous tool:

> My little dildo shall suplye their kinde,
>   A knave that moves as light as leaves by winde;
> That bendeth not, nor fouldeth anie deale,
>   But stands as stiff as he were made of steele,
> And playes at peacock twixt my leggs right blythe.

The poem concludes with Tomalin's tirade against the usurping 'Eunuke
dilldo', and a rueful sense of impaired *machismo* – 'I am not as was
Hercules the stout, That to the seaventh iournie could hould out'.
Tomalin pays off the *madame* and takes his leave, looking 'leane and
lank as anie ghost'.

Nashe's poem is more often mentioned than described or examined.
As a piece of pornography (which by the yardsticks of the day it was)
it is thoroughly wholesome: ribald rather than decadent, naughty rather
than nasty. It is an Elizabethan *Eskimo Nell*. For all its notoriety, it is
not a tenth as dirty as Shakespeare can be – the Falstaff comedies, the
seamy undertones of *Hamlet*, *Troilus* and *Lear* – or Marston, or Jonson
at his most anatomical. Nashe's 'Dildo' is an erotic *vignette*: comic,
titillating, full of cartoon-like visual touches. It would seem that penning
lewd poems became something of a profitable 'line' for Nashe. In 1596,
responding to jibes about him 'prostituting' his pen like a 'Curtizan', he
says:

> Well, it may and it may not bee so, for neither will I deny it nor will
> I grant it: onely thus farre Ile goe with you, that twise or thrise in a
> month, when *res est angusta domi*, the bottome of my purse is turnd
> downeward, & my conduit of incke will no longer flowe for want of
> reparations, I am faine to let my Plow stand still in the midst of a
> furrow, and follow some of these new-fangled *Galiardos* and *Senior
> Fantasticos*, to whose amorous *Villanellas* and *Quipassas* I prostitute
> my pen in hope of gaine.[39]

Has the *Valentines* anything to tell us about Nashe's own sexuality?
Not a lot, perhaps: its purpose and circumstance, its avowed naughtiness,
actually limit its sexual expression. One thing is clear, though: the man
who wrote it was certainly no virgin. Though the poem has its models
(more of which in a minute) there is nothing second-hand in its evoca-
tions of sex. Perhaps the theme of sexual failure, the cartoon of 'weake-
ling' Tomalin and his insatiable lady, catch a reflection of boyish, beard-
less Tom Nashe, ill-fed, skinny, prone to catarrhs and agues. But then
so too must the huge heterosexual gusto which courses through the

poem. If the *Choise of Valentines* is in any way a 'case-book', then the patient is pronounced 'normal'. Of Nashe's love-life nothing is known. It was not, probably, extensive: one gets little impression of Nashe as a ladies' man – perhaps the 'trulls' of Shoreditch kept him happy. Apart from Marlowe, he is the only one of the Wits who never, as far as we know, married.[40] We hear a whisper of some teenage romance in the *Anatomie*, written (he claims) in a fit of 'pensivenes' after some disappointment in love – 'Gentlemen that know what it is to encounter with ingratitude in the forme of Cupid' will readily 'ayme at' his feelings in the matter.[41] Other than this he gives nothing away: no confessions, no names. There are literary elements in this silence: Nashe stood deliberately, and refreshingly, aside from the whole 'love-writing' craze of the time, refusing to pamper the reader's sweet tooth. But also there is a lack, a missing emotional dimension. We hear so much of the men in his life, so little of the women. There is just one really: Diamante, Jack Wilton's Italian lover in *The Unfortunate Traveller*. She is a fiction, of course, but drawn with such warmth and buoyancy that we might almost think we have in her a portrait of Nashe's own lover. Certain suspicious resemblances to another 'Dark Lady' of the time suggest, however, that her provenance is more complex.

Aside from its interest as a specimen of Elizabethan *erotica*, the *Choise of Valentines* opens up an unsuspected cache of literary connections. For the poem has a model, or at least a literary context. In the dedicatory sonnet to Strange, Nashe apologizes that

> ... my Muse devorst from deepest care
> Presents thee with a wanton Elegie,

and in the concluding sonnet he says:

> Yett Ovids wanton Muse did not offend:
> Hee is the fountaine whence my streames doe flowe.

Nashe is clearly claiming a comparison with the *Elegies* of Ovid, known as the *Amores*, and so with the recent and brilliant translation of them by Marlowe. One of the *Elegies* ('*ab Amica receptus, cum ea coire non potuit*') has the same theme of sexual incapacity as Nashe's poem. Ovid's lover describes his detumescence as, in Marlowe's version, 'like as if cold hemlocke I had drunke': Nashe recalls this when he says the drooping Tomalin is 'lyke one with Ovids cursed hemlock charm'd'.[42] In stylistic terms this connection leads nowhere: Nashe's bawdy romp has little in common with the sleek sexuality of Marlowe's Ovid. But as a historical connection it is fascinating, for we know that Marlowe was, on his own evidence, 'very well known' to Lord Strange in early 1592, and also that his *Jew of Malta* was being performed by Strange's Men at the Rose in March 1592.[43] The link between Marlowe's and Nashe's 'wanton elegies' may well be that both were presented to Lord Strange at around this time. When Nashe observes that 'Ovids wanton Muse did not offend', he perhaps refers to Strange's favourable reception of Marlowe's *erotica* and hopes that his own effort will be likewise applauded. If so, Marlowe's Ovid is not so much the model as the precedent for Nashe's Dildo.

These hints, suggesting the apposition of Marlowe and Nashe in Lord Strange's circle in 1592, broaden into a connection startlingly obvious and yet hitherto unnoticed: a connection between *Dr Faustus* and *Pierce Penilesse*, both written in 1592 and both pivoting on the idea of making a 'supplication to the Devil'. There has been much controversy over dating the composition of *Faustus*, but 1592–3 is most strongly indicated, both on the grounds of poetic maturity and because the English source-book which Marlowe frequently echoes – *The Historie of the Damnable Life and Deserved Death of Doctor Iohn Faustus* – was not published until 1592. The first edition of this, now lost, probably appeared in May 1592; it was published by Abel Jeffes, who four months later was the printer of *Pierce Penilesse*.[44] It is possible Marlowe was at work on *Faustus* in exactly the same summer months of 1592 that Nashe was compiling *Pierce*. The two productions are obverse and reverse of the same diabolic coin. In *Faustus*, the devil is invoked by a full-blown Renaissance magus thirsting after infinite knowledge; in *Pierce*, by a skint young scribbler who wants to strike up a profitable deal. Faustus' invocation is resonant of dark necromantic ritual:

> Valeat numen triplex Iehovae, Ignei, Aerii, Aquatici, Terreni spiritus salvete: Orientis princeps Lucifer, Belzebub inferni ardentis monarcha, et Demogorgon, propitiamus vos ut appareat et surgat Mephostophilis.

Pierce's is, by a marvellous twist, a florid, fulsomely correct dedication:

> To the high and mightie Prince of Darknesse, Donsell dell Lucifer, King of Acheron, Stix and Phlegeton, Duke of Tartary, Marquesse of Cocytus, and Lord high Regent of Lymbo.[45]

Thus 'most humbly sueth unto your sinfulnes, your single-soaled orator, Pierce Penilesse' – note the pun: 'single-soled' means 'broke' (shoes in need of repair, as in 'down at heel') but also refers to the single soul of man, that cherished possession that Faustus pawns: '*Consummatum est*: this byll is ended, and Faustus hath bequeath'd his soule to Lucifer'. To assist his diabolic enterprise Faustus conjures up Mephistophilis, 'servant to great Lucifer', amid thunder and apparitions of dragons. Pierce's demon appears, by contrast, in Paul's Walk, 'thrusting himselfe abruptly into my companie, like an Intelligencer'; he is a 'neat pedantical fellow, in forme of a Cittizen'; he claims to be 'a spirit in nature and essence', and promises to despatch Pierce's supplication to the 'Low-countries', but he seems a rather unreliable demon. 'Go beare these tydings to great Lucifer', commands Faustus. 'When do you think you could send next to your Master?' asks Pierce more tentatively.[46] Later Faustus asks, 'Tell me, where is the place that men call Hell?' So does Pierce: 'acquaint me with the state of your infernall regiment, and what that hel is, where your Lord holdes his throne'.[47] And when Faustus challenges Mephistophilis with 'I thinke Hel's a fable', he gets an apparent rebuke from Pierce as well: 'some phantasticall refyners of philosophie will needes perswade us hell is nothing but error'.[48]

Such parallels could be continued, but by now the general point is clear. Marlowe and Nashe have started from the same notional springboard – the invoking of forbidden supernatural forces to accomplish earthly ambitions – but have leapt in precisely opposite directions. Marlowe has made something huge and thunderous, full of sensationalist 'magick' and existential turmoil. Nashe has defused the thing, made it jokey, quotidian, mercenary. Marlowe has made much of the murky mid-European setting: Germany was the heartland of Renaissance occultism, the home of Agrippa, Trithemius, Reuchlin and Paracelsus. Nashe's locale is everyday London, where the 'over-reacher' is a pot-hunting social climber, not a Faustian challenger of cosmic authority; where sin is an amusing *peccadillo*, not a 'hellish fall' to damnation. Given the temperaments of the two men, they have reacted typically: tragedian and comic, mythologizer and cartoonist. It would be wrong, though, to suggest that these two works make up a dialogue or dialectic about the power and purpose of the occult. Marlowe's play contains a dialectic in itself, articulating both the thrilling grandeur of Renaissance magic ('A sound magitian is a Demi-god' . . . 'Tis magick, magick that hath ravisht me') and the orthodox theological condemnation of it (beware of 'unlawfull things' which entice you 'to practise more then heavenly power permits').[49] This condemnation is not just a moral pointed at the end, but is implied in the whole portrayal of Faustus as a daemonic conjurer. As Frances Yates has pointed out, Marlowe's treatment of Faustus is cunningly anachronistic: he paints Faustus as a Renaissance magus in the Agrippan mould, but then smothers him in the old 'mediaeval anti-sorcery formula'.[50] For all Marlowe's ambivalence, the message of *Faustus* is anti-magian: in the debate on magic then current, Marlowe's line is that of the Catholic reactionary, the witch-hunter. The great difference between *Faustus* and *Pierce* is one of treatment: in terms of attitude they are not dissimilar. Given the notion of invoking supernatural power, Marlowe's attitude is hostile, if fascinated, Nashe's is jocular if – as the later *Terrors of the Night* shows more clearly – a touch fearful.

This kinship between *Faustus* and *Pierce* throws out some interesting sidelights. The first touches on the vexed question of the comic prose scenes in *Faustus*. These have long been recognized as entirely untypical of Marlowe, but when and by whom they were written is uncertain. Textually *Faustus* is extremely tangled, with two very different quartos (1604 and 1616) and certain unspecified revisions by William Birde and Samuel Rowley, whom Henslowe paid £4 for 'adicyones in doctor fostes' in November 1602.[51] It has been argued that Nashe was the main author of the comic scenes, and that he added them, after Marlowe's death, for a revival of the play by the Admiral's Men in October 1594.[52] The argument is plausible and the phraseological parallels numerous, but an actual reading of the scenes has left most critics unconvinced. There seem to be flashes of Nashe amid a welter of witless knockabout. What does seem possible, though, is that beneath the corruptions and accretions of the *Faustus* texts there lies an original sharing of material between Marlowe and Nashe in 1592. The first comic scene in the 1604 text opens with Wagner's description of the 'clowne', Robin:

> Alas poore slave, see how poverty jesteth in his nakednesse: the vilaine is bare and out of service, and so hungry that I know he would give his soule to the Divel for a shoulder of mutton, though it were blood rawe.[53]

This is redolent of penniless Pierce, the jesting pauper, who does indeed pawn his soul to fill his stomach. A little later in the scene comes a joke which would be entirely lost but for *Pierce Penilesse*. Wagner summons two devils to frighten Robin: he calls them 'Balioll and Belcher'. Why is the conventional spirit name Belial spelt 'Balioll'? Pierce provides the answer when he calls gluttons 'fleshly minded Belials', adding, 'or rather Belly-als, because all their minde is on their belly'.[54] The joke (such as it is) becomes clear: Wagner's demons are called 'Belly-all and Belcher'. 'Balioll' is just a misleading attempt to orthographize the pun. The whole bantering tone of Pierce's diabolism filters into the *Faustus* comedy: 'I pray ye, good Mounsier divel' . . . 'Good devil, forgive me now'. Parallels in the treatment of the Seven Sins could also be noted. This kind of approach may help to explain the traces of Nashe discernible in *Faustus*. He did not *write* the comic scenes – even his hack-work was better than that – but he may well have influenced them. The *Faustus* text perhaps retains a submerged memory of Marlowe and Nashe in some chamber or tavern in 1592, sparking off comic ideas on supernatural themes.

From such jottings, the bulk of the comic material may have been elaborated in rehearsal and early performance, and only written down by some hack hand later.

Another angle on this scenario is provided by some scribbled marginalia in Nashe's hand (Document 8). These appear in a copy of John Leland's *Principum in Anglia Virorum Encomia* (1589) which bears Nashe's signature on the fly-leaf. (The actual book is irrelevant: with paper dear, Elizabethans used blank spaces in their books for jottings of all sorts – Harvey's marginalia, an afforestation of every spare inch in his library, now fill a stout volume.) On the last two leaves of the book Nashe has written: 'Faustus: Che sara sara devinynitie [*sic*] adieu'; and 'Faustus studie in indian silke'; and again, almost illegibly, 'devynitie adieu'. These are fascinating fragments of Nashe's response to *Faustus*. His mind is playing on Faustus' first thrilling moment of renunciation –

> What doctrine call you this? *Che sera, sera*:
> What will be, shall be: Divinitie adiew.
> These Metaphisicks of Magitians
> And Negromantick bookes are heavenly

– and on Faustus' wish to 'fill the publique Schooles with silke, Wherewith the Students shall be bravely clad', an exotic whim that doubtless appealed to one who had spent seven years in the black-gowned ranks at the 'Schools'.[55] In dwelling on the Faustian 'adieu' to religion these doodles seem to capture Nashe at some candlelit moment of disquiet and speculation, the kind of brooding anxiety he taps in his *Terrors of the Night*:

> When Night in her rustie dungeon hath imprisoned our ey-sight, and that we are shut seperatly in our chambers from resort, the divell keepeth his audit in our sin-guilty consciences . . . and all our thoughts are nothing but texts to condemne us.[56]

The moment that is caught on the pages of this randomly reached-for book was perhaps sometime in 1592, when Marlowe's necromantic desperado was much on Nashe's mind. On the title-page of the *Encomia* he has scrawled more broken phrases – 'printed bookes in these' and 'thinges thought uppon' and, very faintly, 'Faustus' – unintelligible in themselves but somehow part of this sense of collusion between Marlowe and Nashe in 1592.

With the fragmentary evidence of this collusion now gathered – the connection between Marlowe's *Elegies* and Nashe's *Valentines*; the shared devil-conjuring theme of *Faustus* and *Pierce*; the traces of Nashe in the comic scenes of *Faustus*, and the traces of *Faustus* in the marginal scribbles of Nashe; the shared position in the literary circles around

Lord Strange; the shared connection with the printer Abel Jeffes; and all this on top of a friendship between Marlowe and Nashe which goes back as much as ten years before this – we yet and still do not quite know what lies *behind* the collusion. Why are they writing in concert like this, playing variations on a diabolic theme? Are they just two 'modern' young writers seizing on a topic simultaneously and exchanging impressions, or is there something more behind these coincidences? If there is something more, it seems likely that Lord Strange holds the key. He was a patron to both writers in 1592; *Pierce Penilesse* was dedicated to him; *Faustus* may have been composed for his troupe of players to perform, though there is no record of any public performances by them.[57] If Strange was a scholar with a penchant for the occult, he must have been stimulated – to say the least – to receive a tragedy by Marlowe and a pamphlet by Nashe on the subject. If we look more closely at *Pierce Penilesse* we will find further light on this, and on a great deal besides. Approached right, the pamphlet reveals a rich vein of comment on certain political and philosophical movements abroad in 1592. Wisecracking Pierce Penniless proves also to be investigative Pierce Politic, and to his insights we now turn.

8

PIERCE POLITIC

'. . . insisting in the experience of our time'

Pierce Penilesse

Pierce Penilesse was an instant success. Registered by publisher Richard Jones on 8 August 1592, it was on the bookstalls a month later. Two further editions followed in 1592, another in 1593 and a fifth edition in 1595. Nashe says it was 'maimedly translated into the French tongue' in about 1593, but no trace of this remains.[1] 'Pierce' became Nashe's nickname, used by friend and foe alike, with puns on 'purse' and *'per se'* abounding ('Pierce' was then pronounced 'purse', as it still is in America). Harvey's great onslaught on Nashe was called *Pierces Supererogation*, 'and yet not so much to quirke and crosse me thereby, as to blesse himselfe and make his booke sell, did hee give it that title'.[2] More than a nickname, 'Pierce' was Nashe's *persona*, his public image: the angry young man, the 'discontented Scholler' who 'tost his imagination like a dogge in a blanket' for ways to relieve his desperate poverty, spraying out satire, jokes, gossip and downright abuse as he did so. In style, Pierce is quick and light, a garrulous figure buttonholing the reader, but his prose has a metaphoric and psychological range which extends it far beyond mere banter. As such the pamphlet's appeal outlived immediate topicality. A snatch of dialogue from Samuel Rowlands' *Tis Merry when Gossips Meet* shows it was still a talking-point in 1602:

Gentleman	What's that with Nashes name to it there?
Prentice	Marry sir, 'tis *Pierce Penny-lesse*, sir; I am sure you know it: it hath beene a-broad a great while sir.
Gentleman	Oh, I, thou say'st true, I know't passing well.[3]

Nashe had casually promised, 'I might haps (halfe a yeare hence) write the returne of the Knight of the Post from hel, with the Devils answer to the Supplication'. He never did, but after his death no less than three works appeared – Middleton's *Blacke Booke* (1604), the anonymous *Returne of the Knight of the Poste* (1606) and Dekker's *Newes from Hell* (1606) – each professing to be the sequel or answer to Pierce's 'Supplication'.[4]

For the reading public in the summer of 1592, *Pierce Penilesse* was
something brash and exciting. It was snapped up like some new magazine
that precisely caught the 'experience of our time'. There was already a
satirical tradition of sorts – Gascoigne, Hake, Harvey, Gosson, Stubbes
and, of course, Martin – but it tended to be Puritan-minded and sermon-
ical: Martin had jazzed up the tone but retained the Puritan base. Two
recent works suggested a new potential for topical social comment –
John Florio's *Second Fruites* (1591), ostensibly a language-manual but
with consciously journalistic elements in its dialogues, and Greene's
Quip for an Upstart Courtier, published a month or so before *Pierce* –
but neither had Nashe's range and agility.[5] Pierce was the roving eye
about London, ubiquitous and inquisitive, hobnobbing with courtiers
and captains, Inns of Court benchers and pettifoggers, surgeons and
apothecaries, butchers and brewers, alewives and victuallers, colliers and
hackney-men, box-keepers and pandars, porters and car-men. In a series
of vivid cameos he sketches in the follies, affectations and seamy pleasures of the city. There is the love-sick poet:

> hee will be an *Inamorato Poeta*, & sonnet a whole quire of paper in
> praise of Lady Swin-snout, his yeolow fac'd Mistres, & weare a
> feather of her rainbeaten fan for a favor, like a fore-horse.

The phoney cosmopolitan:

> you shall see a dapper Iacke, that hath been but over at Deepe, wring
> his face round about, as a man would stir up a mustard pot, & talke
> English through ye teeth, like Iaques Scabd-hams or Monsieur Mingo
> de Moustrap.

The demurely respectable merchant's wife, that

> iets it as gingerly as if she were dancing the Canaries: she is so finicall
> in her speach, as though she spake nothing but what shee had first
> sewd over in her Samplers, and the puling accent of her voyce is like
> a fained treble, or ones voyce that interprets to the puppets.[6]

These and other such sketches – the 'counterfeit Polititian', the 'prodigall yoong Master', careerist 'drudges', and so on – present conventional
satirical types in up-to-the-minute modern guise. Pierce has not dispensed
with the old moralizing – the homiletic Seven Deadly Sins and the
humanist Ship of Fools are shaping factors for his pamphlet – but he
has applied and 'specialized' his Vices so vividly that they begin to
overstep the confines of their exemplary function. Sin and vice are too
intrinsic to Pierce's literary performance for him to sustain any censo-

rious attitude convincingly. The description of Greed,[7] the seminal vice of the pamphlet, is a case in point. It begins with a lurid, mock-heraldic vision of 'Greedines' in its 'ugly habitation'. At the door, 'Famine, Lent and Dessolation sit in onyon skind iackets'; within is disclosed Greed himself, a weird paper-monster, usury personified, 'attyred in a Capouch of written parchment, buttoned downe before with Labels of wax', his breeches bombasted with 'statute Marchants and forfeitures'. Next to him sits Dame Niggardize, his wife,

> in a sedge rug kirtle that hath beene a mat time out of minde, a course hempen raile about her shoulders, borrowed of the one end of a hop-bag, an apron made of Almanackes out of date (such as stand upon Screens, or on the backside of a dore in a Chandlers shop), and an old wives pudding pan on her head, thrumd with the parings of her nailes.

Various comic descriptions of their stinginess ensue, and then suddenly the focus shifts, and we are sympathizing with 'the verie spiders and dust-weavers' who had to move out to the country for lack of any pickings, and hearing a Disney-like tale of how the emaciated rats and mice

> went a Boothaling one night to Sinior Greedinesse bed-chamber, where finding nothing but emptines and vastitie, they encountred (after long inquisition) with a cod-peece, wel dunged and manured with greace. . . . Uppon that they set, and with a couragious assault rent it cleene away from the breeches, and then carried it in triumph, like a coffin, on their shoulder betwixt them.

By now any moralistic point is long-lost. The 'vice' was a trigger which touched off a whole gamut of responses, variously expressed through grotesque fantasy, comic anecdote and harsh, tactile descriptiveness. Nashe's free-wheeling status, the instability of his reactions, is what made *Pierce Penilesse* so new and refreshing. Pierce's is a satirical voice freed from the singularity of an attitude. This is partly a formal restlessness: Nashe's satire, says Rhodes, bespeaks 'an uneasy relationship between sermon and festive comedy, priest and clown', and his 'associative, rhapsodic technique' is born out of that ambiguity.[8] It is also to do with Nashe's involvement in his material. In translating the Seven Sins into a London *comédie humaine*, Nashe places himself (or at least 'Pierce') in the midst of it all. The journalist, unlike the moralist, is there on the scene. Nashe's reputation – Bohemian wit, penner of bawdy rhymes, friend of the hell-raisers Greene and Marlowe – must have made his deploring of drunkenness, quarrelsomeness and prostitu-

tion somewhat ironic. Throughout *Pierce*, his fascination for the squalors
and dark corners of Elizabethan London, his 'syving of muckhils and
shop-dust', is paramount. He gives us sin from street-level, not even
apologizing for his involvement on the grounds of journalistic impera-
tive, as Greene does in the 'conny-catching' tracts ('odd madcaps I have
been mate to, not as a companion, but as a spy to have an insight into
their knaveries').[9] And when it comes to setting up examples to aspire
to, we hear little of virtue, purity and religion. Instead we hear of the
'quick-witted Italians', of 'divine Aretino', of poets and players, and of
the carefree young 'unthrift' whose *joie de vivre* exempts him from moral
opprobrium:

> Which is a more evill man, of him that is an idle glutton at home, or
> a retchlesse unthrift abroad? The glutton at home doth nothing but
> engender diseases, pamper his flesh unto lust, and is good for none
> but his owne gut: the unthrift abroad exerciseth his bodie at daucing
> schoole, fence schoole, tennis and all such recreations: the vintners,
> the victuallers, the dicing houses and who not, get by him. Suppose
> he lose a little now and then at play, it teacheth him wit: and how
> should a man know to eschew vices, if his own experience did not
> acquaint him with their inconveniences? *Omne ignotum pro*
> *magnifico est*: that villany we have made no assaies in, we admire.
> Besides, my vagrant Reveller haunts Plaies, & sharpens his wits with
> frequenting the company of Poets: he emboldens his blushing face by
> courting faire women on the sodaine, and looks into all Estates by
> conversing with them in publike places. Nowe tell me whether of
> these two, the heavie headed gluttonous house-dove, or this livelie,
> wanton, yoong Gallant, is like to proove the wiser man, and better
> member in the Common-wealth?[10]

This is Nashe *in propria persona*, this the 'moral base' of *Pierce Penilesse*:
the urban delights of movement and action, getting and spending, skill
and experience, conversation and *camaraderie*. Nashe preaches the
virtues of 'being there'.

These are some of the reasons why a discerning reader, browsing
among the stalls of St Paul's on 8 September 1592, would recognize in
Nashe's new pamphlet something fresh and quintessentially 'modern'.
The jazzy style, the 'low' urban landscapes, the secular morality, the
insatiable comic appetite, the restless shifts of tone, the relishing of
ambiguity and quiddity, and (above all) the creation of an authorial
voice that has behind it a whole private psychology, rather than a mere
crop of attitudes, a life rather than a stance – in all these *Pierce Penilesse*
is 'very 1590s'.

All part of the pamphlet's novelty is the liberal 'cup' of actual topical news Pierce offers, the glances – open or covert, amicable or libellous – at real contemporary figures. For latest comment on the literary scene the reader might turn to the '*encomium H Smithi*', a generous elegy on the 'silver tongu'd' preacher, Henry Smith, who had died earlier in the year; or to the 'due commendation of Ned Allen' and of Shakespeare's 'Harry the Sixth'; or to the long '*Aquafortis* & Gunpowder' harangue against Richard Harvey, in answer to the aspersions he had cast on Nashe in *The Lamb of God*.[11] He might note in the sketch of the 'prodigall yoong master' those telling echoes of the career of Thomas Lodge, *littérateur* and 'unthrift'. Another of Pierce's butts turns out to be Anthony Munday, the scribbler and government agent whom Nashe had met during the anti-Martinist campaign. Munday's recent translation, *Archaioplutos* (1592), is draughtily received: not bad 'for a man that stands upon paines and not wit'; he 'hath performd as much as any Storie dresser may doo, that sets a new English nap on an old Latine Apothegs'. Elsewhere Munday's lost ballad, 'The Exployts of Untrusse', earns him the appellation of 'grosse brain'd Idiot'. His line in ceremonial pieces for London civic occasions may be glanced at when Nashe has a go at tedious 'lay Chronigraphers' who 'write of nothing but of Mayors and of Sheriefs': Munday, an affiliated member of the Drapers' Company, would be the 'stutting Townsman' whose unpoetic efforts are derided. As a draper's son, he might also figure in Nashe's paradigm of the would-be – 'All malcontent sits the greasie son of a Cloathier, & complaines (like a Decaied Earl) of the ruine of antient houses.'[12] A throwaway remark about a writer who had nothing but thanks for 'three yeares worke' turns out to refer to the topographer, John Stow. In his *Annals* (1592) Stow relates that in 1562 the Earl of Leicester had commissioned him to make a 'summary of the chronicles of England': the *Summary* was duly published in 1565, dedicated to Leicester, 'in reward whereof I alwaies received his hearty thankes, with commendations, and not otherwise'.[13]

These threads of literary gossip and dispute are what we – and the reader of 1592 – would expect of Nashe. Far more interesting are the motifs of political comment, ingeniously concealed beneath the pamphlet's jocular veneer. These are what give Nashe's journalism its hard edge: Pierce Penniless may have ruffled some feathers with his satire, but Pierce Politic was playing an altogether more dangerous game. An obvious instance is the fable of the Bear and the Fox: this is quite openly offered as a political allegory – a 'parlous tale', as Harvey called it.[14] We shall turn to this soon. A better place to start is with the 'tale of one Fryer Charles',[15] which tells us much about Nashe's methods of subterfuge in presenting risky topical material, and which leads us to an illustrious and powerful figure who lurks elsewhere in the pamphlet. On

the surface it seems a harmless anecdote about a 'foule mouthde knave'
and the comeuppance he received, a jest-book piece like the 'merry tale
of a Butcher and his Calves' or the 'tale of a wise Iustice' a few pages
earlier. It begins: 'Not farre from Chester, I knewe an odde foule
mouthde knave called Charles the Fryer.' It relates the various insults
Charles heaped on noblemen, likening some to 'guilded chines of beefe',
another to a 'Spanish codpisse', and so on. Thereupon, a certain 'great
personage' challenged him to a verbal duel at 'rayling': Charles 'so far
outstript him in vilainous words' that the great man sought vengeance.
He had Charles seized, and 'brickt him up in a narrow chimney' where
'he fed him for fifteene dayes with bread and water, letting him sleep
standing up if he would, for lye or sit he could not'. Thus the 'venemous
toothd Cur' was taught 'to rule his tongue'.

Those in the know would quickly spot that this is no simple punitive
'merry tale', and that Charles the Friar dwelling near Chester was in
fact a Catholic named Charles Chester, who was in some trouble at this
time.[16] Chester was arrested on 19 June 1592, on the orders of Lord
Admiral Howard and Sir Robert Cecil, and committed 'close prisoner
to the Gatehouse at Westminster'. At his lodgings were found 'some
score of vain and papistical books' in Spanish, and various other Catholic
'trumpery'. Writing from prison in July, Chester denies all connection
with the Jesuits or 'any against this realm', and claims he is a 'relapse'
(a lapsed Catholic). He reveals a chequered career as soldier, privateer,
intelligencer and Muscovy trader, but also pleads some powerful
acquaintances: Sir Walter Ralegh had once helped him; he had been 'in
favour' with the Lord Admiral; he had kept company 'this two years'
with Sir George Carey. In particular he says that one malicious enemy
has caused his imprisonment, and he prays that God will 'turn both
your honours' [Cecil's and Howard's] hearts in the hatred of him that
hath caused me this languishing and hidden death'. Nashe's tale
opaquely mirrors these events. Charles is called a friar, i.e. a Catholic.
The punishment he receives, being bricked up in a 'narrow chimney',
reflects Chester's 'close' confinement in the gatehouse. Of the various
grades of imprisonment, 'close' was the worst, not to be shrugged off
like one of Nashe's spells in the Counter. Chester's letters speak feelingly
of 'this cage of misery' where he is kept, 'this afflicted place of close
prison'. Nashe's image of immurement is apt enough. Chester also
complains he is suffering from 'dropsy' because 'of meat and drink I
have none': Nashe tells of Charles fed nothing but bread and water
'through a hole' for fifteen days. This begins to sound like straight
journalistic fact.

What is interesting is that, beneath the apparent disparagement of
Charles, Nashe seems to be relating the affair rather from Chester's own
angle. The joke is by no means all on Charles. The bullying figure of

the 'great personage', using his power to salve his wounded pride, comes
out badly:

> The name of sport could not perswade him patience, nor containe
> his furie in any degrees of ieast, but needs hee must wreake himself
> uppon him: neither would a common revenge suffice him, his displea-
> sure was so infinite (and, it may be, common revenges he tooke
> before, as far as the whipcord would stretch, upon like provokements)
> wherefore he caused his men to take him, and brickt him up. . . .

This ties in with Chester's own claim — that he was innocent of any
subversive Catholic connections, and that his arrest was solely due to
one man's malice. Chester's powerful enemy and Nashe's vengeful 'great
personage' must be one and the same. Who was this man? A possible
answer is found in Aubrey's *Brief Lives*.[17] Here too Charles Chester the
railer turns up: Aubrey calls him a 'bold impertenent fellowe', a 'perpetuall talker' that 'made a noyse like a drumme in a roome'. Aubrey also
claims that Chester was the original of Carlo Buffone, the mocker in
Ben Jonson's *Every Man out of his Humour* (1599), and he particularly
refers to the scene where Puntarvolo silences Carlo by sealing up his
mouth with wax.[18] So the Chester story has another refraction: Charles
bricked up and Carlo with his lips sealed are two versions of Chester
suppressed in 1592. And, most important, Aubrey names the other party
involved, whose treatment of the real Charles Chester gave Jonson the
idea: 'one time at a taverne, Sir W. R. beates him and seales up his
mouth, i.e. his upper and neather beard, with hard wax'. Just visible
beneath the Jonsonian accretions is a core of historical fact. The man
who engineered Chester's imprisonment, the 'great personage' who had
him shut away, was Sir Walter Ralegh.

Though teasingly opaque, Nashe's, Jonson's, Aubrey's and indeed
Chester's versions of events all point to one idea: that Chester was being
silenced by Ralegh. This may well tie in with Ralegh's own parlous
circumstances in the summer of 1592. The previous year he had secretly
married one of the royal maids-of-honour, Elizabeth Throckmorton, an
act virtually sacrilegious in the Virgin Queen's court. Their son, Damerei,
was born in March 1592, but it was not until about May that the
Queen's displeasure finally began to bite and Ralegh's long 'disgraces'
began. On 31 May he was notified that he was formally in the custody
of Sir Robert Cecil; June and July he spent under house arrest at Durham
House awaiting his fate; on 7 August he and his Bess were dispatched
to the Tower.[19] Throughout those months, Ralegh was fighting to clear
his name, to appeal to the Queen *via* the good offices of Cecil, and to
stem the tide of gossip and rumour. 'S.W.R., as it seemeth, have been
too inward with one of Her Majesty's maids,' wrote an anonymous

court wit: 'all is alarm and confusion at this discovery of the discoverer, and not indeed of a new continent but of a new incontinent'.[20] Chester was arrested, on Cecil's orders, on 19 June: was this a desperate attempt by Ralegh to stop the mouth of a leading malicious gossip, Chester the 'foul mouthde knave' and 'perpetuall talker'? On his own evidence, Chester was known in Ralegh's circle. Another contact Chester mentions might link in here – Sir George Carey. His father was Henry Carey, Lord Hunsdon, the Queen's Lord Chamberlain. As the official in charge of the Queen's entourage, including her Maids of Honour, Hunsdon investigated the Ralegh marriage thoroughly – in early June he took Bess Ralegh into custody, and on the 10th he questioned her brother, Sir Arthur Throckmorton.[21] It is possible that some of Chester's blabbings about the Ralegh marriage were passed on by Sir George Carey (himself the Queen's Knight Marshal) to his father. This connection with Carey may also lead us back to Nashe. Carey was the friend and brother-in-law of Nashe's current patron, Lord Strange, and himself became Nashe's patron in late 1593. Nashe may have already been introduced to his circle, and this is perhaps how he has the 'inside story' of the Chester affair.

An unwise marriage was not the only cause of Ralegh's fall in 1592. There was also the charge of atheism. The specific source of this was a wildly propagandist Catholic pamphlet, *An Advertisement by an Inglish Intelligencer*, issued in 1592 by 'Andreas Philopater' (in fact the indefatigable Jesuit, Robert Parsons). This spoke darkly of 'Sir Walter Rauleys schoole of Atheisme', and of 'the Coniurer that is M[aster] thereof' teaching his scholars 'to spell God backwarde'.[22] Despite its dubious provenance, the smear stuck. The term 'atheism' covered a multitude of sins: in this case it fuelled suspicions about Ralegh's *coterie* of friends – the 'Durham House set' – and its enthusiasm for scientific and occult pursuits. Ralegh's companions in this circle were Henry Percy, 9th Earl of Northumberland, the 'Wizard Earl' as he was known; and three leading scientists – Thomas Hariot, Walter Warner and Robert Hues – later known as Northumberland's 'three Magi'. Hariot is undoubtedly the conjuror referred to in Parsons' pamphlet. The group is a classic expression of late Elizabethan occultism: the mood was free-thinking and speculative, the philosophic tendency Hermetic and neo-Platonic, the subjects discussed mathematics and astronomy, alchemy and medicinal 'chymistry' (both Ralegh and Northumberland were enthusiastic chemists).[23] Also associated with the set were the great magus, Dr John Dee, and the poets Matthew Roydon and George Chapman. Marlowe himself was also connected. In early 1592, in the same document that links him with Strange, Marlowe claimed he was also 'well known' to the Earl of Northumberland. In 1593, Thomas Kyd named Hariot, Warner and Roydon as among Marlowe's familiar company, 'such as he conversed

withal'. The informer Richard Baines reported Marlowe as saying that
Moses 'was but a Jugler & that one Heriots being Sir W. Raleighs man
can do more than he'. And from another source, one Richard Cholmeley,
we learn that Marlowe 'hath read the Atheist lecture to Sr Walter
Raliegh & others'.[24]

Not surprisingly, the portrait of the Durham House clique as a nest
of atheists and conjurors finds its way into *Pierce Penilesse*. This is a
time, says Nashe, when 'Atheists triumph and reioyce, and talke as
prophanely of the Bible as of Bevis of Hampton'. They 'deride our
Ecclesiasticall State, and all Ceremonies of devine worship, as bug-beares
and scar-crowes'. To the reader of 1592, this sounded like the Ralegh
coterie – Parsons made the same allegation, that 'both Moyses and our
Savior, the olde and new Testamente, are iested at' in Ralegh's atheistic
'schoole'. Still more pointedly, Nashe adds:

> I heare say there be Mathematitions abroad that will proove men
> before Adam: and they are harboured in high places, who will main-
> tain it to the death, that there are no divels.

These heretical mathematicians suggest Hariot, Warner and Hues. A
later remark of Nashe's implies that Hariot particularly is meant: in
Christs Teares Nashe speaks of atheists that 'impudently' assert 'that
the late discovered Indians are able to shew antiquities thousands before
Adam'.[25] Hariot was indeed a keen student of the 'late discovered
Indians': he had sailed with Ralegh's Virginia expedition in 1585,
learned the Algonquian language and studied the Indians' religious
beliefs. He published his findings as *A Briefe and True Report of the
New Found Land of Virginia* in 1588. This touches on Indian creation-
mythology, though it says nothing in particular about 'men before
Adam'. Where did Nashe get that bit from? The obvious answer is
Marlowe, who was Hariot's friend, and who himself asserted (*teste*
Baines) 'that the Indians . . . have assuredly writen of about 16 thousand
yeares agone, whereas Adam is proved to have lived within 6 thousand
yeares'. It seems likely that Marlowe had this, verbally, from Hariot.
This heresy would no doubt interest the Durham House circle, for it
chimed in with occultist speculation: Paracelsus held views on pre-Adam-
itic races, and the neo-Platonist, Francesco Giorgi, touched on the subject
in his *Problemata in Sacram Scripturam* (1536). An epigram on the
subject – 'Menn before Adame' – was written by Francis Thynne,
another of Ralegh's acquaintances, though sometime later than this.[26]
Nashe's remark in *Pierce Penilesse* seems to be the first printed reference
to the idea in England. Thus he spices his general attack on the Ralegh
circle with an entirely new instance of their unorthodoxy: another little
anti-Ralegh scoop for Pierce Politic. Nashe may also have Ralegh in

mind when he speaks elsewhere of courtly 'Peacocks' who, 'like mightie mens sepulchers, have nothing but Atheisme, schisme, hypocrisie & vainglory, like rotten bones lurking within them'. He adds: 'how my soule abhors these buckram giants' – buckram was cloth stiffened with paste, hence figuratively someone whose strength is brittle and false. A 'buckram giant' is an idol with feet of clay: apt enough for the great courtier suddenly fallen, the bold explorer now, in his own words in July 1592, 'like a fish cast on dry land, gasping for breath'.[27]

Somehow connected with this covert anti-Ralegh material in *Pierce Penilesse* is a glancing reference to the poet George Chapman, hitherto unnoticed. Chapman was the friend of Marlowe, whose *Hero and Leander* he completed after Marlowe's death, and of Roydon, the 'good Mat.' to whom he dedicated *The Shadow of Night* (1594) and *Ovids Banquet of Sence* (1595). His admiring reference to 'deepe-searching Northumberland', his praise of Ralegh's Guiana expedition (*De Guiana Carmen Epicum*, 1596) and his eulogy of Thomas Hariot (appended to *Achilles Shield*, 1598) all suggest his involvement in the Ralegh *coterie*.[28] His *Shadow of Night* – a long, obscure, compelling meditation on the occult and inspirational benefits of night – seems to express the atmosphere of daring magico-scientific speculation that prevailed behind the closed doors of Durham House. In the preface he speaks of 'an exceeding rapture of delight in the deepe search of knowledge', and the poems themselves – two 'hymnes', to Night and to Cynthia (the moon/Queen Elizabeth) – aspire to a trance-like *furor* which will

> . . . loose my working soule,
> That in her highest pitch, she may controule
> The court of skill, compact of misterie,
> Wanting but franchisement and memorie
> To reach all secrets . . .

'Shameless day', the time of trivial terrestrial activity, 'doth marble us in ill', but night is the time of contemplation, magic, power, when the moon ascends 'inchantress-like', circled with 'charms and incantations That ride huge spirits'. It is generally agreed that Chapman's poem is connected with the Ralegh circle, and that both its message and its mode – difficult to the point of being 'for initiates only' – express that circle's esoteric dedication to the 'deepe search of knowledge'. It is to men like Ralegh, Northumberland and Hariot – and, perhaps, Marlowe – that Chapman says:

> All you possest with indepressed spirits,
> Indued with nimble and aspiring wits,
> Come consecrate with me to sacred Night
> Your whole endevors, and detest the light.[29]

Chapman's nocturnal was not registered for publication until 31 December 1593: it appeared early in 1594. It was, however, substantially written by May 1593, for Marlowe read it before his death: Chapman spoke of Marlowe's 'late desires' that he should publish the poem, 'and to light surrender My soules darke ofspring'.[30] I believe that the poem was in fact circulating, or at least known about, by the summer of 1592, and that Nashe was, once more, the first to refer to it in print. In his panegyric of 'Amyntas' (i.e. Lord Strange) Nashe pauses to criticize Spenser for not having included him in 'that honorable catalogue of our English Heroes' in The Faerie Queene (the 'catalogue' being seventeen eulogistic poems addressed to 'several noblemen, &c': Lord Strange is indeed missing). On this theme of Spenser's omission, Nashe has 'happened to frame a sonnet'. Its opening quatrain runs:

> Perusing yesternight, with idle eyes,
>   The Fairy Singers stately tuned verse,
> And viewing after Chap-mens wonted guise,
>   What strange contents the title did rehearse . . .

The cognoscenti would spot two names folded into this. Looking for 'strange contents' in the Faerie Queene also means looking for Lord Strange in Spenser's 'catalogue' of noblemen. And reading the poem 'after Chap-mens wonted guise', which openly means 'like a chapman, or merchant', also means reading it like George Chapman, nocturnalist and occultist, would. The lines tell us what that type of reading would be: nocturnal ('perusing yesternight'), trance-like ('with idle eyes', comparable to Chapman's 'binding my senses . . . in blissful trance') and esoteric (searching for 'strange contents').[31] This glance at Chapman's poetic and philosophic stance is aptly made in the context of the Faerie Queene, which is shot through with occultist and neo-Platonic themes. Spenser described the poem as a 'continued Allegory or darke Conceit', and Harvey praised it in terms – 'some sacred fury hath enricht thy braynes'; 'fyres divine' infusing 'high conceites' – which parallel Chapman's inspirational themes. Harvey also says:

> So moughtst thou now in these refyned layes
>   Delight the daintie eares of higher powers.
> And so mought they, in their deepe skanning skill,
>   Alow and grace our Collyns [Spenser's] flowing quill.[32]

These 'higher powers' with 'deepe skanning skill' who will reward Spenser's poem are once more the noblemen and scholars of the Ralegh clique, for it is to Ralegh that the Faerie Queene is addressed – 'humbly craving the continuance of your honorable favour towards me . . . Yours most humbly affectionate, Ed. Spenser'. Ralegh had befriended Spenser in Ireland: his own long poem, largely lost, The Ocean's Love to

Cynthia, is related to the 'Luna' episode in the *Faerie Queene*, as it is to
Chapman's '*Hymnus in Cynthiam*' in the *Shadow of Night*.[33] Spenser's
'catalogue' of worthies does include Ralegh – Spenser urges him to
publish his poem of 'faire Cinthia's praises' – and also Northumberland.
Thus Nashe's apparently irrelevant tangent about Spenser's 'forgetfulnes'
turns out to be a densely allusive reference to the literary face of the
Ralegh 'schoole': nocturnal *furor*, esoteric allegory, the 'strange contents'
of occultism.

If *The Shadow of Night* was written, or at least taking shape, by
summer 1592, we now have a third variation on supernatural themes
to set beside *Dr Faustus* and *Pierce Penilesse*. The three works run the
gamut of reactions. At either end are Chapman and Nashe, devotee and
sceptic: Chapman immersed in occult study, dedicated to 'invocation,
fasting, watching'; Nashe out and about in the daily world, reacting to
the idea of invocation with the spoof diabolism of Pierce's 'supplication'.
And somewhere between the two, oscillating and ambiguous, is Marlowe,
poetically 'ravisht' by the aspirations and ethos of 'magick', yet thumping
home the orthodox line that invocation is black, unlawful and damnable.
It seems all the clearer that some kind of debate on the value of occultism
is going on here, and that Lord Strange is as central to the debate as the
more famous Ralegh, whose esoteric leanings are well known. When he
came to prepare *The Shadow of Night* for publication, in late 1593,
Chapman penned a dedicatory epistle to Matthew Roydon. Here he
praises three scholar-noblemen who have 'profitably entertained learning' and generously contributed 'to the vitall warmth of freezing
science'. First on this list of occult enthusiasts – for that is basically what
Chapman means by 'learning' and 'science' – is none other than 'most
ingenious Darbie', i.e. Lord Strange, who succeeded as 5th Earl of Derby
in September 1593. We begin to see that *Pierce Penilesse* contains
elements of discrete propaganda. It is dedicated to Lord Strange; it jokily
deflates the supernatural theme; it is rife with anti-Ralegh rumours. It
is not an attack, as such, on his patron's occultist leanings: patrons did
not support writers who attacked them. It is a genial, witty wooing-
away from the occultist cause. There is no doubt, from other writings,
that Nashe was an out-and-out sceptic on these matters. In *Summers
Last Will*, perhaps with an eye on the Ralegh *coterie*, he debunks 'skie-
measuring Mathematicians' and 'golde-breathing Alcumists',

> Both which are subtill witted humorists,
> That get their meales by telling miracles,
> Which they have seene in travailing the skies:
> Vaine boasters, lyers, makeshifts they are all,
> Men that, removed from their inkehorne termes,
> Bring forth no action worthie of their bread.[34]

Alchemy is a perennial target for him:

> Our English Apes, who, striving to warme themselves with the flame
> of the Philosophers stone, have spent all their wealth in buying
> bellowes to blowe this false fire . . .

> The fire of Alchumie hath wrought such a purgation or purgatory in
> a great number of mens purses in England, that it hath cleane fired
> them out of al they have . . .

> They may verie well picke mens purses, like the unskilfuller cousning
> kind of Alchumists, with their artificiall and ceremoniall Magicke,
> but no effect shall they atchieve thereby . . .[35]

A popular branch of alchemy in the 1590s was the 'chymicall' preparation of medicines, practised by the followers of Paracelsus. This too
receives satiric treatment from Nashe. The description of a Jewish physician's niggardliness ingeniously converts into a recipe-book of absurd
Paracelsist extracts:

> Of the ashie parings of his bread, he would make conserve of chip-
> pings. Out of bones, after the meate was eaten off, hee would alchu-
> mize an oyle, that hee sold for a shilling a dram. His snot and spittle
> a hundred times hee hath put over to his Apothecarie for snow water.
> Anie spider he would temper to perfect Mithridate. His reumaticke
> eies . . . dropt as coole allome water as you could request. . . . The
> licour out of his shoes hee would wring, to make a sacred Balsamum
> against barrennes.[36]

To mathematicians, alchemists and Paracelsians may be added
astrologers:

> I thank heaven I am none of their credulous disciples, nor can they
> cousen or seduce me with anie of their iugling coniecturalls, or
> winking or tooting throgh a six penny Iacobs Staffe; their spells, their
> characters, their anagrams, I have no more perswasion of. . . .[37]

The list could go on. Nashe's stance is consistently anti-occultist, anti-
magian, anti-contemplative: 'innumerable monstrous practises hath
loytring contemplation brought forth'.[38] He stands diametrically
opposed to Chapman, and it is scarcely surprising to find Chapman
inserting into the preface to *The Shadow of Night*, on the same page as
his praise of Strange, a series of barbed allusions to Nashe. Nor is it
surprising to find Chapman, Nashe and Lord Strange all featuring in

Shakespeare's topical revue of 1593, *Loves Labors Lost*. These later sparks of the occultist controversy will be dealt with in due time.

The 'Tale of the Beare and the Foxe' in *Pierce Penilesse* was undoubtedly intended as a political fable. It was instantly accepted as such by Harvey – he could 'give a shrewd Gesse at a courtly allegory' – and others.[39] It caused Nashe a good deal of trouble: as late as 1598 he speaks of the litigations and dangers it brought after the 'interpreters' got hold of it and 'fisht out such a deepe politique state meaning, as if I had al the secrets of court or commonwealth at my fingers endes'.[40] The story tells of the villainy and overbearing ambition of the Bear, 'chief Burgomaster of all the Beasts under the Lyon'. To bolster his 'Authoritie', the Bear 'beganne to prye and to smell through every corner of the Forrest for praye'. He plots against a 'fat Cammell' (horse): with the connivance of an Ape, who envied the Horse's 'lordly' power, the Bear traps him in a pit where he can 'seaze on him at his pleasure'. He poisons the Deer, tears out the Unicorn's heart, and stirs up dissent among the 'lesser beasts' of the forest. His enemies suppressed, the Bear conceives a 'newfangled lust' and begins to long for honey. He plans to persuade the countrymen that Bees are idle parasites – 'what should such idle Drones doe with such stately Hyves, or lye sucking at such pretious Honnycombes' – and that they should be dispossessed, their honey 'distributed equally abroad', and their place in the hives taken by Wasps, who would 'humme and buzze a thousand times lowder than they'. To 'broach this device' the Bear engages the cunning Fox, promising 'to have his Pattent seald to be the Kings Poulterer for ever, if he could bring it to passe'. The Fox and his sidekick, 'an old Camelion', travel the country, persuading the 'silly Swaines' that the Bees' honey is 'poysonous and corrupt'. Many are convinced, and take what they say as 'canonical', but at length their 'secret driftes are laide open'. For one day, 'as these two Devisers were plotting by themselves', a Fly passed by and 'heard all their talke'. Out of malice to the Fox, who had 'murdred so many of his kindred with his flail-driving tail', the Fly 'went presentlie and buzd in *Linceus* eares the whole purport of their malice' (Lynceus, the far-sighted Argonaut, here represents authority: 'lynceous' also means 'lynx-like', so in the fable's bestiary, authority is a Lynx). The plotters were 'apprehended and imprisoned'. The Bear, meanwhile, had died, 'impatient of delaies and consumed with an inward greife'.

The Bear is undoubtedly the late Robert Dudley, Earl of Leicester, whose crest was the bear and ragged staff, and who was so-called by writers both libellous and laudatory. Nashe's attempt to deny the identification later in 1592 – 'now a man may not talke of a dog, but it is surmised he aimes at him that giveth the dog in his crest' – shows it was readily recognized.[41] Of all the anti-Leicester libels then current, the most virulent and popular was *Leycesters Commonwealth*, another of Father Parsons' Catholic polemics, printed abroad and widely dispersed in England despite the Queen's express interdict in June 1585. It presented Leicester as a Machiavellian schemer, murderer and usurper, bent on turning England into '*Leycestrensam rempublicam*, a Leycestrian common wealth'. Leicester is said to 'play the Beare' with Burghley; the Queen dares not 'bark at the Beare'; a loyal subject is said to value 'the Lyon before the Beare', i.e. the Queen above Leicester.[42] The general setting of Nashe's fable is clear. The blood-thirsty Bear presents Leicester in the same rabidly hostile light as the Parsons libel. The Lion, whose 'chief Burgomaster' he is, is the Queen: when Nashe says that the Bear grew to be hated by all except 'the Lyon, whose eyes he could blinde as hee list', he is making a *risqué* comment on the Queen's infatuated favouring of Leicester. The Bear's various victims represent Leicester's enemies and alleged victims. The Horse is the Catholic, Thomas Howard, Duke of Norfolk, whose execution in 1572 was partly the result of Leicester's machinations. As Parsons' *Commonwealth* relates it, Leicester had a 'secret desire to pull downe' Norfolk and 'by a thousand cunning devices' drew him into that plan to marry Mary Queen of Scots, 'which afterward was the cause or occasion of his ruine'. The Ape who assists Nashe's Bear is no doubt Sir Nicholas Throckmorton, Leicester's accomplice in his dealings against Norfolk. They 'were at that time both friends and of a faction,' says the *Commonwealth*, and Throckmorton's letters to Norfolk helped plunge the latter 'over the eares in suspition and disgrace' so 'he should never be able to draw himselfe out of the ditch againe'.[43] Parsons' imagery is echoed by Nashe, who has the Horse 'stumbling' into the 'pit' dug by the Bear and the Ape. The Bear's next 'treacherous Conquest' is to poison the Deer. Here Nashe rehearses the widespread rumour that Leicester had poisoned Walter Devereux, 1st Earl of Essex, in 1576, before secretly marrying his widow, Lettice. The Essex crest is a deer. The Deer's premonition – 'prophesying his neere approching mishap' – nicely glances at the poem, 'The Compleynt of a Sinner', supposed to have been written by Essex on the eve of his death. What exactly Nashe means by the Bear's third victim, the Unicorn, is unclear: he may be alluding to the crest of the Scottish royal family and hence to Leicester's supposed murder of Lady Lennox, a Scots lady of royal blood.[44]

In the first half of his fable, Nashe does little more than jump on the anti-Leicester bandwagon, which had been gathering momentum since the Earl's death in 1588. He had clearly read *Leycesters Commonwealth* and he probably also knew Thomas Rogers' poem, circulated in MS, 'Leicesters Ghost'.[45] It is the second half of the fable that contains the

nub, for here Nashe moves into more familiar territory, attacking Leicester as the leading champion and protector of the Puritans. Though he
refused to admit that the Bear was Leicester, he was happy enough to
identify the Fox: 'Let it be Martin if you will, or some old dog that bites
sorer than hee'.[46] The old Puritan dog-fox, whose bite is even worse
than Martin's, is obviously Thomas Cartwright. In 1586, Leicester had
installed Cartwright as Master of his hospital at Warwick, adding to its
annual stipend a personal annuity of £50. This is precisely allegorized
by Nashe – the Bear promises the Fox a 'Pattent' to be the 'Kings
Poulterer for ever': so Leicester gave Cartwright the 'patent' of the
Mastership 'for life'. Nashe had already referred to Cartwright as 'the
idoll of Warwick' in the *Almond*.[47] The fable's anti-Puritan message is
ingeniously delivered. The 'great store' of honey which the Bear craves
is the wealth of church living. The Bees he plans to dispossess are the
Bishops (Martin's 'L Bb', or 'Lord Bees'). The Wasps are the Puritan
ministers who will replace them and 'humme and buzze' (i.e. preach) 'a
thowsand times lowder'. Leicester is thus charged with championing
Puritan reform in order to feather his own nest with episcopal wealth:
a common and not implausible charge against Puritan-tending noblemen.
To this end the Bear engages the Fox, Cartwright, and his accomplice, the
Chameleon. The latter is probably John Penry, alias 'Martin Marprelate',
aptly epitomized as the 'Camelion, that could put on all shapes and
imitate any colour'. Among these shapes, he appeared 'sometime like an
Ape to make sport, and then like a Crocodile to weep': 'martin' was an
Elizabethan word for an ape, as in the anti-Martinist *Whip for an
Ape*; the crocodile tears perhaps refer to the plangent tones of Penry's
'supplications' on behalf of the Welsh. The pair travel the country,
dispensing propaganda against the established Bees: Leicester is thus
implicated in the Martinist campaign. Their discoverer, the Fly who
'buzd' their sedition in authority's ear, may well be Tom Nashe himself,
the anti-Martinist sleuth and pamphleteer. To make of himself an insect,
busy and inquisitive, is somehow typical of Nashe. In *Strange Newes*
Nashe says, *à propos* the deeper meanings of his fable, 'Who but a
Foppe wil labour to anatomize a Flye?'[48] In late 1593, Shakespeare hit
on the name 'Moth' for his caricature of Nashe.

Having grasped something of the 'politique state meaning' of Nashe's
fable, one now wonders why – why, in a pamphlet so urgently topical
as *Pierce* – did he wish to attack Leicester, who had been dead for four
years, and connect him with the Martinist campaign, which had
collapsed at the end of 1589? One answer is that the anti-Puritan
message was still as relevant in 1592. Nashe ends the fable with a
throwaway line about the Fox and Chameleon – 'How they scapte I
know not, but some saie they were hanged, and so weele leave them.'
His point, perhaps, is precisely that the leaders of Puritan dissent –

Cartwright, Penry, *et al.* – had *not* been brought to justice, let alone 'hangd'. Cartwright had in fact been arrested in summer 1590, and committed to the Fleet prison, but repeated interrogations before the High Commission and the Star Chamber failed to convict him. He refused to take the oath *ex officio*, debated the court's prerogatives, stalled, quibbled and theologized. In March 1592, after eighteen months in prison, the authorities were forced to release him.[49] When Nashe wrote *Pierce Penilesse*, Cartwright the Fox was a free man: he had beaten the Establishment at its own game. His sidekick, Penry the Chameleon, was also at large, preaching with impunity in Calvinist Edinburgh; his old Martinist partner, Robert Waldegrave, was also there. The English government had persuaded King James to issue a writ of banishment on Penry, but the powerful Scots clergy sheltered him. This gives us, at least, a motive to start from: Nashe's fable renews his polemic against the Puritans, and glances pointedly at the slackening and failure of official moves against them. The recent fate of a third Martinist, John Udall, takes us further down this line. In June 1592, after over two years locked up under sentence of death, Udall received an official pardon. This booted him little, for he died a few days later, but it throws an interesting sidelight on Nashe's fable. For Udall's pardon was largely thanks to the effort and influence of one powerful man, who 'bore good will to him', persuaded him to redraft his submission for clemency, and himself presented it to the Queen in February 1592. This protector of the Puritans, this latter-day Leicester, was none other than Sir Walter Ralegh.[50] He fits in here well enough: he had begun his courtly career as a *protégé* of Leicester's and, despite inevitable jealousies towards the end, they had remained allies. His sympathies undoubtedly lay with the Puritans, though from an intellectual, 'eirenical', non-doctrinaire stance. Ralegh is fleetingly present in the first part of Nashe's fable as well, for the reader who identified the envious Ape as Leicester's friend, Sir Nicholas Throckmorton, would be instantly reminded of the current Ralegh scandal, for Throckmorton was the father of Ralegh's Bess, the secret bride for whom he had jilted the Queen. A third member of the family, cousin to Sir Nicholas and Bess, is Job Throckmorton, yet another unpunished Martinist. The configurations beneath Nashe's 'courtly allegory' grow more complex.

Nashe's fable, then, is not just a belated smear against Leicester, a safe assault on a dead giant. It has other, more pointed comments to make – about the government's failure to muzzle the Puritan leaders, and about the continued championing, *à la* Leicester, of Puritanism in high places. Leicester is, in a sense, Nashe's epitome of the vested interests and heavy political muscle behind Puritanism. Ralegh's is one name the reader might ponder on, having already discerned other material against him in the pamphlet, but there are others this cap would fit. In this context, it is interesting to find angry remarks about *Pierce Penilesse* in a letter written by a Puritan member of the Privy Council, Robert Beale. Beale was Clerk of the Council, brother-in-law of Sir Francis Walsingham, and an outspoken critic of episcopal power. It is possible he was the author of the anonymous *Abstract of Certain Acts of Parliament* (1583), which argued an existing constitutional base for Puritan reform.[51] In the turbulent parliament of February 1593, **Beale** spoke heatedly against the bishops, supporting Attorney Morice's bill to ban the Commission's oath *ex officio*. This, along with his opposition to the current Subsidy Bill, earned him the Queen's displeasure, whereupon he wrote to Lord Burghley the long letter of self-justification, dated 17 March 1593, which contains the reference to *Pierce*. He argues that the Establishment itself is to blame for current religious 'dissensions', and that its anti-Puritan propagandists have only served to increase 'hatred and strife', both in England and with 'our neighbors, the Churches of France, Geneva, the Low Countries and Scotland'. By way of example, he says

> that one of these subjects, in his book entitled *A Supplication to the Devil*, so reviled the whole nation of Denmark, as everyone who so bore any due respect to her Majesty and her friends, might be sorry and ashamed to see it. The realm hath otherwise enemies enough, without making any more by such contumelious pamphlets. Wherefore such invectives could not but serve the enemy's turn whatsoever was pretended otherwise. And that although he [i.e. Beale] had of late years very little dealt with any foreign causes, yet if this course came not from Rome, he had heard it reported that it was well liked of in Rome by the Pope and his adherents, and all the English Jesuits, Seminaries and traitors abroad, who by such divisions thought the sooner to bring to pass their intended purposes, which he trusted the Lord would never permit. But that in the mean time, the cause being so dangerous, he prayed to God that we be not abused by such partial and sinister tales and pretences; and that by too much credulity and security the remedy were not too long delayed.[52]

Beale is no all-powerful Bear – no Leicester or Ralegh – but it is fascinating to find *Pierce* getting this hostile Puritan feedback from government circles. The 'remedy' Beale recommends at the end presumably included the stopping of Nashe's mouth and the suppression of his 'contumelious' pamphlet: if so, Burghley wisely ignored it. Nashe had indeed been rude about the Danes – 'bursten-bellied sots' . . . 'arrogant Asse-headed people' – and particularly about their militant brand of Calvinism: 'Byshopricks, Deanries, Prebendaries, why they know no such functions: a sort of ragged ministers they have, of whom they count as basely as

water-bearers'. He also glanced at the Danish church in his fable, where
the Fox and Chameleon urge the people to emulate those superior
'Gardners' who have rooted out the episcopal Bees, 'as for example,
Scotland, Denmarke, and some more pure parts of the seventeene
Provinces [i.e. the Netherlands]'.[53]

It is possible that Beale's talk of 'sinister tales and pretences' particularly refers to Nashe's anti-Puritan fable. A close colleague of his in the
government would certainly have had cause to note it – Sir Francis
Knollys, Treasurer of the Household. Not only was Knollys another
zealous Puritan within the Privy Council, and an open supporter of
Cartwright's cause in 1591–2, but he was also the Earl of Leicester's
father-in-law (his daughter Lettice, Essex's widow, married Leicester in
1578).[54] As someone closely connected with both the Bear and the Fox
in the early 1590s, Nashe may well have had Knollys somewhere in
mind when he wrote his fable. If Beale knew about *Pierce*, it is a safe
bet Knollys did too. And if one wants to know who tipped them the
wink, the answer is probably Gabriel Harvey, for in *Strange Newes*,
written in the last months of 1592, Nashe tells us how busy Gabriel has
been trying to 'informe authoritie against me' and 'incense men of high
calling against me'.[55] Harvey had himself been a satellite of Leicester's
back in the 1570s, and so may have had some contact with Knollys
already. Newly returned to London in September 1592, what could
better serve his turn than a discrete word in Knollys' ear about Nashe's
'parlous Tales of Beares and Foxes'?

Much the most serious charge Beale levels at Nashe is that his
pamphlet serves submerged Catholic interests, may even be part of a
sinister 'course' emanating 'from Rome'. Nashe the anti-Puritan polemicist becomes Nashe the Catholic *agent provocateur*, fomenting controversy for subversive ends. This is, of course, a typical doctrinaire argument of Beale's – anything the Puritan disliked was 'papist' – but the
charge is by no means idle. Nashe had, after all, read that banned Jesuit
tract, *Leycesters Commonwealth*: the first half of his fable is a digest of
its allegations against Leicester, a portrait imported wholesale from
Catholic propaganda. Nashe's treatment of the Leicester-Norfolk affair
suggests his total sympathy with the betrayed Catholic nobleman, the
'lordly' Horse who is tricked and devoured by the Bear: 'Alas, goodly
Creature,' Nashe says, 'What availeth thy gentlenes, thy prowesse, or
the plentifull pasture wherein thou wert fed, since malice triumphs over
all thou commaundest?' The reader who identified the Horse as Norfolk
would find this a curiously poignant epitaph for a Catholic who had been
executed for treason. Nashe had, we remember, grown up in Norfolk, at
a church whose previous rectors had been chaplains to the ill-fated Duke.
Who knows what dangerous loyalties he might have formed back then?
Nor is this Duke, Thomas Howard, the only member of the family

Nashe praised: the poet Henry Howard, Earl of Surrey – Thomas's father – is featured prominently and approvingly in *The Unfortunate Traveller*. Beale could not have known about the latter in March 1593, but he was well placed to spot the Norfolk sympathies in Nashe's fable. As one of Walsingham's *amanuenses* he was involved in government efforts to arraign Norfolk's son – Philip, Earl of Arundel – for Catholic sedition. Memoranda in Beale's hand, relating to Arundel, are still extant.[56] His charge against Nashe – of Catholic sympathies, if not of out-and-out subversion – begins to stick: Nashe's fable does have – both in itself and by association with other anti-Leicester libels – a strongly Catholic flavour. The anti-Ralegh motifs in the pamphlet might be similarly scrutinized – how Nashe takes up yet another piece of Jesuit propaganda when he treats the Ralegh coterie as atheists; how he raises questions about Charles Chester, in prison as a suspected Catholic agent. Indeed, one suddenly begins to see that Catholic sympathy might well be a key position from which to view this whole tangle of material I have been teasing out in the last two chapters – Nashe's relations with Lord Strange, scion of a powerful Catholic family not dissimilar from the Howards; his association with Marlowe, whose ambiguous Catholic connections go back to his university days and still seem to haunt the moral landscape of *Faustus*; the whole anti-occultist line which Nashe takes in *Pierce* and elsewhere, whether through general satire or with particular reference to men like Ralegh, Chapman and, indeed, Harvey: the clue to all these may well be Catholicism. We have perhaps stumbled – via the petulant strictures of a minor government official – on a new and central truth about Nashe. For now this must remain a straw in the wind: Beale has 'heard it reported' that Nashe is working for covert Catholic interests, that his 'invectives' tend to 'serve the enemy's turn, whatsoever was pretended otherwise'. Certain events and writings of 1593 will bring these allegations into sharper focus.

One last name, one last piece of Nashe's anti-Leicester jigsaw, remains to be mentioned – Leicester's famous niece, Mary Herbert, Countess of Pembroke. This takes us back into the literary world, for after Leicester's death the Countess became the focus and figurehead for many writers who had admired Leicester and looked to him for support, just as she was the focus for the continuing adulation of her dead brother, Sir Philip Sidney. There was, Rosenberg shows, a discernible literary 'movement', its aim 'to revive the memory of the Dudleys and the Sidneys, and to celebrate the Countess of Pembroke as the chief surviving member of the line'.[57] If so, it is a safe bet that Nashe was aware of it, and that there is a literary, as well as a politico-religious, angle to his anti-Leicester fable. A glance at Spenser's poem, 'The Ruines of Time', published in *Complaints* (1591), confirms this. The poem is a paramount expression of this Leicester-Sidney revival. It is dedicated to the Countess of

Pembroke and, **Spenser** says, 'speciallie intended to the renowming of that noble **Race** from which you and he [Sir Philip] sprong, and to the eternizing of some of the chiefe of them late deceased'. Prominent among the noble deceased is Leicester:

> A mighty prince of most renowmed race,
> Whom England high in count of honour held,
> And greatest ones did sue to gaine his grace;
> Of greatest ones, he greatest in his place.

Spenser laments the surge of anti-Leicester feeling after his death: 'evill men . . . his deeds upbraid' and 'Spite bites the dead, that living never baid'. In one of the visions at the end of the poem Spenser sees

> . . . two Beares, as white as anie milke,
> Lying together in a mightie cave,
> Of milde aspect, and haire as soft as silke,
> That salvage nature seemed not to have,
> Nor after greedie spoyle of bloud to crave,
> Two fairer beasts might not elsewhere be found.

The two Bears are Leicester and his brother, Ambrose Dudley, Earl of Warwick, another of the 'noble Race' whose death Spenser mourns. Spenser's vision is, clearly, the diametric opposite of Nashe's fable. It celebrates Leicester as the gentle, honourable, White Bear, purified of all savage nature and greed for 'bloud'. Every attribute Spenser gives him is upended in Nashe's portrait of the Bear as a 'savadge blood-hunter' possessed of a 'greedy, bestiall humour'. And when Spenser praises Leicester's loyalty and honesty –

> [He] sate in the bosome of his Soveraine,
> And *Right and Loyall* did his word maintaine

– Nashe retorts with a picture of scheming Machiavellianism that makes a mockery of that Leicestrian motto. There are probably personal motives in this – not against Spenser (whom Nashe, to his credit, invariably treats with respect) but against the Countess of Pembroke. Nashe was involved, we remember, in the first edition of Sidney's *Astrophel* in 1591, and he spoke fulsomely of the Countess in his preface. His edition was swiftly supplanted and his overtures ill-received. 'If I bee evill intreated', warns Pierce, 'or sent away with a Flea in mine eare, let him looke that I will raile on him soundly.'[58] It is no surprise to find Nashe settling his score with the Countess in *Pierce Penilesse*. He does so at one remove, by railing on her beloved uncle and by viciously refuting the heraldic celebration of him which Spenser had dedicated to her the previous year.

Some confirmation of this is found in the poetic anthology called *The*

Phoenix Nest, published in the autumn of 1593. This is again a product of the Leicester-Pembroke literary axis. Its editor – 'R.S. of the Inner Temple, gent' – prefaces the book with a frantically pro-Leicester polemic entitled 'The Dead Mans Right'.[59] He castigates the 'wicked Libellors', who have 'forged millions of impieties' against Leicester; defends him from charges of 'ambition and aspiring minde'; approves his Puritan principles; attests his loyalty and political wisdom; and concludes that all in all Leicester behaved 'not as a man',

> But as a God, whose heavenlie wit inspir'd,
> Wrought hie effects, yet vertues courses held.

In denouncing the 'defamatorie libels' against Leicester, editor 'R.S.' distinguishes two types. There is the mainstream of Catholic propaganda, printed anonymously and abroad, 'without reache and feare of authority'. This is typified by *Leycesters Commonwealth*: its author, Parsons, is referred to by puns on his Catholic dignities – 'the *father* of this pestilent invention', 'the capitall and *Cardinall* libellor'. Stirred up by the Jesuit's 'scurilous Cartels', the editor goes on, a second wave of defamation has followed Leicester's death:

> The toongs of men, irritated to envie by the instruments of those libellors, being without fear of controulment sith his death, are become over-scandalous and at too much libertie. It shall not be amisse to perswade more modestie and pietie of speech.

Prominent in the editor's mind must be Nashe's libel, dispersed far and wide in a pamphlet that had by then gone into three editions. The *Phoenix Nest* preface is a fair gauge of reactions to Nashe's slander in pro-Leicester literary circles, just as Beale's waspish letter gives us a glimpse of reactions in Puritan political circles. Both have some powerful kin of Leicester's lurking on the sidelines – Knollys and the Countess – and both imply that Nashe's political pamphleteering has a pro-Catholic base.

Precise details are lacking, but it seems clear that some kind of legal reprisals followed *Pierce Penilesse*. Six years later, writing *Lenten Stuffe*, Nashe recalls what happened after certain of 'Gods fooles' had 'fisht out' political meanings from 'some discourses of mine'. He writes:

> Talke I of a beare, O it is such a man that emblazons him in his armes, or of a woolfe, a fox or a camelion, any lording whom they do not affect it is meant by. The great potentate, stirred up with those perverse applications, not looking into the text it selfe, but the ridiculous comment, . . . straite thunders out his displeasure, & showres downe the whole tempest of his indignation on me, and, to

amend the matter and fully absolve himselfe of this rash error of misconstruing, he commits it over to be prosecuted by a worse misconstruer then himselfe, *videlicet* his learned counsaile, (God forgive me if I slander them with that title of learned, for generally they are not,) and they, being compounded of nothing but vociferation and clamour, rage & fly out they care not how agaynst a mans life, his person, his parentage, . . . and in the first three wordes of his Apology, with impudent exclamations interrupt him.[60]

The 'discourses' in question are clearly the *Pierce Penilesse* fable. The indignant 'potentate' might be Sir Francis Knollys, or possibly the Earl of Pembroke, acting on behalf of his wife's family. A third candidate – Leicester's heir apparent, Sir Robert Dudley – is superficially attractive but in fact unlikely: he was illegitimate and his claim to the title never recognized; he was at this time a wild and disreputable teenager; and he shared none of his father's Puritan connections, eventually embracing Catholicism and living in exile.[61] A related passage in *Lenten Stuffe* may also refer to the litigious aftermath of *Pierce*. Here Nashe speaks of an 'infant squib of the Innes of Court' who peruses one of his pamphlets and,

> to approve hymselfe an extravagant statesman, catcheth hold of a rush, and absolutely concludeth it is meant of the Emperour of Ruscia, and that it will utterly marre the traffike into that country, if all the pamphlets bee not called in and suppressed, wherein that libelling word is mentioned.[62]

This seems close to Beale's letter to Burghley, complaining that Nashe's remarks about Denmark will offend a friendly nation at a time when 'the realm hath otherwise enemies enough'. All in all, there were troubles in store for 'Pierce Politic' as his book rolled off the presses in September 1592. Nor were they long in coming. Nashe must have felt the first rumbles within weeks, for by November he had cause to complain:

> in these ill-eide daies of ours, every man delights with Ixion to beget children of clouds, digge for Pearles in dunghils, and wrest oyle out of iron. Poore *Pierce Penilesse* have they turnd to a coniuring booke, for there is not that line in it with which they doo not seeke to raise up a Ghost.[63]

9

GREENE AND HARVEY

'Small sparkles of dissention have kindled horrible fires of faction'

GABRIEL HARVEY *Foure Letters*

Robert Greene died at his last lodgings, a shoemaker's house in Dowgate, on 3 September 1592. He was buried on the 4th, 'in the New-churchyard neere Bedlam'. His landlord, the 'poore Cordwainer' Master Isam, bore the cost of the funeral, 10s 4d.[1] In a letter written the following day, and immediately published as a six-leaf 'butter-fly Pamphlet',[2] Gabriel Harvey recounted the desperate story of Greene's last days: he lay in a lice-infested bed, pitifully calling for 'a penny pott of Malmesy'; he pawned his doublet, hose and sword, and 'was faine' to borrow Master Isam's shirt 'whiles his owne was a washing'; he was deserted by all but his devoted landlady, who 'loved him derely', and his 'sorry ragged' mistress, sister of 'Cutting' Ball and mother of his boy, Fortunatus. In respect of his dying wish, Mistress Isam crowned his corpse with a garland of bays. She herself showed Harvey the letter Greene had scrawled the night before he died, begging his ex-wife, Doll, to repay the good shoemaker £10 he had borrowed: 'if hee and his wife had not succoured me, I had died in the streetes'.[3] From Cuthbert Burby, the publisher of one of Greene's posthumous pamphlets, we learn that he had been sick for about 'a moneths space', the cause 'a surfet which hee had taken with drinking'. He had been 'continually scowred' with purgatives, 'yet still his belly sweld, and never left swelling upward, untill it sweld him at the hart and in his face'.[4] Throughout his illness, Burby adds, 'he continually called upon God'. The pamphleteer to the last, Greene dashed off prayers and exhortations and fragmentary, remorse-laden autobiographies. These the stationers seized on – 'this happened into my hands' – and cobbled up into the 'deathbed' pamphlets, *Greenes Groatsworth of Wit*, *Greenes Vision* and *The Repentance*. Thus 'the king of the paper stage' (as a friend of Harvey's put it) 'played his last part'.[5]

From the lurid publicity surrounding Greene's death – including Nashe's own *Strange Newes*, partly written to avenge his dead friend's memory – we learn something of the relations between Greene and Nashe in 1592. After their close acquaintance at the time of *Menaphon* and Martinism, 1589, the pair seem to have drifted apart. Nashe says that for a stretch of 'two yeares together', after 'I first knew him about town', they had scarcely seen one another 'any more than for a carowse or two'.[6] During Greene's last months, however, they became closer again. Harvey automatically associates them, calling Nashe Greene's 'sworne brother', his 'inwardest companion', his 'fellow writer'. In the early summer of 1592, Greene referred in print to 'one of Pierce penilesse fraternity', suggesting he knew of *Pierce*, verbally or in MS, before it was published.[7] Both were whetting their pens against the Harveys at this time: Nashe's assault on Richard Harvey in *Pierce* had been written by mid-June, while Greene's *Quip for an Upstart Courtier*, containing his skit on the Harvey family, was registered on 20 July.[8] They no doubt compared anti-Harvey notes. Both were reacting to the same provocation – Richard Harvey's 'arrogantly censoriall' preface to *The Lamb of God*, wherein, Nashe explains,

> not mee alone did he revile and dare to the combat, but . . . mistermed all our other Poets and writers about London, piperly make-plaies and make-bates. Hence Greene, being chief agent for the companie (for hee writ more than foure other, how well I will not say: but *Sat cito, si sat bene*) tooke occasion to canvaze him a little in his Cloth-breeches and Velvet-breeches [i.e. the *Quip*].

According to Nashe, Greene's position as the 'chief agent' of the London literary set made him honour bound to answer Harvey's aspersions. Plausible enough: Greene implies much the same in a marginal note in the *Quip*, warning Harvey to 'looke to it' and 'reconcile' himself, or else 'all the Poets in England will have a blow at your breech for calling them poperlye makeplaies'.[9] Greene's rather jovial sketch about the rope-maker and his three sons is nothing compared to Nashe's long vitriolic harangue on Richard Harvey, but nevertheless Greene decided to cancel the offending passage from subsequent issues of the *Quip*. Gabriel claimed this was because of Greene's 'great feare to be called *Coram* [i.e. brought to court] for those forged imputations'. Nashe gave a different reason, that Greene's physician, ministering to him 'in his sicknesse', had urged him 'either to mittigate it, or leave it out: not for any extraordinarie account hee made of the fraternitie of fooles, but for one of them [John Harvey] was proceeded in the same facultie of Phisicke hee profest'.[10] Either may be true, though Nashe's has the tone of personal knowledge.

In the first week of August, a month before Greene died, he and Nashe dined together. They drank Rhenish wine and ate pickled herring. Harvey called it 'that fatall banquet', believing that Greene's sickness was the result of his over-indulgence at this party. Publisher Burby also speaks of a 'surfet' of drinking 'about a moneths space' before he died.

Nashe confirms the occasion – but not its fatality – in *Strange Newes*.
He adds the name of another guest, 'one of my fellowes, Will Monox'.
Nothing is known of Monox beyond Nashe's aside, offered slightly
menacingly to Gabriel, 'Hast thou never heard of him and his great
dagger?'[11] This was possibly the last time Nashe saw Greene alive.
Harvey makes much capital of Nashe having deserted Greene in his last
sickness: he 'came never more at him, but either would not, or happily
could not, performe the duty of an affectionate and faithfull frend'. This
has often been held against Nashe, but the probable reason is simply
that he had left town. He was certainly 'in the Countrey' – in fact, as
we shall see, in Croydon – when *Pierce Penilesse* first appeared on 8
September. Writing to the printer, Abel Jeffes, he complains that *Pierce*
'was abroad a fortnight ere I knewe of it', that it had appeared 'uncorrected and unfinished' while he was away, and that 'fear of infection' –
the raging plague of 1592 – still 'detained' him.[12] It is quite probable
he had left London sometime in August, and that his absence from the
dying Greene's side was a simple 'could not' rather than a callous 'would
not'.

Among Greene's last writings is that fraught appeal to his 'fellowe
Schollers about this Cittie' which appears in *Greenes Groatsworth of
Wit*.[13] The passage is famous for its snarl at Shakespeare (or 'Shake-
scene') as an 'upstart Crow' masquerading in plumage plagiarized from
the University Wits. Greene addresses three of his 'Quondam acquaintance', Marlowe, Nashe and – very briefly – George Peele. Marlowe –
'thou famous gracer of Tragedians' – is abjured to forsake his 'Diabolicall Atheisme' and 'pestilent Machivilian pollicie'. This is the time of *Dr
Faustus*; of Marlowe's connections with Ralegh's atheistic 'schoole'; of
The Jew of Malta, with its prologue spoken by the ghost of 'Machevill'.
Greene ends on a prophetic note, bidding Marlowe not to 'defer' his
repentance 'till this last point of extremitie, for little knowest thou how
in the end thou shall be visited'. In less than a year, Marlowe too would
be dead, 'visited' by a knife in the head. Next comes Nashe:

> With thee I ioyne young Iuvenall, that byting Satyrist, that lastlie with
> mee together writ a Comedie. Sweete boy, might I advise thee, be
> advised and get not many enemies by bitter words: inveigh against
> vaine men, for thou canst do it, no man better, no man so wel: thou
> hast a libertie to reproove all, and name none; for one being spoken
> to, all are offended, none being blamed no man is iniured. Stop
> shallow water still running, it will rage, tread on a worme and it will
> turne: then blame not schollers vexed with sharpe lines, if they reprove
> thy too much libertie of reproofe.[14]

As Marlowe is warned of diabolical atheism, Nashe is warned of dangerous libel. Generalized satire is alright – 'none being blamed no man is iniured' – but specific 'bitter words' spell trouble. 'Schollers vexed with sharpe lines' suggests Nashe's onslaught on Richard Harvey, confirming that Greene knew *Pierce* in manuscript. He admonishes Nashe in the same mood of conciliation that moved him to retract his own anti-Harvey passage in the *Quip*. One notes also, in contrast to his words to Marlowe, the affection in his tone. Nashe may be the ferocious Elizabethan Juvenal, but to Greene he is still the 'sweete boy' whose 'too much libertie' needs checking for his own good.

These last words of Greene's to Nashe, set down in August 1592, also pose a riddle. What was this 'Comedie' which they had recently ('lastlie') written together? The glib answer is that it is some lost or unassigned play, some piece of theatrical hack-work cobbled up between them. Simpson suggested *A Knack to Know a Knave*, played by Strange's Men in June 1592, with Alleyn in the lead role and a 'merriment' at the end by Will Kemp.[15] The play is too crude, however, and it would hardly have been published anonymously, as it was in 1594, if it were in fact by two such saleable authors as Greene and Nashe. McGinn takes another tack, pointing out that although the context suggests play-writing, the comedy referred to need not be a play: Nashe describes his own *Have with you to Saffron-Walden* as a 'Comodie'. On this basis, McGinn argues that Nashe had collaborated with Greene on the *Quip for an Upstart Courtier*, and had actually written the anti-Harvey sketch which Greene later removed.[16] This might tie in with the message of moderation Greene gives Nashe in the *Groatsworth*, but once again the cons outweigh the pros. The passage does not sound like Nashe: it is too bluff, too static, its pretended yokel dialogue too well sustained (Nashe would show through). In *Strange Newes* Nashe often refers to the *Quip*, always as Greene's; he categorically denies having yet written anything against Gabriel or his father; and he makes a slip – the expurgated passage was twenty-two lines long, not 'some seaven or eight lines' – which he would hardly make if he had written the lines himself.[17] I have a new suggestion to offer: that the comedy Greene and Nashe hatched together was *The Defence of Conny-Catching*, issued in the spring or summer of 1592, under the pseudonym of 'Cuthbert Cunny-catcher'.

Much of Greene's last year was devoted to what many consider his most impressive work: the series of 'conny-catching' tracts, cataloguing the villainous practices and bizarre slang of the Elizabethan underworld. A 'conny-catcher' was a confidence-trickster or hustler, especially a card-sharp: he caught 'coneys' or rabbits, i.e. naive fools. The subject was tailor-made for Greene. He could play the moralist, rooting out these 'vultures' that infect the 'flourishing estate of England'; and the intrepid journalist, 'sore threatened' that 'if I set their practises in print, they will cut off that hande that writes the pamphlet'.[18] His material lay near at hand, in the shady resorts he knew too well, in the company of men like 'Cutting' Ball the cutpurse, who ended 'trussed under a tree'. The first of Greene's tracts, *A Notable Discovery of Coosnage*, appeared at the end of 1591, shortly followed by *The Second Part of Conny-catching*. These contained anecdotes and *exposés* of such crooked arts as 'cross-biting' (using prostitutes to lure victims), 'versing' (using counterfeit gold), 'vincent's law' (hustling at bowls), 'curbing' (hooking goods out of windows), and the various wiles of the 'nip' (cutpurse), 'foist' (pick-pocket), 'apple-squire' (pimp), 'prigger' (horse-thief), etc. The pamphlets were an instant success, and both were reprinted in the spring of 1592. Milking the market to the full, Greene hurried out a series of sequels – *The Thirde and Last Part of Conny-catching, A Disputation betweene a Hee Conny-catcher and a Shee Conny-catcher*, and *The Blacke Bookes Messenger*. Somewhere in among them appeared the curious and witty *Defence of Conny-Catching*, ostensibly offering 'a confutation of those two iniurious Pamphlets published by R.G. against the practitioners of many nimble-witted and mysticall Sciences'. It was registered at Stationers' Hall on 21 April 1592 and probably published soon after. Since it mentions just two previous pamphlets it seems to have appeared before the other sequels.[19]

Few commentators have taken this supposed 'confutation' at face value. It savours too much of good publicity for Greene. It advertises his first two 'conny-catching' pamphlets on the title-page and in the text, bandies his name about on every page, and even manages to preview a forthcoming work in the series – 'it is informed us that you are in hand with a booke named *The Repentance of a Conny-catcher*, with a discovery of secret villainies, wherein you meane to discourse at ful the nature of the Stripping Law'.[20] There are sallies against Greene, but all suspiciously harmless:

> I began to enquire what this R.G. should bee. At last I learned that hee was a scholler, and a Maister of Artes, and a Conny-catcher in his kinde, though not at cards, and one that favoured good fellowes, so they were not palpable offendors in such desperate lawes.

This is kid-glove stuff – if anything, it makes Greene sound rather attractive: the *louche*, easy-going 'scholler'. Nor would he much mind his own 'conny-catching' of the players being exposed (even if true) – how he sold *Orlando Furioso* to the Queen's Men for twenty nobles, 'and when they were in the country, sold the same play to the Lord

Admirals men for as much more'. All in all, it is generally suspected that Greene 'had a hand in' the *Defence* (Grosart) or was at least 'privy to the publication' of it (Lee).[21] This implies a co-writer, but no-one has actually asked who. On circumstantial evidence alone, Nashe would be a plausible answer, both as a close crony of Greene's and as a writer apt for such literary *jeux d'esprit*. The *Defence* itself confirms it.

First there is the pseudonym – like many, it is only partially opaque, an in-joke. Those who knew that Nashe was the 'Cuthbert Curryknave' who confuted Martin in the *Almond* could give a shrewd guess at the identity of 'Cuthbert Cunny-catcher'. The jokey tone of the title-page, vaunting 'conny-catchers' as adepts practising 'mysticall Sciences', and Cuthbert himself as 'licentiate in Whittington Colledge' (i.e. Newgate prison, founded by Dick Whittington), is characteristic enough of Nashe. So is the way Cuthbert relentlessly pursues the joke in his introduction, comparing himself to Plato, no less, in his quest 'to search the deapth of those liberall Artes wherein I was a proffessour', and telling how he had grown so famous in his 'facultie' that

> the learned Philosopher Jacke Cuttes, whose deepe insight into this science had drawne him thrise through every gaole in England, meeting of mee at Maidstone, gave mee the bucklers as the subtellest that ever he sawe in that quaint and mysticall forme of Foolosophie. . . . My principles grew authenticall, and I so famous, that had I not beene crost by those two peevish Pamphlets, I might at the nexte Midsommer have worne Doctor Stories cappe for a favor.

Wearing Dr Story's cap means going to the gallows – the execution of the Catholic John Story, on 'a new payre of Gallowes made in triangle maner', is punningly compared to the three-cornered biretta worn by Romish priests. Cuthbert's is the earliest known allusion to 'Doctor Stories cappe'. Shakespeare takes up the association in *Loves Labors Lost* – 'Thou makest the triumpherie, the corner-cap of societie, The shape of Loves Tiburne.'[22] Nashe could certainly have written this introduction, with its comic hyperbole, mock-scholasticism and ingenious puns. It is hardly vintage Nashe, just something cooked up over a pint of wine, but other passages in the pamphlet are similarly distinctive:

> There bee ... about London, certayne quaint, pickt and neate companions, attyred in their apparel eyther *alla mode de Fraunce*, with a side Cloake and a hat of a high blocke and a broad brimme, as if hee could with his head cosmographize the world in a moment; or else *allespanyole*, with a straight bombasta sleeve like a quaile pipe, his short Cloake and his rapier hanging as if he were entering the List to a desperate Combate; . . . his moustachies after the lash

of Lions, standing as stiffe as if he wore a Ruler in his mouth, or else
nickte off with the Italian cut, as if he meant to professe one faith
with the upper lippe and an other with his nether lippe.[23]

This magnifying glass on contemporary fashions, each detail pinned
down with a simile, is typical of Nashe: compare Jack Wilton's dandified
apparel in *The Unfortunate Traveller*, or the absurd garbs foisted on
Gabriel Harvey. Cuthbert's dandy is full of phoney travel stories, boasting of foreign 'novelties' and showing off 'a superficiall insight into
certaine phrases of everie language', when in fact 'his only travaile hath
been to look on a faire day from Dover Clifts to Callis'. He sounds like
a prototype for the 'dapper Iacke' of *Pierce Penilesse*, who 'hath been
but over at Deepe' yet affects to 'talke English through ye teeth, like
Iaques Scabd-hams'. Another of Cuthbert's London types – one of 'a
crew of terryble Hacksters in the habite of Gentlemen', with a 'locke
worne at theyr lefte eare' and a 'Poynado pendent ready for the stab' –
seems to be echoed in the prowling figure in *Pierce*, who looks 'like one
of the cursed crue', with 'his nittie love-lock' and 'his stabing dagger'.[24]
Cuthbert's description of a 'pure Martinist' catches the mocking tone of
Nashe's *Almond*:

> he was a kind of Scholastical panyon, nourst up onely at Grammer
> Schoole, least going to the Universitie, through his nimble witte, too
> much learning should make him mad. So he had past *As in praesenti*,
> and was gone a proficient as farre as *Carmen Heroicum*: for he
> pronounst his wordes like a bragout, and helde up his head like a
> Malt-horse, and could talke against Bishops, and wish very mannerly
> the discipline of the Primitive Church were restored.

As well as these 'types', there are many fleeting touches redolent of
Nashe. The lecherous old man, hoping for 'an amorous wehe or two,
as olde Jades wynnie when they cannot wagge the tayle'. Thomas
Deloney with his 'braines beaten to the yarking up of Ballades'. The
half-concealed name: 'I knew not farre from Fleetbridge a Haberdasher:
it were a good deed to take *Paine* to tel his name.' The comic phrases:
'farewel, good honest prickelouce'; 'this bowical huffe snuffe'; 'the *Poli-
gamoi* or bel-swaggers'. The specificity: not just a dog but 'a little
prickeard Shault'; not just a night at the inn but 'ostrey, faggots and
faire chambring'.[25]

Much of *The Defence of Conny-catching* is probably Greene's. He
was certainly capable, as Grosart says, 'of resorting to such an expedient'
to 'call the more attention to his "conny-catching" pamphlets'. But he
needed someone else to touch it into life, to give it an identity distinct
from his own. That someone was surely Nashe. The overall conception

may well be Nashe's, for the main point of Cuthbert's confutation is that Greene's pamphlets have exposed only the obvious, small-time crooks of Elizabethan London, and left untouched the *real* 'conny-catchers', the big fish masked by respectability and wealth:

> You decypher poore Conny-catchers, that perhaps with a tricke at cardes winne fortie shillings from a churle that can spare it, and never talke of those Caterpillers that undoo the poore, ruine whole Lordships, infect the common-wealth, and delight in nothing but in wrongfull extorting and purloyning of pelfe, whenas such be the greatest Connycatchers of all.[26]

Thus deftly Cuthbert switches the targets. Greene's journalistic *exposé* of the criminal class becomes Nashe's satirical anger at the middle class, 'those fox-furd Gentlemen' that hide their rapacity 'under their gownes faced with foynes'. The first of Cuthbert's salvoes is against usurers and commodity-brokers, whose 'cossenage and Conny-catching' is more 'daily practised' and 'more hurtfull then our poore shifting at Cardes'. Nashe makes the same point, *in propria persona*, in *Christs Teares*: 'never in any Citty', he says, 'was ever suffered such notorious cosonage and villany as is shrouded under thys seaventie-fold usury of commodities: it is a hundred parts more hatefull then Conny-catching'.[27]

The Defence of Conny-catching was a stunt, a literary hoax, a 'Comedie' which Greene and Nashe 'writ together' for the hell of it. One can also see that 'Cuthbert Cunny-catcher' is a useful warm-up for that more complex and authentic *persona*, 'Pierce Penniless', hence the passages in the *Defence* that sound like early, diffuse versions of Pierce's satirical sketches. Cuthbert's defiance – 'they be wealthy, but Cuthbert Cunny-catcher cares for none of them' – is put to the test in Pierce's more risky political sorties. The *Defence* is not the only piece of comic prose to betray Nashe's presence and influence in 1592. There are fragmentary traces of him, we remember, in the comic scenes of *Dr Faustus*. In both cases the bulk of the writing is commonplace but shot through with Nashe's enlivening comic touch. Nashe is not the only common denominator between the *Defence*, *Dr Faustus* and *Pierce Penilesse*. Abel Jeffes, the disreputable printer whose various 'disorders' and imprisonments feature in Stationers' Company records, is another. He printed the *Defence* in April or so, *The Damnable Life of D. Iohn Faustus* in May, and the second edition of *Pierce Penilesse* in early October. It was to him Nashe wrote from 'the Countrey', complaining that the first edition of *Pierce* had appeared prematurely. The letter – 'a private Epistle of the Author to the Printer', prefixed to the second edition – is signed 'Your friend, Tho. Nashe'. Nashe is everywhere, voluble and busy, the buzzing Fly of the *Pierce* fable. He knows all the

back ways, 'lookes into all Estates by conversing with them', is at home
in the opulent apartments of Lord Strange and the shabby printing-
shops of Jeffes and his kind. He is the man at hand when the literary
stars of the day – Marlowe and Greene – need a bit of comic inspiration.

The flare of publicity around Greene's death sheds some light back on
Nashe in the early summer of 1592. It also casts a harsher light forward,
for it is at this point that the baleful figure of Dr Gabriel Harvey steps
into Nashe's life. Harvey was at home in Saffron Walden when a copy
of Greene's *Quip* reached him, probably sometime in August. In it he
found the sketch where the collier and the ropemaker converse, the latter
obviously portraying his father ('I dwel in Saffron Waldon, and am
going to Cambridge to three sons that I keep there at the schoole'). He
found himself mocked as a poetaster – 'the first that invented the English
Hexamiter' – and as a troublemaker who had been 'clapt in the Fleet'.
Richard was called a 'vaine glorious ass', a 'limb of the devill' who stole
'holy kisses' from his female parishioners; John a 'Physitian or a foole'
who has 'spoiled himselfe' with astrologizing.[28] Harvey's reaction to all
this was intensified by the recent death of John, the brother to whom
he was closest, in late July. Gabriel had been with him at King's Lynn
when he died, and wrote poignantly: 'I . . . can never forget that sweete
voice of the dying Cignet', nor 'his meager and ghastly countenance, that
I cannot rehearse without some fit of compassion'.[29] The righteousness of
Gabriel's cause, at least at the outset, must be granted. His father's
honour and his brother's memory were uppermost in his desire to
counter Greene's 'mote-spying Malice'. As always with Harvey, though,
his overbearing sense of self soon muddied any purer motives.

On about 1 September Harvey arrived in London. He bore a letter of
introduction from a Walden worthy, Christopher Bird, recommending
him to Bird's friend, Emmanuel van Meteren (or Demetrius), a
prosperous Dutch merchant and historian living on Lime Street. Harvey
is introduced as 'an excellent generall Scholler'. He is keen to view
Demetrius' collection of 'antiquities and monuments' and to discuss the
'state of forraine countries'. Bird is shocked by the 'intollerable Invectives' he has read by that 'odious leawd fellow' Greene, with their abuse
of Gabriel's father, 'an auncient neighbour of mine' who has held 'the
chiefest office in Walden' (Treasurer of the Corporation).[30] We see the
Harvey world in all this: provincial worthies and cultured, politic busi-
nessmen. Demetrius was kinsman to Daniel Rogers, a poet and diplomat
closely involved with Leicester, Sidney and Spenser: Harvey still clings
to the edges of the old Leicester circle.[31] Harvey was in his early forties
now, vigorous, intellectually insatiable, gnawed at by thwarted ambi-

tions, and about to hazard his fading reputation in the hard and fast world of the London pamphleteers.

Ostensibly, it was legal business that brought him to London. There was the administration of brother John's estate to attend to. His dealings therein do not reflect well on him. Administration was granted him on 11 October, whereupon – according to the statement of John's widow, Martha – he 'expulsed her from possession of all goods and chattels, and made sale presently of a great part thereof'. Nashe picked up on this – 'Gabriel, under pretence of taking out an Administration' has tried to 'circumvent' his sister-in-law of 'al she hath'.[32] No doubt the Doctor of Civil Law was within his legal rights: it is not so much dirty dealing, as Gabriel's overbearing desire to organize everybody, that lies behind the wrangling. Greene too was originally to be dealt with through the courts, according to Harvey, and 'called *Coram*' for his 'diffamation' of the family. It was only when Greene's death deprived Harvey of 'remedy in Law' that he decided, with great show of reluctance, to air his grievances in print. In this course he was probably persuaded by John Wolfe, a successful and sharp-eyed printer-publisher who had cornered the market in fashionable foreign authors (Aretino, Machiavelli) and 'news letters', and was to become Printer to the City of London in 1593.[33] Wolfe was to publish all of Harvey's diatribes against Greene and Nashe. According to Nashe, Harvey actually lodged with Wolfe at his printing-house, 'over against' the South Door of St Paul's, all the while he was 'ink-squittring and printing against me'. Earning his keep as editor and printer's reader, Harvey remained there 'three quarters of a yere' while the plague raged around him and 'there died above 1600 a week'.[34]

From Wolfe's press on about 7 September came Harvey's 'butter-fly Pamphlet' against Greene, which now survives as the second of Harvey's *Foure Letters and Certaine Sonnets*. As we have seen, it reviles Greene's 'dissolute and licentious living', and rehearses Greene's 'woefull and rascall Estate' at his death. All this is wrapped in a pretence of moral purpose – 'O Lord, what a pregnant occasion were here presented, to display leaud vanity in his lively coullours.' Public duty pricks him on:

> every private excesse is daungerous, but such publike enormities incredibly pernitious and insuportable: and who can tell what huge outrages might amount of such quarrellous and tumultuous causes? Honour is precious, worship of value, fame invaluable: they perillously threaten the Commonwealth, that goe about to violate the inviolable partes thereof.[35]

The pamphlet doubtless sold well, and some disapproved enough of Greene to applaud it, but by and large Gabriel's sanctimonious tirade did little for his reputation. Posterity has agreed with Nashe's splutter of contempt:

> Out uppon thee for an arrant dog-killer: strike a man when he is dead? So Hares may pull dead Lions by the beards.[36]

Nashe is scarcely mentioned in this first salvo, except to be called Greene's 'fellow-writer' and the 'principall guest at that fatall banquet of pickle herring'. He is treated with avuncular leniency: 'I spare his name and in some respectes wish him well'. He has been led astray by Greene's bad company, but will prove 'a proper yong man if advised in time'.[37] On 8 September, however, Harvey began another public letter, addressed 'to every Reader, favourablie or indifferently affected', combining further assaults on 'vile Greene' with long passages of self-justification. Halfway through this letter Harvey breaks off: *Pierce Penilesse* has hit the bookstalls —

> Whilest I am bemoaning his [Greene's] over-pitteous decay, & discoursing the usual successe of such ranke wittes, Loe all on the suddaine, his sworne brother, M. Pierce Penni-lesse, (still more paltery, but what remedy? we are already over shoes and must now goe through) Loe his inwardest companion, that tasted of the fatall herringe, cruelly pinched with want, vexed with discredite, tormented with other mens felicitie, and overwhelmed with his own misery; in a raving and franticke moode, most desperately exhibiteth his supplication to the Divell.[38]

The remainder of the letter is aimed at Nashe, an 'od wit', a 'mad hooreson', a 'mightie lashing Gentleman'; and at *Pierce*, a 'pack of vanity', 'as childish & garish stuffe as ever came in print'. Harvey plays the wise academician ticking off the upstart pupil:

> A Poets or Painters licence is a poore security to privilege debt or diffamacion. I woulde wish the burned child not to forget the hot Element, and would advise over-weening youthes to remember themselves, and the good auncient oracle of sage Apollo. There is a certaine thing called Modestie, if they coulde light upon it: and by my young Masters leave, some pritty smacke of discretion would relish well.

He scoffs at Nashe's 'Grammar-schoole witte', and says his style is a patchwork of plagiarism, 'interlaced with divers new-found phrases of the Taverne'. Among Nashe's literary debts Harvey mentions 'Tarltons surmounting Rhetorique', 'Euphuisme and Greenesse', 'the fantastical mould of Aretine or Rabelays' and 'the pittifull historie of Don Lazarello

de Thoemes': this is a shrewd list of influences, though Harvey exagger-
ates Nashe's indebtedness.[39]

What particularly galled Harvey about *Pierce Penilesse* was its vicious
assault on his brother Richard, whom Nashe calls a 'great babound', a
'Pigmie Braggart', a 'shame-swolne toad', etc. Richard had twitted Nashe
in *The Lamb of God* and now Nashe snapped back:

> Poor Slave, I pitie thee that thou hadst no more grace but to come
> in my way. Why, could not you have sate quiet at home and writ
> Catechismes, but you must be comparing me to Martin? . . . I have
> reade over thy Sheepish discourse of the Lambe of God and his
> enemies, and entreated my patience to be good to thee whilst I reade,
> but . . . I could not refraine but bequeath it to the Privie, leafe by
> leafe as I read it, it was so ugly, dorbellicall and lumpish. . . . Thou
> hast skumd over the Schoolemen, and of the froth of theyr folly made
> a dish of divinitie Brewesse which the dogges will not eate. . . . The
> Lambe of God make thee a wiser Bell-weather then thou art, for else
> I doubt thou wilt be driven to leave all and fall to thy fathers occupa-
> tion, which is, to goe and make a rope to hang thy selfe.[40]

Gabriel's response to all this is surprisingly restrained. He says that
Richard rests secure in 'the knowen truth of his approoved learning &
living'. He claims that 'everie page' of Richard's *Astrologicall Discourse*,
'under correction of inspired and supernaturall conceits', shows 'more
Arte and Iudgement then the whole *Supplication*'. 'Pierce' is 'a man
better acquainted with the divels of Hell then with the starres of Heaven',
and his pamphlet is a 'notorious Diabolicall discourse'.[41] Above all,
Harvey contrives to present Nashe as shrill and infantile, his 'shamefull
complaints scarcely beseeming the rascallest siser in an University'; his
'ratling termes' no more than typical of 'this Martinish & counter-
Martinish age'; his 'trifling discourses' pleasing 'none but the printers &
idle creatures, the onely busy readers of such Novellets'. The likes of
Nashe and Greene are mere troublemakers. They 'backbite and deprave
every person that feedeth not their humourous fancy'; they 'dominiere
in Tavernes and Stationers Shops'; they would 'rather goe to Hell in iest
then to Heaven in earnest'.[42]

Towards the end of the letter Harvey strives to rise above the squabble
– 'no man loather then my self to contend with desperate malecontents
or to overthwart obstinate Humoristes'. He hopes that 'fellow-writers
may bee made friendes with a cup of white wine and some little familiar
conference'. He urges Nashe: 'Good sweet Oratour, be a devine Poet
indeede, and use heavenly Eloquence indeede, and employ thy golden
talent with amounting usance indeede.' He protests: 'it was not thy
person that I any-way disliked, but thy rash and desperate proceeding

against thy well-willers'.[43] But by now he has droned on too long and too patronizingly to extricate himself. The gauntlet is down and he cannot retrieve it. Within a few days of completing this letter it was on the bookstalls, the third of *Three Letters and Certaine Sonnets*: the first is Bird's letter to Demetrius; the second the 'butter-fly Pamphlet' against Greene; the sonnets are twenty-two poems under the title 'Greenes Memoriall', plus an old commendatory poem, dated 28 July 1586, of Spenser's to Harvey. Even while this was printing Harvey was at work on a fourth letter, 'extorted after the rest' (Nashe glossed: 'a letter whereof his invention had a hard stoole').[44] It continued in much the same vein, on the one hand perpetuating the strife between himself and 'beggarly Pierce-Pennylesse', and on the other lamenting the degradation of his true stature 'to entangle my selfe with trifling businesse, or any-way to accrew to the most contemptible fellowship of the scribblinge crew'. Nashe and his fellow pamphleteers – 'our new-new writers, the Loadstones of the Presse' – are, says Harvey, a positive danger to civil order and degree, individualism run amok:

> Every Martin Iunior and Puny Pierce a monarch in the kingdome of his owne humour: every pert and crancke wit, in an odde veine or other, the onely man of the University, of the Citty, of the Realme, for a flourish or two: who but he, in the flush of his overweening conceit? Give him his peremptory white rod in his hand, and God-night all distinction of persons and all difference of estates: his Pen is his mace, his launce, his two-edged sword, his scepter, his Hercules club.[45]

This fourth letter was completed on 12 September. Together with a preface, dated 16 September, it was added to the original compilation, which was newly issued as *Foure Letters and Certaine Sonnets* towards the end of the month. The great 'flyting' had begun. Nashe's pen, that 'peremptory white rod', would soon be retaliating.

10

'IN THE COUNTREY'

'I lurke in no corners, but converse in a house of credit'

Strange Newes

As we saw, Nashe had left London sometime before the appearance of *Pierce Penilesse*, and he was still out of town when Harvey's broadsides against him were published. Writing to Abel Jeffes at the end of September, he says that *Pierce* had appeared 'uncorrected and unfinished' because 'the feare of infection detained mee with my Lord in the Countrey', and that at the time of writing the plague still holds him 'prisoner in the Country'.[1] He has heard of Greene's death, and of Harvey's assault on Greene. He says he has written an epistle 'to the Ghost of Robert Greene, telling him what a coyle there is with pamphleting on him after his death'. There is 'other news I am advertised of' – that certain 'obscure imitators' are hawking a spurious 'second part' of *Pierce* around Paul's Churchyard; that the 'antiquaries' are offended by his satirical passage about their 'mustie vocation'; and that Greene's deathbed pamphlet, the *Groatsworth of Wit*, 'is given out to be of my doing'. His angry denial that he was 'any way privie' to the latter is later confirmed by Harry Chettle, who had transcribed it from Greene's papers: 'I protest it was all Greenes, not mine nor Maister Nashes, as some uniustly have affirmed.'[2] There is no indication that Nashe yet knew of Harvey's third and fourth letters, denouncing him as a 'mad hooreson'. He issues a threat – 'write who wil against me, but let him look his life be without scandale' – but this seems chiefly aimed at the troublesome political allusion-hunters, rife in 'this moralising age, wherein every one seeks to shew himselfe a Polititian'. The whole letter breathes a tetchy, frustrated sense of isolation. He is a 'prisoner' in the country, itching to be back in London.

The 'Lord' with whom Nashe was staying in September 1592 was Archbishop Whitgift. The place was the Archbishop's palace at Croydon. There Nashe composed, and no doubt helped to produce, his 'shewe', *Summers Last Will and Testament*.[3] Various topical references in the play point to its composition in September-October. 'The horses lately sworne to be stolne' refers to an incident in late August involving the retinue of Count Mömpelgard at Windsor. The 'naked channell' of the

135

Thames refers to its drying up on 6 September. The 'want of Terme' refers to the postponement of the Michaelmas law term due to plague: this was decided on by the Privy Council on 1 October, the term eventually commencing in November at Hertford.[4] The whole play, revolving round the 'death' of summer, suggests a performance in early October:

> Forsooth, because the plague raignes in most places in this latter end of summer, Summer must come in sicke: he must call his officers to account, yeeld his throne to Autumne, make Winter his Executour.

Nashe's allusions to the Queen's summer progress help to pinpoint the date of performance more precisely. At the beginning Summer says he would already have 'dyde' but that 'Eliza' had bidden him to 'live and linger' until 'her ioyfull progresse was expir'd'. At the end he dies, bequeathing to Eliza 'all my faire dayes remaining . . . To waite upon her till she be returnd'. The Queen returned to Hampton Court on 10 October. Whitgift himself attended Privy Council meetings there on the 11th and 12th.[5] With the plague raging and the Queen off on progress, he had probably spent most of the summer at his Croydon residence: he had attended no Privy Council meetings since 6 August. News of the Queen's imminent return would have signalled the end of the long summer recess, and provided the occasion for Nashe's elegiac entertainment – 'Weepe heavens, mourn earth, here Summer ends'. It seems likely, then, that *Summers Last Will* was first performed, in the Great Hall of Croydon Palace, sometime during the first week of October 1592.

The Archbishop's manor house at Croydon (Figure 8(a)) – it was Whitgift who first called it a 'palace' – was a convenient rural retreat some ten miles from Lambeth Palace. Whitgift spoke of 'the sweetness of the place' in summer-time, though its low-lying grounds, girded with streams and ponds, were not to every taste. Henry VIII complained that it 'standeth low and is rheumatick' and he could never be there 'without sickness'. Whitgift's predecessor, Grindal, called it 'no wholesome place'. Francis Bacon remembered it as an 'obscure and darke place' surrounded by an enormous wood.[6] Nashe himself called it 'this lowe built house', and it is perhaps ironically that Summer bequeaths

> My pleasant open ayre and fragrant smels
> To Croydon and the grounds abutting round.[7]

The Queen periodically visited Whitgift, her 'little black husband', there, though there were complaints that the 'lodgins' were inadequate, there being insufficient 'romes with chymeneys' for her ladies-in-waiting. In some such a chimney-less nook, 'a Closet no bigger than would holde a Church Bible', we may imagine Nashe billeted, his status in the household hovering ambiguously between guest and employee, scholar and showman. His presence may well have been thanks to Richard Bancroft, who became Whitgift's private chaplain in 1592. Nashe had worked under Bancroft's *aegis* in the anti-Marprelate team; Bancroft is known to have been an *aficionado* of the drama, and when he himself became Archbishop he was wont, according to Bishop Hacket, to 'recreate himself with such diversions at Lambeth'.[8] It was perhaps he, rather than the aloof Whitgift, who commissioned Nashe's show. Whitgift was noted for the 'feudal magnificence' of his household. He 'maintained an army of retainers' and travelled 'with a princely retinue' on his episcopal visitations: 'is seven score horse nothing', chided Martin senior, 'to bee in the traine of an English Priest?'[9] Nashe was simply a temporary part of the retinue. We get a glimpse of him as such in an undated letter from the eccentric Puritan scholar, Hugh Broughton, who wrote to Lord Burghley complaining of various 'injuries' he had received from Whitgift, among them: 'how his brother misused me most deadly in his owne hearing; how his Nash gentleman skoffed my Ebrew studies; how Hutton, his preferred, raged and rayled upon my Daniel'.[10] Here we find Nashe in the company of George Whitgift, an officer in his brother's household, and Matthew Hutton, later Archbishop of York. Their scoffing and railing is done to please Whitgift, long exasperated by Broughton's controversial theologizing. Broughton thinks of Nashe as Whitgift's 'gentleman'.

The night of *Summers Last Will* drew near. Nashe was busy with rehearsals, props, costumes, music, dances. He complains of his lack of 'leysure' in the letter to Jeffes. A sense of rush and amateurish chaos is incorporated into the opening of the play, where the clown-chorus, Will Summer, stumbles on with 'his fooles coate but halfe on', grumbling that his costume was 'but now brought me out of the Lawndry', and that with all the 'turmoyle' and 'care of being perfit' (i.e. learning his lines) he has 'not yet supt to night'.[11] The chief part of Will Summer was played by a well-known professional comic called Toy, perhaps a friend of Nashe's, no doubt glad of an engagement now that the London play-houses were shut due to plague. The rest of the cast were probably members of the household — we hear of Ned the Fool, of Harry Baker playing Vertumnus, of actors named Hall and Butcher, of Dick Huntley the prompter: these names would hardly be mentioned if they were not familiar to the audience.[12] The morris dancers are introduced with 'Now for the credit of Wostershire' — they were perhaps a troupe engaged by Whitgift when he was Bishop of Worcester (1577–83). 'A couple of pratty boyes' lead the opening songs, their 'voyces as cleare as Christall' — pages of the household, or possibly choristers. There are 'Musitians' mentioned. The famous lyric, 'Adieu, farewell earths blisse', is sung to the accompaniment of a lute. The venue for the show was undoubtedly the Great Hall, a magnificent building nearly 60 ft long, with a dizzying roof of arched braces and collar beams, and coats of arms hung round the walls (Figure 8(b)). The archbishop's dais stood at the west end of the hall. Here 'my Lord' and some of his 'Honourable Trayne' would probably have sat, with the rest of the audience ranged round on stools and trestles. The stage would have been erected at the eastern end, in front of the screens passage, with the doors to kitchen, pantry and buttery serving as entrances.[13] The dances were performed on the floor of the hall – the Hobby-horse of the morris is warned, 'goe not too fast, for feare of wearing out my Lords tyle-stones with your hob-nayles'. We must imagine torches, candles, the fire flickering in the hearth, the comfortable post-prandial chat of the audience, the general air of festivity ('a hundreth to one' that the players 'will all be drunke e're they go to bedde'). Nashe is somewhere there, for Will Summer calls out to the 'beggarly Poet that writ it' – 'Repayre to my chamber, poore fellow, when the play is done, and thou shalt see what I shall say to thee.'[14]

The whole show is typical Nashe. The nucleus is ancient: harvest home, the seasonal cycle, growth and decay. Around it Nashe weaves his topical and particular tone. The plague of 1592 is a haunting presence, deepening the intimations of autumn. The figure of Will Summer – the 'ghost' of Henry VIII's famous jester – is the *pièce de résistance*, enlivening the conventional masque format with a Rabelaisian commentary. He is supposed merely to deliver the prologue, but to be 'reveng'd' on 'the Idiot our Playmaker' he stays onstage throughout – 'Ile sit as a Chorus, and flowte the Actors and him at the end of every Sceane: I know they will not interrupt me, for feare of marring of all.' He becomes the authorial voice, the master of ceremonies:

> Actors, you Rogues, come away, cleare your throats, blowe your noses, and wype your mouthes ere you enter, that you may take no occasion to spit or to cough when you are *non plus*. And this I barre, over and besides: that none of you stroake your beardes to make action, play with your cod-piece poynts, or stand fumbling on your buttons when you know not how to bestow your fingers.[15]

In his personification of times and seasons – Summer the ailing Lord, Vertumnus the fussy court official, Ver the flighty young gallant, Sol the ambitious courtier, Harvest the miserly churl, Backwinter the railing malcontent, Christmas the stingy Puritanical 'snudge', etc. – Nashe shows his facility for catching characteristic gesture, attitude, psychological ambiance. We are a long way from that special Shakespearean empathy which speaks from inside a character's skin, but not so far from the 'comedy of humours' which Ben Jonson made so popular with the Everyman plays at the end of the decade. *Summers Last Will* is the only whole piece of Nashe's play-writing extant, also the only sustained instance of his blank verse skills: competent enough but clearly not his medium. Backwinter's lines merit a mention as a deliberate echo of Marlowe's 'mighty line':

> Would I could barke the sunne out of the sky,
> Turne Moone and starres to frozen Meteors,
> And make the Ocean a dry land of Yce;
> With tempest of my breath turne up high trees,
> On mountaines heape up second mounts of snowe,
> Which, melted into water, might fall downe,
> As fell the deluge of the former world.

Marlowe makes him think of hell and Faustian demons –

> Ile beate down the partition with my heeles,
> Which, as a mud-vault, severs hell and thee.
> Spirits come up; 'tis I that knock for you . . .

– and a few lines later, 'I see my downefall written in his browes' echoes Marlowe's 'I see my tragedie written in thy browes' in *Edward II*.[16]

Nashe's show is full of little touches that remind us of his perhaps rather precarious position in the clerical circles of Croydon Palace. A remembering of decorum: 'Fye, drunken sot, forget'st thou where thou art?' A hasty qualification amid a dispraise of learning: 'All bookes, divinitie except, Are nought but tales of the divels lawes.' A deferent note in Sol's claim –

> What do I vaunt but your large bountihood,
> And shew how liberall a Lord I serve?

– and in Summer's bequest of

> My shady walkes to great mens servitors,
> Who in their masters shadowes walke secure.[17]

There is, perhaps, some expediency in the creation of Will Summer. The traditions of the jester, the 'all licensed Fool', sanction Nashe's comic language. Some of Will's raunchier remarks may have raised an episcopal eyebrow, but his 'fooles apparell' vindicated him and 'the Idiot our Playmaker'.

It is probable that Nashe remained in the Archbishop's service – 'his Nash gentleman', as Broughton has it – throughout the autumn and early winter of 1592. In *Strange Newes*, written at the end of the year, Nashe answers Harvey's attack on him as 'base' and 'shifting' by saying:

For the order of my life, it is as civil as a civil orenge; I lurke in no corners, but converse in a house of credit, as well governed as any Colledge, where there bee more rare quallified men and selected good Schollers than in any Noblemans house that I knowe in England. If I had committed *such abhominable villanies,* or were *a base shifting companion*, it stoode not with my Lords honour to keepe me.[18]

The 'Lord' who is keeping him is almost certainly Whitgift. This description of Whitgift's scholarly household is amply confirmed by Sir George Paule, 'Comptroller of his Graces Householde', who asserts:

his home, for the lectures and scolastic exercise therein performed, might justly be accounted a little academy, and in some respects superior and more profitable.[19]

Whitgift's main 'home' was Lambeth Palace, but with the plague continuing unabated throughout the last months of 1592 it is probable that he kept Croydon as his headquarters. He was certainly there on 30 October and on 3 November, when he dated letters from there.[20] Nashe's duties would have been of a secretarial nature, possibly in connection with the Archbishop's board of censors, which scrutinized all books submitted to the Stationers' Company for licensing. Being intimately involved in the Elizabethan publishing scene, Nashe would make a useful 'reader'. It may seem ironic in view of his own skirmishes with censorship, but these were hard times – 'from Winter, plague & pestilence, good Lord deliver us', sang the company as they bore Summer out of the hall – and Nashe was no freedom-fighter anyway. His description in *Strange Newes* of Harvey's book as 'foure Lightors of Letters, cleane cast away on the rocks called the Bishop & his Clarks' gains added point from his own position as one of the Archbishop's 'clerks'.[21]

In this rather incongruous clerical setting Nashe set to work on his withering retort to Gabriel Harvey, fully titled *Strange Newes of the intercepting certaine Letters and a Convoy of Verses, as they were going Privilie to victuall the Low Countries* – the conventions of the news pamphlet title-page turned into a lavatory joke ('low countries' = nether regions). It is possible to date the composition of *Strange Newes* quite precisely. For a start, the work was printed piecemeal, with Nashe sending portions to the printer, John Danter, as he wrote. This is shown by the fact that Nashe had seen the title-page while he was still writing the latter part of the text: he complains, on signature I2, that 'it hath pleased M. Printer' to 'intaile a vaine title to my name' (i.e. 'Gentleman').[22] If the title-page was already printed up, so too were the 'Epistle Dedicatorie' to William Beeston, and the address 'to the Gentlemen readers' which fill the remainder of sheet A. This implies that

Nashe had, unusually, written the prefatory matter before the main bulk of the text. And since he refers in his epistle to Beeston to the time 'when this last Terme was remooved to Hartford', he cannot have been writing it before 3 November, which is when the relocated Michaelmas term began. It seems clear that the mounting of *Summers Last Will* at Croydon, and whatever other duties he had in Whitgift's employ, kept him too busy to begin on *Strange Newes* until at least early November. He speaks in his address to the readers of having to 'breake my daye with other important busines I had' before getting down to 'answering the Doctor'. Further dating evidence is provided by Henry Chettle, whose *Kind Harts Dreame* was published in early December. In it Chettle includes an exhortation from the 'ghost of Robert Greene' to 'Pierce Pennilesse', reproaching him for being 'most slacke' in failing to answer Harvey:

> Pierce, more witlesse than pennilesse; more idle than thine adversaries ill imployde; what foolish innocence hath made thee (infantlike) resist-lesse to beare what ever iniurie Envie can impose? . . . The longer thou deferst, the more greefe thou bringst to thy frends, and givest the greater head to thy enemies. What canst thou tell, if (as my selfe) thou shalt bee with death prevented? And then how can it be but thou diest disgrac'd, seeing thou hast made no reply to their twofold Edition of Invectives?[23]

Obviously Nashe's reply to Harvey's 'invectives' had not been published when Chettle wrote this. There is evidence, however, that it was imminent, for Chettle curiously says that Greene's ghost 'had *once* intended thus to have exclaimed' and, again, 'all this had I intended to write'. These sound like last-minute insertions, as if Chettle now knew that his exhortation was unnecessary because Nashe's reply was about to appear. Chettle had briefly been in partnership with Danter in 1591 and he prepared the copy of *Greenes Groatsworth* for Danter in September 1592. It is even possible he set up *Strange Newes*: he signs a letter written to Nashe sometime between 1593–6, 'Your old compositer, Henry Chettle'.[24] At any rate, he was clearly in a position to know the circumstances of *Strange Newes*, and we can accept his evidence, oblique though it is, that Nashe's pamphlet was nearing completion when his own *Kind Harts Dreame* went to press on about 8 December. *Strange Newes* probably appeared sometime later in the month. It was not entered at Stationers' Hall until 12 January 1593, but the entry describes it as 'The Apologie of Pierce Pennylesse'. This was the wording on the title-page of two later issues, apparently published after March 1593: the first issues had probably appeared before being licensed, as sometimes happened, especially with catchpenny printers like John Danter. In conclusion, *Strange Newes* was written over a period of about six weeks in November-December 1592 and, being printed piecemeal, it could be on the bookstalls almost as soon as the writing was finished. The swift appearance of subsequent issues shows its popularity. Since Nashe's reference to the 'house of credit' in which he 'converses' appears in the penultimate sheet (L) of the pamphlet, we can infer that Nashe was still enjoying Whitgift's patronage, probably at Croydon, as late as December.[25]

From the very first page of *Strange Newes* Nashe identifies his position, draws up the battle-lines against Harvey. Dedicating the pamphlet to William Beeston, he praises him as a 'famous persecutor of Priscian', sworn to 'love poetry, hate pedantisme', admirable for his 'wonted Chaucerisme', his 'pure sanguine complexion', his 'pleasant wittie humour', his fondness for 'new Wine' as opposed to 'small Beere'.[26] To borrow this air of boozy good-fellowship, of poetry as an ingredient in *joie de vivre*, is all Nashe asks of his 'pottle-pot Patron' – 'I coniure thee to draw out thy purse, and give me nothing for the dedication of my Pamphlet: thou art a good fellow I know, and had rather spend ieasts than monie'. In similar vein Nashe invokes the balladeers of the day. Noting that Harvey had called the dead 'balletmaker' William Elderton a 'drunken rimester', he cries:

> Hough Thomas Delone, Phillip Stubs, Robert Armin, &c. Your father Elderton is abus'd. Revenge, revenge on course paper and want of matter, that hath most sacriligiously contaminated the divine spirit & quintessence of a penny a quart. Helter skelter, feare no colours, course him, trounce him, one cup of perfect bonaventure licour will inspire you with more wit and Schollership than hee hath thrust into his whole packet of Letters.

He also suggests that Will Kemp should perform some 'merriment' on the theme of the 'clownish' Harveys.[27] It is part of Nashe's anti-Harvey tactic to go resolutely downmarket, to counter the worthy-wealthy base of the *Foure Letters* – Bird, Demetrius, Spenser – with this motley army of tipplers, clowns and rimesters. Nashe hits below the belt, a guttersnipe antagonist who cares nothing for the rules of the polemical game. Where Harvey had remonstrated and patronized, Nashe ridicules and abuses:

> Why, thou arrant butter whore, thou cotqueane & scrattop of scoldes, wilt thou never leave afflicting a dead Carcasse? . . .

> This bile on the browe of the Universitie, this bladder of pride new-blowne . . . this indigested Chaos of Doctourship and greedie pothunter after applause . . .

Take truths part, and I wil prove truth to be no truth, marching out
of thy dung-voiding mouth . . .

Gaffer Iobbernoule, once more well over-taken, how dost thou? how
dost thou? hold up thy heade, men, take no care; though Greene be
dead, yet I may live to do thee good . . .[28]

'Gaffer Iobbernoule' — a version of 'Hobbinol', Spenser's pastoral name
for Harvey — is only one of the fantastic nicknames Nashe cooks up:
Gamaliel Hobgoblin, Gilgilis Hobberdehoy, Gregory Habberdine,
Gabriel Hangtelow, Timothy Tiptoes, Braggadochio Glorioso, Infractis-
sime Pistlepragmos, Gibralter, Galpogas, Gabrielissime, etc. Arrayed
in these carnival masks, Harvey is paraded through the pamphlet, his
embarrassments and disappointments revived, his buffooneries embroid-
ered, his literary pretensions dissected.

There were many who felt that, however amusing, Nashe's harangue
showed him in a poor light. As he says, 'I know there want not welwillers
to my disgrace, who say my onely Muse is contention'.[29] They had a
point: the reader of Nashe is often prey to disappointment, so much
talent squandered on essentially negative utterance. Anyone who wished
to defend Strange Newes could make, perhaps, three salient points
(leaving aside a fourth, no less valid: that the pamphlet is often very
funny). The first and most obvious is the pamphlet's partial motive to
defend the memory of the dead Greene:

In short tearmes, thus I demur upon thy long Kentish-tayld declaration
against Greene.

He inherited more vertues than vices . . .

Why should art answer for the infirmities of maners? Hee had his
faultes, and thou thy follyes.

Debt and deadly sinne, who is not subiect to? With any notorious
crime I never knew him tainted (& yet tainting is no infamous surgerie
for him that hath beene in so many hote skirmishes).

A good fellowe hee was, and would have drunke with thee for more
angels then the Lord thou libeldst on [the Earl of Oxford] gave thee
in Christs Colledge . . .

Hee made no account of winning credite by his workes, as thou dost,
that dost no good workes, but thinkes to be famosed by a strong
faith of thy owne worthines.[30]

This is the opposite of shrill. It has a clarity and balance perhaps unusual in Nashe. He resists any temptation to glorify his friend: Greene, he says, was a man, no better and no worse than men should be, and it is no business of others to go around moralizing on his faults. We get Nashe's underlying strengths in this: beneath the rather manic hurly-burly of his usual *persona*, over-reacting and often over-writing, we hear someone tolerant, morally relaxed, emancipated from the claustrophobic conventions. 'Debt and deadly sinne, who is not subiect to?' – it is the tone of Hamlet to Polonius, 'use every man after his desert, & who shall scape whipping?'[31] There is a lot of Polonius in Harvey – sententious, interfering, righteous – and, perhaps, not a little of Hamlet in Nashe.

The second point to make about *Strange Newes* is its championing of the satirist's freedoms and rights. Harvey said that 'Invectives by favour have bene too bolde, and Satyres by usurpation too-presumptuous', and that they threatened 'all good Learning and civill Governement'. Nashe takes this up: 'as touching the libertie of Orators and Poets, I will conferre with thee somewhat gravelie', and indeed he does, in good scholarly vein. Cicero, he says, is best remembered for his *Philippics*, 'sound Physick applide to a body that could not digest it': but for these he would 'have beene sentenced by a generall verdit of histories for a timerous time-pleaser'. Aristophanes is praised as one who mingled 'delight with reprehension'. The satires of Horace, Perseus and Juvenal are 'excellently medicinable', though perhaps too 'harsh in the swallowing': their 'Phrigian melodie, that stirreth men up to battaile and furie' should have been tempered with 'the Dorian tune, that favoreth mirth and pleasure'. The poet must be resolute: 'fawning and crouching are the naturall gestures of feare'; he must boldly 'infamize vice and magnifie vertue', and counter 'the generall abuses of the time'. In classical Rome, 'it was lawful for Poets to reprove that enormitie in the highest chairs of authoritie, which none else durst touch'. The writer that shirks this task 'haply may tickle the eare, but never edifies'.[32] Nashe's muck-raking invective is not, perhaps, the best instance of the writer as moral critic, but one might say that its very indecorousness is in part a challenge to the whole notion of permitted literary limits. As he says to Harvey, 'if I scolde, if I raile, I do but *cum ratione insanire*' – rant with a reason.

The third and final point is stylistic. The satirists whose 'too-presumptuous' liberty Harvey deplores have, says Nashe, 'broght in a new kind of a quicke fight, which your decrepite slow-moving capacitie cannot fadge with'. This idea of nimbleness and linguistic agility is absolutely central to Nashe: it is his stylistic *credo*. Harvey is character-ized as ponderous, ill-equipped, 'flourishing about my eares with his two-hand sworde of Oratory and Poetry', yet managing only to shake 'some of the rust of it on my shoulders'. He is 'an unweldy Elephant', an 'olde mechanicall meeter-munger'. He writes 'pan-pudding prose' and verses that 'run hobling like a Brewers Cart upon the stones'.

> I wote not how it fals out, but his invention is overweapond; he hath some good words, but he cannot writhe them and tosse them to and fro nimbly, or so bring them about that hee maye make one streight thrust at his enemies face. Coldly and dully *idem per idem*, who cannot indite? But with life and spirite to limne deadnes it selfe, *Hoc est Oratoris proprium*.

'Over-weaponed' is a marvellous description of Harvey's syntax, with its unwieldy symmetries and over-extended metaphors. There is, as Nashe says, something almost contagious about its mental atmosphere:

> A bots on thee for mee for a lumpish, leaden heeld letter-dawber, my stile, with treading in thy clammie steps, is growne as heavie gated as if it were bound to an Aldermans pace. . . . Ere I was chained to thee thus by the necke, I was as light as the Poet Accius, who was so lowe and so slender that hee was faine to put lead into his shooes for feare the winde should blowe him into another Countrie.[33]

It is not only that Nashe has the light touch so woefully absent in Harvey. With the lightness comes versatility. Nashe's prose is a more pliable, more sensitive instrument: it registers shifts and nuances while Harvey's only bangs out a self-righteous tympany. In *Strange Newes* Nashe scarcely uses this instrument to the full: perhaps he never did. But he knew its potential power, and the more so by contrasting it with Harvey's 'pan-pudding' syntax. The dog-fight with Harvey, as with Martin, gave Nashe a sense of his own literary and psychological outline, indeed much of his satirical aggression has this self-defining urge behind it. This may sound like insecurity, but it gives his prose a psychological dimension, a 'new kind' of authenticity, which Harvey the *rhetor* was powerless to answer:

> Thy soule hath no effects of a soule, thou canst not sprinkle it into a sentence, & make everie line leape like a cup of neat wine new powred out, as an Orator must doe that lies aright in wait for mens affections.[34]

Like many of Nashe's pamphlets, *Strange Newes* offers sudden mirrored glimpses of himself at work on it — 'trip and goe, turn over a new leafe' . . . 'quods, quods, give me my Text pen againe, for I have a little more

Text to launce' . . . 'bee it spoken heere in private'. He is in some
cramped little study at Croydon, 'here on our prating bench in a close
roome', with 'none in company but you, my approoved good frendes,
Four Letters and Certain Sonnets'. It is winter: 'the weather is cold and
I am wearie with confuting'. He falls sick: 'even in the packing up of
my booke, a hot ague hath me by the back' – a burning fever, perhaps
influenza, no doubt to be blamed on the '*malaria*', or bad air, of marshy
Croydon. But he remains resolute: 'maugre sickness worst, a leane arm
put out of the bed shall grind and pash every crum of thy booke into
pin dust'. A few pages on, still ill, '*feci, feci, feci*, had I my health, now
I had leysure to be merry, for I have almost washt my hands of the
Doctour'.[35] It is all expressive of Nashe's nervous, jabbing, adrenal
energy: burning hot, pinched with cold, working on the brink of exhaustion and disquiet. These burning fevers, he says in *The Terrors of the
Night*, bring delirious dreams 'of frayes, lightning and thunder, of skirmishing with the divell, and a hundred such like'.[36] On this note of distem-
perature and skirmish we enter the stormier waters of 1593.

If Nashe returned at all to London in the winter of 1592–3 he has
left no traces of his visit. The next we hear of him is in February 1593:
he is still in the country, but no longer at Croydon. 'It was my chance
in Februarie last', he writes in *The Terrors of the Night*, 'to be in the
Countrey some threescore myle off from London.' He describes the
surroundings as 'low marish ground', with 'almost as rotten a Clymate
as the Lowe Countreyes, where their mystie ayre is as thicke as mould
butter, and the deaw lyes like froathie barme on the ground'. It is a
'quarter not altogether exempted from witches'. It has been convincingly
shown that the area Nashe is describing is Conington in Huntingdonshire; that he was the guest at Conington manor of the illustrious scholar,
Robert Cotton; and that while there he composed the first draft of *The
Terrors of the Night*.[37] Conington fits in every respect. It is about seventy
miles from London. It is in fen country, standing by the marshlands of
Whittlesey Mere, the largest lake in southern England. Camden describes
the area in his *Britannia* of 1594:

> These Quarters, considering the ground lying so low, and for many
> moneths in the yeare surrounded and drowned, in some places also
> floting (as it were) and hoven up with the waters, are not free from
> the offensive noisomnesse of Meres and the unwholesome aire of the
> Fennes.[38]

This accords precisely with Nashe's topography of 'low marish ground'
and a 'rotten' misty climate. Nashe's reference to witchcraft in the area
also figures, for eight miles from Conington was the village of Warboys,
home of the 'Three Witches of Warboys' – John, Alice and Agnes

-ILLUSTRATIONS-

But fee, what art thou heere ? *lupus* in *fabula*, a lop in a chaine ? Nowe firra haue at you, th'art in my fwinge. But foft, fetterd ? thou art out againe : I cannot come neere thee, thou haft a charme about thy legges, *no man meddle with the Queenes* prifoner, now therefore let vs talke freendlye , and as *Alexander* fayd to hys Father *Phillip* , who beeing forely wounded in the thigh in fight, and hardly efcaping death, but could

E 2   not

1 Portrait of Thomas Nashe, 1597

2 St Margaret's, Lowestoft

3 All Saints', West Harling

4 Christopher Marlowe, supposed portrait, 1585

Lord of *Oxford*, but in the single-soald pumpes of his aduersitie, with his gowne cast off, vntrussing, and readie to beray himselfe, vpon the newes of the going in hand of my booke.

The picture of Gabriell Haruey, as hee is readie to let fly vpon Aiax.

If you aske why I haue put him in round hose, that vsually weares Venetians? It is because I would make him looke more dapper & plump and round vpon it, wheras otherwise he looks like a case of tooth pikes, or a Lute pin put in a sute of apparell. Gaze vppon him who list, for I tell you I am not a little proud of my workmanship, and though I say it, I haue handled it so neatly and so sprightly and withall ouzled, gidumbled, muddled, and drizled it so finely, that I forbid euer a *Hauns Boll, Hauns Holbine,* or *Hauns Mullier* of them all (let them but play true with the face) to amend it or come within fortie foote of it. Away away, *Blockland, Trusser, Francis de Murre* and the whole generation of them will sooner catch the murre and the pose tenscore times ere they doo a thing one quarter so masterly. Yea (without *Kerry merry buffe* be it spoken) put a whole million of *Iohannes Mabusiusses* of them together, and they shall not handle

5 Gabriel Harvey, woodcut portrait, 1596

6 The ghost of Robert Greene, woodcut, 1598

7 Lord Strange, *c.* 1593

8 (a) Croydon Palace

8 (b) The Great Hall, Croydon

9 Sir Robert Cotton at age 54

10 Sir George Carey by Hilliard, 1601

Samuel. They were very much in the news at this time. 'Mother Samuel' was interrogated before the Bishop of Lincoln in December 1592, under suspicion of causing a series of local deaths through witchcraft, notably that of Lady Cromwell the previous July. All three Samuels were tried at Huntingdon Assizes in April 1593, found guilty and executed.[39]

Central to the *Terrors of the Night* is a 'strange tale' Nashe heard while at Conington. In an 'unluckie house' in these parts, a 'Gentleman of good worship and credite' had recently died in curious circumstances. Suddenly falling sick, he had a series of 'miraculous waking visions' in which he wrestled with devils and naked temptresses. He was briefly revived by a 'precious extract quintessence' sent by a 'Knight of great honour thereabouts', but within a few hours lapsed into 'trifling dotage' and 'raving dyde within two daies following'. Nashe's source for the story was a certain 'great Man of this Land', to whom the dying man had confidentially 'avouched' his experiences. Nor, Nashe protests, 'have I one iot abusde my informations', except to 'welt and garde' (i.e. embroider) a little what would otherwise be a 'course home-spunne tale'. The story was, furthermore, the starting-point for the *Terrors*: 'upon the accidental occasion of this dreame or apparition ... was this Pamphlet (no bigger than an old Praeface) speedily botcht up and compyled'.[40] It seems likely that this tale of delirium and death is connected with local rumours surrounding the Warboys witches. Sir Henry Cromwell of nearby Hinchingbrooke Priory, whose wife allegedly died by enchantment, may well be the 'Knight of great honour' who sent medication to the dying man. The 'great man' whose 'informations' Nashe is retailing is probably Robert Cotton himself. The identity of the actual victim, whose death sparked off the *Terrors*, is less clear. It has been argued that it was Cotton's own father, Thomas, who had died at Conington on 30 May 1592, but this must remain a moot point. Admittedly Nashe only says that he *heard* the story in February 1593, but he certainly implies that the events themselves were more recent than eight months previously. Also, an essential part of the story is the suddenness of the gentleman's death: the whole thing took just four days (the visions occurred on 'the second day of his lying downe' and he was dead two days later) and it is this abruptness which was so 'suspitious' and bred such 'admiration and wonder' round about. There is no evidence that this was the case with Cotton senior, who was already ill enough 'about the beginning of May' to summon his brother John and make an alteration to his will.[41] Nevertheless, it is still possible that rumours had accrued around Thomas Cotton's death at the height of the Warboys enchantments, and that in *The Terrors of the Night* Nashe gave the supposed 'full story' straight from the horse's mouth. It is Robert Cotton's version of events he is reporting, and whether true or false, whether concerning his father's death or merely some close neighbour's, Cotton's 'informations' are decidedly newsworthy.

It may well be that Nashe's original report on the affair is lost. The official account of the Warboys enchantments – *The Most Strange and Admirable Discoverie of the Three Witches of Warboys* – was registered at Stationers' Hall on 30 June 1593, the very same day that John Danter entered his copy of *The Terrors*. The Warboys pamphlet appears on the Register with this authentication: 'recommended for matter of truthe by master Judge Ffenner under his handwrytinge shewed in a Court or assemblie holden this Daye'. In the preface to the pamphlet, the author thanks Fenner for his 'crossing' of other works which recounted the matter 'partly or confusedly'. It is possible that Nashe's *Terrors* was one of these suppressed pamphlets. It did not actually appear until late 1594, and then Danter took the very unusual precaution of registering it for a second time (on 25 October). Nashe himself says, in the preface, that the work had 'line suppressed by mee' for 'a long time' after it was written.[42] There may have been much more material about the Warboys affair than appears in the printed text – Nashe certainly added some passages during 1594; he may well have deleted some as well.

Whatever the precise circumstances, we find Nashe at gloomy, fog-bound Conington in the early months of 1593, in an atmosphere seemingly saturated with witchcraft, hallucination and death. It is an apt setting for *The Terrors of the Night*. The house seems to have been similarly unsettling ten years later, when Ben Jonson was a guest there (a refugee, like Nashe, from the plague). Jonson told how he was 'in the Country at Sr Robert Cottons house with old Cambden' – William Camden, under whom both Jonson and Cotton studied at Westminster school – when

> he saw in a vision his eldest sone (then a child and at London) appear unto him with ye Marke of a bloodie crosse on his forehead as if it had been cutted with a suord, at which amazed he prayed unto God, and in ye morning he came to Mr Cambdens chamber to tell him, who persuaded him it was but ane appreehension of his fantasie at whiche he should not be disjected. In ye mean tyme comes there letters from his wife of ye death of that Boy in ye plague.[43]

This is a potent coincidence. Two famous literary guests at Conington: one writes a brooding 'Discourse of Apparitions' (as the *Terrors* is subtitled); the other has just such an apparition.

Though only just turned twenty-two, over three years Nashe's junior, Cotton was well worthy Nashe's description of him as a 'great Man', both as a scholar of huge repute and as lord of the considerable estates he inherited from his father.[44] He was already a founding member of the Society of Antiquaries, and had begun to amass that 'inestimable library' of manuscripts that became the Cottonian collection. He was the intimate friend of scholars like Camden, Janus Gruter and Dr John Case. Nashe may have first met him at Cambridge: they were almost exact contemporaries, Cotton matriculating at Jesus College in November 1581. From 1588 to 1591, Cotton was enrolled at the Inns of Court, a *milieu* in which Nashe moved socially in London. Nashe's allusion to 'Iohn Davies Soule' in *Strange Newes* shows he knew Sir John Davies' poem *Nosce Teipsum* in MS: it was not published till 1599. This again brings him near to Cotton, who was Davies' close friend and chamber-fellow at the Middle Temple.[45] It is also noticeable that of all the butts in *Pierce Penilesse*, the only ones to receive an apology from Nashe were the antiquaries:

> The Antiquaries are offended without cause, thinking I goe about to detract from that excellent profession, when (God is my witnesse) I reverence it as much as any of them all, and had no manner of allusion to them that stumble at it. I hope they will give me leave to think there be Fooles of that Art as well as of al other.

Perhaps Cotton, their leading light, was one who 'stumbled at' – objected to – Nashe's sortie. Cotton was certainly not one of the dusty old types Nashe was aiming at, those whose 'rusty witte' dotes on 'worme-eaten Elde', nor of the phoney antique-dealers who 'blow their nose in a boxe & say it is the spettle that Diogenes spet in ones face'.[46] He was, to coin a phrase, a scholar and a gentleman: the term 'antiquary' encompasses the historian, archaeologist, palaeographer, genealogist and bibliophile. As well as Nashe, Jonson and Davies, his literary friends included Donne, Lyly, Hugh Holland and Tom Coryat the travel-writer. The latter, writing to Cotton from India, calls him 'the High Seneschal of the right worshipfull Fraternitie of Sirenical Gentlemen, that meet the first Fridaie of every moneth at the sign of the Mere-maide in Bread-street'.[47] No doubt Cotton counted Shakespeare, another member of the Mermaid 'club', among his familiar acquaintances. All this was later than when Nashe knew him, but serves to show that Cotton was as fond of wine and wit as of the 'dark industry' of antiquities. He was 'sweet Robin', of a jovial 'ruddy complexion', as well as *'dignissimus doctissimus Cottonus'*.[48] His portrait, engraved at age fifty-four, shows an affable, strong, full-blooded face (Figure 9). One thin, graceful hand, unadorned but for a wedding-ring, touches on an old text; the other rests lightly on his chest in a gesture both self-affirming and welcoming.

All was not so well with him in early 1593, however. This we learn from letters written him by his friend and physician, John Case. The previous October, Case had warned him that his constitution tended dangerously towards melancholy, and that he should beware of allowing this 'Hydra' to settle in him. Case prescribed various potions to evacuate the liver and spleen, and Cotton visited him at Oxford for treatment. In late December it appears he was still in poor spirits. His father's death, litigation over the will, bookish studies and Conington's 'rotten' climate all contributed. Among the antidotes to melancholy recommended by Dr Case were good company, 'respectable' recreations and a rest from scholarly labours.[49] Nashe's visit was probably intended as therapeutic: he was there as a professional wit, to jolly the brooding scholar out of his dumps. The *Terrors* itself was doubtless written for Cotton's benefit – to 'satisfie some of my solitary friends heere in the Countrey', Nashe begins it, 'I have hastily undertooke to write of the wearie fancies of the Night.' Hence Nashe's constant recurrence to the dangers of melancholy:

> The grossest part of our blood is the melancholy humor, which in the spleene congealed, whose office is to disperse it, with his thick steaming fennie vapours casteth a mist over the spirit, and cleane bemasketh the phantasie.

The melancholic is 'foggie-braind', his mind benighted in a 'mist' of vapours. As always, Nashe soaks up his surroundings. The *Terrors* breathes winter in the fens as richly as *Pierce* smells of summer in the city. Various kinds of melancholy, moreover, are named as the prime cause of apparitions and hallucinations:

> This slimie melancholy humor still still thickning as it stands still, engendreth many misshapen obiects in our imaginations . . .

> From the fuming melancholly of our spleene mounteth that hot matter into the higher Region of the braine, whereof manie fearfull visions are framed . . .

> Melancholy . . . corrupteth all the blood and is the causer of lunacie . . .

> When all is said, melancholy is the mother of dreames, and of all terrours of the night whatsoever.[50]

Nashe does not deny the possibility of 'true apparitions or prodigies' but warns 'how easily we may be flouted, if we take not great heed, with our own anticke suppositions'. Nor does he deny the power of witchcraft, though he does try to minimize it. 'The exploytes and strategems of witches', he says, may well astonish a little at first sight, but if a man have the least heart or spirite to with-stand one fierce blast of their bravadoes, he shall see them shrink faster than Northren cloath, and outstrip time in dastardly flight.[51]

As for Cotton's tale of the dying man's visions – itself perhaps a symptom of his unsettled mind – Nashe deliberately suspends judgment. It is a 'strange tale', but 'whether of true melancholy or true apparition, I will not take upon me to determine'.

In treating the causes of dreams as physiological and psychological, Nashe pursues a rationalist, rather than occultist, line. Dreams can result from bad diet, illness, discontent, noises in the night. They are mechanical by-products of everyday conscious life – the 'bubling scum or froath of the fancie, which the day left undigested', the 'Eccho of our conceipts in the day'. They are not supernatural or portentous, merely confused little private dramas:

> On those images of memorie whereon we buyld in the daye, comes some superfluous humour of ours, lyke a Iack-anapes in the night, and erects a puppet stage.[52]

But as he rambles on in this vein we lose sight of the melancholy Cotton, and find ourselves in a hyper-active mental world that is first and foremost Nashe's:

> As the firmament is still mooving and working, so uncessant is the wheeling and rolling on of our braines; which everie hower are tempring some newe peece of prodigie or other, and turmoyling, mixing and changing the course of our thoughts.[53]

Nashe's reflecting on dream-states and their mental causes becomes a fragmentary, almost unwitting session on the psychiatrist's couch:

> Our cogitations runne on heapes like men to part a fray ... the confused giddie action of our braines ... our thoughts intensively fixt all the daye time upon a marke wee are to hit, are now and then over-drawne with such force that they flye beyond the marke ... our thoughts troubled & vexed when they are retyred from labor to ease, from skirmishing to surgerie ... wee are agasted and terrified with the disordered skirmishing and conflicting of our sensitive faculties ...

So insistent is this theme of psychic agitation that one begins to wonder about Nashe's own state of mind. It is as if, in seeking to dispel Robert Cotton's neuroses, he had instead raked up his own. Above all it is when he writes about, and probably during, the night that we hear a new note of morbid anxiety:

> When Night in her rustie dungeon hath imprisoned our ey-sight, and that we are shut seperatly in our chambers from resort, the divell keepeth his audit in our sin-guilty consciences . . .

> The table of our hart is turned to an index of iniquities, and all our thoughts are nothing but texts to condemne us . . .

> The only peace of minde that the divell has is despaire, wherefore we that live in his nightly kingdome of darknes must needs taste some disquiet . . .

> This cursed raven, the night, pecks out mens eies in the valley of death. It hindreth them from looking to heaven for succor, where their Redeemer dwelleth.[54]

Nashe is striving for literary effect – an Elizabethan Poe – but the mood is deeper than that. This is the first time he has openly expressed any sort of spiritual struggle or *angst*. He had dabbled in diabolism in *Pierce Penilesse*, and he had issued pious denunciations of sectarians and atheists, but there is nothing like this before. It is the first hint of the religious crisis of the summer to come, as recorded in *Christs Teares*. Once on the theme of sin and bedevilment, Nashe flits from image to image, fear to fear. The devil is like a 'cunning fowler' spreading 'his nets of temptation in the darke'. To the sick and crazy he 'boldly revealeth the whole astonishing treasurie of his wonders'. At night you can hear him 'busie in churchyards': 'the boanes of the dead the divell counts his chief treasurie, and therfore is he continually raking amongst them'. Then suddenly the picture fragments and multiplies:

> What do we talke of one divel? There is not a roome in anie mans house but is pestred and close packed with a campe royall of divels. . . . No place (bee it no bigger than a pockhole in a mans face) but is close thronged with them. Infinite millions of them wil hang swarming about a worm-eaten nose. Don Lucifer himselfe, their grand Capitano, asketh no better throne than a bleare eye to set up his state in. Upon a haire they will sit like a nit, and over-dredge a bald pate like a white scurffe. . . . In Westminster Hall a man can scarce breath for them, for in every corner they hover as thick as moates in the sunne. The Druides that dwelt in the Isle of Man, which are famous for great coniurers, are reported to have beene lousie with familiars.

Had they but put their finger and their thumbe into their neck, they could have pluckt out a whole neast of them.[55]

He tries to make this playfully hyperbolic, to recapture the jaunty tone of *Pierce Penilesse* ('Don Lucifer', etc.). But just behind the joking one senses an obsession. He dwells as if enforced on this close-up view of teeming vermin and diseased flesh. The signs of syphilis – pockmarks, raddled nose, scurfy baldness – link the vision back to the tremors of 'sin-guilty conscience'. Nashe the urban journalist, the fascinated siever of 'muckhils and shop-dust', is now on a different trail. He is finding a 'low-life' inside himself, like the 'wearie traveller' a few pages earlier, who lays down 'unawares on a loathsome neast of snakes'. Here, perhaps, is a genuine nightmare of Nashe's: an insect dream; a malevolent swarming and smothering ('a man can scarce breath'); a nexus of disease, sex and sin.

All in all, Nashe's spell 'in the Countrey' seems to have been a decidedly unsettling period. Deprived of the bustle and business of literary London, he turned in on himself, his voluble fidgety temper bottled up, his inquisitive mind aggravated into neurotic self-doubt. At damp, 'lowe built' Croydon he clowned for the clerics. In the throes of a fever he confuted the Doctor. At Conington he was enveloped in fog, melancholy and hauntings. In both houses he must have been drawn to think of his childhood – the churchy ambiance of Croydon, the low marshy landscape round Conington – and some remembrance of early shadows and fears seems to surface in *The Terrors of the Night*. The dominant mood of the pamphlet is nocturnal, oppressive, jumpy:

Fie, fie, was ever poore fellow so farre benighted in an old wives tale of divells and urchins. Out upon it, I am wearie of it, for it hath caused such a thicke fulsome Serena to descend on my braine, that now my penne makes blots as broad as a furd stomacher, and my muse inspyres me to put out my candle and goe to bed.[56]

One hopes, but doubts, he slept well.

11
JACK WILTON

'Do you play the flouting Jack, to tell us Cupid is a good hare-finder?'

WILLIAM SHAKESPEARE *Much Ado about Nothing*

'*Post tenebras dies*' is the motto on the title-page of the *Terrors* – 'after darkness, the day' – and in the spring of 1593 we find Nashe at work on the sunniest of all his writings, his romance of *The Unfortunate Traveller*. In the dedication to the Earl of Southampton, he gives this modest account of the work and its motives:

> All that in this phantasticall Treatise I can promise, is some reasonable conveyance of historie & varietie of mirth. By divers of my good frends have I been dealt with to employ my dul pen in this kinde, it being a cleane different vaine from other my former courses of writing. How wel or ill I have done in it I am ignorant: the eye that sees round about it selfe, sees not into it selfe.[1]

There is a sense of renewal and relief in this: the new vein of writing, the encouragement of friends. The eye that had looked too much into itself of late is once more roving, prying, observant and bright. One suspects he is back in London; he is certainly back on form. It was to be a brief respite before the storms of the summer.

What kind of book had his friends urged? Perhaps, as McKerrow suggests, 'a romance of the type of Greene's', the end-product being altogether different as a result of 'Nashe's peculiar genius'.[2] Nashe variously describes it as a 'chronicle' and a 'historie'. It has elements of the jest-book in it, and of the 'picaresque' tale as typified by *Lazarillo de Tormes*, translated from the Spanish in 1586, though whether Nashe's hero Jack Wilton is a fully-fledged *pícaro*, or rogue, is questioned by more fastidious critics. It is also, as Agnes Latham shows, a showcase for burlesques of current 'literary themes and modes'.[3] Whether one calls it a romance or a chronicle or (as many do) a prototypical novel, *The Unfortunate Traveller* is essentially a rattling good yarn. This is partly what Nashe means when he promises 'some reasonable conveyance of historie', though this is also a claim, entirely unreliable, of historical authenticity. He throws in something for everyone – action, humour,

154

love, war, rape, executions, romantic Italian settings, and a gorgeous dark-eyed girl called Diamante. In the character of Jack Wilton, the hero and narrator, Nashe creates his most charming *persona*. After the malcontent poet Pierce Penniless and the ribald jester Will Summer comes the waggish page-boy Jack Wilton, a 'rascall', an 'ingenious' young man 'of the age of eighteene, of stature tall, straight limd', with a 'beardles face that had in it no ill signe of physiognomie'. He is a prankster and a cheat, a dab-hand with a 'paire of false dice':

> I had the right vayne of sucking up a die twixt the dints of my fingers; not a crevise in my hand but could swallow a quater trey for a neede; in the line of life manie a dead lift did there lurke.

He is an inveterate flirt, a 'proper apple-squire', a 'fantasticall amorous yonkster': he out-woos his noble master for the hand of Diamante. He is, when employment and the dice permit, the flashiest of dressers:

> I had my feather in my cap as big as a flag in the fore-top; my French dublet gelte in the bellie as though (like a pig readie to be spitted) all my guts had bin pluckt out; a paire of side paned hose that hung downe like two scales filled with Holland cheeses; my longe stock that sate close to my docke, and smoothered not a scab or a leacherous hairie sinew on the calfe of the legge; my rapier pendant like a round sticke fastned in the tacklings for skippers the better to climbe by; my cape cloake of blacke cloth, overspreading my backe like a thorne-backe, or an Elephantes eare, that hanges on his shoulders like a countrie huswives banskin which she thirles hir spindle on; & in consummation of my curiositie, my hands without glooves, all a more French, and a blacke budge edging of a beard on the upper lip, & the like sable auglet of excrements in the rising of the anckle of my chin.[4]

This is classic Nashe – a superabundance of reactions, a foliage of metaphor sprouting up from the retinal image – yet the effect is also controlled, and one senses a cooler mannerist irony in the use of meta-phoric vehicles – stuck pigs and cheeses, sailors and countrywomen, elephants and fishes, and the old joke on excrement (literally 'out-growth') – which suffuse the subject, a Hilliardesque young dandy, with contradictory atmospheres.[5]

There is in Jack Wilton more than a touch of wish-fulfilment. He is a younger, prettier, more carefree, even a taller version of Nashe. Also one sees that Nashe, in his opportunist way, is using his own experience over the past year or so, that Jack as page-boy is partly a sardonic reflection of his own status in the entourages of Lord Strange and

Archbishop Whitgift (not so much Cotton, where he was more an equal).
Jack is 'no common squire, no undertrodden torch-bearer', he is even a
'gentleman' of sorts, but he is an underling, a hanger-on; as he puts it
with mock-precision, 'a certain kind of an appendix or page, belonging
or appertaining in or unto the confines of the English court'.[6] Nashe
must have felt himself just such an 'appendix' in these great households,
his province essentially the back-stairs, outyards and chimney-less closets
of the serving class. He probably found this duality congenial, the gossip
at the 'common table' a relief after more formal repartee in my Lord's
apartments. This flavour of back-stairs subculture is caught in Nashe's
'induction', addressed to 'the dapper Mounsier Pages of the Court':[7]

> Gallant Squires, have amongst you: at Mumchaunce I mean not, for
> so I might chaunce come to short commons, but at *novus, nova,
> novum*, which is in English, newes of the maker. A proper fellow
> Page of yours called Iack Wilton by me commends him unto you,
> and hath bequeathed for wast paper here amongst you certaine pages
> of his misfortunes.

Nashe neatly puffs his pamphlet's broad appeal: here is a piece of
superior pulp-fiction 'to stuffe Serving mens pockets' *à la* Greene.
'Mumchance' is a card game; 'novum' puns on 'news' and the dice game
'novem'. The pamphlet is another such amusement, strictly for pleasure.
These are the pages' pages, to do what they like with: the recommended
uses of literature are to stock the privy, to 'drie & kindle Tobacco' on,
to 'wrap velvet pantofles in', to 'play with false dice in a corner on the
cover' and to 'pawne in the times of famine and necessitie'. In return all
he asks is that the pages be ready with their 'ponyardes' to defend his
pamphlet, and that they 'put of theyr hats' and 'make a low legge' when
they pass a bookseller's stall, 'in regard their grand printed Capitano is
there entombd'. Here is Nashe the entertainer, the 'king of pages',
entering hotfoot with news and gathering his audience around him –
'heigh passe, come aloft: everie man of you take your places'.

The tale is set in the time of Henry VIII, 'the onely true subiect of
Chronicles'. It opens at the English battlecamp in France, 'when Turwin
lost her maidenhead and opened her gates to more than Iane Trosse
did', i.e. at the siege and capture of Térouanne in August 1513. Here we
encounter 'yong Wilton', living off his wits among the camp-followers:
'amongest this chaffe was I winnowing my wittes to live merrily'. His
various tricks, jokes and 'scutcherie' are recounted, anecdotes of the jest-
book variety, with strong 'conny-catching' emphasis. Back in England,
he survives an epidemic of sweating sickness. He returns to Europe as
a soldier of fortune, and gives a gory account of the Battle of Marignano
(1513). Traversing twenty years without a hiccup – Nashe's use of

historical material, notably the chronicles of Lanquet and Sleidan, is cavalier to say the least – Jack witnesses the slaughter of John Leyden's Anabaptists at Münster. At Middleburgh he meets 'the right honorable Lord Henrie Howard, Earle of Surrey', who becomes his master. They travel together to Rotterdam, where they converse with 'superingenious' Erasmus and 'merrie' Sir Thomas More. At Wittenberg they hear 'solempne disputations' between Luther and Carolostadius, and witness magical feats by the 'greatest coniuror in christendome', Cornelius Agrippa. In Venice they are tricked and imprisoned, and there Jack meets his Diamante:

> As glad were we almost as if they had given us libertie, that fortune lent us such a sweete pue-fellow. A pretie rounde faced wench was it, with blacke eie browes, a high forehead, a little mouth and a sharpe nose, as fat and plum everie part of her as a plover, a skin as slike and soft as the back of a swan, it doth me good when I remember her. Like a bird she tript on the grounde, and bare out her belly as maiesticall as an Estrich. With a licorous rouling eie fixt piercing on the earth, and sometimes scornfully darted on the tone side, she figured forth a high discontented disdaine.[8]

They are released through the good offices of 'Monsieur Petro Aretino', and journey to Florence, where the Earl mounts a chivalric tourney in honour of his love, Geraldine. In Rome Jack is framed for murder and once more cast in prison; with the rope around his neck and a farewell ballad entitled *Wiltons wantonnes* on his lips, he is rescued by a 'banisht English Earle'. He falls into the clutches of Doctor Zachary, the Pope's physician, who plans to use him for his annual anatomy demonstration. After further escapades involving the lascivious Countess of Mantua, Jack and Diamante escape to Bologna. Penitent after so many close shaves, 'I married my curtizan, performed many almes deedes, and hasted so fast out of the Sodom of Italy.'

I leave out the half of it, as Nashe would say. *The Unfortunate Traveller* gains its effect through a profusion of incidents, a sense of life as a series of episodic fragments: 'good Lord, see the changing chances of us knights arrant infants'. This being Nashe, there is also plenty going on beneath the narrative surface. It has been argued, for instance, that Jack's gulling of a decayed 'Lord' in the English battle-camp, 'a cavelier of an ancient house', is an obscure hit at Edward de Vere, 17th Earl of Oxford, signalled when Jack calls him 'my welbeloved Baron of double Beere' (= deux beer = de Vere).[9] Jack tells him, 'it is buzzed in the Kings head that you are a secret frend to the Enemie', and have 'furnisht the Enemie' with 'letters of discoverie'. This may echo gossip about Oxford's sudden recall from the Netherlands in 1585. Oxford was an erratic, ambiguous character: widely suspected as a closet Catholic, he nevertheless received an annuity of £1000 out of secret service funds.[10] A hit at him would not be out of place in this pamphlet, for it was dedicated to the young Earl of Southampton. For some years he had been resisting the efforts of his guardian, Lord Burghley, to marry him off: chief among Burghley's candidates was Elizabeth de Vere, daughter of the Earl of Oxford. Southampton's intransigence cost him dear: in about 1594 he was forced to pay £5000 to Burghley, to compensate Lady de Vere for breach of promise.[11] Nashe may have thought to please Southampton with a joke at his uninvited father-in-law's expense.

The main mode of comment in *The Unfortunate Traveller* is not, however, the submerged topical reference *à la Pierce*, but the historical parallel. By placing his chronicle in the bygone days of Henry VIII Nashe is able to wrap his comments in the protective clothing of the past. There are obvious instances. The description of the Anabaptist uprising at Münster is a vehicle for renewed anti-Puritan polemic. Passages on Erasmus, More and Aretino celebrate the humanist tradition of scepticism and satire. The account of Luther disputing at Wittenberg, on the other hand, conveys a rather lukewarm attitude: 'A masse of wordes I wote well they heapte up agaynst the Masse and the Pope, but further particulars of their disputations I remember not. . . . They uttered nothing to make a man laugh, therefore I will leave them.'[12] So much for the Protestant reformation. Most interestingly, Nashe chooses the historical Earl of Surrey to be Jack's noble master. He praises Surrey unstintingly: a 'right noble Lord, liberalitie it selfe', a 'Prince in content because a Poet without peere', a man abounding in a 'supernaturall kind of wit' and in 'admirable airie and firie spirites, full of freedome, magnanimitie and bountihood'. His achievements as a poet are also celebrated. As a chivalrous young nobleman-poet cut off in his prime – he was executed at the age of 30 – Surrey was very much the Tudor prototype of Sir Philip Sidney. But if so, he was a Sidney within a Catholic context.[13] More specifically, he was a Howard, the father of Thomas, the Duke of Norfolk executed for treason in 1572. We remember that Nashe had grown up in Norfolk territory, and that he had celebrated the latter Duke, under the guise of the Horse, in the anti-Leicester fable in *Pierce Penilesse*. *The Unfortunate Traveller* further elaborates Nashe's favourable opinion of this great Catholic family. Those who had sniffed a 'popish' vein in *Pierce Penilesse* – the Puritan Beale and editor 'R.S.' of *The Phoenix Nest*, for instance – would probably find one in Nashe's 'chronicle' also. At one point, certainly, Jack's admiration of Rome as a city shades riskily into an apology for Romish religion:

O Rome, if thou hast in thee such soul-exalting obiects, what a thing is heaven in comparison of thee, of which Mercators globe is a perfecter modell than thou art? Yet this I must saie to the shame of us protestants: if good workes may merite heaven, they doe them, we talke of them. Whether supersticion or no makes them unprofitable servants, that let pulpits decide. But there you shall have the bravest ladies, in gownes of beaten golde, washing pilgrimes & poore souldiers feete. . . . Their hospitals are more lyke noble mens houses than otherwise, so richly furnished, cleane kept and hot perfumed . . . .

Knowing Nashe's feelings on the virtues of charity, his praise of the Catholic emphasis on 'good workes' sounds suspiciously sincere. From another angle, consider this:

I would spend my soule willingly to have that triple headed Pope, with all his sin-absolved whores and oilegreased priests, borne with a blacke sant on the divells backes in procession to the pit of perdition. Would I might sink presently into the earth, so I might blow up this Rome, this whore of Babilon, into the aire with my breath.[14]

An enthusiastic anti-Catholic broadside? Well, hardly. The speaker is the greedy, scheming Jew, Zadoch, who has just sold Jack to the anatomist and stripped and scourged Diamante. We are not invited to sympathize with his hysterical outburst. Zadoch also threatens to poison Rome's 'springs and conduit heades'. Here Nashe is echoing another famous Jew, Marlowe's Barabas in *The Jew of Malta*, who is said to 'go about and poison wells'. Marlowe in turn, it has been suggested, was thinking of his shady acquaintance, Richard Baines, who infiltrated the Catholic seminary at Rheims in the 1580s and then suggested to his English spy-masters that he should poison the community well.[15] Both Nashe and Marlowe may be implying their feelings about extreme anti-Catholic agitators by placing their more dastardly stratagems in the mouths of murderous Jews.

It would be foolhardy to call *The Unfortunate Traveller* a pro-Catholic book. Nashe had no desire to find himself, as Jack Wilton does, with the hangman's knot under his ear. But as with *Pierce Penilesse*, it is hard to ignore its discrete Catholic tinge. If Surrey is a historical *exemplum*, then the pattern of nobility Nashe urges is cultivated, bountiful and Catholic. This seems to be confirmed by the dedicatee Nashe chose for his romance: the Earl of Southampton, a young nobleman who precisely fitted all these requirements. His obstinate loyalty to Catholicism was well-known: he was, as a secretary of Lord Burghley's put it, nursed 'with the warm milk of Error'.[16] He had, moreover, friendly connections with the Howards of Norfolk. His father, the 2nd Earl, had been close to the 4th Duke of Norfolk, part of that concentration of Catholic

interests round the Queen of Scots: the same purge which cost Norfolk
his head consigned Southampton to the Tower for eighteen months. The
young Earl, Nashe's dedicatee, was actually conceived in the Tower: he
was born in October 1573, five months after his father's release. On his
father's death in 1581, another Howard – Charles, Lord Howard of
Effingham – was nominated his 'committie' or guardian.[17] To complete
the picture, Surrey's 'Geraldine' was in reality Elizabeth Fitzgerald,
Southampton's great-grandmother on his mother's side. Nashe no doubt
hoped his *fantasia* on Surrey and Geraldine – it is purely his own
invention, interpolated from Surrey's famous sonnet, 'The Description
and Praise of his love Geraldine' – would please the young Earl.[18] Since
the dedication was withdrawn from all subsequent editions, he seems to
have been disappointed, but the intention itself is interesting enough.
The 'ingenuous honorable Lord' whose 'authorized commendation'
Nashe seeks is a young Catholic nobleman, and this throws the Catholic
hints in his 'historie' into sharper relief.

Nashe's address to Southampton brings us close to Shakespeare. In
April of this year, 1593, Shakespeare's *Venus and Adonis* was licensed
for publication. It appeared with a graceful but tentative dedication to
Southampton – 'I know not how I shall offend in dedicating my unpol-
isht lines to your Lordship', it begins. Unlike Nashe, Shakespeare did
win his place in the Earl's favour, as the dedication of *Lucrece* the
following year unmistakably shows:

> The love I dedicate to your Lordship is without end: wherof this
> Pamphlet without beginning is but a superfluous Moity. The warrant
> I have of your Honourable disposition, not the worth of my untutord
> Lines, makes it assured of acceptance. What I have done is yours,
> what I have to doe is yours, being part in all I have, devoted yours.[19]

It is almost certain that Shakespeare's *Sonnets* were also written for
Southampton at this time, and that the Earl is the 'fair youth' they
celebrate. If Shakespeare was Southampton's poet at this time, Nashe is
doubtless thinking of him when he says to Southampton:

> A dere lover and cherisher you are, as well of the lovers of Poets, as
> of Poets themselves. Amongst their sacred number I dare not ascribe
> my selfe, though now and then I speak English.[20]

I am no Shakespeare, Nashe seems to say, but people listen to me too:
'of your gracious favor I despaire not, for I am not altogether Fames
out-cast'. There were probably other poets in his mind: Barnabe Barnes,
for instance, whose *Parthenophil and Parthenophe*, published in May
1593, included a florid sonnet to Southampton:

Receave (sweet Lord) with thy thrice sacred hande,
Which sacred muses make their instrument,
These worthless leaves which I to thee present . . .[21]

And there is the poet of whose rivalry Shakespeare speaks in the *Sonnets*:

Was it his spirit, by spirits taught to write
Above a mortal pitch, that struck me dead?
No, neither he, nor his compeers by night
Giving him aid, my verse astonished.
He nor that affable familiar ghost
Which nightly gulls him with intelligence,
As victors, of my silence cannot boast.[22]

This sounds much like the poet of occult inspiration and nocturnal *furor*, George Chapman. If Shakespeare and Nashe were, to some extent, rivals for Southampton's favour, they may have been united in their distrust of Chapman and all he stood for.

Also written for Southampton, it is generally thought, was Shakespeare's topical comedy, *Loves Labors Lost*. It is unmistakably a coterie piece, and the allusions in it point to 1593, the year of Shakespeare's known involvement with Southampton. It was probably first performed over Christmas 1593–4, in the 'playhouse room' at Titchfield, the Earl's country seat in Hampshire.[23] There is no doubt that in the character of Moth Shakespeare presents an affable caricature of Tom Nashe. We shall look at this more closely later, but it is clear from the outset how close Shakespeare's portrayal of Nashe is to *The Unfortunate Traveller*. Moth is Nashe in the guise of a 'knavish page', just as Jack Wilton is. He is called a 'prettie ingenius', a 'well-educated infant': Jack is similarly an 'ingenious infant'. None of this would be lost on Southampton, for whom both play and pamphlet were written. Both authors seem to be striving for a broadly similar appeal: plenty of laughter, love-interest and topical spice. They trade in the same romantic commonplaces – Nashe's Cupid is 'sole King and Emperour of pearcing eyes' and 'cheefe Soveraigne of soft hearts'; Shakespeare's is

Th'annoynted soveraigne of sighes and groones,
Liedge of all loyterers and malecontents,
Dread Prince of Placcats, King of Codpeeces,
Sole Emperator and great generall
Of trotting Parrators.[24]

They embed the same kind of Petrarchan love-sonnets in the action, with the same facile neo-Platonic imagery of light, eyes and souls. They even give their heroines the same demeanour: Nashe's Diamante is a 'black browd' Italian beauty with a 'licorous rouling eie'; Shakespeare's

Rosaline is a 'whitly wanton with a velvet brow' and 'two pitch balles stucke in her face for eyes'. The famous 'dark lady' of the *Sonnets* sounds much the same, with her 'raven black' eyes and her hair like 'black wires'.[25] All of this doubtless reflects the fashionable tastes, literary and sexual, of the Southampton circle.

According to the date at the end of the text, Nashe completed *The Unfortunate Traveller* on 'Iune 27 1593'. It was not published till 1594, however, probably in April or May.[26] If Shakespeare knew it when he wrote *Loves Labors Lost*, as the connections between Moth and Jack Wilton suggest, then he knew it in MS. Soon after publication, Nashe tetchily refuted the 'busie wits' who sought to 'anagrammatize' some of its references. He wrote:

> Not so much as out of mutton and potage but they wil construe a meaning of Kings and Princes. Let one but name bread, they will interpret it to be the town of Bredan in the low countreyes; if of beere he talkes, then straight he mocks the Countie Beroune in France.[27]

The curious point about this is that it was not Nashe but Shakespeare who had taken the name of 'the Countie Beroune' – Armand de Gontaut, Duc de Biron – in vain. The central character of *Loves Labors Lost* is Berowne, a follower of the King of Navarre, as was the historical Biron.

For all its panache and charm, *The Unfortunate Traveller* has its darker side. The blood-and-guts battle scenes are just set-pieces, cynical crowd-pleasers, but the events which overtake Jack in Rome signal a distinct change of mood. It is the plague that begins it, ostensibly the Roman plague of 1522 but in reality London, 1593:

> So it fel out that it being a vehement hot summer when I was a soiourner there, there entered such a hotspurd plague as hath not bin heard of: why, it was but a word and a blowe, Lord have mercie upon us, and he was gone . . .

> To smell of a nosegay that was poisond, and turne your nose to a house that had the plague, it was all one. The clouds, like a number of cormorants that keepe their corne til it stinke and is mustie, kept in their stinking exhalations till they had almost stifeled all Romes inhabitants . . .

> All daye and all night long carre-men did nothing but go up and downe the streets with their carts and cry, **Have you** anie dead to

burie, have you anie dead to burie: and had many times out of one house their whole loding. One grave was the sepulchre of seven score, one bed was the alter whereon whole families were offered. The wals wer hoard and furd with the moist scorching steame of their desolation.[28]

Earlier in the book Jack had skipped through a plague of 'sweating sicknes' with jokes about fat men and hothouses. This is a 'cleane different vaine' of writing: for Nashe, intensely direct. He is dealing with the horrors of the plague at first hand – according to Stow over 10,000 Londoners fell victim in 1593[29] – and humour is not a possibility. Heat and putrefaction, an eerie claustrophobic haze, seep from the London streets into the romance world of Jack Wilton.

One death in particular touched Nashe in the early summer of 1593. On the evening of 30 May, Christopher Marlowe died in a knife-fight at Deptford on the south-eastern outskirts of London.[30] The circumstances are, not surprisingly, shady. Ten days earlier, he had been called before the Privy Council on unspecified charges, and 'commaunded to give his daily attendaunce on their Lordships'. On the day of his death he was in the company of three unsavoury characters – Ingram Friser, Robert Poley and Nicholas Skeres – all involved in government intelligence work, and all connected with the Walsinghams, Sir Thomas and Lady Audrey, at whose house in Kent Marlowe had recently been staying.[31] The four men spent the day closeted together at the house of Eleanor Bull in Deptford Strand, probably a tavern or lodging-house. They conversed 'in quiet sort', dined in a private room, walked around in the garden. After supper – so the official coroner's version runs – there was a dispute over 'le recknynge'. Ingram Friser and Marlowe exchanged 'divers malicious words'. Marlowe was lying on a bed, Friser sitting with his back to him, playing 'tables' – backgammon – according to one account. Suddenly Marlowe leapt up, snatched Friser's dagger from its sheath and slashed him twice about the head. Friser struggled,

and so it befell in that affray that the said Ingram, in defence of his life, with the dagger aforesaid of the value of 12d, gave the said Christopher then & there a mortal wound over his right eye, of the depth of two inches.

Of this wound Marlowe 'instantly died'. In Nashe's words above, 'it was but a word and a blowe, Lord have mercie upon us, and he was gone'. He was just twenty-nine years old.

News of Marlowe's death must have quickly reached Nashe. Some reaction, surely, is to be found in *The Unfortunate Traveller*, completed just four weeks later.[32] It has been suggested that some of Nashe's remarks about Surrey contain elegiac reflections on Marlowe:

> Destinie never defames hir selfe but when shee lets an excellent Poet die: if there bee anie sparke of Adams Paradized perfection yet emberd up in the breastes of mortall men, certainelie God hath bestowed that his perfectest image on Poets.

Surrey's 'supernaturall kinde of wit', his 'admirable airie and firie spirites' of freedom, may also be meant for Marlowe. Other contemporaries called him 'that pure Elementall wit', and declared that 'his raptures were all air and fire'. Nashe's long commendation of Aretino has also been combed for sidelong tributes to Marlowe's restless, outspoken temper – he was 'no timerous servile flatterer of the commonwealth'; his words were 'lyke a burning glasse to set on fire all his readers'; his life 'he contemned in comparison of the libertie of speech'.[33] These fit well as oblique epitaphs for Marlowe, but they tell us little of Nashe's feelings about Marlowe's actual death, so violent and so questionable. Something of its impact may perhaps be glimpsed in Nashe's account of the death of Heraclide. Immediately following that vivid description of the plague, this is a gruesome saga of murder, rape and suicide, seven close-printed pages of torrid violence and hysterical lamentation.[34] There is nothing remarkable in this: Shakespeare's *Titus Andronicus* had packed in the crowds on this ticket. But throughout it one seems to get fragmentary images of Marlowe's sudden end – a 'rigorous compelled death', a 'reprobate soule' and its 'troubled departure', a 'dissolute homicide'. We glimpse the knife – 'point, pierce; edge, enwiden' . . . 'my knife shall manumit mee out of the horrour of minde I endure'. We get Faustian fears of damnation – 'the Angells shall hisse at me, the Saints and Martyrs flye from me, yea God himselfe'. We see 'a comfortlesse corse, a carrionly blocke', lying 'stone cold on the dewie floor'. When Heraclide's ravager is brought to execution, he begs them to 'digge out my blasphemous tongue with a dagger'. Again this sounds like Marlowe's death in dramatic shorthand: a blasphemous tongue silenced by a dagger. Repentantly, the guilty man cries: 'Murther is a house divided within it selfe . . . . His soule (beeing his accuser) brings foorth his two eyes as witnesses against him; and the least eie-witnesse is unrefutable.' Is there an accusation hidden in this? The key words are 'murder' and 'witness'. In the days following 30 May Nashe doubtless tried to get at the truth of Marlowe's death, obscured as it was by rumour, Puritan propaganda and government silence. To stem any awkward questions, the authorities were quick to tidy the affair away. On 28 June, the day after Nashe finished *The Unfortunate Traveller*, Ingram Friser received the Queen's pardon. He had killed his man in self-defence: his two eye-witnesses, Poley and Skeres, were no doubt 'unrefutable'. On the 29th, the records show, Friser was back at work for the Walsinghams. Some still believe that he was 'at work' for them on that fateful summer night in Deptford, and that the silencing of Marlowe was indeed, as Nashe perhaps hints, a case of 'murther'.

We must be content with these subterranean responses, for Nashe's actual elegy on Marlowe is unfortunately lost.[35] It was 'prefixed' to certain copies of Marlowe's *Dido, Queene of Carthage*, which Nashe prepared for publication in 1594. Two eighteenth-century bibliophiles, Thomas Warton and Bishop Tanner, saw it. Tanner, in his *Bibliotheca Britannico-Hibernica* (1748), speaks of Nashe praising Marlowe '*in Carmine Elegiaco tragediae Didonis praefixo in obitum Christoph. Marlovii*'. This may give the actual title of the poem, *Carmen Elegiacum*, or, as Tanner is writing in Latin anyway, the original title may have been something like *An Elegiacall Song*. Warton merely describes it as an 'elegy on Marlowe's untimely death'. Of its contents we are told nothing except that it mentions five of Marlowe's plays and that it 'utters many things in praise of Marlowe' ('*multa in Marlovii commendationem adfert*'). Leaving aside *The Unfortunate Traveller*, Nashe's first extant reference to Marlowe after his death is not until the summer of 1594, when he mentions 'poore deceassed Kit Marlow' as one of the 'quiet senseless carkasses' that Gabriel Harvey has 'vilely dealt with'.[36] He is referring to Harvey's poem, 'Gorgon', which describes Marlowe as a man that 'nor feared God, nor dreaded Div'll, Nor aught admired but his wondrous selfe'. Harvey crows:

> Weepe Powles, thy Tamberlaine voutsafes to dye.
> The hugest miracle remaines behinde,
> The second Shakerley Rash-swash to binde.[37]

Translated, this means: Marlowe is dead and Nashe is next on the list.

12

THE CRACK-UP

'Discende into the closet of thyne owne conscience . . .'

Christs Tears over Ierusalem

The intrusion of plague and death into the romance of Jack Wilton sets the mood for summer 1593. With *The Unfortunate Traveller* completed at the end of June, Nashe began to mine yet another 'cleane different vaine'. The result was his brooding, apocalyptic, religious lament entitled *Christs Tears over Ierusalem*. 'These be the dayes of dolour and heavinesse', he announces, wherefore 'it shall not be amisse to write something of mourning.' He warns the reader:

> *Nil nisi flere libet*, Gentles, heere is no ioyfull subiect towardes: if you will weepe, so it is. I have nothing to spend on you but passion.

He bids 'a hundred unfortunate farewels to fantasticall Satirisme', on which 'heere-to-fore have I mispent my spirite and prodigally conspir'd against good houres'. He prays to Christ:

> Mine owne wit I cleane disinherite: thy fiery Cloven-tongued inspiration be my Muse. Lende my wordes the forcible wings of the Lightnings, that they may peirce unawares into the marrow and reynes of my Readers. Newe mynt my minde to the likenes of thy lowlines: file away the superfluous affectation of my prophane puft up phrase, that I may be thy pure simple Orator.

Purity and simplicity are hardly the keynote of a work shot through with such lines as:

> Yea, theyr Firmament-propping foundation shal be adequated with the Valley of Iehosaphat: whose sublimity (whiles it is in beheading) the skie shall resign . . .

> Those ruddy investurings and scarlet habilements, from the clowde-climing slaughter-stack of thy dead carkases, shall they exhalingly quintessence . . .[1]

The style is throughout fevered and baroque: it is the longest and least readable of Nashe's works. It attracted much criticism, as he notes in the preface to the second edition: 'the ploddinger sort of unlearned Zoilists about London exclaim that it is a puft-up stile, and full of prophane eloquence'; others object to 'the multitude of my boystrous compound wordes, and the often coyning of Italionate verbes which end all in Ize'. He replies that he wrote in a 'high ravishte Spirite' appropriate for a 'devine subiect', that all oratory with 'force to confute or perswade' must be 'swelling and boystrous'. As for his neologizing, he claims he is enriching 'our English tongue' which 'of all languages most swarmeth with the single money of monasillables'.[2]

Through the long hot summer of 1593 we find Nashe hunched over his bibles, both the 'Geneva' and the 'Bishops' versions; over Joseph ben Gurion's *History of the Latter Times of the Jews' Commonweal*, translated by Peter Morvyn in 1558; and over the sermon by John Stockwood of Tonbridge, published in 1584, describing 'the moste lamentable destruction of Ierusalem, and the heavy iudgementes of God executed uppon that people'. Harvey suggested that Nashe had also 'a little mused upon the *Funerall Teares* of Mary Magdalene', a tract by the imprisoned Jesuit, Robert Southwell.[3] *Christs Teares* is essentially a sermon, its text being *Matthew*, chapters 23 and 24, specifically the verses where Christ says:

O Ierusalem, Ierusalem, which killest the Prophets, and stonest them that are sent unto thee. How often would I have gathered thy Chyldren together, as the Henne gathereth her Chickins together under her wings, and ye would not.

Therefore your habitation shall be left desolate.

Round this Nashe frames his message of 'repent for the end is nigh', hammering on the word 'desolate' with an almost mantric insistence. The work falls into three main sections. The first interpolates on the text, imagining a continued 'collachrimate oration' delivered by Christ to the Jerusalemites. The second is a lurid description of the fall of Jerusalem, to 'manifest, as it were in a dead-marche, her untimely interment'. The third and longest is, as promised on the title-page, 'a comparative admonition to London':

Now to London must I turne me, London that turneth from none of thy left-hand impieties. As great a desolation as Ierusalem hath London deserved. Whatsoever of Ierusalem I have written, was but to lend her a Looking-glasse. Now enter I into my true Teares, my

Teares for London, wherein I crave pardon though I deale more searchingly then common Soule-Surgions accustome.

He ranges through the sins of the city – pride, his 'principall ayme', and its various 'sons' (ambition, vain-glory, atheism, contention) and 'daughters' (disdain, gorgeous attire and delicacy). The moral terrain is much the same as *Pierce Penilesse* but the treatment unrecognizably different. The satirical jester has turned tub-thumping preacher, the 'soul-surgeon'. The plague is seen as God's punishment: He has 'smitten thee and strooke thee' in the 'misty night of thy mounting iniquities'. The work closes with a plague prayer:

Comfort us Lord; we mourne, our bread is mingled with ashes, and our drinke with tears. With so manie funerals are wee oppressed, that wee have no leysure to weepe for our sinnes for howling for our Sonnes and Daughters. O hear the voyce of our howling, withdraw thy hand from us, & we will draw neere unto thee.[4]

How are we to take all this? Is it a merely literary performance, another experimental *essai*, another pamphleteering cry of 'Newe herringes, new!'? He is certainly writing within a definable tradition, the 'literature of warning' as it is called.[5] Jerusalem as London's 'looking glass' is reminiscent of Greene and Lodge's *Looking Glass for London*, with its admonitory parallels with ancient Nineveh. When he bids fare-well to 'fantasticall Satirisme' and his former 'spleanative vaines of wantonnesse', we hear an echo of Greene's popular repentance-tracts. Yet for all this, it is impossible not to feel the febrile intensity, the genuine *cri de coeur*, in *Christs Teares*. The soured, jumpy, guilt-ridden tone of *The Terrors of the Night* foreshadows it. Dabblings in fashion-able occultism, months among the theological scholars at Croydon, scary nights at Conington: all these play their part, working on a mind predisposed to agitation, reared up from the cradle in the oppressive shadow of the Church. The deaths of his friends – Greene and Watson the previous autumn, and now Marlowe – press in on him, and behind them the relentless horror of the plague. Death haunts *Christs Teares* like a refrain:

Your dayes are as swyft as a post, yea, swifter then a Weavers shettle, they flye and see no good thing: yet flie you swifter to Hell then they . . .

In the marrow of your bones snakes shall breede. Your morne-like christall countenaunces shall be netted over and (Masker-like) cawle-visarded with crawling venomous wormes. Your orient teeth Toades

shall steale into theyr heades for pearle; of the ielly of your decayed
eyes shall they engender them young . . .

Wee see great men dye, strong men dye, wittie men dye, fooles dye,
rich Merchants, poore Artificers, Plowmen, Gentlemen, high men,
low men, wearish men, grosse men, and the fairest complexiond men
die . . .

A dualistic Elizabethan, Nashe's access of piety entails a sickened recoil-
ing from the bodily world: 'What hath immortalitie to do with muck?'
. . . 'Black and cindry (like Smithes-water) are those excrements that
source downe my cheekes, and farre more sluttish then the uglie oous
of the channell' . . . 'Make not your bodies stincking dungeons for
diseases to dwell in: imprison not your soules in a sinck.'[6]
  Reading into *Christs Teares*, one quickly realizes that 'religious crisis'
is a limiting label, that the pamphlet's most urgent message is more
pathological than devotional. What one is witnessing, through the veil
of 'holy complaint', is an actual nervous breakdown, of which the whole
work is a product and certain passages a precise account:

My heart ranne full-butt against my breast to have broken it open,
and my soule fluttered and beate with her ayrie-winges on every side
for passage. My knees crackt and the ground fledde back . . .

I that have poor'd out myne eyes upon bookes, & wel-nie spit out al
my braine at my tongues end this morning, am dumpish, drousy, &
wish my selfe dead . . .

The zeale of thee distraughteth me, and some essentiall parte of my
life seemeth to forsake me and droppe from mee . . .

I have crackt mine eye-strings with excessive staring . . .

When thou shalt lie in thy bedde as on a Racke stretching out thy
ioynts; when thine eyes shall start out of thy head & every part of
thee be wrung as with the wind-chollick; in the midst of thy furie
and malady, when thou shalt laugh and trifle, folter with thy tongue,
rattle in thy throate, be busie in folding and doubling the clothes, &
scratching and catching whatsoever comes neere thee . . .[7]

These are, surely, authentic glimpses of Nashe *in extremis*: melodramatic
but arising out of some real and harrowing crack-up. In the dedicatory
epistle, Nashe describes the circumstances in which *Christs Teares* was
composed:

My woe-infirmed witte conspired against me with my fortune. My impotent care-crazed stile cast of his light wings and betooke him to wodden stilts. All agility it forgot, and graveld it selfe in grosse-braind formallitie. Nowe a little is it revived, but not so revived that it hath utterly shooke of his danke upper mourning garment. . . . That which my Teare-stubbed penne in this Theological subiect hath attempted, is no more but the course-spun webbe of discontent: a quintessence of holy complaint extracted out of my true cause of condolement.[8]

He clearly stresses the private back-drop – 'woe', 'care', 'mourning', 'condolement' – behind the tract. Perhaps most expressive of Nashe's *bouleversement* is a simple remarkable fact. With *Christs Teares* completed, he published no new work for three years. What appeared in 1594 was either previously written (*The Terrors* and *The Unfortunate Traveller*) or mere editorial work (Marlowe's *Dido*). There was nothing in 1595, then *Have with you to Saffron-Walden* in autumn 1596. *Christs Teares* brings to a sudden close a period of marvellous fecundity. In just fifteen months Nashe had written no less than six original works (five prose pamphlets and *Summers Last Will*). Mental exhaustion, the outpouring of copy to keep the wolf from the door, may be one more factor in the crack-up. All in all, we can say that in summer 1593 Thomas Nashe hit bottom. That he clawed up out of it is clear, but he never quite regained his former gusto.

Christs Teares was finished by early September. It was registered at Stationers' Hall on the 8th by Alice Charlewood, widow of John, who had printed Nashe's *Anatomie of Absurditie* and some of the anti-Martinist tracts. It probably arrived on the book-stalls in early October. Ironically, considering its fervid moral tone, it caused more official outrage than any of his previous pamphlets. In the preface to the second edition he speaks of 'the heavie penance my poore Teares here have endured'. Its detractors have 'got salt Catars in their throats with vehement railing upon it'; they 'condemne me all to vineger for my bitternesse'. The fact is that in his self-appointed role as moral scourge, 'prosternating and enforrowing the frontiers of sinne', Nashe offers a more biting critique of the powerful and wealthy than he had as satirist *per se*. He lashes the London citizens whose only religion is 'love of money'; the magistrates that 'will have theyr eyes put out with gyfts'; the avaricious worthy who diverts money from 'the poore and impotent' to 'purse it up into his owne coffers'; the law-givers that frame 'burdenous lawes to oppresse and keepe under the Communalty'; the 'rich chuffes' that ignore the 'cryes of the fatherlesse and the widowe' and say,

> Tut, tut, almes-houses will make good stables and, let out in Tenements, yeelde a round summe by the yeare. A good strong bard hutch is a building worth twenty of those Hospitals and Almes-houses.[9]

There is no doubt that Nashe's cry of corruption in high places – 'oppression is the price of bloode; into your treasuries you put the price of blood' – ruffled a few feathers. One passage in particular caused offence, for in the second edition it was cancelled and substituted with something altogether milder. In its original form, it began:

> London, thou art the seeded Garden of sinne, the Sea that sucks in all the scummy chanels of the Realme. The honestest in thee (for the most) are eyther Lawyers or Usurers. Deceite is that which advauncest the greater sorte of thy chiefest: let them looke that theyr ritches shall rust and canker, being wet & dewed with Orphans teares. The Lord thinketh it were as good for him to kill with the Plague, as to let them kill with oppression. He beholdeth from on hie al subtle conveiances and recognisances. He beholdeth how they pervert foundations, and will not bestow the Bequeathers free almes, but for brybes or for friendship.[10]

Considering the prevailing limits on political comment, this is fairly strong stuff. Its principal target seems to be the Court of Orphans, essentially a trust-fund administered from the Guildhall by the Lord Mayor and Aldermen. In the cancel-leaf inserted in the 1594 edition, as well as toning down the attack, Nashe adds this careful rider:

> I speake not this for I know any such, but if there be anie such, to forewarne and reforme them. Many good men, many good magistrats are there in this City, diverse godly & wise counsellers hath she to provide for her peace; them no part of any reproofe of mine concerneth, how ever it may be otherwise thought.

This is clearly intended to pacify the municipal authorities: the Mayor, Sir Cuthbert Buckle, the magistrates and the counsellors of the Council of London. It would seem that Gabriel Harvey played some part in stirring up the trouble, for in *Have with you to Saffron-Walden* Nashe speaks of Harvey's

> incensing my L. Mayor against me that then was, by directing unto him a perswasive pamphlet to persecute mee, and not let slip the

advauntage hee had against mee; and reporting certaine words I shuld speake against him that Christmas at a Taverne in London.

A leading alderman at this time was Sir Richard Martin: he was a Saffron Walden man, so Harvey may well have been using local leverage against Nashe. What form the persecution took is not clear, but it was still fresh in Nashe's mind in 1596: writing of official measures against the theatre companies, he says that 'the players as if they had writt another Christs tears ar piteously persecuted by the L. Maior & the aldermen'.[11]

Penning 'perswasive' letters to the Lord Mayor was not, by a long chalk, Harvey's only move against Nashe in 1593. Ever since the appearance of *Strange Newes* at the end of 1592, Harvey had been preparing his answer, the mammoth *Pierces Supererogation* (or 'A New Prayse of the Olde Asse'). The bulk of this was completed on 27 April; the prefatory matter is dated 16 July. In September, now back in Saffron Walden, Harvey wrote a further tract, the *New Letter of Notable Contents*. These two works – the *Supererogation* and the *New Letter* – were issued by John Wolfe in October, shortly after the appearance of *Christs Teares*. They were published together, or at least in quick succession, for Nashe refers to Harvey's diatribe as 'six and thirty sheetes of mustard-pot paper', which is the length of the two works together.[12] It was probably Wolfe, rather than Harvey himself, who actually decided to publish them, for they appeared at just the time when Nashe had made honourable and public amends for his previous slanders of Harvey. During the summer of 1593, it seems, private efforts had been made to reconcile the two adversaries. Nashe speaks of 'termes of truce' drawn up between them, through the 'intreatie' of mutual friends, 'trouch-men and vantcurriers betwixt us'. Though the two never met – Harvey claims he 'craved personall conference' but Nashe would only communicate through 'interposed persons' – peace seems to have been patched up, and in the preface to *Christs Teares*, as paramount proof of his reformed personality, Nashe published a generous apology:

Nothing is there now so much in my vowes, as to be at peace with all men, and make submissive amends where I have most displeased. . . . Purely pacifycatorie suppliant, for reconciliation and pardon doe I sue to the principallest of them, gainst whom I profest utter enmity. Even of Maister Doctor Harvey I hartily desire the like, whose fame and reputation . . . I rashly assailed: yet now better advised, and of his perfections more confirmedly perswaded, unfainedly I entreate of the whole worlde, from my penne his worths may receive no impeachment.[13]

Though Harvey makes some mention of *Christs Teares* in his *New Letter*, he had not actually seen a copy. He repeatedly demands a public apology from Nashe: 'till a publique iniurie be publiquely confessed, and Print be confuted in Print, I am one of S. Thomas disciples: not over-prest to beleeve but as cause causeth'. Obviously he had not seen Nashe's apology when he wrote this. Other references to *Christs Teares* in the *New Letter* are vague enough to confirm that he only knew of it by repute. He doubts the sincerity of Nashe's supposed transformation: 'a Spring of rankest Villany' followed by 'a Harvest of ripest Divinity'. He cannot believe that the 'Divels Oratour' can so suddenly become 'Christes Chauncellor', that

> he that penned the most desperate and abominable Pamflet of *Straunge Newes*, and disgorged his stomacke of as poisonous rancour as ever was vomited in Print, within few moneths is won, or charmed, or inchaunted (or what *Metamorphosis* should I terme it) to astonish carnall mindes with spirituall meditations.

He fears, in short, that 'the *Teares of Christ*' will prove to be 'the *Teares of the Crocodile*'.[14] Nowhere does he show any knowledge of the text itself; only an incredulity – understandable enough – at its title and intention. What he knew of it he probably had from John Wolfe, who had written him a letter in early September (the *New Letter* is addressed to Wolfe in reply). Wolfe would be well placed for news of Nashe's forthcoming work, registered on 8 September.

To the general public, however, and to Nashe himself, no such mitigation of Harvey's actions was apparent. The chronology seemed clear: Nashe had apologized, and Harvey had retorted a few weeks later with vilification and abuse. As Nashe put it, 'I thought to make my foe a bridge of gold, or faire words, to flie by; he hath used it as a high way to invade me.' In the second edition of *Christs Teares*, the apology was withdrawn and a bitter threat substituted:

> Thrice more convenient time I wil picke out to stretch him forth limbe by limbe on the racke, and a field as large as Achilles race to baite him to death with darts, according to the custome of bayting buls in Spaine. Never more let him looke to quench wilde fire with milke, or mitigate the matter with mild termes.[15]

It was not until autumn 1596 that the threat was made good. But when it came it was the *coup de grâce*, and no more was heard of Dr Harvey thereafter.

The predominant impression of *Pierces Supererogation* is one of hugeness and weight, the relentless sprawl (more than 250 pages) of

Harvey's indignation.. It is, as Nashe says, an 'unconscionable vast gorbellied Volume', a 'gargantuan bag-pudding' of a book: 'scarce a whole Elephants hyde & a halfe would serve for a cover to this Gogmagog Iewish *Thalmud* of absurdities'. In a comic scenario, Nashe describes how the book was first delivered to him – it has cracked 'three axeltrees' of the carrier's cart on the way here; the carrier begs him to take it, if only to 'make mud walls with'; he struggles in with it – 'I was faine to lift my chamber doore of the hindges, onely to let it in' – and wonders if he should call in a cooper to 'hoope it about'; he thinks the royal guard might 'trie masteries' with it, 'in stead of throwing the sledge or the hammer, to hurle it foorth at the armes ende for a wager'. He even finds an apt typographical error: Harvey must be 'asham'd of the incomprehensible corpulencie thereof himselfe, for at the end of the 199. page hee begins with one 100. againe, to make it seeme little'.[16] This clowning is no more than Harvey deserves: even his biographer, Virginia Stern, admits that the *Supererogation* 'tends sometimes to become tedious' and that 'the reader is occasionally lulled into inattention and near insensitivity'.[17] 'Sometimes' and 'occasionally' are charitable indeed.

It is hard to marshal any coherent argument out of *Pierces Supererogation*, though its scholarly and rhetorical trappings make one feel there ought to be one somewhere. Harvey's painstaking progress is a matter of obsession rather than argumentation. His favourite grammatical mode is 'paratactic': a stacking-up of phrases and clauses to reiterate and exemplify, but seldom develop, an idea. What is Harvey saying about Nashe, except that he is an 'unmannerly puppy' and a seedy dissolute? One motif he returns to frequently is 'St Fame'. Taking up Nashe's cry at the beginning of *Strange Newes* – 'Saint Fame for mee, and thus I runne upon him' – Harvey ridicules Nashe as the devotee and 'young darling' of this saint, indeed the title-page announces that the *Supererogation* is only 'a preparative to certaine larger Discourses, intutuled *Nashes S. Fame*'. The point is to suggest Nashe as the slave of catchpenny commercialism, writing solely to please the crowd and line his pockets, and to infer that behind the showman's flourishes Nashe has absolutely nothing to say:

> It is the destiny of our language to be pestred with a rablement of botchers in Print: but what a shamefull shame is it for him, that maketh an Idoll of his owne penne, and raiseth-upp an huge expectation of paper-miracles, (as if Hermes Trismegist were newly risen from the dead, and personally mounted upon Danters Presse) to emproove himselfe as ranke a bungler in his mightiest worke of Supererogation, as the starkest Patch-pannell of them all.

The title of Harvey's work ties in with this. 'Supererogation' is a Catholic theological term meaning the performance of more 'good works' than are individually required, a kind of banking-up of spiritual assets (Latin *supererogatio*, over-payment). Harvey partly means, I think, that Nashe's shrill performance in *Strange Newes* is a kind of verbal 'supererogation', over-zealous and hyper-active: 'if vaunting or craking make thee singular, thy Art is incomparable, thy Wit superexcellent'. He warns that Nashe

> must either accomplish some greater worke of Supererogation, with actual achievement, (that is now a principall point), or immortalize himselfe as the prowdest Vaine sott that ever abused the world with foppish ostentation.[18]

A trifling, childish railer, his gestures empty and his motives entirely negative: this is the image of Nashe that Harvey wishes us to take away from *Pierces Supererogation*. Two tactical blunders tend to blunt his indictment: first, his own attempts to match Nashe's coarser, racier style; second, the fact that *Pierces Supererogation* appeareed just after Nashe had apologized.

Harvey akes much of th idea thatNashe is part o a literary 'gang'. Tarlton, Greene and Marlowe are mentioned – the latter still alive when the *Supererogation* was written – but Harvey's old enemy John Lyly is especially singled out. Sandwiched between assaults on Nashe is Harvey's *Advertisement for Papp-hatchett*, written against Lyly in 1589 and now first published. As a kind of counterpoint to the old comic triplicity of the Harveys – 'a perfect pariall', Nashe called them, 'pair royal' being three of a kind at cards – we get this disreputable trio of pamphleteers:

> Nash, the Ape of Greene; Greene, the Ape of Euphues; Euphues, the Ape of Envie: the three famous mammets of the presse, and my three notorious feudists, drawe all in a yoke.

It was a motley army: Greene was past caring and Lyly never bothered to answer Harvey in print, despite Nashe's urgings ('for Master Lillie, who is halves with me in this indignitie that is offred, I will not take the tale out of his mouth').[19] Harvey in turn had been gathering his own posse of accomplices. His epistle before the *Supererogation* is addressed to 'my very gentle and liberall frendes, M. Barnabe Barnes, M. Iohn Thorius, M. Antony Chewt', and each of these writers contributes poems and letters in praise of Harvey and scorn of Nashe. Barnes was an excitable, eccentric young poet, the son of the Bishop of Durham; his first volume, the atmospheric *Parthenophil and Parthenophe*, appeared in 1593. Thorius was an Oxford man, a linguist, translator of de Corro's *Spanish Grammar* and compiler of a Spanish dictionary (1590). Anthony

Chute is variously described as a sailor, a lawyer's clerk and a scholar in heraldry: he is best known for his poem, *Shores Wife* or 'Beawtie Dishonoured' (1593). All of the works mentioned were published by John Wolfe, so here is a little clique of minor authors, presided over by *cher maître* Harvey, penning (as Nashe sneers) 'their curteous Letters and commendatorie Sonnets, writ to him from a farre, as namely out of the hall into the kitchin at Wolfes, where altogether at one time they lodged'.[20] All three have a tilt at Nashe. Thorius does so mildly enough, and he later wrote a letter to Nashe calling him his 'very good friend', claiming the poems assigned to him were forgeries, and saying he was 'exceedingly ashamed' of his whole involvement in the *Supererogation*.[21] Barnes and Chute enter the fray with more gusto. Barnes' sonnet, 'Nash, or the Confuting Gentleman', calls him

> Envies vile champion; slaunders stumblingblock;
> Ground Oratour of Cunny-catchers crew;
> Base broaching tapster of reports untrue;
> Our modern Viper, and our Countryes mocke . . .

Chute – 'the bawlingest of them all', says Nashe – contributes 'The Asses Figg', characterizing him as a down-and-out drunken railer:

> So long the Rhennish furie of thy braine,
> Incenst with hot fume of a Stilliard Clime,
> Lowd-lying Nash, in liquid termes did raine,
> Full of absurdities and of slaundrous ryme.

A fourth author, the Frenchman Jean de Fregeville, author of *The Reformed Politicke* (1589), contributes a sonnet in praise of 'le tres-docte & tres-eloquent Docteur'. This touches only remotely on Nashe, yet earned Fregeville his place in *Have with you* ('that prating weazell fac'd vermin' . . . 'vile friggers or Fregeviles').[22]

Two other unnamed figures lurk in the *Supererogation*. The first is the mysterious 'Gentlewoman', whom Harvey introduces as his 'patronesse' and 'Championesse in this quarrel'. In three spirited sonnets she calls Nashe the 'bombard goblin', the 'super domineering Elfe' and asks:

> Ist possible for puling wench to tame
> The furibundall Champion of Fame?

After one of these she signs herself *Ultrix accinta flagello*': the avenging woman armed with a whip. Harvey lards his text with fulsome praise of her: she is 'an enchaunting Angell', her pen 'runneth like a winged horse, governed with the hand of exquisite skill', she has bestowed much 'largesse' and 'hyperbolicall curtesie' on Gabriel. He refuses to name her – 'I dare not particularise her Description . . . without her licence' – and tells us nothing about her motives except that she was moved by 'the Equity of my cause'.[23] It used to be thought that she was the Countess of Pembroke, or at least, as Grosart says, 'that Harvey wished to convey that idea'. McKerrow's main objection to this – that 'Gentlewoman' is an incorrect address – is unsound: if she wished to remain anonymous, she would hardly want Harvey to call her 'the Countess'.[24] But it is unlikely she would get involved in a scrap of this sort, however strong her dislike of Nashe, and it is hard to imagine her penning such lines as

> Il'e leade the gagtooth'd fopp a new-founde daunce:
> Deare howers were ever cheape to pidling me.

By keeping her nameless, Harvey invokes a vague aura of wealthy, powerful backing. Yet he also plays, once more, into Nashe's hands, for an anonymous backer can be abused with impunity: 'Yea, Madam Gabriela, are you such an old ierker? then Hey ding a ding, up with your petticoate, have at your plum tree.' It is not impossible that, as Nashe suggests, she is a figment of Harvey's imagination, 'a meere copy of his countenaunce', brought in 'to breed an opinion in the world that he is such a great man in Ladies and Gentlewomans bookes that they are readie to run out of their wits for him'.[25]

The other unnamed contributor to Harvey's pamphlet is brought on in *defence* of Nashe and all he stands for. Just 'this other day', Harvey explains, this gentleman 'soberlie commended some extraordinary giftes in Nashe'. His speech is supposedly given in full. He praises Nashe as a writer brought up in the school of real life rather than cloistered Academe, a champion of 'sanguine Witt' over 'melancholy Arte'. 'You may talke your pleasures of Tom Nash', he says,

> but assure your selves, if M. Penniles had not bene deeply plunged in a profound exstasie of knavery, M. Pierce had never written that famous worke of Supererogation that now stayneth all the bookes in Paules-churchyard, and setteth both the Universities to schoole. . . . Pardon me though I prefer one smart Pamflet of knavery before ten blundring volumes of the nine Muses. Dreaming and smoke amount alike: Life is a gaming, a iugling, a scoulding, a lawing, a skirmishing, a warre, a Comedie, a Tragedy: the sturring witt, a quintessence of quicksilver; and there is noe dead flesh in affection or courage. You may discourse of Hermes ascending spirit; of Orpheus enchanting harpe; of Homers divine furie; of Tyrtaeus enraging trumpet; of Pericles bounsinge thunderclaps; of Platos enthusiasticall ravishment; and I wott not what marvelous egges in mooneshine: but a flye for all your flying speculations, when one good fellow with his odde iestes, or one madd knave with his awke hibber-gibber, is able to putt

downe twentye of your smuggest artificiall men, that simper it so
nicely and coylie in their curious pointes.

Nashe sets, he claims, a pattern for all that 'intende to be fine companion-
able gentlemen, smirking wittes and whipsters in the world'. He possesses
the 'Archmistery of the busiest Modernistes', which is 'a certayne prag-
maticall secret called Villany'.[26]

One might take all this as ironic – however street-wise Nashe wished
to appear, 'knavery' and 'villany' are dubious compliments – were it not
that the man whose opinions are here voiced was someone whose own
writings suggest he really was an admirer of Nashe. He was, as Frances
Yates has conclusively shown, one John Eliot.[27] Another of Wolfe's
writers, Eliot was a Francophile and French linguist: as well as the
Survay of France (1592) and *Ortho-epia Gallica* (1593), he no doubt
hacked out many of the French 'news-letters' that were one of Wolfe's
specialities. The *Ortho-epia Gallica* is a curious and colourful work:
ostensibly a language-manual, of the type very popular in cosmopolitan
London, it turns out on closer inspection to be a lampoon of other
language-manuals and of the foreigners who wrote them. Its subtitle –
'Eliots First Fruits for the French' – points to a particular target, John
Florio, whose Italian manuals were entitled the *First* and *Second Fruites*
(1578, 1591). Further jibes in the text confirm this, and other language
teachers like William Stepney and Claudius Hollyband are also satirized.
Eliot's preface, 'To the learned professors of the French tongue', sets the
flippant tone:

> I retired my selfe among the merrie muses, and by the worke of my
> pen and inke, have dezinkhornifistibulated a fantasticall Rapsody of
> dialogisme, to the end that I would not be found an idle drone among
> so many famous teachers and professors of noble languages.

These learned professors are, he concludes, all asses: 'I will be breefe,
and shake you straight by the hands, but because here are three or foure
asses, I shall shake them first by the eares'.[28] This is echoed in Eliot's
'speech' in the *Supererogation*, where he talks of 'having shaken so many
learned asses by the eares, as it were by the hands'. The preface to the
Ortho-epia is dated 18 April 1593; the date at the end of the *Supererogation* is 27 April. Eliot's praise of Nashe as 'villanist' is thus closely linked
with his own venturing into the realm of satire and burlesque. Judging
from his own 'fantasticall Rapsody', his fondness for Nashe's 'smart
pamflet of knavery' is completely sincere. His dialogues consist of little
urban scenarios – 'The Pawne', 'The Apoticarie', 'Dicing', etc. – which
smack of Nasheian journalism. He affirms an admiration for Rabelais,
'that merrie grig', which Nashe shared. And since the language teachers

he pokes fun at were mostly Protestant immigrants, his satire is believed
to have a Catholic tinge of the sort discernible in Nashe. John Eliot is
a somewhat duplex figure in this quarrel: at once close to Nashe in spirit
and to Harvey in fact. That Harvey counted Eliot his friend is confirmed
by some marginal notations in his own copy of Florio's *First Fruites*:
'Florio & Eliot, mie new London companions for Italian & French, two
of the best for both'. This jotting must date from 1593 or later, as
another on the same page refers to Eliot's *Ortho-epia*, which Harvey
found 'fine' and 'pleasant'.[29] It is possible that in John Eliot, hack
translator and fantastical rhapsodist, we have one of the mutual friends
who attempted to reconcile Nashe and Harvey in the summer of 1593.

Harvey's onslaught was not the only ill-will to confront Nashe in the
autumn of 1593. The *Phoenix Nest* anthology also appeared around
this time: it was registered on 8 October. Nashe must have recognized
himself among the anti-Leicester libellers castigated by the editor, 'R.S.'.
He must also have sensed some power behind the counter-blast, for the
Phoenix Nest is no collection of needy scribblers. Its title-page vaunts the
contributors as 'noblemen, worthy knights, gallant gentlemen, masters of
arts and brave scholars'. The tone is that of an aristocratic coterie work:
most of the poems are anonymous, but among the known authors are
the Earl of Oxford, Sir Walter Ralegh, Sir Edward Dyer and probably
Sir Fulke Greville.[30] The whole work is, we remember, an attempt to
revive the Leicester-Sidney ethos, with the Countess of Pembroke as
figure-head. With Ralegh in there as well – also Matthew Roydon, whose
elegy on Sidney opens the volume – it is a movement which epitomizes
the Puritan-esoteric axis attacked in *Pierce Penilesse*. One possible identification of 'R.S.' is Richard Stapleton, who has commendatory verses
before Chapman's *Ovids Banquet* (1595) and whom Chapman later
called 'my most ancient, learned and right noble friend'.[31] Chapman
himself was penning, sometime after September 1593, the preface to his
Shadow of Night. This features a veiled but piquant attack on Nashe.
Having spoken of his own devotion to the 'deepe search of knowledge',
Chapman turns to attack his shallow-brained critics. They are 'passion-
driven men', slaves to 'great mens fancies'. They 'take upon them as
killing censures as if they were iudgements Butchers'. That Nashe is
foremost among these opportunist carpers is quickly made clear. Two
key words identify him:

Now what a *supererogation* in wit this is, to thinke skil so mightily
pierst with their loves, that she should prostitutely shew them her
secrets, when she will scarcely be lookt upon by others but with

invocation, fasting, watching; yea not without having drops of their soules like an heavenly familiar. Why then should our *Intonsi Catones* with their profit-ravisht gravitie esteeme her true favours such questionlesse vanities . . . ? Good Lord how serious and eternall are their idolatrous platts for riches![32]

This is a curious and difficult passage, but it seems probable that Chapman's main target is *Christs Teares*. Nashe, the 'passion-driven' *dilettante*, has aspired to treat weighty matters of divinity and metaphysics, to 'pierce' the 'skill' which is Chapman's own preserve. The phrase '*intonsi Catones*' – long-haired Catos – sums up Chapman's scornful attitude. The Roman philosopher Cato was associated with Stoic austerity and high moral rigour. In *Christs Teares*, Chapman suggests, Nashe plays the moralizing Cato, a preposterous role in view of his loose life-style: he is a long-haired Cato, a yob masquerading as a preacher. A similar charge is contained in the phrase 'profit-ravisht gravitie': that Nashe's new-found seriousness is motivated by greed for 'profit', that *Christs Teares* is a commercial rather than religious venture. It is a mere 'platt' – plot or plan – to get rich, however 'serious and eternall' its subject. There is real animosity in this. The opposition hinted at in *Pierce Penilesse* – occultist and satirist, Ralegh's poet and Strange's wit – here surfaces fully into print. Meanwhile, over at court, another poet was sharpening his quills against Nashe – Sir John Harington, the Queen's 'witty godson', whose opinion of him is expressed in an epigram addressed 'To Doctor Harvey of Cambridge':

> The proverbe sayes, Who fights with durty foes
> Must needs be soyld, admit they winne or lose.
> Then think it doth a Doctors credit dash,
> To make himselfe Antagonist to Nash?[33]

This is Nashe in the autumn of 1593. After the crack-up comes the back-lash. At his lowest ebb – psychologically shaken, 'woe-infirmed', haunted by death and plague – he finds himself 'piteously persecuted' by the civic authorities and harassed by a whole regiment of detractors – Harvey, Barnes, Chute, Fregeville, the 'Gentlewoman', the Countess, 'R.S.', Chapman and Harington. It was at this point that Nashe turned for help to Sir George Carey and his family. His call was heard. As he later said of Carey, with feeling: 'in my most forsaken extremities, right graciously hee hath deigned to revive and refresh mee'.[34]

13

THE CAREYS

'The royall descended Familie of the Careys, but for whom my spirit
long ere this had expyred, and my pen serv'd as a puniard to gall my
owne hart'

The Terrors of the Night

In Sir George Carey Nashe had found an influential and wealthy
benefactor. His father was Henry, 1st Lord Hunsdon, the Queen's first
cousin and her Lord Chamberlain, a bluff, soldierly figure of 'stout
heart', known for his 'downright' manner of 'swearing and obscenity',
his lavish hospitality at Hunsdon House, and his beautiful mistress, the
Italian musician's daughter, Emilia Bassano. In this year 1593, Emilia
got pregnant and 'was for colour married to a minstrel', Will Lanier.[1]
As Chamberlain, Hunsdon championed the players against the civic
authorities: his own troupe, the Lord Chamberlain's Men, reformed in
summer 1594 and swiftly established itself as the top company of the
day, with Shakespeare its poet, Richard Burbage its star and Will Kemp
its comic.[2] As ever we find Nashe close to the literary heartbeat of the
1590s – close also to its intrigues, for Hunsdon's discarded paramour,
Emilia, is a convincing candidate for the real 'dark lady' of Shakespeare's
Sonnets.[3] If the *Sonnets* do describe genuine entanglements, then Emilia
may have been the lover of both Shakespeare and his noble young
master, Southampton. It is a small step to find her reflected in Nashe's
black-eyed beauty, Diamante, wooed by both Jack and his master,
Surrey. If so, Nashe is the first into print with it, the gossip columnist
par excellence, sniffing out a trace of courtly scandal and letting it play
through his innocuous 'historie'.

Born in 1547, Sir George inherited his father's forceful personality,
and followed his footsteps as loyal soldier and civil servant. He served
as Knight Marshal, charged with judicial control within the Queen's
'house and verge': his men, Nashe says, 'naile up Mandates at the Court
gate, for annoying the Pallace with filth or making water'.[4] From 1582
Carey was Captain-General of the Isle of Wight, a key military post in
view of the naval threat from Spain and a useful base for his own
privateering interests. On the Isle he won a reputation for authoritarian
vigour. He was, a later Deputy-Lieutenant recalls,

a man beyond all ambitions, whoe, if owre forefathors had not stoode

181

stiffly to itt, woold have browght us in subiection. Hee was ye fyrst
that assumed ye name of Gouvenour, and caused ye Lecturor soe
to stile him; he bore himselfe soe by reason his fathor was Lorde
Chamberlen.

Islanders who chafed at his rule were swiftly despatched, as Sir Robert
Dillington to the Fleet prison in 1588. When an attorney came to settle
on Wight, a story ran, he was 'hunted owt of ye Island' at Carey's
command, 'with a pownd of candels lyghted hanginge att his breeche'
and 'belles abowt his legges'.[5] Others more powerful felt the force of his
temper – we hear of his 'storm of discord' with Sir Robert Cecil in 1593;
of bitter litigation with his youngest brother, Sir Robert, later the same
year; of his huffiness at the Pembroke family in 1595, after his daughter's
match with the future Earl had been broken off.[6] Not surprisingly this
blustery knight features often in official records as an interrogator of
political suspects. More personal glimpses slightly soften the stern
impression. In a letter to his wife Elizabeth he playfully addresses her as
'my sweet pugge'; his extant letters to the Queen, his cousin, are graceful
and humorous. The Hilliard miniature (Figure 10), painted two years
before his death, shows a tough, broad-browed man, but there is a wry
glint in the eye and a half smile behind the beard. Like many Elizabethans, Carey expressed his power through flamboyant display. He
sported magnificent jewelry: a 'Topas orientall sett about with
diamonds', a 'great Aggate wherein is inclosed the portraiture of Perseus
and Andromache'. He entertained sumptuously at Carisbrooke – 'ye
best hospitalitie at ye Castel as evor wase or will be', according to Sir
John Oglander. There is a touch of the ageing *bon viveur* in the Hilliard
portrait: the sitter was already suffering from the syphilis which eventually killed him.[7] Most important for Nashe in 1593, however, was
that Carey's liberality was frequently extended to scholars and artists.
This drew dedications like a magnet, and among their grateful admirers
Sir George and Lady Elizabeth could count the poets Spenser, Roydon,
Chapman and William Warner; the mathematician, Thomas Heath; the
popular occultist, Simon Forman; the chemist, James Forester; and the
prince of Elizabethan musicians, John Dowland.[8]

The first firm connection between Nashe and the Careys is the dedication of *Christs Teares* to the 'vertuous beautified Ladie, Ladie Elizabeth
Carey, wife to the thrice magnanimous and noble discended Knight, Sir
George Carey'. This was patently written after *Christs Teares* itself; it
was also the last portion of the pamphlet to be printed up, for the same
sheet also contains a list of *errata*. It was probably written in late
September or early October, and this ties in neatly with what we know
of the Careys' movements at this time. Having passed the plague-ridden
summer on the Island, Sir George travelled up in early October

'expressly' to conduct a 'business in law', a property dispute with his dashing young brother, Sir Robert.[9] The latter awaited Sir George's arrival at St Albans, where the Michaelmas law-term was to be held due to plague, with trepidation. His lawyers, he recalls, scarcely 'durst follow the cause, they were so bitterly threatened by my brother's agent, who did assure them my brother would be there himself . . . and then they should see who durst appear to contradict him'. Reaching the outskirts of St Albans, Sir George learned from his 'agent' that brother Robert was there before him, lodged in 'the same house that he was to lie in'. At this news he 'was much troubled, and stood musing with himself a good space; at last, of a sudden he turned his horse's head and came not all to St Albans'. Instead he went to Windsor, where the Queen was holding court in preparation for the Accession Day tilts of November. If she was not already with him, Lady Elizabeth would certainly have joined him at Windsor: this 'excellent accomplisht Court-glorifying Lady' was not one to be left pining in distant Carisbrooke, where, we are told, she 'regarded but three ladies in the island' (Mistresses Oglander, Meux and Hobson) as worthy of her company.[10] At Windsor, it seems likely, Nashe presented his dedication to Lady Elizabeth and was received into the Carey circle. The list of *errata* in *Christs Teares* confirms he was not in London while it was printing, otherwise he would have corrected them in proof. The lodging houses of Windsor, we learn, were packed with 'hangers-on and would-be courtiers', clinging to the fringes of the dislocated court.[11] Among them, probably, Thomas Nashe, sheltering from the plague, 'cleaning out' after the traumas of the summer, pursuing his perennial 'had I wist' hopes of employment and patronage.

It is possible that the man described as Sir George's 'agent' in his law-suit against Robert was one William Cotton.[12] In 1597 we find him acting in a similar legal capacity on Carey's behalf in matters of property. He is described as 'a gent wholly depending' on Carey. He was certainly in Carey's service by 1593, for in that year Carey nominated him MP for Newport. He also performed military duties at Carisbrooke – he is 'Captain William Cotton' in a Privy Council letter of 1596 – and he later served as Esquire of the Body at court, after Carey succeeded as 2nd Lord Hunsdon and Lord Chamberlain. And if Cotton was with the Careys at Windsor this autumn of 1593, it may well have been he who provided Nashe his introduction to the Carey entourage. For it is to 'my worshipfull good freinde Mr William Cotton' that Nashe's only surviving autograph letter is addressed. Written in about September 1596, it begins: 'Sir, this tedious dead vacation is to mee as unfortunate as a terme at Hertford or St Albons to poore cuntry clients' – a recollection, three years later, of this very time when the law-term was removed to St Albans – and concludes, after much legal back-chat and extremely coarse gossip, 'yours in acknowledgement of the deepest bond . . .'. The 'bond' Nashe acknowledges is, perhaps, that Cotton first gained him his *entrée* to the Careys. William was, moreover, a distant relative of Robert Cotton, Nashe's host earlier in the year: this may explain his helping Nashe. Robert Cotton himself was associated with the Careys, though later than this: in 1601 he was one of Carey's nominees to parliament, and a letter of 1608 was addressed to him 'at the Lady Hunsden's lodgings' in Blackfriars.[13] One glimpses the circuitous gathering of contacts, the 'discontented idle trudging from place to place', the hanging around and the swallowed pride, which the writer endured in his quest for patronage: out from his 'Studie or Closet at Court' steps the potentate, 'a goodlie tall fellow that shineth in his silkes', only to tell the attendant scribbler that 'his booke is prety, but at this time he is not provided for him'. When next the writer calls on him, 'his Page shall saie he is not within, or else he is so busie with my L. How-call-ye-him and my L. What-call-ye-him, that he may not be spoken withall'. These are, says Nashe, the 'common courses' of the writer's world.[14]

This time, however, Nashe struck lucky. Another connection may have helped to recommend him to Lady Carey: the eldest daughter of Sir John Spenser of Althorp, she was thus sister-in-law to Lord Strange, Nashe's patron of the previous year. She had already shown 'excellent favours' to Edmund Spenser, who dedicated his *Muiopotmos* (1590) to her and praised her in the 'catalogue' of sonnets before the *Faerie Queene*. To this Nashe gracefully refers: 'Fames eldest favorite, Maister Spenser, in all his writings hie praiseth you'. Nashe asks her to pardon his presumption and to vouchsafe his pamphlet 'benigne hospitalitie in your closet, with slight enterview at idle houres'. He believes she will 'recompence learning extraordinarilie', not like certain other 'female braggarts that contend to have all the Muses beg at their doores' yet have 'Barbarie purses which never ope to any but pedanticall Parasites' (a hit, surely, at the Countess of Pembroke and her 'pedanticke' toady, Hugh Sanford). He promises to devote his 'choisest studies' to 'the eternizing of the heroycall familie of the Careys'. He makes much of Lady Elizabeth's supposed piety: 'to write in Divinitie I would not have adventured, if ought els might have consorted with the regenerate gravitie of your iudgement: your thoughts are all holy, holy is your life'.[15] The fulsome seriousness of the dedication, together with Cotton's good offices and the Strange connection, paid off. As the outcry against him in London swelled, Nashe was packing his bags for the Isle of Wight. He presumably travelled down in the Carey retinue: he later recalled the journey as the best of his life – he 'never had good voyage in his life but one, & that was to a fortunate blessed Iland nere those pinacle rocks called the Needles'. He spent Christmas 1593 'and a great while after' at Carisbrooke Castle.[16]

There Nashe found a brief, rare tranquillity, far from the civic outrage and literary mud-slinging that had threatened to engulf him. The Isle was totally remote. The locals 'seldom or never went out of ye Island', thinking the journey 'a East India voiage'. There was no regular mail-service, letters being carried by the 'coneyman' who came to buy rabbits for the London market. Litigation was almost unheard of – 'in ye Queenes tyme', recalls Sir John Oglander, 'wee had not 6 wrytes in a yeare, nor one *nisi prius* in 6 years'.[17] Nashe looked back on his stay on the Island as a fairy-tale of peace and plenty. It was a place 'fit to seat another Paradise', a 'purified Continent'. The countryside – downs, cornfields, forests and cider orchards, so different from the flat fenny lands he grew up in – was a 'fertil plot', a 'sovereign plenteous scituation', 'so delightfull and pleasaunt'. Newport, the busy fishing town down below the Castle, perhaps tugged at childhood memories of Lowestoft. There was an air of sportsmanship at the Castle – hawking, coursing, wildfowling; bowls on St George's Down – and of liberality: here, he said, 'or in no place, the image of the ancient hospitalitie is to be found'.[18] The Careys no doubt celebrated Christmas in style, so perhaps Nashe was called on to 'fadge up' some entertainment, as he had for Whitgift at Croydon. There would be music in the great hall – not only was Carey an early patron of John Dowland, who dedicated his *First Book of Songs and Ayres* (1597) to him, but we also hear of him taking on an apprentice to be 'enstructed in the arte of music'. The young man was Robert Johnson, son of a Queen's musician: he may have been a kinsman of Lord Hunsdon's ex-mistress, Emilia, whose father was also a Queen's musician and whose mother was born Margaret Johnson.[19] The tunes Dowland wrote for the Careys – 'My Lady Hunsdon's Puff', 'My Lord Chamberlain's Galliard', etc. – give us something of the atmosphere of Carisbrooke revelries.[20]

For all the gravity of *Christs Teares* and its dedication, it is probable that Nashe's prime function was to enliven the company at Carisbrooke. He was the entertainer, the clerk of the drolleries, the racy London wit to offset the tinkling conversation of the three good wives of Wight and the practical chat of Carey's deputies, Dinglie and Leigh. He doubtless had more specific literary-cum-secretarial duties. Lady Elizabeth fancied herself as a poetess – as Nashe flatteringly puts it, 'into the Muses societie her selfe she hath lately adopted, & purchast divine Petrarch another monument in England'[21] – so he probably acted as literary adviser, offering discrete encouragement in her efforts as sonneteer. Another assignment may be hinted at in Nashe's promise to write something wholly devoted to the 'heroycall familie of the Careys' and their 'high allied house'. He speaks of a 'complete historie' he is intending to 'goe through with': 'some longer lyved Tractate I reserve for the full blaze of his [Sir George's] virtues, which here only in sparkes I decypher'.[22] If he wrote it, it has vanished, but it is not implausible that the Careys (typical Tudor *parvenus*: their 'royal' descent stretched back to Ann Boleyn) commissioned him to write some genealogical account of the family — the 'blaze of his virtues' suggesting the 'blazon' of heraldic arms. Nashe the scholar, the friend of Robert Cotton, could easily hack up something convincing: his history and description of Great Yarmouth in *Lenten Stuffe* shows how he could touch dry, factual chronology into life. As well as all this, it is highly likely that Nashe acted as tutor to the Careys' daughter Elizabeth. 'Littel Bes', as her father called her, was seventeen when Nashe arrived at Carisbrooke. She was intended for William Herbert, heir to the Earl of Pembroke, but the match was later 'broken off by his not liking': she married the 7th Lord Berkeley's son, Thomas, in 1596.[23] It was to young Elizabeth that Nashe dedicated his *Terrors of the Night* when it was finally published in autumn 1594. She is a 'high Wonder of sharpe Wit and sweete Beautie', an 'exquisite Mistris' outshining 'all vulgar deep flattred mediochritie'. He speaks of his 'much thankfulnesse', of 'the dutie that I owe', of the 'manie fervent vowes and protestations' she has already 'extracted'. One fancies, amid the hyperbole, a touch of sincere affection, and a poignant fall in the sign-off:

> No more I crave in requitall, but that you would put me in the checke-roule of your remembrance, and not salute me as a stranger.

Acres of social distance stretch between the brisk 'checke-roule' — a list of household servants — and the more private 'remembrance'. Salutation and estrangement: the ups and downs of a hired wit.

It is unclear how long Nashe spent on the Isle of Wight. He simply says he was there at Christmas 'and a great while after'. A remark in *Lenten Stuffe* implies that he was 'present at the arraignment of Lopus' — the trial of the Portuguese physician, Roderigo Lopez, on charges of conspiring to poison the Queen. This took place at the Guildhall on 28 February 1594, so it seems that Nashe was back in London by then.[24] Certain details of the printing of *The Unfortunate Traveller* tend to confirm this. On signature A3 is a *corrigendum* in which Nashe corrects errors 'in the leaves of C and D'. These had slipped through 'in my absence, through the Printers oversight and my bad writing'. It is natural to assume from this that he was on hand for the rest of the printing, and able to correct the sheets in proof. Sheets B, C and D, it seems, had been set up before his departure for the Island, but only B corrected. These three sheets, including the uncorrected C and D, were then printed off during his absence, and it was not until his return to London that the remaining eleven sheets (E to O, and A containing the preliminary matter) were set up, properly corrected and printed. Since *The Unfortunate Traveller* was published in April or May, we might expect production to have resumed on it by March at the latest.[25] Thus glimpsed at the Guildhall and at Thomas Scarlet's printing-shop, the news goes round that Tom Nashe is back in town.

It is clear that Sir George Carey continued to support Nashe through the spring and summer of 1594. There is a passage in praise of Carey inserted into the *Terrors of the Night*: it cannot have been added long before publication – autumn 1594 – for it mentions and quotes the new 'repollished edition' of Camden's *Britannia*, which seems to have been published in September or October.[26] In it Nashe speaks of his stay on the Island in the past ('the continued honorable bountie that I *saw* there') but of Sir George's patronage in the present. In a positive fervour of gratitude, he sums up his position as *protégé*:

Whatsoever minutes intermission I have of calmed content, or least respite to call my wits together, principall and immediate proceedeth from him. Through him my tender wainscot Studie doore is delivered from much assault and battrie: through him I looke into, and am lookt on in the world, from whence otherwise I were a wretched banished exile. Through him all my good (as by a conduit head) is conveighed unto me; and to him all my endevours (like rivers) shall pay tribute as to the Ocean.[27]

There is something more than craven cliché in this. It gives out genuine warmth, and contrasts instructively with the satirical picture of 'the patron' – stingy, snooty, ignorant – that Nashe often gives. No other of his benefactors – Beeston, Strange, Whitgift, Cotton – is so roundly thanked as Sir George Carey and his family. It is possible Nashe lived for a while at Carey's London residence in the Blackfriars, just near the converted refectory where Lyly's comedies had been played by the Chapel Children and where Shakespeare's last plays would have their premières fifteen and more years later. This was a chic part of town, cosmopolitan and well-to-do: it would suit Nashe, as it later did Ben Jonson, who lodged there, and Shakespeare, who bought a house near Puddle Wharf (price £140) in 1613.[28] Nashe would find it convenient for Richard Field's printing-house, also 'in the Black-friers': here the new preface and the cancel-leaf for the second edition of *Christs Teares* were printed, probably in June 1594. Field's other productions for 1594 included James Forester's Paracelsist handbook, *The Pearle of Practise*, dedicated to Carey, and Shakespeare's *Lucrece*, dedicated to Southampton.[29] It was a small world. Casting his *Have with you to*

Saffron-Walden in dialogue-form, Nashe asks us to imagine it as an 'honest conference' being held 'in some nooke or blind angle of the Black-Friers'.[30] His Italianate wits – 'Senior Importuno', 'Domino Bentivole', and so on – are no doubt Blackfriars 'types'.

Nashe would have been a useful man for Sir George to have around in April 1594, when events took place which touched them both. On Friday 5 April, the 5th Earl of Derby, Lord Strange as was, fell sick up in Lancashire. He vomited 'rusty matter with blood', his spleen swelled, he was suffused with 'yealowe jaundies' and racked by a 'vehement hickock' – and yet, mysteriously, his pulse remained as 'good and perfect' as 'in time of his best health'. His physicians tried clysters and catheters, 'bezars stone' and 'unicornes horne': still the Earl weakened. Only an old 'homely woman' with a 'iuyce of certaine herbes' had any success with his symptoms, but she was soon sent packing by the official doctors, among them Robert Cotton's physician, Dr John Case. On 11 April, Strange's wife wrote to Sir Robert Cecil that there was little hope of his recovery. On the 16th, at five o'clock in the afternoon, he died. It was a tragic loss, in his mid-thirties, of a cultivated nobleman-scholar. It was also a sensation, for rumours were rife that Strange had been murdered, either by poison or witchcraft. According to the chronicler John Stow, who later pieced together an account of his death, Strange himself believed he was bewitched: 'in all the time of his sicknesse [he] cryed out that the Doctors laboured in vaine, because he was certainely bewitched.'[31]

Strange's widow, it would seem, immediately turned to Sir George Carey – her efficient, influential brother-in-law – to get to the bottom of the matter. On 21 April we find him visiting Sir Thomas Egerton, Master of the Rolls, bringing with him Messrs Goulborne and Leigh, 'late servants of the Earl of Derby deceased'. Egerton was also well known to Lady Strange – six years later, in fact, he married her. The four men 'conferred' and drew up a list of five of the Earl's former servants 'fittest to be employed' in investigating his death. The following day Carey wrote to his wife, from his Blackfriars house, telling her that Strange had died by 'vilanous poysoning wichecraft'. The poisoning, he says, was 'made manifest by the judgement' of Dr Case and his fellow-physicians, the witchcraft by the confession of a 'wiche apprehended in prison for hit'. The chief evidence of 'enchantement' was 'the finding of his picteur framed in wax, with on of his owne heares prict directly in the hart therof'.[32] This touch of Elizabethan voodoo is corroborated in Stow's account: the figurine was found in Strange's bed-chamber, with hair 'twisted through the belly thereof, from the navell to the secrets'. The investigations continued. On 28 April Carey wrote to Cecil that the enquiry has produced 'greater presumptions that the Earl of Derby was bewitched'. Chief suspect in the matter, thanks to 'a letter found by chance', is one Richard or Robert Dowtie, younger brother of the late Earl's secretary. This Dowtie is 'now in London'. Carey requests a warrant for his arrest and interrogation: 'Dowtie can discover much of the matter, if he be well examined.'[33] What the outcome of this was we do not know. Here the records fade, and Stow's later account throws no light on the matter.

Though he was himself a former 'servant' of Strange's, it is unlikely that the troublesome Nashe was on the official list of investigators drawn up by Carey and Egerton. But unofficially, how useful he could be. He had known Strange, moved in his London circle, been privy to some of its secrets. He was a journalist with contacts in every corner of town. If there was something unsavoury to be sniffed out, Nashe was the man. It is curious, too, how the death of Lord Strange, with its lurid suspicions of 'wichecraft' and 'enchantement', seems to link back to the time of Nashe's involvement with Strange; to those months in 1592 when Nashe was writing *Pierce*, Marlowe *Dr Faustus* and, probably, Chapman *The Shadow of Night*; when all the talk was of devil-raising, atheism and the occult. The more one looks at Strange's career, the more traces one finds of two unorthodoxies, two dangerous 'isms' that have cropped up often, if enigmatically, in the previous chapters: occultism and Catholicism. It is time to consider the case of Lord Strange more closely, as Nashe himself probably did in April 1594.

Lord Strange was born into a family with strong Catholic traditions, and grew up in an area notorious as a stronghold of Catholic reaction. In Lancashire alone, in 1590, some 700 recusants were presented; among the gentry, only ten out of seventy-one were considered reliable supporters of the Anglican establishment.[34] Strange's father, the 4th Earl of Derby, was suspected of overmuch leniency: he was probably a practising Catholic himself. Prominent local Catholics – Hesketh,s Southworths, Pooles, Everards, Molyneux, *et al.* – were frequent guests at Knowsley and Lathom. Some of these had shielded Campion and other seminarists during the doomed Jesuit missions of the 1580s. The notorious turncoat, Sir William Stanley, who surrendered the Dutch garrison of Deventer and defected to the Spaniards, was related to the Derby Stanleys. Strange's brother, Sir Edward Stanley, appears on a Privy Council list of Lancashire recusants and 'dangerous persons' in 1592. A daughter of Sir Rowland Stanley married the Catholic subversive, John Poole, of whom more later. A spy reported in 1589 that the brother of the Jesuit activist, William Holt, was 'one of the Earl of Darbies men, a Romish felow and a secret Papist'.[35] Thus immersed in the old religion, we might expect to find in Strange himself another instance of the young Catholic nobleman, like the Earls of Southampton, Northumberland, Arundel, etc. Whether he actually was a Catholic is a moot point: he seems to have wavered somewhat – he is described in

1593 as 'of no religion' – and when under pressure from the government and the Puritan Bishop Chadderton, he made a show of zeal in enforcing Anglican conformity in Lancashire. What is clear, though, is that his own circle was, like his father's, predominantly Catholic. The Derby 'household books' show him dining, conversing and hunting with Catholic gentry. In his retinue he kept two sons of the renegade Sir William Stanley, and protected them from official interference. Thomas Langton, charged in 1593 with harbouring seminary priests, was a close friend and 'follower of his lordship'. Another man who 'served Lord Strange', Edward Bushell, was implicated in a Jesuit plot to assassinate the Queen in 1594.[36] It is, perhaps, the type of associate Strange had, rather than Strange himself, that this story is about. Two of his associates were Nashe and Marlowe. While not necessarily implicated, they at least rubbed shoulders with this shadier Catholic element around Strange.

Not surprisingly, the government kept a wary eye on Strange, but it was not so much his English circle, as his foreign admirers, that aroused suspicions. As a man of royal blood and deep Catholic root-stock, Strange was the perfect figurehead for English Catholic exiles in their master-plan to topple the Queen and, with Spanish assistance, place a Catholic King on the throne. A partly coded letter from the Jesuit Father Parsons, dated 13 April 1591, is of particular interest. The letter was intercepted, and its codes are explained in the margin, presumably by a government intelligencer. Parsons writes:

> The form in the which you may advertise me may be this, and I pray you note it: Your cousin the baker is well inclined and glad to hear of you, and meaneth not to give over his pretence to the old bakehouse you know of, but rather to put the same in suit when his ability shall serve.

In the margin the intelligencer explains that the words 'baker' and 'bakehouse' signify 'my lord Stra. [i.e. Strange] and the title they would have him pretend when her Majesty dieth'. Again Parsons writes, 'I request you that my cousin's matter be dealt in secrecy, lest it may turn the poor man to hurt', and again this is glossed: 'by his cousin is meant my lord Straunge'. In a superscript, probably addressed to Cecil, the intelligencer says that the letter shows 'it was no matter framed of my own head that which they pretend of my Lord Stra.'.[37] Other documents bear him out on this. A Catholic interrogated in September 1592 asserts that the 'rebels beyond sea' are looking to certain of the English nobility to further their cause: he names Lord Strange as one of the nobles, 'much alienated by discontent', who would be 'easily moved to follow the Spaniard'. In summer 1593, a spy in Rome is asked by an English priest for news of Strange, 'with this interrogation: There is not any words of his interest?' At about the same time, Sir William Stanley was trying to arrange 'some priest that might gain access to Lord Strange'. He too cherished hopes of Strange: with the Queen assassinated, 'he would go to Scotland with his regiment, make it strong, and go to the Earl of Derby, as would all the English.'[38]

These fragmentary records give no hint as to Strange's own feelings about his 'interest' in the throne. Far better documented, and somewhat more compromising for Strange himself, is the 'Hesketh plot' of late 1593.[39] Organized by English exiles in Prague, this was another attempt to enlist Strange as the figurehead of a Catholic *coup* against Elizabeth. Their original target was Strange's father, upon whose death they switched their attentions to the new Earl. Spearhead of the mission was one Richard Hesketh, a 'yellow haired' Lancashire Catholic who had been in Prague since about 1590. He arrived in England in late September 1593. His way to the Earl was smoothed by certain Catholic members of the retinue – his letter of introduction delivered by Sir Edward Stanley; he himself brought before the Earl by Thomas Langton. Strange certainly knew the Hesketh family: Richard's father and brother, Sir Thomas and Bartholomew Hesketh, were frequent guests at the Derby seats, and there is some evidence that Strange had known Richard himself.[40] The meeting, it seems, went well. In letters dated 2 October Hesketh wrote that his fears of how Strange 'would accept of my coming' had proved groundless. 'Having seen my passport', the Earl 'hath taken such a liking of me, that for his recreation I must needs keep him company to London or the court.' Two weeks later, however, Hesketh was not at court but in prison, being interrogated about his accomplices and about 'how far forth he hath proceeded with the Earl of Derby further than he hath declared'. It appears that Strange himself had turned Hesketh in – that was *his* version, anyway: 'my Lord of Derby, being by him [Hesketh] moved &c, did presently apprehend the party and made it known to her Majesty.'

Despite his apparently honourable dealings, Strange had not heard the last of this matter. On 9 November he wrote to Cecil from Lancashire, complaining that one of Hesketh's brothers, a lawyer, is trying to 'crosse me and win himself some credit'. This Hesketh is now in London, 'at the term', and Strange asks that he be prevented from 'going about in malice as he doth, to draw the government from me to himself'. Did this trouble-maker have some information which Strange wished suppressed, some evidence that might 'draw' government suspicions? Others more powerful added their doubts. Sir Thomas Heneage, Vice-Chamberlain, told Cecil he had 'good experience' of this Hesketh, and he was 'sorry my Lord [i.e. Strange] should conceive ill opinion' of him. Most pointedly of all, shortly before Hesketh's trial on 28 November, Lord Keeper Puckering wrote to Cecil requesting some explanation of Strange's role in the affair. 'Mr Attorney', he writes, believes that Strange has acted honourably but he has no proof: he 'desireth to be advertised from you of some other that knoweth this to be so'; he has 'no ground as of himself, either of his own knowledge or by examination, to affirm it'. Clearly there were still doubts about Strange in high places. One inference from this is that the government had never shared with Strange its knowledge about Catholic designs on him: it had waited to see which way he would jump. With help from his powerful ally Cecil, the 'Hesketh affair' was tidied away. At his trial Hesketh 'did confess the indictment and acknowledge all'; there 'needed no other testimony'. On 29 November he was hanged at St Albans. The next day Strange's wife wrote to Cecil in thanks: 'it is no little comfort to me, my good cousin, that my Lord finds you so good a friend.' Yet even now she fears that her husband's name is not altogether cleared, that he will encounter more 'malice' and 'be crossed in his court and crossed in his country'.[41] In the light of all this, it is no wonder that Strange's untimely death a few months later caused comment. Had he – the rumour-mongers perhaps asked – been more seriously implicated in the Hesketh plot than appeared? Was he murdered by Catholics, in revenge for his shopping of Hesketh, or because he knew too much about Catholic conspiratorial plans?[42] The fugitive Dowtie, hunted by Sir George Carey in the weeks after Strange's death, no doubt knew the answers. And Tom Nashe, I am sure, knew a good deal more than we do. These later events cast a curious light back on Nashe and Strange in 1592. One recalls the pro-Catholic touches in *Pierce Penilesse*, dedicated to Strange. One hears again Beale's remarks about *Pierce* – such 'contumelious' pamphlets are 'well liked' by the Pope and by 'the English Jesuits, Seminaries and traitors abroad'.

Tracking through the penumbra of the Strange circle, certain connections emerge between this militant Catholic element and some of the more dubious forms of occultism. These too suggest something of the atmosphere out of which *Pierce, Faustus* and the *Shadow of Night* emerge. From Hesketh's confessions, and subsequent government enquiries, we know something of the circle of English exiles in Prague which set up the ill-fated *coup*. Among those involved were the Jesuit priest, Thomas Stephenson; a goldsmith named Tankard; Henry Leigh, a Lancashire man known to Strange; and Thomas Kelley. This last name rings a bell, for he was the brother of Edward Kelley, the alchemist, spiritualist and magical showman who enjoyed a huge notoriety at this time.[43] Kelley was himself in Prague in 1593, though probably in prison. He had grown famous as the accomplice of Dr John Dee. Together they toured central Europe in the 1580s, performing alchemical transmutations and 'angelic conferences'. Kelley won great favour with Emperor Rudolf II, a devotee of the occult, whose court at Prague was the 'headquarters of adepts and adeptship'. He was knighted, incorporated into the Imperial Privy Council and granted lands 'yeilding £1500 yerely'. By 1591, however, the Emperor had tired of him. Spells of imprisonment and torture followed. News of his death reached England in 1595.[44] This daemonic figure was undoubtedly involved with the Catholic plotters in Prague. Leigh had travelled there in 1591 expressly 'to seek some favour of Sir Edward Kelley'. Stephenson and Tankard, we are told, 'did divers times resort to' Kelley's house in Prague. Hesketh in prison wonders if 'Mr Dear' – Sir Edward Dyer, the poet and diplomat closely involved with Kelley – knows of his capture, 'for if it be bruited amongst his men or followers, they will straight write to my lady Kelley [Joan, wife of Edward] or Mr Thomas Kelley'. These twin threads – Catholicism and occultism – meet in Rodolfine Prague, the seat of the Holy Roman Empire and the 'metropolis of magic'.

It is possible that Strange actually knew Edward Kelley, before the latter left for Bohemia in 1583. Kelley's early career is a tissue of crooked exploits – fraud, coining, black magic – and from the resulting records it appears he was up in Lancashire, Strange's country, in the early 1580s. At Lancaster in about 1580 he had his ears cropped for coining base money. He was also in trouble for digging up corpses, for necromantic purposes, at Walton-le-Dale. This brings us close to Strange, for at Walton the local squire, the spuriously titled 'Baron of Walton', was Thomas Langton, Strange's close friend and follower. One wonders if there was some odd little coterie up there, involving Langton and Strange, both in their early twenties, with the charismatic Kelley. We know from Camden that Strange's mother was an enthusiast of 'astrology and divination'. We hear of the great screen hanging at Lathom, decorated with zodiacal devices and verses 'garnisht' from 'astronomy and astrologie'. We see the portrait of another companion of Strange's younger days, Thomas ffarington, with its studied, scholarly melancholy.[45] It is not hard to imagine Strange and his friends falling under the spell of Kelley, drawn to dabble in occult rituals, even such as required a fresh supply of corpses from Walton churchyard. Richard Hesketh was himself still in Lancashire in the early 1580s. Thomas Langton certainly knew him, indeed in 1589 both men were involved in the killing of one Houghton. Hesketh fled to Prague (because Kelley was there?) but Langton stood his ground. No-one was more energetic in his defence than Lord Strange: in April 1590, the 'household books' record, 'My L. Strandge wente towardes the Assizes in Lanc. concerning Mr Baron of Walton's cawses.'[46] When Hesketh returned on his mission in 1593, it was Langton who brought him into Strange's company. In November, with Hesketh under interrogation, Langton was himself arrested on charges of harbouring Catholic priests. It begins to look as if the seeds of the Hesketh plot had been sown back in Lancashire in the 1580s, and that Kelley is a lurking presence at every stage of its growth. One looks again at the rumours of 'enchantement' surrounding Strange's death, as recounted by Stow. We hear of troubled nights, when Strange 'sodainely cryed out, started from his bed, called for helpe, sought about the chamber', and of trances when he was 'not able to moove hand, head or foot'. There was an apparition, 'a tall man with a ghastly and threatening countenance': when this 'shaddow' appeared to him, Strange 'fell sicke and there vomited thrise'. There was the episode of the figurine, stabbed through with one of his hairs. It is hard to resist hearing echoes of Kelley in all this: the necromancer of nearby Walton, the plotters' host in distant Prague. In Strange's highly suscep- tible mind, at least, one suspects this connection was made. Whatever the true cause of his death, it seems likely that the names of Kelley, Langton and Hesketh cropped up often during Carey's subsequent investigation.

A different story reveals a similar pattern. The scene now switches to Newgate prison, July 1587, where one John Poole lies languishing in the dungeon known as 'the Limboes'.[47] He had been arrested 'upon suspicon of Coigninge', though he also claimed he had been mistakenly taken for a Catholic priest because he wore a shaven crown. One night he conversed on state matters with one Humphrey Gunston: Gunston was a plant, and delivered a full account of Poole's 'traitorous speeches' to the authorities. As well as confirming Poole's guilt as a coiner, they show him to be a militant Catholic malcontent. He discourses enthusias- tically on the 'straunge and rare matter' he has read in Father Parsons' *Leycesters Commonwealth*. He defends Sir William Stanley's treason in delivering Deventer to the Spanish and casts aspersions on Stanley's chief enemy, Ralegh. He boasts he has 'persuaded with divers to goe ynto Ireland', an action associated with fractious Catholics. Poole's original offence – coining counterfeit money – was the crime that had cost Kelley his ears at Lancaster. It was the crooked branch of alchemy. A coiner arrested in 1570, one Bedo, drew his recipes from the alchemical sections of della Porta's *Magia Naturalis*. Paracelsus' *De Natura Rerum* describes how to 'sublimate copper and reduce it to a fixed substance, as white as Luna [silver]'. When 'other subtill shifts doe faile', says Thomas Lodge, alchemists 'fall to coyning' and find themselves dancing 'through hempen windowes'.[48] We are back in that same curious underworld, where the grubbier forms of 'magick' mingle with clandestine Catholic aspirations. And once again it leads back to Lord Strange, for this Poole was a Cheshire gentleman almost certainly known to him. He was married to a daughter of Sir Rowland Stanley: the traitor Sir William was therefore his brother-in-law, and Strange his noble kinsman. In October 1587, moreover, we find Poole's father, 'Jhon Pole', and 'one other of the Poles' dining with Strange and his father at Knowsley.[49]

This was just three months after John Poole junior had been shooting his mouth off in Newgate. As always, we cannot quite put the finger on Strange. Poole is just another dubious customer hovering round the edges of his circle.

We meet Poole again, still in Newgate, in September 1589, entertaining a young fellow-prisoner with his crooked chemistry and subversive sentiments. This was none other than Christopher Marlowe, imprisoned with Tom Watson after the Hog Lane brawl. Among Marlowe's 'damnable' opinions, drawn up for the Privy Council by the informer Baines, was the claim

> that he had as good Right to Coine as the Queene of England, and that he was acquainted with one Poole a prisoner in Newgate who hath greate skill in mixture of mettals, and having learned some thinges of him, he ment through help of a Cunninge stamp maker to coin ffrench Crownes, pistoletes and English shillinges.

In the same document, we remember, Marlowe's Catholic sympathies are voiced: 'if there be any God or any good Religion, then it is in the Papistes'. Marlowe's meeting with Poole in Newgate leads us naturally to another scenario, another of Marlowe's brushes with the law. We are now in Vlissingen, or Flushing, in Holland.[50] On 26 January 1592, the Governor of the town, Sir Robert Sidney, sent over his 'ancient' to England. With him were the ubiquitous Richard Baines and two prisoners under escort – a goldsmith named Gifford Gilbert and a 'scholer' named 'Christofer Marley'. The charge against them was coining. According to Baines, who says he was Marlowe's 'chamber-fellow' at Flushing, Marlowe had persuaded the goldsmith into it in order to test his 'conning'. It was his intention 'to practis yt heerafter' – he seems to have been intent on putting those 'thinges' he learned from Poole into practice – but the plan was nipped in the bud by Baines' exposure. They had made, in fact, just one coin, a Dutch shilling, and that a poor counterfeit – 'I do not think', wrote the Governor, 'that they wold have uttred many of them, for the mettal is plain peuter and with half an ey to be discovered.' And together with this charge of coining – as we have almost come to expect – is an accusation of seditious Catholicism. According to Baines, Marlowe had 'intent to goe to the Ennemy or to Rome'. The 'enemy', here in war-torn Holland, means the Spanish army fighting the Anglo-Dutch Protestant forces – the regiment under the command of Sir William Stanley, perhaps, which had been in action at Nijmegen a few months earlier. It was under questioning at Flushing that Marlowe claimed, in his defence, that he was 'very wel known to both the Earl of Northumberland and my Lord Strang'. Here Strange is coupled with another patron, the Catholic and occultist Northumberland, amid this

dubious aura of seditious coining. Nor were Poole and Marlowe the
only members of Strange's circle involved in this type of enterprise.
Another nest of Catholic coiners surfaces in August 1594, charged with
the theft of '£1800 worth of plate from Winchester church to turn into
coin'. The plate, 'melted and coined' in the chambers of Sir Griffin
Markham, was to finance yet another *coup* against the Queen. Among
those under arrest was Edward Bushell, who had formerly 'served Lord
Strange'.[51]

Apart from Marlowe's brief career as a coiner, there is no actual
documentary evidence to link the literary side of Strange's circle with
the conspiratorial Catholic side. How much Marlowe and Nashe knew
of the latter is uncertain. Marlowe has a long history of ambiguous
Catholic connections, dating back to the affair over his MA; among his
companions were agents like Baines, Poley and Friser, his killer. His
involvement in the Catholic manoeuvrings around Strange is not improbable. With Nashe we can only say that he exhibits Catholic attitudes
from time to time, and that he was the sort of man who knew what
was going on around him. At the least this tangle of conspiracy seems
to provide a secret historical backdrop for *Dr Faustus* and *Pierce Penilesse*, with their Catholic tones and occultist themes. Nashe's political
butts in *Pierce*, the work he dedicated to Strange, are Leicester and
Ralegh, the same two men that Poole less discreetly denounced in
Newgate. The conjuring of devils in both works may contain traces of
the necromantic Kelley and his connections with Strange. Nashe makes
a joke of the occultist dream, a genial satirical deflation. Lord Strange
found the whole business less funny in late 1593, when his dubious
connections brought him into political danger, and in April 1594, when
they possibly cost him his life.

Is there anything in Nashe's writings *post* Strange's death that reflects
on these events? Possibly. Though he wrote no new work in 1594, we
know that he revamped *The Terrors of the Night* for publication: the
fact that it was registered anew by Danter implies it was altered substantially from the original version of 1593. The praise of Carey and the
dedication to his daughter are additions: so too, it has been argued, is
the long, self-contained description of the 'cunning-man' and his rise to
high places.[52] At one point, this phoney magician 'sets up a coniuring
schoole, and undertakes to play the baud to Lady Fortune'. His
prescience wins him powerful friends:

> Great peeres entertaine him for one of their privie counsaile, and if
> they have anie daungerous enterprise in hand, they consult with him

about successe. All malcontents entending anie invasive violence against their Prince and Countrey runne headlong to his oracle. Contrarie factions enbosome unto him their inwardest complots, whilest he like a craftie Iacke a both sides, as if he had a spirite still at his elbow, reciprocallie embowelleth to the one what the other goes about; receiving no intelligence from anie familiar but their own mouths. I assure you most of our chiefe noted Augurers and Soothsayers in England at this day, by no other Arte but this gaine their reputation. They may verie well picke mens purses, like the unskilfuller cousning kind of Alchumists, with their artificiall and ceremoniall Magicke, but no effect shall they atchieve thereby, though they would hang themselves: the reason is, the divell of late is growen a puritane, and cannot away with anie ceremonies.

Fraudulent alchemy, ceremonial magic, devil-raising: this sounds much like our friend Edward Kelley. One of the 'great peeres' who entertained him might be Lord Strange. The magician's involvement in 'invasive violence' against the realm would refer to the Hesketh plot, hatched by Kelley's friends in Prague. There is an equation, at the end of the passage, between 'ceremoniall Magicke' and the ceremonial nature of Catholicism. The element of duplicity – a crafty 'Jack-of-both-sides' – may well be an accurate picture of Kelley's involvement in the affair. We know that Kelley was in constant touch with Lord Burghley, via Dyer, in the early 1590s. Placed at the heart of the Catholic Imperial court, he may easily have been feeding information back to England. Was it his duplicity, rather than alchemical disappointments, that led Emperor Rudolf to arrest both him and Dyer in 1591? There are other touches of Kelley in Nashe's cunning man. These magicians get their grounding as 'Apothecaries prentises': Kelley began his career as an apothecary's apprentice in Worcester. They first set up their operation 'farre North' or in 'some such rude simple countrey', as Kelley did in Lancashire. As so often with Nashe, a seemingly general portrait throws out teasing specificities.

Kelley is not the only real person glanced at in Nashe's sketch. There is another of 'these great famous Coniurers' that the reader of 1594 might recognize in it – Simon Forman. In fact the general reader, unaware of the Kelley-Strange connection, might see it primarily as a burlesque of Forman. Nashe speaks of 'our chiefe noted Augurers and Soothsayers in England at this day', and the chiefest of them was not Kelley, now incarcerated in Bohemia, but the astrologer-physician Forman. The interesting point about this is that one of Forman's patrons was Sir George Carey. Considering the strongly admonitory tone of the passage, I suspect that Nashe is playing off these two portraits, of Kelley and Forman, for Sir George's benefit; that the Kelley-Strange hints are there as a kind of warning about Carey's harbouring the likes of Simon Forman.

At some points, Nashe's burlesque biography serves Kelley and Forman alike. Forman was also an 'Apothecaries prentise', bound to Master Commin of Salisbury in the 1560s. He also began his career as a country cunning-man, not 'farre North' but in the 'rude simple countey' of Wiltshire. Elsewhere, Forman's own diary shows how right Nashe has got his picture. In 1579, in Wiltshire, Forman wrote: 'This year I did prophesy the truth of many things which afterwards came to pass; the very spirits were subject unto me; what I spake was done; and I had a great name'. Nashe says: 'with their vaunting and prating, and speaking fustian in steede of Greeke, all the Shyres round about do ring with their fame'. From at least 1580, Forman was 'curing sick and lame folk' and 'practising physic and surgery' at Salisbury. Nashe: 'they rake some dunghil for a few durtie boxes and plaisters, and of tosted cheese and candles endes temper up a fewe oyntments and sirrups'. In 1589, Forman settled in London: 'very poor and without a penny, I took a chamber at James Ash's in Barbican'. Nashe: 'having pickt up theyr crummes thus pretely well in the Countery . . . at length into London they filtch themselves prively'. One of Forman's early associates in London was Emery Molyneux the globe-maker, at whose house in Lambeth he stayed in 1591. Forman claimed to have taught Molyneux 'the longitude': his own *Grounds of Longitude* was published later that year. Molyneux is perhaps reflected in the accomplice Nashe gives his cunning-man, a 'dappert Mounsier Diego' who has 'a little skill in his Iacobs staffe and hys Compasse, being able at all times to discover a new passage to Virginia'. In among the sexual puns is an apt hit at the celebrated compass- and globe-maker, whose 'exact terrestrial Globe' incorporated the 'secretest and latest discoveries' in the Americas. Nashe mentions 'Molenax great Gloabe' (completed in 1592) elsewhere in the *Terrors*. Molyneux may well have introduced Forman to wealthy clients, as Nashe's 'dappert Mounsier' does here.[53]

It is particularly Nashe's emphasis on the cunning-man as physician which chimes in with Forman. Kelley no doubt included healing in his magical repertoire – there is a letter from Lord Burghley asking him for some 'receipt' (i.e. recipe) against 'my old enemy, the gout' – but it was not a speciality of his. It certainly was with Forman, whose physic grew famous in London during the plague of 1592–3. In these years, he wrote, 'I did many notable cures and began to be known', and 'I distilled my strong water, for the which I got much money'. By 1596 he was earning £300 *per annum* and attracting a fashionable clientele, whose secrets – medical and otherwise – he recorded in his case-books. As his mention of 'strong water' suggests, Forman embraced the fashionable Paracelsist medicine, with its 'chymicall' extracts and magical overtones. We hear of his 'compound waters', his *aqua vitae*, his electuary of sweet roses for the 'hectical and tabid' (i.e. consumptive). He diagnosed astrologically: 'as Saturn doth cause the black plague, so Mars doth cause the red', he wrote in 1593. He announced himself a healer guided 'according to the course of heaven and nature'. He decried the medical orthodoxy of Galen; the Royal College of Physicians, staunchly Galenist, retorted by fining and imprisoning this 'intruder into the profession of physic', so 'notorious an imposter'.[54] In 1594, when Nashe composed this portrait, Forman was probably the leading popular practitioner of Paracelsist medicine in London. This is exactly the type of physician Nashe is satirizing:

This newe Phisition . . . rayleth on our Galenists, and calls them dull gardners and hay-makers in a mans belly, compares them to dogs, who when they are sick eate grasse . . .

His horse-leach will leap over the hedge & ditch of a thousand Dioscorides and Hippocrates, and give a man twentie poysons in one, but he would restore him to perfit health . . .

The hungrie druggier . . . speaks nothing but broken English like a French Doctor, pretending to have forgotten his naturall tung by travell . . .

He . . . will sweare he can extract a better Balsamum out of a chip than the Balm of Iudaea: yea, all receipts and authors you can name he syllogizeth of, & makes a pish at, in comparison of them he hath seen and read . . .

This is most certaine, if he be of any sect he is a mettle-bruing Paracelsian, having not past one or two Probatums for al diseases.

As a 'noted augurer', a 'metal-brewing Paracelsian' and a *protégé* of Sir George Carey, Simon Forman is a strong candidate for the original of Nashe's cunning-man in *The Terrors of the Night*.

The earliest record of Carey's association with Forman is 22 December 1587, when Forman visited him at Carisbrooke. In 1588, William Monson, captain of one of Carey's privateering vessels, consulted with Forman to know 'how he should speed in his voyage for Sir George'. Another of Carey's seamen at this time was Stephen Michell, Forman's half-brother and his sometime 'scryer' (spirit-medium). In 1596, battling with the Royal College of Physicians, Forman wrote to Carey for help. In 1601, Carey's sister – Margaret, Lady Hoby – consulted Forman on her brother's behalf: he was suffering from syphilitic palsy.[55] His disability is referred to in an anonymous court lampoon of about 1601, which says of him:

> Foole hath he ever bin
> with his Joane silverpin
> She makes his cockescombe thin
> and quake in everie limme
> Quicksilver is in his head
> but his wit's dull as lead.

'Quicksilver' refers to the mercurial preparations prescribed by Paracelsians – and probably by Forman – for syphilis: 'mercury sublimed' (as Nashe puts it) 'is a good medicine for the itch'.[56] In July 1602, a gossipy letter relates, Carey dined too liberally, whereupon

> he called his apothecary to make him a suppositer, which wrought such alteration that he sounded [swooned] and continued dead 3½ hours; but a servant remembering a water which my Lord used, called spirit of sack, poured some into his mouth, which revived him.

This 'spirit of sack' would be a 'distilled water' or *aqua vitae* of the type Forman dealt in. The Earl of Northumberland's distiller, Roger Cook, brewed a similar sack-based 'distillacone' called '*spiritus dulcis*'.[57]

Forman was not the only Paracelsian favoured by Carey. In this year, 1594, James Forester dedicated his *Pearle of Practise* to 'his honorable good Patrone, Sir George Carey', praising him as one who bears 'so good and liberall a minde to learning and learned workemen'. 'Workman' in this context means 'chemist': it is a literal translation of Latin '*laborator*'; the alchemist's laboratory is similarly called a 'work-house'. Forester asks Carey to shield his book from 'the venemous darts of carping toungs' that decry 'Paracelsicall phisicke' – he had perhaps crossed paths with Nashe at Sir George's house, or at Richard Field's printing-house. Forester himself lived in the Blackfriars, where he signed the prefatory epistle to the *Pearle*, 19 January 1594.[58] Forester is not actually portrayed in Nashe's burlesque in *The Terrors* – he was a Cambridge man, a divinity scholar, not a country wizard made good – but it is interesting, in the general context of this chapter, to find charges of religious subversion hanging over Forester as well. He was not a Catholic, but a Puritan extremist, and in March 1593 he was indicted at the Old Bailey for his part in publishing works which 'cry down the church of England and the Queen's prerogative'. These were the pamphlets of the 'Independents', Barrow and Greenwood, smuggled out in 'slips and fragments' from the Fleet prison. In the dock Forester disavowed their 'sharpe maner of writing' and was pardoned.[59] Barrow and Greenwood were hanged in April, part of the same clean-up which saw the execution of the Martinizer, John Penry. Again we probe into the occult world and find seditious religious connections. The anti-Paracelsist elements of Nashe's cunning-man sketch, though primarily aimed at Forman, take in Forester as well.

We now have a full reading of this complex, witty passage. Its message is directed to Sir George Carey, Nashe's patron and protector. It reminds him of the heinous Kelley and of the dangers that Lord Strange brought on himself by associating with him. It points a finger at his own favoured occultist, Simon Forman, as a potential Kelley. Such men are dangerous, Nashe is saying. They will entangle you in darkness and conspiracy: they will bring you, in fact, the 'terrors of the night', such as Strange himself suffered in the last days of his life. Indeed the whole pamphlet, with its apparitions and nocturnal superstitions, seems appropriate in the aftermath of Strange's death, especially since Carey had himself investigated the matter. This may be hinted at in Nashe's dedication to Carey's daughter Elizabeth, also added in 1594. He says to her: 'you partly are acquainted from whose motive imposition it [*The Terrors*] first proceeded, as also what strange sodaine cause necessarily produced that motion.' It sounds as if Nashe is saying that the 'motive imposition', or commissioning, of the pamphlet came from Sir George, and the 'strange sodaine cause' for it was the sudden death of Strange. We know that the pamphlet had originally been written, in Huntingdonshire, some eighteen months before it was published. Strange's death would offer a topical peg to hang it on, and it may well be true that *The Terrors*, with its troubled but essentially rationalist treatment of 'apparitions', was revamped at the request of Carey. The occult pursues Nashe wherever he goes. It was the great Elizabethan enthusiasm, a gamut ranging from the refined Hermetic reformism of Bruno and Dee to the underworld of coiners and gimcrack necromancers. Nashe despised and attacked it, almost obsessively so, a hostility born out of fear. We remember the little boy in Norfolk, listening spellbound to the old wives' witchcrafts. The enemies he chose in later life – Leicester, Ralegh, the Pembroke circle, the Harveys, Chapman – were all enthusiasts of occultism in its more intellectual aspects. In the preface to the *Shadow of Night*, Chapman praises Carey as 'skill-imbracing heire of Hunsdon', placing him alongside 'ingenious' Strange and 'deepe searching' Northumberland, the so-called Wizard Earl. The 'skill' Carey embraced was probably alchemy, especially in its therapeutic Paracelsist form. We see the debate, the tug of war: Chapman luring Carey into the role of occultist patron, Nashe pulling him away with this warning burlesque. Shakespeare treads this path a few years later, in *The Merry Wives of Windsor*. In the comic French physician, Dr Caius, we get another guying – somewhat gentler than Nashe's – of the fashionable Paracelsians. The play was first performed by the Lord Chamberlain's Men at the Garter Feast of April

1597. It was almost certainly commissioned by the troupe's new patron, who was one of the Garter Knights installed that year: Sir George Carey.[60]

14

MASTER MOTH

'When thou with rebukes dost correct man for iniquity, thou makest his
beauty to consume away like a moth'

Psalm 39

By a curious oversight, the greatest of Nashe's literary contemporaries
is the one never mentioned by name in his pamphlets. This is partly
a trick of perspective: during Nashe's brief reign as a commentator,
Shakespeare was only one talent among many. With the status of the
playwright still questionable, his serious reputation rested largely on his
'sugred' love poetry – *Venus*, *Lucrece*, and such of the sonnets as filtered
out in manuscript. We have Nashe's generous 'puff' for *Henry VI* – the
first printed reference to a Shakespeare play, even if Shakespeare is not
named – and we have his glancing reference to 'the Countie Beroune'
in the summer of 1594, probably reflecting Shakespeare's Berowne in
Loves Labors Lost. But apart from these, nothing. All is not lost,
however. Though older by three years, Shakespeare was Nashe's literary
junior in the early 1590s: it is he who reflects Nashe, not *vice versa*. His
early plays – notably *The Taming of the Shrew*, *Loves Labors Lost* and
the Falstaff comedies – are full of stylistic and atmospheric echoes of
Nashe, and the character of Moth in *Loves Labors Lost* is an unmistakable portrait of him. These help us piece something together about the
relationship of these two writers, who must often have met in London
literary circles and through their shared interest in the favours of Strange,
Southampton and Sir George Carey.

The Taming of the Shrew is Shakespeare's first recognizably Shakespearean comedy. His other early comedies – *The Two Gentlemen* and
The Comedy of Errors – are stiffer, more cautiously close to their
models, pastoral and Plautine. In the *Shrew* Shakespeare achieves a
richer, seamier language, the first hints of Falstaff. There are strong
indications that the play was first composed in about 1589–90, though
it may well have been worked over later. The earliest authentic text
appears in the Folio of 1623, but it is now thought that the anonymous
Taming of a Shrew (1594) contains memories of an earlier version of
Shakespeare's play, now lost. Another curiosity is the list of Shakespeare's comedies drawn up by Francis Meres in 1598. Meres does not
include the *Shrew*, but he does mention a comedy called *Loves Labours*

Wonne. This is either an unknown play or, more likely, an alternative title for the *Shrew*, in which a love is indeed hard-won.¹ If so, it seems possible that the *Shrew* was in some way 'twinned' with *Loves Labors Lost*. Of these more later: we first turn to the authentic *Shrew* and its bearings on Nashe.

The Taming of the Shrew, though it has its emotional subtleties, is essentially straightforward. It is a comedy of confrontation: one central duel with various peripheral rivalries and *rapprochements* around it. The eponymous shrew, Katherina, a 'brawling scold' full of 'loud alarums', finally meets her match in the opportunist young gallant, Petruchio. He is variously described as a 'mad-cap ruffian and swearing Jack', a 'mad brain'd rudesby full of spleen', a 'frantic fool hiding bitter jests in blunt behaviour'. The dominant tone – indeed, the monotone – of the play is one of raillery, insult, verbal violence. The gallants and their henchmen are 'quick-witted folks', they 'butt together well'. They thrive on repartee, back-chat, wit-combats – 'have at you for a bitter jest or two' . . . 'a good swift simile, but something currish' . . . 'the jest did glance away from me, 'tis ten to one it maimed you'. The play is, in short, soaked with the volatile, contentious tones of the 'University Wits'. The verbal 'rope-tricks' of Petruchio and Kate go together, in time and mood, with the scoffs of Nashe and the quips of Greene, the 'froth of witty Tom Watsons jests' and the 'merry conceited jests of George Peele'. Petruchio threatens to 'throw a figure in her face and so disfigure her with it that she shall have no more eyes to see withal than a cat' – his rhetorical 'figures' are a caustic splash of derision, just as Nashe threatens Richard Harvey: 'I have tearmes laid in steepe in *Aquafortis*' . . . 'I squirt inke into his decayed eyes.' Kate in turn promises

> To comb your noddle with a three-legged stool
> And paint your face and use you like a fool.

– a boisterous verbal belabouring of the kind offered by Nashe: 'swinge him with Sillogismes' . . . 'spurgalling an Asse' . . . 'off with thy gowne and untrusse, for I mean to lash thee mightily'.²

It is not just as witty railers that the characters in the *Shrew* echo the London Wits. They catch them also in social manner and status. Lucentio arrives in Padua as a young gentleman-scholar in pursuit of 'ingenious studies' in philosophy: clearly a university man. He worms his way into the Minola household as a tutor. His attire is 'mean' but he seems a youth of 'learning and behaviour fit' and 'well-read in poetry and other books'. This is the Wits' world again, the threadbare scholar moving among the moneyed, touting his learning. He is presented to his employer as a 'young scholar that hath been long studying at Rheims' and is 'cunning in Greek, Latin and other languages'. This sounds much like 'witty Tom Watson', who had indeed studied at the Catholic seminary

at Douai (which removed to Rheims in 1578); who was prized as a
linguist and translator from Greek, Latin and Italian; and who was
employed as a tutor in the early 1590s by the Cornwallises of
Bishopsgate, an area of London Shakespeare himself lodged in. While
there, Watson was involved in romantic intrigue, helping his brother-in-
law, Thomas Swift, to woo the eldest Cornwallis daughter, Frances.
There were elements of fraud in this – Frances apparently signed a
marriage contract thinking it was another document entirely – and
Cornwallis *père* fulminated furiously about Watson's 'fictions and knaveryes'.[3] Much the same romantic disguisings and disruptions dog the
Minola household after Lucentio and Petruchio arrive. There is a
substratum of reality in the *Shrew*'s manic intrigues. We remember too
Watson's gulling of old Mistress Burnell, the *soi-disant* daughter of the
King of Spain. This more unpleasant tone is in the *Shrew* as well: the
mentality is hard, the humour has victims. The Wits lived close to
physical violence: Kyd spoke of Marlowe's 'attempting soden privy iniuries to men'; Nashe recalled Greene forcing a bailiff to 'eate his citation,
waxe and all, very handsomly serv'd twixt two dishes'; Watson left
William Bradley dead in a ditch on Hog Lane.[4] Petruchio has the same
over-excitable temper, the same hint of psychosis: he is 'half-lunatic',
some 'odd humour pricks him'. At his wedding he fetches the priest a
hearty 'cuff', he 'stamps and swears' and 'calls for wine':

> . . . A health, quoth he, as if
> He had been aboard, carousing to his mates
> After a storm; quaff'd off the muscadel
> And threw the sops all in the sexton's face.

Shakespeare's primary 'model' for the *Shrew* is not, as in his earlier
comedies, a formal one. It is his own habitat, the fractious literary
London of the late 1580s, where rival poets, like the rival suitors in the
Shrew, 'quaff carouses' together of an afternoon,

> And do as adversaries do in law,
> Strive mightily, but eat and drink as friends.[5]

As a member of this skirmishing literary crew, the most notoriously
'shrewd' of them all, Nashe contributes to Shakespeare's sense of raillery.
At the end of their first 'flyting', Kate sarcastically asks Petruchio, 'Where
did you study all this goodly speech?', and Petruchio answers, 'It is
extempore, from my mother wit.' He is a wit in the spontaneous Nashe
style, 'the man whose extemporall veine in any humour will excell our
greatest Art-maisters deliberate thoughts'.[6] Many of the linguistic tricks
typical of Nashe surface in the language of the *Shrew*. The jovial interjections, 'now, my spruce companions' . . . 'come hither, crack-hemp' . . .
'skipper, stand back'; the garnish of Latinisms, *ergo* and *imprimis*; the

printing-house joke, 'take your assurance of her *cum privilegio ad impri-mendum solum*', with a bawdy undertone; the glimpses of seedy low-life, 'an old trot with ne'er a tooth in her head', a 'meacock wretch', a 'rascal fiddler', 'cunning men'.[7] If the main part of the *Shrew* dates back as far as 1589–90, we might guess that Shakespeare had recently read Nashe's *Almond for a Parrat*, which has just this racy, abrasive tone. The whole Marprelate controversy, in fact, provides a stylistic backdrop for the *Shrew*, as it does for the Jack Cade scenes in *Henry VI*. But most specifically Nashe-like of all is Shakespeare's portrait of Petruchio in his down-at-heel wedding gear: his 'old breeches thrice turned', his 'boots that have been candle-cases', his 'rusty sword ta'en out of the town-armoury'. His lackey wears

> a linen stock on one leg and a kersey boot-hose on the other, gartered with a red and blue list, an old hat and the humour of forty fancies pricked in't for a feather.

His horse is fitted with an 'old mothy saddle' and a 'woman's crupper of velure, which hath two letters of her name fairly set down in studs', and the animal itself is

> possessed with the glanders and like to mose in the chine, troubled with the lampass, infected with the fashions, full of windgalls, sped with spavins, rayed with the yellows, past cure of the fives, stark spoiled with the staggers, begnawn with the bots, swayed in the back and shoulder shotten.

The whole vignette adds up to 'a monster, a very monster in apparel'.[8] Critics have noted how close this is to Nashe's type of *grotesquerie*: the blend of sharp detail and absurd distortion; the relishing in scuffed and mangy textures; the wresting of disease into hyperbolic comedy. The closest parallels in Nashe – the Greed scenario in *Pierce Penilesse*, the Anabaptist army in *The Unfortunate Traveller* – are probably too late to be specific influences on this passage in the *Shrew*, but it is clear that in the early 1590s the two writers were stylistically very close, exploring those imaginative possibilities of comic prose first opened up by the seditious jester, Martin.

It is curious to note in the Induction of the *Shrew* certain hints of Lord Strange. A humorous young nobleman, coming upon Christopher Sly the tinker in a drunken stupor, resolves to play a trick on him. Sly is to be convinced that he himself is a Lord, suffering from a 'lunacy' that deludes him into thinking he is a tinker. He is swathed in 'sweet clothes' and washed in 'distilled waters'. When he awakes, fractious and baffled, solicitous attendants soothe him:

> Heaven cease this idle humour in your honour!
> O that a mighty man of such descent,
> Of such possessions and so high esteem,
> Should be infused with so foul a spirit . . .
> Hence comes it that your kindred shuns your house,
> As beaten hence by your strange lunacy.
> O noble lord, bethink thee of thy birth,
> Call home thy ancient thoughts from banishment
> And banish hence these abject lowly dreams.[9]

Your 'strange lunacy': our ears have been sharpened by Nashe for this kind of hint, as in looking for 'strange contents' in Spenser's sonnets. Here, perhaps, is another of Nashe's techniques echoed in the *Shrew*: the cleverly veiled topicality. As with Nashe, once the signal is noticed the whole concealed message becomes clear. Shakespeare decks Sly out as a mock Lord Strange, a 'thrice noble' lord, a 'mighty man of such descent, of such possessions'. He is dragged down by a 'lunacy', an 'idle humour', 'abject, lowly dreams', these referring to the real Strange's entanglement in occultism and conspiracy. When a page-boy is brought on as his 'wife', Sly wonders how to address her: 'Madam', he is told; 'Alice madam or Joan madam?' he asks. Alice was indeed the name of Lady Strange. Together they settle down to watch the play –

> Seeing too much sadness hath congeal'd your blood
> And melancholy is the nurse of frenzy,
> Therefore they thought it good you hear a play

– just as the real Lord and Lady Strange must often have done. The play is *The Taming of the Shrew* – singularly appropriate, because we happen to know that Lady Strange *was* something of a 'shrew'. Her second husband, Sir Thomas Egerton, tells us so unequivocally in a cautionary tale he penned for his son, 'An unpleasant declaration of thinges passed betwene the Contesse of Derby and me since our marriage.'[10] He pitifully complains of her 'cursed rayling and bytter tongue'; never until 'this my last mariage' had he been 'acquaynted with such tempests and stormes'; he had suffered in silence for fear of becoming *'fabula vulgi'*, the object of tittle-tattle. The pursed, pointed features in the Countess's portrait – probably dating from her wedding to Egerton in 1600 – do not contradict him, though there is a wicked humour in her too. Whether she was as 'shrewd' in her younger days with Lord Strange we do not know. Strange's young brother, William, who succeeded as 6th Earl, certainly felt the force of her tongue in certain legal disputes that arose after Strange's death.[11] She lived on to a ripe old age: she is the 'Countess Dowager of Darby' for whom Milton wrote his *Arcades* (*c.* 1632).

All this demands a context: playwrights did not normally indulge in satirical skits on noblemen like Strange. The influence of Nashe is a stylistic context, but that is not enough. Some bearings are provided here, unexpectedly, by the anonymous *Taming of a Shrew*, issued in 1594. This is essentially a 'bad quarto' – an unauthorized text based on actors' reconstructions – but it diverges much more from the authentic text than is common with these piracies, and it is thought to be based on an earlier Shakespearean version of the *Shrew* which has since perished. References to *Dr Faustus* in *The Taming of a Shrew* suggest that the latter was compiled sometime after mid-1592. To summarize the probable story: Shakespeare wrote an early version of the *Shrew* in *c.* 1590; it was still current, and popular enough to merit piracy, in *c.* 1592; sometime later – but not, on stylistic grounds, much later – he worked over the play, altering names and scenes, trimming it down to the version eventually printed by the Folio editors in 1623.[12] I would suggest 1593 as a convenient date for the rewriting. The play-houses were shut throughout that year, and Shakespeare's fortunes lay with Southampton, to whom he dedicated his poetic volumes, *Venus* (1593) and *Lucrece* (1594). It is almost certain that Shakespeare put on *Loves Labors Lost* for Southampton and his guests during the Christmas festivities of 1593–4. Why not the revamped version of the *Shrew* as well? This would certainly explain why Meres refers to the play as *Loves Labours Wonne*: the two comedies belong together under Southampton's patronage. The title may just be theatrical jargon, or it may be an authentic alternative, distinguishing the genuine article from the mangled reconstruction issued in 1594.

Shakespeare's original treatment of the Sly Induction – inasmuch as it is reflected in *The Taming of a Shrew* – was very different. There are certainly none of the hints of Strange that appear in the later version. This is not conclusive – *lacunae* in a 'memorial reconstruction' may simply be lapses of memory – but it argues strongly that the satirical material on Strange was inserted during the rewriting of the Induction. This, then, is our context. It was for the Southampton circle – a refined, private audience – that Shakespeare cooked up this Nashe-like political *badinage*, dressing up a tinker as 'Lord Sly', jesting about his 'lunacy' and 'lowly dreams', and setting him down before a comedy about a railing shrew. The rudiments of the Sly story are as old as the hills; the hits at Strange are a highly topical garnish. There seems to be no external evidence as to the relations between Southampton and Strange, but one connection is, yet again, Catholicism. Southampton was a confirmed Catholic, but he kept himself well clear of any seditious associations.

The troubles suffered by his father made him wary. If he knew of the conspiratorial dealings Strange was involved in – wittingly or otherwise – in 1593, he might well consider them a 'strange lunacy', an infusion of 'foul spirit' into a 'mighty man'. 'Lord Sly' is told that his 'kindred' shuns his house because of his lunacy. This may mean that Strange's spiritual 'kindred' – fellow Catholic noblemen like Southampton – deeply distrusted him after the Hesketh affair of 1593. Lady Strange speaks of her husband being 'crossed in his court and crossed in his country'. And, she perhaps could have added, crossed onstage by Southampton's poet, Shakespeare.

Some confirmation of this is close at hand, for these hints of Strange in the *Shrew* are writ large in *Loves Labors Lost* itself. Most – but not all – agree that this is a play which 'bristles throughout with topical allusions', and critics since Warburton in the mid-eighteenth century have been busy unearthing the characters and events which might lie beneath it.[13] That Moth is a sketch of Nashe is widely accepted; that Holofernes the pedant is John Florio, Southampton's Italian tutor, is also plausible. Both these belong to the 'sub plot', to which we will turn in a moment. A leading character in the main plot – in theory *the* leading character, though Berowne overshadows him – is Ferdinand, King of Navarre. Critics have tentatively suggested that he has some relationship with Ferdinando, Lord Strange, especially since Strange's accession to the Earldom of Derby in 1593 brought with it a whole convoy of titles, including King of the Isle of Man.[14] But beyond this nominal connection little has been discovered. Why should King Ferdinand of Man appear in *Loves Labors Lost* as King Ferdinand of Navarre? With the benefit of the new material on Strange in the previous chapter, we can now see why. There was a real King of Navarre in 1593. He was not Ferdinand, but Henry of Navarre: he was, furthermore, King Henri IV of France. And one of the talking-points of 1593 was Henry's dramatic conversion, on 25 July, to Catholicism. An expedient move to unite war-torn France, the news was greeted with horror in Protestant England: their staunchest European ally had switched sides overnight. 'The French King's apostasy', wrote the pragmatic Carey on 2 August, will win him friends in neither religious camp but 'make him hateful as of no religion to them both'. It will bring him 'torment to his conscience much greater than the gain of such a kingdom'. This was the Navarre of 1593: a treacherous Catholic king. The Princess he woos in *Loves Labors Lost* sums up the current attitude to him:

> O heresie in faire, fit for these dayes . . .
> Glorie growes guyltie of detested crimes,
> When for Fames sake, for praise, an outward part,
> We bend to that the working of the hart.[15]

It seems clear that Shakespeare's conflation of Strange with Navarre hinges on the Hesketh plot of autumn 1593, whose aim was precisely to place Strange on the throne as a Catholic King, an English Navarre. In an intercepted letter from one of the Prague plotters, Father Stephenson, we read: 'I hear no news of the French King: all rumours are wist. Our Lord send us a king and some more comfort after so many surging waves.'[16] Here, in the words of one of the conspirators, is the hope that King Ferdinand of England will soon stand beside Henri of France in Catholic unity. Out of the rumours flying around in late 1593, Shakespeare makes this pointed connection between Strange and Navarre in the character of King Ferdinand.

Other little clues surround this equation. The Princess beloved by Navarre is referred to as 'the strange queen', ostensibly meaning 'foreign', but perhaps suggestive of Lady Strange as the Queen of the conspirators' dreams. Other phrases, such as 'moon-like men of strange inconstancy' and 'strange without heresie', contain miniature comments on Strange. Much of Shakespeare's portrait of Strange has probably been lost. There is strong evidence of revision in the text, and the first known edition of the play (1598) is described as 'newly corrected and augmented'. The revisions perhaps mark the play's transition to the public stage, where such political motifs would be unwise. The death of Strange in April 1594 would anyway place him beyond the satirical pale. The all-important clue – that Shakespeare originally called his Navarre Ferdinand – only survives, perhaps by oversight, in a few speech headings.[17]

This nomenclature presses Lord Strange into the centre of *Loves Labors Lost*, and here we find further echoes of his penchant for occultism. As is well-known, Shakespeare's story of Navarre and his three followers is essentially a skit on noblemen-scholars, and on the fascination for *esoterica* so rife in the early 1590s. We first meet Ferdinand and his lords planning to retreat from the world in monastic scholarly seclusion:

> Our Court shall be a little Achademe,
> Still and contemplative in lyving Art.

They are to be bound by 'strickt observances' of self-discipline for three years: 'the minde shall banquet though the body pine'. Thus they will achieve 'the ende of study', which is knowledge of 'things hid & bard ... from common sense'. To attain these occult secrets is 'studies god-like recompense'.[18] Navarre's 'little academy' sounds much like the kind of esoteric coterie associated with Ralegh and company. Many think it *is* the 'Durham House set' that is satirized in the play; that there are specific hits at the astronomy of Hariot and the nocturnalism of Chapman; and that Shakespeare reflects or invents a popular name for the clique in the lines, 'Blacke is the badge of hell, The hue of dungeons and the Schoole of night.' Parsons called it a 'Schoole of Atheisme', it is argued; Shakespeare dubs it the 'School of Night'. The trouble with this is that by late 1593 the Durham House clique was dispersed. Ralegh was a disgraced courtier living in semi-retirement on his Dorset estates. Hariot was still nominally his Chief Steward, but his future lay with the Earl of Northumberland: he received a gift of £24 from the Earl in 1593 and an annual pension from 1598 until his death. Chapman may have written *The Shadow of Night* under the Ralegh *aegis*, but he was pragmatic enough to omit all mention of Ralegh in his preface, penned in late 1593: it is to 'ingenious Darbie' and 'deepe searching Northumberland' that he appeals. If Shakespeare had an occult 'schoole' in mind, I suspect that its chief patron was not Ralegh but Lord Strange, Shakespeare's Navarre.[19]

With Strange at its heart, Shakespeare's spoof in *Loves Labors Lost* takes up the same humorous anti-occultist territory as Nashe in *Pierce Penilesse* and in the cunning-man burlesque of *The Terrors*. For both writers, this stance entails some enmity with, or at least confutation of, George Chapman. It has long been recognized that some of Berowne's lines pointedly rebuff Chapman's nocturnalism. Chapman writes,

> No pen can anything eternal write
> That is not steept in humour of the night

Berowne counter-claims,

> Never durst Poet touch a pen to write
> Until his Incke were tempred with Loves sighs.

Chapman speaks of the 'rapture of delight in the deepe search of knowledge'. For Berowne, 'universal plodding poysons up The nimble spirites in the arteries'. On Chapman's 'invocation, fasting, watching' Berowne scornfully comments: 'To fast, to study. . . : flat treason gainst the kingly state of youth'. Via Berowne, Shakespeare gives us a '*hymnus in diem*', a paean to light, love and experience, as against night, seclusion and study. He also uses the same pun of Chapman's name that Nashe has in the *Pierce Penilesse* sonnet: 'Beautie', says the Queen in *Loves Labors Lost*,

> . . . is bought by iudgment of the eye
> Not uttred by base sale of chapmens tongues.[20]

The play is too subtle, too *chiaroscuro*, to be called propaganda. But played before the young Catholic noble, Southampton, in the winter of 1593–4, it has a message for him. Avoid the gloomy esoteric bent of those other Catholic nobles, Strange and Northumberland. Pursue real experience, not 'leaden contemplation'. It is the same message glimpsed in the Induction to the *Shrew*, with its lunatic 'Lord Sly'. It is the same message playing through *Pierce Penilesse*, the *Terrors*, and even – in its ambiguous way – *Dr Faustus*, all of them linked in some way to Lord Strange.

Nashe has connections with the main plot and he has his fitting place in the sub-plot, genially guyed as Master Moth, page to the fantastical Armado. The clues Shakespeare threw out to his courtly audience, that here was tart Tom Nashe, are many and varied.[21] 'Moth' is, first, an anagram: 'Thom' was a common variant of 'Tom'. It is also a descriptive name, suggesting Nashe's flittering, busy, irritant presence, the 'buzzing fly' of the Bear-Fox fable, the 'moth' of 1593. Moth as a 'pretty knavish page' echoes, as we have seen, Jack Wilton, the 'little page' of *The Unfortunate Traveller*. The whole portrait catches Nashe's physical presence: small, skinny, mercurial, piquant. Moth is a 'bolde wagg', a 'handfull of wit', a 'deere imp': he is 'little', 'volable', 'quick', 'acute', 'well-educated'. Jokes abound about his smallness – he is a 'mere consonant', a 'sweet ounce of mans flesh'. In the Worthies show got up by Armado, Moth plays Hercules, an absurd bit of casting since 'he is not quantitie enough for that Worthies thumb'. They decide he shall present Hercules 'in minoritie':

> Great Hercules is presented by this Impe,
> Whose clubb kilde Cerberus, that three-headed Canus,
> And when he was a babe, a childe, a shrimp,
> Thus did he strangle serpents in his manus.

Here is Nashe the satirist, a pint-sized Hercules cudgelling the three-headed Harvey monster.

Other hints suggest Shakespeare's knowledge of the Greene-Harvey-Nashe broil of 1592–3. At their first appearance, Armado calls Moth 'my tender Iuvenall'; the name is repeated three times in the next few lines, and again in Act III, where Moth is a 'most acute Iuvenall'. This clearly echoes the nick-name Greene gave Nashe in the *Groatsworth of Wit*, 'young Iuvenall, that byting Satyrist', punning on 'juvenile' and Juvenal, the Roman satirist. Shakespeare had doubtless lingered on this passage in the *Groatsworth*, since 'young Iuvenall' is one of the 'schollers' that Greene warns about upstart players like William 'Shake-scene'. Also a literary echo are the puns on 'purse' and 'penny' that crop up around Moth. Costard calls him a 'half pennie purse of wit', a 'pigeon-egg of discretion'. The first phrase evokes *Pierce Penilesse*, the second perhaps glances at Harvey's ironic request in the *Supererogation*, 'let him publish *Nashes Penniworth of Discretion*'. When Armado asks,

'How hast thou purchast this experience?', Moth replies, 'By my penne [i.e. penny] of observation': this suggests Nashe's pamphlets as a 'penni-worth of observation', like Greene's 'groatsworth of wit'. Holofernes' absurd quibble on 'parson', 'person' and 'pierce one' is part of the same motif. So too is his phrase, 'persing [i.e. piercing] a hoggeshead': this is Elizabethan slang for getting drunk, but it is also another echo from the *Supererogation*, where Harvey speaks of 'Pierce, the hoggeshead of witt'.[22] Armado's doggerel about 'the fox, the ape and the humble bee' seems to recall the anti-Leicester bestiary in *Pierce*. Finally, on the literary side of Shakespeare's portrait of Nashe, there may be a reference to *Christs Teares* in this exchange:

Costard Well, if ever I do see the merrie dayes of desolation that I
            have seen, some shall see —
Moth   What shall some see?
Costard Nay, nothing, Master Moth, but what they looke upon.[23]

Costard's curious phrase seems to have touched some nerve in Moth. The 'merrie dayes of desolation' is, perhaps, Shakespearean shorthand for the incongruities of *Christs Teares*, the comic pamphleteer turning prophet of doom. Young Juvenal, Pierce Penniless, Jack Wilton and the looker upon desolation: Shakespeare touches on each of Nashe's literary guises of 1592–3 to underscore his caricature. It is, unlike some others in the play, a totally affable sketch. As Dover Wilson says, 'the portrait is rather complimentary than otherwise: had the original recognized it on the stage he might have felt flattered'.[24] He is 'represented as an ally': like Berowne in the main plot, he is an agent rather than a butt of the play's satire. Moth's one long speech in the play — about how to win the ladies — is clearly written in imitation of Nashe's style:

Iigge off a tune at the tongues ende, canarie to it with your feete, humour it with turning up your eylids, sigh a note and sing a note, somtime through the throate (as if you swallowed love with singing love), sometime through the nose (as if you snuft up love by smelling love); with your hat penthouse-like ore the shop of your eyes; with your armes crost on your thinbellies doublet (like a Rabbet on a spit); or your handes in your pocket (like a man after the olde painting); and keepe not too long in one tune, but a snip and away: These are complements, these are humours; these betraie nice wenches . . .[25]

If Moth is Nashe, his master, the ridiculous Armado, is surely Harvey. Some have suggested this, though there are other rival identifications of Armado, notably Ralegh and Antonio Perez. If we look at the descrip-tions of Armado that Shakespeare gives us, we find Gabriel Harvey drawn to a 'T'. Armado is, first and foremost, the play's 'Braggart', just as Holofernes is its 'Pedant'. Speech headings in both the quarto (1598) and folio (1623) texts constantly name them as such: these are *commedia dell'arte* notations, comic types imported straight into this topical *revue*.[26] Armado is also a Spaniard: this enforces his status as braggart – Nashe expresses the current lore when he says, 'Pride is the disease of the Spaniard, who is borne a Bragart in his mothers wombe.' Navarre describes Armado as

> One who the musique of his own vaine tongue
> Doth ravish like inchaunting harmonie,
> A man of complements, whom right and wrong
> Have chose as umpier of their mutenie.

Boyet calls him 'a Phantasime, a Monarcho, and one that makes sport To the Prince and his Book-mates'. And Holofernes says of him:

> His humor is loftie, his discourse peremptorie, his tongue fyled, his eye ambitious, his gate maiesticall, and his general behaviour vaine, rediculous & thrasonicall. He is too picked, too spruce, too affected, too od. . . . He draweth out the thred of his verbositie finer then the staple of his argument. I abhorre such phanatical phantasims, such insociable and point-devyse companions.[27]

At every turn we recognize Gabriel's 'singuler giftes of absurditie and vaineglory'. Armado the braggart is the Harvey whom Nashe calls a 'professed poeticall braggart', a 'vaine Braggadochio', notorious for 'intollerable boasting' and 'horrible insulting pride'. Holofernes calls Armado 'thrasonicall', referring to the bragging soldier, Thraso, in Terence's *Eunuchus*. Nashe also calls Harvey 'this Thraso' in *Strange Newes*, and speaks of 'his Thrasonisme' in *Have with you*. Boyet calls Armado a 'Monarcho', comparing him to the well-known court buffoon whose name was a byword for 'phantastick humours'. Nashe makes the same comparison: Harvey is 'an insulting Monarch above Monarcha, the Italian that ware crownes on his shoes'. Throughout the play Armado is the chief butt of the court, one that 'makes sport to the Prince and his Book-mates'. This is the picture Nashe gives of Harvey in his courtly days, how the courtiers would 'plague him for his presumption', how he was 'bad stand by for a Nodgscombe', how his patron, Leicester, found 'he was more meete to make sport with than anie way deeply to be employed'.[28] Nashe's whole account of Harvey's 'revelling and domineering' at Audley End is very close in atmosphere to Armado's florid foolery at Navarre's court. It appears in *Have with you to Saffron-Walden*, not published till 1596. Shakespeare cannot be 'borrowing' from it as such: if there is shared material, it was verbally shared.

The Spanishness of Armado, as well as invoking the pride of the Spaniard, has other suggestions of Harvey. The Elizabethans, careless of Spanish genders, often called the naval Armada an 'armado', so here is that idea of Harvey as a lumbering, 'over-weaponed' antagonist, a 'decrepite slow-moving' mind incapable of 'quicke fight'. Nashe indeed compares his own onslaught on the Harveys to the English defeat of the Armada:

The Spanyards called their invasive fleet agaynst England the Navie invincible, yet it was overcome. Lowe shrubbes have outliv'd high Cedars. One true man is stronger than two theeves. Gabriell & Richard, I proclaime open warres with you.

This same naval metaphor is found in Fuller's famous description of the 'wit-combates' between Shakespeare and Ben Jonson. Jonson was like a 'Spanish great Gallion', 'built far higher in Learning, solid, but slow in his performance'. Shakespeare, 'the English man of War', was 'lesser in bulk but lighter in sailing', and could 'tack about and take advantage of all winds, by the quickness of his Wit and Invention'.[29] Harvey as Armado is this same unwieldy galleon of learning, Shakespeare and Nashe the sprightly men o' war. Spanishness had also another connotation: absurdly over-elaborate courtesy. This the 'picked' and 'spruce' Armado, the 'man of complements', epitomizes. His 'new devisde cursie' (i.e. courtesy) provides constant amusement in this courtly comedy. This too is another strand in Nashe's burlesque of Harvey, the 'finicaldo fine' *poseur*, Timothy Tiptoes, with his 'curious finicall complement'. Harvey receiving a visitor – 'downe he came, and after the *bazelos manus*, with amplifications and complements hee belaboured him till his ears tingled' – is just such a Spanish-style fantastic (*besar las manos*, to kiss the hand). And again: 'no Usher of a dauncing schoole was ever such a *Bassia Dona* or *Bassia de umbra de umbra des los pedes*, a kisser of the shadow of your feetes shadow, as he is'.[30] We are edging here towards a visual element in Shakespeare's portrait: Armado catches Harvey's actual manner – florid, punctilious, 'huffty tuffty in his suite of velvet'. He may even reflect Harvey's actual features, the Mediterranean cast he was so proud of after the Queen had told him he looked 'something like an Italian'. Nashe describes Harvey's complexion as 'of an adust swarth chollericke dye, like restie bacon, or a dride skate-fish'. His skin is 'riddled and crumpled like a peice of burnt parchment' and has more wrinkles 'than there be Fairie circles on Salsburie Plaine'. Harvey's rugged Latin looks certainly qualify him for this 'knight from tawny Spain', this Shakespearean Quixote. The jesting about Armado being 'cleane timberd' (brawny, well-built), with a leg 'too bigge', must be sarcastic, since Harvey was notably lean: 'he looks like a case of tooth-

pikes, or a lute pin put in a sute of apparell'.[31] All this reminds us of
the lost visual dimension of Shakespeare's comedy, the extent to which
verbal hints in the text were writ large in visual terms – gait, gesture,
accent, costume, wigs, props. What had most struck Nashe about the
Cambridge lampoon of Harvey, *Pedantius*, was the actuality of the
portrait:

> not the carrying up of his gowne, his nice gate on his pantoffles, or
> the affected accent of his speach, but they personated. And if I should
> reveale all, I thinke they borrowd his gowne to playe the part in, the
> more to flout him.

A similar exactitude is urged by Lyly: Martin should be shown onstage
'in a cap'de cloake' and whatever clothing he would wear 'on some
rainie weeke daie'.[32] Every possible medium was used in these satirical
shows. The textual clues in *Loves Labors* are only part of the presentation, though in this richly linguistic play, this comedy of meanings and
meaninglessness, they are a vital part.

It is also a very literary play, so Shakespeare's caricature has specific
jokes about Harvey as *littérateur*. There is, first, much ado about
Armado's letter-writing. Before we even meet him, we hear his orotund
tones in his letter to Navarre, and further absurdities are revealed in his
letter to Jaquenetta. This of course hits at Harvey the epistler, author
of two volumes of letters to Spenser, four letters against Greene and
Nashe, and, most recently, the *New Letter of Notable Contents*. Nashe
calls him the 'Nunparreille of impious Epistlers', a 'letter-dawber', a
'letter-leaper', a 'letter-munger', and so on. The characters react to
Armado's letters as real-life wits might have done to Harvey's – 'What
a plume of fethers is he that indited this letter?' scoffs the Princess,
'What vaine? What wethercock?' Or:

> King   A letter from the magnificent Armado.
> Berowne   How low soever the matter, I hope in God for high
>   words.
> Longaville A high hope for a low heaven. God grant us patience![33]

Low matter in high words: an apt epitome of Harvey as controversialist.
When Constable Dull delivers the letter to Navarre, he says, 'Signeour
Arme, Arme, commendes you: Ther's villanie abrod! This letter will tell
you more.' He cannot get his tongue round the Spaniard's name, but he
expresses the letter's subject succinctly enough. 'There's villainy abroad!'
Precisely Harvey's cry in the *Foure Letters* and the *Supererogation*,
harping on Nashe as 'villanist' and on his own duty not to let 'abhominable villany passe unlaunced'. Another literary aspect of Armado is his

eccentric vocabulary, particularly his love for coining new words: he has, says the King, 'a mint of phrases in his braine'; he is 'a man of fier new wordes'. This echoes Harvey's penchant for neologizing, the 'hermaphrodite phrases' and 'newe ingendred fome of the English' that Nashe swoops on in *Strange Newes*. The strangest Nashe lists – 'effectuate', 'polimechany', 'addoulce' – are nothing compared to the exotic hybrids to be found in Gabriel's marginalia, such as 'megelander', 'stoicheologia', 'axiozelis', all his own coinages. Harvey's orthographic interests are also glanced at when Holofernes complains about Armado,

> I abhorre . . . such rackers of orthographie, as to speak 'dout' fine, when he should say 'doubt'; 'det' when he should pronounce 'debt'. . . . He clepeth a calfe, 'caufe'; halfe, 'haufe'; neighbour *vocatur* 'nebour'.

Harvey was a great believer in the simplifying of English spelling. This is evident in his own writings, and in his annotations on Smith's *De Linguae Anglicanae Scriptione* (1568) and Hart's *Orthographie* (1569). Hart's precept that 'a writing is corrupted when any worde or sillable hath more letters than are used of voyces in the pronunciation' sums up Harvey's stance. He did indeed write – and so, evidently, pronounce – 'debt' as 'det', as Holofernes complains, and he would no doubt have written 'nebour' for 'neighbour', as he did 'endevur' for 'endeavour'.[34] Thus another of Harvey's hobby-horses is touched on. There are other such small glances – Armado's greeting of 'Chirrah!', for instance, is a corruption (either malapropist or a printer's bodge) of the Greek salutation, χᾶἶρε (chaere). This refers to the opening title of Harvey's Audley End panegyric – *Gabrielis Harveii χᾶἶρε, vel Gratulationis Valdinensis Liber Primus* ('Gabriel Harvey's All Hail, or the First Book of the Walden Well-wishing').[35] Shakespeare's caricature is meticulous in detail; it is also just in its wider judgments. A man 'ravished' with 'the musique of his own vaine tongue', one who 'draweth out the thred of his verbositie finer then the staple [rough wool] of his argument' – those who have travailed through Harvey's pamphlets know how right this is. He 'whom right and wrong Have chose as umpier of their mutenie' – here is Harvey the great moral arbiter, the interferer, the Polonius. And at the end, when Armado takes on the role of Hector in the Worthies antic, Shakespeare throws in a final irony. Faced with a jeering audience, Armado begs them to respect the valiant Hector's memory:

> The sweete war-man is dead and rotten. Sweete chucks, beat not the bones of the buried. When he breathed, he was a man.[36]

Even Harvey, the notorious vilifier of the dead Greene, would have blushed at that.

Thus Moth and Armado, Nashe and Harvey, the zany and the braggart of 1593. And all part of Shakespeare's treatment is the fact that they are *twinned* like this. Though Moth teases and taunts Armado, they are essentially a pair, the 'boy' and his 'master'. As well as the comedy of caricature there is the comedy of their kinship – the benign, avuncular Harvey patting Nashe on the head, calling him 'deare Imp' and 'tenderness of years'. When Moth cries, 'My fathers wit and my mothers tongue assist me', Armado dotingly burbles, 'Sweet invocation of a child! Most pretty and patheticall' – a far cry from the real Harvey's remarks to Nashe about 'thy mothers gutter and thy fathers kennel'. The effect of this twinning is to turn these sworn enemies into a little vignette, a literary sideshow, a Punch and Judy double-act:

> Armado ath toon side: O, a most daintie man!
> To see him walke before a Lady and to beare her fann . . .
> And his Page atother side, that handfull of wit!
> Ah heavens, it is a most patheticall nit.[37]

This idea of comic pairing may be repeated in the other duo of the subplot, Holofernes and Sir Nathaniel. There are ample reasons for believing that the polyglot pedagogue Holofernes contains a satirical portrait of Iohn Florio, linguist and lexicographer, currently Southampton's Italian tutor. The name is ingenious: it recalls Holoferne, the 'docteur sophiste' in Rabelais' *Gargantua*; and it is also an anagram, best expressed as

I, HOLOFERNES = IOHNES FLOREO

There are echoes of Florio's Italian proverbs, of his famous Italian-English dictionary, of his interest in Montaigne. The very title of the play was probably suggested by an adage in Florio's *First Fruites*, 'it were a labour lost to speake of Love'. Since Florio seems to have been used by Burghley as a Protestant snoop in Southampton's Catholic retinue, Shakespeare felt free to satirize him for the Earl's amusement.[38] If Holofernes is Florio, then perhaps his toady, the parson Sir Nathaniel, is some real-life enemy of Florio's, and Shakespeare makes the same comic inversion of enmity into kinship as he does with the Moth-Armado pairing. Could Sir Nathaniel possibly be Hugh Sanford, the Countess of Pembroke's secretary, whose official edition of the *Arcadia* in. 1593 denounced the former 'blemished' edition which Florio had himself edited in 1590? So when Nathaniel oilily commends Holofernes' style – 'your epithets are sweetly varied, like a scholler at the least' – we get the same polar inversion of reality as Armado calling Moth his 'deare Imp'. There is not space to develop this possibility, but the cap fits

Sanford pretty well. As a heinous old pedant, Sir Nathaniel reflects contemporary assessments of Sanford, as described by Florio ('grammarian-pedante') and by Rowland Whyte ('my feare is that Mr Sanford will in his Humor persuade my Lord to some Pedantike Invention').[39] Sanford's pedantic 'humor' extended into theological realms: his posthumous publication, *De Descensu ad Inferos* (1611), is a markedly Puritan contribution to the scriptural controversy first fomented by Hugh Broughton (he whose 'Ebrew studies' Nashe scoffed at in Croydon). Sanford the Puritan theologizer becomes Sir Nathaniel the quavering country parson, a godly, sychophantic 'hedge priest'. Sanford was another of Nashe's enemies: he is probably the 'pedanticall parasite' Nashe has in mind in the *Christs Teares* dedication, written in autumn 1593, and there is a sarcastic glance at 'H.S.' and his 'Maid-marrian' (i.e. the Countess of Pembroke) in *Lenten Stuffe*. This later reference, probably written in early 1599, ties in with Florio's own assault on Sanford in the preface to his Italian dictionary (1598).[40] These are further sparks of the squabble Shakespeare reflects, and ironically reconciles, in Holofernes and Nathaniel. When these two and Armado pontificate together, the knowing courtly audience chuckles at this vision of Florio, Sanford and Harvey in learned conflab, and at Moth's, or Nashe's, mischievous aside: 'they have been at a great feast of Languages, and stolne the scraps'.

In the festive, intricate comedy of *Loves Labors Lost*, where puns and in-jokes fly like confetti, we find such figures as Strange and Chapman, Nashe and Harvey, Florio and Sanford. Insofar as Shakespeare's attitude can be inferred, it is remarkably close to Nashe's. He jests at the scholarly, esoteric, nocturnalist aura associated with Ralegh and, most prominently in 1593, with Lord Strange. In the aftermath of the Hesketh affair, his equation between Strange and Navarre points to the Catholic conspiratorial taint on Strange. If he does make fun of Hugh Sanford, this draws another occultist-minded clique – the Countess of Pembroke's – into the satiric arena. On a more personal level, Shakespeare's treatment of the Nashe-Harvey dispute argues his sympathy with Nashe, the sprightly knave with a 'sweet tutch of wit', as against the ornate Harvey fulminating amid a 'smoke of rhetoric'. Shakespeare's knowledge of the quarrel is intimate and acute: he had clearly read the warring pamphlets and he probably knew Nashe, personally and professionally, in the early 1590s. It is even possible that Shakespeare was somehow involved in the mediations between the two antagonists in mid-1593, one of those 'interposed persons' through whom they communicated. His portrait of the pair in *Loves Labors Lost* is indeed a comic envisaging of Nashe and Harvey reconciled. One looks again at the passage in *Have with you* where we hear of those Hispanic '*bazelos manus*' courtesies of

Harvey's which sound so much like Armado's. Nashe was not describing
his own experience of Harvey, but reporting a friend's account of him:

> A Gentleman, a frend of mine, that was no straunger to such bandy-
> ings as had past betwixt us, was desirous to see how he lookt since
> my strappadoing and torturing him: in which spleene he went and
> enquird for him.

The caller was told that Harvey was 'but new risen' and asked to
wait. 'Two houres good by the clocke he attended', while Harvey was
'currying & smudging and pranking himselfe' in his private chamber.
Finally the great man descended to belabour him with compliments 'till
his ears tingled and his feet ak'd'. The date of this visit must have been
1593 – it was not long after Nashe's 'strappadoing and torturing'
Harvey, i.e. the appearance of *Strange Newes*. It must have been before
September 1593, for Harvey was back in Saffron Walden by then.[41] It
is not impossible that this gentlemanly friend of Nashe's was Shakespeare, and that his experience of Harvey's absurd Hispanic flourishes
was not only retailed to Nashe but worked up in his own portrait of
Harvey as Armado, the 'man of complements'. Shakespeare's movements
in 1593 are obscure, but he was almost certainly in London in the
spring, overseeing the printing of his *Venus and Adonis*, registered on
28 April.[42] Sometime around then, perhaps, he spent two hours of a
spring morning hanging around to meet 'his Gabrielship', presumably
chez Wolfe at Paul's Churchyard, where Harvey was 'billetted'. It would
be generous of the socially-conscious Nashe to describe Shakespeare as
a 'gentleman', but again not impossible. Around the time *Have with you*
was published, Shakespeare's father, John – or probably Shakespeare on
his behalf – successfully applied for a coat of arms: draft documents
assigning the family shield are dated 20 October 1596. If Shakespeare
was not technically a 'gent' when Nashe actually wrote the passage, he
soon would be. Harry Chettle's impression of him in 1592 – 'his
demeanour no lesse civill than he excelent in the qualitie he professes',
'divers of worship have reported his uprightnes of dealing' – certainly
describes, in the wider sense, a gentleman.[43] So perhaps, after all, Shakespeare *is* mentioned in Nashe's pamphlets, in this most casual and human
guise of 'a Gentleman, a frend of mine'.

15

A SILENCE

'discontented idle trudging from place to place, too and fro, and prose-
cuting the meanes to keep mee from idlenesse . . .'

Have with you to Saffron-Walden

'What, Tom, thou art very welcome', says Signor Importuno, 'where
hast thou bin this long time?'[1] With this imagined remonstration Nashe
begins *Have with you to Saffron-Walden*, published in the autumn of
1596 after a long and uncharacteristic silence. In 1594 he remained in
the public eye by virtue of publishing works previously written, *The
Unfortunate Traveller* and *The Terrors of the Night*. His name appeared
beneath Marlowe's on the title-page of *Dido*, and his elegy on Marlowe
was inserted before some of the copies. He wrote a preface for the new
edition of *Christs Teares*, giving notice that Harvey was once more in
his sights. There was a second edition of *The Unfortunate Traveller*,
'newly corrected and augmented', its small repolishings presumably
Nashe's own. For a man of his garrulous energies, it was a year of bits
and pieces. In 1595 and the first half of 1596 there was nothing save a
solitary re-issue of *Pierce*, its fifth and final edition.[2] He is, chides the
colloquist Importuno, a 'disgraced and condemned man' while 'Harvey
thus lives unanswered'. His public wonders 'what means he to be thus
retchles of his fame', and 'whether he be dead or no, or forbidden to
write, or in regard he hath publist a treatise in Divinitie makes a
conscience to meddle any more in these controversies'. The shadow of
Christs Teares seems still to hang over him. Importuno thinks he has
been hiding away 'in Saint Faiths Church under ground' — St Faith's,
beneath the choir of St Paul's, served as parish church for the stationers,
and no doubt for pamphleteers who had got religion. A sense of aimless
discontent pervades these years. In one of the late passages added to the
Terrors he speaks of 'manie embers of encumbraunces' smothering the
'bright flame of my zeale', of 'turbulent cares' sitting 'at the stearne of
my invention'.[3] Importuno says 'he is idle and new fangled, beginning
many things but soone wearie of them ere hee be halfe entred'. We get
a sense of the 'dark side' of Nashe; as Lewis suspects, the adrenal vigour
of his writing 'is by no means the whole story, may indeed be only the
"manic" peak, balanced in private by a "depressive" trough'. Occasionally — in *Christs Teares* and parts of the *Terrors* — this surfaces into the

text: a 'thicke fulsome Serena' descends on him: he is dumpish, drowsy and wishes himself dead.[4]

According to Nashe, his delay in answering the Doctor was due to a depression less mental than financial. Poverty had always been his element – 'many a faire day agoe have I proclaimed my selfe to the world Piers Pennilesse' – but now it seems to envelop and dissipate him. To Importuno he retorts: 'there is no newfanglenes in mee but povertie, which alone maketh mee so unconstant to my determined studies'. He admits he has frittered time away on 'vain hopes and had I wist Court humours', and on penning 'toies for private Gentlemen':

> twise or thrise in a month, when *res est angusta domi*, the bottome of my purse is turnd downeward, & my conduit of incke will no longer flowe for want of reparations, I am faine to let my Plow stand still in the midst of a furrow, and follow some of these new-fangled *Galiardos* and *Senior Fantasticos*, to whose amorous *Villanellas* and *Quipassas* I prostitute my pen in hope of gaine.

The galliard and the 'qui (or che) passa' were fashionable dances, the villanelle a rhyming verse-form associated with dance tunes. If we take him literally he has been writing lyrics for Elizabethan pop songs, but the terms may be euphemistic and the 'toys' more bawdy rhymes along the lines of *Nashes Dildo*. Whatever they were, they kept the wolf from the door. Confutations of Harvey, he grumbles, did not: '*Patentia vestra*, there is not one pint of wine more than the iust Bill of costs and charges in setting forth, to be got by anie of these bitter-sauced Invectives.' He swears that after this 'Cock-fight' is over he will write only what carries 'a present rich possibilitie of raysing my decayed fortunes, and Cavalier flourishing with a feather in my cappe (hey gallanta) in the face of envie'. He speaks bitterly of the scant rewards of professional authorship:

> Some foolish praise perhaps we may meete with, such as is affoorded to ordinarie Iesters that make sport: but otherwise we are like those fugitive Priests in Spaine and Portugall, whom the Pope (verie liber-ally) prefers to Irish Bishoprickes, but allowes them not a pennie of any living to maintaine them with, save onely certaine Friers to beg for them. High titles (as they of Bishops and Prelates), so of Poets and Writers we have in the world, when, in stead of their begging Friers, the fire of our wit is left as our onely last refuge to warme us.[5]

The fugitive priest and the hard-bitten pamphleteer: the comparison is somehow indicative of Nashe's mood at this time.

We know a little of the 'private Gentlemen' who contributed to Nashe's coffers. In about June 1594, we learn, Nashe was 'excessively

beholding' to Sir Roger Williams, the flamboyant Welsh soldier-scholar
believed to be a model for Shakespeare's Fluellen. He lived at Paul's
Wharf, a few doors down from James Forester's distillery 'at the signe
of the Furnaises'. A truculent, witty figure, a noted 'plain-speaker', one
can well imagine him valuing Nashe's company.[6] Another of Nashe's
benefactors – 'none of my coldest well-wishers' – is described in *Have
with you*. Nashe calls him a 'young Knight'. At his 'chamber in the
Strand' one day, Nashe met Sir Thomas Baskerville. This Knight may
well be Sir Robert Carey, youngest brother of Sir George, who was
indeed living on the Strand in mid-1595. He arrived in London in the
early summer, his *Memoirs* relate, and 'got lodging' at Arundel House,
one of the noble riverside houses along the south side of the Strand. The
house belonged to the Howard family but Carey's father, Lord Hunsdon,
had 'the keeping' of it. As the brother of Nashe's patron of 1593–4 he
is plausible enough. Greene had dedicated his *Orpharion* (1590) to him,
and he had been a good friend of Lodge's at Oxford.[7] It is fitting to find
him entertaining Sir Thomas Baskerville: both were veterans of Essex's
French campaign of the early 1590s (Carey was knighted by Essex at
Dieppe in 1591). So we get a glimpse of Nashe in salubrious quarters –
on either side stood Essex House and Somerset House; just up river was
Durham House, where the Ralegh clique had met. The company is
courtly and military: he praises Baskerville as 'one of the most tryed
Souldiers of Christendome'. The time is somewhere before the end of
July 1595, by when Baskerville was down in Plymouth preparing for
the Drake-Hawkins expedition to the West Indies.[8] While in London Sir
Robert says he 'went daily to court' and revelled 'merrily' there: he was a
dashing, cavalier figure who had won the Queen's heart as the 'Forsaken
Knight' in the tilts of 1593. It was as one of his followers, perhaps, that
Nashe's courtly fancies were briefly but unavailingly tickled. Another
'honourable Knight . . . about Court yet attending' is mentioned and
praised in *Have with you*. An erstwhile 'companion' to Sir Philip Sidney;
a poet who has 'repurified Poetrie from Arts pedantisme' and 'instructed
it to speak courtly'; a rich man with a firm grasp on the 'fore lockes of
Fortune': this is almost certainly Sir Fulke Greville, later Baron Brooke.
He too had his residence on the Strand: Giordano Bruno describes a
philosophical evening there, with fellow-guests Sidney and Florio, in his
Cena de le Ceneri ('The Ash-Wednesday Supper').[9] It is not clear whether
Nashe's lauding of him – he promises to 'invent some worthy subject
to eternize him' – is in gratitude for benefits received or in hope of
benefits to come. It all seems part of those 'had I wist court humours'
that he mocks in himself in *Have with you*.

   This covey of knights – Sir George Carey in the Blackfriars, Sir Robert
on the Strand; Williams, Baskerville, Greville – represents the aspirant
upper reaches of Nashe's world at this time. For his daily bread we

move more familiarly downmarket. For much of this period Nashe was lodging with, and probably working for, the printer-publisher John Danter. He had been associated with Danter's 'scar-crowe Presse' ever since the printing of *Strange Newes* in late 1592. In *Pierces Supererogation*, Harvey dubs him 'Danters gentleman', a sarcastic reference to the styling, 'Tho. Nashe, Gentleman', on the title-page of *Strange Newes*. 'Printers take hede how ye play the Heralds', Harvey chides, shrugging off Nashe's satire as an upstart's snobbery:

> If ever Esquier raved with conceit of his new Armes, it is Danters gentleman, that mightily despiseth whatsoever hee beholdeth from the high turret of his creast.[10]

In a separate passage, Harvey talks of 'Danters Maulkin', the 'onely hagge of the Presse', a 'daggletaild rampalion' with a 'moodie tongue'. Carefully read, it is clear he is speaking of 'St Fame', the supposed patroness of Nashe's gutter-press products. In *Have with you*, however, Nashe takes it as an insult to Mistress Danter: 'my Printers Wife too hee hath a twitch at . . . and makes a *maulkin* & a shoo-clout of her, talkes of her *moody tung*', etc. Rising to her defence, Nashe says: 'in all the time I have lyne in her House, and as long as I have knowen her, I never saw anie such thing by her'. So we learn, circuitously, that Nashe was 'lying in', i.e. lodging at, the Danters' house on Hosier Lane for some period before the appearance of *Have with you*, also published by Danter.[11] Hosier Lane ran west out of Smithfield, down towards Holborn Bridge. Smithfield, the site of London's great horse and cattle market, was a rough, brawling, smelly part of town. Nashe speaks of the 'Smithfield ruffianly swashbuckler' and his 'harsh hell-breaking Othes'. There are plenty of kings here, he says, for 'any man may weare a silver crowne, that hath made a fray at Smithfield & lost but a peece of his braine-pan'.[12] From time to time this wide open space, originally 'Smoothfield', was a venue for executions and religious burnings. Most famously it housed the great three-day fair at the feast of St Bartholomew (24 August), celebrated by Ben Jonson in *Bartholmew Fayre* (1614). Here flocked the drovers, horse-coursers and pig-women, the jugglers, cutpurses and gingerbread-sellers, Little Davy the pimp, Kindheart the tooth-drawer and Nightingale the balladeer. Jonson conjures it up in a language that 'savours of Smithfield, the Booth and the Pig-broath', and presents it in a public play-house 'as dirty as Smithfield and as stinking every whit'. Something of this idea of literary pungency, a language with the raunchy 'savour' of London at its roughest, seems relevant to Nashe on Hosier Lane. Close to the east end of the street was the haunt known as Pie Corner: here Jonson's Subtle hung out in his days as a ragged cunning-man — 'Do but collect, Sir, where I met you first: . . . at Pie

Corner, Taking your meale of steeme in from cookes stalls.' Nashe too
mentions a 'Cookes shop at Pye-corner'.[13] One imagines him dropping
down there for a hasty meal, a 'rasher on the coals' or a 'bag-pudding'
and a pint of 'small beer'.

While living at Danter's Nashe would almost certainly have worked
for his keep, probably in the job known as 'corrector' or 'overseer' of
the press. For a man of his accomplishments, this would mean general
reader, editor and adviser on MSS, as well as more menial proof-reader.
The original role of the 'learned corrector' was to supervise foreign
language texts: the martyrologist John Foxe was Latin corrector for
John Day; the Florentine exile Petruccio Ubaldini oversaw Wolfe's Italian
productions.[14] Gabriel Harvey's status at Wolfe's printing-shop is probably close enough to Nashe's at Danter's. Harvey was 'billetted' on
Wolfe, according to Nashe, for 'seaven and thirtie weekes space
together'. While there he acted as literary adviser, 'pressing upon' Wolfe
the works of his own admirers, Chute and Barnes; he composed an
'eloquent post-script' for the weekly plague-bills issued by Wolfe in
1593; he prepared copies for press, witness his handwritten corrections
in, ironically, Greene's *Perimedes*; and he ran up an enormous bill for
his 'diet' which he left unpaid. The hack Iudicio in the Cambridge
comedy, *The Returne from Parnassus (Part II)*, speaks bitterly of the
drudgery involved in the job. 'What ere befall thee, keepe thee from the
trade of corrector of the presse', he warns:

> would it not grieve any good spirritt to sit a whole moneth nitting
> over a lousy beggarly Pamphlet, and like a needy Phisitian to stand
> whole yeares tooting and tumbling the filth that falleth from so many
> draughty inventions as daily swarme in our printing house?[15]

This is probably not far from Nashe on Hosier Lane, for Danter aimed
resolutely for the popular end of the market. His staples were ballads,
plays and hair-raising homilies, and he had a reputation for unscrupulous
piracy – even as an apprentice in the 1580s he was had up for printing
the patented *Grammar* and *Accidence*. But 'popular' meant also Shakespeare – Danter's quarto of *Titus Andronicus* (1594) was the first ever
printing of a Shakespeare play – and it meant plays by Greene and
Lodge, love poems by Tom Watson, and three pamphlets by Nashe.[16]

Looking through the titles registered by Danter in the years 1594–6
one gets some inkling of Nashe's presence at the printing-house. A ballad
lamenting the death of Lord Strange catches the eye – 'A Dolefull Adewe
to the last Erle of Derby', to be sung to the tune of 'Bonny Sweete
Robin'. Works by Rabelais, Sir Roger Williams and Thomas Lodge may
suggest Nashe's taste and influence as 'overseer'. Most interesting of all,
perhaps, are two surreptitious Catholic texts issued by Danter at this

time. The first was *Marie Magdalenes Love*, published in 1595. It is
ascribed on the title-page to Nicholas Breton, and bound up with a
genuine Breton piece, *A Solemne Passion of the Soules Love*, but it is
almost certainly by another, unknown hand. The Breton poem may have
been useful 'cover', for despite its Romish tinge *Marie Magdalenes Love*
was duly licensed at Stationers' Hall on 20 September 1595.[17] In 1596
Danter pressed his luck, and clandestinely published a book of Catholic
devotions called *Iesus Psalter*. For this, in about June or July, his press
was ordered to be seized. Stationers' Company documents record the
ensuing small drama:

> for taking of Danters man and i forme and i heape brought to the
> hall and expences that nighte . . . 1s 8d
> for fetching him out of the Compter . . . 3s
> for fetching Danters presse to the hall withe porterage and other
> charges . . . 3s 6d

Nashe would not be the 'man' of Danter's hauled off to the Counter
prison – this was probably a print-worker or prentice – but he may well
have been at Hosier Lane on the night of the raid. He was in town all
that summer, as his letter to William Cotton makes clear. Danter's
Romish tracts of 1595–6 seem to be further evidence of Nashe's religious
leanings: they suggest that his favoured printer had Catholic sympathies
and that these were aggravated into action during Nashe's spell as
'overseer' of the press. It all fits well with the rather neurotic, restless
tone of these years for Nashe. It is a short step from *Christs Teares* to
Marie Magdalenes Love: Harvey had compared the former to
Southwell's *Funerall Teares of Mary Magdalene*, another Catholic treatise. Nor is it hard to imagine Nashe poring nocturnally over the section
in *Iesus Psalter* entitled 'A Wholesome Doctrine how to resist and overcome the ghostly temptations of the Fende.'[18] Wherever Nashe goes the
tempo quickens: he brings disruption and intrigue into the room, as well
as tonic laughter.

Somewhere between the *dolce vita* of the Strand and the sweat
smudges of the printing-shop, Nashe pursued his perennial literary
round. A particular colleague at this time was John Lyly, who lived with
his wife Anne in the precincts of St Bartholomew's Hospital, a short
walk across Smithfield from Hosier Lane. The dapper wit of old had
fallen on hard times: the Paul's Boys were disbanded, his delicate style
outmoded, his hopes for the Mastership of the Revels frustrated. Plain-
tively he petitioned the Queen: 'thirteen yeares your Highnes servant,
butt yett nothinge', he wrote, 'a thousand hopes, butt all noethinge'; he
had just 'three Legacyes' left, 'Patience to my Creditors, Mellanchollie
without measure to my frindes, & Beggerry without shame to my

familye'.[19] Lyly is frequently mentioned in *Have with you*. Harvey's inclusion of the 'Advertisement for Papp-hatchett' in *Pierces Supererogation* made Lyly 'halves with me in this indignitie that is offred'. Nashe clearly hoped Lyly would 'march' with him against Harvey, and it seems that Lyly had actually composed something: 'The Paradoxe of the Asse M. Lilly hath wrought uppon, as also to him I turne over the Doctors Apothecarie tearmes'. Nashe also recalls Lyly's 'immoderate commending' of the great preacher, Lancelot Andrewes, whereupon 'by little and little I was drawne on to bee an Auditor of his'. This must have been a private remark of Lyly's since he left no printed allusion to Dr Andrewes. Nashe praises Andrewes warmly – 'an Orator and a Poet', the 'absolutest Oracle of all sound Divinitie'. One glimpses him in the congregation, perhaps at St Paul's where Andrewes was prebendary, an appreciative 'auditor' of the preacher's 'incomparable gifts'.[20]

Another of Nashe's associates at this time was Henry Chettle, whose *Kind Harts Dreame* had urged him on against Harvey back in 1592. While Nashe was compiling *Have with you* Chettle penned him an extremely courteous letter, refuting Harvey's claim that Nashe had in some way 'abusde' him:

> I hold it no good manners (M. Nashe), being but an Artificer, to give D. Harvey the ly, though he have deserv'd it by publishing in Print you have done mee wrong, which privately I never found. . . . Your booke being readie for the Presse, Ile square & set it out in Pages, that shall page and lackey his infamie after him (at least) while he lives, if no longer.
>
> Your old Compositor,
Henry Chettle

Chettle was himself a printer, and was briefly – in 1591 – a partner of Danter's: 'your old Compositor' may mean he had helped to set up *Strange Newes*, or it may just be printing-house jargon for 'your old friend'. An immensely prolific penny-a-liner – no less than forty-eight plays are associated with him in Henslowe's theatrical accounts – Chettle was described by Thomas Dekker as an 'old acquaintance' of Nashe, Marlowe and Greene. Dekker sketches him in with a single brush-stroke: 'in comes Chettle, sweating and blowing by reason of his fatnes'.[21] This amiable, portly printer-scribbler fits in well with the Nashe of Hosier Lane. So too does Humfrey King, the dedicatee of *Nashes Lenten Stuffe*, a poet of sorts but best known as a devotee and connoisseur of tobacco. Anthony Chute's panegyric, *Tabaco* (1595), is dedicated to him: 'What your experience is in this divine hearbe, al men do know, and acknowledge you to bee The Sovereigne of Tabacco'. Nashe also calls him 'King of the Tobacconists *hic & ubique*' – a 'tobacconist' then meant a user, not a seller, of tobacco. He was a small man – Nashe styles him 'little Numps' and 'your diminutive excelsitude' – and a generous dispenser of 'good fellowshippe'. Nashe hopes for a 'Kanne of strong ale', with toast, sugar and nutmegs, 'to entertaine mee everie time I come by your lodging'. What better way to start the day than 'the best mornings draught of merry-go-downe in your quarters'?[22] King's poem, *The Hermits Tale*, appeared in about 1599. In a prefatory sonnet, an unnamed friend of King's swears a 'solemne oath':

> By the red Herring, thy true Patronage,
> And famous Nash, so deere unto us both.
> By all the bowers we have reveld in,
> Our merry times that gallop hence so fast . . .[23]

This is redolent of Nashe as sheer good company. He was undoubtedly a smoker, as were Marlowe and Lyly and probably most of this 'scribbling crew'. Tobacco was the fashionable drug of the day, expensive enough to be a luxury, disapproved enough to be a gesture. It was bought in dark, moist 'cakes', dried, and smoked in long shallow-panned clay pipes. A smoke toned Nashe up for the day's literary labours: 'Saint George and a tickling pipe of Tobacco, and then pell mell, all alone have amongst them'. It helped to dampen hunger and 'expell cold'. They were hard times indeed when he had 'not so much as a pipe of Tabacco to rayse my spirites and warme my braine'.[24]

Another name connected with Nashe in the mid-1590s is that of Thomas Campion, poet, musician and physician. Campion was the same age as Nashe and they were contemporaries at Cambridge: Campion was at Peterhouse, but being a Catholic he took no degree. Whether they knew one another is unproved, but they certainly admired one another. In his Latin volume of 1595, *Poemata*, Campion included a stirring tribute '*Ad Nashum*'. He praises 'that bitter brilliance of your spirit' ('*istudque ingenii tui acre fulmen*') which makes the 'feeble and dull' ('*insipidis & inficetis*') quake. He urges him to rout his enemies with 'bloody words' ('*cruenta verba*') and 'wounding scoffs' ('*vulnificos sales*'). He cannot get enough of Nashe's satiric frenzies:

> Nunc oro rogoque improbos ut istos
> Mactes continuis decem libellis:
> Nam sunt pitudili atque inelegantes

(I beg and pray that you plague these unworthies in ten continuous pamphlets, for they are addled and ungainly creatures)

It is clear that Harvey and his crew are meant, though Campion also mentions Nashe's anti-Puritan polemic. A few epigrams later, Campion mounts a hostile attack on George Chapman, and elsewhere is a deroga-

tory epigram '*In Barnum*', about Harvey's florid young admirer, Barnabe
Barnes. The Catholic Campion clearly shared Nashe's attitudes and
antagonisms. Nashe returned the compliment in *Have with you*, with a
puff for 'that universall applauded Latine poeme of Master Campions'.[25]

Sometime in 1595, Nashe left town on a trip to Lincolnshire, for what
reason we do not know. He mentions the road 'betwixt Stamford and
Beechfeeld', which is 'all up hill and downe hill', and talks of 'a horse
plunging through the myre in the deep of winter'.[26] We know, at least,
of one incident on his return journey. 'Comming out of Lincolnshyre, it
was my hap to take Cambridge in my waye, where I had not been in
sixe yeare before.' He took a room at the Dolphin Inn. There, 'by
wonderful destinie', lodged in the 'very next chamber to mee, parted but
by a wainscot doore that was naild up', was none other than Gabriel
Harvey. Nashe was thrown into a lather of uncertainty:

> What a stomacke I had to have scratcht with him, but that the nature
> of the place hindred mee, where it is as ill as pettie treason to look
> but awry on the sacred person of a Doctour.

Harvey apparently sent an invitation for Nashe to join him in a 'conference' over dinner, 'wherein all quarrells might be discust and drawne to
an attonement'. But 'I had no fancie to it, for once before I had bin so
cousend by his colloging'. The *Supererogation* was still unanswered, a
'publique wrong in Print', not to be 'so sleightly slubberd over in private
with Come, come, give me your hand, let us bee frends, and thereupon
I drinke to you'. And what if the invitation were a trap, a plot to poison
him?

> If I had (I say) rusht in my selfe, and two or three hungrie Fellowes
> more, and cryde, Doo you want anie guestes? What, nothing but bare
> Commons? it had beene a question (considering the good-will that is
> betwixt us) whether he wold have lent me a precious dram more than
> ordinarie, to helpe disgestion.

And so they never met. Nashe displays all the hesitancy of a timid lover.
It is untypical and therefore revealing. He seems anxious to protect his
own image and idea of Harvey: he had lived so long with it, in these
lean years it was a *raison d'écrire* to cling to. He did not want the actual
human Harvey to dislodge that cherished cartoon-figure, which served
as the butt of more angers than one man could possibly warrant.

A deal of controversy, both for and against Nashe, emanates from

Cambridge in the late 1590s. There was, naturally, keen interest there
in the Harvey-Nashe war: it was a Cambridge controversy, a 'chapter'
of disputation, fought out in a national arena. In his *Polimanteia* (1595),
William Covell treats it in just this way, and urges:

> Cambridge make thy two children friends [in margin: D. Harvey. M.
> Nash], thou hast been unkinde unto the one to weane him before his
> time; and too fond upon the other to keepe him so long without
> preferment. The one is ancient & of much reading, the other is young
> but ful of wit: tell them both thou bred them and brought them up:
> bid the ancient forbeare to offer wrong; tell the younger he shall
> suffer none.[27]

Clearly Covell hoped the university could influence its two 'children' to
patch up their differences – Nashe certainly valued his reputation there:
he cares not 'what Hoppenny Hoe & his fellow Hankin Booby thinke'
so long as 'those whom Arte hath adopted for the peculiar Plants of her
Acadamie' hold him in some 'tollerable account'[28] – but nothing is
recorded of any official effort to do so. Cambridge was happy enough
to let the entertainers 'flyte' on. Their presence in Cambridge in 1595 –
Nashe there for the first time in six years – no doubt stirred up the
factions anew.

In the Harvey corner, for instance, was the Puritan divine, Joseph
Hall, a fellow of Emmanuel College. In 1597 he ventured into the
burgeoning field of verse-satire with his *Virgidemiarum* ('A Harvest of
Scourges'). In it are several hits at Nashe. He is undoubtedly the 'too
licentiate' poet of whom Hall says,

> Arts of Whoring, stories of the Stewes,
> Ye Muses will ye beare, and may refuse?
> Nay let the Divell, and Saint Valentine
> Be gossips to those ribald rymes of thine.

The 'Divell' refers to Pierce's 'supplication', and St Valentine to the
Choise of Valentines. Hall also calls Nashe 'Balbus', the stammerer,
referring to his failure to answer Harvey:

> But why doth Balbus' dead-doing quill
> Parch in his rusty scabbard all the while,
> His golden fleece o'ergrown with mouldy hoar,
> As though he had his witty works foreswore?
> Belike of late now Balbus hath no need,
> Nor now belike his shrinking shoulders dread
> The catch-poll's fist: the press may still remain
> And breathe, till Balbus be in debt again.[29]

Here Nashe is styled a literary mercenary: the 'catch-poll' is the bailiff
and Hall suggests – quite wrongly – that Nashe is silent because financi-
ally secure. Hall is clearly part of the Harvey faction. His literary idol
was Harvey's friend, Spenser, and the founder of his college, Sir Walter
Mildmay, was an early patron of Harvey's. Hall was later to follow in
Harvey's steps as University Praelector in Rhetoric. He doubtless knew of
Nashe's scoffing at Cambridge Puritanism, and at his college, Emmanuel,
which Nashe called 'S. Lawrence his monastery', referring to its Puritan
Master, Laurence Chaderton.[30]

Rich testimony of the esteem Nashe enjoyed in undergraduate circles
is found in the three college comedies known as the *Parnassus Plays*.
These were played at Nashe's old college, St John's, over three Christmas
holidays: *The Pilgrimage to Parnassus* in 1598–9, the first part of *The
Returne to Parnassus* in 1599–1600, the second part of *The Returne* in
1601–2. The author is anonymous – two Johnsmen, William Dodd and
Owen Gwyn, have been suggested – but whoever he was he knew
Nashe's works intimately. Phrases from them are scattered *verbatim*
throughout the plays and the whole tone is modelled on Nashe's refrac-
tory wit. Written by 'earnestly modish' Elizabethan students, says
Rhodes, the plays are a 'sensitive pointer to fashionable literary trends'.
Trendiest of all, they show, is satire, and in particular 'Nashe and
Nasheian invective'.[31] The character of Ingenioso is clearly intended as
a portrait of – 'an allusion or tribute to' – Nashe. As a student he is a
'mad greeke', a 'ladd of mettall', a 'tattered prodigal'. He resolves to
forsake the 'region of Philosophy' and seek his literary fortune: 'To
London Ile goe, Ile live by the Printinge house.' He becomes a prolific
popular hack, puts his wit 'out to interest' and makes it 'returne two
Phamphlets a weeke'. He is perennially penniless – 'fidlinge thy
pamphlets from doore to doore, like a blind harper for bread & chease'
– and indulges in much cursing on stingy philistine patrons: 'yonders a
churle thinckes it enough for his favoure to shine like a sunn on the
dunghill of learning'; 'it pleased my witt yesternighte to make water,
and to use this goutie patron in steed of an urinall'.[32] All this traces,
humorously but accurately, the outline of Nashe's early career. One of
Ingenioso's patrons is Gullio, a vapid courtly *inamorato* who has him
pen poems to his mistress. Ingenioso speaks bitterly of the servitude of
his 'freer spirit' while he

> . . . applauded bragging Gullio,
> Applyed my veyne to sottishe Gullio,
> Made wanton lines to please lewd Gullio.

Here is the Nashe of the *Valentines*, wasting his talents on cosmetic
'toies for private Gentlemen'. This Gullio is a fervid admirer of Shakespeare's love-poetry – 'O sweet Mr Shakespeare, Ile have his picture in

my study at the court.' There may be a touch of Southampton in him, his disdainful treatment of Ingenioso echoing Southampton's rejection of Nashe in 1594.[33] More specifically, Ingenioso's publisher is Danter – whose dubious status allows him to appear in the play undisguised, as do the players Burbage and Kemp – and we are treated to a marvellous vignette of them haggling over the copy of Ingenioso's latest pamphlet, entitled *A Chronicle of Cambridge Cuckolds*:

Ingenioso	I tell thee this libel of Cambridge has much salt and pepper in the nose: it will sell sheerely underhand, whenas these bookes of exhortations and Catechismes lie moulding on thy shopboard.
Danter	It's true; but good fayth, M. Ingenioso, I lost by your last booke, and you know there is many a one that payes me largely for the printing of their inventions. But for all this you shall have 40 shillings and an odde pottle of wine.
Ingenioso	40 Shillings? A fit reward for one of your reumatick poets, that beslavers all the paper he comes by, and furnishes the Chaundlers with wast papers to wrap candles in: but as for me, Ile be paid deare even for the dreggs of my wit. Little knowes the worlde what belongs to the keeping of a good wit in waters, dietts, drinckes, Tobacco, &c . . .

As a portrait of Nashe, Ingenioso is largely a *collage*, a textual patchwork: in this last speech alone are one straight quote and two other echoes from Nashe's pamphlets.[34] But when the pastiche relents we get something more informing: another pair of eyes, Nashe as viewed by a young Elizabethan intellectual who deeply admired him and may perhaps have met him. When they are not plagiarisms, Ingenioso's words are well-informed guesses, imagined fragments of Nashe's actual conversation:

Ile now to Paules Churchyard, meete me in an hour hence at the signe of the Pegasus in Cheap-side, and Ile moyst thy temples with a cuppe of Claret, as hard as the world goes . . .

Such barmy heads wil alwaies be working, when as sad vineger witts sit souring at the bottome of a barrell . . .

There is no foole to the Sattin foole, the Velvet foole, the perfumede foole. . . . Ther's no knave to the barbarous knave, the mooting knave, the pleading knave . . .

Ile marche on with a light purse & a nimble tongue, and picke a quarell with his doore . . .

O fustie worlde, were there anie commendable passage to Styx and Acharon, I would goe live with Tarleton, and never more bless this dull age with a good line . . .

I see wit is but a phantasme. . . , the idle follower of a folorne creature. Nay it is a devill that will never leave a man till it hath brought him to beggerie, a malicious spirit that delightes in a close libell or an open Satyre.

These catch Nashe's moods: busy, gregarious, splenetic, a cavalier tone tinged with deep bitterness. Nashe's literary presence, the multiplicity of his appeal, is also well caught. He is in part just a joker, the crazy scribbler with a bundle of 'dissolute papers' in his pocket, begged by his friends to 'drinke of a sentence to us, to the health of mirth and the confusion of Melancholye'. Yet the Grub Street entertainer is also the 'truth telling' satirist, the scourge of social abuses:

> I, Iuvenall: thy ierking hand is good,
> Not gently laying on, but fetching bloud.

He is, above all, the Elizabethan journalist of immense acuity and power:

Why man, I am able to make a pamphlet of thy blew coate and the button in thy capp, to rime thy bearde of thy face, to make thee a ridiculous blew sleevd creature, while thou livest. I have immortalitie in my pen, and bestowe it on whome I will.[35]

During his visit to Cambridge, Nashe probably crossed paths with Richard Lichfield, the eccentric barber-surgeon of Trinity College. When Have with you finally appeared in 1596, Nashe prefaced it with a long, gymnastic dedication to 'olde Dicke of Lichfield', whom he hails as

the most Orthodoxicall and reverent Corrector of staring haires, the sincere & finigraphicall rarifier of prolixious rough barbarisme, the thrice egregious and censoriall animadvertiser of vagrant moustachios, chiefe scavenger of chins, and principall Head-man of the parish wherein he dwells.[36]

Barber-surgeons were college servants, rather than academics: the 'barbi-tonsor' at St John's received 6s 8d a quarter. They acted as rudimentary doctors and dentists as well as hairdressers. The traditional barber's pole recalls their role as 'phlebotomists' (blood-letters), the red and white

stripes signifying the blood and the tourniquet.[37] Nashe speaks of Lichfield's 'sharpe pointed launce' to 'let bloud with', his 'keene Palermo
rasour' and his 'knacking' scissors. He pictures him in his 'narrow' little
shop, with its 'painted may-pole' and a rotten tooth in the window; or
bustling 'bluntly' into some Fellow's room with his 'washing bowle' and
'nursecloutes'. Nashe may have known him from his own undergraduate
days. He says Lichfield has performed 'in the crowne office' throughout
'this sixteene yeare': this takes us back to the early 1580s, when Nashe
came up. Lichfield was still living in Cambridge in 1630, when he died
at a ripe old age.[38]

These Cambridge barbers had a reputation as merry 'grigs' and fantastic mock-scholars. Nashe mentions one Williamson, 'thy fellow Barber',
who 'hath long borne the bell for finicall descanting on the *Crates*'
(probably a style of beard). A letter of Harvey's also refers to the 'rowling
tongue' of 'M. Williamson, over-fine Cambridge barber'. Another loqua-
cious local character mentioned by both Nashe and Harvey is Tom
Tooley, probably also a barber.[39] Among this fraternity of antic orators
Dick Lichfield apparently reigned supreme, and so it is Nashe bids him
be his 'paraphrasticall gallant Patron', and apply his skills, surgical and
linguistic, on the Harveys – 'phlebothomize them, sting them, tutch
them, Dick' . . . 'If thou wilt have the Doctour for an Anatomie, thou
shalt' . . . 'I am the man will deliver him to thee to be scotcht and
carbonadoed.' He also composes a mock 'Grace' on the Harveys, for
Lichfield to broadcast 'this winter at an Evening tearme', among some
'honourable assembly of sharpe iudiciall fierie wits'.

So far, so good: Nashe counts this *magister* of the barber's shop a
powerful ally, who will whip up support among the fun-loving elements
of the university. In this, however, he would seem to have badly
misjudged, for in the spring of 1597 Lichfield set to work, not on a
'phlebotomy' of the Harveys, but on a vicious assault on Nashe. He
called it *The Trimming of Thomas Nashe*.[40] He complains of Nashe's
'foule Epistle', addressed to him without permission: 'you might have
said By your leave, Sir'. He claims: 'had I but knowne of this Cockatrice
whilst twas in the shell, I would have broken it, it never should have
beene hatcht by my patronage'. It is on Nashe that his fantastic pedan-
tisms are heaped: 'right glossomachicall Thomas' . . . 'the polypragmati-
call, parasituprocriticall and pantophrainoudendeconticall puppie,
Thomas Nashe'. It is Nashe who is to be 'carbonadoed' and his bones
speared 'on my launce-point' to 'hang at my shop windowe'.[41]

Lichfield's furious retort to 'malevolent Tom' makes one look anew
at Nashe's address to him, and the intentions behind it. One finds, with
hindsight, the veins of sarcasm and provocation. For all his 'dexteritie',
says Nashe, Lichfield has received no 'requitall' except for 'some few
french crownes, pild Friers crownes drie-shaven': these 'crowns' are not

the coins so-named, but familiar slang for syphilitic boils and buboes.[42]
Nashe's talk of the 'lousy naprie' that barbers 'put about mens neckes'
is hardly complimentary. A typographical prank turns Lichfield from a
'notable' benefactor into a 'not able' benefactor. Above all, the humour
is double-edged when Nashe says that Lichfield's 'inkhornisme' is a mere
shadow of Harvey's. Compared to that *maestro* of absurdities, Dick
talks 'plodding and dunstically, like a clowne of Cherry-hinton'; his 'few
scraping ceremonies' only reveal his 'non-proficiency in the Doctors
Paracelsian rope-rethorique'. Perhaps, says Nashe, you are incapable of
answering Harvey; perhaps, even, you are an *admirer* of his:

> I feele thy pulses beat slowly alreadie, although thou beest fortie mile
> off from mee, and this impotent answer (with much adoo) droppes
> from thee, even as sweate from a leane man that drinks sacke: namely,
> that thou thinkest there cannot much extraordinarie descant be made
> of it, except it be to say, such a one [i.e. Harvey] hath an admirable
> capacitie, an incomparable quick invention and a surmounting rich
> spirit above all men. Hah, ha, a destitute poore fellow art thou, and
> hast mist me nine score: goe, goe, get thee a candle and keepe thy selfe
> warme in thy bed, for out of question, thy spirit is in a consumption.

This clearly is needle. These ironies can easily be missed amid the general
romp of the dedication, but Lichfield himself did not miss them. 'Of
Epistles some be denuntiatorie', he says, and Nashe's is obviously one
of them. It is an affront from one whose 'convicious' mouth utters
'nothing but noysome and ill-saverd vomites'. Lichfield evidently felt he
was the target, rather than the accomplice, of Nashe's 'Hah ha'.

A separate mention of Lichfield, in the main text of *Have with you*,
throws a little more light on the matter. Here Nashe describes him as
an 'ingenuous odde merry Greeke, who (as I have heard) hath translated
my *Piers Pennilesse* into the Macaronicall tongue, wherein I wish hee
had been more tongue-tide'.[43] This perhaps is the clue: that Lichfield
had himself composed some anti-Nashe burlesque. Macaronics – the
comic mingling of English words with Latin formations – were a popular
literary diversion. The *locus classicus* was Coccaeus' *Liber Macaronices*;
Tom Coryat's *Crambe* (1611) included various 'Macaronick Dishes'.
Whether Nashe uses the term strictly, or simply means Lichfield had
made some 'paraphrasticall' parody of *Pierce*, is hard to say. Lichfield's
puns and nonce Latinisms in the *Trimming* – 'Nas hum. Mitto tibi
Nashum prora N. Puppi humque carentem'; 'Choroebus quasi chori
bos' – help us imagine such a *pastiche*.[44] It was probably a verbal rather
than written performance, reported to Nashe (hence 'as I have heard').
Nashe's vaunting of Lichfield as an 'aenigmaticall Linguist', a noted

professor of 'Neoterick tongues' (i.e. neologisms), takes on an ironic coloration.

This whole business has never been examined. The old chestnut that Lichfield was just a pseudonym for Harvey has long been discarded, but nothing has been said about Nashe's relations with the real Lichfield, and about why his ostensibly good-humoured dedication plucked on this snarling reply. Nashe was, essentially, 'trying it on' with Lichfield. He may have met the comical barber while an undergraduate, or crossed swords with him on this later visit. He knows that Lichfield has made some 'macaronicall' mockery of *Pierce*, that he is in his odd-ball way a Harveyesque figure. Back in London, he pens not so much an 'Epistle Dedicatorie' as an 'Epistle Provocatorie'.[45] It is a shot in the dark: Lichfield could jump either way. A new friend or a new foe, no real matter: in the politics of pamphleteering, freshness is all. Nashe cannot have been much pleased by the *Trimming*, but he was probably not much surprised by it either. He announced in 1599 that he had 'a pamphlet hot a brooding' in reply. It will be called *The Barbers Warming Panne*. 'Stay till Ester Terme', he promises, 'and then, with the answere to the *Trim Tram*, I will make you laugh your hearts out.'[46] On this note of imminent merriment the matter rests, for no such pamphlet appeared. This whole episode suggests Nashe's professional instinct for trouble-making. Whichever way Lichfield reacted, hostilities would be prolonged, more controversial copy assured. As he travelled back down to London, in 1595 or early 1596, Nashe left a carefully stirred-up nest of factions behind him, the buzzing of which can be heard in Hall's *Virgidemiarum*, in Lichfield's *Trimming*, and in the plays of the young 'Parnassian' of St John's. Even he, Nashe's staunch supporter, knows that the Juvenalian satirist – 'surgean-like thou dost with cutting heale' – is also a wanton *provocateur*. 'What, Ingenioso, carrying a Vinegar bottle about thee, like a great schole-boy giving the world a bloudy nose?'[47]

In August or September 1596, from London, Nashe wrote to his 'worshipfull good freinde' William Cotton, Carey's man, presumably down on the Isle of Wight. It is his only personal letter to have survived in manuscript (Document 10). He complains of 'this tedious dead vacation', slack time for the entertainers. Though 'earnestly invited elsewhere', he has stayed in town 'upon had I wist hopes, & an after harvest I expected by writing for the stage and for the presse'. Things have not worked out, however. 'The players as if they had writt another Christs tears, ar piteously persecuted by the L. Maior & the aldermen.' The company he was writing for must have been the Lord Chamberlain's Men, now

Carey's troupe, for he says that 'however in there old Lords tyme they thought there state setled, it is now so uncertayne they cannot build upon it'. This refers to the death of their old patron, Henry, Lord Hunsdon, on 23 July 1596, and to the rivalries between Carey and Lord Cobham that followed: of this more later. As for the printers, Nashe continues, 'there is sutch gaping amongst them for the coppy of my L. of essex voyage & the ballet of the thre score & foure knights' – for news, that is, of Essex's expedition to Cadiz, which returned on 10 August, and for ballads about the gaggle of knighthoods conferred by Essex – that the writer with anything else to sell will not get 'a scute or a dandiprat', not even 'the price of all Harveys works togither', for his pains. Next he tosses in a bit of gossip about Sir John Smythe – an old Catholic soldier currently in the Tower for treason – but he has swift second thoughts about touching on 'state matters' and heavily scores through the whole passage. Just decipherable is: 'Sr Iohn Smith himselfe . . . shold make another supplement or second pt of his fooles bolt . . . soone shot as I cold say of both of his.' These refer to Smythe's tracts on warfare: he advocated the old archery, hence 'fooles bolt'. One of these had been officially suppressed, as likely to 'breed discredyt to divers of greater Accownt than hymself'. Among its targets was Nashe's *bête noire*, Leicester. In June 1596 Smythe announced to a platoon of startled soldiers at Colchester: 'The common people have been oppressed and used as bondmen these thirty years, but if you will go with me I will see a reformation.' He was arrested and thrown in the Tower. He pleaded that his treason was due to having supped too liberally the night before, but he spent twenty months in the Tower and many years thereafter under house-arrest.[48] This quixotic old Catholic flits into Nashe's thoughts and then is prudently expunged. The letter had a long way to travel, and the 'mice-eyed decipherers' were everywhere.

If he censored himself on political matters, Nashe compensated with other improprieties. Sir John Harington had recently published *The Metamorphosis of Ajax*, which combined a quirky 'cloacinian satire' with actual descriptions and diagrams of his newly invented flushing lavatory (the title puns on a 'jakes', or privy).[49] Harington had spoken sniffily of Nashe – his 'Epigram to Dr Harvey' warned him of fighting such 'durty foes' as 'Nash' – and Nashe in turn had doubtless scoffed, with a touch of envy, at this courtly jester who sparred with the Queen. Turning now to the *Metamorphosis*, and the stir its publication has caused, Nashe rattles off a stunningly coarse tirade against Harington:

Only Mr Harrington of late hath sett up sutch filthy stinking iakes in pouls churchyard, that the stationers wold give any mony for a cover for it. What should move him to it I know not, except he meant to bid a turd in all gentle readers teeth, or whereas Don Diego &

Brokkenbury beshitt poules, to prevent the like inconvenience, he hath revived an old innes a court tricke of turning [?turds] out in a paper, & framed close stooles for them to carry in there pockets as gentlewomen do there spunges. . . . He should have sett for ye mott or word before it Fah, and dedicated it to the house of the shakerlies that give for there armes thre doggs turds reaking. For my parte I pitty him & pray for him that he may have many good stooles to his last ending . . . for otherwise it is to be feared . . . he will dy with a turd in his mouth at his last gaspe & bee coffind up in a iakes farmers tunne, no other nosewise christian for his horrible perfume being able to come nere him.

This may begin with dislike, and a pretence of shock at Harington's literary stunt, but it quickly becomes something else. Nashe warms compulsively to the lavatorial theme: if Harington wants to get dirty Nashe has – in a private letter at least – a few tricks to show him. There is a real love of dirt here, a *nostalgie de la boue*: here, the psychologist might say, is the infantile raw stuff of Nashe as 'low life' journalist and satirical mud-slinger. In its relentless smuttiness is also a social anger, a dragging-down of distinctions into the common denominator of defeca-tion. As he splutters on one gets the feeling that in summer 1596 Nashe was off the rails somewhat, close to an edge, or close – in the Elizabethan way of thinking – to one of those polar psychological points between which one shuttled. 'What hath immortalitie to do with mucke?' 'Better beseeming a privie then a pulpit' – these phrases of Nashe's express real tensions. 'To vex me contraries meet in one', said John Donne, and Nashe the pamphleteer milked the contraries for every drop of copy: *Christs Teares* and the *Valentines*, the preacher and the pornographer. Even in the confines of this letter the contraries appear, for just before this anal rhapsody on Harington is a touching moment when a mention of Thomas Churchyard's *Chippes* calls to his mind a picture hanging at Carpenters' Hall, where the boy Christ is painted gathering up wood-chips while 'Ioseph his father stands hewing a peice of timber & Mary his mother sitts spinning by'. A sudden moment of simplicity: Nashe is moved by this Caravaggian picture of Christ in daily surroundings. As suddenly as it swelled, the tirade against Harington passes. We are back in the day-to-day world, scratching for cash:

Well some men for sorrow singe as it is in the ballet of Iohn Carelesse in the booke of martirs, & I am merry when I have nere a penny in my purse. God may move you though I say nothing, in wch hope that that wch wilbee shalbe, I take my leave.

On this hopeful note, a cadge made graceful with years of practice,

Nashe signs off. The letter is itself a commodity, a gift which he hopes will elicit some return: words into money, the hack's alchemy. Cotton was far from the action, toiling down at Carisbrooke, starved of metropolitan gossip. It was not everyone who got their cup of news straight from Tom Nashe.

The letter is still to be read today, grubby and threadbare – inherently so, perhaps, as well as through four centuries of handling. It is a moment of the real Nashe, caught in the dead city summer, leaving a trail of fast spiky gestures across the paper. The speed and vigour of the writing is unmistakable: he writes *in currente calamo*, spontaneously himself, undisguised and uncontrolled. He fills up every inch of paper, the lines packed, 'close pestered' as he would say, and stretching right to the edge of the page. Here is Nashe occupying his personal patch of Elizabethan England, filling it with fidgety gestures, chafing at its boundaries. Though hurried the hand is not, by Elizabethan standards, unclear. The 'middle zone' – letters with no upper or lower strokes – is smallish and simply formed; the dots are in place over the i's; there is acuity and concentration, Nashe's marvellous eye for detail, in all this. But the intelligence is always a threatened one, disrupted by strange obsessive gestures, in particular that wide low scooping movement in the 'y', '&' and long-tailed 'h'. Here is the sieving of 'muckhils and shop-dust', the gutter-level reportage, the anal fixation. This scooping stroke tends to mingle with the line below it: graphologically this suggests an invasion of 'lower' forces into the precincts of the ego. Another telling feature is an interruptedness, the fast horizontal flow of the hand held up in patches and blotches of ink: a moment of brooding, pressure, a sudden thicket of tension. Perhaps most apt of all is Nashe's personal 'I', taken by graphologists as a virtually pictorial image of the self. His is perfect: it carries a thin sharp cross-stroke, like a *picador* with his lance, the satirist with his quill. This flimsy leaf of paper is Nashe in miniature; cluttered, grubby, rapid and passionate, shadowed with tensions but teeming with life.

In the autumn of 1596, *Have with you to Saffron-Walden* finally rolled off Danter's press. It cannot have been out before October, since there is a passing reference to the death of the old Countess of Derby, Strange's mother, which occurred in late September.[50] It had been composed in fits and starts over 'this two or three yeare'. Much of it was written before his trip to Lincolnshire: one of his reasons for avoiding a *rapprochement* with Harvey was that he would waste the 'paines' he had already taken 'in new arraying and furbishing him'. Apart from some minor additions, it was probably complete by summer 1596, for he says the manuscript 'hath gone abroad with his keeper any time this quarter of this year'.[51] Though over-long and tangential, *Have with you* has a centre-piece – an exhaustive mock-biography of Harvey – which is one of the masterpieces of English satire. The episode of Harvey's committal for debt may have been in Shakespeare's mind when he wrote the scene of Malvolio's imprisonment in *Twelfth Night*. For all its surreal fantasies and unsubstantiated innuendoes, Nashe's burlesque biography is a also fine piece of journalism, a detailed *exposé*. Harvey made no answer to it, in fact the *Suprerogation* and *NewLetter* of 1593 prove to be his last ventures into print. He had destroyed himself, perhaps, with his own elephantine posturings, but *Have with you* administered the *coup de grâce*. As Nashe's subtitle put it, 'Gabriel Harveys Hunt is up'.

To break up the relentless satirical assault, Nashe frames *Have with you* as a kind of judicial discussion of the rights and wrongs of the quarrel, and he introduces the comments and arguments of four'*interlocutores*', with himself – 'Piers Pennilesse Respondent' – puttig his case to them. These characters are, he insists, not 'fained', but four real people who 'have dealt with me in the same humour that heere I shaddow'.[52] The leading figure is 'Senior Importuno', a 'gentleman of good qualitie, to whom I rest many waies beholding'. Thus casually described he is hard to identify. He could possibly be Lyly, or some other fellow-writer like Lodge, or Peele, or the just-gentlemanly Shakespeare; he could be his 'worshipfull' friend, William Cotton, or the 'copious Carminist', William Beeston. He must remain a mystery. The second is called 'Grand Consiliadore'. Under this name, says Nashe, 'I allude to a grave reverend Gimnosophist, *Amicorum amicissimus*, of all my Frends the most zealous.' This surely is Robert Cotton, '*dignissimus doctissimus Cottonus*', the great scholar who had been Nashe's host in 1593. Consiliadore's 'Chamber' is called an 'Oracle or Convocation Chappell of sound counsaile for all the better sort of the sonnes of understanding about London'. This is exactly the reputation of Cotton's town-house, in Old Palace Yard, Westminster. With its vast library, it was 'the meeting place of all the scholars in the country', men like Dee, Camden and Bacon, and it was often the venue for meetings of the Society of Antiquaries. Consiliadore takes on the role of 'censor or moderator' in Nashe's *colloquium*: apt for the learned young Cotton, already acknowledged as a 'master of precedents', fit to adjudicate in ticklish matters of international protocol.[53] The last two characters – 'Domino Bentivole' and 'Don Carneades de Boune Compagniola' – both appear to be military men, 'retainers to Madame Bellona' (the goddess of war). The stylings 'Domino' and 'Don' suggest knightly figures. The former has a 'ripe pleasant wit in conversing', and has 'ennobled his name extraordinarie' through his 'resolution and valure'. This could be Sir Robert Carey, who was knighted during Essex's French campaign, and won royal favour in the Accession Day tilts. 'Don Carneades', a soldier full of 'mirthfull sportive conceit' and 'ingenuous Apothegs and

Emblemes', sounds rather like the eccentric soldier-scholar, Sir Roger Williams. The fact that he had died in December 1595 does not really preclude him. Nashe's characters were probably drafted before then, and the portrait was too vague to be withdrawn for propriety's sake. These are mere conjectures, but Cotton, at least, seems fairly certain as one of Nashe's supporters, and his house at Westminster one of Nashe's venues, during the mid-1590s. But as *Have with you* draws to a close, Nashe says:

> I . . . shall . . . steale out of your companie before you bee aware, and hide my selfe in a Closet no bigger than would holde a Church Bible, till the beginning of Candlemas Terme, and then, if you come to Paules Church-yard, you shall meet me.[54]

Again the downbeat note of these years: tiptoeing away, holing up in a tiny room, lurking in St Faith's church underground. The milling of friends and enemies around him does not disguise a mounting sense of bitterness and isolation.

16

THE *ISLE OF DOGS* AFFAIR

'Schollers are pryed into of late, and are found to bee busye fellowes, disturbers of the Peace. Ile say no more . . .'

ANON   *The Returne to Parnassus* (II)

In the spring of 1597, according to Richard Lichfield, Nashe was in prison. 'But see, what art thou heere?' gloated the barber: a 'lop' (flea) in chains, a 'cunny-catching weasell insnared in the Parkers net'. He dwells on Nashe's discomforts: he must 'crinch' himself up on a cold hard couch, dreaming of 'faire lodgings and softe beds'; he must listen at every step to his 'shackles crying clinke'. The 'demi-hell' of prison is a 'darksome laborynth out of which thou canst never passe'. His fairweather friends – 'they would come to eat up thy meat, and sawce it with fine talk' – have all deserted him. They 'leave their iester desolate in the winter of his affliction'. There is no evidence to corroborate Lichfield's claim, but much of his information on Nashe is sound, and he may well be right.[1] We know that Nashe was no stranger to debtors' prison – 'unthrifts consistorie', as he called it – and we know that he had 'nere a penny' in his purse the previous summer. Whatever 'after-harvest' *Have with you* had provided was doubtless long since spent. It is not improbable that he had felt 'the catch-poll's fist' on his shoulder, and been hauled off to the Counter or some such 'melancholy habitation'.

Another dubious note in early 1597 is the appearance of the first quarto of Shakespeare's *Romeo and Juliet*, printed by John Danter. This is clearly a piratical publication, textually corrupt and vilely printed: it was supplanted by a second edition, 'corrected, augmented and amended', in 1599. Danter's text is some 700 lines shorter than the authentic text: the early part of it is mostly correct but the second half mangled and crudely paraphrased. In view of this inconsistency, Harrison argues it was 'the work of a reporter', but that he 'must have been helped either by someone who knew the play intimately or else had seen a playhouse copy of the script'.[2] On circumstantial evidence, at least, Nashe might be suspected of involvement. He was associated with *both* the Lord Chamberlain's Men and John Danter in 1596, perfectly placed for such dealing in 'stolne and surreptitious copies'. Would he have treated Shakespeare, and his own former patron's troupe,

in this underhand way? It is not impossible. As his old friend Greene
put it, 'Poverty is the father of innumerable infirmities'.

These rumours of piracy and imprisonment, though they are only
rumours, serve as a fitting prologue to the main action of 1597, for in
the summer Nashe ran into the biggest trouble of his career – 'such a
heavie crosse laid upon me as had well neere confounded mee' – when
his satirical comedy, *The Isle of Dogs*, was reported to the authorities
as a 'lewd plaie' full of 'seditious and sclanderous matter'. Nashe only
part-wrote the play. His collaborator was a little-known young player,
a former bricklayer's apprentice named Ben Jonson. Nashe later called
it 'an imperfit Embrion of my idle houres', and claimed he had composed
only 'the induction and the first act', and that the remaining four acts
'without my consent, or least guesse of my drift or scope, by the players
were supplied'. Certainly writers did hand over portions of a play in
return for 'redey mony', but it seems likely that Nashe is expediently
understating his contribution. Its satiric sting doubtless originated with
him – official proceedings credit Jonson only as 'maker of parte of the
said Plaie'. Whoever was the more responsible, *The Isle of Dogs*
provoked an immediate storm of outrage in official circles. It went on
in late July 'at one of the plaie howses on the Bancke side'. The evidence
is not conclusive, but it was probably played by the Pembroke's Men at
the Swan theatre in Paris Gardens. News of its dangerous contents
quickly reached Richard Topcliffe, chief of the Elizabethan secret police.
Writs for arrest were issued by the Privy Council. Three of the principal
players – Gabriel Spenser, Robert Shaa and Ben Jonson – were arrested
and despatched to the Marshalsea prison. Nashe's lodgings were raided,
and some of his 'papers' seized, but he himself managed to escape. He
had given birth to a 'monster', he later said, and 'it was no sooner borne
but I was glad to runne from it'.[3]

While Nashe took to his heels, the machinery of suppression rolled
into action. On 28 July, the Council ordered the closure of all the
theatres in London, due to the 'great disorders' caused both 'by lewd
matters that are handled on the stages, and by resorte and confluence
of bad people'. This 'restraint', impresario Henslowe testily recorded in
his account-books, 'is by the meanes of playinge the Jeylle of dooges'.[4]
On 15 August, meeting at Greenwich, the Council directed Richard
Topcliffe to interrogate the imprisoned players (Document 11). Many
years later, Jonson recalled 'the tyme of his close imprissonment': how
'his judges could gett nothing of him to all their demands but I and No';
and how 'they placed two damn'd Villans to catch advantage of him',
but he was 'advertised' of them by his keeper. According to Drummond,
Jonson penned 'ane Epigrame' about these informers. It is presumably
Epigram LIX, 'Of Spies', but there may be another reference in Epigram

CI, where a friend is invited to supper with a promise of free and frank conversation:

> And we will have no Pooly or Parrot by;
> Nor shall our cups make anie guiltie men.

Both Pooly – assuming he is Robert Poley – and Parrot were known prison informers. We find the latter at work in Newgate in 1598. It is possible these were the two 'Villans' planted on Jonson to wheedle out information on *The Isle of Dogs*.[5] Once again the sinister figure of Robert Poley, one of the men present at Marlowe's death, moves round the edge of Nashe's world, the edge where literature shaded dangerously into politics.

Nashe, meanwhile, had disappeared. In their instructions of 15 August the Privy Council urged Topcliffe to track down those responsible for 'the devysing of that sedytious matter'. They must 'receave soche punyshment as their leude and mutynous behavior doth deserve'. Nashe was presumably top of the wanted list. The Council also instructed Topcliffe 'to peruse soch papers as were fownd in Nash his lodgings, which Ferrys, a Messenger of the Chamber, will deliver'. These papers probably included his personal note-books – 'of my note-books and all books else here in the countrey I am bereaved', he later complained; 'a workman is nothing without his tooles'.[6] This suggests just how suddenly he had to leave town.

What was in this play that stung the authorities so sharply? No copy of it survives. We know only the title, the authors, and the aftermath. We also know it was a comedy, for Nashe refers to the affair as 'the straunge turning of the Ile of Dogs from a commedie to a tragedie'. The Isle of Dogs was, and is, an actual London location, not strictly an island but a low, marshy isthmus jutting down into the Thames at the bend between Limehouse and Blackwall reaches. The name may originate from the kennels kept there in mediaeval times, for the royal hunt at Waltham Forest, or it may be a corruption of 'Isle of Ducks', the marshland abounding in wild fowl. In Elizabethan times, the Isle was known as an unsavoury location, haunted by outlaws and fugitive debtors, and the repository of sewage and detritus washed downriver from the city. Thus in *Strange Newes*, Harvey

> will carrie your occupations handsmooth out of towne before him, besmeare them, drowne them; down the river they go Privily to the Ile of Dogges with his Pamphlets.[7]

This suggests – 'besmeare', 'privily' – an Elizabethan sewage dump as the destination for Harvey's pamphlets. Another point about the Isle of Dogs is that it lay plumb opposite the royal palace at Greenwich, scene of many lavish Elizabethan entertainments. Thus we get our first whiff from the play, the glimmerings of a satirical theme in this nasty, swampy, lawless place so pointedly proximate to the royal court. Eight years after the *Isle of Dogs* affair, Ben Jonson part-wrote another stage comedy, *Eastward Hoe* (1605), which also earned him a spell in prison. It works according to a sort of moralized London topography. 'Eastward ho!' leads to the court at Greenwich, 'Westward ho!' to the gallows at Tyburn, the twist being that too much ambition for the one will probably lead to the other: 'Eastward Hoe will make you go Westward Hoe'. At one point in the play, the phoney knight, Sir Petronel Flash, sets off on a merchant-venture to Virginia, only to founder in a storm and beach up on the Isle of Dogs. He thinks he is in France but two gentlemen accost him and tell him he is 'on the coast of Dogs'. There follows some *badinage* about upstart knights – 'I ken the man weel: he's one of my thirty pound knights' – which hits at King James' habit of boosting revenues with the indiscriminate sale of knighthoods. It was this particular insolence, couched in the royal Scottish accent, which resulted in Jonson's arrest.[8] There is an equation in this – the Isle of Dogs + satire on the royal court = imprisonment – that may be relevant to *The Isle of Dogs*.

An aroma of sewage and a spotlighting of courtly abuses: thus far the associations seem apt for Nashe. It is tempting to take this a stage further, and to think of the Isle of Dogs not just as an actual place but as a metaphorical *topos*. Another of Nashe's allusions to the Isle, found in *Summers Last Will*, seems relevant here:

> Here's a coyle about dogges without wit. If I had thought the ship of fooles would have stayde to take in fresh water at the Ile of dogges, I would have furnisht it with a whole kennell of collections to the purpose.[9]

This continues the sewage association – 'kennel' meaning a gutter or channel, as well as a doghouse – but it also hints at this more emblematic reading of the Isle of Dogs. Brandt's famous *Narrenschiff* (Ship of Fools), to which Nashe refers, made of that vessel a satirical emblem of society. Nashe and Jonson, perhaps, did the same with the Isle of Dogs. It suggests an image of society as bestialized, savage, a nexus of 'dog fights' and 'doggedness' (the latter, to Elizabethans, meaning 'envy' rather than, as now, 'tenacity'). This again is apt for both Nashe and Jonson: the predatory, acquisitive, competitive nature of society is a constant theme in both. The eponymous 'Isle of Dogs', in short, may be England itself.

The passage quoted from *Summers Last Will* mentions the Isle of Dogs in connection with the character of Orion, the dog-star. This brings in another interesting association: that of the 'dog days'. The ascendance of Orion in July was believed to bring on these hot, plaguey *'caniculares dies'*, a time of enervation, disease and 'mellancholicke imaginations'. Dogs ran mad, wine was soured, crops blasted: *'canicula pestilens est omnibus sidus'*, the dog-star is a blight on all things. Autumn sums up the effects of Orion in *Summers Last Will*:

> With those venome-breathed curres he leads,
> He comes to chase health from our earthly bounds:
> Each one of those foule-mouthed mangy dogs
> Governes a day, (no dog but hath his day),
> And all the daies by them so governed,
> The Dog-daies hight . . .

In view of the political furore caused by *The Isle of Dogs*, the word 'governes' catches the eye. Was this the rash satirical message conveyed by the play, that just as certain days were 'governed' by astrological dogs, so England was an isle governed by political dogs? It was, of course, during the 'dog days' of July 1597 that *The Isle of Dogs* was produced – a point not lost on Richard Lichfield, who taunts Nashe:

> Woe to the dog-daies, for in those thou wroughtest that which now works thy woe. . . . What all the whole yeere could not bring to passe, and all the Country long have expected, that is thy confusion, these dog dayes by thine owne words have effected.[10]

There is a political context for all this, for the play went out at a time of economic crisis and social unrest. Heavy trading losses, soaring inflation, the debilitations of plague and continual war with Spain: to these were added a run of disastrous harvests, 1594–8. This was the time of the 'dearth': Nashe refers to 'this deare yeare' in *Have with you* ('dearth' means literally the 'dearness' of things). There were food riots in Southwark in 1595: the authorities responded with whip and pillory. Famine appeared in several districts in 1596. In the summer of 1597, wrote John Stow, 'by reason of much rain and great floods', corn again 'waxed scant'. Wheat was selling in London for 10s a bushel, in remoter towns for as much as 18s. In the autumn, twenty-five died of starvation in the streets of Newcastle. In the face of the emergency, parliament set about framing a new Poor Law, laying down statutory regulations for the maintenance of the 'honest poor': employment schemes, endowment of hospitals and work-houses, compulsory welfare contributions of 2d per parish, etc. The law of 1598, amended slightly in 1601, became the basis of state welfare clear through to the nineteenth-century Reforms.[11]

Was this background of hardship, hunger and unrest part of the *Isle of Dogs*? Was its seditious content some goading critique of government complacency and corruption? Were there accusations of profiteering and 'engrossing' (stock-piling) in high places, as there were in *Summers Last Will*?

> No almes, but unreasonable gaine,
> Disgests what thy huge yron teeth devoure:
> Small beere, course bread, the hynds and beggers cry,
> Whilest thou withholdest both the mault and flowre,
> And giv'st us branne and water, fit for dogs.[12]

Here too we hear a howling of dogs and beggars, a populace subsisting on a diet 'fit for dogs': a foretaste, perhaps, of England as the 'Isle of Dogs'. If so, Nashe and Jonson were not the first to run into trouble for strident comments on 'the dearth'. In 1596, Thomas Deloney, the Norwich weaver and balladeer, had a ballad about the dearth suppressed, because it 'brought in the Queen speaking to her people Dialoguewise, in very fond and undecent sort'. Nashe refers to this suppression in *Have with you*: the 'ale-house' muse of this 'balletting Silke-weaver' has ever lived off 'a penny a quart' (cheap beer), but 'this deare yeare, together with the silencing of his looms, scarce that'.[13]

These hints throw up something of the atmosphere of this vanished play. The real Isle of Dogs, the foul-smelling badlands under the very nose of the court; the metaphoric 'Isle of Dogs', an England of bestial struggle and capitalistic 'dog eat dog'; the back-drop of famine and beggary and greedy politicians with 'huge yron teeth' – out of these ingredients, perhaps, Nashe and Jonson brewed up their pungent satirical cocktail. At this point, we might turn to the one contemporary work which contains some genuine comment on *The Isle of Dogs*. Not to Lichfield's *Trimming* – where the treatment of Nashe's 'infamous, most dunsicall and thrice opprobrious worke' is highly generalized – but to the Cambridge comedy, *The Returne from Parnassus (Part II)*. All the allusions here to the Isle of Dogs undoubtedly refer to Nashe's play. The scene in question begins with Ingenioso hurriedly preparing for flight:

> Faith, Academico, it's the feare of that fellow, I meane the signe of the sergeants head, that makes me to be so hasty to be gone: to be briefe, Academico, writts are out for me, to apprehend mee for my playes, and now I am bound for the Ile of doggs.[14]

This clear glance at Nashe's escape from London in 1597 is underscored by an association between the Isle of Dogs and dangerous satire – 'we are fully bent to be Lords of misrule in the worlds wide hall', says Ingenioso:

> Our voyage is to the Ile of Dogges,
> There where the blattant beast doth rule and raigne,
> Rending the credditt of whome ere hee please,
> Where serpents tongs the pen men are to write,
> Where cats do waule by day, dogges barke by night:
> There shall engoared venom be my inke,
> My pen a sharper quill of porcupine,
> My stayned paper, this sin loaden earth:
> There will I write, in lines shall never die,
> Our feared Lordings crying villany.

This 'blattant (or blatant) beast' that reigns over the Isle of Dogs comes straight out of Spenser's *Faerie Queene*. The offspring of Cerberus and Chimaera, it symbolizes the spirit of calumny, a 'monster of scandal':

> The Beast . . . gan his hundred tongues apply,
> And sharpely at him to revile and raile
> With bitter termes of shamefull infamy,
> Oft interlacing many a forged lie . . .[15]

Thus the *Isle of Dogs* is associated with scandal and libel, with venomous satiric quills, with defiance in the face of 'feared Lordings' crying 'Villainy!' A few lines later comes a hint as to the full extent of the play's defiance. Ingenioso's friend, the mad poet Furor, resolves to accompany him, threatening: 'When I arrive within the Ile of Doggs, Don Phoebus I will make thee kisse the pumpe.' This image of trampling down the 'sun' (Phoebus) of authority is made more specific when he adds, 'And thou, my sluttishe landresse Cinthia . . . Furor will have thee carted through the dirt.' Ingenioso comments: 'Is not here a true dogge, that dare barke so boldly at the Moone?' Cynthia was, by habitual notation, Queen Elizabeth, as in Ralegh's poem, *The Ocean's Love to Cynthia*, and Chapman's *Hymnus in Cynthiam*. The name emblematically links the moon with the 'Virgin Queen': Cynthia is the Romans' Diana, born on Mount Cynthios, goddess of both the moon and chastity. Trading on these instinctual associations, the author seems to suggest that the *Isle of Dogs* had aimed its anger at the very highest authority – it mocked 'Cynthia' and dragged her 'through the dirt', it barked 'boldly' at the royal Moon, it was the 'blattant beast' of slander snarling at the 'faerie queene' herself – or, at least, that this was how the authorities had viewed it. One recalls Deloney's ballad, suppressed for its 'fond and undecent' treatment of the Queen. If the Isle of Dogs – the 'snarling Iland', as Ingenioso calls it – is England, the authorities could well have construed the play, had they so wished, as a 'seditious' attack on the Queen.

It may be that vehemence alone made *The Isle of Dogs* so scandalous, that the authors simply went too far in their social critique. More likely, however, is that the general satire was spiced with specific libels, and that these served to precipitate the wrath of the government. The Privy Council denounced the play as 'sclanderous' as well as, more vaguely, 'lewd' and 'seditious'. A letter of Ben Jonson's, written during his imprisonment after *Eastward Hoe* in 1605, strengthens this suggestion. Writing apologetically to Cecil, Jonson refers to his earlier imprisonment for the *Isle of Dogs*, saying:

> since my first Error, wch yet is punish'd in mee more wth my shame, than it was then wth my Bondage, I have so attempred my stile, that I have given no cause to any good Man of Greife; and if to any ill, by touching at any generall vice, it hath alwaies bene wth a reguard and sparing of perticular persons.[16]

This implies that in *The Isle of Dogs* – his 'first Error' – he *did* give some 'good Man' cause for 'Greife', that the play was definitely *not* 'sparing of perticular persons'. Strong circumstantial evidence allows us to name at least one of the play's specific butts: Henry Brooke, 8th Lord Cobham. *The Isle of Dogs* is, in fact, a missing link in a whole train of satirical material about the Cobham family in 1596–8.

What drew the Cobhams into the satirical arena was a fairly parochial court rivalry, but one which touched the players nearly. On the death of the 1st Lord Hunsdon in July 1596, his son, Sir George Carey, clearly hoped to succeed him as Lord Chamberlain. Even Cecil assured him he would not 'fayle of succession' to those exalted 'places' his father had occupied.[17] Much to Carey's chagrin, however, the post went to the old Lord Cobham, William Brooke. This was also bad news for the Lord Chamberlain's Men – doubly so: they lost their exalted name and had to be content with styling themselves 'the L. of Hunsdon his Servants' (as they appear on Danter's quarto of *Romeo*); and they found the new Lord Chamberlain, who exercised close control over the Revels offices and hence over the play-companies, considerably less friendly to them than Hunsdon had been. It is precisely this turn of events which Nashe comments on in his letter of August 1596, when he says of the players: 'however in there old Lords tyme they thought there state setled, it is now so uncertayne they cannot build upon it'. Probably the first, and certainly the most famous, rumble of satire against the Cobham family appeared in Shakespeare's 1 *Henry IV*, first performed by the Chamberlain's Men in 1596.[18] As is well known, the character of Falstaff first saw light under the name of Sir John Oldcastle, and as such the old rascal contained a comic allusion to the real Oldcastle, a mediaeval Lord Cobham burned as a heretic in 1417. His noble descendants, the Elizabethan Cobhams, took immediate exception to this. Dr Richard James, apart from mixing up his Henries, gives a succinct account of the affair:

> that in Shakespeares first shew of Harrie the fift, the person with which he undertook to playe a buffone, was not Falstaffe, but Sir Jhon Oldcastle, and that offence beinge worthily taken by Personages descended from his title . . . the poet was putt to make an ignorant shifte of abusing Sir Jhon Falstophe.[19]

According to Nicholas Rowe, in his 1709 edition of Shakespeare, Lord Cobham took his grievance to the Queen, and it was she who ordered Shakespeare 'to alter it'. So he did: Oldcastle became Falstaff, a satiric hit at the Cobhams becoming a punning, detumescent version of his own name. He made the dissociation public in the epilogue at the end of 2 *Henry IV*: 'Falstaff shall die of a sweat, unless already a be killed with your hard opinions; for Oldcastle died martyr, and this is not the man.'[20] Traces of the old identity remain in the texts, as in Hal's 'my old lad of the castle', and an errant speech heading which refers to 'Old.' instead of 'Fal.'.

On 5 March 1597 the old Lord Cobham died, and Sir George Carey, 2nd Lord Hunsdon, duly became Lord Chamberlain. His troupe resumed its title and its 'setled' state. But the satire lingered on, now focused on the new (8th) Lord Cobham, Henry Brooke, an ambitious young courtier and a close friend of Ralegh. In April the Chamberlain's Men played a new Falstaff comedy, *The Merry Wives of Windsor*, at the Garter Feast at Whitehall, where their patron Carey was among the recipients of the Order of the Garter.[21] Enraged at Falstaff's attempts to cuckold him, Master Ford dons a disguise and a pseudonym: it is Brooke, the Cobhams' family name. There is a joke about 'Brooks . . . that oerflow such liquor' – the young Lord Cobham was a noted *bon viveur*. Thus Shakespeare underscores, for Carey's amusement, the old connections between Falstaff and the Cobhams. There was certainly no love lost between Carey and Cobham: in March 1597 they jockeyed for the Wardenship of the Cinque Ports, which Cobham got, and in later years, as Carey's health failed, Cobham lobbied keenly for the Chamberlain's office.[22] Further trouble may have arisen from the *Merry Wives* hit – Brooke is amended to Broome in the Folio text of the play – but by now Cobham was saddled with the fat knight's *sobriquet*. In a letter of

February 1598, the Earl of Essex recounted gossip of romance between Cobham and Margaret Ratcliffe: she is all but 'maryed', he says, 'to Sr Jo. Falstaff'. The original satirical element in the Henry comedies stayed long in the memory: documents dated 1600 and 1639 refer to one or other of them as *Sir John Oldcastle*. In each case it is a Shakespeare play referred to, not the pro-Oldcastle play of that name, hacked together by Munday and others in 1599.[23]

Knowing Nashe's links with Carey and with the Chamberlain's Men, not to mention his relish for piquing the powerful, it would be no surprise to find him and Jonson 'playing a buffone' with the young Lord Cobham in the *Isle of Dogs*, presumably composed in spring or early summer 1597. Primary evidence of this is, of course, lost with the play. But there is strong secondary evidence in the fact that both Nashe and Jonson took the first opportunity after the *Isle of Dogs* affair to toss out covert but unmistakable remarks about Cobham. In September 1598, the Chamberlain's Men (with Shakespeare in the cast) put on Jonson's *Every Man in his Humour* at the Curtain theatre, Shoreditch. As his name suggests, the character of Cob, the water-bearer, is a vehicle for burlesque on Cobham. The menial role of water-bearer jokes on Cobham's recent installation as Lord Warden of the Cinque Ports, with its vital strategic role of controlling the Kent harbours and the English Channel. As Scoufos says: 'Jonson seizes upon the idea of controller of waters, and in comic inversion makes Cob a peddler of water, a humour-ridden clown.'[24] The Oldcastle connection is renewed *via* one of the meanings of the word 'cob', which is 'herring' (a 'red cob' is a kipper). Thus when Cob vaunts of his 'ancient lineage', he says

> The first red herring that was broil'd in Adam and Eves kitchen doe I fetch my pedigree from. . . . His Cob was my great-great-mighty-great-Grand-father.'

The real Cobham's ancestor was, of course, Sir John Oldcastle. In the word 'broil'd', Jonson cruelly mocks at Oldcastle's martyrdom, as a further speech of Cob's makes clear:

> My lineage goes to rack, poore cobs they smoke for it, they are made martyrs of the gridiron, they melt for passion.

The real Oldcastle was 'hanged and burned hanging', according to the chroniclers: Jonson's image of a cob smoked on a grill is gruesomely accurate.

In *Nashes Lenten Stuffe*, written in 1598 and published early the following year, Nashe promises 'a new Play never played before, of the Praise of the Red Herring'. Noting the Cobham-cob-herring motif in

Jonson's *Every Man*, the knowing reader might expect to be treated to some anti-Cobham satire. The work opens with an account of the 'troublesome stir' occasioned by *The Isle of Dogs* 'two summers past' (he must have been writing this in late 1598). The worst of its effects, says Nashe, was not that 'it sequestered me from the woonted meanes of my maintenance', nor the 'deepe pit of despaire wherinto I was falne', but that

> in my exile, and irkesome discontented abandonment, the silliest millers thombe or contemptible stickle-banck of my enemies is as busie nibbling about my fame as if I were a deade man throwne amongest them to feede upon. So I am, I confesse, in the worldes outwarde apparance, though perhappes I may proove a cunninger diver then they are aware. . . . Let them looke to it, for I will put them in bryne, or a piteous pickle, every one.[25]

The identification of his chief enemy in the affair is ingeniously veiled. It is another fishy pun, for the 'miller's thumb' Nashe speaks of is a small freshwater fish, the *cottus gobio*, also known as the 'goby', the 'cobbo' and the 'cob'. In Florio's Italian dictionary, '*bozzolo*' is translated as 'a fish called a millers thumbe or a cob', and Grose's *Provincial Glossary* gives 'cobbo' as 'a small fish called a miller's-thumb'.[26] It is not some contemptible nobody who has been 'nibbling' at Nashe's 'fame'. The 'silliest millers thombe', the mere stickleback, is none other than the 'cob', Lord Cobham. He it is whom Nashe threatens to 'pickle' in satirical brine. In view of this, a passage a few pages later takes on a cast of heavy sarcasm. Here Nashe says he has undergone 'mutch brainetossing' to write something in praise of 'the Baylies of the Cinqueports'. Their 'primordat *Genethliaca*' – a celebration of their birth and origins – was 'dropping out of my inckhorne, with the silver oare of their barronry by William the Conqueror conveyed over to them'. This openly refers to the Cobham family, who had been the Wardens of the Cinque Ports since Queen Mary's time. The current Lord Cobham had been granted the Wardenship in August 1598, despite the rivalry of (*inter alia*) Lord Hunsdon. The family, moreover, did trace its 'barronry' back to William the Conqueror. In mentioning this Nashe touches on a nerve, for the trumpeting of their ancestry had caused the Cobhams some embarrassment. The second edition of Holinshed's *Chronicles* (1585–7) was dedicated to the old Lord Cobham, and included a detailed genealogical treatise on the family. This was swiftly excised from the text by order of the Privy Council, on the grounds that it aggrandized the family unacceptably. Nashe's innocuous promise to pen a '*genethliaca*' of the Cobhams revives this incident.[27] He has decided not to write it after all, he continues – 'to shun spight I smothered these dribblements' – even though he had spent 'a whole moneths minde' preparing it. The key-note of the whole passage is a feigned innocence – the Cobhams could scarcely complain of his bright-eyed enthusiasm, however surely they knew that if Nashe had spent a month cooking up a tract about them, the result would be no heraldic panegyric.

Just how far Nashe proceeds to satirize Cobham in *Lenten Stuffe* is questionable. Alice Lyle Scoufos, who first put much of this material together, gives several possible instances, but it must be said that at the very heart of *Lenten Stuffe* is a celebration of the multiplicity of language, and that a 'Dispraise of Lord Cobham' is only one strand in the myriad 'Prayse of the Red Herring'. Nevertheless, when Nashe starts to talk of the smoking of the first herring in history, he is clearly embarking on the same tasteless joke as Jonson about the burning of Cobham's ancestor, Oldcastle. He relates how this primordial kipper was purchased by the 'Popes caterer' in Rome, and brought to the papal kitchens in great pomp to be cooked:

> All the Popes cookes in their white sleeves and linnen aprons met him middle way, to enterteine and receyve the king of fishes. . . . The clarke of the kitchin . . . would admit none but him selfe to have the scorching and carbonadoing of it, and kissed his hand thrice, and made as many *Humblessos*, ere he woulde finger it, . . . kneeling on his knees and mumbling twenty ave Maryes to hymselfe in the sacrifizing of it on the coales.[28]

This culinary ceremonial – this 'diligent service in the broyling and combustion' of the ancient cob – is another wicked rendition of Oldcastle's martyrdom. He had been burned by the Catholic powers of pre-Reformation England. Hence the papal setting here: the 'Popes cookes' are his Catholic executioners. Upon being put to the fire, Nashe continues, the old herring gave out a 'puissant' and 'pestilent' aroma which 'stunk so over the popes pallace that not a scullion but cried foh'. This 'foggy fume' knocks the Pope clean unconscious. Here Nashe glances at the strident religious controversy which rose up around Oldcastle's martyrdom. This predates the Oldcastle satire in Shakespeare, Jonson and Nashe, and provides an important back-drop for it. As such, it offers further bearings on *The Isle of Dogs* and its lost satire on Lord Cobham.

A Lollard, Sir John Oldcastle was executed as a rebel against Catholicism and a conspirator against Henry V. To the Catholic chroniclers of the fifteenth century – Vergil, Fabyan, Walsingham – he was a heretic and a traitor. With the Reformation, however, his status drastically improved. Protestant propagandists like Tyndale and Bale portrayed him not as a heretic but as a pre-Reformation Protestant martyr. Bale's *Brefe*

Chronicle (*c.* 1544) spoke of him as the 'blessed martir of Christ' and of the 'blody belly-gods' who had murdered him. In 1563 the martyrologist John Foxe completed Oldcastle's rehabilitation, enshrining him in the new Protestant calendar of saints: henceforth 6 February was the saint's day of 'Syr John Ould Castell, Lord Cobham, Martyr'. In return, Catholic counter-propaganda like Nicholas Harpfield's *Dialogi Sex* (1566) denounced Oldcastle anew, while Stow's 1574 edition of Walsingham placed the old denunciations in the public view. By the time Shakespeare and company came on the scene, the Oldcastle legend had become a religious ping-pong ball, enshrined by the Protestants, vilified by the Catholics.[29] And though their targets were the contemporary Cobhams, the satirists annexed this long tradition of dispute – or, more precisely, they annexed the antagonistic, *Catholic* angle on Oldcastle. It would be rash to infer Shakespeare's religious leanings from this – he has been claimed as both a crypto-Catholic and a staunch orthodoxist.[30] But with Nashe and Jonson we are on firmer ground. Time and again, Nashe's satirical stance has a Catholic tinge – the denunciations of Leicester and Ralegh, drawing on Parsons' Catholic invectives; the oblique celebrations of the Catholic Howard family; the involvement with Strange and Southampton, with Marlowe and Watson; the appearance of *Marie Magdalenes Love* and *Iesus Psalter* during his association with Danter; the endless abuse of Puritanism, which won him the suspicion of Puritan officials like Beale and the applause of Catholic poets like Campion. With Jonson we have even clearer evidence of Catholicism. In 1598, a year after the *Isle of Dogs* affair, he openly converted. He was in prison again, this time for killing the actor Gabriel Spenser: there 'took he his Religion by trust of a priest who Visited him'. He remained thereafter '12 yeares a Papist'. In 1603 he was summoned before the Privy Council for his *Sejanus*, '& accused both of popperie and treason'. In 1606 he and his wife were cited for recusancy.[31] If *The Isle of Dogs* contained abuse of Lord Cobham, it seems likely it was noticeably Catholic abuse, drawing on the traditional denigrations of Oldcastle. This, perhaps, is why the man most involved in government moves against the play was Richard Topcliffe, whose speciality was the detection and examination of Catholic suspects. It is Topcliffe to whom the original informer came, Topcliffe who is instructed to 'peruse' Nashe's seized papers and to conduct all further investigations.

There are also Catholic hints in the play's solitary scrap of textual history. It seems that a manuscript copy of the play, or at least part of one, evaded the government crack-down, and was incorporated into a collection of Elizabethan MSS now at Alnwick Castle.[32] The list of this collection's contents, written in an Elizabethan hand, includes:

Ile of doges   frmnt[?]
by Thomas Nashe   inferior plaiers

The fragment – assuming this is meant by the scarcely legible 'frmnt' –
has since vanished, but the company it once kept is interesting. Also
catalogued in the collection are copies of mainstream Catholic works
like *Leycesters Commonwealth* and the 'Earl of Arundells letter to the
Queen'. The contents page also mentions a copy, now missing, of Shakespeare's *Richard II*: this too has an interesting sidelight. The first printed
edition of the play – entered for publication on 29 August 1597, just a
few weeks after the *Isle of Dogs* furore – appeared in expurgated form,
as did two further editions in 1598. Missing was the scene of Richard's
deposition, controversial then and even more so in 1601, when the play
was pointedly staged on the eve of the Essex uprising.[33] One suspects
that this politic excision was inspired by the wrath so recently heaped
on *The Isle of Dogs*. The manuscript copy of the play, that once lay
alongside the *Isle of Dogs* fragment, may well have contained the
suppressed deposition scene. Even around these lost scraps of Nashe's
play suspicions of Catholicism and sedition cluster.

Sifting through the tremors surrounding *The Isle of Dogs*, two major
motifs emerge to account for its persecution – generalized political satire,
perhaps arising from the economic crises of the mid-1590s, perhaps
aggressive enough to constitute a 'seditious' attack on the Queen; and
specific personal libel against Lord Cobham, continuing Shakespeare's
Oldcastle satire, perhaps with too pointed a reminiscence of Catholic
propaganda on the subject. These are only shots in the dark: the play
must remain an enigma. But it was real enough that summer day when
the storm first broke, when the players were taken off to the Marshalsea
and Nashe made his getaway, one jump ahead of Topcliffe's heavies.
He knew what was in it, that he had taken on an adversary larger and
more lethal than a hundred conceited old Doctors. In the first flash of
government reaction, the possibilities of punishment were endless. Nashe
might think of the seditious pamphleteer John Stubbs and his publisher,
taken to Westminster market-place to have their right hands struck off
'by the blow of a butchers knife with a mallet'; or of Stephen Vallenger,
convicted of spreading 'false and slanderous libels', Catholic ones,
condemned to lose his ears in the pillory and spend the rest of his life
in Fleet prison; or of the authors of certain seditious 'placards' of 1593,
whose pursuivants were directed by the Privy Council to 'put them to
torture in Bridewell, and by the extremity thereof . . . draw them to
discover their knowledge'.[34] The macabre ingenuities of rack-master
Topcliffe were well known.

Nashe probably left town immediately, and began threading his way
back East. He was running scared and he was going home: back to the

edge of the 'snarling Iland', back to the coast of his childhood. How he
travelled we do not know: horses were costly to hire, journeying 'on
foot-back' dangerous and exhausting (unless you were Will Kemp, who
danced from London to Norwich for a publicity stunt in 1600). His
own Jack Wilton, fleeing from Rome, sets the mood: 'a theefe, they saie,
mistakes everie bush for a true man; the winde ratled not in any bush
by the way as I rode, but I straight drew my rapier'. No doubt, like
Jack, he edged into towns and villages surreptitiously, took lodgings 'in a
blinde streete out of the waie, and kept secret many daies'.[35] In October,
Lichfield's *Trimming* appeared, gloating over Nashe's latest catastrophe:

> Hearke you, Thomas, the Crier calls you. What, a fugitive? How
> comes that to passe, that thou a man of so good an education, & so
> wel backt by the Muses, shouldst proove a fugitive? But alas, thy
> Muses brought thee to this miserie: you and your Muses maye even
> goe hang your selves. . . .

He imagines Nashe's clandestine movement through the country: 'now
in this thy flight thou art a night-bird, for the day wil bewray thee: the
Bat and the Owle be thy fellow travellers'. He jokes about the 'speedie
carriage' of Nashe's feet: 'thou canst not chuse but in all humilitie offer
thy old shooes for sacrifice to Thetis'. He exhorts the pursuivants to
catch him and 'crop his eares', like 'a dogge that hath done a fault': this
will suit his ruffianly long hair, for crop-ears are 'priviledged to weare
long lockes by ancient charter'.[36]

Finally, Nashe tells us, after many 'knight arrant adventures and
outroades and inroades', he made it to the coast.

> At greate Yarmouth in Norfolke I arived in the latter ende of
> Autumne. Where having scarse lookt about me, my presaging minde
> saide to it selfe, *Hic favonius serenus est, hic auster imbricus*, this is
> a predestinate fit place for Pierse Pennilesse to set up his staffe in.[37]

He also tells us he remained at Yarmouth 'for six weekes first and last,
under that predominant constellation of Aquarius', i.e. in January. He
cannot have arrived there much before December, which just about
qualifies as the 'latter ende of Autumne'. He had been on the run for
four months. Somewhere down the line, on a day in November, he
celebrated his thirtieth birthday.

17

LENTEN STUFF

'Falangtado, falangtado,
My mates are gone, Ile followe'

ELIZABETHAN BALLAD

Back in London the storm blew over. On 3 October the keeper of the
Marshalsea received the Council's warrant 'for the releasing of Beniamin
Johnson' and the other two players. The restraint on the theatres was
lifted and they re-opened.[1] It was business as usual in literary London.
Nashe, however, remained for many months in 'exile and irkesome
discontented abandonment'. Perhaps he was still a wanted man: he
speaks of being 'sequestered' from the 'woonted meanes of my maintenance', which suggests he was officially banned from publishing.[2] Perhaps,
anyway, he needed the rest. Where he lived after leaving Yarmouth in
January or February 1598 is unknown. He may have travelled down to
Lowestoft, where his brother Israel, sister-in-law Ann, and probably
other kin, were still living. It is curious, though, that it is Yarmouth, not
Lowestoft, that Nashe thanks for sheltering and supporting him. Had
he been turned away from his old home-town? Wherever it was, he was
'in the countrey' while writing *Lenten Stuffe*. The work was drafted in
the early spring of 1598 – 'it was most of my study the last Lent' – but
it was clearly written up later in the year, since it refers to the *Isle of
Dogs* affair as 'two summers past'.[3] In September 1598, over a year
after his flight, Nashe had still not returned to London, for in *Palladis
Tamia*, registered 7 September, Francis Meres refers to his continued
'banishment':

As Actaeon was wooried of his owne hounds, so is Tom Nash of
his *Ile of Dogs*. Dogges were the death of Euripedes, but bee not
disconsolate, gallant young Iuvenall. . . . God forbid that so brave a
witte should so basely perish: thine are but paper dogges, neither is
thy banishment like Ovids, eternally to converse with the barbarous
Getes. Therefore comfort thy selfe sweete Tom, with Ciceros glorious
return to Rome.[4]

Meres was a dedicated follower of literary fashion: he is almost certain to be right that Nashe was still missing from London. Or if he had returned, he had done so furtively, not in Ciceronian triumph.

Nashes Lenten Stuffe was his last work. It is not his most readable, probably *The Unfortunate Traveller*; nor his most wittily satirical, *Pierce* or the Harvey lampoons, according to taste; but it is, perhaps, his masterpiece. In this work, as Steane says, 'he is his most fully and distinctively developed self'. The work grew, quite genuinely, out of a desire to thank the town of Great Yarmouth for the 'kind entertainment and benigne hospitality' it had shown him. It is a return gift in his own currency: 'I had money lent me in Yarmouth, and I pay them againe in prayse.' If there is any 'resounding belmettall' left in his pen, 'the first peale of it is Yarmouthes'.⁵ The work opens, as promised on the title-page, with a description and history of the town. Some twenty pages long in the original edition, this is a superb piece of descriptive journalism, a prototypical 'feature article'. Some of it is lifted out of Camden's *Britannia*, but often transformed in the translation: Camden's '*Cerdicus bellicosus Saxo*' becomes 'one Cerdicus, a plashing Saxon, that had reveld here and there with his battleaxe'. There were more detailed, local sources he used. The distant antiquities of Yarmouth, '*An. Do.* 1000 or thereabouts', he claims to have 'scrapte out of wormeaten parchment', and he certainly made full use of a 'Chronographycal Latine table, which they have hanging up in their Guild Hall', which related 'in a faire texte hande' the deeds and worthies of the town and 'all their transmutations since their Cradlehoode'. Camden also mentions this '*tabula Chronographica antiqua*', though he says it was displayed '*in templo*', presumably meaning the church. Nashe transcribed passages from this into his note-books – 'my Tables are not yet one quarter emptied of my notes out of their Table'.⁶ It appears that he also had access to another document, a free English translation from the Latin *tabula* made by a prominent citizen, Henry Manshyp senior, in the 1560s. This manuscript – treating of 'the Foundacion and Antiquitye of the Towne of Great Yermouthe' – is frequently echoed in *Lenten Stuffe*, often *verbatim*. Once again one notes Nashe's instinctive jazzing-up of factual material. Where the Manshyp MS has simply 'marshes and fennes', Nashe substitutes 'the fennie *Lerna* betwixt, that with Reede is so imbristled'. Manshyp blandly recounts how, in the time of William the Conqueror,

> the saide sande did grow to be drye and was not overflowen by the Sea, but waxed in heighte and also in greatnes, in so muche as greate store of people of the Counties of Norff. and Suffolke did resorte thither, and did pitche Tabernacles and Boothes . . . to sell their Herringes, fish and other comodoties.

Nashe puts it like this:

this sand of Yarmouth grew to a setled lumpe, and was as drie as the
sands of Arabia, so that thronging theaters of people (as well aliens
as Englishmen) hived thither about the selling of fish and Herring . . .
and there built sutlers booths and tabernacles, to canopie their heads
in from the rhewme of the heavens.[7]

With a few deft strokes the scene comes to life.

The Manshyp MS seems to have been in the possession of the author's
son, Henry Manshyp junior, a former Town Clerk and a leading member
of the municipal Corporation. Nashe probably got to know him: he
may be the 'gentleman, a familiar of mine' that Nashe speaks of 'commu-
ning' with at Yarmouth, and who seems partly to have inspired *Lenten
Stuffe*.[8] Nashe must have had some *entrée* into municipal circles to
get all the details he retails so punctiliously: Yarmouth's new cannon
emplacement, we learn, is 167 yards in 'compasse about the wall'; 20 ft
6 inches in height; the 'bredth of the foundation' 9 ft; the 'depth within
ground' 11 ft; and so on. Harbour costs 'these last 28 yeares' amount
to £26,256 4s 5d. This latter must come straight out of the Yarmouth
'haven book'.[9] Here is the plausible, enquiring, educated Nashe,
flattering the local worthies with his promise to write up the 'length and
bredth of Yarmouth'. He praises, rather untypically, the 'grave substantial burgers' of the town, their upstanding 'marchantly formallity'. He
left happy memories with Manshyp, who says, in his own *History of
Great Yarmouth* (1619), 'here by way of merriment let me remember to
you an odd conceit of a late pleasant-pated poet, who making a catalogue
of national gods or patrons . . . termeth Red Herring to be the titular
God of Yarmouth'.[10] Nashe made much fuss of his enmities, but a more
pervasive use of his talent for 'getting on' with people. Like the 'vagrant'
young wastrel in *Pierce*, he 'lookes into all Estates by conversing with
them'. And for all the linguistic eccentricities of *Lenten Stuffe*, there is
a rich central celebration of ordinariness. As he says in the preface,
anyone can 'write in prayse of vertue and the seven Liberall Sciences',
but to 'wring iuice out of a flint, thats Pierce a Gods name, and the right
tricke of a workman'. He becomes our voluble 'pleasant-pated' guide:
'I shall leade you a sound walke about Yarmouth'.[11] First, 'looke wistly
upon the walles, which, if you marke, make a stretcht out quadrangle
with the haven'. He spiels off their measurements, notes the sixteen
towers, the ten town-gates, the fortifications 'underfonging and
enflancking them', the cannon to repel 'Diego Spanyard' and 'strike the
winde collicke in his paunch if he praunce to neere them'. We set off
through the town. He has been 'walking in her streetes so many weekes
togither' he knows every inch of them. The main thoroughfares 'are as
long as threescore streets in London', while a warren of little 'lans' and
'scores' — some 140 of them, in fact — criss-cross through the town. We

briefly survey the 'voide ground' and 'liberties' at the edge of town; the
'levell of the marshes' off east to Norwich, 'sixteene mile disiunct'; then
up to the disused, 'gravelled up' harbour at Caister, 'by aged Fishermen
commonly tearmed Grubs haven'; and to Gorleston, a 'decrepite over-
worne village' amid 'slymie plashie fields'. But the topographical life and
soul of Yarmouth is its harbour. Its size, he says, is deceptive:

> A narrow channell or *Isthmus* in rash view you woulde opinionate
> it: when this I can devoutly averre, I beholding it with both my eies
> this last fishing, sixe hundreth reasonable barkes and vesselles of good
> burden (with a vantage) it hath given shelter to at once in her harbour,
> and most of them riding abrest before the Key betwixt the Bridge and
> the Southgate. Many bows length beyond the marke my penne roves
> not, I am certain: if I doe, they stand at my elbow that can correct
> mee. The delectablest lustie sight and movingest obiect, me thought
> it was, that our Ile sets forth, and nothing behinde in number with the
> invincible Spanish Armada, though they were not such Gargantuan
> boysterous gulliguts as they. . . . That which especiallest nourisht the
> most prime pleasure in me was after a storme, when they were driven
> in swarmes and lay close pestred together as thicke as they could
> packe; the next day following, if it were faire, they would cloud the
> whole skie with canvas, by spreading their drabled sailes in the full
> clue abroad a drying, and make a braver shew with them then so
> many banners and streamers displayed against the Sunne on a moun-
> taine top.

This is vivid and oddly moving. The hard-bitten polysyllabic
pamphleteer, the city wit with a chequered past, here jostles happily
with the old salts and fish-wives on the quay – 'they stand at my elbow
that can correct me' – and is rapt by this 'lustie sight' of ships and sails
and 'close pestred' activity. There is nostalgia in it, a sense that the wheel
is come full circle and Nashe is back where he began, the little boy on
the waterfront at Lowestoft. He never quite lost that child's eye: its
magnifications, its sense of suddenness, its fascination slipping into fear.
There is undoubtedly an encomium of his native East Anglia, a *recherche
du temps perdu*, wrapped up in *Lenten Stuffe*.

Central to his description of Yarmouth is an idea of struggle and
effort. The town itself is 'reared and enforced from the sea most mira-
culously'. Like some mythological giant, 'forth of the sands thus strug-
lingly' Yarmouth 'exalteth and liftes up his glittering head'. It is
'rampierd' against the 'fumish waves battry', a hard-won solidity, a
bulwark of human resistance against the 'universall unbounded empery
of surges'. The fishery which is Yarmouth's economic foundation is itself
a constant battle. To be 'in Yarmouth one fishing' is to behold a 'violent

motion of toyling Mirmidons', a 'confused stirring to and fro of a
Lepantalike hoast of unfatigable flud bickerers and foame curbers'. To
plumb 'the captious mystery of Mounsieur herring' is an arduous art.
He puts the fishermen 'to their trumps' and 'scuppets not his benificence
into their mouthes' without a struggle. The 'driftermen' – as herring-
fishers are known – are no 'shorecreepers, like those Colchester
oystermen'. The herring 'keepeth more aloof' and

> those that are his followers, if they will seeke him where hee is, more
> then common daunger they must incurre. . . . Fortie or threescoare
> leagues in the roaring territory they are glad on their wodden horses
> to post after him, and scoure it with their ethiope pitchbordes till
> they be windlesse in his quest and pursuing. . . . Let the carreeringest
> billow confesse and absolve it selfe before it pricke up his bristles
> against them, for if it come upon his dancing horse and offer to tilt
> it with them, they will aske no trustier lances then their oares to beat
> out the brains of it . . .

Nashe's image of the fishermen as warriors, the *chevaliers* of the sea,
elaborates the sense of toil and toughness intrinsic to Yarmouth, and
this whole motif in the pamphlet spills over into a reflection of his own
struggles. 'My state', he says, 'is so tost and weather-beaten that it hath
nowe no anchor holde left to cleave unto.'[12] The hard-edged, palpable
fact of Great Yarmouth, the bravery of its herring-men 'holding their
owne pell-mell in all weathers', become images of survival, lessons in
grace under pressure.

Thus the herring: a 'treasure' won out of dangerous 'profundities',
the economic life and soul of 'this superiminente principall metropolis
of the redde Fish'. The red herring, or kipper, is a prime piece of 'English
marchandise', a national product:

> Of our appropriate glory of the red herring no region twixt the poles
> articke and antartick may, can or will rebate from us one scruple. On
> no coast like ours is it caught in such abundance, no where drest in
> his right cue but under our Horizon; hosted, rosted and tosted heere
> alone it is.

It brings in foreign currency – 'to trowle in the cash throughout all
nations of Christendome, there is no fellowe to the red herring'. Through
trade it converts into 'wine and woades', into 'salt, canvas, vitre and a
great deale of good trash'. It provides employment, 'sets a worke thousands' who would have 'begd or starvd, with their wives and brattes, had
not this Captaine of the squamy cattell so stoode their good Lord and
master'. It is a bulwark of religious observance: but for the pickled

herring, Lent would be 'clean spung'd out of the Kalendar'. It is even a potent medicine, a 'counter-poyson to the spitting sickness', an antidote for 'all rheumatique inundations', and '*ipse ille* agaynst the Stone'. Above all it is nourishment, food for the belly, a 'chollericke parcel' of vitamins, such a 'hot stirring meate' that it makes 'the cravenest dastard proclaime fire and sword' and hardens 'his soft bleding vaines as stiffe and robustious as branches of Corrall'. It is, moreover, food for all, plenteous and cheap, 'every mans money':

> every housholder or goodman Baltrop, that keepes a family in pay, casts for it as one of his standing provisions. The poorer sort make it three parts of there sustenance; with it, for his dinnier, the patchedst Leather piltche *laboratho* may dine like a Spanish Duke, when the niggardliest mouse of biefe will cost him sixpence.[13]

Again we touch the kernel of hard reality within the exotic ornations of *Lenten Stuffe*. It is what it claims to be: a 'prayse of the red herring', the food that sustained him through the hard days of Lent 1598.

Now Nashe begins in earnest his mounting surreal rhapsody on the theme of the red herring. He makes of it an apotheosis of poetic beauty: Helen's face was 'triviall' in comparison with 'our dappert Piemont Huldrick Herring, which draweth more barkes to Yarmouth bay then her beautie did to Troy'. It becomes a monarch, the 'king of fishes', 'Caesarian Charlemaine Herring', 'Solyman Herring' – 'stately borne, stately sprung he is, the best bloud of the Ptolomies no statelier'. Its sovereign splendour draws down planetary influences – 'the lordly sonne, the most rutilant planet of the seven, in Lent when Heralius Herring enters into his chiefe reign and scepterdome, skippeth and danseth the goats iumpe on the earth for ioy of his entrance'. It becomes an icon: it was not an image of Jupiter that Dionysius of Syracuse plundered, 'no such Iupiter, no such golden coated image was there, but it was a plaine golden coated red herring'. The 'true etimologie' of Mortus Alli, worshipped by the Persians, is '*mortuum halec*, a dead red herring'. The herring is a repository of occult wisdom – philosophers claim the Golden Fleece 'to be nothing but a booke of Alcumy'; Nashe will prove 'the redde Herrings skinne to be little lesse: the accidens of Alcumy I will sweare it is'. The curing of the herring is indeed an alchemical *magnum opus*, as the fish undergoes a 'transfiguration *ex Luna in Solem*, from his duskie tinne hew into a perfit golden blandishment'. The kipper is thus the alchemist's vaunted '*aurum philosophicum*' – 'of so eye-bewitching a deaurate ruddie dy is the skincoat of this Lantsgrave, that happy is that nobleman who for his colours in armory can neerest imitate his chimicall temper'.[14] And so it goes on – Nashe wrests the herring to the centre of every conceivable mental enterprise. There are jokes, anecdotes, proverbs, burlesques, fables, political allegories:

> My conceit is cast into a sweating sickenesse with ascending these few steps of his renowne; into what a hote broyling Saint Laurence fever would it relapse then, should I spend the whole bagge of my winde in climbing up to the lofty mountaine creast of his trophees?

That the possibilities are endless is really the point of *Lenten Stuffe*. The herring becomes anything his wit can transform it into. Give me a subject, Nashe says, *any* subject, and I will give you a pamphlet. There are precedents for this:

> I follow the trace of the famousest schollers of all ages, whom a wantonizing humour once in their life time hath possest to play with strawes, and turne mole hils into mountaines.

He gives a long list of the 'wast authors' through history who have 'terleryginckt it so frivolously of they reckt not what'. Homer, for instance, 'of rats and frogs hath heroiqut it'.[15] But it remains a quintessentially Nasheian performance, a hymn to the inexhaustibility of language, a quirky pageant of responses and reverberations. The red herring is, in the axiomatic sense, a complete red herring, and as such it is Nashe's metaphor for life itself. His 'prayse of the red herring' becomes a paradigm for the mind's peripheral agitations around an elusive, perhaps non-existent, core of meaning. And if the red herring tells us life's secret, then that secret is the plain fact of survival. The metaphor doubles back: the herring is food on his plate, the 'stuffe' of life in a hard 'lenten' world. The wits back in London will scoff – 'alas, poore hungerstarved Muse', they will say, 'was it so hard driven that it had nothing to feede upon but a redde herring?' – but the fishermen of Yarmouth will take his meaning. It is for them he prays at the end of the pamphlet – 'No more can I do for you than I have done, were you my god-children every one: God make you his children and keepe you from the Dunkerks' – and to them he appeals, his 'storm-tost' fellows, to drink 'the health of Nashes Lenten-stuffe', and

> let not your rustie swordes sleepe in their scabberds, but lash them out in my quarrell as hotely as if you were to cut cables or hew the main mast over boord, when you heare me mangled and torne in mennes mouths.[16]

Our first clear sighting of Nashe back in London is not until early 1599, some eighteen months after his flight from 'the signe of the seargeants heade'. On 11 January, publisher Cuthbert Burby entered his copy of *Lenten Stuffe* at Stationers' Hall. Nashe's position was still parlous, for the scribe added the words, 'upon Condicon that he [Burby] gett yt Laufully Aucthorised'. This does not prove that Nashe was back in town – he could have sent the manuscript to Burby – but he was certainly in London when he wrote the latest section of the pamphlet, the address 'To his Readers, hee cares not what they be'. This may have been written after the registration on 11 January, but since he bids his readers 'stay till Ester terme' for his next pamphlet (an empty promise, as it turns out), we can assume he was expecting *Lenten Stuffe* to appear during the previous, Hilary or Lent, term. Nashe was, therefore, writing his preface, in London, before the end of the Lent term in mid-February.[17]

Lenten Stuffe duly appeared, presumably 'laufully aucthorised'. In June, however, a new 'crosse' was 'laide upon' our hard-pressed pamphleteer. It was not particularly *Lenten Stuffe* that provoked it: it was a total, blanket suppression. On Friday 1 June 1599, from the familiar precincts of Croydon Palace, Archbishop Whitgift issued a series of 'commaundements' in his capacity as chief censor. He ordered the immediate calling in of various 'unsemely Satyres & Epigrams', including Hall's *Virgidemiarum*, Marston's *Scourge of Villany*, Guilpin's *Skialetheia*, Middleton's *Microcynicon*, Cutwode's *Caltha Poetarum*, Sir John Davies' *Epigrams* and Marlowe's *Elegies*. And, to make a clean sweep of it, he commanded

> that all Nasshes bookes and Doctor Harveyes bookes be taken wheresòever they maye be founde, and that none of theire bookes bee ever printed hereafter.[18]

There is a sidelong tribute in this attempt to erase Nashe totally from the record, an acknowledgment of him as the *fons et origo* of this dissident satirical hubbub. Maybe Nashe felt, also, a bitter satisfaction in having dragged the Doctor down with him into unacceptability. In real terms, however, the prohibition was a catastrophe for him. On the following Monday, 4 June, various books 'presently thereuppon were burnte' at Stationers' Hall. Amid the smoke of the Elizabethan police-state, Nashe begins to fade from view.

There was little time left him. There is a stamp of finality on *Lenten Stuffe*, an intimation of death:

> Some of the crummes of it, like the crums in a bushy beard after a greate banquet, will remaine in my papers to bee seene when I am deade and under grounde . . .

While I have sence and existence I will praise it . . .

Commend thy muse to sempiternity, and have images and statutes
erected to her after her unstringed silent interment . . .

Stay, let me looke about, where am I? In my text or out of it? Not
out for a groate: out for an angell: nay I'le lay no wagers, for now I
perponder more sadlie uppon it, I thinke I am oute indeed. . . .[19]

Lenten Stuffe is Nashe's swan-song, one last desperate 'feate' before the
curtains close. In the new century we hear of him just faintly. *Summers
Last Will* was published in 1600, registered on 28 October, again by
Cuthbert Burby. Apparently the prohibition of 1599 had petered out,
in the manner of these state fulminations. The play had, ironically, been
written for Whitgift himself. Another work issued in 1600 may give us
some clues about Nashe in the last year of his life. This was *The Hospitall
of Incurable Fooles*, published by Edward Blount, a translation from the
Italian of Tommaso Garzoni (*L'Hospidale de' Pazzi Incurabili*). In one
copy of this is a memorandum, in an early-seventeenth-century hand,
which reads: 'Tho. Nashe had some hand in this translation and it was
the last he did as I heare.'[20] The note is signed, 'P.W.'. Whoever this was,
he pitches his assertion convincingly. Not that Nashe *did* the translation,
which might argue a better command of Italian than there is reason to
assign to him, but that he 'had a hand' in it. That it was the last thing
Nashe wrote is also plausible: if he was involved, it would certainly be
his last known piece. The text itself leaves one guessing, but two pieces
in the prefatory matter that are not from Garzoni's original Italian
deserve attention. These are a burlesque dedication by 'Dame Folly' to
her 'special benefactresse, Madam Fortune', and an address, 'Not to the
Wise Reader', signed '*Il Pazzissimo*'. There are moments in these which
could be Nashe, throwing out to the wisest of his foolish readers a rich
hidden irony – the malcontent Pierce fawning on 'Madam Fortune' and
scoffing the 'poore despised Nation of Poets' that

defame and traduce your Ladyshyp with the imputative slanders of
niggardize and instability, when I (which have known you more
inwardly then a thousand of these candle-wasting Booke-wormes) can
affirm you to be the most bounteous, open-handed, firme, unswayed,
constant Ladie under Heaven.

The pieces have a vein of mock self-deprecation, an authorial shrug,
which is typical of Nashe:

This I did carelessly, accept you of it as lightly. . . . Even your Phisicall drams, that are so greedily sought after, suffer a little sophistication at the hands of the Apothecarie. Think not so much therefore, if so tickle and foolish a commoditie as this is be somewhat endamaged by the transportation of it out of Italie.

And again, in the nonchalant sign-off:

There was a true tricke of my selfe now (if you marke it): Folly must have a flurt of lightnesse and ostentation ever. I feare nothing more but that I have beene too grave all this while, & appeer'd like one dancing in a gowne. If I have, pardon me; I beg it with as forced a looke, as a Player that in speaking an Epilogue makes love to the twopennie-roume for a *plaudite*.[21]

Is this Nashe, trailing his forbidden pen under a last pseudonym, '*Il Pazzissimo*', the Fool of Fools? Does he tease the readers with an occasional 'true tricke of my selfe' which they could knowingly 'marke'? Does his claim to be a 'poore traveller' in Italian contain a hinting reminiscence of that 'unfortunate traveller' in Italy, Jack Wilton? There are more possible Nasheian phrasings in the text itself:

Unhappie men, who with a mind puffed up with pride, a noddle lighter than an oake-apple, and more voide of wit than cockles of meate in the waine of the moone, presume notwithstanding ... as the Kings of Fooles, they shall receive an open-mouthed applause of them all, to the ende that while the pipkin boylleth, the smoke that pleaseth themselves so much may forcibly come steaming out at the crowne of their owne hats ...

Minerva to take care of franticke and delirant Fooles; *Iupiter Hospitalis*, of melancholicke and savage; ... the Egyptian Oxe, of those notted, grosse and loblolly-lams; the Samian sheepe, of shallow-pates and ninnie hammers; the Goddesse *Bubona*, of lumpish and loggerheaded ...

These men, who counterfeiting other *Catoes* among the multitude, will in the end appeare to be nothing but Kings of Crickets, Doctor doddipowles, grout-headed Gratians, or cockscombe-like Merlins, as in truth they are ...

This is no two-penie matter, nor no triviall gridiron growt-headrie. . . .

There is a story of a 'testie and fustian' man who wore 'the *Toga Praetexta* or long robe of a Doctor':

Hearing one day a drummer that played but badly upon this instrument, he steps me downe from his chaire of dignitie, and taking the drum in his hand, brased it hard, and in succinct and grave habite went sounding of it into the market place, drawing after him all the whole Frie of boyes, everie one gazing at him with so great laughter.

It sounds not unlike a moral fable for Gabriel, with his tympanic entry into the literary 'market-place'. The discourse on 'Scoffing Fooles' gives us a sound *apologia* for Tom Nashe himself:

Scoffers and iesters are good in this one point, for they make men merrie, and expell melancholy from the heart, neither doe they eate their bread in treacherie, as flatterers doe.[22]

None of this is evidence. It need only show that whoever did compile *The Hospitall* managed, at times, to sound very like Nashe, just as, for instance, the satirical 'Parnassian' of St John's did. Nashe was, quite simply, the touchstone for late Elizabethan humorous prose. But it is nevertheless possible that Nashe is lurking in this text; that he 'had some hand' in it, as 'P.W.' puts it, just as he did in the 'Pasquill' tracts, the *Defence of Conny-Catching*, and possibly the comic scenes in *Dr Faustus*. It would be plausible enough to find Nashe working at Blount's printing-house, 'over against the Great North Door of St Paul's', rather as he had at Danter's a few years earlier. Danter himself had died in 1599.[23] Edward Blount had been a friend of Marlowe's: he was probably one of those 'stationers in Paules churchyard' whom Kyd described Marlowe as 'conversing' with. In his edition of Marlowe's unfinished poem, *Hero and Leander* (1598), Blount speaks poignantly of his dead friend in an Epistle Dedicatory to Marlowe's old patron, Sir Thomas Walsingham. 'Sir,' he writes,

Wee thinke not our selves discharged of the dutie wee owe to our friend, when wee have brought the breathlesse bodie to the earth: for albeit the eye there taketh his ever farwell of that beloved object, yet the impression of the man that hath beene deare unto us, living an after life in our memory, there putteth us in mind of farther obsequies due unto the deceased.

In 1600, Blount was himself the dedicatee of the first edition of Marlowe's translation from Lucan's *Pharsalia*. Fellow-publisher Thomas Thorpe addresses his 'true friend', Ned Blount:

Blount: I purpose to be blunt with you, and out of my dulnesse to

encounter you with a Dedication in the memory of that pure Elementall wit, Christopher Marlowe.

It is probable that Blount had once held the copyright on Marlowe's
Lucan, as he did on *Hero and Leander*, for Thorpe speaks of his 'old
right in it'.[24] Nashe's own rendition of the story of Hero and Leander
in *Lenten Stuffe* was doubtless occasioned by the publication of
Marlowe's poem in 1598: 'two faithfull lovers they were,' he says, 'as
everie apprentise in Paules churchyard will tell you for your love, and
sell you for your money'. There were, in fact, two editions of the poem
in 1598: Blount's was the first, but the second, published by Paul Linley,
contained a continuation of Marlowe's unfinished translation. The poet
who supplied this was Nashe's old enemy, George Chapman.[25] The old
trio of 1592 appears once more, ranged characteristically round this
classic love-story: Marlowe's opening sestiads, fiery and erotic in content,
glacially cool in form; Chapman's sequel, full of fustian philosophizing;
Nashe's prose version, abrasive and over-familiar, roughening and
ruffling the nap of the legend. His version is not, as is sometimes said,
a 'burlesque' of Marlowe; but it may well be a riposte to Chapman.
Let the public choose: me or Chapman, a pamphlet-story or a poetic
meditation. Sheer market-place competitiveness, honed and embittered
by exile, motivates Nashe's superb redaction of the Hero and Leander
romance. Another of Blount's productions in 1598 – John Florio's Italian
dictionary, *A Worlde of Wordes* – is also echoed in *Lenten Stuffe*, when
Nashe briefly tilts at Hugh Sanford and the Countess of Pembroke –
'H.S., that in honour of Maid-marrian gives sweete Margeram for his
Empresse'. This rehearses an old enmity of Nashe's, but it was almost
certainly inspired by Florio's own assault on Sanford in the preface to
his dictionary:

> Horse Stealer, Hob Sowter, Hugh Sot, Humphrey Swineshead, Hodge
> Sowgelder. Now Master H.S., if this doe gaule you, forbeare kicking
> hereafter, and in the meane time you may make a plaister of your
> dride Marioram.[26]

Nashe was 'in the countrey' while he wrote *Lenten Stuffe*. Perhaps news,
or even gifts, of the Marlowe poem and the Florio dictionary were sent
by the publisher himself. It is, at any rate, likely that if Blount called
Marlowe his 'beloved' and 'deere' friend, he also knew Nashe. And it is
not implausible that he offered Nashe support and employment in the
bleak days after the prohibition, and that Nashe did indeed spice up
some more pedestrian translator's version of Garzoni with his brilliant,
if now fading, 'flurt of lightnesse and ostentation'. It is a nice thought:
to get our last glimpse of Nashe in the company of this cultivated,

sanguine publisher, who won his niche in posterity in 1623, as the printer and prime mover of *Mr William Shakespeares Comedies, Histories and Tragedies*, otherwise known as the 'First Folio'.

Where, how and exactly when Nashe died is unknown. Whether it was sudden and violent like Marlowe, lousy and repentant like Greene, of the pox like George Peele, or of the plague like tens of thousands of other Londoners, we do not know. The year was almost certainly 1601. He was thirty-three years old, or at most just turned thirty-four. Two epitaphs appear in this year. In *Affaniae*, published at Oxford, Charles Fitzgeffrey pens an eight-line Latin poem headed '*Thomae Nashe*':

> Quum Mors edictum Iovis imperiale secuta
>   Vitales Nashi extingueret atra faces;
> Armatam juveni linguam calamumque tremendum
>   (Fulmina bina) prius insidiosa rapit,
> Mox illum aggreditur nudum atque invadit inermem
>   Atque ita de victo vate trophaea refert.
> Cui si vel calamus praesto vel lingua fuisset,
>   Ipsa quidem metuit mors truculenta mori.[27]

(Upon the imperial edict of Jove, black death snuffs out Nashe's vital flame. First, insidiously, it seizes those twin thunderbolts, the young man's weaponed tongue and fearsome pen. Then it advances and overruns the naked defenceless man, and so returns in triumph, the poet vanquished. But if either his pen or his tongue had been at his command, he would have struck the fear of death into savage death itself.)

This may be trying to tell us something. One theory is that it means Nashe suffered a stroke, which deprived him of his speech and paralysed his pen-hand, and that he lingered some while in this state before dying.[28] Another possibility connects Nashe's death with the official silencing of him. The '*edictum Iovis*' would be Whitgift's 'commaundements' of June 1599, with the implication that Nashe died in poverty because unable to pursue his 'woonted meanes' of maintenance. Perhaps, after all, it is only a metaphor: the ineluctable victory of death, a young man burnt out in his prime. The idea of Nashe scoffing death itself into a piteous pickle ends the poem, touchingly, on an up-beat. The other epitaph of 1601 comes from Nashe's anonymous admirer and fellow *alumnus* of St John's (Document 12). In the second part of *The Returne from Parnassus*, performed that Christmas, Ingenioso and Iudicio are passing comment on various authors named in the fashionable anthology,

Belvedere (or 'The Garden of the Muses'). They come upon Nashe's name:

> *Ingenioso   Thomas Nash*. I, heer's a fellow, Iudicio, that carryed the
> deadly Stockado in his pen, whose muse was armed with a gag-tooth,
> and his pen possest with Hercules furies.

> *Iudicio*   Let all his faultes sleepe with his mournfull chest,
>   And there for ever with his ashes rest.
>   His stile was wittie, though it had some gall,
>   Some thing he might have mended, so may all.
>   Yet this I say, that for a mother witt,
>   Fewe men have ever seene the like of it.

This is a very human tribute: Nashe's flaws and faults and over-abundant 'gall' are annulled by the joys of his irrepressible 'mother witt'. It has something of the tone of Nashe's own tribute to Greene in *Strange Newes*: here is a personality too big for the sensible confinements of morality. A third epitaph, probably, is found in a miscellaneous Elizabethan manuscript:

> Heer lyes Tom: Dashe, yt notable Raylour,
> That in his lyfe neere payde Shoemaker nor taylor.[29]

Here perhaps is yet another of Nashe's nicknames: speedy Tom Dash.

Over the next few years his literary disciples paid their dues. Both Thomas Middleton and Thomas Dekker, whose pamphlets and 'city comedies' derive from Nashe's satirical journalism, praise him generously. In *Father Hubburds Tales* (1604), Middleton recalls that 'honest soule' who never compromised himself for 'private praise'. He says, truthfully enough,

> Thou wast indeed too slothfull to thy selfe,
> Hiding thy better tallent in thy Spleene.

He laments Nashe's early death, and the adulteration of his purer satiric spirit:

> Thou didst not live thy ripend Autumne day,
> But wert cut off in thy best blooming May . . .
> Thy name they burie, having buried thee,
> Drones eate thy Honnie, thou wert the true Bee.
> Peace keepe thy Soule . . .[30]

Two years later, in *Newes from Hell*, Dekker fervently invokes Nashe's spirit:

> Thou, into whose soule (if ever there were a *Pithagorean Metempsu-*

chosis) the raptures of that firie and inconfinable Italian spirit were bounteously and boundlessly infused, thou sometimes Secretary to Pierce Pennylesse and Master of his requests, ingenious, ingenuous, fluent, facetious T. Nash, from whose aboundant pen, hony flow'd to thy friends, and mortall Aconite to thy enemies. . . . Sharpest Satyre, Luculent Poet, Elegant Orator, get leave for thy Ghost to come from her abiding, and to dwell with me a while, till she hath carows'd to me in her owne wonted ful measures of wit, that my plump braynes may swell and burst into bitter invectives against the Lieftennant of Limbo.

In a revamped version of this pamphlet, issued as *A Knights Conjuring* in 1607, Dekker adds a humorous vision of a scribbler's Elysian Fields. There we spy 'learned Watson, industrious Kyd, ingenious Atchlow'; over in a corner, 'under the shades of a large vyne', sit Marlowe, Greene and Peele. They laugh to see the newest arrival at their 'Colledge', Nashe, 'still haunted with the sharpe and Satyricall spirit that followd him heere upon earth', still railing on 'dry-fisted Patrons' and

accusing them of his untimely death, because if they had given his Muse that cherishment which shee most worthily deserved, hee had fed to his dying day on fat Capons, burnt sack and Suger, and not so desperately have ventur'de his life and shortend his dayes by keeping company with pickle herrings.[31]

There is already the sense of a vanished era in this little *vignette*. This was King James' England now: those flamboyant, fast-burning Wits belonged to another world, a lost Elizabethan moment. Of his fellow Wits only two outlived Nashe. John Lyly died, poor and neglected, at his house in St Bartholomew's in November 1606. Thomas Lodge converted to Catholicism, took a degree in medicine at Avignon in 1600, published various medical and philosophical tracts, and died, substantial Dr Lodge, in 1625.[32] As for Gabriel Harvey, he lingered on at Saffron Walden, with typical tenacity, into his eighties. Apart from a couple of local law-suits, and a tradition that he 'practised physic' at Walden, nothing is heard of his last years. He lived comfortably off the family estates, unmarried, alone with his vast library and his memories. The parish register records the burial of 'Mr Doctr Gabriel Harvey' on 11 February 1631. Down in London, an enterprising publisher rushed out the first printed edition of *Pedantius*, the old college comedy which had so tickled the undergraduate Nashe half a century earlier.[33]

Let Nashe himself sign off. His latest piece of writing – leaving aside whatever fragments may be in *The Hospitall of Incurable Fooles* – is the address to the readers in *Lenten Stuffe*. He 'cares not what they be' so long as they read him. He tosses them this extraordinary work, a mere 'friskin of my witte'. He promises it will be unmistakably his: 'I scorne it, I scorne it, that my woorkes should turne taile to any man.' The reader will say, 'thats Pierce a Gods name'. He explains his style, and himself, one last time:

> Let me speake to you about my huge woords which I use in this booke, and then you are your own men to do what you list. Know it is my true vaine to be *tragicus Orator*, and of all stiles I most affect & strive to imitate Aretines, not caring for this demure soft *mediocre genus*, that is like water and wine mixt togither; but give me pure wine of it self, & that begets good bloud, and heates the braine thorowly: I had as lieve have no sunne, as have it shine faintly, no fire as a smothering fire of small coales, no cloathes, rather then weare linsey wolsey.

The literary alignments – rousing oratory and the Renaissance satire of Aretino – become for a moment a personal manifesto. He is a man who has refused the middle road, the '*mediocre genus*'; he has chosen the risks and extremities of a pamphleteer's life, the delights and agitations of a thoroughly heated brain. But the mood of revelation quickly passes. 'Apply it for me', he says carelessly, 'for I am cald away to correct the faults of the presse, that escaped in my absence from the Printing-house.' With that he leaves us, the words seemingly thrown back over his shoulder, as he goes out of a door, into the London streets, hurrying off – as ever – to the printer's.

DOCUMENTS, NOTES AND BIBLIOGRAPHY

-DOCUMENTS-

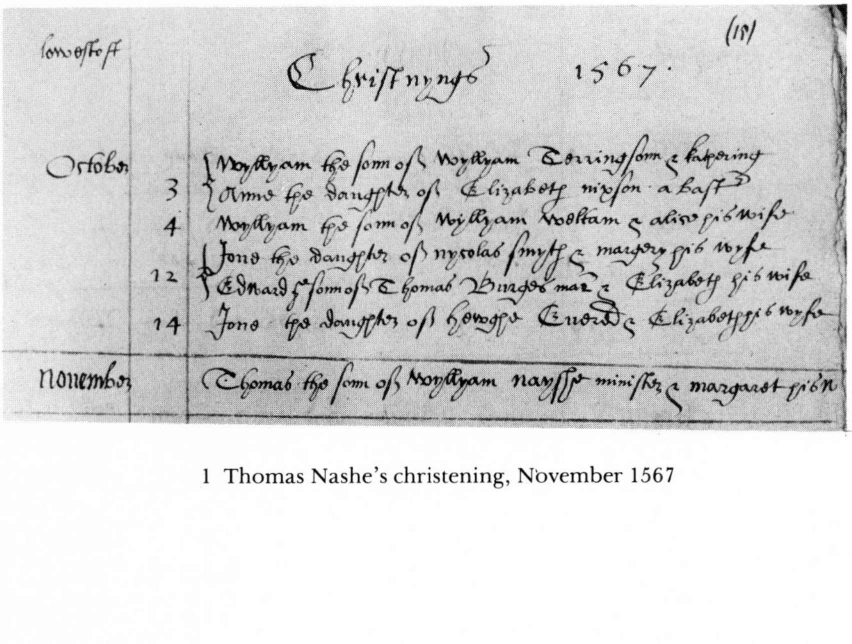
lowestoft (18)

Christnyngs 1567.

October { Wyllyam the sonn of Wyllyam Torringtonn & Katherine
3 { Anne the daughter of Elizabeth nixson a bast
4 Wyllyam the sonn of Wyllyam Woltam & alice his wife
{ Jone the daughter of Nycolas Smyth & margery his wyfe
12 { Edward ye sonn of Thomas Burges mar & Elizabeth his wife
14 Jone the daughter of George Everd & Elizabeth his wyfe

November Thomas the sonn of Wyllyam Nasshe minister & margaret his w

1 Thomas Nashe's christening, November 1567

2 Margaret Nashe's will, 2 December 1589

conteyninge iiij payer of shetes and pillow bers
ij towels a table clothe & a shirt Bond Item
I give unto Elizabeth Blancher my kinswoman
a payer of shetes Item I give unto Elizabeth
the wiefe of mathew wytheringen my kinsman
a payer of shetes Item I give a payer of shetes
unto Stephen wytheringam my kinsman Item I give
and bequeath all my other goods moveables utensiles
... at sote ungiven and bequeathed unto Isaac my
sonne whom I assigne and constitute to be my sole
executor witnesse hereof Stephen Phillipp

signum [mark] wytherens master

Probatum fuit huiusmodi testamentum vicesimo
primo die februarii Anno Dni 1589 apud
[...] coram magro willimo [...] thio
substitut min jo. mophiden desinat Angl
&c Et comissa fuit ado conuas &c
Isaac executori &c Iurat &c
Exhibit est Inuentar
[...]

3 Nashe's matriculation as sizar scholar of St John's, 13 October 1582

4 Nashe's admission as Lady Margaret scholar of St John's, autograph entry, 1584

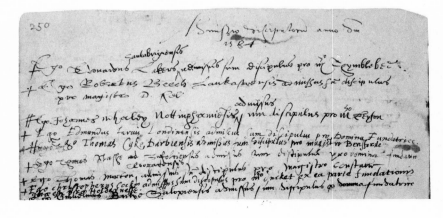

5 Nashe's Latin verses on *Ecclesiasticus,* in text hand, part of a presentation copy by Lady Margaret scholars, 1585

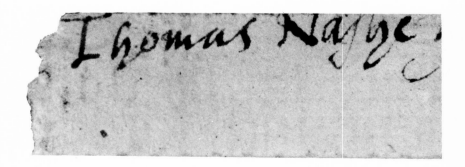

Coll. Johns.
Do. Cook.
Do. Grm.
Do. Starky sen.
Do. Starky ju.
Do Wortley.
Do. Briggs.
Do. Sanders.
Do. Huffam.
Do. Forman.
Do. Nash.
Do. Post.
Do. Bellowes.
Do. Peachy.
Do. Crowder.
Do. Morton.
Do. Pilkinton.
Do. Bate.
Do. Fox.
Do. Beverley.
Do. Matershed.
Do. Lambe.
Do. Faucet.
Do Heblethwait.
Do. Alcock.
Do. Cupper.
Do. Tomson.
Do Orwell.

6 List of students attending philosophy lectures in 1588

7 Signature, probably Nashe's, in a copy of Thomas Phaer, *The Seven First Bookes of the Eneidos of Virgill* (London, 1558)

Thomas Nashe

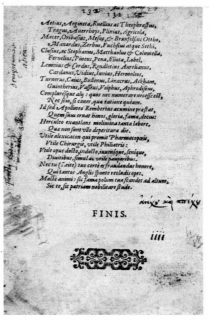

8 Nashe's signature and marginalia, *c.* 1592, in a copy of John Leland, *Principum ac Illustrum in Anglia Virorum Encomia* (London, 1589)

Folie and lacke of naturall witte, oʒ els wãante of honeſtie, geue good matter of myʒthe often tymes. When Scipio beyng Pʒetoʒ, had appoincted vnto a certain Sicilian, one to be his lawier that was of a good houſe, and had an euill wit, little better then halfe a foole. I pʒaie you, quod the Sicilian to Scipio, appoint this lawier foʒ mine aduerſary, and let me haue none at all hardly. |

J.C.

wiſhing.

In ſpeakyng againſt an euill man, and wiſſhyng ſomewhat thereupon, a ieſte ſeme delitefull. When an euill man had accuſed many perſons, and none toke any harme by hym, but rather were acquited from tyme to tyme, and taken the ſoner foʒ honeſtmen: Now would to Chʒiſtes paſſion, quod a naughtie fellowe

Naſh y rayler.

What talke you of ſuche a manne (ſaieth an other) there is an
honeſt manne ye may bee aſſured. Foʒ if a man had neade of one,
he is ready at a pinche, hys body ſwetes foʒ honeſtie; if you come
to hym in a hotte ſommers daie, you ſhall ſe his honeſtie in ſuche
ſoʒte to reeke, that it woulde pitie any Chʒiſtian ſoule liuynge.
He hath moʒe honeſty with hym then he nedes; and therfoʒe both
is able and will lende, where it pleaſeth hym beſte. Beware of
hym aboue all menne that euer you knewe. He hath no fellowe,
there is none ſuche, I thinke he will not liue long, he is ſo honeſt
a manne; the moʒe pitye that ſuche good felowes ſhoulte knowe
what death meaneth. But it maketh no matter, when he is gone,
all the woʒlde will ſpeake of hym, his name ſhall neuer dye, he is
ſo well knowen vniuerſallie.   *Green, & Naſh at his inſ tant.*

Thus we maie mockingly ſpeake well of hym, when there is
not a naughtier fellowe within al England again, & euen as wel
ſette out his naughtines this waie, as though wee hadde in very
dede vttered all his naughtie conditions plainlie, and without te
ſtyng. Emong all that euer were pleaſant in this kinde of delite,
Socrates beareth the name, and maie woʒthelie chalenge pʒaiſe.
*Julian in his Miſopogon finely commendes k. & his foes: Sic
vt s̄ &c.*

9 Harvey's marginalia on Nashe and Greene, *c.* 1592, in a copy of Sir Thomas
Wilson, *The Art of Rhetorike* (London, 1567)

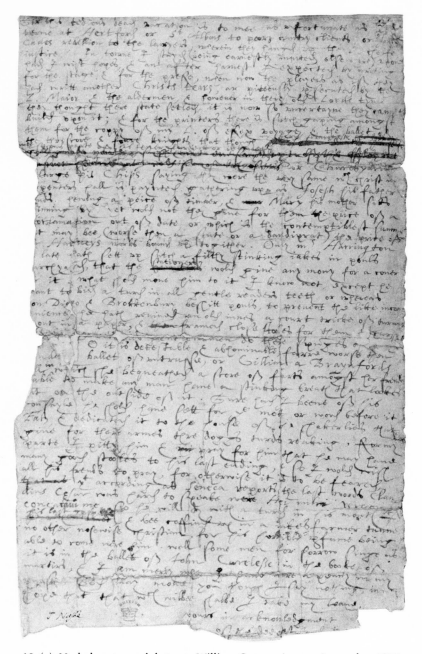

10 (a) Nashe's autograph letter to William Cotton, August–September 1596

10 (b) Address to Cotton and an Elizabethan shopping-list

11 Government directive to Richard Topcliffe *et al.* concerning *The Isle of Dogs* and Nashe's seized papers, 15 August 1597

Ingen: Christopher Marlowe/

Judicio/ Marlow was happy in his buskind muse
Alas vnhappye in his life and end
Pittye it is that witt so ill should dwell
witt lent from heauen, but vices sent from hell.

Ingen: Our theater hath lost: Pluto hath gott
A tragick penman for a driery plotte
Beniamin Johnson.

Judicio/ The wittiest fellow of a Bricklayer in England

Ingeni: A meere Empyrick, one that getts what he hath by obseruation, and makes
onelye nature priuie to what he indites: so slowe an Inuentor, that
hee were better betake himselfe to his ould trade of bricklaying,
A bold whorson, as confident now in making of a booke, as he was
in times past at laying of a Bricke./
william Shakespeare/

Judicio/ Who loves not Adons love, or Lucrece rape?
His sweeter verse contaynes hart throbbing line
Could but a grauer subiect him content
without loves foolish lazye languishment

Ingenioso/ Churchyard/
Hath not Shores wife, although a light skirt shee
Given him a chast long lasting memorye

Judicio/ Noe all his witt goes els our Sir in London wall
A thing right after a poets to know all

Ingenio: Thomas Nashe/ I heare a fellow Judicio that carried y deadly stoc
hade in his penne, whose muse was armed with a gag tooth & his pen
possest with seauen spirits of heuerable furious/

Judicio/ Lett all his faultes sleepe with his mournefull chest
And then forgiue his ashes ashes accost
his life was witty though it had some gall
Some things he might haue mended so may all,

Ingenioso Readers my wish./

Judicio/ As for those, they have some of them beene the outt hodg staffe of y
presse, & some of them are at this instant y bottle o slaunders of y
printinge house. followes y stand onely vpon tearmes to serve y
tearmes with their blotted papes write as men goe to y stoole, for nedle
and roson they write, they write as a beare pisses now & then dropps
a pamphlette/
Sound Solum is dead. God laite lord grant as I doe nothinge.

12 Nashe's epitaph in a manuscript copy of 'The Progress to Parnassus', *c.* 1601

NOTES

Full details of the sources referred to here are given in the Bibliography. For works referred to by acronym – TN, GH, etc. – see Bibliography 1. For works referred to by author's name see Bibliography 2.

1 THE PAMPHLETEER

1 GH II 65.
2 TN II 186.
3 So Nashe titles King in *Lenten Stuffe* (TN III 147), which is dedicated to him. 'Tobacconist' then meant a smoker, rather than seller, of tobacco.
4 Shakespeare, *Loves Labors Lost*, IV i 145.
5 On Nashe and Falstaff, see J. Dover Wilson (ed.), *1 Henry IV* (Cambridge, 1946), pp. 191–6, and 'The Origins and Development of Shakespeare's *Henry IV*'; Rhodes, ch. 6. As late as 1605–6, writing *Macbeth*, Shakespeare makes specific use of a Nashe pamphlet (*The Terrors of the Night*).
6 Leishman (ed.), *1 Returne from Parnassus*, 136–7. On Ingenioso in this play as a portrait of Nashe, see Leishman's introduction, pp. 71–9, and ch. 15 below.
7 TN II 207, III 145.
8 TN I 204.
9 With the exception of Hosier Lane (see TN III 114–15, V 28 on Nashe's residence *chez* Danter) these are general locations rather than addresses: see below ch. 4. On Nashe's association with Coleharbour, see TN III 25, GH III 26; with Pickt-hatch, see Middleton, sigs B3–D2v.
10 TN I 212, 287–8, 310, GH I 162, 194.
11 'Ew. H.' in Brydges, *Restituta* (1815), II 359.
12 TN V 1.
13 Harrison, 'Books & Readers 1591–4', p. 287. News productions entered in the Stationers' Register during those years include 49 pamphlets and 4 ballads on the French wars; 11 pamphlets and 4 ballads on other foreign news; 5 pamphlets and 3 ballads on naval news; 14 pamphlets and 36 ballads on home news.
14 TN III 216–18.
15 The satirical boom of the 1960s – *Beyond the Fringe*, *Private Eye*, *That was the Week that Was*, etc. – is analogous to that of the 1590s. It emanated from the universities, with special emphasis on Cambridge; it was in part a product of the middle-class affluence it criticized; it developed during a

period of deep political and moral readjustment. One major difference is that the penalties for overstepping the limits of satire were considerably harsher in Elizabethan times.

16 TN I 5.

17 John Taylor, *Crop-eare Curried, or Tom Nash his Ghost* (London, 1644), sig. A2v. This is one of three mid-seventeenth-century politico-religious pamphlets using Nashe's 'ghost' in the title. Throughout the seventeenth century, Nashe was primarily remembered for his polemics against 'Martin Marprelate' and the Harveys. See TN V 45–8.

18 RG XII 143; Lodge, *Wits Miserie* (1596), sig. I1; TN I 242. Nashe's references to Aretino are numerous: see especially TN I 285, II 264–6, III 152. On Nashe's actual debt to Aretinian satire see TN V 128–9; Rhodes, pp. 26–36; McPherson.

19 Shakespeare, *As You Like It*, III vii 47–51. Cf. I ii 82–4: 'since the little wit that fools have was silenced, the little foolery that wisemen have makes a great show'. See AS edition (ed. Latham, 1975), pp. xvii, xxvif, on the dating of the play and its possible allusions to the Injunction of June 1599.

20 SR III 677–8.

21 TN II 184, GH II 63. The latter phrase is in fact John Eliot's: he is the 'Gentleman' whose praise of Nashe is inserted by Harvey into *Pierces Supererogation*. See Yates, *John Florio*, pp. 178f.

22 TN III 312.

23 See Rhodes, who traces Nashe's influence as 'the master of this peculiar literary mode' through Shakespeare, Dekker, Middleton and Jonson.

24 Lewis, pp. 410–11.

25 TN I 333.

26 GH II 243, echoed almost *verbatim* in Leishman (ed.), *1 Returne*, 152–4.

27 TN I 192. In Leishman (ed.), *2 Returne*, 344, Danter offers 40 shillings and a 'pottle' of wine to Ingenioso for a pamphlet. Ingenioso's reply suggests this was a basic minimum: '40 shillings? a fit reward for one of your reumatick poets, that beslavers all the paper he comes by.' Cf. George Wither, *Schollers Purgatory*: the publisher 'cann hyre for a matter of 40 shillings some needy Ignoramus'. John Stow received £3 and 40 complimentary copies for his *Survay of London* (1603), Thomas Bastard not much more than £1 for his verses, *Chrestoleros* (1598). See Miller, pp. 150–70; Sheavyn, pp. 72, 101f.

28 TN III 151–3; Leishman (ed.), *1 Returne*, 214.

29 TN I 343–4, III 19.

30 Lewis, p. 410. Prose pamphlets sold at various prices. See RG XI 45: 'I have for 3 pence bought a little pamphlet' (i.e. Greene's *Notable Discovery of Coosnage*).

31 TN I 320.

32 Lewis, p. 416; cf. Knights, p. 258.

33. TN I 162–3, 177, 208, II 150–1, 207, 230, 232, III 9, 88, 261. 'Coney' = rabbit; 'dust-box' = container for sand or dust to dry ink on paper; 'pantofles' = slippers. Using Spurgeon's image classification, Crosten (pp. 97f) analyses the images in *The Unfortunate Traveller* for 'vehicle content': out of 563 images he finds 133 from 'daily life', 70 from 'animals', 68 from 'the body' and 30 from 'domestic'.

34 TN III 174.

35 TN I 255.

36 See Cunnington, pp. 87f. Dekker refers to Jonson as a strolling player in a 'leather pilch' in *Satiromastix*. Aubrey was told by the player Lacey (p. 338)

that Jonson wore 'a coate like a coachman's coate, with slitts under the arme-pitts'. The 'buff jerkin', as worn by soldiers, sergeants, etc., was made of leather, usually ox-hide, 'buffed' to give a velvety surface.

37 GH III 65.

38 Shakespeare, *Hamlet*, II i 78–9; Jonson, Chapman and Marston, *Eastward Hoe*, II 1 82 (s.d.), V v 54.

39 So Jack Wilton's calf as displayed by his tight-fitting 'long stock', TN II 227.

40 RG XII 143; JL III 398–9; Chettle, sig. E2. Lyly does not actually identify the 'little wag in Cambridge' who threatens to '*ergo* Martin into an ague' as Nashe, but it seems likely (as Bond points out). Harvey refers to this same 'Cambridge wagg, a twigging Sophister' in his *Advertisement for Papp-Hatchett* (1589), GH II 129.

41 Shakespeare, *Loves Labors Lost*, V i 109–10; TN III 213, I 283.

42 All these names are given Nashe in *Pierces Supererogation* (1593): all come from Harvey except 'bombard goblin' which occurs in a poem contributed by the anonymous 'Gentlewoman' (GH II 17). Some suspect her to be Harvey anyway.

43 TN II 281, GH I 168, 288.

44 GH III 38–9, 36.

45 TN I 195, III 129, I 292.

46 TN I 312, III 129, I 267, 163, III 7.

47 GH II 225, 18. The latter is another phrase from the 'Gentlewoman'.

48 See OED, s.v. 'gag' (verb 2 sense 3) and 'gag-tooth'.

49 TN I 210.

50 Donne, *Divine Poems*, XIII (*Poems* I 328).

2 CHILDHOOD

1 If zodiacal evidence is acceptable, it was before 21 November. Nashe was surely a sting-tailed Scorpio.

2 TN III 205. The spelling 'Nayshe' may preserve an East Anglian pronunciation of the name. A pun of Richard Lichfield's (GH III 33), however, implies that Nashe rhymes with 'ash'. See TN V 2 n. 1.

3 The earliest reference to him is 6 February 1562, when his daughter Mary was christened. The previous vicar, Thomas Downing, had died in 1559, but the date of William Nashe's appointment, and his exact status at Lowestoft, are unclear. See TN V 3–5, and Appendix E; Lees, p. 163.

4 The connection is mooted by McKerrow (TN V 3 n. 3). He notes that sisters of this John Nash married John and Edward Blomvyle, and that a John Blomvyle (rector of Rollesby, Norfolk) seems to have held the actual living of Lowestoft while William Nashe was 'minister' there. There may be family connections behind this. In saying that William 'sprang from' the Hereford-shire Nashes, not that he actually came from Herefordshire himself, Nashe implies an earlier generation of migrants.

5 TN I 311.

6 TN I 174, 323, III 168.

7 TN I 311–12. He refers to the title-pages of *Pierce Penilesse* and *Strange Newes*. He is also styled 'gent' on the title-page of *Dido* (1594). A gentleman was strictly one 'lawfully entitled to armorial distinction' though not included in any recognized degree of nobility: see John Cussans, *The Handbook of Heraldry* (1868), and other references in OED, s.v. 'gentleman'.

8 TN III 127.

9 Although John Blomvyle resigned the vicarage of Lowestoft in 1555, he apparently regained the living after the death of his successor, Thomas Downing, in 1559, for in 1574 he is described as '*ultimus et nuper Vicarius*' of Lowestoft. On the uniting of Besthorpe and Lowestoft, see Lees, p. 163.

10 TN III 10; Stubbes, *Anatomy of Abuses*, cited Sheavyn, pp. 123–5; VCH Suffolk, II 292 n. 1.

11 The National Grid reference for Thomas Nashe's birthplace is TM 541941 (see Sheet TM 59 in the OS 1:25000 series). The site is in an angle formed by Oulton Road to the south and the old churchyard wall to the west. Some historical material in this paragraph is based on information provided personally to me by Mr Hugh Lees. On the destruction of the vicarage on 6 March 1606, see Lees, p. 238.

12 Psalms 93 v. 5. This was actually the text of the Harvest of the Sea address by Canon Whytehead at St Margaret's, 19 January 1947, transcribed Lees, pp. 206–9.

13 On Annot and his foundation, see Lees, pp. 93–4, Longe, p. 62. Philip was master from 1570 till his death in 1605. He married Mary *née* Witchingham in 1571, and was Parish Clerk from 1584. The population is Longe's computation (pp. 72–3), based on the burial registers and an estimated *per capita* mortality rate.

14 TN III 180–1, 198, I 292, 378–9, 158. The latter refers to the immigrants at Yarmouth rather than Lowestoft, but much of Nashe's treatment of Yarmouth in *Lenten Stuffe* contains memories and attitudes from his Lowestoft childhood. On Dutch refugees at Lowestoft, see Longe, p. 73.

15 TN III 180. The herring fleet is advocated by Robert Hitchcock in his *Politic Plat*: see Rowse, *England of Elizabeth*, p. 160.

16 VCH Suffolk II 199f ('Maritime History'), 289f ('Fisheries').

17 TN III 171, 181, 160, II 84–5. 'Haberdine' = salted cod, 'poor john' = salted hake. Caliban smells like 'a kind of not-of-the-newest poor John' (Shakespeare, *Tempest*, II ii 27).

18 TN I 379, III 158, II 303, 227. The periphrases for the sea are all from *Lenten Stuffe*.

19 TN II 38.

20 The first was buried on 27 April 1571, the second on 14 August 1572. The 'soule bell' (TN III 163) is the passing bell.

21 Historical details of the church and village, and of the Berdewell and Gawdy families, are contained in what Nashe would have called 'Chronographycal Tables' in the church. All Saints is now administered by the Redundant Churches Fund. See also Blomefield, I 297–312; Chambers, II 709.

22 Blomefield, I 307.

23 BM Sloane MS 93 f. 71v–84; GH III 73–97; TN III 129. See C. G. Moore-Smith, NQ, 8 April 1911, pp. 261–3; Stern, pp. 35–7. Philip Howard's uncle Henry, Earl of Northampton, lived at Audley End. His *Defensative against the Poyson of Supposed Prophesies* (1583) was largely aimed at Richard Harvey's *Astrologicall Discourse* (1583). There may have been personal motives in the attack, for on a page of his copy of the *Defensative* Gabriel wrote: 'Iwis it is not the Astrological Discourse, but a more secret mark whereat he shootith'. See Stern, p. 72.

24 TN II 146, 47, I 386, II 61–2.

25 TN I 356–7.

26 Shakespeare, *King Lear*, II iii 17–18; *A Midsummer Night's Dream*, II i 96; *Macbeth*, III ii 50–1.

27 TN III 329, with particular reference to the *Bowre of Delights* (1591), ascribed to (though largely disowned by) Nicholas Breton. See below, ch. 7.
28 TN III 156–72, II 282–5.
29 TN III 280.
30 TN III 262.
31 TN I 376, II 227, 229, 232–3, 327, III 34–5, 94, 264–5, 263.
32 TN I 369.
33 TN III 351, 372–3, 375.
34 On Elizabethan schooling, see Foster Watson, *English Grammar Schools to 1660* (1908); T. W. Baldwin, *William Shakespeare's Petty School* (1943); Rowse, *The England of Elizabeth*, pp. 530–50; Dodd, pp. 91–8; Schoenbaum, pp. 50–9.
35 TN III 156, 351. 'Ruinous and desolate' is a historical rather than topographical description: Thetford had been the ecclesiastical centre of East Anglia until the see was removed to Norwich in the eleventh century. In the parish church, St Cuthbert's, there is a reference to Archbishop Parker's legacy providing 6s 8d *per annum* for a minister to 'preach and declare one sermon at the town of Thetford'. This must have been effective when Nashe knew Thetford (Parker died in 1575) and may be loosely referred to in the phrase 'tenne shillings Sermones'.
36 He is not the same as the Philip Gawdy (1562–1617) whose letters are extant – ed. I. H. Jeayes (Roxburghe Club, London, 1906) – though the latter was also a Norfolk gentleman, and possibly related.
37 He says (TN III 127) of his father: '. . . and (as another Scholler) he brought me up at St Iohns'. McKerrow takes this to mean 'he maintained both me and another scholar at St John's'. It could, however, mean 'he maintained me, as a scholar like himself, at St John's'. While there were traditions, and sometimes obligations, for churchmen to assist in funding parish scholars, the other reading is quite possible.
38 TN II 123–4.
39 TN III 60, 70, 194, I 356.
40 TN III 279–80.
41 TN V 135. McKerrow's analysis of Nashe's reading (V 110–36) is masterful, if a trifle starchy in its judgments on Nashe's intellect ('not once, in however trifling a matter, does he seem to have thought for himself'). He is also unduly sceptical about Nashe's knowledge of Aretino: see references above, ch. 1 n. 18.
42 GH I 195. The line was axiomatic as simple '*amo-amas-amat*' Latin. The pedant Holofernes gets it wrong – '*facile*' instead of '*fauste*' – in *Loves Labors Lost*, IV ii 90.
43 TN V 133: McKerrow notes 38 quotations from the *Amores* and *Ars Amatoria*, 23 from the *Metamorphoses*.
44 TN III 63, 60.

3 CAMBRIDGE

1 Nashe says (TN III 181) he 'took up his inn' at St John's for 'seven yere together lacking a quarter'. Lichfield says (GH III 68) he left Cambridge while a 'batchelor of the third yere', i.e. between March 1588 and March 1589. He sold his first MS to publisher Thomas Hackett, in London, not later than 19 September 1588 (SR II 499). That he came up in late 1581 and left in summer 1588 seems to satisfy the parameters. It was customary

for students to attend university for a couple of terms before formally matriculating.

2 See Venn, I xxvii; OED, s.v. 'sizar'; Sheavyn, p. 106; TN I 198. Standard charges in hall at St John's were 1d a day at the scholars' table, 2d a day at the Fellows' table, 4d a day at the Master's table. See *Eagle* LVI (1954–5), p. 196f; Mullinger, *The University of Cambridge*, II 399–400.

3 Middleton, sig. F2v. 'Cewe' (cue, or in college accounts simply 'q') = a ration worth half a farthing. 'Commons' = standard college rations. 'Gawdy days' = feast days when 'double commons' or 'gaudies' were allowed.

4 Bakeless, I 65–6.

5 The 'prizing books', dating back to 1606, are described in *Eagle*, LVI (1954–5), p. 196f. Cf. Leishman (ed.), *2 Returne*, 944–5: 'when I was in Cambridge, and lay in a Trundlebed under my Tutor'. At St John's, scholars over the age of 14 were not expected to sleep more than two to a bed.

6 Donne, *Satyre* I, 2–4 (*Poems*, I 145).

7 *St John's College Rentals, 1575–99*, f. 225.

8 TN III 197. See, on generally spartan conditions, the sermon by Thomas Lever, *c.* 1550, describing life at St John's, quoted Bakeless, I 57–8.

9 'Salting' required the freshman to amuse an assembly of students in the college hall: if he spoke well and wittily he was rewarded with wine or beer; if not, with salted water or caudle. 'Tucking' was a small incision on the lip or chin which drew blood. Another ceremony required the freshman to swear an oath and kiss an old shoe proffered by the senior college cook. See Mullinger, *The University of Cambridge*, II 400–1. The germs of Nashe's mock dedications and satirical pranks are in these rituals.

10 TN III 317.

11 TN III 122–3.

12 Penry matriculated at Peterhouse in 1580 and transferred to Oxford in 1584–5. See Cooper, *Athenae Cantabrigienses*, II 154–8. On Nashe's 'unmasking' of Penry, see TN III 365f, and ch. 6 below.

13 TN III 355.

14 TN II 251, I 313.

15 Nashe shows his dislike of Ramus in his student piece, *The Anatomie of Absurditie*, TN I 43, 45. See also TN III 313, 368.

16 Marlowe, *Massacre at Paris*, I vii 27–9, 45–6.

17 TN II 246–53, 181–3.

18 Harrison, I 77–8; Cooper, *Annals*, II 360–1; Mullinger, *The University of Cambridge*, II 391–4, 429–36.

19 Greene's parentage is not entirely certain: he was probably the second son of Robert and Jane Greene, baptized at Norwich on 11 July 1558. See Collins, pp. 10–12.

20 RG XII 172.

21 GH III 67.

22 TN III 11, I 313–14.

23 On Digby, see Cooper, *Athenae*, II 146–7; Mullinger, *St John's College*, pp. 78–9. The anti-Ramist tracts were *De Duplici Methodo* (1580) and *Admonitioni F. Mildapetti Responsio* (1580). The latter replied to the pro-Ramist *Admonitio* by 'Franciscus Mildapettus' (i.e. William Temple). Digby also wrote a treatise on swimming, *De Arte Natandi* (1587).

24 On the efflux of English students to Cardinal Allen's English College at Douai and (in 1578–93) at Rheims, see Mullinger, *University of Cambridge*, II 253–62; Eccles, *Christopher Marlowe*, pp. 137–44; Leishman (ed.), *1 Returne*, 1560n.

25 Constable proceeded BA in 1580, but left without an MA. See Mullinger, *St John's College*, p. 83.
26 Bald, pp. 46–7, substantially accepts Walton's statement that Donne transferred from Oxford to Cambridge 'in about his fourteenth year' (*c.* 1586) and studied there three years. No official records exist to confirm this, but as a practising Catholic he would be unlikely to enter college and unable to take any degree. On his desertion of Catholicism and its reverberations in his poetry of the 1590s, see Carey, pp. 15–59.
27 Donne, *Satyre* III, 51–2 (*Poems*, I 156).
28 Despite McKerrow's strictures (TN IV 445–6), it is widely accepted that Marlowe is the main target of Nashe's remarks in the preface to Greene's *Menaphon* (1589), TN III 311–12. See ch. 5 below.
29 TN III 131, 195, 180.
30 See TN II 335–6. Bishop Tanner asserts that Nashe '*perfecit & edidit*' the play after Marlowe's death. This is the earliest statement on the matter (1748), but Malone questions it as an assumption: 'it does not appear from the title page that it was not written in conjunction by him and Marlowe in the lifetime of the former [*sic*; i.e. latter]'.
31 One of many scandalous beliefs ascribed to Marlowe by the informer Richard Baines in 'A Note containing the opinion of one Christopher Marley concerning his damnable Judgment of Religion and scorn of Gods word', BM Harleian MS 6848 f. 185–6 (original note); 6853, f. 307–8 (copy). The note was delivered on Whitsun Eve 1593, i.e. 2 June, three days after Marlowe's death. Most historians accept Marlowe's homosexuality, on artistic evidence as well as the Baines slur.
32 TN II 341–2.
33 TN II 238: Nashe gives Marlowe's version of Ovid's lines on eunuchs (*Elegies* II iii 3–4; CM II 344) *verbatim*. That he took it from an MS cannot be proved, since the first edition of Marlowe's translation – *Epigrammes and Elegies by I. D. and C. M.* – is undated. 'I.D.' is Sir John Davies. The imprint – 'at Middleborough', i.e. Middleburg, Holland – may be a decoy, often used for putting risky books on the market. The date usually assigned to the edition is *c.* 1594–5. See CM II 309–14; Fredson Bowers, 'The Early Editions of Marlowe's *Ovid's Elegies*', *Studies in Bibliography*, XXV (1972), 149–72. The recent discovery that Marlowe actually was in Holland in January 1592 (see Wernham, and ch. 13 below), close to Middleburg, *may* suggest that the 'Middleborough' imprint is genuine and the *Elegies* on sale as early as 1592.
34 Rowse, *Christopher Marlowe*, pp. 37, 40.
35 *Privy Council Register for the Reign of Elizabeth*, VI, 29 June 1587; APC XV 141. This was first related to Marlowe by Leslie Hotson, *The Death of Christopher Marlowe*, pp. 58–9. It is often suggested that Marlowe really did travel to Rheims on government business (see, e.g., Bakeless, I 83, Rowse, p. 30). The wording of the Council directive suggests the opposite to me: they would scarcely seek to allay the rumour of Marlowe's *intentions* to defect to Rheims if there was a far more damaging rumour that Marlowe had *actually* gone there.
36 On Thomas (later Sir Thomas) Walsingham, see Bakeless, I 161–3. On the relations between Watson and Walsingham, as recorded in Watson's dedication of *Meliboeus* (1590), see Eccles, *Christopher Marlowe*, pp. 162–4.
37 Baines' note, ut supra n. 31. See also ch. 7 and n. 23 for another accusation by Baines that Marlowe was a seditious Catholic.
38 TN I 269.

39 *Gratulationum Valdinensum Libri Quatuor* (SR 20 August 1578). The poems are addressed to the Queen, Leicester, Burghley and Sidney: two are transcribed and translated by Grosart, GH I xxxv–xliii.

40 On Harvey's relations with Dyer and Rogers, see Stern, pp. 39 n. 55–6, 61. Harvey's projected volume, 'The Verlayes', was to be dedicated to Dyer. The Harvey-Spenser correspondence was published in 1580 as *Three Proper and Wittie Familiar Letters* and *Two other very Commendable Letters*. Harvey claimed they had been printed without his consent by 'undiscreete friends', but the denial is too typical to carry much weight. Stern discusses the business in detail, pp. 54–68.

41 TN III 80. See *Pedantius*, ed. G. C. Moore-Smith (1905). Nashe elsewhere describes it as 'M. Winkfields Comoedie' (TN I 303) but Moore-Smith shows (pp. xi–xx) that the main author was probably Edward Forsett.

42 On the 'commonplace book', dated 1580, of William Withie, student of Christ's College, Oxford, see RES 23 (1947) 297–309.

43 TN III 73.

44 The account of Harvey at Audley End is TN III 75–8. Monarcho was a fantastical Italian who frequented the court in the 1560s. See TN IV 339, and notes on Shakespeare, *Loves Labors Lost*, IV i 100, where Armado is called 'a Monarcho'. On Armado and Harvey, see below, ch. 14.

45 TN III 79. On Atey, see Rosenberg, pp. 150, 335 n. 27.

46 TN III 67.

47 TN III 81, I 277, III 7, 86, I 330, III 68, 38. McKerrow (IV 321) suggests that the damaged condition of the block, as evidenced by the left-hand leaves, may have been caused by the printer cutting it from an original larger wooduct.

48 Baker MS 36, p. 114, cited DNB, s.v. Harvey. BM Harleian MS 7031, f. 78v–79, cited Stern, pp. 77–8.

49 See Stern 75–6, TN I 278–9.

50 TN I 195–6.

51 TN I 196–7, III 82–3. On Northampton's *Defensative against Supposed Prophesies*, see above, ch. 2, n. 23. Thomas Heath, a disciple of Dee and *protégé* of Sir George Carey, published *A Manifest and Apparent Confutation of an Astrological Discourse* (1583). The Elderton ballad has been tentatively identified by Rollins as one beginning 'Trust not the conjunctions or judgements of men, when all that is made shall be unmade again' (see Stern, p. 70, n. 70). For the reactions of Aylmer and Tarlton we have only Nashe's word.

52 TN III 80–1. There are two possible dates for the show, since Nashe mentions that Dr Perne, Master of Peterhouse, was then Deputy Vice-Chancellor, an office he held in 1580–1 and 1586–7: the latter date seems more likely for *Duns Furens*.

53 TN I 196, 271, 262, III 81.

54 Greene, *Quip for an Upstart Courtier*, sig. E3v (in the suppressed passage found only in the first issue: see ch. 9, n. 10 below); TN III 85.

55 The *Iatromathematica* predates the *Smaragdine Table of Hermes*, which appeared in Roger Bacon (attrib.), *The Mirror of Alchimy* (1597). Harvey's *New Letter* (1593), GH I 275f, is filled with Paracelsist curative lore, and there are passages in praise of Paracelsus in his *marginalia*. A broadsheet advertising John Hester's chemical wares is in the British Library (C 60 o 6), with annotations dated *c.* 1588 in Harvey's hand. Harvey mourns the death of 'oulde Iohn Hester' in 1593, GH II 80. On Hester see Nicholl, pp. 66–7.

56 TN III 81.
57 The 'Lady Margaret', foundress of St John's (1511), was Margaret *née* Beaufort (1443–1509). She married Edmund Tudor, Earl of Richmond, and was the mother of Henry VII. By her third husband – Thomas Stanley, 1st Earl of Derby – she was great-great-grandmother of Nashe's future patron, Lord Strange.
58 GH III 67–8.
59 TN III 13. On the date of *Richardus III* performed at St John's, see G. C. Moore-Smith, MLR III 41.
60 Thomas Heywood, *Apologie for Actors* (Shakespeare Society ed., 1841), p. 28. See G. C. Moore-Smith, *College Plays in the University of Cambridge*.
61 TN II 249–50.
62 Since '*terminus*' is, in logic and chronology, a term for the beginning (*a quo*) as well as the end (*ad quem*) of an argument or duration, the title could be rendered by various permutations – 'The Beginning and not the End', etc. The play went on when Nashe was 'Bachelor of Arte', i.e. after March 1586. As Lichfield says he wrote it to show he was 'not unworthie' of that degree, it was probably not long after his graduation.
63 Episcopal Consistorial Court of Norwich Actbook (1586), f. 120. Transcribed TN V 198.
64 TN I 37.
65 TN I 5, 9. The composition of the *Anatomie* cannot be dated with certainty. In the dedication to Blount Nashe says he was first moved to write the work 'two summers since'. If he wrote the dedication in late 1589, shortly before publication, 'two summers since' is summer 1587. If the dedication was earlier, the previous summer is indicated. The later date is more likely (if the earlier, the passage about his father's death must be an addition). If it was composed in summer 1587 it cannot have been at West Harling, or at least not in the old rectory where William Nashe's successor would now be living.
66 TN III 319.
67 TN I 20. For further satire on Stubbes, see TN III 356–8.
68 GH III 68; TN III 181; William Covell, *Polimanteia* (1595), sig. Q4; TN III 127.
69 *Tamburlaine* was certainly onstage by 16 November 1587, the date of Philip Gawdy's letter (ed. Jeayes, p. 23) recounting a performance. It has been argued that Gawdy saw the Second Part of *Tamburlaine*. If so, assuming the Second Part was written because of the First Part's success, the original play had been on the boards for some months. See Bakeless I 198–9.
70 Marlowe, *Edward II* II i 31–43; CM II 37.

4 LONDON

1 Stow, *A Survey of London*, II 75, 369.
2 Ibid., II 74, I 165; APC XXV 230 (Privy Council directive to the Middlesex magistrates, 1596).
3 Nathan Field, *A Woman is a Weathercock* (1612), sig. G4.
4 Eccles, *Christopher Marlowe in London*, pp. 122–6.
5 Chambers, *William Shakespeare*, II 252 (from Aubrey MS 8 f. 45v).
6 On Marlowe's two brushes with the London Law, see Eccles, chs 1–5; Bakeless I 98–105.
7 On Robert Poley, 'a verie bad felow', see Bakeless I 171–80.

8 Harvey mentions Shoreditch as one of Greene's 'resorts' (GH I 169). On Ball and Fortunatus, see RG XII 135, GH I 169–70, Eccles, *Christopher Marlowe in London*, pp. 124–6.

9 GH III 11.

10 TN I 204.

11 TN I 214, 265, 274, 364, II 150, 160.

12 TN I 319. On Tarlton's death, see DNB, Eccles, pp. 125–6. It is possible that Nashe met Tarlton at Cambridge, though there are no records of Tarlton or the Queen's Men there.

13 TN III 96. This execration of Nashe and Lyly – assuming it actually happened – must have been in about 1594. Nashe says the preacher who delivered it 'lay in the same house in Wood-streete which hee [Harvey] did'. By Nashe's chronology, Harvey was lodging on Wood Street after his return to London from Saffron Walden in late 1593–early 1594, but this whole episode (TN III 97–101) is uncorroborated. The passage seems to imply that the preacher and fellow-lodger was Robert Harvey, rector of St Alban's, Wood Street.

14 Stow, *A Survay of London*, I 225, 324–338, II 316, 348–9; Salgado, *The Elizabethan Underworld*, pp. 22–32; Floyd-Ewin, p. 8; TN I 239.

15 TN I 163, cf. II 393. According to Stow, *A Survay of London*, I 335, the tomb and monument called Duke Humfrey's was actually that of John Beauchamp (d. 1358): Humphrey, Duke of Gloucester, son of Henry IV, was buried at St Albans. See OED, s.v. 'dine' (sense 1b); Partridge, *A Dictionary of Historical Slang*, p. 258.

16 TN III 172.

17 TN I 278. See McKerrow's index (TN V 316) for Nashe's many references to Paul's Churchyard.

18 Eliot, 55–6. From the dialogue headed 'The Booke-seller'.

19 See Harrison, 'Books & Readers, 1591–4', pp. 274–5, for detailed figures and cautions on interpreting them.

20 TN I 239.

21 SR II 449. See Duff, s.v. Hackett, and various entries in SR. The work by Kyd was his translation from Tasso, *The Householders Philosophie*.

22 TN I 3. On the Pope's Head and Lombard Street, see Stow, *A Survay of London*, I 199–205, II 306–7. John Wolfe had a printing-shop in Popes Head Alley; Thomas Kyd was baptized at St Mary Woolnoth.

23 See Duff, s.v. Charlewood. As printer to the Earl of Arundel he also had a press in the Charterhouse. His widow married James Roberts, printer of Nashe's *Christs Teares*. Though the first issue of the *Anatomie* bears the date 1589 it was almost certainly printed after January 1590 (new style), since a second issue dated 1590 was set up from the same blocks. See TN IV 1.

24 Greene dedicated *Alcida* (1588) to Blount. On the dedication fee, see Sheavyn, pp. 17–25; Miller, pp. 110–36. Nat Field declined to dedicate *A Woman is a Weathercock* (1612), 'because forty shillings I care not for, and above, few or none will bestow on these matters'. Miller (pp. 126–8) analyses the dedication fees received by Richard Robinson, as detailed in his *Eupolemia*. Robinson received a total of £24 6s 4d from 31 dedications, or (if reprints are excluded) £20 0s 4d from 20, an average of roughly £1 per book. His highest single reward was £3. George Peele received £3 from the Earl of Northumberland for *The Honour of the Garter* (1593). Much smaller sums were common, of course – down to 2s for Robinson.

25 RG XI 75–6.

26 TN I 255–8. This passage first occurs in the 2nd ed., replacing a more

scurrilous account of Beeston keeping a bevy of 'maides' in his house and getting into trouble with the Archdeacon's Court. Beeston presumably objected to this.

27 Nashe speaks of 'Iohn Davies Soule' as something Beeston holds 'most pretious'. This refers to Davies' *Nosce Teipsum*, a poetic meditation on 'the Soul of Man and the Immortality thereof'. It was not published till 1599, so Beeston and Nashe knew it in MS. On Davies at the Middle Temple, see Harlow, 'Thomas Nashe & Robert Cotton', p. 18.

28 Bald, p. 55, describing Lincoln's Inn when Donne entered (1591).

29 BJ I 22–3. The dedication first appeared in the folio *Works* (1616), but the 'friendship' specifically refers to 'when I wrote this poeme', i.e. 1598–9.

30 TN V 195. The context demands this unsavoury interpretation.

31 TN I 163.

32 TN I 157, 161, 310, 323.

33 GH III 26. Cf. TN III 25, where 'Importuno' accuses Nashe of having been hiding in a 'chamber in Cole-harbour' during his period of silence (1594–6). Nothing is known of Nashe's 'fellowe', Lusher.

34 Middleton, sigs B3–D2v.

35 The 'pickt hatch' was a common name and sign for brothels. It refers to the brothel door, which had, for security, an upper half-door or hatch surrounded by spikes. The famous Pickt-hatch was in Turnmill (or Turmoyle) Street, Clerkenwell. See Partridge, *A Dictionary of Historical Slang*, p. 687, and commentators on *Merry Wives of Windsor*, II ii 17, where Pistol is dispatched to his 'Manor at Pickt-hatch'.

36 Rich, sig. A4v: 'that liquour which I [Greene] was wont to drinke with my Hostesse at the Redde Lattesse in Turmoyle Streete'.

37 Nashe warns us not to take it too literally: 'I was never altogether Peter Poveretto, utterly throwne downe, desperately seperated from all meanes of releeving my selfe, since I knew how to seperate a knave from an honest man', TN I 322. By late 1592, then, he had never been totally derelict: he was of a type, and class, who never quite starve.

5 THE WITS

1 TN III 311–25. *Menaphon* was registered 23 August 1589 (SR II 529).

2 GH I 187.

3 TN I 287.

4 Chettle, sig. A4. He transcribed the *Groatsworth of Wit* from Greene's 'foul papers'.

5 GH I 189, 187; TN I 329; RG XII 195.

6 TN III 312.

7 After *Greenes Mourning Garment* came *Greenes Never Too Late* (1590), *Greenes Farewell to Folly* (1591), and the three posthumous pamphlets, *Greenes Groatsworth*, *Greenes Vision* and *The Repentance* (all 1592). The *Farewell* had actually been written in 1587, so Greene's repentant phase should not be too precisely dated. '*Sero sed serio*' properly means 'late but in earnest'.

8 GH I 168.

9 RG XII 161, 173–4, 177.

10 RG XII 177–8. Dorothy Greene was possibly from Lincolnshire: she went there after Greene deserted her. Two versions of Greene's deathbed letter to her are given, one by Harvey (GH I 171–2) and one by publisher Burby

(RG XII 185). They are basically the same and probably authentic. A third, longer letter, 'founde with his booke after his death', is given in the *Groatsworth* (RG XII 149).

11 TN I 287.
12 Chettle, sig. C1; TN I 287–8.
13 'The Printer to the Gentleman Readers' in *The Repentance*, RG XII 156.
14 RG XII 175–6. On the dating of Greene's 'conversion' and the ballad, see Storojenko, RG I 10–11.
15 RG XII 178.
16 RG VII 7–8. *Perimedes* was registered 29 March 1588. The allusion is to the Second Part of *Tamburlaine*, V iii 42, 'What daring God torments my body thus?' Variants on Marlowe's name include Marlin, Marlyn, Malyn, Marlen, Marley and Morley: see Bakeless, I 96. It is generally accepted that Greene is tilting at Marlowe specifically, but see TN IV 445–6 for caveats.
17 TN III 311–12.
18 TN III 315–16, IV 449–54.
19 See Kyd's letters to Lord Keeper Sir John Puckering, 1593, BM Harleian MSS 6848, f. 154, 6849, f. 218, transcribed Boas, pp. 139–42. The letter was written after Marlowe's death, but refers to them lodging together 'two years since', i.e. *c.* 1591. The troupe referred to is hard to identify: the Lord Admiral's or Lord Strange's seem most likely.
20 TN I 10. On Greene's Euphuistic metaphors, see TN I 319: 'Is my stile like Greenes. . . . Do I talke of any counterfeit birds, or hearbs or stones?' *Penelopes Web* was registered 19 June 1587.
21 TN III 324: 'It may be my Anatomie of Absurdities may acquaint you ere long with my skill in surgery. . .'.
22 TN I 7. Dekker, *Newes from Hell* (1606), sig. C2v, praises 'fluent facetious T. Nash'.
23 RG XII 141. The 'fellow scholars' in question were Marlowe, Nashe and (probably) Peele.
24 On Buc and Acheley, see TN III 323; Horne, pp. 65–70, 83; Eccles, 'Sir George Buc, Master of the Revels', in Sisson, pp. 409–506. As a near-native Buc may have informally attended at Cambridge: he refers to 'a scholler in Cambridge in my tym' but there is no record of him at any college. See MLR XX (1935), 6. Watson also studied law (his title-pages refer to him as '*J.V. studiosus*') but there is no record of him at the Inns of Court. 'J.V.' = 'juris utriusque' = of both laws, i.e. canon and civil law.
25 See Blount's address 'To the Reader' in his edition of *Six Court Comedies by . . . John Lilly* (1632).
26 GH II 132.
27 TN III 46. The Paul's Boys were inhibited sometime before October 1591. In the first ed. of Lyly's *Endimion* (registered 4 October), printer John Charlewood says, 'Since the Plaies in Paules were dissolved, there are certaine Commedies come to my handes by chaunce' (Bond III 17). The conjecture that some of Paul's Boys were in the cast of Nashe's *Summers Last Will* at Croydon in 1592 is unsubstantiated: see TN IV 419.
28 GH II 128, TN I 300, DNB s.v. Lyly, TN III 138, Jones *passim*.
29 GH II 122, cf. I 183–4. The *Speculum Tuscanismi* appears in the *Three Proper Letters* (1580), GH I 84–6. See Stern, pp. 64–6.
30 TN III 126–7, 320.
31 On Watson's continental travels, see his dedicatory verses to the Earl of Arundel before *Antigone* (1581), and Eccles, *Christopher Marlowe in London*, pp. 128–44.

32 William Covell, *Polimanteia* (1595), sig. R3.
33 On Watson and the Cornwallises, see *The Athanaeum*, 23 August 1890 (not 1880, as given in DNB s.v. Watson), and Eccles, *Christopher Marlowe in London*, p. 60.
34 Anon, *Ulysses upon Ajax* (1596), p. 15; Eccles, *Christopher Marlowe in London*, pp. 7–8. It is conceivable that the writer knew of Watson's visits to Paris in the late 1570s but the reference is more probably to Paris Gardens.
35 Eccles, *Christopher Marlowe in London*, pp. 145–61.
36 Kyd, letters to Lord Keeper Puckering, 1593, ut supra n. 19.
37 *Antigone* (1581) was dedicated to Arundel, though Eccles points out this was before the latter's open championing of Catholicism. *Ekatompathia* (1582) was dedicated to Oxford. The French ambassador, Mauvissière, noted Oxford as a Catholic from 1576, but in 1581 he denounced his former co-religionists. See Ward, pp. 207f. *Meliboeus* is an elegy on Sir Francis Walsingham in Latin hexameters.
38 TN III 127.
39 TN III 323.
40 Huanebango's 'O that I might – but I may not, woe to my destiny therefore' (l.674) exactly echoes a line from Harvey's *Encomium Lauri* in the *Three Proper Letters* (1580), GH I 83.
41 See F. P. Wilson, 'The English Jest-books of the Sixteenth and Early Seventeenth Centuries', in *Shakespearian and other Studies*, pp. 285–324.
42 Horne, p. 105. The letter is dated 17 January 1596. In less than a year Peele was dead.
43 Horne, p. 9. Peele married Mary Yates at St Olave's on 26 December 1591.
44 Anon, *The Merry Conceited Jests of George Peele, Gentleman* (London, 1607), pp. 5, 14–15. On the validity of the *Jests*, see Horne, pp. 110–26.
45 TN III 323. See Rollins' edn of *The Phoenix Nest* for details of the MSS of this superb poem.
46 Horne, p. 67. An earlier legal document, cited by Moore-Smith (MLR IX (1914), pp. 97–8) shows that on 6 January 1582, 'Matheus Royden de Davyes [i.e. Thavies] Inne in holborne' was cited for a £40 debt to a London goldsmith (Close Rolls 1144 (24 Eliz) pt 24).
47 See Kyd's letter, ut supra n. 19. He implies that Roydon has left the country at the urging of Marlowe. There may be links here – in Kyd's mind at least – with the Ralegh 'School of Atheism' scandal of 1592 (see below, ch. 8).
48 See Chapman's dedications of *The Shadow of Night* (1594) and *Ovids Banquet of Sence* (1595), and G. B. Harrison (ed.), *Willobie his Avisa*.
49 Greene and Lodge, *A Looking Glass for London and England*, I ii.
50 H. C. Hart, NQ, 17 March 1906; Agnes Latham (ed.), *As You Like It* (AS), p. xxxv.
51 RG I, Appendix 1.
52 TN I 170–1.
53 Sisson, pp. 102–3.
54 Lodge, *Rosalynde*, p. xxix.
55 Sisson, pp. 87–100. Sir Thomas' remarks are quoted on p. 96.
56 Lodge, *Wits Miserie*, sig. I1.
57 Lodge's *Fig for Momus* (1595) uses exactly this form – 'T.L., of Lincolnes Inne, Gent' – on the title-page.
58 Stephen Gosson, *Playes Confuted in Five Actions* (1582), cited DNB s.v. Lodge. This was a counterblast to Lodge's own retort – *A Defence of Playes* (1580) – to Gosson's *The School of Abuse* (1579). The *Defence* was Lodge's

first published work. He defends classical, rather than popular English, drama.
59 TN III 321.
60 TN II 165.

6 CUTHBERT CURRYKNAVE

1 Cited Allen, p. 175. The *Admonition* is generally attributed to John Field and Thomas Wilcox, but it is probable that Cartwright had a hand in it.
2 Leicester patronized Cartwright as early as 1570, and installed him as Master of Warwick Hospital in 1586 with an income of £100 p.a. See Pearson, *Thomas Cartwright and Elizabethan Puritanism*, p. 293. See ch. 8 for Nashe on Leicester.
3 The Whitgift-Cartwright controversy is a polemical ping-pong match. Cartwright published a *Second Admonition to Parliament* in 1572. Whitgift's *Aunswere to a certen Libell intituled an Admonition* (1572), Cartwright's *Replye to an Answere* (1573), Whitgift's *Defense of the Aunswere* (1574), Cartwright's *Second Replie* (1575) and *The Rest of the Second Replie* (1577) followed.
4 JL III 405.
5 Peel, p. xii, n. 3.
6 'Martin Marprelate', *The Protestatyon*, p. 21.
7 Anthony a Wood, *Athenae Oxonienses* (ed. 1813), I 592.
8 John Penry, *The Aequity of an Humble Supplication*, pp. 39–40.
9 Idem, *The Appellation*, pp. 42f. Cf. 'Martin Marprelate', *The Epistle*, pp. 29–30.
10 SR I 528; Pierce, pp. 151–2. The beadle of the Stationers' Company at this time was John Wolfe, future publisher of Harvey's anti-Nashe tracts.
11 Pierce, pp. 152–4; Arber, pp. 39, 81–7; 'Martin Marprelate', *The Epistle*, pp. 42–3.
12 'Martin Marprelate', *The Epistle*, pp. 37, 40.
13 TN III 349.
14 'Martin Marprelate', *Hay any Worke*, p. 41. The raid is described as in 'November last' (i.e. 1588). Cf. 'Martin senior', sigs Aii–Aiiv.
15 On the Fawsley phase, see Arber, pp. 129–30 (Brief held by Attorney General Puckering against Sir Richard Knightley) and pp. 124–5. A portrait of Knightley is the frontispiece of Pierce's *Historical Introduction to the Marprelate Tracts*.
16 Arber, pp. 94–104.
17 Ibid., p. 115.
18 'Martin Marprelate', *The Epitome*, sigs A2–A2v.
19 The proclamation is in Arber, pp. 109–11.
20 R. Coddington, *Life and Death of Robert, Earl of Essex* (ed. 1744), I 214.
21 'Cater' is French *quadré*, square. 'Catercorner' refers to the square hats worn by the episcopacy: Martin frequently calls the bishops 'catercaps'.
22 'Martin Marprelate', *Hay any Worke*, pp. 30, 48.
23 Arber, pp. 99–100.
24 Bancroft, p. xviii. Strype (II 387) renders this inaccurately, giving 'own vain writings' instead of 'own vein in writing'.
25 TN III 348, 354, I 100; JL III 408.
26 TN I 92.
27 TN I 83. 'Pasquill' seems to imply that this *Maygame* was not yet performed,

that it is 'a new worke which I have in hand', but the show is clearly referred
to in *A Whip for an Ape* (JL III 419): 'Now out he runnes with Cuckowe
king of May,/Then in he leapes with a wild Morrice daunce'. And 'Marforius'
says Martin took it 'verie grievouslie, to be made a Maygame upon the
Stage' (*Martins Months Minde*, GTN III 175): a marginal note here gives
'the Theater' as the venue of the show.

28 JL III 421.
29 'Martin junior', sig. D3v. It may be that another William Kemp, a writer on
educational and religious matters, is meant, rather than Kemp the comic.
See DNB, s.v. Kemp, William.
30 On the suppression of the anti-Martinist shows, see Pierce, pp. 222–3.
31 *Mar-martine* was out by mid-July 1589, since it is mentioned in the *Theses
Martinianae*, dated 22 July. 'Marforius' (GTN III 175) implies that the *Whip*
was earlier, for after referring to the *Whip* and the *Maygame* he says Martin
was 'at length cleane Marde', with a marginal note 'Marre-martin'. The
Whip cannot have been earlier than the end of March, as it refers to *Hay
any Worke*, issued about 23 March.
32 Dover Wilson, 'Anthony Munday, Pamphleteer and Pursuivant', p. 484.
33 'Martin senior', sig. A2v.
34 'Martin Marprelate', *Hay any Worke*, p. 41; Pierce, p. 164.
35 TN I 100.
36 'Martin junior', sigs D3v–D4, D1v.
37 'Martin senior', sig. Aii.
38 Arber, p. 102.
39 On Throckmorton and his part, see Arber, p. 134 (Attorney General's brief
against Throckmorton); Matthew Sutcliffe, *Answere to Job Throckmorton*
(1595); Throckmorton's own *Defense*; Dover Wilson, 'Martin Marprelate
and Shakespeare's Fluellen'; McGinn, 'The Real Martin Marprelate'. Dover
Wilson credits Throckmorton as the author behind 'Martin senior'. His
assignation of the first three Martinist tracts to Sir Roger Williams is examined by McKerrow and Pierce in *The Library*, 1912, pp. 345–74.
40 Arber, p. 134.
41 See 'Martin junior', sigs Diii–Diiiv; 'Martin senior', sig. Diiv.
42 TN I 57–64.
43 See TN V 50 for McKerrow's reasons for retracting the attribution to Nashe.
44 TN III 376.
45 TN I 270. Greene is clearly included as an anti-Martinist. Nashe explains
that Greene's satire on the Harveys in *A Quip for an Upstart Courtier* (1592)
was in revenge for Richard Harvey having played 'the Iacke of both sides
twixt Martin and us'. If Greene was not one of 'us' he would not need to
retaliate. Attempts have been made to identify Munday as 'Pasquill' (see
Celeste Turner, *Anthony Munday*). There was undoubtedly much pooling
and collaboration among the anti-Martinists, and the pseudonyms may
conceal various authors. Munday has also been claimed (Dover Wilson,
'Anthony Munday, Pamphleteer and Pursuivant', p. 490) as 'Cuthbert Curryknave', author of the *Almond for a Parrat*; but this was certainly Nashe.
See McGinn, 'Nashe's Share in the Marprelate Controversy'.
46 JL III 396.
47 Arber, p. 135; Pierce, pp. 189–91, 335–9 (Appendix CII, Examination of
Tomlyn and Simmes).
48 Arber, p. 112.
49 'Martin Marprelate', *The Protestatyon*, pp. 3, 10–11, 13.
50 See TN I 101; JL III 410. Pasquill writes: 'yesternight late, olde Martins

Protestation in Octavo was brought unto mee'. According to the date on Pasquill's answering 'Protestation upon London Stone', the *Protestatyon* reached him on the night of 19 October 1589. The brevity of his comments on it suggests his pamphlet was already at the press. Lyly's *Pappe* was out before 5 November, when Gabriel Harvey wrote his *Advertisement for Papp-hatchett*.

51 TN I 100.
52 JL III 408.
53 APC XVIII 214–15; BM Lansdowne MS 60, 47; TN IV 44.
54 TN I 83, 110–12. There is no internal evidence of Nashe in this last Pasquill tract.
55 Bacon's *Advertisement* was not published till 1657. It casts aspersions on the anti-Martinists, with their 'strange abuse of antiques [i.e. antics] and Pasquils'. See transcript in Arber, pp. 146–68.
56 JL III 400–1; GH II 130–1. Harvey is not actually named by Lyly, but references to 'a familiar Epistle about the naturall causes of an Earthquake' (cf. GH I 40–74) and to Harvey falling 'into the bowells of libelling' (*Speculum Tuscanismi* and the Earl of Oxford) are unmistakable. Harvey's *Advertisement* was not published till 1593, sandwiched between assaults on Nashe in *Pierces Supererogation* (GH II 124–221).
57 Richard Harvey, *Plaine Percevall* (*c.* 1590), sig. A2, dedication to 'the new upstart Martin', etc. *The Lamb of God* was registered 23 October 1589. *Plaine Percevall* (not entered in SR) was the first to be actually published (see TN I 270). The *Lamb* appeared sometime after 26 March 1590 (beginning of the old style year).
58 Anon, *A Myrrour for Martinists* (1589), sig. A3. McKerrow rejects Pierce's attribution of the pamphlet to Thomas Thurswell.
59 Nashe describes the pamphlet (TN III 343) as having 'stayed for a good winde ever since the beginning of winter', suggesting it was written soon after the *Protestatyon* appeared but not published till early 1590.
60 TN III 362.
61 TN III 344.
62 TN III 348–9, 360, 363.
63 TN III 350.
64 TN III 369.
65 TN III 343.
66 TN III 341–2.
67 On the fate of the Martinists after the round-up of 1589, see Pierce, pp. 196–219.
68 Arber, pp. 96, 102.
69 See Peel, p. xvii; Job Throckmorton, *The Defence*, sig. Eii; Penry's draft letters to Burghley, spring 1593, Peel, pp. 61–71.

7 LORD STRANGE

1 The will was drawn up by Margaret Nashe on 2 December 1589: the handwriting on the original document is apparently Stephen Philips'. It was proved on 21 February 1590. See Document 2.
2 The epistle occurs in only a few of the extant copies of the *Lamb* (sigs a1–a4v). See McKerrow's transcription, TN V 176–83, from the Bodleian copy. On the dating of the *Lamb* see ch. 6, n. 57.
3 GH I 199.

4 TN I 309, IV 184–5. McKerrow tentatively suggests that a reference in the *Anatomie* to the 'paultry' poetry of 'Cherillus' (TN I 45) may be a scoff at Churchyard.

5 TN I 271.

6 E.g. Sir Sidney Lee, DNB, s.v. Tarlton. See TN V 140.

7 McKerrow prints the *Prognostication* among Nashe's *dubia*. TN III 377–95. 'A booke entituled ffrauncis fayre weather' was entered on Stationers' Register on 25 February 1591: no copy survives. Fowleweather's pamphlet was published before Smellknave's, which mentions it. John Florio refers to pamphlets that 'pronosticate of faire, of foule and of smelling weather' in his *Second Fruites* (1591), sig. A2.

8 F. P. Wilson, *Shakespearian and other Studies*, p. 265. His essay, 'Some English Mock-Prognostications', provides a history and context for 'Fowleweather'. Wilson also shows that Fowleweather's *Prognostication* went into a second edition and was reprinted later in the year (MLR, XII (1918), pp. 84–5).

9 TN III 329–33.

10 See Newman's epistle, to 'his very good Freende, Ma. Frauncis Flower', in the first edition of *Astrophel*; Samuel Daniel's dedication, to 'the Ladie Mary, Countesse of Pembroke', in *Delia* (1592); SR I 555; Kirschbaum, pp. 100, 131–2.

11 Mona Wilson, *Sir Philip Sidney* (1931), p. 168. Newman's 2nd edition is dated 1591 on the title-page. i.e. 'before April 1592' assuming old style dating. McKerrow missed the suppression of the 1st edition recorded in SR, but inferred it from the appearance of this 2nd edition.

12 See Sanford's preface to *The Countesse of Pembrokes Arcadia* (1593); Florio's 'Address to the Reader' in *A Worlde of Wordes* (1598); TN III 147. Yates, *John Florio*, pp. 194–209, convincingly argues that Florio was the editor of the 1st edition of the *Arcadia*, which was apparently commissioned by Sir Fulke Greville. Sanford's remarks about flowers in his preface are probably intended as puns on '*florio*'. On Florio and Sanford, see ch. 14 below.

13 See Hyder Rollins (ed.), *Brittons Bowre of Delights*, pp. xiii–xviii; Breton's preface, to 'the Gentlemen Students of Oxforde', in *The Pilgrimage to Paradise* (1592); SR II 581. On Jones' later dealings with Breton's work see Kirschbaum, pp. 115–16. Breton's other dedications to the Countess include *Auspicante Jehova*, or 'Maries Exercise' (1597); *The Ravisht Soule & the Blessed Weeper* (1601); and 'The Countesse of Pembrokes Passion' (MS).

14 Another 'implied insolence' in Nashe's preface is his derision of the current fashion for alchemy. Enthusiasts are described as 'our English Apes', who strive to 'warme themselves with the flame of the Philosophers stone', and squander their wealth 'buying bellowes to blowe this false fyre'. We know, however, that the Countess was herself a great 'Chymist', who 'spent yearely a great deale in that study' (Aubrey, p. 297). She kept Adrian Gilbert, Ralegh's half-brother, as her 'laborator', and Thomas Moffet, a leading Paracelsian, as her physician. Moffet's Latin biography of Sidney, *Nobilis* (ed. Heltzel and Hudson, 1940), records that Sidney himself had studied alchemy, 'that starry science', under Dr Dee.

15 APC XXII, 550. The actual riot was earlier (Sunday 11 June). The 'Defence of Playes' is TN I 211–15. In Harry Chettle's *Kind Harts Dreame* (1592), the ghost of Tarlton gratefully remarks that Pierce Penniless has defended 'the profession' so eloquently 'that for me there is not any thing to speake'.

16 William Bentley was closely involved with the Wits. In *A Knights Conjuring*

(1607), Dekker mentions 'inimitable Bentley' in the same breath as Watson, Kyd and Acheley, saying that 'tho hee had bene a Player, molded out of their pennes', he was 'their Lover and a Register to the Muses' (sigs K4v–L1). William Knell played Prince Hal in an early Henry V play – either *The Famous Victories of Henry the Fifth* or a lost prototype thereof – at the Bull in Bishopsgate. He was killed in a duel with a fellow-actor, John Towne, at Thame, Oxfordshire, in June 1587. His widow married John Heminges, co-editor of the First Folio of Shakespeare's works (1623). See Mark Eccles, *Shakespeare in Warwickshire* (1961), pp. 82–3, and Schoenbaum, p. 90.

17 Judging from the third of Harvey's *Foure Letters*, dated 8–9 September 1592, *Pierce* appeared on 8 September (see GH I 193–4; TN IV 77–9). It is extremely unlikely that Greene's *Groatsworth* was transcribed, printed and issued within five days of his death, though it was out before the end of the month (see Nashe's letter to Abel Jeffes, TN I 154).

18 See TN Supp. 77; J. Dover Wilson (ed.), *1 Henry VI* (Cambridge, 1952), pp. xxi–xxxi; idem (ed.), *1 Henry IV* (Cambridge, 1946), pp. 191–6; Rhodes, pp. 89–99. In 'The Origins and Developments of Shakespeare's *Henry IV*', Dover Wilson argues that *The Famous Victories of Henry V* is a memorial reconstruction of *two* earlier plays, one of which was the play in which Knell and Tarlton acted at the Bull in the 1580s. He believes that Nashe may have written over some of the comic scenes, 'for revival performances in 1592 by Lord Strange's Men' (p. 11), and that this might explain the echoes of Nashe in Shakespeare's Falstaff comedies of *c.* 1596–8. Wilson believes Nashe's references in *Pierce Penilesse* are to a performance of one of these lost Henry V plays, but this seems unnecessarily conjectural when Nashe's words perfectly fit the death of old Talbot in Shakespeare's *1 Henry VI*, IV vii.

19 On Alleyn and Strange's Men, see Henslowe, II 72, ES II 120–2. The 'plat' of *The Seven Deadly Sins*, a Strange's Men production of 1592, shows Alleyn heading the cast. On the Strange's Men repertoire of 1592 see Henslowe, II 149–57.

20 His father was the great grandson of Henry VII's mother, Margaret, Countess of Richmond (see above, ch. 3, n. 57). His mother, Margaret *née* Clifford, was the daughter of Henry VIII's niece, Eleanor Brandon.

21 Raines, p. iv.

22 ES II 118–19; Henslowe, II 71; Heywood, pp. 11–14.

23 See RG VII 99–101; Peele, *Polyhymnia* (1590), 'describing the honourable triumph at Tylt'; Spenser, *The Teares of the Muses* (1591), dedication; Newton, 'Ad Dominum Strangaeum', one of the 'encomia et eulogia' appended to his edition of Leland's *Principum in Anglia Virorum Encomia* (1589); Barnes, *Parthenophil and Parthenophe* (1593), sonnet to Lady Strange; Chapman, *The Shadow of Night* (1594), dedication (also citing Roydon's admiration of Strange); Covell, *Polimanteia* (1595), cited Heywood, p. 37; Harington, *The Most Elegant and Witty Epigrams* (1618), Bk III, Epigram 47, 'In prayse of the Countesse of Darby'; Lok, *Christian Passions* (1597), sonnet to the Countess of Derby; Davies, *The Holy Rood* (1609), dedication to the Countess of Derby and her three daughters, and *The Scourge of Folly* (1611), p. 253, sonnet to the Countess of Derby; Marston, *The Lord and Lady Huntingdon's Entertainment*, performed at Ashby, August 1607, in honour of the Countess (Lady Huntingdon was Strange's eldest daughter Elizabeth); Heywood, pp. 26–47. Marlowe's mention of Strange was not in a dedication, but in mitigation when under

arrest at Flushing, Holland, in January 1592. See Wernham, p. 345, and ch. 13 below.

24 Spenser, *Colin Clouts Come Home Again* (1595), ll.440–3.

25 The only possible connection of Strange with the Ralegh coterie is his inclusion, along with Northumberland, in Chapman's trio of noblemen-scholars who have sheltered 'freezing science' and pursued 'the deepe search of knowledge' (*The Shadow of Night*, dedication to Roydon). My own investigations (see chs 8, 13, 14) suggest that Strange was an occultist, but not necessarily connected with Ralegh; that he had links with the alchemist Edward Kelley; and that he is satirized as Ferdinand of Navarre in Shakespeare's *Loves Labors Lost*.

26 Raines, pp. 58, 62. 'The Booke of the Weekeley Bryffements [i.e. brevements] of My L. the Earle of Derbies House' shows that on 21 January 1589 'my L. Strandge & La. Strandge' went 'towards London'. He is not mentioned again until 9 July.

27 Ibid., p. 75.

28 Nashe was at Croydon in September 1592, and probably remained in the Archbishop's retinue till at least December. See ch. 10. The theologian Hugh Broughton speaks of Whitgift's 'Nash gentleman' (Strype, III 369; TN Supp. 74).

29 TN I 242–5. Three pointers identify Strange as 'Amyntas'. (1) Spenser uses the name for Strange in *Colin Clout*, see above, n. 24. (2) Nashe further describes Amyntas as 'Ioves Eagle-borne Ganimed', referring to the Derby crest, an eagle carrying up a child, as Jupiter in the guise of an eagle carried off Ganymede. Peele describes Strange's appearance at the Tilts 'strangely embark'd/Under Jove's kingly bird the golden eagle,/Stanley's old crest and honourable badge' (*Polyhymnia*). (3) Nashe puns on Strange's name in l. 4 of the sonnet (TN I 244).

30 TN I 303.

31 Richard Harvey, *Philadelphus* (1593), sig. C1. In his epistle 'to his most loving brother, Master Gabriell Harvey', dated '1592. the 14. of Iune', Harvey says, *à propos* certain 'petite Momes' who 'play the mocking Ape': 'the schollers head without moderation is like the merchantes purse penni-lesse without all credite'. Coupled with a reference to Lyly ('I desire . . . that everie wilde Lilly may be set in his gardens'), this suggests that Harvey had seen, or heard of, the attack on him in *Pierce*. See Sidney Thomas, 'New Light on the Nashe–Harvey Quarrel'.

32 Stow, *A Survay of London*, II 16–17, 359, 102. The 1603 ed. of the *Survay* describes the 6th Earl's residence as 'a stately house now in building'.

33 The portrait has 'Ferdi: E. of Der.' painted above the crest in the top left-hand corner, but questions have been raised on the grounds of costume. The collar style worn by the subject is not known in England before *c.* 1598, four years after Ferdinando's death. This has led some historians to re-identify the sitter as Strange's younger brother William. See, e.g., *Shakespeare Quarter-Centenary Exhibition Catalogue* (1964), p. 78.

34 That 'the right Honourable the lord S.' is Strange is suggested by Nashe's reference to his prowess as a poet ('sweete flower of matchless Poetrie') and his Lancastrian blood ('fairest bud the red rose ever bare'). The latter rules out the only plausible competitor, the Earl of Southampton.

35 GH II 91, cf. TN III 129.

36 Hall, *Virgidemiarum* (1597), I ix. See Salyer; TN Supp. 78; ch. 15 below.

37 Davies, *The Scourge of Folly* (1611), 'Paper's Complaint', 64–70, and sonnet 'To the right noble and most gracefull Lady Alice, Countess of Derby, my

good Lady and Mistresse'. Davies' other reference to 'Nashes choosing Valentines, to wit, his Dildo knowne to every Trull' appears in *Wits Bedlam* (1617), Epigram 206, 'Tis merry when Knaves meet'. See TN V 141, 153, Supp. 78–9; Heywood, pp. 39–42.

38 As of 1958, the three MSS were in the Bodleian (Rawlinson MSS); the Dyce Collection (in cypher); and an unnamed private collection (the only one of the three MSS to bear the dedication to 'Lord S'). The work was first printed in 1899 (ed. John S. Farmer, privately printed). McKerrow's text (TN III 403–15) is based on the anonymously owned MS.

39 TN III 30–1.

40 The Wits' wives were Dorothy Greene; Anne Watson (*née* Swift); Anne Peele (*née* Christian) and Mary Peele (*née* Yates); Joan Lodge and Jane Lodge (widow of Solomon Aldred, at one time an agent of Walsingham's); and Anne Lyly. Nothing is known of Roydon marrying.

41 TN I 5.

42 *Elegies*, III 6. Cf. TN II 238. On the textual history of Marlowe's translation see ch. 3, n. 33.

43 See Wernham. In the letter to Puckering (see above, ch. 5, n. 19), Kyd says his acquaintance with Marlowe 'rose upon his bearing name to serve my Lord'. He adds that 'his Lordship never knewe his [Marlowe's] service but in writing for his plaiers, ffor never cold my Lord endure his name or sight when he heard of his conditions'. Tucker Brooke, *The Life of Marlowe*, p. 47, and Kocher, p. 24, identify this unnamed Lord as Strange, and are sceptical about Kyd's dissociation of the two – an expedient to avoid trouble with Strange, who was 'probably sensitive to the Privy Council's opinion of his religious orthodoxy'. Other patrons of players – the Lord Admiral, the Earls of Pembroke and Sussex – are equally possible candidates, however.

44 W. W. Greg argues strongly in favour of 1592 in his parallel text edition, *Marlowe's 'Doctor Faustus', 1604–1616* (1950), pp. 5–10. See also CM II 123–59; *Dr Faustus*, ed. John Jump (1962), pp. xxii–xxiii; Leo Kirschbaum, 'The Good and Bad Quartos of *Dr Faustus*', *The Library* (n.s.), XXVI (1946), 272–94. The lost first ed. of *The Damnable Life* is inferred from proceedings recorded in the Stationers' Company Court Book, 18 December 1592, which refers to Abel Jeffes having 'claymed' copyright on the book 'about May last'. Since the claim was not in the form of a licensing entry in the Stationers' Register, it must have been in the form of publication. Thomas Orwin's edition appeared later in 1592, 'newly imprinted' and 'with imperfect matter amended', again implying an earlier edition. It was the second edition of *Pierce* which Jeffes printed: the first was the work of Richard Jones.

45 CM II 169; TN I 165.

46 CM II 171; TN I 163–4.

47 CM II 177; TN I 217. Both are close to *The Damnable Life*, ch. xi: 'my Mephostophiles, I pray thee resolve me in this doubt: what is hell, what substance is it of, in what place stands it, and when was it made?'

48 CM II 178; TN I 218.

49 CM II 163, 228.

50 Yates, *The Occult Philosophy in the Elizabethan Age*, pp. 115–21.

51 Henslowe, I 172.

52 See Kocher, 'Nashe's Authorship of the Prose Scenes in *Faustus*'. For various reasons, both texts ('A', 1604; 'B', 1616) are thought to be based on copy that predates the Birde-Rowley revisions, so the simple answer that they were responsible for the comic scenes is untenable.

53 CM II 229 ('A' text, 1604, scene iv).
54 CM II 230–1 ('A' text, 1604, scene iv); TN I 201.
55 CM II 163, 164.
56 TN I 345.
57 The earliest recorded performance of the play is by the Admiral's Men at the Rose theatre on 2 October 1594 (Henslowe, II 168). Middleton's *Blacke Booke* (1604) refers to performances of *Faustus* at 'the old Theater' in Shoreditch: these probably predate the Admiral's Men revival. Strange's Men played *The Jew of Malta* at the Rose in 1592.

8 PIERCE POLITIC

1 On the dating and editions of *Pierce*, see TN I 137–48, III 33, IV 77–9. Richard Harvey's reference to 'purse pennilesse' on 14 June 1592 (see ch. 7, n. 31 above) suggests a slightly earlier date of composition than McKerrow's 'June–August'. Nashe must have been fairly embarked on it by mid-June for Harvey to know its title.
2 TN III 35.
3 Cited TN IV 80.
4 The author of the anonymous *Returne of the Knight* claims to have been an 'intimate and neare companion' of Nashe's. He recalls the 'community and affection' between them, such that 'I cannot chuse but still take much delight in his memory'. He describes the publication of *Pierce* as 'about some tenne yeares agone', so the work may have been written as early as 1602 – very soon after Nashe's death – though not published till 1606. Dekker was ignorant of his identity – 'the Gentleman . . . whom I know not' – and scoffed at his style: 'he strives to speake soberly, gravely and like a Puritane'. Dekker was peeved that the *Returne* had got out before his own *Newes from Hell* (running title, 'The Devils Answere to Pierce Pennylesse'). He remarks: 'now (since Christmas), he [the Devil] has . . . shot 2 Arrowes at one mark'. Assuming old style dating on the title-pages, both works may have appeared in early 1607 (new style).
5 The great outpouring of Elizabethan verse satire is later than this. Donne' satires were probably circulating in MS by *c.* 1593, as were Sir John Davies' epigrams (first published, undated, with Marlowe's elegies). Lodge's *Fig for Momus* (1595) and Hall's *Virgidemiarum* (1597) herald a clutch of satires in 1598–9, both published and performed onstage. The injunction of 1 June 1599 (see ch. 17) ordered 'that noe Satyres or Epigrams be printed hereafter', but the fashion continued for a few years unabated. Apart from Lodge's *Wits Miserie* (1596), the prose pamphleteers who essentially derive from Nashe – Middleton, Dekker, Rowlands – flourished after the turn of the century.
6 TN I 169, 173.
7 TN I 166–8.
8 See Rhodes, ch. 4, 'Nashe and the beginning of Satirical Journalism'.
9 RG X 6.
10 TN I 209–10.
11 TN I 192–3, 215, 212, 195–9.
12 TN I 199, 159, 194, 168. See F. P. Wilson's ingenious identification of Munday's *Archaioplutos* as Nashe's target, TN Supp. 13. Munday's authorship of the 'Ballad of Untruss' is presumed from Nashe's letter to Cotton (TN V 195), where a partly torn line reads '[ ]nday[ ] ballet of untrusse'.

Munday's father was Christopher Munday, draper. Munday calls himself a draper, probably an inherited freedom of the Company. He also served as a stationer's apprentice, bound to John Aldee, October 1576.

13 TN I 242, IV 149; Stow, *Annales*, p. 815.

14 GH I 205: 'some od wittes . . . can tell parlous Tales of Beares and Foxes as shrewdlye as Mother Hubbard'.

15 TN I 190–1.

16 On Chester's arrest and imprisonment, see HMC Salisbury, IV 210–11, 221–2.

17 Aubrey, p. 418.

18 BJ III 582–5. Jonson describes Carlo as 'a publike, scurrilous and prophane Iester that (more swift than Circe) with absurd similes will transforme any person into deformity' (BJ III 423–4). He is clearly one with Nashe's Charles.

19 See Rowse, *Ralegh and the Throckmortons*, pp. 158–63, drawing on the diary of Bess's brother, Arthur Throckmorton. Entries from the diary are reproduced opposite p. 160.

20 Anonymous letter, 1592, cited Lacey, p. 189.

21 Lacey, p. 186.

22 'Andreas Philopater' (i.e. Robert Parsons or Persons), *An Advertisement written to a Secretarie of my L Treasurers of Ingland by an Inglish Intelligencer . . . concerning an other Booke*, p. 18. This pamphlet was essentially a publicity exercise by Parsons, to advertise the 'other Booke', namely his *Responsio ad Elizabethae Reginae Edictum contra Catholicos* (1592). The charges against Ralegh also appear there, in Latin (pp. 49–50, transcribed Bakeless, I 130).

23 Hariot was in Ralegh's service as early as 1580. He was official surveyor on the Virginia voyage (1585) and served as Ralegh's Chief Steward. He received a gift of £24 from Northumberland in 1593 and an annual pension from him, 1598–1621. Warner was in the Earl's service by February 1591. Hues was a close associate of Hariot, who contributed to Hues' *Tractatus de Globis*, though he does not appear on Northumberland's accounts till 1615. See Shirley, pp. 52–9, and the documents there cited. More general accounts of the Durham House set abound: see bibliography under Strathmann, Bradbrook; Lacey, ch. 15. Contemporary accounts of their magico-scientific pursuits, more useful than Parsons', include: George Peele, *The Honour of the Garter* (1593), which describes Northumberland's devotion to 'mathesis', 'the stars and zodiac', 'Trismegistus and Pythagoras' and 'divine science and philosophy'; Ralegh, *The History of the World* (1614); George Chapman, 'To my admired and soul-loved friend, M. Harriots', in *Achilles Shield* (1598); the Earl of Northumberland's undated essay on the superiority of learning to love, calendared in CSP (Dom) 1603–10, p. 187, transcribed by Yates, *Study of 'Love's Labour's Lost'*, Appendix 3. See also Aubrey, pp. 281, 416, 420–2, 475; Rattansi, 'Alchemy & Natural Magic in Ralegh's *History of the World*'.

24 Wernham, p. 345; Kyd's letter to Lord Keeper Puckering (see ch. 5, n. 19); Baines' 'Note' (see ch. 3, n. 31). A spy's report, 'Remembraunces of wordes & matter againste Rich. Cholmeley' (BM Harleian MS 6848, f. 190), contains the allegation about Marlowe's 'Atheist lecture'. According to the report, 'Marloe' himself had told Cholmeley he had read the lecture to Ralegh. Baines' 'Note' corroborates that Marlowe knew 'one Ric. Cholmley', and adds that the latter was 'persuaded by Marloe's Reasons to become an Atheist'.

25 TN I 172; 'Philopater', p. 18; TN II 116.

26 TN IV 236, Supp. 12, 29–30. McKerrow cites Thomas Erastus, *Paracelsus* (1572), I 244, II 137, and Francis Thynne's epigram 'Menn before Adame', in *Emblemes and Epigrames*, ed. Furnivall, EETS, p. 81.

27 TN I 242 (following ed. 1592A); Ralegh, letter to Sir Robert Cecil, cited Rowse, *Ralegh and the Throckmortons*, p. 162.

28 Chapman, *Works*, pp. 3, 50–5. *De Guiana* was prefixed to Lawrence Keymis, *A Relation of the Second Voyage to Guiana* (1596).

29 Ibid., pp. 4, 8.

30 See Chapman's completion of *Hero and Leander*, Sestiad III, ll. 195–8 (CM II 462). This was published in 1598 (see ch. 17).

31 TN I 244. Shakespeare uses the same pun to jibe at Chapman in *Loves Labors Lost* (II i 15–16): 'Beautie is bought by iudgement of the eye,/Not uttred by base sale of chapmens tongues'.

32 'Hobynoll' (i.e. Gabriel Harvey), 'To the Learned Shepheard', prefixed to Spenser's *Faerie Queene* (1590).

33 See Spenser's epistle to Ralegh, dated 23 January 1590, before the *Faerie Queene*. The work is actually dedicated to Queen Elizabeth. On the philosophical connections between Spenser, Ralegh and Chapman, see Yates, *The Occult Philosophy in the Elizabethan Age*, ch. IX, 'Spenser's Neoplatonism and the Occult Philosophy', and ch. XIII, 'Agrippa and Elizabethan Melancholy'.

34 TN III 276–7.

35 TN III 333, 52, I 367.

36 TN II 306. The burlesque of the cunning man in *The Terrors* (TN I 363–7) is also full of Paracelsist references. See Nicholl, pp. 70–1.

37 TN III 83.

38 TN III 277.

39 GH II 54. Nashe's fable is TN I 221–6.

40 TN III 214. Cf. TN I 154–5, 259–61.

41 TN I 260–1. 'Him that giveth the dog in his crest' suggests the Earl of Shrewsbury, whose family name of Talbot was represented by the dog of that breed, but the general meaning is that the bear of his fable has been equated with that of the Leicester crest. Cf. TN III 214. Collier and McKerrow note that the bear is Leicester (TN IV 139–40), and more detailed correspondences have been worked out by McGinn, 'The Allegory of the "Beare" and the "Foxe" in Nashe's *Pierce Penilesse*'. I have followed McGinn's identifications.

42 *Leycesters Commonwealth*, ed. F. J. Burgoyne (1904), pp. 29, 63, 208, 236. The *Commonwealth* appears to have been circulating in England by September 1584. The actual title of the pamphlet is *The Copie of a Leter wryten by a Master of Arte of Cambridge to his Friend in London concerning some talke past of late ... about ... some proceedinges of the Erle of Leycester and his Friendes in England*. It was also known as 'Father Parsons Greencoat'.

43 Ibid., pp. 200–2; McGinn, pp. 439–41; see also 'Howard Traditions in *Leycesters Commonwealth*' in Pollen, *The Venerable Philip Howard, Earl of Arundel*, pp. 57–66.

44 'The Compleynt of a Sinner' is ascribed to Essex in *The Paradise of Dainty Devises* (1585). On Lady Lennox, see McGinn, pp. 444–5.

45 See Franklyn B. Williams (ed.), 'Leicester's Ghost', *Harvard Studies & Notes in Philology and Literature*, XVIII (1935), and 'Thomas Rogers of Bryanston, an Elizabethan Gentleman of Letters', *Harvard Studies*, XVI (1934).

46 TN I 321.

47 TN III 360 (cf. III 356, 'the aged champion of **Warwicke**'); Pearson, *Thomas Cartwright and Elizabethan Puritanism*, pp. 293–4.

48 TN I 260. McGinn is surely wrong in saying that Harvey calls Nashe the 'iolly Fly' in Sonnet IV of *Foure Letters* (GH I 240). The whole sonnet is about Greene, not Nashe.

49 Cartwright was summoned before the High Commission in August 1590. The 31 articles against him are dated 1 September. In March and May 1591 he appeared before the Star Chamber, and he was also interrogated by Bancroft and others at the Bishop of London's house, 'secretlie kept lest any that favoured his cause . . . should come in'. The petition by four Cambridge University heads (27 February 1592) and Cartwright's own petition to Burghley and Whitgift (1 March) secured his release. See Strype, II 22–8, 70f, III 242f; CSP (Dom) 1591–4, vol. CCXXXVIII, no. 102; Cartwright's *Answer to the Bil in the Star Chamber* (1591). His letter to Burghley, 4 October 1590 (Strype, III 231–2), shows his stung reaction to the anti-Martinist pamphlets – 'divers books of Antimartinus' wherein his name is 'slanderously rent and torn in pieces'. Nashe's sorties against him in the *Almond* must have been prominent in his mind.

50 Strype, II 96–102; CSP (Dom) 1591–4, vol. CCXLIV, no. 64. Essex was also active on Udall's behalf.

51 Beale himself claimed (Strype, II 130–1) that various Puritan 'libels' had been laid at his door, including works by Stubbes, Penry and 'the new Martin'. The attribution of *The Abstract* to him may be accurate, however: its arguments precisely accord with Beale's own in the letter to Burghley.

52 Strype, II 140–1. One of McKerrow's rare lapses, uncorrected by F. P. Wilson, is to assert that Beale's letter is undated (TN V 142). The date given by Strype (II 141) shows the letter to be 1593 (new style), not 1592 as McKerrow catalogues it.

53 TN I 177–9, 225.

54 On Knollys' Puritan agitation, see Strype, I 597f, II 71–3, 120f. He supported Cartwright's cause during the Star Chamber proceedings of May 1591, arguing to both Burghley and the Queen that the 'claimed superiority of the Bishops might be discussed lawfully' (i.e. that Cartwright's critique was not *per se* an offence). He spoke in favour of Morrice's bill against the oath *ex officio* in the parliament of February 1593.

55 TN I 307, 320.

56 See the 'Collection touchinge the Attainder of Phillip Howard, Earl of Arundell' in Beale's hand, in Pollen, *The Venerable Philip Howard, Earl of Arundel*, pp. 175–7. See also pp. 172, 199, 206, 210. Beale was still active in anti-Catholic work in 1594, one of the interrogators of the Jesuit Henry Walpole on 4 June. See Pollen, *Unpublished Documents relating to the English Martyrs*, pp. 251–2.

57 Rosenberg, p. 350.

58 TN I 195. The threat is specifically aimed at Richard Harvey.

59 *The Phoenix Nest*, ed. Rollins, pp. 5–8.

60 TN III 214–15.

61 On Sir Robert Dudley, see Rosenberg, pp. 24, 353; Yates, 'John Eliot's *Ortho-Epia Gallica*', p. 11; DNB.

62 TN III 213.

63 TN I 259.

9   GREENE AND HARVEY

1 GH I 171. The expenses were 4s for the winding sheet and 6s 4d for the burial. Harvey's account of Greene's death (GH I 170–3) is substantially accurate, probably, if exaggerated in its more lurid particulars. His chief source was Greene's landlady, Mistress Isam (I 171).

2 No copy of this individual issue survives. It is inferred from Nashe's references to Harvey's 'first butter-fly Pamphlet against Greene' (TN III 130) and his 'short pamphlet of six leaves' (TN I 263). The pamphlet reappeared as the second of the *Three Letters*, and then of the *Foure Letters*, issued later in the month. See TN V 81, IV 152–3, and bibliography under F. R. Johnson.

3 Cf. the letters to Doll printed in Greene's *Repentance* (RG XII 185) and *Groatsworth* (RG XII 149). The former is close to Harvey's version, the latter rather differently worded.

4 RG XII 184–5.

5 GH I 167.

6 TN I 303, 330.

7 GH I 193–4, 170; RG X 203. Greene puts the phrase into the mouth of Lawrence, a 'foist' (pickpocket), in *A Disputation between a He-conny-catcher and a Shee Conny-catcher* (*c.* April–June 1592). On the dates of the 'conny-catching' tracts, see below, n. 19.

8 On the dating evidence in Richard Harvey's letter to Gabriel (14 June 1592) in *Philadelphus* (1593), see ch. 7, n. 31 above.

9 TN I 271; Greene, *Quip* (1592, first issue), sig. E4. The misprint 'poperlye' for 'piperly' is interesting.

10 GH I 162, TN I 279–80. Harvey also says Greene offered the printer 20s 'to leave out the matter of the three brothers'. The first, unexpurgated issue of the *Quip* was only rediscovered in 1919. See TN Supp. 75–6; McKerrow, *An Introduction to Bibliography for Literary Students*, p. 228.

11 GH I 170, TN I 287–8. Nashe says he was 'in company' with Greene 'at that fatall banquet of Rhenish wine and pickled hearing (if thou wilt needs have it so). . .'. For a very long shot at Will Monox, there was a George Monox who owned the Pope's Head tenements in 1553 (Stow, *A Survay of London*, II 307). A younger Monox, growing up round there, might know the young Thomas Kyd (baptized at St Mary Woolnoth) and the publishers like Hackett and Wolfe who had shops at the Pope's Head, and hence Nashe.

12 TN I 153–5.

13 RG XII 141–6.

14 Most accept that 'young Iuvenall' is Nashe, but attempts have been made to show it is Lodge. This sacrifices just about every hint in the passage in order to identify the recent 'Comedie' as *The Looking Glass for London*. See TN V 143–4.

15 Simpson, *School of Shakespeare* (1878), II 382–3.

16 See McGinn, 'A Quip from Tom Nashe'.

17 TN I 269–71. To reject McGinn's actual attribution is not to deny that Nashe may have helped, informally, to shape Greene's skit.

18 RG X 12.

19 The precise chronology of the 'conny-catching' tracts is elusive. *The Notable Discovery* and the *Second Part* were both registered, to different publishers, on 13 December 1591, and probably appeared that month. The *Third Part*, though registered on 7 February 1592, did not appear until at least 26 March. The *Defence*, registered 21 April, only mentions two earlier tracts, so the *Third Part* may not have been issued till early May, a little after the

Defence. The *Disputation* and the *Black Bookes Messenger* seem to be later, as they promise the forthcoming *Black Booke*, which never appeared. If Greene was preparing the *Quip* for the press in July (registered 20 July) and was terminally sick in August, June 1592 is the latest date of composition for the last two tracts. This is highly tentative and assumes old-style dating on the title-pages. The *Defence* is RG XI 39–104.

20 RG XI 103–4. 'Stripping law' is the 'abuse' and 'extorting bribery' practised by certain prison officers – Cuthbert mentions Newgate and the Marshalsea – and also by 'counterfaite keepers' who arrest people with 'unlawful warrants'.

21 RG XI 47, 75–6; Grosart's introduction, RG I 30, n. 27; Sir Sidney Lee, DNB, s.v. Greene. Grosart failed to correct a contradictory assertion (RG XI 40) that even the 'most superficial reading' of the *Defence* 'would have shown it is against, not by, Greene'.

22 RG XI 43–4; Shakespeare, *Loves Labors Lost*, IV iii 51–2; F. P. Wilson, *Shakespearian and other Studies*, pp. 127–8.

23 RG XI 72.

24 RG XI 72, 74, 76–7; TN I 169–70.

25 RG XI 80, 59, 49, 78, 98–9, 85, 65. 'Thos Payne the haberdasher' is mentioned in a letter of Father Parsons', dated 10 February 1592. See CSP (Dom Eliz) 1591–4, vol. CCXLI, no. 41.

26 RG XI 51–2.

27 TN II 95.

28 Greene, *Quip* (1592, first issue), sig. E3v.

29 GH I 188; Stern, p. 94.

30 Bird's letter appears as the first of the *Foure Letters*, GH I 159–61. The sonnet supposedly by Bird is almost certainly Harvey's. On Demetrius, see TN IV 161; E. J. Worman, *Alien Members of the Book Trade* (Bibliographical Society), pp. 41–4.

31 On Demetrius and Rogers, see Stern, p. 95, n. 53. Rogers was a member of the 'Areopagus' group, with Sidney, Spenser and Dyer. Harvey and Spenser corresponded about the group (GH I 7, 20), on which see Peter French, *John Dee* (1972), ch. 6, 'John Dee and the Sidney Circle'; James Phillips, *Daniel Rogers: a neo-Latin Link between the Pleiade and Sidney's 'Areopagus'* (Los Angeles, 1965).

32 Stern, pp. 98–101; TN III 81. Martha Harvey's petition against Gabriel is dated 9 May 1593.

33 On Wolfe, see McKerrow, *A Dictionary of Printers and Booksellers in England, 1557–1640*, s.v. Wolfe; Hoppe, 'John Wolfe'; Stern, pp. 101–3.

34 TN III 87–91, 96–9.

35 GH I 165, 168.

36 TN I 271. The latter phrase is proverbial: see Kyd, *Spanish Tragedy*, I ii 172; Shakespeare, *King John*, II i 137–8.

37 GH I 170.

38 GH I 193–4.

39 GH I 195, 202, 206, 218. The Spanish picaresque romance *Lazarillo de Tormes* (1554) was translated by David Rouland in 1586. Alpert (Penguin ed., 1969, p. 8) ascribes the work to the satirist Diego Hurtado de Mendoza.

40 TN I 197–8.

41 GH I 199. Harvey's condemnation of *Pierce* as a 'diabolicall' work may just be over-literal, a confusion of subject with intent, or it may glance at the Strange–Ralegh–Marlowe–Chapman motifs argued in chs 7 and 8. Harvey was well informed about the new occultism, an admirer of Dee, Agrippa and

Paracelsus. In this passage, Richard's *Astrologicall Discourse* and Pierce's 'diabolicall discourse' appear to epitomize, somewhat in motley, the polarities of Elizabethan magic – white and black, astral and necromantic, angelic and daemonic, etc.

42 GH I 203–5, 215.

43 GH I 214–15, 217, 219–20.

44 TN I 266. Nashe's equation between literary products and excreta is frequently deployed against Harvey. See, e.g., TN III 133, where one of the 'lenvoys' (short concluding stanzas, French *'l'envoi'*) in Harvey's poem 'Gorgon' (1593) is likened to 'a fart after a good stoole'.

45 GH I 222, 233.

10　'IN THE COUNTREY'

1 TN I 153–5: 'A Private Epistle of the Author to the Printer' in the 2nd ed. of *Pierce*. Nashe is writing in reply to a letter from Jeffes ('You write to me my book is hasting to the second impression'). On the date of Nashe's letter (*c.* end September) see TN IV 77–9.

2 Chettle, sig. A4.

3 On the evidence for Croydon Palace as the venue for *Summers Last Will* see B. A. Nicholson's article, GTN VI xxviii–xxx; TN IV 416–19. Lee's suggestion of Beddington, near Croydon (DNB, s.v. Nashe), arises from a confusion between the Carews, who lived there, and the Careys, who later sheltered Nashe.

4 TN III 241, cf. ES, III 452, and Shakespeare, *Merry Wives of Windsor*, IV v 78; TN III 250, cf. Stow, *Annales*, p. 765; TN III 292, cf. APC XXIII 221 (1 October 1592).

5 TN III 235, 237, 291; IV 418, 422.

6 On Croydon Palace – now the Old Palace School for girls – see bibliography under Oswald and Fleay. I am indebted to Mr Roberts, the school Bursar, for a personal tour of the buildings in April 1981.

7 TN III 291–2.

8 Raines, p. 190.

9 DNB s.v. Whitgift; 'Martin senior', sig. Bi. Sir George Paule, Whitgift's first biographer, describes the Archbishop visiting Dover in 1583–4, 'attended with an hundred of his own servants at least, in livery, whereof there were forty gentlemen in chains of gold'. His total 'train' was then 'above five hundred horse'. See Pierce, *An Historical Introduction to the Marprlelate Tracts*, p. 360.

10 BM Lansdowne MS 107, no. 30, f. 52; transcribed Strype, III 369. Strype vaguely catalogues the letter under 1597, which Wilson apparently accepts (TN Supp. 74), but a close reading of Strype's earlier account of the controversy (II 220f), together with evidence in Simon Forman's case-books (Rowse, *The Case Books*, pp. 156–60), suggest that Broughton wrote it in 1594. The argument is not worth setting out in full because the clash with Nashe and company was already in the past when he wrote, and other of the 'injuries' he relates go back as far as the mid-1580s. That the fracas occurred in 1592, during Nashe's spell at Croydon, is made more likely by Hutton's raging against Broughton's 'Daniel'. Earlier in 1592 Archbishop Whitgift expressly 'sent to the Stationers' to 'hinder the printing' of this work, a controversial exposition of the prophesy of the seventy weeks in the Book of Daniel (Strype, II 117). Nearly twenty years later, Ben Jonson

likewise 'scoffed' Broughton's Hebrew studies. Doll's rantings in *The Alchemist* (IV iii 1f) are a wicked pastiche of Broughton's *Concent of Scriptures*. She has 'gone mad with studying Broughton's works./If you but name a word touching the Hebrew,/She falls into her fit'.

11 TN III 233.
12 There are three internal references to Toy (TN III 233, 267, 294). His fame as a comic is suggested by Harvey calling Greene 'the second Toy of London' (GH I 189). It has been argued that members of the Paul's Boys company acted in the show, and that the remark in the Prologue – 'we . . . have ceased to tune any musike of mirth to your eares this twelvemonth' (III 234) – refers to the inhibition of the company in or shortly before October 1591. The dates are neat but McKerrow (TN IV 419) and Chambers, ES II 19 n. 1, argue against it.
13 The range of kitchens and offices at the east end of the great hall was demolished in 1810, but the doorways are still visible in Blore's drawings (Figure 8). My conjectured reconstruction of the setting for *Summers Last Will* is partly based on parallels, e.g. the staging of Thomas Campion's wedding masque for Lord Hay, performed in the banqueting hall at Whitehall on 6 January 1607. See ES I 203f, 219f, III 240; and Ernest Law's reconstructions of staging at Whitehall and Hampton Court (*London Topographical Record*, VII 41; *The Times*, 3 December 1912). Play scenes in *A Midsummer Night's Dream*, *Hamlet*, Middleton's *A Mad World, My Masters*, etc., help to give us the flavour of the first night.
14 TN III 244.
15 TN III 236.
16 TN III 289–90, cf. Marlowe, *Edward II*, V v 71 (CM II 92).
17 TN III 249, 278, 291.
18 TN I 329. The italicized words are quoted from Harvey's *Foure Letters*.
19 Cited DNB, s.v. Whitgift.
20 CSP (Dom Add) 1580–1625, p. 341; Strype, II 149.
21 TN I 333. There are real rocks so called West of Scilly and on the Pembrokeshire coast.
22 TN I 311–12, IV 86.
23 Chettle, sigs E1v–E2. The 'two-fold Edition of Invectives' is Gabriel's *Three Letters* and *Foure Letters*. Chettle's pamphlet was entered on SR on 8 December 1592.
24 TN III 131.
25 The basis of this dating of *Strange Newes* is found in F. R. Johnson, 'The First Edition of Harvey's *Foure Letters*', and Harlow, 'Nashe's Visit to the Isle of Wight and his Publications of 1592–4', pp. 228–30.
26 TN I 255–8.
27 TN I 280, 287.
28 TN I 282, 286, 299, 301–2, 305.
29 TN I 259.
30 TN I 287–8.
31 Shakespeare, *Hamlet*, II ii 505–6. The 1604 quarto's 'shall' is replaced by 'should' in the Folio (1623).
32 GH I 164, TN I 281, 284–6.
33 TN I 283, 262, 275, 282, 322.
34 TN I 307.
35 TN I 276, 331, 305, 320–2, 326.
36 TN I 369.
37 TN I 378, 382. I have followed C. G. Harlow's ingenious argument – see

'Thomas Nashe, Robert Cotton the Antiquary, and *The Terrors of the Night*' – in most particulars. On Conington, see also Mirlees, pp. 16–17, 30–2; VCH Huntingdon III 144.

38 Cited Harlow, p. 10, from Holland's trans. of *Britannia* (1637).

39 See Harlow, pp. 10–11; anon, *The Most Strange and Admirable Discoverie of the Three Witches of Warboys* (1593); W. Notestein, *A History of Witchcraft in England* (1911).

40 TN I 378–83. As Harlow points out, there are three strata of composition in the published text of the *Terrors* – (1) In its original form, the tract was 'botch up and compyled' in or shortly after February 1593. (2) It was written over for publication, probably in the early summer of 1593: Danter entered his copy at Stationers' Hall on 30 June, though the work remained unpublished. (3) Further additions were made in 1594, including the eulogy of Sir George Carey and the dedication to Elizabeth Carey: a reference to the 'last repollished edition' of Camden's *Britannia* (TN I 374) cannot have been written before *c.* September–October 1594, when the enlarged (fourth) edition of *Britannia* appeared. The *Terrors* was finally published in late October or November 1594: Danter's second registration of the work on 25 October suggests that publication was imminent.

41 See the memorandum concerning Thomas Cotton's will, and the litigation between Robert Cotton and his sister Dorothy Bawde, Mirlees, p. 43.

42 TN I 341.

43 BJ I 139–40.

44 Cotton's estates amounted to some 6,000 acres of land. His father also left a handsome £33,000 to be shared among the eleven children. See Mirlees, p. 42.

45 TN I 257–8; Harlow, 'Thomas Nashe, Robert Cotton and *The Terrors*', p. 19. See Davies' letter to Cotton, Mirlees, p. 50.

46 The satirical 'Commendation of Antiquaries' is TN I 182–3. The apology is in the letter to Jeffes prefixed to the 2nd ed. (TN I 154).

47 See letters (Mirlees, pp. 47–8) to Cotton from 'your honest assured friend' John Donne (February 1601); from Hugh Holland (*c.* 1603); and from Lyly (too badly burned to be legible). Mirlees's references to Nashe' letter to Robert Cotton (p. 48) must be ignored. The letter in question is addressed, in Nashe's own hand, to William Cotton (see Document 10 and ch. 13). Thomas Coryat wrote to the Mermaid club from Agra in November 1615: see BJ I 49.

48 'Sweet Robin' to Sir John Davies (Mirlees, p. 50); '*dignissimus doctissimus*' to Dr John Case (Harlow, 'Thomas Nashe, Robert Cotton and *The Terrors*', p. 14).

49 Harlow, 'Thomas Nashe, Robert Cotton and *The Terrors*', pp. 18–19, citing four unpublished letters from Case in British Library MS collections. Nashe himself recommends 'well moderated recreations' as an antidote to melancholy (TN I 357).

50 TN I 354, 357.

51 TN I 378, 383–4.

52 TN I 355–6.

53 TN I 378.

54 TN I 345–6.

55 TN I 349–50.

56 TN I 384.

11   JACK WILTON

1 TN II 201.

2 TN V 23.

3 See bibliography under Latham and Berryman. McKerrow argues sternly against describing the story as 'picaresque' (TN V 23) and Hibbard follows suit. It should be noted that Harvey himself likens Nashe's style to that of *Lazarillo de Tormes* (GH I 206), though not with reference to *The Unfortunate Traveller*.

4 TN II 217, 227. A 'quater trey' is a dice loaded to turn up fours and threes (as opposed to a 'barred quater trey' which turned up everything but fours and threes). Jack's other false dice (II 218) are 'high men' and 'low men', weighted to turn up high and low numbers; 'langrets', apparently the same as 'quater treys'; and 'fullams', or 'fulhams', dice weighted at the corner to ensure high or low throws.

5 On the interplay of metaphoric 'vehicle' and 'tenor' (i.e. subject) in Nashe, see Crosten, p. 91f. This passage is typical of Nashe in that 'the "vehicle" part of the image propagates of its own accord, extending far beyond the original idea'.

6 TN II 209, 227.

7 TN II 207–8.

8 TN II 261.

9 TN II 210–16; J. B. Hunter, NQ, 17 February 1951, pp. 75–6. The nominal pun is ingenious but much of Hunter's argument shaky.

10 See Ward, pp. 206f, 251f, 257f. The annuity, granted by the Queen in 1586, is still unexplained, but everything about it suggests secret government work. He is still thought of as a potential supporter of Spain in 1592: see CSP (Dom Eliz) 1591–4, pp. 268–70.

11 Stopes, pp. 85–6. A letter of Henry Garnet's (Foley, *English Jesuits*, IV 49) says: 'The young Earl of Southampton, refusing the Lady Vere, payeth £5000 of present payment.' In January 1595, Elizabeth de Vere married William Stanley, 6th Earl of Derby (Lord Strange's younger brother and successor).

12 TN II 249–50.

13 That Surrey 'rigidly adhered to the old religion' was one of the charges against him at his trial for high treason. His sister, the Duchess of Richmond, testified against him on this point. He was executed in January 1547. See DNB, s.v. Howard, Henry. Nashe's commendation of Surrey is TN II 241–3.

14 TN II 285, 310–11.

15 See F. S. Boas, 'Informer against Marlowe', *Times Literary Supplement*, 16 September 1949; Rowse, *Christopher Marlowe*, p. 95.

16 John Clapham, *Narcissus* (1591). The work is addressed to Southampton, and contains veiled exhortations concerning his Catholic 'error' and his refusal to marry (hence 'Narcissus'). See also Yates, *A Study of Love's Labour's Lost*, pp. 28–32, on Southampton's Catholic upbringing, and his tutor Swithin Welles, who was executed in December 1591.

17 On the Southamptons and the Howards, see Akrigg, pp. 21–2; Stopes, pp. 5, 57, and Addendum III (pp. 499–528) where the Southamptons' Catholic connections are fully documented. According to Stopes, Southampton rejected Nashe's dedication because 'he was intimate with the Howards and . . . would know that the whole story of the Earl of Surrey was false and disparaging'.

18 TN IV 271. By her second marriage Elizabeth Fitzgerald became Duchess of Lincoln. She died in 1589. See Akrigg, pp. 3f.

19 Shakespeare's two dedications are reproduced in facsimile in Schoenbaum, figs 92, 94. *Venus* was registered on 18 April 1593. It was certainly on sale by 12 June, when one Richard Stonley recorded purchasing a copy of 'the Venus and Adhonay pr Shakspere'. For this and a copy of John Eliot's *Survay of France*, Stonley paid 12d. See Stonley's diary (Folger Library MS Va 460 f.9), Schoenbaum, pp. 131–2. *Lucrece* was entered on 9 May 1594. Both works were printed by Richard Field, who also printed additional matter for Nashe's *Christs Teares* in summer 1594.

20 TN II 201–2. Stopes says (p. 57): 'it is evident from this dedication that Nashe knew of Shakespeare's [in *Venus and Adonis*] when he wrote it'.

21 Stopes, p. 55. There are six commendatory sonnets before *Parthenophil*: the others are addressed to the Earls of Northumberland and Essex, the Countess of Pembroke, Lady Strange and Lady Manners.

22 The literature on the 'rival poet', referred to in Sonnets 78–86, is vast. Barnes, Marlowe, Chapman and Thomas Edwards have all been advanced. These lines (Sonnet 86, 5–11) strongly suggest Chapman, who is also glanced at in *Loves Labors Lost* (II i 15–16). The final couplet of Sonnet 21, 'Let them say more that like of hearsay well/I will not praise that purpose not to sell', has been glossed as punning on 'hearsay' = 'heresy', and 'salesman' = 'chapman'. Arthur Acheson, *Shakespeare and the Rival Poet* (1903), was the first to present Chapman's case.

23 The even vaster literature on *Loves Labors Lost* is reviewed below, ch. 14 n. 13. On the 'playhouse room' see Akrigg, p. 15.

24 TN II 243; Shakespeare, *Loves Labors Lost*, III i 163–7.

25 Compare the opening quatrains of Surrey's sonnet (TN II 254) with Navarre's (*Loves Labors Lost*, IV iii 25–8). For the dark ladies, see TN II 261, 313; *Loves Labors Lost*, III i 177–8; Sonnets, 127, 130.

26 I date the publication of *The Unfortunate Traveller* as follows. (1) It had recently appeared when Nashe wrote the epistle for the 2nd edition of *Christs Teares*: he refers to its reception (TN II 181–3). (2) In *Have with you* Nashe says, 'I have been big with childe of a common place of revenge [against Harvey] ever since the hanging of Lopus' (TN III 18). Roderigo Lopez was hanged on 7 June 1594. The threats referred to cannot be in *Strange Newes*: they must be those issued in the new epistle before *Christs Teares*. (3) June 1594 is thus a *terminus ad quem* for the publication of *The Unfortunate Traveller*. (4) Assuming old style dating, the title-page date (1594) gives a *terminus a quo* of 26 March 1594. This deduction accords with Nashe's known movements, and with peculiarities in the printing of the first edition. See below, ch. 13; Harlow, 'Nashe's Visit to the Isle of Wight and his Publications of 1592–4', pp. 234–5.

27 TN II 182.

28 TN II 286. The car-men's cry is from the 1st edition, not the 2nd which is McKerrow's exemplar.

29 Stow's exact figure is 10,675 dead between 29 December 1592 and 20 December 1593 (Schoenbaum, p. 126). This is a conservative figure. Nashe says that over 1600 Londoners died each week during the 'ragingest furie of the last Plague' (TN III 87). The period referred to is *c*. April–June 1593. Nashe was familiar with the 'Plague Bills' which Wolfe printed (TN III 89): his figure may be accurate for the worst weeks.

30 Hotson gave the first full account of Marlowe's death in *The Death of Christopher Marlowe* (1925). The major documents are to be found there. See also Bakeless I 151–8.

31 For details of Poley, Skeres, Friser and the Walsinghams, see Bakeless I 161–89.

32 On the 'Marlovian echoes' in the Surrey and Aretino passages in *The Unfortunate Traveller*, see bibliography under Feasy.

33 TN II 242, 264–5; Thomas Thorpe's dedication to Blount, prefixed to his edition of Marlowe's *Lucan* (1600), CM II 279; Michael Drayton, *Of Poets and Poesy*.

34 TN II 288–95, cf. II 323.

35 See TN II 335–7; Thomas Warton, *History of English Poetry* (1774–81), III 435; Thomas Tanner, *Bibliotheca Britannico-Hibernica* (1748), s.v. Marlovius. According to Malone, a copy of *Dido* containing the elegy was on sale at Osborne's bookshop in 1754.

36 TN II 180–1.

37 The poem appears at the end of Harvey's *New Letter of Notable Contents*, GH I 295. The letter itself is dated 16 September 1593.

12   THE CRACK-UP

1 TN II 12, 15, 48–9.

2 TN II 183–4; cf. TN V 202 (Appendix F6: 'The Vocabulary and Style of *Christ's Tears*').

3 GH I 273. On Nashe's use of ben Gurion and Stockwood, see TN IV 212–13.

4 TN II 80, 174. On the relationship between 'preaching and satire' in Nashe, see Rhodes, pp. 50–5.

5 See E. D. Mackerness, '*Christs Teares* and the Literature of Warning', on the pamphlet's predecessors and successors. Among the latter are the lost *Destruction of Jerusalem* (*c.* 1598), possibly the work by Thomas Deloney later published as *Canaans Calamity* (1618); Lodowick Lloyd's *Stratagems of Jerusalem* (1602); Thomas Wilson's *Christs Farewell to Jerusalem* (1614); Francis White's *Londons Warning by Jerusalem* (1619); and John Jones' *London Looking-Back to Jerusalem* (1633).

6 TN II 90, 138–9, 36, 154.

7 TN II 37, 89, 51, 92.

8 TN II 10. On the dedicatee, Lady Elizabeth Carey, see ch. 13 below.

9 TN II 92–108. Nashe usually uses 'hutch' to mean a 'chest' or 'trunk', but the sense here (II 107) seems to be 'prison'.

10 See TN II 158–9 for both versions (sig. X3 in the original text). The cancel leaf was printed on sheet 2*4 of the 2nd edition, following the new epistle 'To the Reader' (sigs *4v–2*3v). There are extant copies of the 2nd edition where the cancel leaf is still found in this position, with the original sig. X3 also still in place.

11 TN III 95–6, V 25–6, 194. Nashe answered the charge of mutinous language against the Mayor by pointing out that he was not in London that Christmas, but in the 'Ile of Wight'. This is only a partial refutation, and Harvey may well have been reporting a genuine incident, but confusedly as to the exact date when it happened. Harvey's 'perswasive pamphlet' and his 'reporting certaine words' seem to be two separate *communiqués* to the authorities, the first shortly after the appearance of *Christs Teares*, the second in early 1594. See Harlow, 'Nashe's Visit to the Isle of Wight and his Publications of 1592–4', pp. 226–7, 232–3. Harlow convincingly shows McKerrow's

errors in interpreting this passage, as also his larger error of dating Nashe's visit to the Isle of Wight Christmas 1592, rather than 1593.

12 TN III 180. Cf. TN III 36, where Nashe refers to *Pierces Supererogation* and then to 'one Epistle thereof, to Iohn Wolfe the Printer', as though the *New Letter* were simply part of the *Supererogation*. The *New Letter* was registered on 1 October 1593; the *Supererogation* was not registered.

13 TN II 179, III 92–3, 118; GH I 286–7; TN II 12.

14 GH I 273, 287–9.

15 TN II 179, 181.

16 TN III 33–6.

17 Stern, p. 104.

18 GH II 272, 280–1, 117. On the intellectual drift on the *Supererogation*, see TN V 88–95, Stern, pp. 103–6, and the articles by McPherson and Perkins listed in the bibliography.

19 GH II 222; TN III 137. According to Nashe (III 139) Lyly had actually 'wrought uppon' Harvey's 'Paradoxe of the Asse' – one of the motifs in the *Supererogation* – but whatever he wrote remained unpublished.

20 Nashe's treatment of this trio – TN III 102–10 – is superbly contemptuous. On Barnes, see Eccles, 'Barnabe Barnes'. Other discreditable incidents in Barnes' career give some credence to Nashe's charge that he stole 'a Noble-mans Stewards chayne at his Lords enstalling at Windsore'. The lord was probably the Earl of Northumberland, the occasion the Garter ceremony of 25 June 1593. On Thorius, see Stern, p. 106. On Chute, see Kane's article in the bibliography. Chute's pamphlet *Tabaco*, thought to be the earliest work devoted to the drug, was published posthumously in 1595.

21 Nashe printed the letter in *Have with you* (TN III 135). Thorius claims that the 'Sonet' (GH II 336) was nothing to do with him, and that the 'Stanzaes' (II 343–4), though his, had been 'altred to your [Nashe's] disgrace in some places'.

22 GH II 23, 338, 345; TN III 134, 136.

23 GH II 16–18, 318–30.

24 See TN IV 356, V 89–90, GH III xxiii.

25 TN III 110–14. Cf. II 180, 'his vaineglorie, which some take to be his gentlewoman. . .'.

26 GH II 62–4.

27 See Yates, *John Florio*, pp. 178f, and *A Study of 'Love's Labour's Lost'*, pp. 73f.

28 Eliot's preface is pp. 19–21 of Lindsay's reprint (1928). On Eliot's satiric intentions, see the articles by Yates ('John Eliot's *Ortho-Epia Gallica*' and 'Italian Teachers in Elizabethan England') in the bibliography.

29 See Huffman, NQ (July 1975), pp. 300–2; Stern, pp. 43, 156.

30 *The Phoenix Nest* (ed. Rollins), pp. xvii–xx.

31 See ibid., pp. xxi–xxxi, on the various candidates for 'R.S. of the Inner Temple'. Stapleton is plausible in view of his literary connections with Chapman, though the only student of that name at the Inner Temple was admitted in February 1534. He would have been about seventy-five when *The Phoenix Nest* was published, and well into his nineties when Chapman praised him in the preface to the 1616 edition of his complete *Homer*. This might seem to stretch Stapleton's career to an unlikely length, but Chapman does describe his friend as 'most ancient' and indeed as the 'first most desertfull mover in the frame of our *Homer*'. Stapleton may also be the 'R.S.' who wrote one of the poems in praise of Spenser before *The Faerie Queene* (1590). This praises Spenser for his 'hye drifts' and 'deepe conceites',

just as Stapleton praises Chapman for 'philosophick strains' suitable for 'aspiring sprights' (Sonnet before *Ovids Banquet*). If these are all one and the same man, he is another link in the Chapman–Ralegh–Spenser–Leicester–Pembroke chain in *Pierce Penilesse*.

32 Chapman's preface must have been written after 25 September 1593, since it refers to Lord Strange as the Earl of Derby. The registration of *The Shadow of Night* on 31 December provides an approximate *terminus ad quem*. Because of the connections, chronological and dialectic, between *The Shadow of Night* and *Loves Labors Lost*, the preface has been frequently glossed as a sortie against Shakespeare. This seems 'bardocentric' in the extreme: why should 'pierst' and 'supererogation' make the reader of 1594 think of Shakespeare? There may be some continued anti-Nashe quibbling in Stapleton's sonnet before *Ovids Banquet*, where Chapman's Muse 'sings/Sweet philosophick straines that Feends might pierse'.

33 Sir John Harington, *The Most Elegant and Witty Epigrams* (1618), II, Epigram 36. This is the earliest known appearance of the epigram, but it was presumably composed in or about 1593.

34 TN I 374–5.

13   THE CAREYS

1 Naunton, pp. 46–7; Rowse, *The Case Books of Simon Forman*, pp. 110–26, and *Shakespeare the Man*, pp. 102–9.

2 Schoenbaum, pp. 135–6. The earliest record of the newly formed company is in June 1594, when they played at Newington Butts. Hunsdon refers to his 'nowe companie of Players' in a letter to the Lord Mayor dated 8 October. Shakespeare, Kemp and Burbage, 'servauntes to the Lord Chamberleyne', appear on the royal accounts for 15 March 1595, jointly receiving £13 6s 8d for performances at court the previous Christmas.

3 See Rowse, *Shakespeare the Man*, pp. 102f. Rowse was forced to retract a key aspect of his original identification. Simon Forman describes Emilia not as 'brown' (i.e. dark) but as 'brave' (i.e. beautiful, with a hint of tarty). See the article by Stanley Wells, *Times Literary Supplement*, 11 May 1973. Nor have Rowse's later pronouncements on the subject strengthened his case. In 'Shakespeare and the Tell-tale Sonnet' (*The Times*, 23 April 1980) he adduces evidence about Emilia and Shakespeare from a sonnet in *The Passionate Pilgrim* anthology (1599). He omits to mention that the sonnet is not by Shakespeare at all. Some in the anthology are, but this one is by Richard Barnfield. It appears in his *Poems in Divers Humors* (1598), addressed 'to his friend, Maister R.L.', and has nothing whatever to do with Emilia Lanier. For all this she remains the most plausible Dark Lady yet, and a brilliant discovery by Rowse.

4 TN I 194. On the Knight Marshal, see OED, s.v. 'marshal', sb 6b. The royal 'house and verge' was defined as the area within a twelve-mile radius of the royal palace.

5 Oglander, pp. 4–5, 21.

6 HMC Salisbury, IV 346; Carey, pp. 26–7; HMC Penshurst, II 194.

7 DNB, s.v. Carey; Jeayes, pp. 259, 312–16, 330; Oglander, pp. 4–5, 128 n. 1. The jewels are itemized in Carey's will, drawn up 10 May 1599. For references to Carey's illness see below, n. 55.

8 See the dedications of Edmund Spenser, *Muiopotmos* (1590); George Chapman, *The Shadow of Night* (1594); William Warner, *Albions England*

(1586); Thomas Heath, *Manifest Confutation of an Astrological Discourse* (1583); James Forester, *The Pearle of Practise* (1594); John Dowland, *First Book of Songs and Ayres* (1597). On Carey and Forman, see Rowse, *The Case Books of Simon Forman*, pp. 49, 192.

9 Robert Carey describes the events in his *Memoirs*, pp. 26–7. The exact dates of the Michaelmas term 1593 are not known, but as early as 2 October a ballad lamenting London's 'losse of the terme' (i.e. the removal of the term to St Albans) was entered in the Stationers' Register. In normal years the Michaelmas term began in the second week of October.

10 Oglander, p. 4, n. 4.

11 See Harlow, 'Nashe's Visit to the Isle of Wight and his Publications of 1592–4', pp. 232–3.

12 On William Cotton, whom McKerrow could not identify, see Mackerness, 'Thomas Nashe and William Cotton', and Harlow, 'Thomas Nashe and William Cotton, MP'. Mackerness is uncertain that William Cotton gent and Captain William Cotton are the same, but it seems likely. The suggestion that Cotton is the 'agent' referred to by Robert Carey is my own. For Nashe's letter to Cotton, see Document 10, and TN V 194–6.

13 See BM MS Cotton Julius C III, f. 122v. Mirlees, p. 72, prints a short letter from Sir George to Robert Cotton, dated 18 December 1600. Carey sent two 'meddangles' (i.e. medallions), asking Cotton to 'try' them and to translate their inscriptions. Cotton was MP for Newton, Isle of Wight, in the parliament of 1601.

14 TN I 241, III 8, 31.

15 TN II 9–11.

16 TN I 374, III 96. An apparent interruption of the printing of *The Unfortunate Traveller* suggests the suddenness of Nashe's departure. Production had almost certainly begun on the pamphlet before he left. It was registered on 17 September, and in the preface to *Christs Teares* (late September–early October) Nashe says, 'two or three triviall Volumes of mine at this instant are under the Printers hands, ready to be published' (TN II 13). These are presumably *The Unfortunate Traveller* and *The Terrors of the Night*. In an ingenious conjecture Harlow argues that sheets B, C and D had been set up before Nashe left, and that he disappeared having corrected only sheet B in proof: see n. 25 below and text.

17 Oglander, pp. x, 20–1.

18 TN I 374.

19 Deed of Apprenticeship, dated 29 March 1596, catalogued by Jeayes. Emilia's mother is described as 'Margaret Bassany alias Margaret Johnson' in the will of Baptista Bassano, Emilia's father, who died in May 1576. See Rowse, *The Case Books of Simon Forman*, pp. 110, 113.

20 Both pieces appear in Dowland's *Second Book of Songs and Ayres* (1601), and both titles use stylings not applicable before 1596–7, but the tunes themselves may be earlier.

21 TN I 342. Nothing is known of her poems, though possibly some appeared anonymously in one of the anthologies of the day. A closet drama, *The Tragedie of Miriam, the faire Queene of Iewry* by 'Lady Elizabeth Carey', was published in 1613. Chambers assigns this to the Careys' daughter, Elizabeth, and dates composition *c.* 1602–5, but it is almost certainly the work of another Lady Elizabeth Carey, the 1st Lady Falkland.

22 TN II 10, I 375.

23 She was born in 1576, not 1586 as Chambers gives. On her prospective

marriage to William Herbert, see HMC Penshurst, II 163, 173, 188, 194. See also Jeayes, pp. 259, 330.

24 TN III 215–16; CSP (Dom Eliz) 1591–4, vol. CCXLVII, nos 97, 100–3; A. Dimock, 'The Conspiracy of Dr Lopez', EHR IX (1894), pp. 440–72.

25 TN II 203; Harlow, 'Nashe's visit to the Isle of Wight', pp. 234–5. On production rates in Elizabethan printing see R. B. McKerrow, 'Edward Allde as a Typical Trade Printer', The Library, 4th Series, X (1929), pp. 142–3. As a rule of thumb, an efficient compositor could set up one sheet (eight quarto pages) per day.

26 TN I 374. The enlarged fourth edition of Britannia had recently appeared when John Stradling wrote to Camden on 13 November 1594. See Harlow, 'Nashe's Visit to the Isle of Wight and his Publications of 1592–4', p. 236.

27 TN I 375.

28 On Elizabethan Blackfriars, see ES IV 475f, with sketch map, and the scale model at the Museum of London. Carey's house abutted upon the modern Printing House Lane. The King's Men – as the Chamberlain's Men became – acquired the lease of Blackfriars theatre in August 1608: see Schoenbaum, pp. 213–16. Ben Jonson and his wife were living in the parish of St Anne's, Blackfriars, in January 1606, and in 'the Precinct of the blackffreers' in May 1610 (see BJ I 220, 228). For facsimiles of conveyance and mortgage documents concerning Shakespeare's Blackfriars house, see Schoenbaum, figs 182–3.

29 TN Supp. 27. Forester's Pearle was registered on 11 December 1593, Shakespeare's Lucrece on 9 May 1594.

30 TN III 21.

31 On Strange's death, see Stow, Annales, pp. 767–8; John Goulborne, 'A Trewe Reporte and Observaunce of the Sicknes and Death of F. late Erle of Derby', Jeayes, p. 335; letter from Strange's wife to Cecil, 11 April 1594, HMC Salisbury IV 508.

32 Letter from Egerton to Heneage, 22 April 1594, HMC Salisbury IV 515; letter from Carey to his wife, 22 April 1594, Jeayes, p. 335.

33 Letter from Carey to Heneage and Cecil, 28 April 1594, HMC Salisbury IV 517. Another 'Mr Doughtie' was Clerk of the Kitchens in the Derby household in 1587.

34 Rowse, The England of Elizabeth, pp. 84–90; CSP (Dom Eliz) 1591–4, vol. CCXLIII, nos 11, 51–2.

35 On these various families see Raines, passim; on Edward Stanley, see 'Instructions for proceeding, touching recusants in Lancashire', October 1592, HMC Salisbury IV 240–2; on Holt, see letter from Richard Scholfield, a government spy, 7 May 1589, Raines, p. 180.

36 On the Stanley sons, see HMC Salisbury IV 411; on the charges against Langton, see ibid. IV 428; on Bushell, see n. 51 below.

37 Parsons' letter (HMC Salisbury IV 104) is written to two English priests, John Sicilio and John Fixerro, then at Lisbon. The identity of the intelligencer is uncertain. He may possibly be the Captain William Morgan who claimed, in 1595, that he 'gave warning that the late Lord Strange should be dealt with for practices against the state': see CSP (Dom Eliz), 1595–7, pp. 19–20. This may be the same as the Captain Morgan, 'a tall man with one eye', who once served in Sir William Stanley's regiment (HMC Salisbury IV 500).

38 Examination of George Dingley (alias Thomas Christopher, alias James Young), 14 September 1592, CSP (Dom Eliz), 1591–4, vol. CCXLIII, no. 11. Dingley also names the Earls of Oxford and Cumberland, and Lord Percy, as pro-Catholic nobles. On the priest in Rome, see William

Goldsmyth's report on the 'treacherous speech of Philip Woodward', 11 July 1593, HMC Salisbury IV 335. On Sir William Stanley's designs on Strange, see CSP (Dom Eliz) 1591–4, vol. CCXLIX, nos 12, 63 (confessions of Henry Walpole and Edmund Yorke).

39 The principal documents on which this account of the Hesketh plot is based are as follows (unless otherwise stated, references are to Cecil's MSS calendared in HMC Salisbury IV). (1) Hesketh's letters: to his wife Isabel and to his brother Thomas, both 2 October 1593, p. 381; to Cecil, 15 October 1593, pp. 389–90; to William Waad, 4 November 1593, pp. 407–8. (2) Other letters: Thomas Stephenson to Richard Hesketh and to Henry Leigh, both 28 November 1593, pp. 424–5; Henry Leigh to Cecil, 21 February 1594, pp. 480–1. (3) Statements of Bartholomew Hesketh, 4 November 1593, p. 408; of Richard Baylye, 5 November 1593, pp. 408–9; of Richard Hesketh, 7 November 1593, p. 409; of Henry Leigh, December 1593, pp. 450–2; of Edward Pemberton, 9 December 1593, CSP (Dom Eliz) 1591–4, vol. CCXLVI, no. 29; of William Polwhele, December 1593, ibid., no. 49; of Hugh Owen, March 1594, ibid., vol. CCXLVIII, no. 53. (4) Official proceedings: 'Interrogations unto Richard Hesketh', 15 October 1593, p. 390; Waad's description of Hesketh's arraignment, 28 November 1593, pp. 423–4; charges against Thomas Langton, November 1593, p. 428; confiscated paper containing 'Heskeths instructions for treating with the Earl of Derby', undated, pp. 461–3.

40 On the Hesketh family, see Raines, pp. 124–6. Bartholomew Hesketh, 'a zealous friend of Campion the Jesuit', dined at Lathom on 29 May 1587. Sir Thomas, imprisoned as a 'disaffected Papist' in 1581, was a guest there in early June. Lord Strange dined at Rufford, the Hesketh family home, in March 1590. In April 1590, Strange returned from a visit to Sir Richard Molyneux (another local Catholic): with him was 'Mr Hesketh'. This may well be Richard before his departure to Prague. He and Thomas Langton were at this time charged with the murder of Mr Houghton, and a few days after this Strange attended Lancaster Assizes to plead Langton's cause.

41 Strange to Cecil, 9 November 1593, HMC Salisbury IV 411–12; Heneage to Cecil, 29 November 1593, ibid., p. 425; Lord Keeper Puckering to Cecil, c. 24 November 1593, ibid., pp. 421–2; Lady Strange to Cecil, c. 30 November 1593, ibid., pp. 427–8.

42 For a parallel revenge, see Pollen, *Philip Howard*, p. 199, where a priest named Bennet is 'thought to have been empoisoned' for having 'declared his knowledge' of a Catholic conspiracy.

43 For a brief account of Kelley's career, see Nicholl, pp. 19–22. On Dee and Kelley in Bohemia, see Elias Ashmole (ed.), *Theatrum Chemicum Britannicum* (1652), pp. 478–84; Dee's diaries, ed. J. O. Halliwell (1842); Sargent, pp. 97–122.

44 Dee's diary, 25 November 1595, records the news that Kelley was 'slayne' (see Ashmole, ut supra, p. 484). He is said to have died from a fall while trying to escape prison. Evans (pp. 227–8) asserts he was still alive in 1597, and that the Paracelsian Oswald Croll visited him at Most Castle.

45 Raines, pp. lxxxiii–xci. Thomas ffarington, son of the Derbys' clerk-controller, was born in 1560 (about a year after Strange) and grew up on the Derby estates. Raines describes his portrait (dated 1593) as showing a 'careworn' countenance, dark eyes and a 'sombre' doublet. A book of madrigals is open before him, showing the music of '*Non nobis Domine*' by the Catholic composer William Byrd. The astrological screen was designed by Henry Parker, Yeoman of the Wardrobe, in 1576. A copy of its verses is in

BM Harleian MS 1927, f. 10. On Strange's mother's bent for astrology see Heywood, p. 20.

46 Raines, pp. 72–80, 202–3. Hesketh's implication in the killing is asserted by Henry Leigh, HMC Salisbury IV 481: 'Mr Heskett . . . said he left Lancashire for the slaughter of Mr Howghton'. According to Bartholomew Hesketh (ibid., p. 408), Richard left England in about autumn 1590.

47 On John Poole, see Mark Eccles, 'Marlowe in Newgate', *Times Literary Supplement*, 6 September 1934, and *Christopher Marlowe in London*, pp. 36–7; Raines, p. 150. The Captain Poole, a Cheshireman accused of absconding with 'church plate' in 1593, may be the same. See HMC Salisbury IV 458.

48 Nicholl, pp. 10–13; Lodge, *A Fig for Momus* (1595), sig. I2v.

49 Raines, p. 41.

50 On Baines' 'Note', see ch. 3, n. 33 above; on Marlowe at Flushing, see bibliography under Wernham.

51 See CSP (Dom Eliz) 1591–4, vol. CCXLIX, nos 64, 87, 103. The ringleader of this plot was one Richard Williams. Bushell was 'at the Winchester robbery', and was named as one of the accomplices in Williams' plan to assassinate the Queen. The warrant for Bushell's arrest is dated 16 August. Having formerly 'served' Strange, he was at the time of his arrest a 'servant to Lady Strange'.

52 TN I 363–7. Harlow argues that it is a late addition ('Nashe's Visit to the Isle of Wight', p. 236). He believes Nashe's cunning-man was meant for Dr Lopez, the supposed poisoner executed in June 1594.

53 See Forman's 'autobiography', Rowse p. 276, and his diary, 1564–1602, ibid., pp. 284–304. On Molyneux, see TN I 379, IV 209; E.G.R. Taylor, *The Mathematical Practitioners of Tudor and Stuart England*. He had links with the Ralegh circle, which had keen interests in geography and navigation.

54 Astrological diagnosis (see Forman's unpublished 'Discourse of the Plague', 1593, cited Rowse, *The Case Books of Simon Forman*, p. 57), guidance by '*lumen naturae*', and rejection of Galen are all typically Paracelsist. Other Paracelsians who fell foul of the Royal College of Physicians include Robert Fludd, Francis Anthonie and Arthur Dee.

55 Rowse, *The Case Books of Simon Forman*, pp. 49, 172, 178–9, 240–1. See p. 192 for a consultation on Carey's behalf in April 1598, relating to the purchase of 'merchandise'. Rowland Whyte's letters to Sir Robert Sidney (HMC Penshurst II 448–9, 453–4, 459, 466, 471, 484) refer to Carey's ill-health from 1599 on, as do Carey's own letters to the Queen. He travelled to Bath in spring 1600 to take the waters.

56 TN III 47. On the lampoon, see Stopes, pp. 235–7. For mercury as a treatment for syphilis, see Philip Hermann, *An Excellent Treatise how to Cure the French-Pockes*, trans. John Hester (1590).

57 Sir William Browne to Sir Robert Sidney, 7 July 1602, HMC Penshurst II 598. On Northumberland's '*spiritus dulcis*' and other alchemical preparations, see Shirley, pp. 60–3.

58 Forester, sig. *ii, and 'Epistle to the Reader'.

59 DNB, s.v. Forester.

60 Hotson's highly plausible argument – see *Shakespeare versus Shallow* (1931) – is followed by Oliver (*Merry Wives*, AS, pp. xlv–xlix). The first recorded performance – before King James at Whitehall in November 1604 (ibid., p. x) – is obviously a late one: the play had been published, in mangled form, two years earlier. *The Merry Wives* has many references to Garter ceremonial (not least the setting in Windsor, where the actual Garter installations took

place). Curious jokes about a 'Duke de Iamanie' and 'cosen garmombles' may allude to Count Mömpelgard, Duke of Württemberg, who was also elected to the Order of the Garter in 1597.

14 MASTER MOTH

1 On *Loves Labours Wonne*, see Schoenbaum, pp. 140–1, and T. W. Baldwin, *Shakspere's 'Love's Labor's Won'* (1957). Baldwin's candidate – a lost early version of *All's Well that Ends Well* – is rejected by Schoenbaum.

2 Shakespeare, *Taming of the Shrew*, I ii 113–15, i 64–5; TN I 195–9, 262; JL III 398, referring (probably) to Nashe's threats against Martin.

3 On Watson and the Cornwallis family, see ch. 5, n. 33 above. Shakespeare was living in the parish of St Helen's, Bishopsgate, by 1596 at the latest and probably earlier (see Schoenbaum, pp. 161–4). This was inside the city walls, but convenient for the Shoreditch theatres, north of Bishopsgate Ward Without. Watson had lodgings in St Helen's, Bishopsgate, in 1587, and in the 'liberty' of Norton Folgate, between Bishopsgate and Shoreditch, in 1589.

4 Kyd's letter to Lord Keeper Puckering (see ch. 5, n. 19 above); TN I 271.

5 Shakespeare, *Taming of the Shrew*, III ii 160f, I ii 278–9.

6 Ibid., II i 263–4; TN III 312.

7 '*Cum privilegio ad imprimendum solum*' was the Elizabethan formula for copyright. The joke is that marriage gives the husband the sole right to 'print' or 'press' his wife. Partridge does not give this reference (*Shrew*, IV iv 92), but see his *Shakespeare's Bawdy*, s.v. 'press', 'print' for parallels.

8 Shakespeare, *Taming of the Shrew*, III ii 48–73.

9 Ibid., Induction, ii 14–17, 30–4.

10 *Calendar of the Ellesmere Manuscripts*, Huntingdon Library, I no. 213. See Bald, pp. 110–11. Egerton's secretary at the time of the marriage was John Donne: through this connection two of Strange's daughters – Frances and Elizabeth, later Countess of Huntingdon – became Donne's friends and patronesses.

11 Her portrait (artist unknown) hangs at Stoneleigh Abbey. A reproduction is in the *Shakespeare Quater-Centenary Exhibition Catalogue* (1964), p. 82. Her 'bytter tongue' is fleetingly heard in reaction to rumours of her brother-in-law's marriage to Lady Vere: 'how true the news is I know not, only I wish her a better husband' (HMC Salisbury, IV 527).

12 The new AS edition of the *Shrew* (ed. Brian Morris, 1981, pp. 12–50) admirably summarizes the complex debate about the relations between these two plays. A convenient edition of *The Taming of a Shrew* is in Bullough, I 69f. The Induction scene in the latter is followed by four Sly 'interludes' and an Epilogue: these were apparently ditched when Shakespeare rewrote the play.

13 J. Dover Wilson (ed.), *Love's Labour's Lost* (1962), p. xxxiv. Warburton, *The Works of Shakespear* (1747), II 227–8, declared that 'by Holofernes is designed a particular character, . . . one John Florio'. Reams of scholarship and speculation have followed. Editions by Dover Wilson (Cambridge, 1923, revised 1962) and Richard David (AS, 1951) summarize the various interpretations of the play. For studies of the play, see bibliography under Yates, Schrickx, Campbell, Taylor, Spens. Bradbrook, *The School of Night* (1936), Strathmann, *Sir Walter Ralegh* (1951) and Oakeshott, *The Queen and the Poet* (1960), ch. 4, 'Ralegh and *Love's Labour's Lost*', should also be read,

though the stress they place on Ralegh is, I believe, something of a red herring. The alternative argument – that the play has no topical dimension at all – is equally venerable. In the notes to his edition of Shakespeare (1765), Dr Johnson was 'inclined to doubt' that Holofernes was Florio, 'notwithstanding the plausibility of Dr Warburton's conjecture'. The sceptics' case is too often founded on a bardolatrous premise that Shakespeare would not 'descend' to personal satire. See, e.g., Anne Barton, 'A Source for *Love's Labour's Lost*', *Times Literary Supplement*, 24 November 1978: 'it no longer seems necessary to justify the play in terms of its supposed topical allusions'.

14 See Spens, pp. 333–4, Yates, *A Study of 'Love's Labour's Lost'*, pp. 9, 173, 201, on Strange and Navarre. After September 1593, Strange's full title was Prince Ferdinand, Earl of Derby, King of the Isle of Man, Viscount Kenton, Baron Stanley of Lathom, Strange of Knocking, Mohun of Dunster, Lacy, Woodville and Bassett. See Abraham Darcie and Thomas St Leger, *Honors and Vertues Monument* (1633), an elegy on Strange's daughter, Elizabeth.

15 HMC Salisbury IV 346; Shakespeare, *Loves Labors Lost*, IV i 22, 31–3. Dover Wilson and David both interpret the passage as a 'direct allusion to the conversion of Henry IV'.

16 Stephenson to Richard Hesketh, 28 November 1593, HMC Salisbury IV 424.

17 In the surviving text, the name Ferdinand does not appear in the dialogue. Both quarto (1598) and folio (1623) have the name in the stage directions and speech headings of I i, and the speech headings of II i 126–54. Elsewhere the headings are 'Navar' or 'Nav.', and 'King'. On the evidences of revision, see Dover Wilson's 'The Copy for *Love's Labour's Lost*, 1598 and 1623', pp. 98–135 of the Cambridge edition, and David's introduction to the Arden edition, pp. xviii–xxiii.

18 Shakespeare, *Loves Labors Lost*, I i 1–159.

19 On the Durham House set, see sources referred to in ch. 8, n. 23 above. The best-known study of Ralegh and *Loves Labors* – Bradbrook's *The School of Night* – is marred by distortions and vagueness. It is true that rumours persisted about Ralegh's 'schoole' after his disgrace and exile, and it was not until March 1594 that the commission to investigate his beliefs convened, at Cerne Abbas. Its findings were laughably tame, however, and Ralegh's circle in Dorset was, apart from Hariot, decidedly non-intellectual. As a type, the Ralegh *coterie* was doubtless in Shakespeare's mind, but more topical sting attaches to Strange in 1593, especially in view of the Catholic overtone suitable for Southampton. In supposing a hypothetical 'Strange *coterie*', one is merely shifting figure-heads from Ralegh to Strange: the main luminaries – Northumberland, Hariot, Chapman, etc. – remain constants. Strange *may* have been an original member of the Durham House set anyway. It is frequently stated that he was, but this is a syllogistic deduction from the Chapman preface. There is no actual evidence at all to link Strange with Ralegh.

20 Shakespeare, *Loves Labors Lost*, IV iii 330–1, 297–8, 290–1, I ii 15–16; Chapman, *The Shadow of Night*, in *Works*, pp. 3, 8; TN I 244.

21 Fleay, 'Shakespeare and Puritanism' (*Anglia*, 1884, VII, 223–31), was the first to identify Nashe as Moth, though he dated the play *c.* 1590 and thought the context was the Marprelate controversy. His identification has been consistently accepted since – '*aut Nashe aut nullus*', as Dover Wilson puts it – with the context realigned to 1592–3. Weighing up the current interpretations of the play, David (AS, p. xli) says that 'the key' to its

interrelations – 'if we could only grasp it' – is 'that elusive and engaging person Thomas Nashe'.

22 Shakespeare, *Loves Labors Lost*, I ii 8f, 137–41; III i 25, 82; IV ii 84; V i 66–7, 107f; V ii 579f. Cf. RG XII 144; GH II 75, 91.

23 Ibid., III i 82–95, I ii 149–53.

24 J. Dover Wilson, Cambridge edition, p. xiv.

25 Shakespeare, *Loves Labors Lost*, III i 9–20.

26 On the *commedia dell'arte* influence on the play, see bibliography under Campbell, and Yates, *A Study of 'Love's Labour's Lost'*, ch. 10, 'The Characters of *Love's Labour's Lost* and Italian Comedy'. The Harveian aspects of Armado, noticed by many critics, have been overshadowed by arguments that Armado = Ralegh and that Holofernes rather than Armado is the portrait of Harvey. Taylor's full analysis of the allusions to Harvey and Nashe is weakened by his attempt to date the play after *Have with you* (1596), an unnecessary inference. Stern, p. 145n., describes Armado as 'a character in some but not all respects suggestive of Harvey'. The *prima facie* case for Antonio Perez is strong – a real-life fantastical Spaniard known in England in the early 1590s – but the point is surely to make Harvey a Spaniard *like* Perez, just as Nashe compares him to a similar court buffoon, the Italian, Monarcho. Perez is part of the caricature, not its subject.

27 Shakespeare, *Loves Labors Lost*, I i 165–8, IV i 99–101, V i 9–13, 16–19; TN I 176.

28 TN I 257, 276, 317; II 181; III 76–9, 135. On Monarcho see TN IV 339 and the commentators on *Loves Labors Lost*, IV i 100.

29 TN I 298; Thomas Fuller, *History of the Worthies of England* (1662), 'Warwickshire', p. 126.

30 TN III 91–2.

31 TN III 38, 93; Shakespeare, *Loves Labors Lost*, V ii 631–2.

32 TN III 80; JL III 408.

33 TN I 257, 309, 317, 322; Shakespeare, *Loves Labors Lost*, IV i 95–6, I i 189–92.

34 TN I 265, 316; Shakespeare, *Loves Labors Lost*, V i 19–23; Stern, pp. 144–7; GH I 103–5.

35 Shakespeare, *Loves Labors Lost*, V i 31; GH I xxxv.

36 Shakespeare, *Loves Labors Lost*, V ii 653–5. Two other antagonists whom Gabriel 'vilely dealt with' after their death were Dr Andrew Perne and Marlowe (TN II 180–1).

37 Shakespeare, *Loves Labors Lost*, IV i 145–6, 148–9.

38 See Yates, *A Study of 'Love's Labour's Lost'*, pp. 13–17, 27–49. De Chambrun, *Giovanni Florio* (1921), p. 127, was the first to spot the anagram. Another confirmatory anagram may lurk in the text. Holofernes' baffling doggerel about the deer-hunt concludes with the lines, 'Of one sore I an hundred make by adding but one more l'. If we treat this as a clue, and follow its directions, we add the letter 'l' to 'of one sore I' and get an anagram of 'Iones Floreo'. This, we are told, makes a hundred sores – a pun, perhaps, on 'saws' or proverbs. This would be apt for Florio, whose *Second Fruites* (1591) appeared together with his *Gardine of Recreations*, containing 'six thousand Italian proverbs'. One of his 'saws' in the *First Fruites* provided Shakespeare's title; another, '*Venetia, chi non ti vede, non ti pretia*', is quoted by Holofernes. Shakespeare's riddle thus spells out Florio and calls him 'the man of a hundred saws'. Supposed Shakespearean anagrams have shored up some extremely silly arguments and no real weight

can be attached to them, but to find *two* anagrams of one name in a topical play seems worthy of comment.

39 Florio, *A Worlde of Wordes* (1598), 'Address to the Reader'; Arthur Collins, *Letters and Memorials of State collected by Sir Henry Sydney* (1746), II 215 (letter from Rowland Whyte to Sir Robert Sidney, 26 September 1600).

40 TN II 11, III 147; Yates, *John Florio*, pp. 192f.

41 It is assumed that Harvey wrote the *New Letter*, dated 16 September, from Saffron Walden. He was, at any rate, somewhere outside London. He must have left town sometime after 16 July, when he signed the prefatory epistle of *Pierces Supererogation* 'at London'.

42 Rowse, *Shakespeare the Man*, pp. 56–7, observes: 'the proofs [of *Venus* and *Lucrece*] were very well corrected, and no doubt the poet was in and out of Blackfriars'.

43 On the Shakespeare coat of arms and its subsequent controversies, see Schoenbaum, pp. 166–73; Stephen Tucker, *The Assignment of Arms to Shakespere and Arden, 1596–1599* (1884). Chettle's complimentary remarks about Shakespeare (*Kind Harts Dreame*, 'To the Gentleman Readers') followed some protest by Shakespeare about the slur on him in Greene's *Groatsworth*, which Chettle had prepared for the press.

15   A SILENCE

1 TN III 25.

2 The copyright on *Pierce* was transferred from John Busby to Nicholas Ling some time after the 4th edition (1593) appeared. The printer of the 5th edition, 'T.C.', is probably Thomas Creede. On the relation between the two editions of *The Unfortunate Traveller*, see TN II 189–97.

3 TN III 26, I 375.

4 Lewis, p. 414; TN I 384; II 89.

5 TN III 18–19, 30–1.

6 TN III 108. Nashe dates Sir Roger's kindness to him 'a yeare and a halfe before his death', which was in December 1595. On Williams, see DNB, Dover Wilson, 'Martin Marprelate and Shakespeare's Fluellen', pp. 148–50.

7 See TN III 107–8; Carey, p. 32. On Arundel House, see Stow, II 92, 97; Prockter and Taylor, Map 17 F5. Lodge's dedication of *Rosalynde* to Lord Hunsdon (ed. Greg, p. xxvii) speaks of his friendship with both Robert and Edmund Carey at Oxford.

8 Baskerville was 'daily expected' at Plymouth on 16 July, but had not yet arrived. He was there twelve days later, when he wrote to the Privy Council. See CSP (Dom Eliz) 1595–7, vol. CCLIII, nos 19, 41. The expedition sailed on 27 August.

9 TN III 76–7; Yates, *Giordano Bruno and the Hermetic Tradition*, pp. 235f.

10 GH II 41–2.

11 GH II 229–30, TN III 114–15. For Danter's address see various editions of *Strange Newes* (not the 1st): 'Iohn Danter, dwelling in Hosier Lane neere Holburne Conduit'. This locates the printing-house down the western end of the street. See Prockter and Taylor, Map 6 J3–4, where Holborn conduit is Well W15.

12 TN II 148, III 285; Stow, II 28–33 *et passim*.

13 Ben Jonson, *Bartholmew Fayre*, Induction 135–6, 144–5; *The Alchemist*, I i 25–6; TN III 101.

14 On correction in the printing-house, see McKerrow, *Introduction to Biblio-*

graphy for Literary Students, pp. 205–8, 240f; Sheavyn, pp. 103–4. McKerrow quotes the informative letter from publisher William Jaggard, prefaced to Augustine Vincent, *Discoverie of Errours* (1622). On Ubaldini, see Hoppe, pp. 242–3. In the first edition of Sidney's *Arcadia* (1590), 'the division and summing of the chapters was not of Sir Philip Sidneis dooing, but adventured by the over-seer of the Print, for the more ease of the Readers'. The 'overseer' was probably Florio. See Yates, *John Florio*, pp. 194–209, and ch. 7 above.

15 TN III 89, 96; Leishman (ed.), *2 Returne*, 139–46. Stern, p. 101, notes that the Bodleian copy of *Perimedes* has 'proof reader's corrections in a hand that resembles Harvey's'.

16 See SR for Danter's entries of *Titus Andronicus* (6 February 1594), Lodge's *Wounds of Civil War* (24 May 1594), Watson's *Tears of Fancy* (11 August 1593). Danter held the copyright on Greene's *Orlando Furioso* till December 1593, when he assigned it to John Busby, retaining the right to print it (SR II 650). He later printed the first quarto of *Romeo and Juliet* (1597): see ch. 16 below.

17 The Strange ballad was licensed on 26 April 1594, ten days after his death. Danter had earlier published 'Lankeshiers Lamentacon for the Deathe of the noble Erle of Derbie', i.e. Henry, 4th Earl, Strange's father. On *Marie Magdalenes Love*, see DNB, s.v. Breton. The work is a prose commentary on St John X 1–18.

18 On the seizure of Danter's press, see SR I 580. On *Iesus Psalter*, see Southern, *English Martyrs*, pp. 413–14, 523–6. *Certaine Devout and Godly Petitions commonly called Iesus Psalter* was first published by the Catholic exile, John Fowler (Antwerp, 1575). It is sometimes known as 'Fowler's Psalter'. Another edition appeared in 1599: its Calais imprint probably disguises a secret press in England. The 'Wholesome Doctrine' is sigs D5v–7v of the 1575 edition.

19 Lyly's Second Petition (1598), BM Harleian MS 1323, f. 250; JL I 70–1.

20 TN III 137–9, 105–7.

21 Dekker, *A Knights Conjuring* (1607), sig. L1v. Nashe printed Chettle's letter in *Have with you* (TN III 131). Harvey had said (GH II 322) that Nashe 'odiously misuseth every frend', naming 'M. Apis Lapis' (Beeston), Greene, Marlowe and Chettle as injured parties. Nashe's description of *Greenes Groatsworth*, which Chettle had edited, as a 'scald, trivial, lying pamphlet' (TN I 154) may have been in Harvey's mind, but in general his charge is idle.

22 TN III 147–50, 'To his worthie good patron, Lustie Humfrey'; Anthony Chute, *Tabaco* (1595), sigs A2–A3, 'To the Heroicall minded Gentleman, Maister Humphrey King'. See Kane, pp. 152, 156–8. The *Tabaco* dedication was actually written by the printer, Adam Islip, following Chute's last 'immutable decree' before he died.

23 Humfrey King, *The Hermits Tale* (1613), sig. B2. This, the 3rd impression, is the earliest extant. When Nashe wrote the *Lenten Stuffe* dedication, in early 1599, he was 'expecting your sacred Poeme of the *Hermites Tale*, that will restore the golden age amongst us' (III 150). This suggests imminent publication, though it must have appeared after *Lenten Stuffe*, which the prefatory sonnet refers to ('the red Herring').

24 TN III 32, 220.

25 TN III 110. In the 'Epigrammatum Liber' in Campion's *Poemata*, 'Ad Nashum' is epigram 88; 'Ad Ge. Chapmannum' is epigram 94; and 'In Barnum' is epigram 80.

26 TN III 7, 92–3, 95. 'Beechfeeld' is now Bitchfield. Lord Burghley's family seat, Burghley House, was a few miles from Stamford. Nashe could conceivably have travelled there on business. Lord Strange's brother, William, married Burghley's granddaughter in January 1595; Sir Robert Carey's property dispute with his brother John was adjudicated by Burghley around this time. These are shots in the dark.

27 William Covell, *Polimanteia* (1595), sigs Q4–Q4v.

28 TN III 63.

29 Joseph Hall, *Virgidemiarum* (1597), I ix, Vi i. See Salyer, pp. 154, 168, TN Supp. 78.

30 TN III 368.

31 Rhodes, p. 70. On the dating and authorship of the *Parnassus Plays*, see Leishman's introduction, pp. 24–34. On Gwyn, see Reyburn and Thomas, 'A Note on Owen Gwyn', PMLA LXXVI (1961), pp. 298–300.

32 Leishman (ed.), *1 Returne*, 142–382. On Ingenioso and Nashe, see Leishman's introduction, pp. 71–9, TN V 149. The character of Luxurio contains touches of Harvey.

33 Leishman (ed.), *1 Returne*, 835–1040, 1101–1215, 1353–1474; introduction, pp. 80–2.

34 Ibid., *2 Returne*, 337–51. Cf. TN I 287, 306, III 35, 330.

35 Ibid., *1 Returne*, 165–71, 203–12, 235–7, 249–53, 269–71; *2 Returne*, 87–8, 158, 332–5, 1575–6, 1580–1.

36 The dedication is TN III 5–17.

37 *St John's College Rentals*, 1575–99, f. 266r; Brewer, *Dictionary of Phrase and Fable*, pp. 77–8.

38 Lichfield's will, at least, was proved in that year: see *Calendar to Cambridge Wills, 1501–1765*, p. 51. This seems to be the only documentary record of Lichfield. Unlike the *St John's College Rentals*, where we hear of 'George the goldsmith', 'Ellis the chaundler', etc., the Trinity College Muniments do not identify College servants by name. I am grateful to Mr Trevor Kaye of Trinity College library for help in tracing Lichfield.

39 On Williamson, see Harvey's undated letter (*c.* 1579?) in *Letter Book*, p. 71. In a letter to Spenser (GH I 79) Harvey speaks of discriminating between 'learned and unlearned, Tully and Tom Tooly'.

40 Lichfield styles himself 'Don Richardo de Medico Campo', a rebus for Richard Leech-field (*medicus* = doctor = 'leech'). The bulk of the *Trimming* was 'bred in Lent' (*c.* March 1597), but a passage dealing with Nashe's *Isle of Dogs* (sigs E4v–G1v, GH II 51–63) must have been added in August or later. The *Trimming* was registered on 11 October 1597. See TN V 107–9, 175.

41 GH III 13–14, 37, 42.

42 See Partridge, *A Dictionary of Historical Slang*, s.v. 'French crown'; *Shakespeare's Bawdy*, s.v. 'piled for a French velvet'. The latter phrase (*Measure for Measure*, I ii 33–5) puns on pile = nap of velvet and = haemorrhoid. Nashe's 'pild Friers crownes' refers to syphilitic eructations, as well as to loss of hair from syphilis.

43 TN III 33. Perhaps this is why Lichfield says, 'his [Nashe's] Epistle I expected any time these three yeares' (GH III 5). This would give us *c.* 1594 as the date of Lichfield's 'macaronicall' rendition of *Pierce*.

44 GH III 13, 28; OED, s.v. 'macaronic'; Brewer, *Dictionary of Phrase*, pp. 668–9. 'Choroebus' = '*chori bos*' = 'the very bull-heade of all the troope of pamphleters'.

45 Nashe was 'forty mile off from' Lichfield when he wrote the dedication (TN

III 17), which strongly suggests he was back in London. According to Harrison, the London–Cambridge road was 44 miles via Ware or 46 miles via Saffron Walden (TN IV 310).

46 TN III 151, 153.

47 Leishman (ed.), *2 Returne*, 118–20. The author mentions 'Leichfildes trimming of Nashe', as well as other satires – Lodge's *Fig for Momus* (1595), Marston's *Scourge of Villany* (1598) and Bastard's *Chrestoleros* (1598). See *Pilgrimage*, 209–12. So as not to polarize the factions too rigidly, the *Parnassus* author was an admirer of Joseph Hall (see introduction, pp. 52, 57, 82–92), though efforts to credit Hall with part-authorship of the plays seem dubious.

48 On Smythe, see DNB, TN Supp. 56. His suppressed tract – *Discourses concerning divers sorts of Weapons* (1590) – is probably the work in praise of 'the browne bill and the long bowe' mentioned by Nashe in *Lenten Stuffe* (TN III 177). Nashe's blotted lines are partly deciphered, as given here, by W. W. Greg, *English Literary Autographs, 1550–1650*, I xx.

49 An earlier pun on Ajax and 'jakes' is in Shakespeare's *Loves Labors Lost*, V ii 571–2. Nashe captions the woodcut of Harvey in *Have with you* (TN III 38), 'Gabriell Harvey, as hee is readie to let fly upon Aiax'. Harington was banned from court after the *Metamorphosis* appeared, but the Queen is said to have installed a Harington privy in Richmond Palace.

50 TN III 77; CSP (Dom Eliz) 1595–7, p. 289.

51 TN III 18, 32.

52 TN III 20–3.

53 See DNB, s.v. Cotton. Cotton was consulted as an expert on precedents in 1600, to decide the precedence of the English and Spanish ambassadors at the Anglo-Spanish talks at Calais, and by Henry Howard, Earl of Northampton, in 1602.

54 TN III 133.

16   THE *ISLE OF DOGS* AFFAIR

1 GH III 43–50. The passage dealing with Nashe's imprisonment is from the earlier section of the *Trimming*, composed during Lent 1597. The later section describes Nashe as on the run, rather than in prison, following *The Isle of Dogs*. See ch. 15, n. 40 above. Lichfield's information is authentic as to Nashe's Cambridge career (III 67–8) and his authorship of *The Choise of Valentines* ('your Dildoe', III 63).

2 G. B. Harrison (ed.), *Romeo and Juliet* (Penguin, 1953), p. 18.

3 The documentary sources relating to *The Isle of Dogs* are few. (1) Privy Council *communiqué* to Topcliffe *et al.*, 15 August 1597, *Privy Council Register*, XXII 346 (APC XXVII 338). (2) Council warrant for release of Jonson, Spenser and Shaa, 2 October 1597, *Privy Council Register*, XXIII 13 (APC XXVIII 33). (3) Nashe's own account in *Lenten Stuffe*, TN III 153–4. (4) Jonson's letter to Cecil, undated (1605), *Cecil Papers*, CXIV 58 (BJ I 194–6). That Topcliffe was the official who initiated proceedings against the play is shown by his letter to Cecil, 10 August 1597, recommending an unnamed bearer as 'the first man that discovered to me that seditious play called *The Isle of Dogs*' (HMC Salisbury VII 343). On the Pembroke's Men as the players involved, see Chambers, ES, III 453–5: Spenser and Shaa were definitely with this troupe earlier in 1597. Though Nashe was involved with the Chamberlain's Men in 1596, they were apparently playing at the

Theatre in Shoreditch in summer 1597, whereas *The Isle of Dogs* was played at one of the theatres on the 'Bancke side'.

4 APC XXVII 313; ES IV 321–3; Henslowe, I 203.

5 BJ I 139, XI 573–4; Eccles, 'Jonson and the Spies'. Herford's original assumption (BJ I 18–19), that the imprisonment referred to was Jonson's spell in 1598 for the killing of Spenser, is superseded by Eccles' article.

6 TN III 175–6.

7 TN I 280–1.

8 Jonson *et al.*, *Eastward Hoe*, IV i 133–171. His co-authors were John Marston and George Chapman. Letters from Jonson and Chapman, relating to their imprisonment in mid-1605, are extant: see BJ I 190–200; Petter (ed.), *Eastward Ho!* (1973), Appendix III. Jonson said that Sir James Murray, probably one of the knights jested at, 'delated' him to the King. See BJ I 140, 164.

9 TN III 257–8. Lee (DNB, s.v. Nashe) suggests that this passage was inserted after the *Isle of Dogs* affair – *Summers Last Will* was not published till 1600 – but there is no evidence to support this. The comment arises naturally out of the dialogue on dogs between Orion and Summer.

10 GH III 58–9; TN III 253–4, cf. I 20, III 256–7, IV 21; Brewer, *Dictionary of Phrase*, pp. 332–3. The particular date of the dog days was 3–11 July.

11 On the dearth, see Stow, *Annales*, pp. 768–9, 782–4; Dodd, p. 137; Black, pp. 409–10; TN III 84, 136; Shakespeare, *Midsummer Night's Dream*, II i 82f. On the Poor Law (1598), see Black, pp. 265–7; E. M. Leonard, *The Early History of English Poor Relief* (1900).

12 TN III 260.

13 TN III 84, IV 343. On Deloney, see A. Chevalley, *Thomas Deloney* (1926); *Works*, ed. Mann (1967). He wrote several ballads, as well as *Jack of Newbury* and *Thomas of Reading*, often classed along with *The Unfortunate Traveller* as early 'novels'. He died poor in 1600.

14 Leishman (ed.), 2 *Returne*, 2062–2223.

15 Spenser, *Faerie Queene*, Book VI, xii 33; cf. i 7ff. See Leishman's notes on the correspondences between Canto xii and Ingenioso's speech.

16 Jonson to Cecil, *c.* May–September 1605, BJ I 195.

17 Cecil to Carey, 25 July 1596; Jeayes, p. 334.

18 On the dating of *1 Henry IV* and the Falstaff–Oldcastle connections, see A. R. Humphreys (ed.), *1 Henry IV* (AS, 1960), pp. xi–xxi; Dover Wilson, 'The Origins and Development of Shakespeare's *Henry IV*'; Hotson, *Shakespeare's Sonnets Dated*, pp. 147–60; Clark, p. 242f; Scoufos.

19 Richard James to Sir Henry Bourchier, *c.* 1625, Bodleian MS James 34. A facsimile of the letter is in Schoenbaum, p. 143. James was Robert Cotton's librarian.

20 Shakespeare, *2 Henry IV*, Epilogue 30–2; Nicholas Rowe, *Works of Shakespeare* (1709), I viii; Scoufos, p. 307.

21 On the date and venue of *The Merry Wives*, see ch. 13, n. 60 above.

22 HMC Penshurst II 243, 448, 459.

23 Letter from Essex to Cecil, *c.* 25 February 1598, cited Hotson, *Shakespeare's Sonnets Dated*, p. 148; letter from Rowland Whyte to Sir Robert Sidney, 8 March 1600, HMC Penshurst II 446; performance of 'ould Castel' by the King's Men at court, 29 May 1639, cited Chambers, *William Shakespeare*, II 353. Munday's co-authors in *The true and honorable Historie of the Life of Sir John Oldcastle* were Drayton, Hathaway and Wilson. The play was acted by the Admiral's Men in 1599 and published in 1600.

24 See Scoufos, pp. 319–23, for a full account of Jonson's allusions to Cobham.

25 TN III 153.
26 Scoufos, pp. 310–11; Florio, *A Worlde of Wordes*, p. 152; OED, s.v. 'cob', 'miller's thumb'. The 'Falstaff' and 'cob' motifs are linked in a letter from the Countess of Southampton to her husband, 8 July 1599, HMC Salisbury XV 175–6. Apparently referring to the birth of a son to Cobham, she says 'Sir John Falstaff is by his Mrs Dame Pintpot made father to a godly milers thum, a boy that is all heade and veri litel body'. See Stopes, p. 160.
27 TN III 167–8; Scoufos, p. 313.
28 TN III 208.
29 Scoufos, pp. 307–8, 315–16. The Protestant propagandist view of Oldcastle was most easily accessible to Shakespeare and his contemporaries in Holinshed's *Chronicles* (1585), a favourite source-book, dedicated to William, Lord Cobham. The older Catholic version survived in Stow's *Annales* (1592), pp. 550–1, as well as in his edition of Walsingham.
30 See Schoenbaum, pp. 41–50; Rowse, *Shakespeare's Globe*, pp. 180f; J. H. de Groot, *The Shakespeares and 'the Old Faith'* (1946); Peter Milward, *Shakespeare's Religious Background* (1973).
31 BJ I 139, 141, 151, 220–3. Entries in the *Book of Corrections or Presentments of the Consistory Court of London, 1605–6*, ff. 23v, 321v, 329, 334v, cite Benjamin and Anne Jonson for failing to attend 'divyne servis', and the former as 'a seducer of youthe to popishe religion'. In 1619 Drummond described Jonson as 'for any religion, as being versed in both'.
32 See bibliography under Burgoyne. The collection mainly comprises minor works by Francis Bacon, including his *Advertisement touching the Controversies of the Church of England*, written during the Marprelate controversy. The name 'Nevill' occurs twice on the contents page, which is full of scrawls and broken phrases. Burgoyne suggests the collection was compiled for Bacon's nephew, Sir Henry Neville. Of the pieces included to which a date of composition can be assigned, *The Isle of Dogs* is the latest. The compilation may date back as far as 1597: some of the *Baconiana* included were published in this year and it is unlikely they would be copied out in MS if available in print.
33 On *Richard II* and the Essex rebellion, see Schoenbaum, pp. 158–60. The Chamberlain's Men received 40 pieces of silver from one of the conspirators, Sir Gilly Meyrick, for their performance in May 1601. The 'Earl of Arundells letter to the Queen', now also missing from the collection, is presumably that of April 1585, printed in Pollen, *The Venerable Philip Howard, Earl of Arundel*, pp. 99–108. There are many extant MSS of this eloquent Catholic complaint.
34 On Stubbes, see Sutherland, *Oxford Book of Literary Anecdotes*, pp. 8–9. On Vallenger, see Southern, pp. 279–82, 376–9; TN I 297. His 'slanderous libels' were Alfield's *True Report of the Martyrdom of M. Campion* (1582), which he helped to print. On the seditious 'placards' – the 'Dutch Church libel' which Kyd found himself involved in – see APC XXIV 222.
35 TN II 319.
36 GH III 51, 53, 61.
37 TN III 154.

17 LENTEN STUFF

1 BJ I 218; ES I 299.
2 TN III 153. It is also to be noted that Nashe says, complaining of his lack

of note-books, 'had I my topickes by me instead of my learned counsell to assist me . . .' (TN III 176). This suggests he was still under threat of legal reprisals in 1598.

3 TN III 151–3, 176.

4 Meres, *Palladis Tamia* (1598), sigs Oo6–Oo6v.

5 Steane, p. 14; TN III 151, 156.

6 TN III 160–1, IV 372–3. A transcript of this *tabula* is given by Thomas Hearne in his edition of Leland's *Collectanea* (1770), VI 285–8. He describes the table as hanging '*in Aula communi*', which agrees with Nashe rather than Camden. Palmer describes it as 'written in black letter with rubricated initials, painted on folding boards'.

7 TN III 174; Manshyp senior, p. 8.

8 TN III 174. On Henry Manshyp junior, see TN IV 373, and Palmer's introduction to his edition of Manshyp's *History of Great Yarmouth*.

9 TN III 166, 170.

10 Manshyp junior, p. 120. The 'catalogue' he refers to, and quotes from, is the concluding sentence of *Lenten Stuffe*, TN III 226.

11 The description of Great Yarmouth is TN III 156–75.

12 TN III 156, 181–3, 185.

13 TN III 179–80, 183, 191, 221.

14 TN III 185, 189, 194–5, 221.

15 TN III 151, 176, 178, 226.

16 TN III 225.

17 The phrasing at the end of the preface – he is 'cald away to correct the faultes of the presse' – shows he was in London when he wrote it. The faults had 'escaped in my absence from the Printing-house', which may suggest that the MS of *Lenten Stuffe* had been sent to Burby, and that printing had commenced while Nashe was still out of town. The Lent law term usually ended on 12–13 February. Nashe describes the bulk of the pamphlet as having been composed 'the last Lent' (i.e. 1598) which is further evidence that the preface was written at least before the end of Lent 1599 (i.e. Easter day, which fell on 8 April). While the indications are that Nashe *expected* the pamphlet to appear before the end of Lent term, the date on the title-page shows (assuming old-style dating) that it did not actually appear till after 26 March. This does not affect the probable date of composition for the preface.

18 SR III 677.

19 TN III 154, 175, 219.

20 See TN V 140–1.

21 Garzoni, sigs A2–A2v, a2. The collation of the text is curious, with 'Not to the Wise Reader' appearing on two leaves (a1–a2v) which look like a late insertion.

22 Ibid., sigs A3–A3v, A4v, P1–P1v, O1.

23 On Blount, see McKerrow, *Dictionary of Printers*, s.v. On Danter's death, see SR III 54, where 'Widowe Danter' has dealings re the copyright of *Tom o Lincoln*.

24 CM II 279, 430. The copyright of both *Hero and Leander* and *Lucan* originally belonged to John Wolfe (SR 28 September 1593). He seems to have transferred the rights to Blount, though no record remains of this. See W. W. Greg, 'The Copyright of *Hero and Leander*', *The Library* (4th series), XXIV 165f.

25 Nashe's version is TN III 195–201. On the Linley edition, see CM II 425.

Chapman contributed the last four of the poem's six sestiads and an obscurely worded dedication to Lady Walsingham.

26 TN III 147; Florio, *A Worlde of Wordes* (1598), 'Address to the Reader'. The marjoram refers to the emblem chosen by Sanford for the 1593 *Arcadia*. See Yates, *John Florio*, p. 194; Corbett and Lightbown, p. 65.

27 Charles Fitzgeffrey, *Affaniae*, sig. N3.

28 G. C. Moore-Smith, *Times Literary Supplement*, 10 May 1917, p. 225.

29 BM Sloane MS 1489 f. 23.

30 Middleton, *Father Hubburds Tales*, sig. B3v.

31 Dekker, *Newes from Hell*, sigs C2–C2v; *A Knights Conjuring*, sig. K4v–L1.

32 *The Workes of Iosephus* (1602), *A Treatise of the Plague* (1603), and *A Learned Summary of du Bartas* (1625) are among Lodge's later works. He may be the 'Dr T Lodge' who is in debt to the actor Edward Alleyn in 1619 (see DNB).

33 Stern, pp. 130–4. *Pedantius* was licensed on 9 February 1631, two days after Harvey's death, two days before his burial.

BIBLIOGRAPHY

1 Collections and Serials

TN   *The Works of Thomas Nashe*, ed. Ronald B. McKerrow, revised with supplementary notes by F. P. Wilson, 5 vols (Oxford, 1958).

GTN   *The Complete Works of Thomas Nashe*, ed. Alexander B. Grosart, 6 vols (London, 1883–5).

GH   *The Works of Gabriel Harvey DCL*, ed. Alexander B. Grosart, 3 vols (London, 1884–5).

RG   *The Life and Complete Works in Prose and Verse of Robert Greene MA*, ed. Alexander B. Grosart, 15 vols (London, 1881–6).

CM   *The Complete Works of Christopher Marlowe*, ed. Fredson Bowers, 2 vols (Cambridge, 1973).

JL   *The Complete Works of John Lyly*, ed. R. Warwick Bond, 3 vols (London, 1888–90).

BJ   *Ben Jonson*, ed. C. H. Herford, Percy and Evelyn Simpson, 11 vols (Oxford, 1925–52).

AS   *The Arden Shakespeare*, ed. various (London, 1899–).

SR   *A Transcript of the Registers of the Company of Stationers of London*, ed. Edward Arber, 5 vols (London, 1875–94).

ES   *The Elizabethan Stage*, by E. K. Chambers, 4 vols (Oxford, 1923).

APC   *Acts of the Privy Council, 1542–1604*, ed. J. R. Dasent, 32 vols (London, 1890–1907).

CSP   Calendar of State Papers
HMC   Historical Manuscripts Commission
VCH   Victoria County Histories
DNB   Dictionary of National Biography
OED   Oxford English Dictionary
RES   Review of English Studies
PMLA   Publications of the Modern Language Association of America
NQ   Notes and Queries
MLN   Modern Language Notes
MLQ   Modern Language Quarterly
MLR   Modern Language Review
SP   Studies in Philology
EETS   Early English Text Society
EHR   English Historical Review
PQ   Philology Quarterly

2   Select Sources

Akrigg, G. P. V., *Shakespeare and the Earl of Southampton* (London, 1968).

Allen, J. W., *A History of Political Thought in the Sixteenth Century* (London, 1949; revised 1960).

Anon., *The Parnassus Plays* – see Leishman.

Arber, Edward, *An Introductory Sketch to the Martin Marprelate Controversy* (London, 1895).

Aubrey, John, *Brief Lives*, ed. Oliver Lawson Dick (London, 1949).

Bakeless, John, *The Tragical History of Christopher Marlowe*, 2 vols (Cambridge, Mass., 1942).

Bald, R. C., *John Donne: A Life* (Oxford, 1970).

Bancroft, Richard, *Tracts ascribed to Richard Bancroft*, ed. Albert Peel (Cambridge, 1953).

Berryman, John, 'Thomas Nashe and *The Unfortunate Traveller*', in *The Freedom of the Poet* (New York, 1977).

Black, J. B., *The Reign of Queen Elizabeth* (Oxford, 1959).

Blomefield, Francis, *A Topographical History of the County of Norfolk*, 11 vols (London, 1805–10).

Boas, Frederick S., *Marlowe and his Circle* (Oxford, 1929).

Bradbrook, Muriel, *The School of Night: a Study in the Literary Relationships of Sir Walter Ralegh* (Cambridge, 1936).

Brenan, G., *History of the House of Percy* (London, 1902).

Burgoyne, Frank J., *Collotype Facsimile and Type Transcript of an Elizabethan Manuscript preserved at Alnwick Castle* (London, 1904).

Bullough, Geoffrey, *Narrative and Dramatic Sources of Shakespeare*, vol 1 (London, 1957).

Byrne, Muriel St Clare, *Elizabethan Life in Town and Country* (London, 1941).

Campbell, O. J., '*Love's Labour's Lost* Re-studied', in *Studies in Shakespeare, Milton and Donne* (Michigan, 1925), pp. 3f.

Campion, Thomas, *Poems*, ed. Perceval Vivian (Oxford, 1909).

Caraman, Philip, *The Other Face: Catholic Life under Elizabeth I* (London, 1960).

Carey, John, *John Donne: Life, Mind and Art* (London, 1981).

Carey, Sir Robert, *Memoirs*, ed. F. H. Mares (Oxford, 1972).

Chambers, E. K., *William Shakespeare*, 2 vols (Oxford, 1930).

Chambrun, Clara Longworth de, *Giovanni Florio* (London, 1921).

Chapman, George, *Works*, ed. A. C. Swinburne (London, 1875).

Chettle, Henry, *Kind Harts Dreame* (1592), ed. G. B. Harrison (London, 1923).

Clark, Eleanor Grace, *Ralegh and Marlowe: a Study in Elizabethan Fustian* (New York, 1941).

Collins, John Cherton, *The Plays and Poems of Robert Greene*, 2 vols (Oxford, 1905).

Cooper, C. H., *Annals of Cambridge*, 5 vols (Cambridge, 1842–1908).

Cooper, C. H. and T., *Athenae Cantabrigienses*, 2 vols (Cambridge, 1858–61).

Corbett, Margery, and Lightbown, R. W., *The Comely Frontispiece: the Emblematic Titlepage in England 1550–1660* (London, 1979).

Crosten, A. K., 'The Use of Imagery in Nashe's *The Unfortunate Traveller*', RES XXIV (1948), pp. 90f.

Cunnington, C. Willet and Phillis, *A Handbook of English Costume in the Sixteenth Century* (London, 1970).

Dodd, A. H., *Life in Elizabethan England* (London, 1961).

Donne, John, *The Poems*, ed. H. J. C. Grierson, 2 vols (Oxford, 1912).

Duff, E. Gordon, *A Century of the English Book Trade* (London, 1905).

Eccles, Mark, *Christopher Marlowe in London* (Cambridge, Mass., 1934).

Eccles, Mark, 'Barnabe Barnes', in Sisson, pp. 165f.

Eccles, Mark, 'Sir George Buc, Master of the Revels', in Sisson, pp. 409f.

Eccles, Mark, 'Jonson and the Spies', RES XIII (1937), pp. 385f.

Eliot, John, *The Parlement of Pratlers*, abridged reprint of *Ortho-epia Gallica* (1593), ed. Jack Lindsay (London, 1928).

Evans, R. J. W., *Rudolf II and his World* (Oxford, 1973).

Feasy, Lynette and Eveline, 'Nashe's *The Unfortunate Traveller*: some Marlovian Echoes', *English* VII 39, pp. 125f.

Fleay, F. G., 'Shakespeare and Puritanism', *Anglia* VII (1884), pp. 223f.

Fleay, F. G., *Queen Elizabeth, Croydon and the Drama* (London, 1898).

Floyd-Ewin, David, *St Paul's Cathedral* (London, 1975).

Forester, James, *The Pearle of Practise* (London, 1594).

Garzoni, Tommaso, *The Hospitall of Incurable Fooles* (London, 1600).

Gillingwater, Edmund, *History of Lowestoft* (Lowestoft, 1790).

Gray, Austin K., 'Some Observations on Christopher Marlowe, Government Agent', PMLA (1928), pp. 682f.

Greg, W. W., *English Literary Autographs, 1550–1650*, 2 vols (Oxford, 1925–32).

Greg, W. W., *Marlowe's 'Doctor Faustus', 1604–16* (London, 1950).

Harlow, C. G., 'Thomas Nashe and William Cotton, MP', NQ (November 1961), pp. 424–5.

Harlow, C. G., 'Thomas Nashe, Robert Cotton the Antiquary, and *The Terrors of the Night*', RES XII (1961), pp. 7f.

Harlow, C. G., 'Nashe's Visit to the Isle of Wight and his Publications of 1592–4', RES XIV (1963), pp. 15f.

Harrison, G. B., 'Books and Readers, 1591–4', *The Library* (4th series) VII (1927), pp. 273f.

Harrison, G.B., 'Books and Readers, 1599–1603', *The Library* (4th series) XIV (1933), pp. 1f.

Harrison, William, *A Description of England*, ed. F. J. Furnivall, 3 vols (London, 1877–1908).

Henslowe, Philip, *Diary*, ed. W. W. Greg, 2 vols (London, 1904–8).

Heywood, Thomas, *The Earls of Derby and the Verse Writers of the Sixteenth and Seventeenth Centuries* (Stanley Papers I; Manchester, 1853).

Hibbard, G. R., *Thomas Nashe: a Critical Introduction* (London, 1962).

Holmes, M. R., *Moorfields in 1559* (London, 1963).

Hoppe, Harry R., 'John Wolfe, Printer and Publisher, 1579–1601', *The Library* (4th series) XIV (1933), pp. 241f.

Horne, David H., *The Life and Minor Works of George Peele* (Newhaven, 1952).

Hotson, J. Leslie, *The Death of Christopher Marlowe* (London, 1925).

Hotson, J. Leslie, *Shakespeare versus Shallow* (London, 1931).

Hotson, J. Leslie, *Shakespeare's Sonnets Dated and other Essays* (London, 1949).

Huffman, Clifford Chalmers, 'Gabriel Harvey on John Florio and John Eliot', NQ (July 1975), pp. 300f.

Hunter, G. K., *John Lyly: The Humanist as Courtier* (London, 1962).

Hunter, J. B., '*The Unfortunate Traveller* of Thomas Nash as a Sidelight on Elizabethan Security', NQ (February 1951), pp. 75f.

Jeayes, I. H., *A Catalogue of the Muniments at Berkeley Castle* (London, 1892).

Jenkins, Harold, *The Life and Works of Henry Chettle* (London, 1934).

Johnson, Francis R., 'The First Edition of Gabriel Harvey's *Foure Letters*', *The Library* (4th series) XV (1934), pp. 212f.

Johnson, Francis R., 'Gabriel Harvey's *Three Letters*', *The Library* (5th series) I (1946), pp. 134f.

Jones, Deborah, 'John Lyly at St Bartholomew's', in Sisson, pp. 363f.

Jourdan, John C., *Robert Greene* (New York, 1915).

Judges, A. V., *The Elizabethan Underworld* (London, 1930).

Kane, Robert J., 'Anthony Chute, Thomas Nashe and the first English Work on Tobacco', RES VII (1931), pp. 151f.

Kirschbaum, Leo, *Shakespeare and the Stationers* (Columbus, Ohio, 1955).

Knights, L. C., *Drama and Society in the Age of Jonson* (Harmondsworth, 1962).

Kocher, Paul H., 'Some Nashe Marginalia concerning Marlowe', MLN LVII (1942), pp. 45f.

Kocher, Paul H., 'Nashe's Authorship of the Prose Scenes in *Faustus*', MLQ III (1942), pp. 17f.

Kocher, Paul H., *Christopher Marlowe: A Study of his Thoughts, Learning and Character* (London, 1946).

Lacey, Robert, *Sir Walter Ralegh* (London, 1975).

Latham, Agnes, 'Satire on Literary Themes and Modes in *The Unfortunate Traveller*', *English Studies* (1948), pp. 85f.

Lees, Hugh D. W., *The Chronicles of a Suffolk Parish Church* (Lowestoft, 1949).

Leishman, J. B. (ed.), *The Three Parnassus Plays* (London, 1949).

Lewis, C. S., *English Literature in the Sixteenth Century* (*Oxford History of English Literature*, vol. VII; Oxford, 1954).

Lichfield, Richard, *The Trimming of Thomas Nashe* (London, 1597).

Lodge, Thomas, *Rosalynde* (1590), ed. W. W. Greg (London, 1907).

Lodge, Thomas, *Wits Miserie* (London, 1596).

Longe, Francis D., *Lowestoft in Olden Times* (Lowestoft, n.d.).

McGinn, Donald J., 'The Real Martin Marprelate', PMLA LVIII (1943), pp. 84f.

McGinn, Donald J., 'Nashe's Share in the Marprelate Controversy', PMLA LIX (1944), pp. 952f.

McGinn, Donald J., 'The Allegory of the "Beare" and the "Foxe" in Nashe's *Pierce Penilesse*', PMLA LXI (1946), pp. 431f.

McGinn, Donald J., 'A Quip from Tom Nashe', in Bennet, Cargill and Hall (eds), *Studies in the English Renaissance Drama* (London, 1959), pp. 172f.

Mackerness, E. D., 'Thomas Nashe and William Cotton', RES XXV (1949), pp. 342f.

Mackerness, E. D., '*Christs Teares* and the Literature of Warning', *English Studies*, XXXIII (1952), pp. 251f.

McKerrow, Ronald B., *A Dictionary of Printers and Booksellers in England, 1557–1640* (London, 1910).

McKerrow, Ronald, B., *An Introduction to Bibliography for Literary Students* (Oxford, 1927).

McPherson, David C., 'Aretino and the Harvey–Nashe Quarrel', PMLA LXXXIV (1969), pp. 1551f.

Manshyp, Henry (senior), *A Booke of the Foundacion and Antiquitye of the Towne of Great Yermouthe*, ed. C. J. Palmer (Great Yarmouth, 1847).

Manshyp, Henry (junior), *The History of Great Yarmouth* (1619), ed. C. J. Palmer (Great Yarmouth, 1854).

'Marprelate, Martin', *Oh Read over D. Iohn Bridges* [*The Epistle*] (East Molesey, 1588).

'Marprelate, Martin', *Oh Read over D. Iohn Bridges* [*The Epitome*] (Fawsley, 1588).

'Marprelate, Martin', *Certaine Minerall and Metaphysicall Schoolpoints* (Coventry, 1589).

'Marprelate, Martin', *Hay any Worke for Cooper* (Coventry, 1589).

'Marprelate, Martin', *The Protestatyon of Martin Marprelat* (Haseley, 1589).

'Marprelate, Martin', *The Marprelate Tracts*, ed. William Pierce (London, 1911).

'Martin junior', *Theses Martinianae* (Wolston, 1589).

'Martin senior', *The Iust Censure and Reproofe of Martin Iunior* (Wolston, 1589).

M., T. (Middleton, Thomas), *The Blacke Booke* (London, 1604).

Miller, Edwin H., *The Professional Writer in Elizabethan England* (Cambridge, Mass., 1959).

Mirlees, Hope, *A Fly in Amber: an Extravagant Biography of the Romantic Antiquary, Sir Robert Bruce Cotton* (London, 1962).

Moore-Smith, G. C. (ed.), *Pedantius* (London, 1905).

Moore-Smith, G. C. (ed.), *Gabriel Harvey's Marginalia* (Stratford-upon-Avon, 1913).

Moore-Smith, G. C., 'Matthew Roydon', MLR IX (1914), pp. 97–8.

Moore-Smith, G. C., *College Plays in the University of Cambridge* (Cambridge, 1923).

Mullinger, James Bass, *The University of Cambridge from the Royal Injunctions of 1535 to the Accession of Charles I* (Cambridge, 1884).

Mullinger, James Bass, *St John's College* (London, 1901).

Naunton, Sir Robert, *Fragmenta Regalia: Observations on the late Queen Elizabeth, her Times and Favourites*, ed. E. Arber (London, 1870).

Nicholl, Charles, *The Chemical Theatre* (London, 1980).

Oglander, Sir John, *Memoirs*, ed. W. H. Long (London, 1888).

Onions, C. T., *A Shakespeare Glossary* (Oxford, 1919).

Oswald, Arthur, 'The Old Palace, Croydon', *Country Life*, 8 and 15 April 1965.

Partridge, Eric, *Shakespeare's Bawdy* (London, 1955).

Partridge, Eric, *A Dictionary of Historical Slang* (Harmondsworth, 1972).

Pearson, F. Scott, *Thomas Cartwright and Elizabethan Puritanism* (Oxford, 1925).

Pearson, F. Scott, *Church and State: Political Aspects of Sixteenth Century Puritanism* (Cambridge, 1928).

Peel, Albert (ed.), *The Notebook of John Penry, 1593* (London, 1944).

Peele, George, *Life and Works*, ed. Charles T. Prouty, 3 vols (Newhaven, 1952–70).

Perkins, David, 'Issues and Motivations in the Harvey–Nashe Quarrel', PQ XXXIX (1960), pp. 224f.

Pierce, William, *An Historical Introduction to the Marprelate Tracts* (London, 1908).

Pollen, John H., *Unpublished Documents relating to the English Martyrs*, vol. I, 1584–1603 (Catholic Record Society V; London, 1919).

Pollen, John H., *The Venerable Philip Howard, Earl of Arundel* (Catholic Record Society XXI; London, 1919).

Porter, H. C., *Reformation and Reaction in Tudor Cambridge* (Cambridge, 1958).

Prockter, Adrian, and Taylor, Robert, *The A–Z of Elizabethan London* (London Topographical Society CXXII; London, 1979).

Raines, F. R. (ed.), *The Household Books of Edward and Henry, 3rd and 4th Earls of Derby* (Stanley Papers II; Manchester, 1853).

Rattansi, P. M., 'Alchemy and Natural Magic in Ralegh's *History of the World*', *Ambix* XIII (1965), pp. 122f.

Reyce, Robert, *A Breviary of Suffolk* (London, 1618).

Rhodes, Neil, *Elizabethan Grotesque* (London, 1980).

R., B. (Rich, Barnabe), *Greenes Newes from Heaven and Hell* (London, 1593).

Rollins, Hyder (ed.), *The Phoenix Nest* (Cambridge, Mass., 1931).

Rosenberg, Eleanor, *Leicester, Patron of Letters* (New York, 1955).

Rowse, A. L., *Ralegh and the Throckmortons* (London, 1962).

Rowse, A. L., *The England of Elizabeth* (London, 1973).

Rowse, A. L., *The Case Books of Simon Forman* (London, 1976).

Rowse, A. L., *Shakespeare the Man* (London, 1976).

Rowse, A. L., *Christopher Marlowe: a Biography* (London, 1981).

Rowse, A. L., *Shakespeare's Globe* (London, 1981).

Ryan, M. junior, *Thomas Lodge, Gentleman* (Hamden, Conn., 1959).

Salgado, Gamini (ed.), *Cony Catchers and Bawdy Baskets: an Anthology of Elizabethan Low Life* (Harmondsworth, 1972).

Salgado, Gamini, *The Elizabethan Underworld* (London, 1977).

Salyer, Sandford M., 'Hall's Satires and the Harvey–Nashe Controversy', SP XXV (1928), pp. 149f.

Sargent, Ralph, *At the Court of Queen Elizabeth: The Life and Lyrics of Sir Edward Dyer* (London, 1935).

Schoenbaum, S., *William Shakespeare: A Documentary Life* (Oxford, 1975).

Schrickx, W., *Shakespeare's Early Contemporaries: the Background of the Harvey–Nashe Polemic and 'Love's Labour's Lost'* (Antwerp, 1956).

Scott, E. J. L. (ed.), *The Letter Book of Gabriel Harvey, 1573–80* (London, 1884).

Scoufos, Alice Lyle, *Shakespeare's Typological Satire: A Study of the Falstaff–Oldcastle Problem* (Athens, Ohio, 1979).

Scoufos, Alice Lyle, 'Nashe, Jonson and the Oldcastle Problem', *Modern Philology* LXV (1968), pp. 307f.

Sheavyn, Phoebe, *The Literary Profession in the Elizabethan Age*, revised J. W. Saunders (Manchester, 1967).

Shirley, John William, 'The Scientific Experiments of Sir Walter Ralegh, the Wizard Earl and the Three Magi in the Tower, 1603–17', *Ambix* IV (1948), pp. 52f.

Sisson, Charles J. (ed.), *Thomas Lodge and Other Elizabethans* (Cambridge, Mass., 1933).

Southern, A. C., *Elizabethan Recusant Prose, 1559–82* (London, 1950).

Spens, Janet, 'Notes on *Love's Labour's Lost*', RES VII (1931), pp. 331f.

Steane, J. B. (ed.), *The Unfortunate Traveller and Other Works* (Harmondsworth, 1972).

Stern, Virginia F., *Gabriel Harvey: His Life, Marginalia and Library* (Oxford, 1979).

Stopes, Charlotte C., *The Life of Henry, Third Earl of Southampton* (Cambridge, 1922).

Storojenko, Nicholas, *Robert Greene: his Life and Works* (1878), trans. E. A. B. Hodgetts, in RG I 1f.

Stow, John, *Annales, or Generall Chronicle of England* (London, 1631).
Stow, John, *A Survay of London* (2nd edn, 1603), ed. Charles L. Kingsford, 2 vols (Oxford, 1908).
Strathmann, Ernest A., *Sir Walter Ralegh: a Study in Elizabethan Scepticism* (New York, 1951).
Strype, John, *The Life and Acts of John Whitgift DD*, 3 vols (Oxford, 1822).
Summersgill, Travis L., 'The Influence of the Marprelate Controversy upon the Style of Thomas Nashe', SP XLVIII (1951), pp. 145f.
Taylor, Rupert, *The Date of 'Love's Labour's Lost'* (London, 1932).
Thomas, Sidney, 'New Light on the Nashe–Harvey Quarrel', MLN LXIII (1948), pp. 481f.
Venn, John and J. A., *Alumni Cantabrigienses*, 4 vols (Cambridge, 1922–7).
Ward, B. M., *The Seventeenth Earl of Oxford* (London, 1928).
Wernham, R. B., 'Christopher Marlowe at Flushing in 1592', *English Historical Review*, April 1976, pp. 344–5.
'Willoby, Henry', *Willobie his Avisa* (1594), ed. G. B. Harrison (London, 1926).
Wilson, F. P., *The Plague in Shakespeare's London* (Oxford, 1927).
Wilson, F. P., *Shakespearian and other Studies* (Oxford, 1970).
Wilson, J. Dover, 'Anthony Munday, Pamphleteer and Pursuivant', MLR IV (1909), pp. 484f.
Wilson, J. Dover, 'Martin Marprelate and Shakespeare's Fluellen', *The Library* (3rd series) X (1912), pp. 113f.
Wilson, J. Dover, *The Fortunes of Falstaff* (Cambridge, 1943).
Wilson, J. Dover, 'The Origins and Development of Shakespeare's *Henry IV*', *The Library* (5th series) I (1945), pp. 2f.
Wilson, J. Dover, 'The Marprelate Controversy', in Ward and Waller (eds), *The Cambridge History of English Literature* III (Cambridge, 1964).
Wright, Celeste Turner, 'Anthony Munday', *University of California Publications in English* II (1928).
Wright, Celeste Turner, 'Munday and Chettle in Grub Street', *Boston University Studies in English* V (1961), pp. 129f.
Yates, Frances A., 'John Eliot's *Ortho-Epia Gallica*', RES VII (1931).
Yates, Frances A., *John Florio: an Italian in Shakespeare's England* (London, 1934).
Yates, Frances A., *A Study of 'Love's Labour's Lost'* (Cambridge, 1936).
Yates, Frances A., 'Italian Teachers in Elizabethan England', *Journal of the Warburg and Courtauld Institutes* I (1937), pp. 103f.
Yates, Frances A., *Giordano Bruno and the Hermetic Tradition* (London, 1964).
Yates, Frances A., *The Occult Philosophy in the Elizabethan Age* (London, 1979).

INDEX

Accession Day tilts, 57, 88, 183, 223, 240

Acheley (or Atchlow), Thomas, poet, 54, 56, 58, 271

Admiral's Men, 87, 96, 126–7

Aesop, 52, 86

Agrippa, Heinrich Cornelius, 4, 21, 37, 95, 157

All Hallows', Cambridge, 33

All Saints', West Harling, 15–17, 37, 117, Figure 3

Allen, Robert, parish clerk of Lowestoft, 11

Allen, Cardinal William, 30

Alleyn, Edward, player, 38, 86–7, 103, 125

Alnwick Castle, Northumberland, 254

Althorp, Northants, 88

Alvey, Henry, of St John's, Cambridge, 25

Andrewes, Lancelot, 227

Annot, Thomas, merchant of Lowestoft, 13, 19

Aretino, Pietro, 4, 60, 131, 132, 157, 158, 164, 272

Aristophanes, 144

Aristotle, 26, 35

Armada, 1, 41, 215, 260

Armin, Robert, 142

Arundel, Earl of, see Howard, Philip

Arundel House, Strand, 223

Ascham, Roger, 24

Ash, James, of Barbican, 198

Ashford, Kent, 72

Atey, Arthur, secretary to the Earl of Leicester, 33

Aubrey, John, 40, 105

Audley End, Essex, 16, 31–3, 214

Aylmer, John, Bishop of London, 34

Babington plot, 31

Bacon, Sir Francis, 24, 45, 74, 75, 136, 240

Baines, Richard, informer, 31, 107, 159, 195–6

Baker, Harry, of Croydon, 137

Baker, Thomas, 34

Bale, John, 253

Ball, 'Cutting', cutpurse, 40, 122, 126

Ball, Em, of Shoreditch, 40

Ball, mistress of Robert Greene, 40, 122

Ballard, John, conspirator, 31

Bancroft, Richard, Canon of Westminster, 24, 63, 66, 67, 69, 137

Barbican, London, 44, 198

Barnes, Barnabe, 2, 88, 160–1, 175–6, 180, 225, 229

Barrow, Henry, sectarian, 82, 200

Bartlemew, merchant of Great Yarmouth, 14

Baskerville, Sir Thomas, 223

Bassano, Emilia, see Lanier, Emilia

Bassano, Margaret, 185

Bayley, official of St John's, Cambridge, 24

Beale, Robert, Clerk of the Privy Council, 116–18, 120–1, 158, 192, 254

Beccles, Suffolk, 13, 15

Bedlam, see St Mary Bethlehem

Bedo, William, coiner, 194

Beechfield (or Bitchfield), Lincs, 229

Beeston, Christopher, player, 40

Beeston, William, 7, 40, 44–5, 140–2, 187, 240

Belvedere, anthology, 88, 270

Bentley, William, player, 86

Berdewell, Elizabeth, of West Harling, 16

Berdewell, William, 16

Berkeley, Sir Thomas, 186

Besthorpe, Norfolk, 12

Bifield, Northants, 72

Bindo and Richardo, lost play, 87

Bird, Christopher, of Saffron Walden, 130, 134, 142

Birde, William, 96

Bishopsgate, London, 39, 56, 205

Blackfriars, London, 184, 187–8, 200

Blackwall reach, London, 244

Bland, Tobias, polemicist, 69

Blomevyle, John, rector of Rollesby, Norfolk, 12

Blount, Sir Charles, 44

331

Blount, Edward, publisher, 54, 265, 267–9
Blue Boar Inn, Spitalfields, 44
Boleyn, Ann, 186
Bow bells, 51
Bradley, William, of Holborn, 40, 205
Brandt, Sebastian, 245
Bread Street, London, 149
Breton, Nicholas, 85, 226
Bridewell, London, 255
Bridges, Dr John, Dean of Sarum, 64
Brooke, Henry, 8th Lord Cobham, 2, 249–55
Brooke, William, 7th Lord Cobham, 237, 249–50
Broughton, Hugh, theologian, 25, 137, 139, 219
'Brownbread', see Newman, Humfrey
Brownists, sect, 82
Bruno, Giordano, 201, 223
Buc, George, 54
Buckle, Sir Cuthbert, Mayor of London, 171
Bull, Eleanor, of Deptford, 163
Bungay, Suffolk, 15
Burbage, James, theatre manager, 40
Burbage, Richard, player, 40, 181, 232
Burby, Cuthbert, publisher, 50, 122, 123, 264, 265
Burghley, Lord, see Cecil, William
Burnell, Anne, of Bishopsgate, 56–7, 205
Bushell, Edward, servant to Lord Strange, 190, 196
Buxton, Derbyshire, 12

Caister, Norfolk, 260
Cambridge university, 1, 12, 19, 20, 23–38, 51, 62, 63, 76, 97, 149, 200, 216, 229–36; Christ's College, 31, 143; Clare Hall, 27, 35; college plays, 29–30, 32, 34–7, 216, 225, 231–3, 236, 247–8, 267, 269–70, 271; Corpus Christi College, 23, 29, 31;

Emmanuel College, 230–1; Jesus College, 149; Lady Margaret Foundation, 35–6, Documents 4, 5; Pembroke Hall, 31, 34; Peterhouse, 34–5, 37, 228; Queen's College, 35; St John's College, 23–5, 27, 28, 33, 35–8, 231, 233, 236, Documents, 3, 6; Trinity College, 7, 28, 32, 62, 233; Trinity Hall, 31, 33, 34
Camden, William, 6, 146, 148, 149, 187, 193, 240, 258
Campion, Edmund, missionary, 189
Campion, Thomas, poet and musician, 228–9, 254
Canterbury, 29, 52
Carey, Elizabeth, daughter of George Carey, 182, 186, 196, 201
Carey, Lady Elizabeth, wife of George Carey, 182–5
Carey, George, 2nd Lord Hunsdon, 2, 104, 106, 180–9, 194, 196, 197, 199–202, 203, 209, 223, 236–7, 249–52, Figure 10
Carey, Henry, 1st Lord Hunsdon, 106, 181–2, 185, 223, 227, 249
Carey, Sir Robert, brother of George Carey, 182–3, 223, 240
Carisbrooke Castle, Isle of Wight, 2, 182–6, 239
Carolostadius, 157
Carpenters' Hall, London, 238
Cartwright, Thomas, 25, 62, 67, 114–15, 117
Case, Dr John, physician, 149–50, 188
Cato the Elder, 180
Cecil, Sir Robert, 104, 105, 182, 188, 191–2, 249
Cecil, William, 1st Lord Burghley, 24, 58, 62, 65,

73, 79, 83, 113, 116, 158, 159, 197, 198, 218
Chadderton, William, Bishop of Chester, 190
Chaderton, Laurence, Master of Emmanuel, Cambridge, 231
Chamberlain's Men, 1, 181, 201–2, 236–7, 242, 249–51
Chapman, George, 2, 9, 58, 88, 106, 108–11, 118, 161, 179–80, 182, 189, 192, 201, 210–11, 228, 248, 268
Charlewood, Alice, printer, 170
Charlewood, John, printer, 43–4, 170
Chaucer, Geoffrey, 142
Cheke, Sir John, 24
Cherry Hinton, Cambs, 235
Chester, Charles, suspected Catholic, 103–6, 118
Chettle, Henry, 1, 8, 50, 135, 141, 220, 227
Cholmeley, Richard, informer, 107
Christopher Inn, St Albans, 71, 72
Churchyard, Thomas, 2, 81, 238
Chute, Anthony, 2, 175–6, 180, 225, 227
Cicero, 21, 25, 144
Cinque Ports, 250–2
Clapham, John, secretary to Lord Burghley, 159
Clarke, Captain, 60
Cleaton, Ralph, curate of Buxton, 12
Clerkenwell, London, 46–7
Cliff, Cuthbert, cobbler, 76
Cobham, Lords, see Brooke, Henry and William
Coccaeus, 235
Coke, Thomas, of St John's, Cambridge, 36, Document 4
Colchester, Essex, 237
Coleharbour, London, 2, 46
Colonthus, 30
Commin, Matthew, apothecary, 198

Conington, Cambs, 2, 17, 146–8, 150, 153, 168
'conny-catching', see 'Cunny-catcher, Cuthbert'; Greene, Robert, 'conny-catching' tracts
Constable, Henry, poet, 28–9
Cook, Roger, distiller, 200
Cooper, Thomas, Bishop of Winchester, 66
Cornwallis, Frances, daughter of William Cornwallis, 205
Cornwallis, William, of Bishopsgate, 56, 205
Corro, Antonio de, grammarian, 175
Coryat, Thomas, travel-writer, 149, 235
Cotton, John, uncle of Robert Cotton, 147
Cotton, Robert, 2, 45, 146–51, 156, 184, 186, 187, 240–1, Figure 9
Cotton, Thomas, father of Robert Cotton, 147
Cotton, William, servant to George Carey, 183–4, 226, 236, 239, 240, Documents 10(a) and 10(b)
Counter prison, 2, 45, 82, 104, 226, 242
Court of Arches, London, 34
Court of High Commission, 63, 115, 116
Court of Orphans, London, 171
Covell, William, 38, 88, 230
Coventry, 66
Crane, Elizabeth, 64
Crane, Nicholas, preacher, 64
Cranmer, Thomas, Archbishop of Canterbury, 24
Cromwell, Sir Henry, 147
Croydon Palace, Surrey, 2, 89, 124, 135–42, 146, 153, 185, 264, Figures 8(a) and 8(b)
Cross Keys Inn, Gracechurch St, 74

'Cunny-catcher, Cuthbert', 125–9, 267
'Curryknave, Cutbert', see Nashe, Thomas, Almond for a Parrat
Curtain theatre, Shoreditch, 39–40, 251
Curtis, Meg, of Shoreditch, 41
Cutwode, Thomas, poet, 264

Damnable Life of D. Iohn Faustus, 94, 129
Daniel, Samuel, 83–5
Danter, John, printer, 1, 34, 140–1, 148, 174, 196, 224–6, 227, 232, 239, 242, 249, 254, 267
Danter, Mistress, 224
Davies, John, of Hereford, 88, 90
Davies, Sir John, poet, 44, 149, 264
Day, John, printer, 225
Dee, Dr John, 24, 106, 192, 201, 240
Dekker, Thomas, 6, 42, 99, 227, 270–1
Deloney, Thomas, balladeer, 128, 142, 247, 248
Demetrius, Emmanuel, see Meteren, Emmanuel van
Deptford, London, 163, 165
Derby, Earls of, see Stanley, Ferdinando, Henry and William
Derby House, Paul's Wharf Hill, 90
Deventer, Holland, 189, 194
Devereux, Robert, 2nd Earl of Essex, 57, 66, 223, 237, 240, 251, 255
Devereux, Walter, 1st Earl of Essex, 113, 117
Dexter, Robert, publisher, 6
Dickenson, John, 50
Dieppe, France, 100, 128, 223
Digby, Everard, of St John's, Cambridge, 28, 37
Dillington, Sir Robert, 182
Dioscorides, 199

Diss, Norfolk, 15
Dixie, Wolston, Mayor of London, 57
Dodd, William, of St John's, Cambridge, 231
Doleta, John, prognosticator, 37
Dolphin Inn, Bishopsgate, 39
Dolphin Inn, Cambridge, 229
Donne, John, 10, 24, 29, 45, 149, 238
Douai, Catholic seminary, 56, 205, see also Rheims
'Double V', see Lyly, John
Dover, Kent, 128
Dowgate, London, 122
Dowland, John, 182, 185
Dowtie, Richard (or Robert), conspirator, 189, 192
Drake, Sir Francis, 43, 57, 223
Draper, Thomas, informer, 64
Drapers' Company, 103
Drummond, William, of Hawthornden, 243
Dudley, Ambrose, Earl of Warwick, 119
Dudley, Lettice, Countess of Leicester, 113, 117
Dudley, Robert, Earl of Leicester, 2, 31, 33, 62, 103, 112–21, 130, 179, 196, 201, 237, 254
Dudley, Sir Robert, son of Earl of Leicester, 121
Duns Furens, college play, 34–5
Duns Scotus, 34
Durham House, Strand, 105, 223
'Durham House set', 88, 106–10, 210–11, 223
Dyer, Sir Edward, 31, 179, 193, 197

East Cheap, London, 82
East Molesey, Surrey, 64–5, 66
Edinburgh, 78, 115
Egerton, Sir Thomas, Master of the Rolls, 188–9, 207
Elderton, William, balladeer, 34, 142

Eliot, John, linguist, 178–9
Elizabeth I of England, 14,
    31–2, 54, 63, 66,
    105–6, 113, 115, 116,
    136, 164, 181–2, 190–1,
    215, 223, 226, 247,
    248–9
Ely, Cambs, 54
Erasmus, Desiderius, 4, 37,
    157, 158
Eskimo Nell, 92
Essex, Earls of, *see*
    Devereux, Robert and
    Walter
Essex House, Strand, 223
Exeter, Devon, 6

Fabyan, Robert, chronicler,
    253
Falcoln Inn, Cambridge,
    33
Fawsley, Northants, 65, 72
'Fayreweather, Francis',
    prognosticator, 81
Fenner, Judge, 148
Ferrys, Messenger of the
    Chamber, 244,
    Document 11
ffarington, Thomas, 193
ffarington, William,
    steward to the Earls of
    Derby, 88
Field, John, preacher, 62
Field, Richard, printer,
    187, 200
Finsbury Fields, London,
    39, 41
Fitzgeffrey, Charles,
    obituarist, 269
Fitzgerald, Elizabeth, 157,
    160
Fleet bridge, London, 128
Fleet prison, London, 57,
    130, 182, 200, 255
Florio, John, 84, 100,
    178–9, 209, 218–19,
    223, 252, 268
Flushing (or Vlissingen),
    Holland, 195
Forester, James, chemist,
    182, 187, 200–1
Forman, Simon, astrologer
    and physician, 182,
    197–201
'Fowleweather, Adam',
    prognosticator, 81–2
Foxe, John, 225, 254
Fregeville, Jean, 176, 180

Friser, Ingram, spy, 163–5,
    196
Fuller, Thomas, 215
Fulmerston, Sir Richard,
    20

Galen, 199
Garzoni, Tommaso, 265,
    268
Gascoigne, George, 45,
    100
Gawdy, Anne, of West
    Harling, 15
Gawdy, Bassingbourne
    (junior), 20
Gawdy, Bassingbourne
    (senior), 15
Gawdy, Philip, 20
'Geraldine', *see* Fitzgerald,
    Elizabeth
Gilbert, Gifford,
    goldsmith, 195
Giorgi, Francesco, 107
Golding, Arthur,
    translator, 43
Gontaut, Armand de, Duc
    de Biron, 162
'Goodfellow, Robin', 81
Gorleston, Norfolk, 260
Gosson, Stephen, 37, 61,
    100
Goulborne, John, servant
    to the Earls of Derby,
    188
Great Jane of Ipswich, 19
Great Yarmouth, Norfolk,
    6, 14, 17, 19, 186, 256,
    257–63
Greene, Dorothy, wife of
    Robert Greene, 49–50,
    122
Greene, Fortunatus, son of
    Robert Greene, 40, 122
Greene, Robert, 1, 2, 4–6,
    8–9, 27–9, 31, 35, 37,
    40–1, 44, 48–54, 55–7,
    59, 63, 68, 72–3, 86–7,
    100–1, 122–7, 128–32,
    134–5, 143–4, 154, 168,
    175, 204–5, 212–13,
    216, 218, 223, 225,
    227, 243, 269, 270,
    271, Figure 6;
    *Alphonsus, King of
    Aragon*, 52, 57;
    Arbasto, 37; *Ciceronis
    Amor*, 56–7, 88; 'conny-
    catching' tracts, 5, 6, 49,

125–30; *Euphues his
    Censure*, 48; *Greenes
    Groatsworth of Wit*, 50,
    87, 122, 124–5, 135,
    141, 212–13; *Greenes
    Mourning Garment*, 49,
    72; *Greenes Vision*, 122;
    *Looking Glass for
    London*, 59, 168;
    Mamillia, 27;
    Menaphon, 48, 51–5,
    57–8, 72, 122; *Orlando
    Furioso*, 44, 126–7;
    Orpharion, 223;
    Pandosto, 48; *Penelopes
    Web*, 37, 53; *Perimedes
    the Blacke-smith*, 51,
    225; *Quip for an
    Upstart Courtier*, 49,
    100, 123, 125, 130–1;
    Repentance, 23, 27, 49,
    122; *Spanish
    Masquerado*, 48, 59, 72;
    Tullies Love, see
    Ciceronis Amor
Greenwich, London, 243,
    245
Greenwood, John,
    sectarian, 200
Greepe, Thomas, 43
Gresham, Sir Thomas, 24
Greville, Sir Fulke, 179,
    223
Grindal, Edmund,
    Archbishop of
    Canterbury, 24, 63, 136
Grosart, Alexander,
    127–8, 177
Gruter, Janus, 149
Guildhall, London, 171,
    186
Guilpin, Everard, satirist,
    45, 264
Gunston, Humphrey,
    prison informer, 194
Gurion, Joseph ben, 167
Gwyn, Owen, of St John's,
    Cambridge, 231
Gylian, servant to the
    Nashe family, 12

Hackett, Thomas,
    publisher, 43–4, 52
Hake, Edward, poet, 100
Hales, John, of Coventry,
    66–7
Hall, Joseph, 2, 90, 230–1,
    236, 264

Hampton Court, 136
Hanmer, Meredith, vicar of Shoreditch, 39
Harington, Sir John, 2, 56, 88, 180, 237–8
Hariot, Thomas, scientist, 106–7, 108, 210–11
Harpfield, Nicholas, polemicist, 254
Harrison, William, topographer, 6, 27
Harry of Cornwall, lost play, 87
Hart, John, Mayor of London, 68, 74
Hart, John, orthographer, 217
Harvey, Dr Gabriel, 2–6, 8–9, 11, 16, 20, 21, 31–5, 40, 50, 54–5, 57, 74–5, 81, 90, 97, 99, 100, 109, 112, 117–18, 122–5, 130–5, 139–46, 153, 165, 167, 171–80, 201, 212–20, 221–2, 224–31, 234–7, 239–40, 264, 267, 271, Figure 5; Advertisement for Papp-hatchett, 74–5, 175; Foure Letters, 50, 122–4, 130–4, 140–6, 216; Latin works, 31, 33, 217; New Letter of Notable Contents, 165, 172–3, 216; Pierces Supererogation, 9, 172–9, 216, 227, 229; Speculum Tuscanismi, 55
Harvey, John (junior), brother of Gabriel Harvey, 2, 35, 123, 130–1, 201
Harvey, John (senior), father of Gabriel Harvey, 31, 123, 130
Harvey, Martha, wife of John Harvey (junior), 131
Harvey, Mercy, sister of Gabriel Harvey, 16
Harvey, Richard, brother of Gabriel Harvey, 2, 12, 26, 34–5, 37, 75, 80–2, 89, 103, 123, 125, 130, 133, 201, 204; Astrologicall Discourse, 34, 81–2,

133; Lamb of God, 75, 80–1, 123, 133; Plaine Percevall, 75, 81
Hasely, Warwickshire, 70
Hatton, Sir Christopher, Lord Chancellor, 65, 69
Hawkins, Sir John, 223
Heath, Thomas, mathematician, 34, 182
Helliott, sub-constable of Shoreditch, 40
Heneage, Sir Thomas, Vice-Chamberlain, 191
Henry IV of France, 162, 209–10
Henry V of England, 253
Henry VIII of England, 16, 136, 138, 156, 158
Henslowe, Philip, impresario, 87, 96, 227, 243
Herbert, Henry, 2nd Earl of Pembroke, 121, 186
Herbert, Mary, Countess of Pembroke, 2, 82–5, 118–21, 177, 179–80, 184, 201, 218–19, 268
Herbert, William, 3rd Earl of Pembroke, 83, 182, 186
Hertford, 136, 183
Hesketh, Bartholomew, brother of Richard Hesketh, 189, 191
Hesketh, Richard, conspirator, 189, 191–4, 197, 209–10
Hesketh, Sir Thomas, father of Richard Hesketh, 189, 191
Hester, John, chemist, 35
Higgins, John, lexicographer, 9
Hilliard, Nicholas, 155, 182
Hindon, Wiltshire, 54
Hippocrates, 199
Hobson, Mistress, of Isle of Wight, 183
Hoby, Lady Margaret, 199
Hodgkins (or Hoskins), John, printer, 70, 72, 78–9
Hog Lane, Shoreditch, 40, 195, 205
Holborn, London, 54, 224
Holinshed, Raphael, chronicler, 252

Holland, Hugh, 149
Hollyband, Claudius, linguist, 178
Holt, Fr William, 189
Holywell Street, Shoreditch, 40
Horace, 21, 144
Hosier Lane, Smithfield, 224–7
Howard, Catherine, wife of Henry VIII, 16
Howard, Charles, Lord Effingham, 104, 160
Howard, Henry, Earl of Northampton, 34
Howard, Henry, Earl of Surrey, 16, 118, 157–60, 164, 181, 254
Howard, Philip, Earl of Arundel, 16, 56, 118, 189, 255
Howard, Thomas, 4th Duke of Norfolk, 16, 56, 113, 117–18, 158, 159–60, 254
Hoxton Fields, London, 40
Hues, Robert, geographer, 106, 107
Hunsdon, Lords, see Carey, George and Henry
Huntley, Dick of Croydon, 137
Hutton, Matthew, Archbishop of York, 137

Iesus Psalter, Catholic tract, 226, 254
Inns of Court, 44–5, 54, 59–60, 121, 149; Gray's Inn, 45; Lincoln's Inn, 60; Middle Temple, 44, 149
Ipswich, 19
Isam, Mistress, 122
Isam, shoe-maker of Dowgate, 122
Isle of Dogs, London, 244–5, 247

James I of England and VI of Scotland, 58, 78, 115, 245, 271
James, Dr Richard, librarian, 250
Jeffes, Abel, printer, 94, 98, 124, 129–30, 135, 137

Johnson, Margaret, *see*
    Bassano, Margaret
Johnson, Robert, musician,
    185
Jones, Richard, printer, 85,
    99
Jonson, Ben, 1, 2, 6–7, 40,
    42, 45, 55, 79, 92, 105,
    138, 148, 149, 187,
    215, 224, 243–5, 247,
    249, 251–4, 257;
    Alchemist, 224–5;
    Bartholmew Fayre, 224;
    Eastward Hoe, 8, 245,
    249; *Every Man in his
    Humour*, 138, 251, 252;
    *Every Man out of his
    Humour*, 45, 55, 105,
    138; *Isle of Dogs*, 1, 6,
    242–9, 251–6; *Sejanus*,
    254
Juvenal, 4, 124–5, 144,
    212, 233, 236

Kelley, Edward, magician,
    192–4, 196–8, 201
Kelley, Joan, wife of
    Edward Kelley, 193
Kelley, Thomas, brother of
    Edward Kelley, 192–3
Kemp, Will, comic, 1, 68,
    77–8, 89, 125, 142,
    181, 232, 256
King, Humfrey, tobacco-
    buff, 1, 227–8
Kings Lynn, Norfolk, 2,
    35, 130
Kingston, Surrey, 64–5
Knack to Know a Knave,
    anonymous play, 125
Knell, William, player, 86
Knewstub, John, of St
    John's, Cambridge, 25
Knightley, Sir Richard,
    65–6
Knollys, Sir Francis, 117,
    120–1
Knollys, Lettice, *see*
    Dudley, Lettice
Knowsley, Lancashire, 87,
    189
Knox, Eleazar, of St
    John's, Cambridge, 28
Kyd, Thomas, 43, 52–3,
    56, 58, 106, 205, 267,
    271

Lambeth, London, 44, 198

Lambeth Palace, London,
    63–4, 71, 136–7, 140
Lancaster, 193, 194
Langton, Thomas, Baron
    of Walton, 190, 191,
    193–4
Lanham, John, player, 68
Lanier, Emilia, 181, 185
Lanier, Will, minstrel, 181
Latham, Agnes, 154
Lathom, Lancashire, 87,
    89, 189, 193
Lawson, Margaret, of St
    Paul's, 76
Lazarillo de Tormes,
    132–3, 154
Legge, Thomas, 36
Leicester, Earl of, *see*
    Dudley, Robert
Leigh, Henry, of
    Lancashire, 192–3
Leigh, Thomas, servant to
    the Earls of Derby, 188
Leland, John, 97,
    Document 8
Lewis, C. S., 5, 6, 221
Leycesters Commonwealth,
    see Parsons, Fr Robert
Leyden, John, sectarian,
    157
Lichfield, Richard, barber-
    surgeon of Trinity,
    Cambridge, 7–9, 28,
    36–7, 38, 41, 45–6,
    233–6, 242, 246–7, 256
Lilly, William,
    grammarian, 20
Lime Street, London, 130
Limehouse reach, London,
    244
Little Downham, Norfolk,
    19
Livers, Mother, fortune-
    teller, 41
Lloyd, Lodowick, 37
Lodge, Lady Anne, mother
    of Thomas Lodge, 59
Lodge, Sir Thomas, father
    of Thomas Lodge,
    59–60
Lodge, Thomas, 4, 45, 54,
    59–61, 103, 168, 223,
    225, 240, 271
Lodge, William, brother of
    Thomas Lodge, 60
Lok, Henry, poet, 88
Long, Valentine (or Fol),
    fencer, 6

Lopez, Dr Roderigo,
    physician, 186
Lowestoft, Suffolk,
    111–15, 20, 80, 185,
    257, 260
Lucan, 30, 267–8
Lusher, companion of
    Nashe, 45
Luther, Martin, 157–8
Lyly, Anne, 226
Lyly, John, 1, 8, 41, 54–6,
    63, 72–5, 88–9, 149,
    175, 187, 216, 226–8,
    240, 271; as 'Double V',
    68–9, 72–5, 227;
    Euphues, 17, 27, 37,
    48–9, 53–4, 59, 75,
    132, 175; *Mother
    Bombey*, 55

McGinn, Donald, 125
Machiavel, lost play, 87
Machiavelli, Niccolo, 76,
    87, 124, 131
McKerrow, Ronald B., 3,
    72, 154
Manchester, 73, 89
Manshyp, Henry (junior),
    259
Manshyp, Henry (senior),
    of Great Yarmouth,
    258–9
Mantuanus, Giovanni
    Battista, 21
'Marforius', 68, 73
Marie Magdalenes Love,
    Catholic tract, 226, 254
Markham, Sir Griffin, 196
Marlowe, Christopher, 1,
    6–7, 26, 29–31, 35, 38,
    40–1, 51–6, 58, 69, 86,
    88, 93–8, 101, 106–8,
    110, 118, 124, 130,
    139, 159, 163–5, 168,
    189, 195–6, 205, 227–8,
    254, 264, 267–9, 271,
    Figure 4; *Dido, Queene
    of Carthage*, 29–30,
    165, 170, 221; *Edward
    II*, 38, 139; *Faustus*, 94–
    8, 110, 118, 124, 129,
    189, 192, 196, 208,
    212, 267; *Jew of Malta*,
    94, 124, 159; *Massacre
    at Paris*, 26; poems, 30,
    93–4, 97, 264, 267–8;
    Tamburlaine, 38, 51, 53,
    57, 165

'Mar-Martin', 67–9, 70–1
'Marprelate, Martin', 25,
   62, 64–79, 80–1, 82,
   87, 100, 114–15, 127,
   145, 206, 216; *Epistle*,
   64–5; *Epitome*, 65–6;
   *Hay any Worke for
   Cooper*, 66–7, 73;
   Mineralls, 66; *More
   Work for the Cooper*,
   73; *Protestatyon*, 73,
   75–6, 78
Marshalsea prison,
   London, 243, 255, 257
Marston, John, 88, 92,
   264
Martial, 4
'Martin junior', 69–71,
   134
'Martin senior', 69, 137
Martin, Sir Richard,
   alderman of London,
   172
Mary I of England, 90,
   252
Mary, Queen of Scots, 16,
   113, 160
Mathew, ship, 14
Mayde, Katherine, 15
Melbancke, Brian, 37
Meres, Francis, 203–4,
   208, 257–8
Meriton, George, of St
   John's, Cambridge, 28
Mermaid tavern, Bread
   Street, 149
Meteren, Emmanuel van,
   merchant, 130, 134, 142
Michael, servant to Robert
   Dexter, 6
Michell, Captain, of
   Lowestoft, 14
Michell, Stephen, scryer,
   199
Middle Harling, Norfolk,
   15
Middleton, Thomas, 6, 23,
   46–7, 99, 264, 270
Mildmay, Sir Walter, 231
Milton, John, 208
Molyneux, Emery, globe-
   maker, 198
Molyneux, Sir Richard,
   189
Mömpelgard, Friedrich,
   Duke of Württemberg,
   135

Monarcho, court fantastic,
   32, 214
Monox, William,
   companion of Nashe,
   124
Monson, Captain William,
   199
Moorfields, London, 39,
   41
More, John, of Norwich,
   50
More, Sir Thomas, 157–8
Morice, James, attorney,
   116
Morocco, performing
   horse, 6
Munday, Anthony, 68–9,
   71–2, 78, 103, 251
Myrrour for Martinists, 75

Nag's Head Inn,
   Cheapside, 57, 60
Nash, John, of
   Swainsthorpe, 11
Nash, William, of
   Swainsthorpe, 11
Nashe, Ann, wife of Israel
   Nashe, 257
Nashe, Israel, brother of
   Thomas Nashe, 11, 15,
   80, 257, Document 2
Nashe, Margaret, mother
   of Thomas Nashe,
   11–12, 15–16, 37, 80,
   Documents 1, 2
Nashe, Martha, sister of
   Thomas Nashe, 11, 15
Nashe, Mary, half-sister of
   Thomas Nashe, 11, 15
Nashe, Rebecca, sister of
   Thomas Nashe, 11, 15
Nashe, Thomas,
   1 PERSONAL: birth,
   11, Document 1;
   boyhood, 15–22, 117,
   153; Cambridge, 12, 19,
   23–38, 76, 229–36;
   Catholic leanings, 16,
   28, 30–1, 117–18, 120,
   158–60, 167, 189–97;
   225–6, 228–9, 237,
   253–5; in the country,
   16–18, 35, 146–8, 150,
   153, 185, 229, 251;
   death, 264–5; 269–71;
   dreams, 17, 146, 148,
   151, 153, 194;
   handwriting, 36, 97,

239, Documents 4, 5, 7,
   8, 10; illness, 24, 92,
   146, 150–1, 168–70;
   infancy, 11–15, 153,
   256, 260; and London,
   2–3, 38–47, 60–1,
   100–2, 154, 162–3,
   167–8, 170–2, 187–8,
   222–8; obsessive traits,
   16, 17, 151–3, 168–70,
   205, 221–2, 237–8, 241,
   262–3; parentage,
   11–12, 37, 80,
   Documents 1, 2;
   physical characteristics,
   7–10, 58, 92, 145–6,
   155, 212; poverty, 5,
   44–7, 99, 222, 224–5,
   238, 242; prison, 2, 7,
   45, 104–5, 242, 244–5,
   Figure 1; schooling, 19–
   22; and the sea, 14–15,
   258–63; sexuality, 9, 16,
   90–3, 152–3, 157, 161–
   2, 177, 198; social
   mobility, 11–12, 61,
   130, 136–7, 140, 142,
   155–6, 222–9, 238; and
   tobacco, 5, 55, 227–8,
   232
   2 CAREER: and
   alchemy, 35, 44, 106,
   110–11, 192–7, 262;
   and antiquaries, 135,
   149, 240–1; and
   astrology, 34–5, 81–2,
   111, 262; and the book-
   trade, 1, 5, 42–4, 82–5,
   94, 124, 129–30, 135,
   140–2, 170, 186–7,
   224–6, 227, 232, 236–7,
   242–3, 264–5, 267–9;
   and censorship, 3, 4,
   77–8, 86, 116, 140,
   144, 148, 170–2, 243–9,
   255–7, 264; on the
   Danes, 6, 116–17; on
   the devil, 94–6, 133,
   151–3, 197; as
   ecclesiastical
   propagandist, 62–3,
   67–8, 71–2, 75–9, 89;
   and the Inns of Court,
   44–5, 54, 121, 149;
   law-suits, 112, 120–1,
   131, 183; literary
   quarrels, 1–2, 51–3,
   59–60, 80–1, 103, 109–

10, 118–20, 123, 131–4, 140–5, 172–80, 211–12, 214–20, 229–31, 233–6, 268; and medicine, 35, 68, 106, 111, 123, 144, 149–50, 157, 188, 198–202, 262; and the occult, 18, 94–6, 98, 106–11, 133, 146–8, 150–1, 188–9, 192–202, 207, 210–12; and his patrons, 2, 44–5, 87–90, 93–4, 98, 130, 135–41, 159–62, 180–7, 222–3, 231–2, 240–1; political motifs, 3, 103–8, 112–21, 135, 157–8, 164–5, 196–202, 206–12, 237, 244–55; and the Puritans, 18–19, 25, 28–9, 37, 62, 68, 75–8, 86, 114–17, 158; and the satirical vogue, 4, 51–3, 60, 62, 76, 99–102, 124–5, 142–5, 168, 174, 230–1, 233, 238–40; 249–53, 264, 270–1; on the Spanish, 24–5, 219–20, 259–60; and the theatre, 29, 36–7, 44, 68, 86–7, 94–8, 124, 135–9, 161–2, 181, 203–20, 224–5, 236–7, 242–51
3 WRITINGS: *Almond for a Parrat*, 3, 18–19, 25, 47, 68, 72, 75–8, 79, 82, 89, 114, 127–8, 206; *Anatomie of Absurditie*, 4, 37–8, 43–4, 47, 53, 79, 93, 170; *Choise of Valentines*, 6, 30, 80, 90–4, 97, 222, 230, 231, 238; *Christs Teares over Ierusalem*, 14, 17, 129, 152, 166–73, 180, 182–3, 185, 213, 219, 221, 226, 236, 238; *Have with you to Saffron-Walden*, 3, 16, 32–3, 125, 170–2, 187–8, 214, 221–4, 227, 233–6, 239–42, 246–7, 258; *Nashes Dildo, see Choise of Valentines*; *Nashes Lenten Stuffe*, 1,

42, 84, 121, 186, 219, 251–3, 257–65, 268, 271–2; *Pierce Penilesse*, 1, 2, 21, 42–3, 45–7, 59–60, 81–2, 86–7, 89–90, 94–8, 99–121, 123–5, 128–9, 132–5, 152–3, 155, 158, 168, 180, 189, 192, 196, 206, 211–12, 221, 230, 235, 258, 265; preface to Greene's *Menaphon*, 4–5, 48, 51–5, 57–8, 72, 122; preface to Sidney's *Astrophel*, 82–5, 119; *Strange Newes*, 6, 41, 45, 50, 117, 122, 125, 139–46, 172–3, 214, 217, 220, 224, 227, 244, 258; *Summers Last Will and Testament*, 17–18, 21, 110, 135–9, 141, 155, 170, 245–7, 265; *Terrors of the Night*, 17–18, 96–7, 146–53, 154, 168, 170, 186–7, 196–201, 211–12, 221; *Unfortunate Traveller*, 26–7, 30, 36–7, 93, 128, 154–64, 170, 181, 186–7, 206, 212, 221, 258, 266
4 ATTRIBUTIONS AND LOST WORKS: *Astrologicall Prognostication, see* 'Fowleweather, Adam'; *Countercuffe given to Martin Iunior, see* 'Pasquill'; *Defence of Conny-catching, see* 'Cunny-catcher, Cuthbert'; *Dido, Queene of Carthage, see* Marlowe, Christopher; elegy on Marlowe, 6, 29, 165; *Hospitall of Incurable Fooles, see* Garzoni, Tommaso; *Isle of Dogs*, 1, 6, 242–9, 251–6, 257; *Pasquils Apologie, see* 'Pasquill'; *Returne of Pasquill, see* 'Pasquill'; *Terminus & non Terminus*, 36–7
Nashe, Thomas, butler of Pembroke Hall, Cambridge, 80

Nashe, William, father of Thomas Nashe, 11–13, 15, 20, 37, Document 1
Navarre, Henry of, *see* Henry IV of France
Newcastle-upon-Tyne, 65, 246
Newgate prison, 40, 56, 64, 127, 194–6, 244
Newman, Humfrey, cobbler, 65, 69, 78
Newman, Thomas, publisher, 83–4
New Park, Lancashire, 87–8
Newport, Isle of Wight, 183, 185
Newton, Thomas, 88
Nicholls, constable of Shoreditch, 40
Norfolk, Duke of, *see* Howard, Thomas
Northampton, Earl of, *see* Howard, Henry
Northumberland, Earl of, *see* Percy, Henry
Norton Folgate, London, 40
Norwich, 19, 37, 256, 260

Oglander, Sir John, Deputy Lieutenant of Isle of Wight, 181–2, 185
Oglander, Mistress, 183
Oldcastle, Sir John, 250–1, 253–5
Old Palace Yard, Westminster, 240
Old Swan Inn, Bankside, 82
Ovid, 4, 21, 30, 37, 93–4, 97
Oxford university, 23, 32, 34, 54–5, 63, 223

Paine, Thomas, haberdasher, 128
Paracelsians, 35, 111, 198–202
Paracelsus, Philippus Aureolus, 35, 95, 107, 111, 194, 235
Paris Gardens, Bankside, 56, 243
'Parnassus Plays', college plays, 225, 231–3, 236, 247–8, 267, 269–70
Parrot, prison informer, 244

Parsons (or Persons), Fr
  Robert, 106–7, 113,
  117–18, 120, 190, 194,
  211, 254–5
'Pasquill', 67–9, 71–5, 78,
  267
Paternoster Row, London,
  42
Paule, Sir George, servant
  to Archbishop Whitgift,
  140
Paul's (or Powles), see St
  Paul's Cathedral and
  Churchyard
Paul's Boys, children's
  company, 54–5, 226
Paul's Wharf, London, 90,
  223
Pedantius, college play, 32,
  216, 271
Peele, Anne, first wife of
  George Peele, 57
Peele, George, 54, 56–8,
  86, 88, 124, 204, 240,
  269, 271
Peele, Mary, second wife
  of George Peele, 58
Pegasus Inn, Cheapside,
  232
Pembroke, Countess and
  Earls of, see Herbert,
  Henry, Mary and
  William
Pembroke's Men, 243
Penry, John, 25, 63–8,
  69–70, 73, 75, 77–9,
  114–15, 201
Percy, Henry, 9th Earl of
  Northumberland, 57,
  106, 108, 110, 189,
  195, 201, 211
Perez, Antonio, courtier,
  213
Petrarch, Francesco, 185
Phaer, Thomas, translator,
  29, Document 7
Philip II of Spain, 56
Philip, Stephen, school-
  master of Lowestoft, 13
'Philopater, Andreas', see
  Parsons, Fr Robert
Phoenix Nest, anthology,
  58, 119–20, 179
Pickt-hatch, Clerkenwell,
  2, 46–7
Pie Corner, Smithfield,
  224–5
plague, 40–1, 61, 124,

131, 135–7, 148, 162–3,
  198–9, 225, 269
Plato, 127, 177
Plautus, 21, 36
Playfere, Thomas, of St
  John's, Cambridge, 28
Pliny, 17
Plymouth, Devon, 223
Poe, Edgar Allen, 152
Poley, Robert, spy, 40,
  163, 165, 196, 244
Poole, John (junior),
  coiner, 189, 194–6
Poole, John (senior), 189,
  194
Pope's Head tavern,
  Lombard St, 43
Porta, Giovanni Battista
  della, 194
Prague, 191–4, 197
'Prince of Purpoole' revels,
  45
Priscian, 25, 142
Private Eye, magazine, 3
Privy Council, 3, 30–1, 56,
  74, 86, 136, 163, 183,
  195, 243–4, 254,
  Document 11
Puckering, Sir John, Lord
  Keeper, 191–2
Puddle Wharf, Blackfriars,
  187

Queen's Men, 44, 126

Rabelais, François, 78,
  132, 178, 225
Ralegh, Damerei, 105
Ralegh, Elizabeth, 105–6,
  115
Ralegh, Sir Walter, 2,
  58–9, 88, 104–10,
  115–16, 118, 124,
  179–80, 194, 196, 201,
  210–11, 213, 248, 250,
  254
Ramus, Peter, 26, 28, 34,
  37
Rankins, William, satirist,
  43
Ratcliffe, Margaret, 251
Red Lattice Inn,
  Clerkenwell, 47, 60
Reuchlin, Jacob, 95
Revels Office, 54, 226
Rheims, Catholic seminary,
  28, 159, 204
Rhodes, Neil, 101, 231

Rogers, Daniel, poet and
  diplomat, 31, 130
Rogers, Thomas, of
  Bryanston, 113
Rollesby, Norfolk, 12
Roscius, Roman actor, 86
Rose theatre, Bankside, 2,
  58, 87
Rosenberg, Eleanor, 118
Rowe, Nicholas, editor,
  250
Rowlands, Samuel,
  pamphleteer, 99
Rowley, lecturer at
  Cambridge university,
  38
Rowley, Samuel, 96
Royal College of
  Physicians, 199
Roydon, Matthew, 45, 54,
  56, 58–9, 88, 106, 108,
  179, 182
Rudolf II, Holy Roman
  Emperor, 192–3, 197

'S., R.', editor of Phoenix
  Nest anthology, 120,
  158, 179–80
Saffron Walden, Essex, 31,
  130, 172, 220, 271
St Albans, Herts, 71–2,
  183, 192
St Andrew's, Norwich, 19,
  50
St Bartholomew's Hospital,
  Smithfield, 55, 226, 271
St Faith's, under St Paul's
  Cathedral, 221, 241
St Helen's, Bishopsgate, 56
St Leonard's, Shoreditch,
  39–40
St Margaret's, Lowestoft,
  11–13, 15, 20, 80,
  Figure 2, Document 1
St Mary Bethlehem,
  Bishopsgate, 39, 122
St Mary Woolnoth,
  Lombard St, 43
St Olave, Southwark, 58
St Paul's Cathedral,
  London, 41–2, 66, 221,
  227
St Paul's Churchyard,
  book-market and
  meeting-place, 2, 42–3,
  53, 60, 69, 76, 82, 85,
  95, 102, 131, 135, 165,

220, 232, 237, 241,
  267–8
St Paul's School, *see* Paul's
  Boys
St Thomas a Watering,
  Surrey, 78
Salisbury, Wiltshire, 64,
  198, 215
Samuels, Agnes, of
  Warboys, 146–8
Samuels, Alice, 146–8
Samuels, John, 146–8
Sanford, Hugh, secretary
  to the Countess of
  Pembroke, 84, 184,
  218–19, 268
Savoy Hospital, Strand, 54
Scarlet, Philip, publisher, 7
Scarlet, Thomas, printer,
  187
'School of Night', *see*
  'Durham House set'
Scogin (or Scogan), John,
  jester, 57
Scoufos, Alice Lyle, 251,
  253
Sea-coal Lane, London, 58
Seneca, 52
Shaa, Robert, player, 243
Shakespeare, John, father
  of William Shakespeare,
  220
Shakespeare, William, 1,
  17, 19, 40–1, 52, 55,
  59–60, 79, 86–7, 92,
  103, 114, 124, 127,
  138, 144, 149, 160–2,
  164, 181, 187, 201–20,
  231, 240, 242–3, 250–1,
  254, 269; *As You Like
  It*, 4, 60; *Comedy of
  Errors*, 203; *Hamlet*, 1,
  5, 8, 52, 74, 92, 144; *1
  Henry IV*, 92, 203,
  249–51; *2 Henry IV*,
  92, 203, 250–1; *Henry
  V*, 87; *Henry VI*, 2, 86–
  7, 103, 203, 205; *King
  Lear*, 92; *Loves Labors
  Lost*, 1, 8, 112, 114,
  127, 161–2, 203–4,
  208–20; *Lucrece*, 160,
  187, 203, 208; *Merry
  Wives of Windsor*, 201–
  3, 250; *Richard II*, 255;
  Romeo and Juliet, 242,
  249; *Sonnets*, 160, 162,
  181, 203; *Taming of the

Shrew, 203–9, 212;
  Titus Andronicus, 164,
  225; *Troilus and
  Cressida*, 92; *Twelfth
  Night*, 240; *Two
  Gentlemen of Verona*,
  203; *Venus and Adonis*,
  55, 160, 203, 208, 220
Sharpe, Henry,
  bookbinder, 65–7, 69,
  73, 78–9
Shoreditch, London, 2,
  39–41, 93, 251
Sidney, Mary, *see* Herbert,
  Mary
Sidney, Sir Philip, 31, 55,
  82–5, 118–19, 130, 158,
  179, 223
Sidney, Sir Robert,
  Governor of Flushing,
  195
Simmes, Valentine, printer,
  70, 73
Skelton, John, 57
Skeres, Nicholas, spy, 163,
  165
'Smellknave, Simon',
  prognosticator, 81
Smith, Henry, preacher,
  103
Smith, Sir Thomas,
  orthographer, 217
Smithfield, London, 2, 55,
  224, 226
Smythe, Sir John, soldier,
  237
Society of Antiquaries,
  148–9, 240
Somerset House, Strand,
  223
Southampton, Earl of, *see*
  Wriothesley, Henry
Southwark, London, 2, 58,
  86, 246
Southwell, Fr Robert, 167,
  226
Southworth, Sir John, 189
Spenser, Alice, *see* Stanley,
  Alice
Spenser, Edmund, 31–2,
  88, 109–10, 118–19,
  130, 134, 142–3, 182,
  184, 207, 216, 231, 248
Spenser, Elizabeth, *see*
  Carey, Lady Elizabeth
Spenser, Gabriel, player,
  40, 243, 254

Spenser, Sir John, of
  Althorp, 88, 184
Stamford, Lincs, 229
Stanley, Alice, Lady
  Strange, Countess of
  Derby, 88, 188, 192,
  207–10
Stanley, Sir Edward, 189,
  191
Stanley, Ferdinando, Lord
  Strange, 5th Earl of
  Derby, 2, 87–90, 93–4,
  97–8, 106, 109–11, 118,
  130, 155, 180, 184,
  187, 188–97, 201, 203,
  206–12, 225, 254,
  Figure 7
Stanley, Henry, 4th Earl of
  Derby, 73, 87–9, 189,
  191
Stanley, Margaret,
  Countess of Derby, 193,
  239
Stanley, Sir Rowland, 189
Stanley, Sir William,
  189–91, 194–5
Stanley, William, 6th Earl
  of Derby, 90, 207–8
Stanyhurst, Richard,
  translator, 29
Stapleton, Richard, 179
Star Chamber, 115
Stationers' Company, 43,
  64, 83, 129, 140, 226
Stationers' Hall, London,
  43, 83, 89, 126, 141,
  148, 226, 264
Stationers' Register, 53,
  83, 225, 255, 264
Steane, J. B., 258
Stephenson, Fr Thomas,
  conspirator, 192–3, 210
Stepney, William, linguist,
  178
Stern, Virginia, 174
Stillyard (or Steelyard) Inn,
  London, 44
Stockwood, John, of
  Tonbridge, 167
Story, Dr John, 127
Stow, John, 6, 39, 103,
  188–9, 194, 246
Strand, London, 54, 223,
  226
Strange, Lord and Lady,
  see Stanley, Ferdinando
  and Alice

Strange's Men, 68, 74, 87–8, 98, 125

Stubbes, Philip, pamphleteer, 12, 37, 100, 142

Stubbs, John, pamphleteer, 255

Summer, Will, jester, 138

Surrey, Earl of, see Howard, Henry

Sutcliffe, Matthew, ecclesiastical propagandist, 78

Swan theatre, Bankside, 243

Swift, Thomas, brother-in-law of Thomas Watson, 205

Taming of a Shrew, anonymous play, 203, 208

Tankard, Richard, goldsmith, 192–3

Tanner, Thomas, Bishop of St Asaph, 165

Tarlton, Richard, comic, 1, 34, 40–1, 57, 77–8, 81, 86, 132, 175, 233

Tarrarantantara Turba Tri-Harveyorum, college play, 35

Tasso, Torquato, 52, 55

Terence, 21, 214

Theatre play-house, Shoreditch, 39–40, 60, 68

Thetford, Norfolk, 20

Thompson, Sir John, rector of West Harling, 16

Thompson, Sir Thomas, rector of West Harling, 16

Thorius, John, linguist, 175–6

Thorpe, Thomas, publisher, 267–8

Throckmorton, Sir Arthur, 106

Throckmorton, Elizabeth, see Ralegh, Elizabeth

Throckmorton, Job, 70, 73, 78–9, 115

Throckmorton, Sir Nicholas, 113, 115

Thynne, Francis, 107

Titchfield, Hampshire, 161

tobacco, 1, 29, 55, 61, 227–8

Tomlyn, Arthur, printer, 70, 73

Tom Nash his Ghost, 4

Tooley, Tom, of Cambridge, 234

Topcliffe, Richard, government investigator, 69, 243–4, 254–5, Document 11

Tower of London, 73, 237

'Toy', comic, 137

Travers, Walter, 25, 62

Trimming of Thomas Nashe, see Lichfield, Richard

Trithemius, Johannes, 95

Turnmill (or Turmoyle) Street, Clerkenwell, 47

Tyndale, William, 253

Ubaldini, Petruccio, corrector at Wolfe's press, 225

Udall, John, of Kingston, 64–6, 75, 78–9, 115

Vallenger, Stephen, publisher, 255

Vaux, of Lambeth, 44

Vere, Edward de, 17th Earl of Oxford, 54–7, 143, 157–8, 179

Vere, Elizabeth de, daughter of Edward de Vere, 158

Vergil, Polydore, chronicler, 253

Virgil, 26, 29, 31

Waldegrave, Robert, printer, 63–5, 67, 69, 78, 115

Walsingham, Lady Audrey, wife of Sir Thomas, 163, 165

Walsingham, Sir Francis, spy-master, 24, 31, 62, 116

Walsingham, Sir Thomas, cousin of Sir Francis, 31, 56, 163, 165, 267

Walsingham, Thomas, chronicler, 253

Waltham Forest, 244

Walton, Baron of, see Langton, Thomas

Walton-le-Dale, Lancashire, 193–4

Warboys, Cambs, 146–8

Warner, Walter, scientist, 106, 107

Warner, William, poet, 182

Warton, Thomas, 165

Warwick, 70, 114

Watson, Thomas, 1, 31, 40–1, 54–8, 69, 168, 195, 204–5, 225, 254, 271

West Harling, Norfolk, 15–21

Westminster, 63, 82, 90, 104, 148, 152

Whip for an Ape, 68–9, 114

Whitehall, London, 250

White Hart Inn, Bishopsgate, 39

Whitgift, George, brother of Archbishop Whitgift, 137

Whitgift, John, Archbishop of Canterbury, 2, 62–5, 67–70, 73, 77, 89, 135–42, 156, 185, 187, 264, 265, 269

Whittington, Dick, 127

Whittlesey Mere, Cambs, 146

Whyte, Rowland, servant to Sir Robert Sidney, 219

Widdowes, Mistress, wife of the butler of St John's, Cambridge, 33

Wigginton, Giles, preacher, 69

Wight, Isle of, 2, 181–7, 236

Wilcox, Thomas, preacher, 62

Williams, Sir Roger, soldier, 223, 225, 240–1

Williamson, barber at Cambridge, 234

'Willobie, Henry', 59

Wilton House, Wiltshire, 83

Winchester, 66, 196

Windsor, 183

Wingfield (or Winkfield), Anthony, Public Orator at Cambridge, 32

Witchingham, Margaret,
  see Nashe, Margaret
Wittenberg university, 26,
  157–8
Wolfe, John, publisher, 3,
  131, 172–3, 176, 178,
  220, 225
Wolston Priory,

Warwickshire, 67, 70, 73
Worcester, 137, 197
Wright, Leonard,
  polemicist, 69
Wriothesley, Henry, 2nd
  Earl of Southampton,
  159–60
Wriothesley, Henry, 3rd

Earl of Southampton, 2,
  154, 159–62, 181, 187,
  189, 203, 208–9, 232,
  254
Wychingham, Edmund de,
  16

Yates, Frances, 95, 178